THE GREEK
of the
SEPTUAGINT

A SUPPLEMENTAL LEXICON

The Greek of the Septuagint

A Supplemental Lexicon

Gary Alan Chamberlain

An Essential Addition *to any*
Greek New Testament Lexicon

The Greek of the Septuagint: A Supplemental Lexicon

© 2011 Hendrickson Publishers Marketing, LLC
P. O. Box 3473
Peabody, Massachusetts 01961-3473

ISBN 978-1-56563-741-2

All rights reserved. No part of this book may be reproduced or transmitted in any form or by any means, electronic or mechanical, including photocopying, recording, or by any information storage and retrieval system, without permission in writing from the publisher.

Printed in the United States of America

Second Printing — November 2016

Library of Congress Cataloging-in-Publication Data

Chamberlain, Gary Alan, 1945–
    The Greek of the Septuagint : a supplemental lexicon / Gary Alan Chamberlain.
      p. cm.
    Includes indexes.
    ISBN 978-1-56563-741-2 (alk. paper)
    1. Greek language, Biblical—Dictionaries—English. 2. Greek language, Biblical—Glossaries, vocabularies, etc. 3. Bible. O.T.
    Greek—Versions—Septuagint. I. Title.
    PA781.C43 2011
    487'.403—dc22
                        2011015150

Table of Contents

Preface	vii
Introduction	xi
Abbreviations	xxxi
Lexicon	1
Appendix I: Word Lists	187
Appendix II: Comparative Index of Words in This Lexicon and BDAG	203
Appendix III: Septuagint—English Bible Parallels	251

Preface

The Design and Use of This Lexicon

I have envisioned this lexicon as a supplement to BDAG,[1] the standard NT lexicon, much as the standard Patristic lexicon[2] is constructed as a supplement to Liddell/Scott/Jones (LSJ),[3] the standard lexicon of classical Greek. I prepared it by reading through the Septuagint (LXX), comparing the texts of the Rahlfs (Ra) and, where available, the Göttingen (Gött) edition, and assessing the variant readings in Ra, as well as working through Hatch & Redpath (HR), the standard LXX concordance.[4] BDAG served as my primary lexical resource, augmented by very frequent reference to LSJ (with its Supplements) and, as the work has developed and they have appeared, two other lexica of the LXX itself.[5]

In general, the result is that often I have offered no treatment of the most common words (e.g., ἀγαθός, βασιλεύς, γίνομαι, διά, εἰμί, καί, οὗτος, ποιέω, τίθημι, and ὥς; cf. the list of the most common LXX words in the Introduction, p. xi, n. 13), since the range of meanings for these words is essentially no different from that found in BDAG. Also, the NT uses a great many less common LXX words in precisely comparable senses; as Bauer himself says: "As for the influence of the LXX, every page of this lexicon shows that it outweighs all other influences on our literature."[6] Thus when the user with even a modest command of the Greek NT encounters the LXX's most common words, he or she is likely to need no lexicon at all. With less common words, as long as they occur in early Christian literature in the LXX sense, he or she can almost always find in BDAG a typical sense that fits the specific LXX context, often with a citation in BDAG that refers to the particular verse under

---

[1] F. Bauer, F. W. Danker, et al., eds., *Greek-English Lexicon of the New Testament and Other Early Christian Literature* (3rd ed., Chicago: University of Chicago Press, 2000). Danker has based this work on Bauer's German lexicon (6th edition, edited and revised by K. and B. Aland) and on the previous English renderings by Arndt, Gingrich, and himself. But in many ways it is new in format and method, with particular attention to the distinction between definitions and translation equivalents.

[2] G. W. H. Lampe, *A Patristic Greek Lexicon* (Oxford: Oxford University Press, 1961–68).

[3] E. Hatch and H. A. Redpath, *A Concordance to the Septuagint* (Oxford: Clarendon, 1897; reprinted Graz: Akademische, 1975).

[4] H.G. Liddell and R. Scott, *A Greek-English Lexicon* (9th ed. with revised Supplement; H. Stuart Jones, ed.; Oxford: Clarendon, 1996).

[5] J. Lust, E. Eynikel, and K. Hauspie, compilers, *A Greek-English Lexicon of the Septuagint* (rev. ed., 2003); and T. Muraoka, *A Greek-English Lexicon of the Septuagint* (Leuven: Peeters, 2009).

[6] W. Bauer, "An Introduction to the Lexicon of the Greek New Testament," reprinted in BDAG, p. xxii.

consideration. The better the user's command of the ordinary Greek *either* of early Christianity *or* of late classicism (Xenophon, Plato, Euripides), the greater the probability that he or she can begin by consulting my work, proceeding to BDAG only where I have not found it necessary to refer to the particular word or instance under consideration.

When BDAG treats a word, but the LXX has additional meanings, I have often simply supplemented the presentation in BDAG (see ἀγρός, αἰχμαλωσία, ἀκούω, ἐπάνω, καθίστημι, and many others), expanding BDAG's numbering scheme where relevant. With ἀγρός we are dealing with an unparalleled meaning that (if it occurred with any frequency) could be classified as stereotypical translation. In 2 Macc we encounter an unusual (though fundamental Greek) use of ἀκούω not employed anywhere else in the Greek Bible. The common word καθίστημι happens to offer both an unparalleled meaning and an instance of mistranslation. The case of αἰχμαλωσία is more complicated. BDAG offers the two meanings of 1) *a state of captivity* and 2) *a captured military force, prisoners of war*—both of these consistent with the etymological derivation from αἰχμή *spear*. The context in DiodS 20.61.8 (cited in LSJ) involves an enemy commander and supports this narrow definition. But the context of DiodS 17.17.6 (cited in BDAG) refers to civilian captives (women, in fact) for whom captivity is the transition to slavery. The LXX contexts (generally) refer not only to military personnel but to civilian populations (who are not prisoners of war) being subjected (generally) not to confinement or slavery, but to deportation; hence my supplemental definitions extend BDAG's framework to include (current and former) *exiles* and their communities.

When the LXX word is not in BDAG at all, or when the whole pattern of usage differs substantially from that of the NT (as with περιοχή, where BDAG can cite only one instance, or ἀνίημι, δῆμος, διαστέλλω, and many others, where the LXX occurrences are more frequent and the meanings more varied), I have composed new lexical articles along the following lines:

1. Following the pattern of BDAG, I have given sufficient morphological information to parse any LXX instance. I have added many verbal forms for words cited in BDAG, but I have not always noted adverbs or comparatives and superlatives regularly derived from adjectives in BDAG. I have also assumed that the user is acquainted with such grammatical forms as optatives.

2. Again as with BDAG, I provide some indication of extrabiblical uses of the word. The citations are drawn largely (but not uncritically—I have checked nearly every instance in which I cite a particular text) from LSJ. Where possible, these citations conform to the system of the Loeb edition, which gives the briefest specified context.[7] I have sought to cite an author from the first century in which a word occurs, as well as other authors who are more accessible or whose usage more closely parallels that of the LXX. If the word occurs only in the LXX, it is noted with (LXX). The notation (LXX+) means that the LXX clearly provides the earliest identified instance of the word; if other texts yield but one instance (apart from the medieval lexicographers) I have generally noted that as well (see ἀναζυγή, ἐμπλατύνω, as well as several instances, such as ἀναλημπτήρ, where the only non-LXX instance is from Josephus or Philo and related to a LXX passage). The notation *h.l.* (*hapax legomenon*)

---

[7] This is in contrast to LSJ, from which it is quite tedious to locate citations in Philo, Josephus, or Diodorus Siculus. With the exception of a few papyri and inscriptions, almost all non-biblical texts cited are in Loeb.

3. If there are six or fewer occurrences of a word in the Ra text, all LXX instances are cited (often even in cases, such as ἀβροχία, where BDAG has relevant definitions). Variant readings are seldom explicitly cited unless the meaning differs from all others cited (cf. ἀπολέγω) or where some textual or other issue requires notice (cf. ἀγύνιος). When I have cited every instance in the text of the editions, the entry is concluded with an asterisk (even if the discussion supplements BDAG—as with ἀγκών and ἀδιάκριτος); otherwise, the number of instances in uncontested texts[8] is noted by a number followed by "x" in the initial parentheses (e.g., 32x)

4. Where I have not cited all instances of a word, I have given some indication of the range of usage. In these cases, the first instance in Ra is always cited, and instances are given when possible from the Pentateuch, the Former Prophets (Josh–4 Km), the other historical books, the Psalter, the Wisdom books, and both the Minor and the Major Prophets (with Daniel included among the latter). So, with ἄβατος the user can infer that the word occurs in each group save the Former Prophets, with **ἁγιαστήριον** that the word is unknown outside the Pentateuch and the historical books, and that ἀγαθύνω is absent from the Pentateuch and **ἀκούσιος** from the writing prophets.

5. When a word has two or more substantially different meanings, I have tried to cite these meanings as they occur within the same book; otherwise, the user can infer that all the instances from a cited book have the same meaning (cf. **ἀποικεσία**).

6. Most importantly, words are generally taken to mean what they would have meant to a non-Jewish Hellenistic reader, regardless of the underlying Semitic base (if any). For the principles involved, see the full discussion in the Introduction (pp. xii–xv). Where the Greek context compels us to postulate a meaning with no parallel in classical or secular Hellenistic texts, I have so indicated by use of the sign (no //) and/or by noting the reason for the word being so used—such as stereotypical translation. Here, too, I have sought to indicate the range of such usage (cf. **βασιλεύω**). My insistence on the Greek context as decisive for meaning is the major difference between this work and LSJ, whose renderings of the LXX are notoriously unreliable. While LSJ remains indispensable for classicists, those who consult it with reference the Greek Bible will do well always to check anything unusual that LSJ suggests against this lexicon and BDAG.

7. Where a Hellenistic reader would be at a loss as to how to wrest meaning from the context, I have sought to understand and explain the difficulty, whether it arises from textual difference (in the LXX or its *Vorlage*), stereotypical translation, or mistranslation arising from confusion of meanings (e.g., ἀδικέω, ἀνατολή), roots (e.g., ἀγάπησις, ἀγχιστεία), or even languages (ἀπόσπασμα, διαγράφω). Not only is this necessary information for those who read Greek without any background in Hebrew (such as those working with the classics or Patristic authors), but it is the minimal way to take into account the interplay of lexicography and textual criticism in both Hebrew

---

[8] That is, texts where there is no significant difference between the Ra and Gött editions.

Bible and LXX studies. Since this work is not a treatise on textual criticism, I have not undertaken anything like a systematic comparison of the LXX with its sources. I only indicate textual issues or translation errors when they are needed to explain a confusing text. Even then, we must remember that the Greek world as well as the Jewish community expected oracular or prophetic texts (broader categories for them than for us) to be enigmatic or to suggest singular or symbolic meanings. Where the Greek text, no matter how incorrectly rendered, involves no real lexical problem, I have let it pass unremarked (e.g., David "making music" in 2 Km 6:16). Again, I have treated the issues involved more fully in the Introduction.

Throughout this work I have assumed that the user has sufficient command of ancient Greek to cope with articular infinitives, genitive absolutes, and the varied means of expressing volition and command. The thousand or so most common LXX words should convey relatively few difficulties. On the other hand, I have not assumed that the user will know any Hebrew (let alone other Semitic languages), or for that matter any Latin (apart from common abbreviations), and have translated any non-English terms so as to make this lexicon accessible to a wider circle of students.

At the same time, I have tried to make the work concise but *not* elementary. For example, with respect to textual criticism, I have reviewed (and sought to account for, though, as noted, seldom cited explicitly) all textual variants in the apparatus of Ra where these do not represent mere misspellings or scribal errors. Ra does not consistently distinguish these, though this is often the import of *sic* (e.g., Pr 22:25VL; PsSol 8:16VL) or "cf. Thack" (referring to Thackeray's *Grammar*). Only once (**διαβουλία**, Sir 17:6VL) does Ra simply say, "This word does not exist." More often (Esth 8:12e; 2 Macc 9:24; Sir 43:1) the apparatus does explain transcription errors.[9] Still, in the absence of comprehensive treatments of orthographica and grammatica such as some of the Gött volumes offer for individual books, I have often relied on my own judgment. Naturally, I have taken no note of copyists' mere guesses when the text itself is a transliteration of a Semitic word.

The Introduction and the accompanying multiple Word Lists (see Appendix I) are the heart of the work and the key to assessing many of its details. The user seeking simply to make sense of a LXX pericope need not especially engage them, but will find a preliminary reading (and investigation of a few examples) helpful in navigating the necessarily terse presentation. More advanced scholars should find much here to suggest lines for further research.

Certainly much remains to be done. I hope eventually to complete a full lexicon, with precise parallels (where they exist) for all LXX meanings, coupled with the manner of development employed here for usages that have no secular analogue. The New English Translation of the Septuagint (NETS)[10] will undoubtedly be of great assistance in this endeavor, as will new volumes in the Göttingen edition, recently completed lexical works, and other ongoing scholarship in the Greek Bible and related fields. The LXX itself instructs us both in continued diligence and in humility; as Sirach says:

Ὅταν συντελέσῃ ἄνθρωπος, τότε ἄρχεται,
καὶ ὅταν παύσηται, τότε ἀπορηθήσεται. (Sir 18:7)

---

[9] See also at Esth 8:12g: *alias eiusdem codicis lectiones inanes praetereo* ("other meaningless readings from the same codex I simply ignore").

[10] A. Pietersma and B. G. Wright, *A New English Translation of the Septuagint* (Oxford: Oxford University Press, 2007).

Introduction

The Character of the Septuagint Vocabulary

Consider the opening sentence of the Septuagint: Ἐν ἀρχῇ ἐποίησεν ὁ θεὸς τὸν οὐρανὸν καὶ τὴν γῆν. Every word is what I will call *fundamental Greek*. That is, every word occurs in Homer and/or Herodotus,[11] is used in a variety of genres (drama, history, philosophy) in the Classical period, and persists with similar meanings through Hellenistic and Imperial times in texts such as Polybius, inscriptions, papyri, Plutarch, and the literature of early Christianity. We translate: "In the beginning, God made the sky and the earth," using meanings widely attested in Classical and Hellenistic texts. The sentence makes sense. We have done what lexicographers of any foreign language would do, and our translated sentence provides a solid basis for proposing lexical definitions or translation equivalents.

Of the 120 most common words[12] in the LXX,[13] all but three are fundamental Greek, and even the exceptions (ἐνώπιος, κύριος, and λαλέω) are found in early lyric or the tragedians. These exceedingly common words account for perhaps 70% of the words on a typical LXX page, and the LXX almost always uses them in senses identical with those of earlier and contemporary non-Jewish texts. A good deal of the rest of the LXX vocabulary is also fundamental Greek. Just on the first page of the lexicon we could note ἅ, ἄβατος, ἀβουλία, and ἄβυσσος. While absent from Homer and Herodotus, ἀβασίλευτος, ἀβλαβής, and ἄβρωτος are nonetheless Classical. Further, a cursory survey of BDAG will reveal how often words and usages, whether frequent or uncommon, even in these early Christian

---

[11] Therefore it is not narrowly Attic.
[12] I.e., words occurring more than about 500 times, equivalent to seven or so columns in HR.
[13] ἀγαθός, ἀκούω, ἀλλά, ἄν, ἀνά, ἀναβαίνω, ἀνήρ, ἄνθρωπος, ἀντί, ἀπό, ἀποθνήσκω, ἀποστέλλω, ἀποστρέφω, ἄρχω, αὐτός, βασιλεία, βασιλεύς, βασιλεύω, γάρ, γῆ, γίνομαι, γινώσκω, γυνή, δέ, διά, δίδωμι, δύναμις, δύο, ἐάν, ἑαυτοῦ, ἐγώ, ἔθνος, εἰ, εἶδον, εἰμί, εἶπον, εἰς, εἷς, εἰσέρχομαι, ἐκ, ἐκεῖ, ἐκεῖνος, ἐν, ἐναντίος, ἐνώπιος, ἐξέρχομαι, ἐπί, ἐσθίω-φάγομαι, ἔτι, ἔτος, εὑρίσκω, ἐχθρός, ἔχω, ἕως, ζάω, ἤ, ἡμέρα, θεός, θυγάτηρ, ἱερεύς, ἵνα, ἵστημι, καί, καρδία, κατά, κατοικέω, κύριος, λαλέω, λαμβάνω, λαός, λέγω, λόγος, μέγας, μέσος, μετά, μέν, μή, νῦν, ὁ-ἡ-τό, ὁδός, οἶκος, ὄνομα, ὁράω, ὄρος, ὅς, ὅσος, ὅτι, οὐ, οὐδέ, οὖν, οὐρανός, οὗτος, ὀφθαλμός, παρά, πᾶς, πατήρ, περί, ποιέω, πόλις, πολύς, πορεύομαι, πρό, πρός, πρόσωπον, πῦρ, ῥῆμα, στόμα, σύ, σύν, τίθημι, τίς, τόπος, ὕδωρ, υἱός, ὑπέρ, ὑπό, φυλάσσω, φωνή, χείρ, ψυχή, ὡς. Almost all these words would be familiar to anyone who had read Xenophon's *Anabasis*, and of course all of them are common in the NT.

texts, are fundamental[14] or classical Greek. Hence, well over 90% of the words on a typical page of the LXX would surely be transparent to a Sophocles or a Thucydides.

Of course, the LXX, like the NT, also uses many words that are apparently of Hellenistic origin, reflecting, as Swete had already indicated,[15] such characteristic features as a fondness for compound words. Some, such as ἅβρα and ἀβροχία, are attested in texts earlier than or contemporary with the LXX. Others, such as ἀγαθοποιέω, -ποιός, occur for the first time, so far as we know, in the LXX itself. Here, too, studies of all of "biblical" Greek prove that both the words and their meanings are most often found in earlier or contemporary texts that are neither Jewish nor Christian.[16] That is, words and meanings in Ptolemaic, Seleucid, or Imperial inscriptions and papyri, and in authors from Menander to Plutarch, in most cases precisely parallel LXX and NT instances. In many instances, the LXX use is notably apposite and idiomatic.[17]

Nevertheless, the LXX vocabulary does not consist entirely of classical or Hellenistic words used in senses for which we can find a parallel in secular Greek documents. This lexicon represents the first systematic attempt to acknowledge every word or use that conforms to ordinary expectations for fundamental/classical or Κοινή Greek on the one hand, and on the other hand to account for all the instances in which "in manifold and diverse ways" the LXX vocabulary confronts us with unprecedented challenges. Precisely because we do not subscribe to any form of the hypothesis of a special "Jewish-Greek" dialect, we must account for these divergences not with some overarching theory but with attention to specific instances and contexts. At the same time, what emerged in the course of the work was a taxonomy of a limited number of specific categories which will account for nearly all the exceptions to common usage.

In the sections that follow, I discuss several categories of LXX words. Word Lists for each of these categories is included in Appendix I, and I consider the detailed instances and their overall classification to be the distinctive contribution of this lexicon to LXX studies.

I. Precise Parallels

Within the lexicon, I have cited nearly 140 instances[18] of extrabiblical texts which use a word in ways that are precisely parallel to LXX usage. Most of these are cited by LSJ, but I have checked each against the printed editions. These are often merely illustrative, to show that well-known works by Xenophon, Plato, or Euripides provide many close parallels to LXX usage. But at times the texts cited can suggest how the LXX translators clearly show a strong command of Greek idiom and deploy their resources precisely as a native Κοινή speaker would do. As a perhaps trivial example, in the cases of ἀναδέω, ἀνατέλλω, and

---

[14] In BDAG (as in this lexicon) the equivalent is "Hom+" or "Hdt+."

[15] Swete, *An Introduction To The Old Testament In Greek* (Cambridge, University Press, 1902; 2nd ed. rev. by R. R. Ottley, 1914; repr. New York, KTAV, 1968), 310–313.

[16] Cf. J. A. L. Lee, *A Lexical Study Of The Septuagint Version Of The Pentateuch* (Septuagint and Cognate Studies 1; Chico, Scholars Press, 1983), Bauer's classic essay in BDAG, and the several volumes of *NewDocs* (see particularly G. H. R. Horsley, "The Fiction of 'Jewish Greek'" [*NewDocs* 5: 5–40]).

[17] As shown by Lee, ibid., for the Pentateuch in particular.

[18] See Word List I for the entire list. Most often these instances have been drawn initially from LSJ, but in every cited instance I have checked printed editions of the text.

τρέφω, we can cite specific classical parallels for the use of these verbs with respect to binding or growing one's hair. More substantively, 4 Macc uses εὐνομία with reference to *divine law*, as does Sophocles in the *Ajax*. In the case of εὕρεμα, meaning both *invention, discovery* and *lucky find, windfall*, we can see that both senses were known to writers who just precede the flowering of the Κοινή, just as they were to Sirach. As for ἀβλαβής *without harm*, I observe that Plato's *Republic* uses the word in both active *(harmless)* and passive *(unharmed)* senses, as does the book of Wisdom.

Beyond mere illustration, parallels also give us evidence for text as well as meaning in the LXX: the conjectured reading of ἔνεδρος *inhabitant, indweller* in Pr 14:33 is supported by the parallel in Soph *PHIL* 153.[19] And in a few instances,[20] LXX usage can help us better interpret other texts: ἐπιβάλλω with the dative in 2 Macc 15:1 means *set upon, attack* (someone). Yet the same construction has been misinterpreted in the Loeb translation of DiodS 17. 64. 3. Similarly, παρακλείω *displace, put out of the way* has the extended or figurative meaning *do away with*, i.e., *murder*, not only in 2 Macc 4:34, but also in Polyb 5.39.3. Yet LSJ has misconstrued both texts.[21] If a precise parallel occurs only in a slightly later author such as Epictetus (ἀβοήθητος) or Plutarch (ἀγαθοποιός), that does not in my judgment change the nature of the evidence. The Greeks (and the Romans after them) showed next to no interest in the cultures of Egyptians, Celts, Jews, or any other "barbarians." Accustomed as we are to Herodotus and Caesar, it is easy for us to forget how unusual they were.[22] Almost always, word usage in Greek authors down to Plutarch is innocent of any influence from Jewish literature or culture.

As a final example of normal Greek idiom in the LXX, I cite ἡ κιβωτός as the word for the "ark" of the Covenant.[23] In an inscription from Paros,[24] dated to the second century B.C.E., the civil authorities declare that, to alleviate disputes about civic customs and traditions, they are depositing normative copies of key communal documents εις την κιβωτον την ουσαν εν τωι ιερωι. Obviously, this single instance cannot prove that κιβωτός was the one acceptable word for any container holding a normative text kept in a sacred space. What it does prove, as does *any* single use of a word from sources not influenced by the Bible itself, is that the word could and did occur to a native Greek speaker as the most appropriate rendering of a particular idea, and would be readily and correctly apprehended by most Greek readers. When the LXX parallels such an instance, it is far more likely that the LXX translators or authors were aware of such use than that they happened to choose the same word by chance.

---

[19] I survey several textual questions in relation to Word List VIII below.

[20] Examples are printed in boldface type in the Word List I.

[21] LSJ's errors with respect to the LXX are widely known; unfortunately the new Supplement has done next to nothing to remedy its defects; cf. the extended meaning wrongly suggested for καταποντισμός in Ps 51:6—a mistranslation of the Hebrew.

[22] Cf. A. Momigliano, *Alien Wisdom: The Limits of Hellenization* (Cambridge: Cambridge University Press, 1975). In my opinion, the first classical author who shows familiarity with Jewish traditions or scriptures is Ovid. The opening sections of *Metam.*, dealing with creation and flood (the sequence itself is suggestive), have too many echoes of Genesis for Ovid's independence to seem credible.

[23] G. A. Chamberlain, "Cultic Vocabulary in the Septuagint" (*BIOSCS* 27, 1994), 27.

[24] F. W. Danker once remarked at a Society of Biblical Literature meeting that inscriptions, not papyri, are the best sources for LXX parallels, since (unlike the NT writings) the LXX shares the inscriptions' public and declamatory goals. And unlike the papyri, inscriptions are widely dispersed geographically and most often composed by native Greek speakers.

This, then, is the single dominant characteristic of the LXX vocabulary: *it is normal, idiomatic Greek.*[25] I base my construal of it on this hypothesis whenever I can. I read the text itself, and if it makes sense as a text, then for lexical purposes I know all I need to know.[26] In terms of method, the key principle is that contexts determine meaning—firstly, the context of the word in the LXX Greek sentence, and secondly, the contexts (when available) in the wider world of ancient Greek literature. Etymology and word formation, as well as reference to underlying Hebrew Bible texts or to early citations of or translations from the LXX, can be helpful, but only in supplementing what the contexts teach us. They are never the basis for importing meanings not suggested by the LXX text itself. So, for instance, throughout the LXX, μονόκερως means *unicorn*, as it does in all other ancient Greek texts, no matter what the Hebrew original may mean. The Gallican Psalter[27] confirms this, and the LXX contexts do not pressure us to see a different meaning based on Hebrew[28] or any other factor.

This applies even in cases where, knowing the Hebrew, we are tempted to remove an ambiguity. In 3 Km 22:34 (= 2 Ch 18:33), the Hebrew means that the archer made a lucky shot, and the Greek adverb εὐστόχως can mean that as well. But Hellenistic readers were at least as likely to take word as meaning *well-aimed*, which is the adjective's clear sense in Wsd 5:21. And in the expanded text of Job 18:15, it is likely that the translator took נוה *pasturage > home* as related to נאוה *beautiful*; given the negative context, readers and commentators may well have read τὰ εὐπρεπῆ as *pretences* rather than *attractive things* (the meaning of the underlying Hebrew). So even when we can clarify the *translator's* intent, that does not determine meaning for the *readers* (including Patristic commentators, and the modern scholars who study them). In the Letter to the Hebrews, we rightly translate βραχύ τι as *for a little while*, as the NT author has read it—even though *by a little bit* is the meaning of the Hebrew source and is the translator's probable intended meaning in LXX Ps 8.

But if the LXX as normal, idiomatic Greek is our working hypothesis, how shall we account for the hundreds of instances where the texts present us with words which, in their LXX context, are *not* normal Greek? While these exceptions have drawn much attention from commentators, they have never been systematically assessed in the context of the LXX as a whole. They have misled some into asserting that Hellenistic Jews spoke and wrote Greek in some decidedly Jewish fashion or even dialect—comparable to Yiddish. Construed in context, these exceptions, though numerous, do not suggest an identifiable dialect or even much specialized cultic and cultural jargon. Rather, they consistently fall into a small group of ad hoc translation strategies pointing toward, rather than away from,

---

[25] LXX *syntax*, on the other hand, is, of course, "translator" syntax, strongly shaped by its Semitic sources; ancient critics, had they bothered to comment on it, would surely have called it "barbaric." And certainly some words (ἰδού rendering Hebrew הנה, or ἐνώπιος in its stereotypical rendering of לפני) are far more common in the LXX than they would be in typical Greek texts. But at the level of vocabulary, the evidence does not support any hypothesis of a special Jewish dialect.

[26] For better or worse, LXX Is 7:14 is clearly about a virgin, as is the quotation of it in the Gospel of Matthew. The Hebrew says something different, and that should (and does) matter greatly historically, exegetically, and theologically. But lexically it is irrelevant.

[27] Jerome's revision of an Old Latin rendering of the LXX. Interestingly enough, in his *Psalmi Iuxta Hebraicum*, he renders the Hebrew ראם once as *unicorn* and once as *rhinoceros* (cf. Num 23:22; Job 39:9). In the third instance (a mistranslation in the Greek) he simply transliterates the *Greek* word (even though he is translating the *Hebrew*)!

[28] C. LSJ. The effort to import meanings into Greek words from the underlying Hebrew text is the single most common error in method in LSJ and in many commentators.

the hypothesis that the LXX vocabulary is intended to be normal Greek. Classifying these exceptions, noting how widespread they are among the LXX's many translators and authors, explaining them in ways that are accessible to the widest possible range of scholars and students, is the primary aim of this lexicon and of this essay.

The other Word Lists contain the data whose arrangement and interpretation will test the hypothesis. And it is a testable hypothesis in some specific ways. Most of the LXX is a series of translations, varying in method and skill, but susceptible to *predicting and testing* the translators' intentions against the surviving sources. And the construals of Hellenistic readers can be *predicted and tested* against daughter translations such as the Old Latin, or against extensive commentaries such as those of Philo Judaeus and the early Church Fathers.

This σχῆμα or taxonomy, as I present it, emerged inductively, through the process of reading the texts themselves. In work extending over a quarter-century, doubtless this produces some inconsistencies in assessing individual cases. But the principals and overall structure will prove clear and useful.

II. Transliterations

The most obvious category of LXX words that are not normal Greek is comprised of those which are not Greek at all, but transliterations of Semitic (almost always Hebrew) terms.[29] A few common ones—words that from context and repeated use conveyed their meaning to Greek readers—entered the NT and the language of the Church.[30] A good example is χερουβ, χερουβιν—though LXX σεραφιν is missing from the NT, and is the *only* LXX transliteration that entered Christian liturgical or doctrinal language without appearing in the earliest Christian literature. The LXX transliteration φασεκ for Hebrew פסח *Passover* occurs about twenty times, alongside the more common loanword τό πάσχα which enters the language of the Greek (and English) churches. Similarly, the transliterations εφουδ, -ωδ, -ωθ render the Hebrew אפד *ephod* some fifteen times—all from the translators of Judges and 1 Samuel, while, from Ex 25:7 on, through Sirach and Ezekiel, the appropriate (though probably influenced by similar sound as well) ἐπωμίς, -ίδος is typically the Greek equivalent. Apparently, the translators of Judges and 1 Samuel neither comprehended this relatively common word nor consulted the Greek Pentateuch for possible precedents. Or was the transliteration a cultic transplant in a particular community—as it still is for us? Transliterated μαναα (from מנחה *gift, offering*) also occurs about twenty times, and may have been a "naturalized" term in the translators' worshipping community. Outside of liturgical terms, the Hebrew הין is simply transliterated ιν more than twenty times, but in Lev 19:36 and 3 Km 7:24 (the latter omitted from HR) is more or less correctly rendered by χοῦς (a smaller liquid measure).

Apart from those few exceptions, the other LXX transliterations[31] generally occur only once or twice, and are clearly the result of a baffled translator who simply handed on a word he did not know (such as φελεθθι and χερεθθι, apparently titles or honorifics for the king's "honor guard," which Jerome also simply transliterated and for which we still lack an

---

[29] See Word List II for the complete list; there are about 170 that are not taken up in Christian literature, and so do not occur in BDAG.

[30] This is especially true with liturgical terms, such as *Messiah, hallelujah, hosanna,* and *amen.*

[31] Ra generally does not provide accents (or breathings) for transliterations. These should be distinguished from loanwords, which are generally nouns (and thus declined) and may be as old as Homer (such as χιτών) or more recent (cf. ἀρραβών, νάφθας, νάβλα; βακχύριον is *h.l.*)

interpretation). On the first page of the lexicon, I note αβαρκηνιν, αββους, and αγανωθ. The Hebrew words are typically uncommon, and the transliterations often are, or have, textual variants, suggesting that they were problematic for translators and copyists alike.

There are still some mixed or debatable instances that leave us wondering whether they are translation or transliteration. In some mss. influenced by Origen, the Tetragrammaton appears as πιπι, which resembles the Heb יהוה visually rather than phonetically. The use of τόκος *interest* (on a loan) in Ps 71:14[32] to render Heb תך *oppression, extortion* arises from sound, not meaning, as does σκληρία, σκληρός *hard(ness)* in Ecclesiastes, rendering Heb (סכלות) *foolish(ness)*.[33] The repetition of ἆ ἆ in Judg 6:22 makes it *both* a translation and a transliteration of Heb אהה. Walters' argument [BDF 128.5] concerning ἵλεως σοι in relation to Hebrew חלילה deserves attention, as do his comments on νῖκος (in contrast to νεῖκος *contention, strife*), which renders Hebrew לנצח *forever* both from the Aramaic homograph meaning *glory, victory* and from similarity in sound.[34]

There remain some mixed cases around transliteration vs. loanwords. We find a Hebrew word נזיר *Nazirite* transliterated in one version of Judges, alongside a declined ναζιραῖος in the other version and in Maccabees (neither form is noted in LSJ). Similarly, a word for *harp* is transliterated ναβαλ in a textual variant at 1 Km 10:5, but the corresponding loanword νάβλα not only occurs in the text but is relatively common in the LXX—and is known from Strabo and inscriptions. The oddest example is κοθωνός or χοθωνωθ *chiton(s)*, a loanword and a transliteration of a Canaanite term that was already a loanword from Canaanite (χιτών) that we meet in Homer, which leaves us wondering whether the translator of 2 Esdr even understood the Hebrew word. (Yet how could he *not*, since it is quite common in Hebrew and is the word for Joseph's famous "coat"?)

These transliterations (and some of the loanwords as well) must have baffled anyone who did not know Hebrew, because to the Greek reader (as was often true of the translator) they have no meaning at all. Paradoxically, they offer no lexical difficulty; without imputing meaning in the Greek, we simply explain how they came to be used in the LXX.

III. Hapax Legomena

There can of course be no parallels cited for *hapax legomena (h.l.)*—Greek words that occur, so far as we know, only in the LXX itself. Here I have presented two lists, the first (Word List III.A.) of *h.l.* proper, and the second (Word List III.B.), of words that occur in our texts more than once but nowhere else outside the LXX unless in texts (e.g., Philo Judaeus) directly commenting on the LXX passage,[35] or in the later Greek versions such as Aquila (e.g., ἐξιχνιασμός). These I have designated "LXX" throughout the lexicon.

---

[32] Ra correctly conjectures it as well in Ps 54:12, on the basis of the Sahidic rather than the Greek. Again, the copyists had some difficulties. Something similar was done at LXX Jer 9:5, but cf. Hebrew text (?).

[33] Cf. the discussion of ἐκλείχω in section VI below.

[34] P. Walters, *The Text of the Septuagint* (ed. by D. W. Gooding, Cambridge, University Press, 1973), pp. 34–36.

[35] See Word Lists III and IV. The *h.l.* (there are about 500 of them!) occur only once in the LXX and have no citation in LSJ apart from the LXX instance (about a dozen, printed in **bold**, do not appear in LSJ at all). The Word Lists do not record (though they may appear in the lexicon) dubious words that occur only as variant readings. Nor do the lists include adverbs normally formed from attested adjectives. Words that occur more than once in the LXX itself, but in no other texts of which I am aware, number around 230.

The category of *h.l.* is the most difficult to assess in any orderly way, since we have no evidence apart from the context of a single sentence, supplemented by etymology and word formation. Nevertheless, it is suggestive that from the first forty or so items in Word List III, I can quickly cull the following list:

ἀβατόω, ἀβοηθησία, ἀβουλεύτως, ἀγριομυρίκη, ἀδελφοπρεπῶς, ἀλλόφωνος, ἀμφιβολεύς, ἀναγνεία, ἀνδρογύναιος, ἁπλοσύνη, ἀποδεκατίζω, ἀποκάλλυμα, ἀποπαρθενόω, ἀργυροκοπέω, ἀργυροχόος

From this informal selection, I observe:

1. The meanings in context are just what I *expect* from etymology and word formation, and would present no challenges to anyone literate in Greek.

2. None reflects practices or values that are particularly Jewish.

These characteristics apply to the *h.l.* in general—they are for the most part normally formed, and not notably Jewish or religious. What ancient Greek reader would stumble over words such as these?

δευτερολογέω, ἐκφυγή, ἐλεημοποιός, ἐπιγνωστός, καρπόβρωτος, καταγογγύζω, καταμιμνήσκομαι, λοιμότης, μακροβίωσις, μεγαλοκράτωρ, νηπιοκτόνος, ὀλιγοποιέω, προνουμηνία, συγκατακληρονομέω, συμβόσκομαι, τριμερίζω, ὑπερδυναμόω, φοβεροειδής, χρυσοτόρευτος

I agree with Bauer,[36] that many apparent *voces Biblicae* will surface in secular texts as they are discovered and published, and that many others should be assumed to be normal Greek words for which we simply lack other testimony. Often within the lexicon I cite etymological relationships suggesting that the given words and/or meanings may not be unusual (e.g., ὑποσκέλισμα with a reference to the classical verb occurring seven times in the LXX itself). The otherwise unknown verb περιχαλκόω would offer no challenge for anyone familiar with either περιχρυσόω or περιαργυρόω. Even if these words are unusual, they are easy to understand. Indeed, even if a few are ad hoc coinages, the authors or translators may not have known they were inventing anything. The exceptional case here is the author of 4 Macc, who is obviously striving for effect, and is disproportionately responsible for this list—for instance he contributes four words among the fourteen beginning with "o."

The Hebrew *h.l.* גזבר, a Persian loanword found also in Akkadian, Aramaic, and post-biblical Hebrew, leads to the *h.l.* transliteration γασβαρηνος *treasurer* in 2 Esdr 1:8, taken as a personal name (equivalent to "Caspar") in the Vulgate. Nor should we leave unmentioned the oddity of βακχύριον, a loanword from Hebrew בכורים *first-fruits*—for which the translator would seem to have had both classical (ἀπαρχή) and LXX (πρωτογένημα) alternatives.

The latter term is one of the more common words not known outside the LXX—to which we now turn (see Word List III.B.[37]). The results are similar to those outlined for *h.l.* Most appear only a few times; often only in a single book (ἀληρός only in Jer—but the related

---

[36] W. Bauer, "An Introduction to the Lexicon of the Greek New Testament," republished in BDAG, pp xiii-xxix.

[37] As with some other words in this list, for πρωτογένημα LSJ can cite only Philo—commenting precisely on the texts in question—beyond the LXX itself. I have not checked this list against Patristic sources or against the standard Patristic lexicon (Lampe, *A Patristic Greek Lexicon*); consulting the

ἄλγος is fundamental Greek). An enigmatic instance, not found in HR or LSJ, is παταχρός (or πατραχρόν), from the Persian via the Aramaic פתכרא *statue*, used twice in Isaiah to render *(pagan) god*. (One wonders why the translator did not avail himself of the fundamental Greek ἄγαλμα, which appears in Is 19:3; 21:9). In fact, it is not rare to find a word used more than once but only in a single passage (ἀναφαλάντωμα) or even a single verse (ἀχρειότης). Seldom does the expression or subject seem to arise from Semitic idiom or specifically Jewish practice. Again (though to a lesser degree), we find 4 Macc somewhat overrepresented, but the words (though "impressively" polysyllabic) are normally formed and clear from context and etymology (of which the most numerous example is μιαροφαγέω, -γία). When instances of words from the LXX list are both somewhat numerous and widely distributed across the canon, they are likely words unrepresented elsewhere only by chance; I have in mind ἀμνάς, ἐπικαταράομαι, περισπόριον, φονευτής, and perhaps θνησιμαῖος. And while ὁλοκαύτωσις, with over seventy occurrences, is a "religious" word, it can hardly be specifically Jewish when ὁλόκαυτος, ὁλοκαυτέω, and perhaps the alternative ὁλοκαυτόω, are attested from Xenophon and Callimachus as well as Plutarch.

There are a few exceptions in each list. Occasionally one does find a word that reflects a Hebrew idiom (βαθύγλωσσος, βαθύφωνος) or refers to an Israelite custom (such as καταλιθοβολέω). Yet the latter case is still instructive. The word occurs only twice, while the more common term (taken up by the NT) for the same practice is λιθοβολέω, attested in Diodorus Siculus and Plutarch. On the other hand, the meaning *stone to death* has no parallel outside the communities of Judaism and Christianity. The one word I would take to be a neologism due to Israelite custom as well as Semitic idiom is φυγαδευτήριον (more than fifteen occurrences) for ערי מקלט *(cities of) refuge*.

As for the enigmatic διάψαλμα, appearing only to render (without interpreting) the Psalms' equally enigmatic סלה, it reveals only the translator's helplessness, as surely as that of our modern transliterations, the Gallican Psalter's transliterations of the Greek, and Jerome's later *semper* in his rendering from the Hebrew. As far as I know, the word disappeared in the West, with no literary, liturgical, or theological reference until the Diapsalmata of Kierkegaard's *Either/Or*.

Though they properly fall into subsequent sections of this Introduction, several *h.l.* and LXX words appear even more likely to represent translators' tactics with difficult passages, since they are textually questionable (see Word Lists VIII and IX) or are mistranslations of their *Vorlagen* (see Word List VII). Examples of the first type include ἁγιαστία (more probably, an error for ἁγιστεία Walters, p. 38), and ψαλμῳδός, which appears in our editions only as a variant. For mistranslations, we can point to θελητής, which in 4 Km renders אוב *magician* as if it were related to אבה *to desire*) or πρόσκαυμα. As an instance of both factors, we can perhaps cite ἀκριβασμός.[38]

We must conclude that all this evidence points largely to normal Hellenistic vocabulary or, less often, to ad hoc translation strategies. Nothing in the vocabulary peculiar (with respect to our current evidence) to the LXX requires us to postulate special use of these words in the conversation (or even the worship, apart from reading Scripture) of the Diaspora communities.

---

latter will doubtless show that some words unknown from secular sources down to Plutarch, or from the NT or other early works covered in BDAG, were later taken up into the language of the Church.

[38] For the most egregious instance of a mistranslation involving a word that is *h.l.*, see p. xxiv below.

IV. Words First Found in the LXX (LXX+)

Also very numerous are the words (I list over 500 in Word List IV.A.) that, by the evidence, appear for the first time in the LXX, but are attested in later texts (Imperial papyri and inscriptions, or authors such as Plutarch) that do not seem to be influenced either by the LXX or by the Jewish or Christian communities. These I have designated "LXX+," following BDAG. Perhaps the majority of the words in this category—and certainly many of the most important—do not appear in this lexicon, because in all their LXX meanings they appear in early Christian literature and are adequately treated in BDAG. Most of the words in my list (as with those with no examples outside the LXX itself) will prove to have been normal Hellenistic Greek, employed in their ordinary senses through the Imperial period by the Jewish and Christian communities and by secular Greek speakers and writers alike.

Complications bedevil the dating either of the LXX or of the secular texts involved. It is impossible to be precise here; Plato himself certainly precedes the entire LXX, but the date of some (pseudo-)Platonic dialogues and epistles is unclear. The Hippocratic corpus is extensive and provides many parallels to LXX usage, but it was a developing tradition of which little can be dated with assurance. And dating the various LXX books is often problematic as well. The consensus is that the Torah was translated first, perhaps by the middle of the third century B.C.E. But both the translation of Ecclesiastes and the composition of The Wisdom of Solomon may well date from the Common Era.[39] In general, I have excluded from this category words that appear, with the same meanings,[40] in the substantial Hellenistic corpuses of Polybius, Strabo, and Diodorus Siculus, or in papyri and inscriptions that predate the Common Era. It is highly improbable that any LXX neologism would so quickly penetrate the secular culture.

It is striking how seldom these "new" words occur; fewer than twenty offer as many as eight instances. Even more remarkable, only about fifteen words occur in senses we cannot document from secular texts. Two of these, ἀμνησία and γονορρυής, have come into English as medical terms. One of the more common, περικύκλωι (24x), is an adverb and preposition that can hardly have had a specific Jewish sense.

In Word List IV.B. I present more than fifty words (a few of which are certainly earlier than the LXX) for which LSJ suggests just one other occurrence *anywhere* in pre-Christian Greek. Hippocrates (again, an accumulating corpus difficult to date) offers the only instance of ἑβδομηκοστός. A fragment of the Platonist Numenius in Eusebius preserves the only secular text with ἀγαθόω. Apart from Sirach, κατάπαυμα is known from just one line in Homer, and the διατίλλω of Job would be *h.l.* except for a fragment of Sophocles. As for ἀνίσχυς in Isaiah, I could cite only the same inscription (later than the NT) given in LSJSup, which now also cites an even later inscription testifying to μακροημέρευσις. Found a total of seven times (in the Pentateuch, Proverbs, and the Minor Prophets) ἐμπλατύνω is otherwise known from just one occurrence in Strabo.

All of this simply demonstrates how haphazard and partial our evidence must be. In Num 22:30 we find the word ὑπερόρασις *disdain*. It occurs just this once in the LXX itself, and is cited in LSJ for just one instance elsewhere—in the meditations of the well-known Stoic emperor of Rome, Marcus Aurelius. It is most improbable that the emperor learned

---

[39] D. Winston, *The Wisdom Of Solomon* (AB, Garden City, Doubleday, 1979), argues for the reign of Caligula (p. 23).

[40] I treat at a later point the instances of LXX *meanings* not paralleled in secular texts.

this word from pondering the book of Numbers, so we must assume that the word was a normal Hellenistic term over a span of about three centuries. We must also remark that the formation of the noun is typical in relation to the verb ὑπεροράω, which is fundamental Greek (appearing in Herodotus, Plato, and several later authors). Yet, apart from a single manuscript copied in the tenth century C.E.,[41] the emperor's reflections would be unknown to us, and ὑπερόρασις would be another "biblical" *h.l.*

On the other hand, προσήλυτος appears in this lexicon only because BDAG does not give the meaning *resident alien, stranger* alongside the meaning it bears as a loanword in English. Almost certainly it is a Jewish neologism; no example occurs outside the literature of Judaism and Christianity.[42] Notably, the word also does not occur in any of the LXX books originally *written* in Greek (its sole instance apart from the books of the Hebrew Bible is in the Sinaitic text of Tob). The גר, the "wanderer," was not to Judaism what the βάρβαρος or "foreigner" was to the Greeks and Romans—though the author of 2 Macc was willing to apply the latter term (in its most pejorative sense) *to* the Greeks and their allies (cf. 2 Macc 2:21).

Nevertheless, προσήλυτος is an exception, like the common loanwords—μεσσίας, πάσχα, σάββατος, κτλ.—also taken up into the language of Christianity. And as with the loanwords and a handful of other technical terms, we do well to see them simply as the results of translation, not of Jewish speech patterns in the streets of Alexandria. Similarly, the Hebrew idiom נשׂא פנים *lift up the face > show favor or favoritism* is literally translated πρόσωπον λαμβάνω in the LXX and appears as well in the NT (cf. Lk 20:21; Gal 2:6—neither instance is a quote). This idiom in turn leads to a cluster of related NT terms: προσωπολημπτέω, -λημτής, -λημψία, all unknown outside of Christian literature. Still, the idiom appears not only in the Greek Bible but in Barnabas, Polycarp, the Didache, and various ecclesiastical authors at least into the eighth century C.E. Apparently, as with the common loanwords, frequent use of the Hebrew and LXX idiom rendered these few (but very frequently employed) "translationisms" sufficiently comprehensible in context.

V. Words with No Parallel Meanings Attested in Secular Greek (no //)

The true cruxes of the LXX are the words—common or more unusual, but amply attested in non-Jewish sources—that have *meanings* for which I know of no parallel in secular Greek. For about 450 of these instances, I have simply used the abbreviation "no //."[43] Since the case of ἀναγνώστης is correctly treated in LSJ, it can serve as a model of the type. In secular texts the basic meanings (through Cicero) are of a slave or subordinate who is literate—who can read aloud or (LSJSup) even act as a secretary. A later Christian sense (again, LSJSup) is a reader for the community, or as we would say (using an ecclesiastical Latin loanword), a lector. But unique to the LXX is the sense of one who reads and interprets, of a scholar or presenter able speak from a text as a trained expert, which is not paralleled in the other sources.

Again, I emphasize that these unparalleled meanings are *inferred from the Greek sentences themselves*—not imputed from the translators' Semitic *Vorlagen* (or any other out-

---

[41] A. Lesky, *A History Of Greek Literature* (New York: T. Y. Crowell & Co., 1966), p. 4, uses precisely this example to show our dependence on improbable chances for the survival of so much of our evidence.
[42] C. BDAG, προσήλυτος is *not* found in AppolonRhod.
[43] See Word List V.

side influence). In fact, in many instances the unparalleled meanings are in texts (2 Macc; 4 Macc; Sap) for which Greek was the language of composition.⁴⁴

For many or most of these meanings, new evidence will probably confirm that they are normal Greek. Sometimes this is the implication we can draw from related words. The meaning *made of ruby* for ἀνθράκινος in Esth 1:7 may be unparalleled, but ἄνθραξ can mean either *garnet, ruby* or *coal*. Nor do I know of a secular text in which ἐπονείδιστος bears the active sense *insulting, contemptuous*, but the adverb is so employed in Polybius. Less clear is the case of ἀποστατέω with the meaning *to rebel*; but even if the meanings *rebellion* for ἀπόστασις (attested by Thucydides and Aristotle) and *rebel, deserter* for ἀποστάτης (in Polybius) go back to ἀφίστημι, the transferred meaning for ἀποστατέω is not likely to have originated with the LXX.

The lines are not necessarily clear here. For the most part I have not classified any figurative or metaphorical use as unparalleled—or even as a different "meaning" with its own definition. But, in the case of αἱμοβόρος for instance, is it "unparalleled" when extending the use to humans implies a "beastly" quality in the people described? Or is it "unparalleled" to employ ἀκολουθία in a moral sense? When does a figure of speech (whether from the Hebrew or not) become a "new" meaning?⁴⁵ Or, to anticipate a subsequent section of this essay, when does a pattern become stereotypical translation or a calque—a settled translation equivalent that persists in the literature?

One common type of Hebrew influence is the unparalleled uses of verbs in transitive/causative senses, often (but not always) where the Hebrew employs the hiphil. I can note just one example with ἁμαρτάνω or ἀνομέω, but nine instances of βασιλεύω meaning *install as king* are scattered across much of the canon apart from the Pentateuch. One is surprised to find ζάω in this group, when a translation alternative such as ζωόω *bring to life* (Hippocr+) might have suggested itself—and in the case of the Psalms actually occurs in the same book. Perhaps it is well to point out here that the translators often seem more willing to use a word in an unusual sense than to coin a new word. In the case of these verbs, I might have expected new (causative) formations with -ίζω or -όω. We may wonder whether the *h.l.* σοφόω was just such a new formation or whether it was already available in the Hellenistic vocabulary.

We do find here a very few distinctly Jewish terms. The specific meaning *Exodus (from Egypt)* presents itself in ἐξοδία and ἐξόδιος. Oddly, the plural σκηνώματα in 2 Macc 10:6 alone refers to Succoth; the usual rendering in the Greek Pentateuch for *tabernacle* is σκηνή. Nor should we ignore the unparalleled use of νεός to mean *first fruits* in Numbers and Sirach. The oddity here is that we have already encountered a word with the same meaning—πρωτογένημα—also used in the Pentateuch and Sirach (and unknown, according to LSJ, outside of the LXX and Philo). Yet "first fruits" as an offering to the god is not even a specifically Jewish theme; the practice and the word ἀπαρχή were typically Greek at least since Herodotus—and this normal Greek word itself occurs more than eighty times across the whole Greek Bible from Exodus to Revelation (including, again, Numbers and Sirach).

Generally, we lack explanations for the unparalleled meanings of the words in this section. In many cases I am simply listing facts—and the "fact" is (so far) only a lack of evidence, though as we know, arguments from silence are never definitive and not often even very convincing. In the next two sections we will look closely at unusual meanings (or lack

---

⁴⁴ As examples, see ἀποκοσμέω, ἡμίθνητος, πρώταρχος, στοιχείωσις, ὑποτίθημι, φιλόψυχος.
⁴⁵ Cf. as examples πρόσωπον, ψυχή.

of meaning) for which we can propose clear explanations. But here we can only summarize using broad hypotheses. Sometimes these unparalleled meanings suggest translation difficulties. More often it seems likely that these were normal meanings for which we simply lack evidence. We find unparalleled meanings for two of the most common prepositions, παρά and ὑπό. The same would be true of the odd use of ἀπό in Esth 1:7, except for a single papyrus that shows this meaning was known in the wider world.

VI. Stereotypical Translations

When I began working on this lexicon, the concept of stereotypical translation (designated "s.t." throughout the lexicon) was to my mind the clearest category in this taxonomy. Having read through the entire LXX, I now find it the most indefinite and confusing.

At one pole, we can occasionally be sure that an otherwise-unparalleled meaning is due to the translators' aim consistently to translate the same Hebrew root with the same Greek word-group, regardless of the prior semantic range of the two sets of terms. When stereotypical translation of a particular root is thoroughgoing and widespread across a variety of Jewish texts, we can use the term *calque*. The best example is also well-known from early Christianity, the use of ἀφίημι/ἄφεσις (which in secular Greek refer to remitting a debt or excusing someone from a duty, among varied meanings) to translate סלח and other roots relating to the forgiveness of sins.[46]

Similarly, several oddities of expression in Greek (both in the LXX and in the NT) result from the extremely consistent use of ψυχή to render נפש, one of the least translatable of Hebrew words.[47] My lexical notes merely supplement the extended and generally useful treatment in BDAG, even if I judge that Danker and his predecessors should have given greater weight to the Semitic/translational contexts from the LXX. Just so, in many modern English translations, *soul,* even as a rendering of ψυχή in the NT, is less than appropriate. But as a translation of נפש in the Old Testament, *soul* is generally misleading and wrong. The varied turns of expression around ψυχή, as they arise from the semantic range of נפש, also help to explain some mistranslations and textual issues to which I refer in subsequent sections.

The best (and perhaps the only) example of a calque specific to the LXX is the use of τραυματίας to render חלל. Ordinarily the Greek term (related to English "trauma") means *wounded person*, as it does in the three passages in 2 Macc. But the Hebrew means *someone pierced* (by a weapon), whether wounded or killed, like our military term "casualty." Hence there are numerous passages where the Greek now has an extended meaning *military casualty* (wounded or dead—Judg 9:40; 1 Macc 1:18; Ezk 30:11) and others where the context forces us to translate not as *wounded person* but simply as *corpse* (Gen 34:27; 2 Km 1:25; Ps 87:6, etc).

We also find a cluster of words (ἀδικία, ἁμάρτημα, πλημμέλεια, κτλ) which, via stereotypical translation, receive extended meanings of *the offering or penalty* for sin or

---

[46] The very idea of divine forgiveness is unknown and indeed incomprehensible in Greek culture, where the gods are not moral guardians and are subject, as are mortals, to impersonal standards of conduct and forces of fate. See my concluding remarks to this essay.

[47] To *be* (not *have*) a living נפש (Gen 2:7), I suggest, is to experience one's own life through the complex interactions of vitality, integrity and vulnerability—with no distinction whatever from the life of the body. Most uses of the term in the Hebrew Bible, and many contexts employing ψυχή in the LXX and in early Christian writings, make sense only within some such framework.

offence. Similarly, κρίμα, κρῖσις extend their semantic range from *judgment or custom* to include *pattern or design*. But these extended meanings occur with neither the frequency, nor the range, nor the consistency of true calques. They seem, again, to be *ad hoc* translation tactics by particular translators. Despite its range across Torah, historical books, and the prophet Ezekiel, the extended meaning *task or responsibility* for φυλακή (corresponding to the Hebrew root שמר) is quite infrequent, and does not require us to hypothesize anything beyond the translators' improvisation.

With a few other words, as with ψυχή, sometimes we have difficulty distinguishing between a mere unparalleled meaning (made clear by the context), a stereotyped and sometimes over-literal rendering of a Hebrew idiom (perhaps unintelligible to the reader), and a mistranslation (unintelligible to the *translator*—cf. the following section). This is true of the varied meanings or explanations I offer for χείρ *hand*, as well as δέξιος κτλ *right (left) > south (north)* as terms for geographical direction. At least it *seems* likely that in "translating" ענה (piel) *subdue* (but also *violate, humiliate*) as κακόω, the intended meaning was something like *mortify* (no //), not *mistreat, damage or embitter* (oneself or one's "soul"—ψυχή again). But it is hard to see what sense a Hellenistic (or modern) reader could make of those verses without reference to the Hebrew. Do we discuss these passages here (inferring a meaning from context) or in the next section (implying that the translator himself failed to comprehend the Semitic text)?

What we clearly can see is that the translators faced severe challenges in rendering a few common Hebrew terms for which no equivalent was possible within the framework of Greek language;[48] ultimately, they resorted to *consistent translation expedients* (calques) that made their way into early Christian literature. However, we noted that our only purely LXX example of a calque is a Hebrew term meaning *pierced* (not bludgeoned, stoned, or trampled—but whether alive or dead, unable to continue fighting) linked with a Greek word that anywhere else means simply *wounded* (by whatever means, but still breathing); the common context of the two terms being battle rather than anything particularly Jewish (in terms either of religion or culture), this one example again points away from rather than toward any hypothesis of "Jewish Greek." Otherwise, this section offers the shortest of the Word Lists, and most of the examples are of an occasional nature. Oddly enough, among the more widely attested is the "translation" of ˚jl with ἐκλείχω; the two share the meaning *lick up*, but the stereotypical translation *consume*, which ranges across several books and genres (Num 22:4; 3 Km 18:38; probably Jdth 7:4 and EpJer 19; taken up in Philo), appears to be based on similarity of *sound*. Finally, as an example of what is *not* stereotypical translation, the common word παρατάσσομαι has an unparalleled meaning in Zech1:6; 8:15— but it relates to a different root from the 80 or so other LXX instances, including Zech 10:5.

VII. Mistranslations

Up to this point we have been pondering classes of word use in which readers of Hellenistic Greek (ancient or modern) would have difficulty understanding what an author or

---

[48] Or, I think, within the much broader framework of Indo-European language and culture. With the Greeks as with the idea of karma, your offence against an *impersonal* moral or spiritual order cannot be forgiven by a divine person; sooner or later, someone (you, your descendants, you yourself in another body) will pay. Nor is an immortal soul (either disembodied or reincarnated) compatible with the Hebrew Bible's monistic perception of the human individual.

translator is saying. In this section we specify nearly four hundred cases of words that show the translators themselves misconstruing the meaning of their sources. In all cases, we can specify the nature of the error—confusion of meanings, of words and vocalization, of homographs, of roots, or even of languages.

As an example of the first type of error (of meanings), עוה can mean *do wrong* either in *qal* or *hiphil*, but in *niphal*, as in Is 21:3, the word means *be distressed*. The translator, choosing ἀδικέω, has misunderstood both the word and its sentence.

For a clear instance of the second type (confusion of words), we can see that the translator of Hos 13:3 has misread the consonants ארבה as if they were pronounced '*arbeh (locust)* rather than '*arubah (smokehole)*. Not only does the context of the sentence confirm that the Masoretic vocalization is correct, but some old manuscripts have the variant reading καπνοδοχή, drawn from Theodotion, showing that some early editor had felt and tried to remedy the difficulty in the LXX. The occurrence of αἰχμάλοτος in Job 41:24 is the result of confusing שיבה *gray hair* (with the initial sound *sin*) with שבה *captivity* (with the sound *shin*[49]). As we shall see again in relation to textual criticism, we must keep in mind that the LXX translators worked from unpointed Semitic texts, just as they and the early copyists wrote the uncial script without word separation, accents, or punctuation. Thus we find ἀποκτενέω in Zeph 1:10 because (with no vowel or dagesh pointing) the definite plural noun הדגים *the fish* looked so much like an indefinite plural passive participle הדגים *those who were killed*.

A truly egregious mistranslation through misvocalization occurs in Ps 89:5 (MT 90:5) involving the *h.l.* ἐξουδένωμα. The consonants וזרמתם are construed not as a second-person verb with object suffix *(you bring them to an end)* but as a noun with possessive suffix, as if pronounced precisely as in Ezk 23:20, with the meaning *their phalluses*. The Greek noun (like the Hebrew verb) being *h.l.*, we cannot draw on other uses to suggest meaning. But the word cannot mean *shame* (*pace* LSJ, followed by LEH), the normal formation for which would be ἐξουδένωσις—a word which we find in Ps 30:19 (as well as six other places in the LXX) with the meaning *scorn, contempt*. The meaning *objects of contempt* (so Pietersma in NETS) better accords with the word's formation and at least recognizes the grammatical plural, but neither reflects the euphemistic usage (cf. μεγαλόσαρκος in Ezk 16:26) nor elucidates the source of the difficulty. The correct rendering of the word (should we ever discover a secular text in which the word occurs) will prove to have been *contemptible things*. In this clause, as the translator "understood" the Hebrew, the "things" (i.e., genitals) are compared or linked in some way to "years" (which is itself a mistranslation confusing the words for *year* and *sleep*). "Their contemptible things are years" may make no sense as an English sentence—but the Greek (and the limping Latin rendering of the Gallican Psalter) say nothing different, and this correctly represents the counsel of despair to which the translator was reduced; he could offer only a literal rendering of individual words because the Hebrew words as he construed them made no connected sense either. But Hellenistic translators (and readers) were much more likely than we to let stand enigmatic (and potentially "oracular") statements whose meaning could await a future unfolding.

---

[49] As is well known to Semitists, the Phoenician sound system and alphabet did not distinguish two distinct sibilants as in many Semitic languages (including Hebrew) and some alphabets (such as Ugaritic and Arabic). The graphic distinction was added to Hebrew writing only with the introduction of pointing.

Perhaps the most common type of mistranslation arises from the confusion of roots. A good example is αἰσχύνομαι in, for instance, 2 Esdr 8:22, which renders the less-common root בוש² meaning *delay* as though it were the more common בוש¹ meaning *be ashamed*, while the same translator has similarly confused the homographic roots גאל¹ *redeem* and גאל² *make impure*, as we can see both with the noun ἀγχιστεία and with the related verb ἀγχιστεύω. Occasionally we do not even need access to the Semitic *Vorlage*; in Sir 25:15 (as most modern versions and commentators recognize) the translator has confused the common ראש *head* with the unusual ראש *venom*.

We also find instances where, apparently not knowing the Hebrew word, the translator has tried to use etymology but derived a "meaning" from an unrelated word or root. Such is the case with ἀγάπησις in Hab 3:4, where *h.l.* חיון *covering* has no relation to חבב *to love*, and ἀπειλή in Zech 9:14, where תימן *south* has nothing to do with אימה *dread*. At times when the translators were baffled by the Hebrew, they even fell back on Aramaic—confusing not just roots but languages. We find clear examples with ἀπόσπασμα and διαγράφω.

For the most part, we are not reviewing mistranslations which resulted in a coherent Greek sentence; to identify most of these would require a systematic comparison of the entire Greek text with its Semitic *Vorlagen*, which is far beyond the scope of this work. Too, my primary purpose here is not to assess instances where words had, for the translator, their usual common Greek meanings. As we have argued above, as long as the context of the meaning *unicorn* for μονόκερως results in a clear and ordinary Greek sentence, then lexically there is nothing more to say.

But when a literal translation of the Greek results in something like, "He has built up his sanctuary like a unicorn" (Ps 77:69), we may well suspect that something has gone awry—and it has, for the translator has confused רמים *lofty* with ראם *wild ox* (or, typically in the LXX, *unicorn*). In these cases (as with the transliterations that carried no discernible meaning for the translator) we typically should not offer a definition or translation equivalent at all; κεφαλή never means *poison* and ἀκρίς never means *chimney*. With stereotyped translations, the translator basically understood the Hebrew and the reader can often make sense of the Greek result—even if that result is a kind of malapropism where context forces us to infer a meaning that might otherwise never occur to us. But with these mistranslations, the Hebrew was misconstrued, and the Greek words and/or sentences are usually baffling as a text and fundamentally meaningless as an interpretation of the sources.[50] Naturally, readers must still have *sought* meaning, just as modern English readers have striven to "interpret" texts in the Authorized Version that we now know bear no relation to any meaning of their Hebrew (or Greek) source.[51] Our task, however, is to explain to the modern reader how this word came to be here—not to infer a meaning from a translator's mistake.

It is interesting to note that in at least one case, καθηλόω, LSJ is correct in method—noting the confusion of roots and the resulting mistranslation. And we cited ἀναγνώστης

---

[50] Paradoxically, by the principle of *lectio difficilior*, these misconstruals can provide very valuable textual evidence, showing that the translator was looking at the same unusual or enigmatic text that we confront today. But lexically they evidence nothing beyond a baffled mind.

[51] In my first pastorate, I tried (unsuccessfully) to explain to a parishioner that since Psalm 69:1 (AV) misconstrued the Hebrew, it *presents no meaning* of water in relation to one's "soul" and thus cannot be a typological reference to Christian baptism. The AV in this case of course corresponds to the LXX.

earlier, with respect to unparalleled meanings, as another example of correct method in LSJ. Surely we are entitled to wonder why these correct methods of assessment were not much more widely employed.

VIII. Textual Variants

In no way do I intend the present work as a review of the LXX's textual issues or even as a sampling of text-critical observations. I have, however, noted over two hundred instances where a lexical assessment requires a textual observation. These I have arranged in Word List VIII not in alphabetical word order but by the chapter-and-verse sequence that will, I think, be more useful to the exegete. Especially with very common words, the modern student may otherwise miss a lexical or translation issue and misconstrue an entire verse. A good example is ψυχή in Job 24:7 (a conjecture, certainly correct, in the Gött apparatus); Ra offers no alternative, nor does any manuscript we possess. But the translator clearly must have employed the word ψῦχος, corresponding to Hebrew קרה *cold*—though a very early copyist substituted the more common (and more "religious") word[52] and the corruption became universal. Similarly, in Judg 5:16B the correct reading (missing from the uncials on which Ra relies) must be ἀγελῶν, as HR already knew, and the passage has nothing to do with ἄγγελος, so familiar to any reader of the Greek NT. Users of this lexicon are advised to consult this Word List for any passage to which they turn their attention.

Another good example is Is 17:11. Anyone familiar with the lines along which I have worked could well assume that I might have nothing to say about so common and generally transparent a word as πατήρ. Hardly anyone translating a Greek text would look up the *word* in a lexicon. But as a *sentence* this single verse in Isaiah presents us with three mistranslations, the results of which include a pointless and misleading textual note in BHS.

The majority of these textual observations simply note places where the Ra and Gött texts differ. In a few cases I have asserted that Ra rather than Gött preserves the correct text; with διαξαίνω I believe the decisive points are both sentence context and the reading of the Vulgate. In even fewer cases, neither edition, in my judgment, presents the true reading. In 3 Macc 2:31, I am persuaded that *v.l.* ἐπίβαθρον is correct by the parallel use of the same metaphor in AppolonRhod.

The meaning *embrace* for περιλαμβάνω may be unparalleled (as I have noted), but that must not dissuade us from conjecturing it as the true text (*c*. both Ra and Gött) in La 4:5, especially since the underlying Hebrew חבק permits no alternative. We see how easy the confusion of the aorists (ελαβο-/εβαλο-) could be by looking as well at 2 Esdr 21:1 and Job 22:22. The confusion of ἕτερα and ἑταίρα in Judg 11:2 likewise can be compared to Mt 11:16.

Brevity is a virtue in lexicography, as long as terseness does not become opacity. Yet lest my attempts at economy of expression make me sound dogmatic, I must avow that I am often much less sure of being correct than I am in the examples so far cited, where I really do not see that another conclusion is possible. With ξεστός and ξυστός, on the other hand,

---

[52] It is amusing to note a precisely analogous error in BAGD. In its analysis of πράσσω in 1.b. (dealing with taxes) we find the common and "religious" word "exhort" when clearly what is intended must be "extort." In this case I could prove my conjecture from the underlying German (*erpressen*) and correctly predict that the error would prove to have been corrected in BDAG.

the translators likely were less precise in their idiom (technically, only ξεστός should be used in relation to stone) than modern critics, and the textual variants may well have been felt more as variant spellings.

IX. Words Involving Multiple Factors

If I am far from certain regarding many of the specific lexical and textual assessments proposed in this work, how much more diffident must I be when dealing simultaneously with multiple variables![53]

Sometimes (but not always), the underlying Hebrew text provides an additional variable.[54] So, for instance, we understand the mistranslation θεμελιόω in 2 Esdr 7:9 only when we emend the Hebrew vocalization. Conversely, we can identify the *v.l.* ἐγχειρίζω as the correct reading in Jer 30:10 (Gött 29:17) only when we see how the translator confused two Hebrew roots. In the case of πειροχή in Ob 1:1, I think a meaning equivalent to περιπέτεια (for which LSJ cites only the lexicographer Photius), in the sense of *complete reversal > overturning, upheaval*, connects with the translator's misapprehension of ציר² *messenger* as if it were ציר³ *convulsion, upheaval*.

A number of complications attend the word στήριγμα. In the first place, the translator of 4 Km 25:11 (cf. Jer 52:15//) obviously found אמון *craftsman* in his Hebrew text rather than the Masoretes' המון *army*, though he mistranslated it as if it were related to אמן *be firm, support*, probably influenced by the homograph in the Hebrew underlying 2 Km 20:19. The translator of Ezk 7:11 followed his own precedent from 4:16 and 5:16 to his detriment; the context is obscure, but he would have done better to understand מטה as the usual *staff* rather than *prop*. Ps 71:16 uses στήριγμα for the enigmatic פסת בר, which probably means *abundance of grain*. Does this somehow relate to the bread stacked on a stick or rack we see not only in Ezk but also in Ps 104:16? But for 1 Macc 2:43 (6:18 and 10:23 are completely different), I suggest the possibility (without being able to refer to the Semitic sources) that the translator found המון *army* both in 2 Ki 25:11 (= MT) and in his own *Vorlage*, but appropriated the στήριγμα he found in his copy of 4 Km. Hence 1 Macc 2:42–44 means (with no full stop after 42) that those "mighty" on behalf of Torah were joined by many who were escaping other difficulties, and together they made up a *host/army* (המון) that became (was organized by the Maccabees into) a *military force* (δύναμις, probably rendering חיל). Again, this is not to say that στήριγμα now acquires the meaning *army*, any more than κεφαλή "means" *venom* in Sir. We are simply trying to explain how a Greek word was placed in a context that does not make good sense if we read it as a Greek sentence.

X. Conclusion

Our first—and, I believe, indisputable—conclusion must be that, read straight through, the LXX offers no evidence for any Jewish-Greek dialect in Biblical times. Overwhelmingly,

---

[53] A multiplier effect is working against us here. Suppose I can be 80% confident that I am right about each of four particular factors. As long as they are independent of each other, my chances of being correct about *all four* are only about 40%.

[54] For about thirty places where the lexicon refers to possible variants in the Hebrew, see Word List IX.

the vocabulary is demonstrably normal Hellenistic Greek. Most of those words occurring first or even solely in the LXX are normally formed, clear from the Greek context, and not notably Jewish in cultural or religious terms. As for meanings so far unparalleled from secular sources (which I identify for words constituting less than five percent of the LXX vocabulary), I am predominantly arguing from the silence of LSJ, and I expect that widespread reading, especially of Hellenistic inscriptions and papyri, will considerably reduce my list. Apart from a handful of very common Hebrew terms with no ready equivalent in Greek, the "special cases" generally fall into a few categories of ad hoc translation tactics—transliterating the unknown word, attempting stereotypically to translate from etymology (and not infrequently confusing roots or even languages in the process), or simply rendering a Hebrew phrase word-for-word, whether or not the translator himself is positing a meaningful construction. And even here, such Hebrew idioms as "lifting up the face" migrate (as do the common transliterations and the few true calques) into Byzantine Greek and endure through centuries among Christians who, apart from Scripture and liturgy, are utterly disconnected from Judaism or Hebrew.

The critical implication is that we err whenever we try to infer Hebrew meanings in Greek words apart from their Greek context. That ἄφεσις in many a Greek sentence must have to do with forgiving sins is a literary conclusion forced upon us by the texts themselves. Stereotyped translation is also a workable and sufficient hypothesis for ἀνήρ or ἄνθρωπος rendering Hebrew איש in contexts suggesting the meaning *each*, and any proposal that the idiom was part of a broader spoken dialect is unnecessary and redundant, and is countered by the observation that many contexts (including the Psalter, the longest book in the Hebrew Bible) consistently use the normal Greek ἕκαστος (e.g., Ps 61:13—hence my efforts to observe and cite the range of usage for terms and meanings across the LXX canon).

Yet the importation of "transferred" meanings persists—and not only in LSJ. In 2 Km 11:7, an enquiry about "the peace of the war" is merely odd, and no comment on the semantic range of שלום seems necessary; yet even BDAG proposes "ask after one's *health*" in a comment supposed to relate to εἰρήνη in Lk 14:32 and TestJud 9:7, both of which contexts are unambiguously concerned with cessation of war. Nor, *pace* LEH, do I see anything in the Greek context to turn a *sparrow* (στρουθός, στρουθίον) into an *ostrich* in Lev 11:16 or (with the diminutive!) La 4:3.

I said at the beginning that, as in biology, the test of my "taxonomy" will be its predictive power. I have referred to the Gallican Psalter, the only Latin translation of a complete LXX book for which we possess a complete Hebrew text. As noted, neither the original translator, nor Jerome working without the Hebrew, saw a *wild ox* in μονόκερως or *shame* in ἐξουδενώματα. But it was with the latter—the mistranslation that made no sense in its context—that the translator struggled. The real test of the typology I present, and of the broader theses it supports, should come in two contexts—the study of extra-Biblical Hellenistic Jewish literature and the assessment of the Greek Fathers' comments on specific LXX texts. Certainly the common transliterations, the stereotyped translations that established their extended means in Greek contexts, and even the occasional Hebrew idiom like προσωπολημψία or στόμα μαχαίρης (Lk 21:24, Hb 11:34—neither one a quotation from the OT), will prove comprehensible in both settings. I predict, both for Jewish and Christian readers, that it is the mistakes in translating *phrases and sentences* and the textual corruptions—not the expressions that are clarified by a knowledge of Hebrew—that occasion the bulk of the difficulties, for the elucidation of which this lexicon will prove useful.

In many ways, this lexicon, as Thackeray somewhere says of his own *Grammar,* is the work of a dilettante—that is, it is a labor of love. My sojourns in the strictly academic life now seem brief and long ago. But while I have earned my keep, not in the academy, but in financial services, my interest in understanding the Scriptures is as strong today as ever. For many years I have been reflecting upon and experimenting with the question of what the faithful reading of Scripture *is* in relation to life lived very much "in the world." Both the method and the goal of preparing this lexicon have been the reading of the LXX text itself (alongside the Hebrew Bible, the Greek NT, and not infrequently the Vulgate) with the prayerful attention the Benedictines call *lectio divina*. I have made constant and grateful use of the astonishing resources of biblical and classical scholarship, with an embarrassed and hopeless inability to be in any sense in *command* of those resources. I want simply to apprehend the text, and beyond that to engage the living reality of which the text intends to speak.

Abbreviations

Wherever possible, these abbreviations conform to F. Bauer, F. W. Danker, et al., eds., *Greek-English Lexicon of the New Testament and Other Early Christian Literature* (3rd ed., BDAG, 2000), except that in most cases punctuation has been removed. Abbreviations not listed in BDAG correspond to the *SBL Handbook of Style* wherever possible.

Standard Abbreviations

*	asterisk symbol (see section 3, p. ix)
†	dagger symbol (see App. II, p. 205)
‡	words also treated in BDAG
+	from the time of the indicated writer or version forward
=	having the same meaning (as)
>	leads to, evolves into, becomes
//	parallel in secular Greek literature
abbr	abbreviation
abs	absolute
acc	accusative
act	active
ad loc	*ad locum*, at the place under consideration
add	addenda
adj	adjective
adv	adverb
Akk	Akkadian
al	*alii*, others
alt	alternate(ly)
alw	always
aor	aorist
app	apparatus
appar	apparently
appos	apposition
Aram	Aramaic
archit	architectural
Att	Attic (Greek dialect)
augm	augment(ed)

BCE	before the Common Era (B.C.)
c.	*contra*, against
ca.	*circa*, about, approximately
caus	causative
CE	Common Era (A.D.)
cf.	compare
cj	conjecture
class	classical
cogn	cognate
coll	collective(ly)
comp	comparative(ly)
concr	concrete(ly)
confl	conflation
contr	contracted for, contraction
corr	corrected form
corresp	corresponds to, corresponding to
corrup	corruption, corrupted form
dat	dative
dbl	double
demonstr	demonstrative
dep	deponent
deriv	derivative(s)
dim	diminutive
dir	direct
dub	dubious (lexically or textually)
ed(d)	editor, edition(s)
e.g.	*exempli gratia*, for example
elat	elative
Engl	English
esp	especially
et al	*et alii*, and others
etc	*et cetera*, and the rest
euphem	euphemism, euphemistic
f(f)	and the following verse(s)
f.l(l).	*falsa lectio*, false reading(s)
fem	feminine
fig	figurative
fr	from
fut	future
g	grams
gen	genitive
Gk	Greek
h.l.	*hapax legomenon, -a*, word(s) occurring only once in LXX
Heb	Hebrew
hiph	hiphil (Heb stem)
hit	hitpael or hitpolel (Heb stems)
hoph	hophal (Heb stem)

i.e.	*id est,* that is
impers	impersonal
impf	imperfect
impr	improper
impv	imperative
indecl	indeclinable
indic	indicative
inf	infinitive
ins	inscriptions
interrog	interrogative
intr	intransitive
irreg	irregular
itac	itacism
κτλ	καὶ τὰ λοῖπα, and the rest
l	liter(s)
Lat	Latin
lexicog	lexicographers
lit	literally, literature
m	meter(s)
masc	masculine
metaph	metaphoric
mid	middle
missp	misspelling
mistrans	mistranslation
mistranslit	mistransliteration
ms(s)	manuscript(s)
mus	musical
n.	note, footnote
N DEI	*nomen dei,* name of a god
N GENT	*nomen gentis,* name of people
N LOC	*nomen loci,* name of a place
N PERS	*nomen personae,* name of a person
N PROP	*nomen proprius,* proper name
neg	negative
neut	neuter
niph	niphal (Heb stem)
no //	no parallel in secular Greek
obj	object
oft	often
opp	opposite (of)
opt	optative
orig	original(ly)
p(p).	page(s)
pace	in respectful disagreement with
pap	papyri
pass	passive
pejor	pejorative(ly)

perh	perhaps
pers	person
Pers	Persian
pf	perfect
piel	(Heb stem)
pilpel	(Heb stem)
pl	plural
plpf	pluperfect
prec	preceding
prep	preposition(al)
pres	present
prob	probable, probably
prol	prologue
pron	pronoun
prop	proper(ly)
ptc	participle
q.l.	*quod lege,* which read (indicating a textual correction in a current edition)
q.v.	*quod vide,* which see
qal	(Heb stem)
qual	quality, qualitative
rd	read
RECTE	rightly, correctly (indicating a textual correction)
redupl	reduplication
reflex	reflexive
rel	related
Schol	Scholia (ancient commentaries)
SCIL	*scilicet,* one may understand
Sem	Semitic
seq	*sequens,* following
sg	singular
sim	similar
spat	spatial(ly)
specif	specific(ally)
spur	spurious
s.t.	stereotypical translation
subj	subject, subjunctive
subst	substantive
superl	superlative
superscr	superscript
suppl	supplement, supplied
t.t.	*terminus technicus,* technical term
temp	temporal
trag	tragedians
trans	transitive
transl	translate(s), translation
translit	transliteration

txt	text
Ugar	Ugaritic
unaugm	unaugmented
unexpl	unexplained
usu	usually
var	variant, variation
vb	verb
VEL SIM	*vel simile*, similarly
VL (VVLL)	*varia(e) lectio(nes)*, variant reading(s)
voc	vocative
vs	verse
w.	with
x	indicates the number of occurrences of a Greek word in the LXX

Biblical, Apocryphal, and Pseudepigraphal Books

Ac	Acts
Am	Amos
Bar	Baruch
Bel	Bel and the Dragon
Ch, 1–2	1–2 Chronicles (1,2 Paralipomena)
Da	Daniel
Dt	Deuteronomy
Eccl	Ecclesiastes
EpJer	Epistle of Jeremiah
Esdr, 1	1 Esdras
Esdr, 2	2 Esdras (= Ezra + Nehemiah)
Esth	Esther
Ex	Exodus
Ezk	Ezekiel
Gen	Genesis
Hab	Habakkuk
Hb	Hebrews
Hg	Haggai
Hos	Hosea
Is	Isaiah
Jdth	Judith
Jer	Jeremiah
Job	Job
Joel	Joel
Jon	Jonah
Josh	Joshua
Judg	Judges (Judices)
Km, 1–2	1–2 Kingdoms (1–2 Reges; 1–2 Samuel)
Km, 3–4	3–4 Kingdoms (3–4 Reges; 1–2 Par; 1–2 Kings)

La	Lamentations
Lev	Leviticus
Lk	Luke
Macc, 1–4	1–4 Maccabees
Mal	Malachi
Mi	Micah
Mt	Matthew
Na	Nahum
Num	Numbers
Ob	Obadiah
Odes	Odes (Odai)
OdeSol	Odes of Solomon
Pr	Proverbs
Ps(s)	Psalm(s)
PsSol	Psalms of Solomon
Ro	Romans
Ruth	Ruth
Rv	Revelation
Sir	Sirach (Ecclesiasticus)
SSol	Song of Solomon (Canticles)
Sus	Susanna
Text12Patr	Testaments of the Twelve Patriarchs
TestSol	Testament of Solomon
Tob	Tobit
Wsd	Wisdom of Solomon (Sapientia)
Zech	Zechariah
Zeph	Zephaniah

Bible Codices, Translations, and Editions

A	Codex Alexandrinus (V CE)
A	Rahlfs edition, text family A (in biblical references to Judges)
Aq	Aquila revision of the LXX
AV	Authorized (King James) Version
B	Rahlfs edition, text family B (in biblical references to Judges)
BA	Rahlfs edition, text family BA (in biblical references to Tobit)
BHS	Biblia Hebraica Stuttgartensia, Hebrew Bible
G	Göttingen edition of the LXX (in biblical references)
Gött	Göttingen edition of the LXX
L	Septuagint (LXX) (in biblical references)
Lucian	Lucian revision of the LXX
LXX	Septuagint Greek Version of the Old Testament
MT	Hebrew Masoretic Text
NA	Novum Testamentum Graece, Nestle-Aland, 27th ed.
NETS	New English Translation of the Septuagint

NRSV	New Revised Standard Version
OL	Old Latin Version
R	Rahlfs edition of the LXX (in biblical references)
Ra	Rahlfs edition of the LXX
S	Codex Sinaiticus (IV CE)
S	Rahlfs edition, text family S (in biblical references to Tobit)
Sym	Symmachus revision of the LXX
Theod	Theodotion revision of the LXX
Vulg	Vulgate Latin Version
Θ	Theodotion revision of the LXX (in biblical references)

Ancient Authors and Works

AelAristid	Aelius Aristides (II CE)
Aelian	Claudius Aelianus (III CE)
Nat an	*De Natura Animailum*
Var hist	*Varia Historia*
AeneasTact	Aeneas Tacticus (IV BCE)
Aeschin	Aeschines (IV BCE)
Aeschyl	Aeschylus (V BCE)
Ag	*Agamemnon*
Eum	*The Eumenides*
Sept	*Seven against Thebes*
Suppl	*The Suppliants*
Alcman	Alcman (VII BCE)
AlexAphr	Alexander Aphrodisiensis (c. 200 CE)
AmmoniusGr	Ammonius Grammaticus (=Ammonius Hist.) (I/II CE?)
Anacr	Anacreon (VI BCE)
Andoc	Andocides (V–IV BCE)
AnecdGr	*Anecdota Graeca*
AnthGr	*Anthologia Graeca*
AnthPal	*Anthologia Palatina*
AntiphanesCom	Antiphanes Comicus (IV BCE)
AntiphoOr	Antiphon the Orator (V BCE)
AntiphoSoph	Antiphon the Sophist (V BCE)
AntyllusMed	Antyllus *On Medicine*
ApollonRhod	Apollonius Rhodius (III BCE)
Arat	Aratus (IV–III BCE)
ArchilochusLyr	Archilochus Lyricus (VII BCE)
Aristoph	Aristophanes Comicus (V–IV BCE)
Av	*Aves*
Pax	*Peace*
Thesm	*Thesmophoriazusae*
Aristot	Aristotle
Artem	Artemidorus (II CE)
AsclepiodTact	Asclepiodotus *Tactica* (I BCE)

AthenMech	Athenaeus Mechanicus (I BCE)
Axioch	Axiochus (Pseudo-Platonic dialogue; date uncertain)
Batr	Batrachomyomachia (I CE?)
Bito	Bito Mechanicus (III or II BCE)
Callim	Callimachus (III BCE)
Ep	*Epigrams*
CallixenusHist	Callixenus Historicus (III–II BCE)
CassDio	Cassius Dio (II–III CE)
CatCodAstr	*Catalogus Codicum Astrologorum Graecorum*
Chrysipp	Chrysippus (III BCE)
Clearch	Clearchus (IV–III BCE)
Cl, I	I Clement
Com	Comicorum Atticorum Fragmenta and related comedy fragments
Crates	Crates (poet-philosopher; V BCE)
CratesCom	Crates Comicus (V BCE)
CratinusCom	Cratinus Comicus (V BCE)
CratinusJun	Cratius the Younger (IV BCE)
DemetrPhaler	Demetrius of Phaleron (IV–III BCE)
Democr	Democritus (V/IV BCE)
Demosth	Demosthenes (IV BCE)
Diocles	Diocles of Carystus (IV BCE)
Dinarchus	Dinarchus (IV–III BCE)
DioChrys	Dio Chrysostom (I–II CE)
DiodS	Diodorus Siculus (I BCE)
DiogL	Diogenes Laertius (III CE)
DiogApol	Diogenes of Apollonia (V BCE)
DionysHal	Dionysius of Halicarnassus (I BCE)
DionysThrax	Dionysius Thrax (II BCE)
Diosc	Dioscorides (I CE)
DioscEpig	Dioscorides Epigrammaticus (III BCE)
DiphilusCom	Diphilus Comicus (IV–III BCE)
EphorusCumaeus	Ephorus Cumaeus (IV BCE)
Epicharm	Epicharmus Comicus (V BCE)
Epict	Epictetus (I–II CE)
EpArist	*Epistle of Aristeas* (II BCE)
EtymMag	*Etymologicum Magnum* (XII CE)
EubulCom	Eubulus Comicus (IV BCE)
Eunap	Eunapius (IV–V CE)
Eur	Euripides (V BCE)
Bacch	*Bacchae*
Cycl	*Cyclops*
El	*Electra*
Phoen	*Phoenician Maidens*
Hipp	*Hippolytus*
Ion	*Ion*
EupolisCom	Eupolis Comicus (V BCE)

Eus	Eusebius of Caesarea (IV CE)	
Eustath	Eustathius (XII CE)	
EzkTrag	Ezekiel the Tragedian (II BCE)	
Geopon	Geoponica (X CE)	
Gorgias of Leontini	Gorgias of Leontini (V–IV BCE)	
HecateusMil	Hecateus Milesius (VI–V BCE)	
Hdt	Herodotus (V BCE)	
Heliod	Heliodorus Eroticus (III? CE)	
HermippusCom	Hermippus Comicus (V BCE)	
HermWr	Hermetic Writings	
HeroAlex	Hero(n) of Alexandra (I? BCE/I CE)	
HerodianGramm	Herodianus Grammaticus (II CE)	
Hes	Hesiod (before VI BCE?)	
Hippiatr	*Corpus Hippiatricorum Graecorum* (IX CE)	
Hippocr	Hippocrates, *Corpus Hippocraticum* (V–IV BCE)	
Hipponax	Hipponax (VI BCE)	
Hom	Homer (VIII BCE)	
IL	*Iliad*	
OD	*Odyssey*	
HomHymns	Homeric Hymns (from VII BCE)	
Hyperid	Hyperides	
Iambl	Iamblichus (III–IV CE)	
Isocr	Isocrates (IV BCE)	
Joseph	Josephus (I CE)	
AJ	*Antiquitates judaicae*	
BJ	*Bellum judaicum*	
Lycophron	Lycophron Tragicus (IV–III BCE)	
Manetho	Manetho Apotelesmatidca (IV? CE)	
MAnt	Marcus Aurelius Antoninus (II CE)	
MaximusTyr	Maximus Tyrius (II CE)	
Menand	Menander of Athens Comicus (IV–III BCE)	
MenandRhet	Menander Rhetor (III/IV CE)	
MetrodorusPhilos	Metrodorus Philosophus	
NicophoCom	Nicophon Comicus (IV BCE)	
Orph	*Orphica*	
Ovid		
METAM.	*Metamorphoses*	
Paus	Pausanius (II CE)	
Pherecr	Pherecrates Comicus (V BCE)	
Pherecyd	Pherecydes of Syros (VI BCE)	
PhilemonCom	Philemon Comicus (IV–III BCE)	
PhilippedesCom	Philippedes Comicus (IV–III BCE)	
Philo	Philo (Judaeus) of Alexandria (I BCE–I CE)	
ABR	*De Abrahamo*	
CONGR	*De congressu eruditionis gratia*	

	Decal	De Decalog
	Det	Quod deterius potiori insidari soleat
	Ebr	De ebrietate
	Flacc	In Flaccum
	Her	Quis rerum divinarum heres sit
	Leg	Legum allegoriae (Allegorical Interpretation)
	Legat	Legatio ad Gaium
	Migr	De migratione Abrahami
	Opif	De opificio mundi
	Plant	De plantatione
	Prob	Quod omnis probus liber sit
	Somn	De somniis
	Spec	De specialibus legibus
	Virt	De virtutibus
PhiloMech		Philo Mechanicus (III BCE)
Philod		Philodemus (I BCE)
Philostrat		Flavius Philostratus (II–III CE)
PhilostratJun		Philostratus the Younger (III CE)
PhoenixCol		Phoenix of Colophon (III BCE)
PhrynicusCom		Phrynic(h)us Comicus (V BCE)
Phylarch		Phylarchus (III BCE)
Pind		Pindar (V BCE)
	Nem	Nemean Odes
Pla		Plato
	Apol	Apologia
	Gorg	Gorgias
	Phaedo	Phaedo
	Rep	Republic
PlaCom		Plato Comicus (V–IV BCE)
Plu		Plutarch (I–II CE)
Polyb		Polybius (III–II BCE)
Porph		Porphyry (III CE)
Posidon		Posidonius Apamensis (II–I BCE)
Ps-Callisth		Pseudo-Callisthenes (II–III? CE)
Ps-Pla		Pseudo-Plato
Ptolem		Ptolemaeus
Sappho		Sappho (VII–VI BCE)
SextEmp		Sextus Empiricus (II–III CE)
Simonid		Simonides of Ceos (IV–V BCE)
SopaterCom		Sopater Comicus (IV BCE)
Soph		Sophocles
	Aj	Ajax
	Fr	Fragmentary Plays
	OedCol	Oedipus at Colonus
	OedTyr	Oedipus Tyrannus (= Oedipus Rex)
	Phil	Philoctetes

Stob	Stobaeus (V CE)
Strabo	(I BCE–I CE)
StrattisCom	Strattis Comicus (V? BCE)
Test12Patr	Testaments of the Twelve Patriarchs (II BCE–III CE)
TestJud	Testament of Judah
Theocr	Theocritus Bucolicus (IV–III BCE)
Theognis	(VI BCE)
Theophr	Theophrastus (IV–III BCE)
Theopomp	Theopompus (IV BCE)
TheopompCom	Theopompus Comicus (V BCE)
Thu	Thucydides (V BCE)
Timon	Timon of Phlius (IV–III BCE)
Virg	Virgil
Aen	Aeneid
VettVal	Vettius Valens (II CE)
X	Xenophon (V–IV BCE)
Anab	Anabasis
HG	Historia Graeca
Mem	Memorabilia
Oec	Oeconomicus
ZenP	Zenon Papyri (III BCE)

Modern Literature

AB	Anchor Bible (commentary series; now Anchor Yale Bible). New Haven: Yale University Press, 2008–
Dialekt-Inschr	Sammlung der griechischen Dialekt-Inschriften. 4 vols. F. Bechtel, H. Collitz, et al., eds. 4 vols. Göttingen: Vandenhoeck & Ruprecht, 1884–1915
BDAG	Greek-English Lexicon of the New Testament and Other Early Christian Literature. 3d ed. F. Bauer, F. W. Danker, et al., eds. Chicago: University of Chicago Press, 2000
BDF	A Greek Grammar of the New Testament and Other Early Christian Literature. F. Blass, A. Debrunner, and R. Funk, eds. Chicago: University of Chicago Press, 1961
BIOSCS	Bulletin of the International Organization for Septuagint and Cognate Studies
Gött	Septuatinta. Vetus Testamentum Graecum Auctoritale Academiae Scientiarum Gottigensis editum, Göttingen, 1931–, 20 vols.
Holl	A Concise Hebrew and Aramaic Lexicon of the Old Testament: Based upon the Lexical Work of Ludwig Koehler and Walter Baumgartner. W. L. Holladay. Leiden, Brill, 1988
HR	A Concordance to the Septuagint and the Other Greek Versions of the Old Testament (Including the Apocryphal Books). 3 vols. E. Hatch and H. A. Redpath. Supplement by A. Redpath. 2d ed. Grand Rapids, MI: Baker Books, 1998

LEH	*A Greek-English Lexicon of the Septuagint.* Rev. ed. Compiled by J. Lust, E. Eynikel, and K. Hauspie. Rev. ed. Stuttgart: Deutsche Bibelgesellschaft, 2003
LSJ	*A Greek-English Lexicon.* Originally compiled by H. G. Liddell and R. Scott. 2 vols. 1925–1940. Rev. 9th ed., H. S. Jones and R. McKenzie, eds. Oxford: Clarendon, 1996
LSJSup	*A Greek-English Lexicon, Revised Supplement.* P. G. W. Glare and A. A. Thompson, eds. Oxford: Clarendon Press, 1996
M-M	*The Vocabulary of the Greek Testament Illustrated from the Papyri and Other Non-Literary Sources.* J. H. Moulton and G. Milligan, eds. London: Hodder and Stoughton, 1930. Repr. Grand Rapids, MI: Eerdmans, 1985
NewDocs	*New Documents Illustrating Early Christianity.* Edited by G. H. R. Horsley and S. Llewelyn. North Ryde, N.S.W., Australia: Macquarie Unisversity. 1981–89
OTL	Old Testament Library (commentary series; Westminster John Knox)
Ra	*Septuaginta.* Rev. ed. A. Rahlfs and Robert Hanhart, eds. Deutsche Bibelgesellschaftt, 2006
TOTP	*The Old Testament Pseudepigrapha.* J. H. Charlesworth, ed. Garden City, NY: Doubleday, 1983–85
W	Walters, P. (formerly P. Katz) *The Text of the Septuagint: Its Corruptions and Their Emendation.* D. W. Gooding, ed. London: Cambridge University Press, 1973

Lexicon

A

ἅ (Hom+) interjection of alarm: *alas, woe* (translit of אהה *alas*) Judg 6:22; 11:35B.*

αβακ cf. αββους.

αβαρκηνιν translit of הברקנים *thornbushes* (cf. βαρκοννιμ, βαρακηνιμ) Judg 8:7B.*

ἀβασίλευτος, -ον (Thu+) *without a king* Pr 30:27.*

ἄβατος, -η, -ον (27x, Hdt+) **1.** *empty, deserted, waste* Lev 16:22; 3 Macc 3:29; Ps 62:2; Wsd 5:7; Jer 2:6. **2.** *impassable* Am 5:24; *not to be trodden* Esth 8:12x; 3 Macc 5:43. **3.** (neut subst) *waste place, desert* (no //) Ps 106:40; Job 38:27; Wsd 11:2; Jer 30:7; (fig, of people) Bar 2:4.

ἀβατόω (h.l.) (pass) *be laid waste* Jer 30:14.*

αββους translit of הבוץ *white linen* as if N PERS 1 Ch 4:21VL (A, RECTE; cf. MT).*

αβεδηριν mistranslit of הדברים *words* as if part of N LOC 1 Ch 4:22.*

αβιρα translit of הבירה *capitol, acropolis* as if part of N LOC 2 Esdr 11:1.*

ἀβλαβής, -ές (Aeschyl+) **1.** *harmless* Wsd 18:3 (Pla REP 357b). **2.** *unharmed* Wsd 19:6 (Pla REP 342b).*

ἀβοηθησία, -ας, ἡ (h.l.) *helplessness* Sir 51:10.*

ἀβοήθητος, -ον (Theophr, Polyb+) *helpless* 2 Macc 3:28; Ps 87:5; Wsd 12:6.*

ἀβουλεύτως (h.l.) *recklessly* 1 Macc 5:67.*

ἀβουλία, -ας, ἡ (Aeschyl+) *thoughtlessness, recklessness* Pr 14:17; Bar 3:28.*

ἄβρα, -ας, ἡ (15x, Menand+) *lady in waiting, servant* Gen 24:61; Esth 2:9; Jdth 8:10.

ἀβροχία, -ας, ἡ (Menand+) *drought* Sir 35:24; Jer 14:1; 17:8.*‡

ἄβρωτος, -ον (Aristot+) *inedible*; (subst) Pr 24:22e.*‡

ἄβυσσος, -ον (46x, Aeschyl+) *bottomless* Dt 33:13; (subst) *bottomless source* Dt 8:7; Ps 77:15; (specif) *the sea* (no //; s.t. of תהום (*primal deep, sea*) Ps 32:7; Pr 3:20; Job 41:23; Sir 43:23; Am 7:4; Is 44:27; Ezk 26:19; *(cosmic) deeps, the abyss* (= BDAG) Gen 1:2; Ps 35:7; Job 38:30; Sir 1:3; Da 3:55.‡

αγαθ translit of חתת *be broken* as if N LOC Jer 31:1VL.*

ἀγαθόω (LXX+) *benefit, do good to* (τινί) 1 Km 25:31; (τινά) Sir 49:9; Jer 39:41; 51:27.*

ἀγαθύνω (23x, LXX+) **1.** *treat well* (τινί) Judg 17:13B; Ps 48:19; (τινά) 3 Km 1:47; Ps 50:20. **2.** *do well* 4 Km 10:30; Ps 35:4; (pass) *seem good* 2 Esdr 7:18; 1 Macc 1:12. **3.** *adorn, make attractive* 4 Km 9:30; (pass) Eccl 7:3. **4.** *cheer, encourage* Judg 16:25; (pass) *be cheered* Judg 16:25; Eccl 11:9; *be encouraged* Da 6:24Θ.

ἀγαθῶς (Aristot+) *well, suitably* 1 Km 20:7; Tob 13:11BA; *thoroughly* (no //) 4 Km 11:18.*

ἀγαλλίαμα, -ατος, τό (23x, LXX) *gladness* Esth 4:17k; Is 16:10; Bar 4:34; (pejor, of self-indulgent celebration) Is 22:13; usually of religious joy Ps 31:7; Sir 30:22; cf. Jdth 12:14 (ironic); > *joyful worship* Tob 13:13; Is 35:10.

ἄγαλμα, -ατος, τό (Hom+) *statue (of a god), idol* 2 Macc 2:2; Is 19:3; 21:9; Bar 4:34VL.*

ἄγαν (Hdt+) *very much* 3 Macc 4:11.*

αγανωθ translit of אגנות *bowls* Is 22:24VL.*

ἀγάπησις, -εως, ἡ (11x, Aristot+) *love* Ps 108:5; Pr 30:15; for a friend 2 Km 1:26a; for woman 1:26b; for wisdom Sir 40:20. Of God, for Israel Hos 11:4; of Israel's desire for false gods Jer 2:33. Hab 3:4 mistrans of חביון *covering* as if fr חבב *love*.

ἀγαυρίαμα, -ατος, τό (LXX) *pride, exultation* Job 13:12; Is 62:7; Jer 31:2; Bar 4:34.*

ἀγαυριάομαι (lexicog) *be insolent, strut* Job 3:14.*

ἀγείοχα   2 pf of ἄγω (pap, ins since II BCE; cf. ἀγήοχα).

ἀγελαῖος, -ον   (Hom+) *belonging to the herd;* > (of people) *vulgar, rabble* 2 Macc 14:23.*

ἀγέλη, -ης, ἡ   **2.** *flock* (fig, metaph) *company, assembly* 4 Macc 5:4; (fig, metonymy) *shepherds* (piping) Judg 5:16B (c. Ra; cf. HR, W).‡

ἀγεληδόν   (Hom+) *in droves or crowds* 2 Macc 3:18; 14:14.*

ἀγερωχία, -ας, ἡ   (Polyb+) *youthful impetuosity,* expressed as *arrogance* 2 Macc 9:7; 3 Macc 2:3; as *revelry* Wsd 2:9.*

ἀγέρωχος, -ον   (Hom+) *impetuous, arrogant* 3 Macc 1:25.*

ἀγήοχα   2 pf of BDAG: ἄγω, cf. ἀγείοχα.

ἁγίασμα   **2.** *holy object* Ex 28:36 = Sir 45:12; (as offering) Ezk 20:40; *Judah* (as a people) Ps 113:2. **3.** *holiness* (abstract quality) Ps 131:18.‡

ἁγιαστήριον, -ου, τό   (LXX) *sanctuary, holy place* Lev 12:4; Ps 72:17; 73:7; 82:13.*

ἁγιαστία, -ας, ἡ   (h.l.; W, p 38 ἁγιστεία [Isocr, Pla+], RECTE) *holiness, ritual service* 4 Macc 7:9.*

ἀγκαλίς, -ίδος, ὁ   (Hom+) *arm* Job 24:19.*

ἀγκύλη, -ης, ἡ   (11x, Eur+) *loop* (on tabernacle curtain) Ex 26:4; *hook* (for curtain, no //) 37:15; 38:18.

ἀγκών   **1.a.** *elbow* (Hom+) 4 Macc 10:6; Job 31:22; Sir 41:20. **b.** *wrist* (no //) Ezk 13:18. **2.** (bent) *arm* (of chair) 2 Ch 9:18.*‡

ἀγκωνίσκος, -ου, ὁ   (LXX+) *hook or angle* Ex 26:17.*

ἁγνιασμός, -οῦ, ὁ   (spur) *purification* Num 8:7VL.*

ἅγνισμα, -ατος, τό   (Aeschyl+) *purification* Num 19:9.*

ἀγνοέω   **5.** *be unknown* (act, no //) Wsd 5:12; (ptc subst) 19:14.‡

ἅγνος, -ου, ὁ   (Pla+) *purity tree* (Heb ערבה *willow* or *poplar*) Lev 23:40; Job 40:22.*

ἄγονος, -ον   (Hom+) *sterile, childless* Ex 23:26; Dt 7:14; Job 30:3*

ἀγορανομία, -ας, ἡ   (Aristot+) *regulation of the market* 2 Macc 3:4.*

ἀγορασμός, -οῦ, ὁ   (7x, ins) **1.** *merchandise* Gen 42:19; 2 Esdr 20:32; Pr 23:20. **2.** (act of) *purchase or sale* Sir 27:2; 2 Macc 8:11.

ἀγοραστής, -οῦ, ὁ   (X+) *buyer* Tob 1:13BA.*

αγουρ   (not in HR) translit of עגור *thrush* Jer 8:7G.*

ἀγριαίνω   (Pla+) *become wild or furious* Da 11:11Θ.*

ἀγριομυρίκη, -ης, ἡ   (h.l.) *wild tamarisk* Jer 17:6.*

ἄγριος   **2.b.** (of diseased sores) *malignant* (cf. M-M) Lev 21:20; Dt 28:27.‡

ἄγροικος, -ον   (Aristoph+) *rude, rustic* Gen 16:12; 25:27; 2 Macc 14:30.*

ἀγρός   **4.** *land, territory, nation* (no //) Judg 5:4; Ruth 1:1; 1 Km 6:1.‡

ἄγρωστις, -ιδος, ἡ   (Hom+) *wild grass* Dt 32:2; Hos 10:4; Mi 5:6; Is 9:17; 37:27.*

ἀγυιά, -ᾶς, ἡ   (Hom+) *street* 3 Macc 1:20; 4:3.*

ἀγύναιος, -ον   (LXX+) *unmarried;* (subst) *unmarried person* Job 24:21VL (q.l.; so BSA, MT אלמנה *widow*).*

ἀγχιστεία, -ας, ἡ   (Aristoph+) *responsibility or right of next of kin* Ruth 4:6–8. 2 Esdr 23:29 mistrans of גאל² *make impure* as if גאל¹ *redeem.*

ἀγχιστεύς, -έως, ὁ   (8x, Hdt+) *near-kinsman* with responsibilities and rights of vengeance and inheritance Ruth 3:9; 2 Km 14:11.

ἀγχιστευτής, -οῦ, ὁ   (h.l.) *near-kinsman* Ruth 4:1.*

ἀγχιστεύω   (32x, Eur+) *exercise rights and responsibilities of near-kinsman* Num 5:8; Ruth 2:20; e.g., *inherit property* Num 36:8; *redeem land* Lev 25:25; *avenge* Num 35:12; Josh 20:3; *marry widow of kinsman* Ruth 3:13. 2 Esdr 2:62; 17:64 mistrans of גאל² *make impure* as if גאל¹ *redeem.*

ἄγχω   (Hom+) *squeeze, grip* Ps 31:9; *strangle, throttle* 4 Macc 9:17; 10:7; 11:11.*

ἄγω   **6.** *complete, accomplish* 4 Km 19:25; 1 Ch 29:19; (pass) 1 Esdr 9:17.‡

ἀγωγή   **2.** *policy, program* 2 Macc 6:8; *treatment* (of traitors) 3 Macc 4:10.‡

ἀγωγός, -όν   (Hdt+) *leading, guiding;* (subst) *channel, conductor* Sir 48:17VL.*

ἀγωνιστής, -οῦ, ὁ (Hdt+) *competitor, champion* 4 Macc 12:14.*

ἀδαμάντινος, -η, -ον (Pind, Aeschyl, Pla+) *of steel* Am 7:7; (fig) 4 Macc 16:13.*

ἀδάμας, -αντος, ὁ (Hes+) *steel* Am 7:7f.*

ἀδάμαστος, -ον (Hom+) *unbroken, untamed* Sir 30:8; (fig, of suffering) *unrelenting* 4 Macc 15:13.*

ἄδεια, -ας, ἡ (Hdt+) **1.** *amnesty* (from God) Wsd 12:11. **2.** *license, permission* 2 Macc 11:30 (αδια [VL] spur, itac); 3 Macc 7:12.*

ἄδειπνος, -ον (X+) *without eating* Da 6:19Θ.*

ἀδελφιδός, -οῦ, ὁ (34x, LXX) *lover, companion* SSol 1:13ff; 2:3ff.

ἀδελφιδοῦς, -οῦ, ὁ (Hdt+) *nephew* Gen 14:14VL, 16VL.*

ἀδελφικῶς (adj Aristot+) *like brothers, in brotherly fashion* 4 Macc 13:9.*

ἀδελφοκτόνος, -ον (Hdt+) *fratricidal* Wsd 10:3.*

ἀδελφοπρεπῶς (h.l.) *in brotherly fashion* 4 Macc 10:12.*

ἀδιάκριτος **3.** *mixed, unsorted* Pr 25:1.*‡

ἀδιάλυτος, -ον (Pla+) *non-raveling* Ex 36:30.*

ἀδιάπτωτος, -ον (Hippocr+) *unfailing, faultless* Wsd 3:15.*

ἀδιάστρεπτος, -ον (adv Hippocr) *not to be turned, headstrong* Sir 26:10VL.*

ἀδιάστροφος, -ον (Aristot+) *straightforward, undeterred* 3 Macc 3:3.*

ἀδιάτρεπτος, -ον (LXX+) *undeterred, shameless* Sir 26:10; 42:11; (adv) 26:10VL.*

ἀδιάφορος, -ον (Aristot+) *without profit or gain* Sir 7:18VL.*

ἀδιεξέταστος, -ον (h.l.) *unweighed;* (fig) *unconsidered* Sir 21:18.*

ἀδικέω Is 21:3 mistrans of עוה *be distressed* as if *do wrong.*‡

ἀδικία **3.** *penalty for guilt* (s.t. of עון [penalty for] *guilt* Ezk 44:10.‡

ἄδικος 4 Km 9:12 mistrans of שקר (*"[that's a] lie"*) as if *wrongful act.*‡

ἀδόκητος, -ον (Pind+) *unexpected* Wsd 18:17.*

ἀδολεσχέω (12x, Pla+) **1.** *babble, prate* Ps 68:13; Sir 7:14. **2.** *meditate* (no //; s.t. of שיח *babble, talk, think*) Gen 24:63; Ps 76:4.

ἀδολεσχία, -ας, ἡ (Aristoph+) **1.** *babbling* 3 Km 18:27; 4 Km 9:11; Ps 118:85. **2.** *speech* 1 Km 1:16; Ps 54:3. **3.** *meditation* (no //; cf. ἀδολεσχέω, s.t. of שיח *concern, thought, conversation, babbling*) 3 Km 18:27.*

ἀδοξέω (Eur+) *be despicable* Is 52:14.*

ἀδοξία, -ας, ἡ (Pla+) *ill repute* Sir 3:11.*

ἀδρανής, -ές (LXX+) *impotent, feeble;* (superl ἀδρανέστατος) *utterly impotent* Wsd 13:19.*‡

ἀδρός, -ά, -όν (8x, Hdt+) *strong;* (subst) *leader, warrior* 2 Km 15:18; Job 29:9; Is 34:7.

ἀδρύνομαι aor ἡδρύνθη (8x, Soph+) **1.** *grow up, grow to maturity* Judg 11:2; Ps 143:12. **2.** *be weaned* (no //) Ex 2:10; 4 Km 4:18. **3.** *aggrandize oneself* (no //) 1 Macc 8:14.

ἀδυναμέω (LXX+) *be incapable* Sir prol 20.*

ἀδυναμία, -ας, ἡ (Hdt+) *helplessness, impotence* 3 Macc 2:13; Am 2:2.*

ἀδυνατέω **1.b.** (trans, no //) *be impossible or too difficult for* (τινά) Da 4:9Θ.‡

ἄδυτος, -ον (Hom+) *not to be entered;* (neut subst) *shrine* 2 Ch 33:14VL.*

ᾄδω fut ᾄσω or ᾄσομαι aor ᾖσα.‡

αδων translit of אדן *lord, ruler* Jer 41:5.*

αδωναι voc αδωναιε (Judg 13:8B; 16:28B) translit of אֲדֹנָי *Lord* (title for God) 1 Km 1:11.*

αδωρηεμ or -ημ or -ην translit of אדיריהם *their nobles* as if N GENT 2 Esdr 13:5.*

ἀειγενής, -ές (not in HR; Hippocr, X+) *eternal, everlasting* Sir 24:18(VL).*

ἀεργός, -όν (Hom+) *not working;* (subst) *idle person* Pr 13:4; 15:19; 19:15.*

ἀέρινος, -η, -ον (Aristot+) *"airy," light blue* Esth 8:15VL.*

Ἀζωτιστί (HR as N PROP, not in LSJ, h.l.) *in the Philistine language* (cf. BDAG: Εβραιστι etc) 2 Esdr 23:24.*

ἀθεῖα, -ας, ἡ (LXX+) *impiety* 1 Macc 16:17VL.*

ἀθεσία, -ας, ἡ (Polyb+) *treachery, faithlessness* 1 Macc 16:17; 2 Macc 15:10; Jer 20:8; Da 9:7Θ.*

ἀθετέω **2.b.** *rebel (against), break faith (with)* 3 Km 12:19 = 2 Ch 10:19; 4 Km 1:1.‡

ἀθέτημα, -ατος, τό (pap) *transgression* (alw as cogn acc; ἀθετεῖν ἀθ. *to commit transgression*) 3 Km 8:50; 2 Ch 36:14; Jer 12:1.*

ἀθέτησις **3.** *rebellion, treachery* 1 Km 24:12.*‡

ἀθεώρητος, -ον (Aristot+) *unseen* Wsd 17:18.*

ἄθλιος, -α, -ον (Aeschyl+) *struggling, miserable* (superl ἀθλιώτατος, of person) 3 Macc 5:37; (of expectation) 5:49.*

ἀθλοθετέω (LXX+) *offer a prize* 4 Macc 17:12.*

ἆθλον, -ου, τό (Hom+) *prize* 4 Macc 9:8; Wsd 4:2.*

ἀθλοφόρος, -ον (Hom+) *bearing away the prize, victorious* 4 Macc 15:29; 18:23.*

αθουκιιν translit of עתיקים *handed down from ancient times* as if part of N LOC 1 Ch 4:22.*

ἄθροισμα, -ατος, τό (Pla+) *gathering, assembly* 1 Macc 3:13.*

ἀθρόος, -α, -ον (Hom+) *gathered together* 3 Macc 5:14.*

ἄθυτος, -ον (Pla+) *not (to be) offered* Lev 19:7.*

ἀθῳόω fut ἀθῳώσω fut pass ἀθῳωθήσῃ pf pass ἠθῴωμαι (17; LXX+) *acquit, declare innocent* 3 Km 2:9; Wsd 1:6; Joel 4:21; ptc, for Heb inf abs, Jer 26:28G; *vindicate* Jer 15:15; *forgive, dismiss as harmless* (obj ἀδικία) Jer 18:23; (pass) *be (declared) guiltless, not subject to penalty* Judg 15:3B; Pr 6:29.

αἰγίδιον, -ου, τό (ins, pap) *small goat* (dim of BDAG: αἴξ) 1 Km 10:3.*

αιδαδ Gött αιδεδ (not in HR) translit of הידד *shout, loud cry* Jer 31:33; 32:30.*

αἰδέομαι **2.** *be ashamed* Jdth 9:3; 4 Macc 12:11.‡

αἰδήμων, -ον (Aristot+) *modest* 2 Macc 15:12; 4 Macc 8:3.*

ἀϊδιότης, -τητος, ἡ (Aristot+) *eternity* Wsd 2:23R (RECTE, cf. Philo ABR 55; not in HR).*

αἰεί cf. BDAG: ἀεί.

αἰθάλη, -ης, ἡ (Hippocr+) *soot* Ex 9:8, 10.*

αἰθής, -ές (CratinusCom) *burning* or αἶθος, -εος, τό (ApollonRhod) *fire, burning* 3Rg1:9VL corrup fr λίθος (VEL SIM; ΛΙΘ. > ΑΙΘ).*

αἰθρίζω (dub; not in LSJ) *clear* (ptc) Ezk 41:12VL.*

αἴθριος, -ον (9x, Hdt+) **1.** *in the open, outdoors* 1 Esdr 9:11; Job 2:9. **2.** (neut subst) *atrium, open court* Ezk 9:3; 40:14.‡

αἰκίζομαι pf pass ptc ᾐκισμένος (8x, Aeschyl+) *torture* 2 Macc 7:1; 3 Macc 5:42; (mid ptc) *torturer* 4 Macc 1:11; (pf pass ptc) *tortured* 3 Macc 5:42; (subst) *victims of torture* 2 Macc 8:28.

αιλ, αιλαμ, αιλαμμειν, αιλαμμω(θ), αιλευ (70x) all except Ezk 40:6 (Heb [3] סף *doorsill, threshold*) are translit of איל *doorpost* or אולם/אילם *vestibule* (alw concerning Jerusalem temple) 3 Km 6:3; 2 Ch 3:4; 59x in Ezk 40 and 41; the terms overlap because αιλαμ is used both for the abs pl of איל (pl w. suffix αιλευ) and the sg of אילם (Ezk 40:49 within the same verse); frequent textual problems in MT partly reflected in Kethib-Qere distinctions. Hence αιλαμμω supports the Kethib sg w. suffix; αιλαμμωθ and -μειν are fem and masc pl, the first relegated to VL in Ezk 40:30; the second unreflected in MT.

αἱμάσσω (Aeschyl+) *draw blood, make bloody* Sir 42:5.*

αἱμοβόρος, -ον (Aristot+) *bloodthirsty* (of pers, no //) 4 Macc 10:17.*

αἱμωδιάω (Aristot+) *become numb or tingly* (of teeth) Jer 38:29f.*

αιν translit of עין *spring, fountain* (as N LOC; so HR, 2 Esdr 12:14) 2 Esdr 22:37.*

αἰνετός, -ή, -όν (12x, Aristot) *praiseworthy* Lev 19:24; 2 Km 14:25; Ps 47:2; Odes 14:35; PsSol 3:1; Da 3:26.

αἰνέω **2.** *approve, be content w.* Ps 55:11; Pr 31:30.‡

αἰνιγματιστής, -ές (h.l.) *speaking of mysteries*; (subst) Num 21:27.*

αἰπόλιον, -ου, τό (Hom+) *herd of goats* Pr 30:31.*

αἰπόλος, -ου, ὁ (Hom+) *goatherd* Am 7:14.*

αἴρεμα, -ατος, τό (dub, not in LSJ) *choice* Sir 35:9VL.*

αἵρεσις **3.** *choice* (ἐξ or καθ᾽ αἵρ. *by choice, at one's own discretion*) Gen 49:5; Lev 22:18; 1 Macc 8:30.‡

αἱρετίζω   1 Km 25:35 renders (uniquely) נשא *lift up* (obj "face," i.e., *show favor*; cf. BDAG: προσωπολημψία); transl *choose as a person* (?) or emend to αἴρω.‡

αἱρετίς, -ίδος, ἡ   (h.l.) *partner, confederate* Wsd 8:4.*

αἱρέω   2 fut ἑλῶ mid ἑλοῦμαι 2 aor εἷλον or ἕλον.‡

αἴρω   3rd pl aor ἥροσαν (usually ἦραν) Josh 3:14. Job 21:3 mistrans of נשא *bear, endure* as if *carry, lift*. 2 Km 24:12 = 1 Ch 21:10 (c. HR, listed under αἱρέω; cf. MT BHS note ad loc). La 3:28 mistrans of נטל qal *impose* as if piel (or Aram; cf. Da 7:4) *lift up*.‡

αἰσθητικός, -ή, -όν   (Pla+) *sensitive, conscious, responsive*. Pr 14:10, 30 καρδία αἰσθ. renders קנאה *jealous,* unexpl.*

αἴσθομαι   alt form of BDAG: αἰσθάνομαι, see CORROLARIUM to SSol 5:2 (end of book).

αἴσχιστος   irreg superl of BDAG: αἰσχρός 3 Macc 3:27.

αἰσχύνη   2.b. ἕως αἰσχύνης *"to the point of shame," for an excessive or inordinate period of time* (Heb, no //) 4 Km 8:11.‡

αἰσχύνω   1.b. *be ashamed before* (τινά) Bar 4:15. Judg 3:25B ἕως ᾐσχύνοντο *"until they were ashamed," excessively* (cf. 4 Km 8:11). Judg 5:28B; 2 Esdr 8:22 mistrans of בוש² *delay* as if בוש¹ *be ashamed.*‡

αἰχμαλωσία   1.b. (Babylonian) *exile* Ps 95:1; (Assyrian) Tob 1:3S. 2.b. *community of exiles* 2 Esdr 5:5; Ps 125:1; Is 1:27; Ezk 1:1; 3:11; *of returned exiles* 1 Esdr 5:67; 6:5ff; *of exiles from another land* (Elam) Jer 25:19; (Egypt) Ezk 29:14.‡

αἰχμάλωσις, -εως, ἡ   (dub, h.l.) *community of exiles* 2 Esdr 5:5VL.*

αἰχμαλωτίς, -ίδος, ἡ   (Soph+) *captive woman* Gen 31:26; Ex 12:29.*

αἰχμάλωτος   Job 41:24 mistrans of שיבה *grayhaired,* > *old person* as if שׁבה *captivity.*‡

ἀκάθεκτος, -ον   (LXX+) *ungovernable* Job 31:11VL.*

ἀκάλυπτος, -ον   (Soph+) *uncovered, without a veil* Tob 2:9BA, EpJer 30; (adv) *without veil or covering* 3 Macc 4:6.*

ἄκαν, -ανος, ὁ   (VL ἡ; h.l.) *thornbush* 4 Km 14:9.*

ἀκάρδιος, -ον   (Theophr) *heartless, mindless* Pr 10:13; Jer 5:21; (subst) *foolish person* Pr 17:16; Sir 6:20.*

ἀκαριαῖος, -ον   (Demosth, Aristot+) *momentary, brief* 2 Macc 6:25.*

ἀκαρπία, -ας, ἡ   (Aeschyl, Aristot+) *barrenness, fruitlessness* Pr 9:12.*

ἀκαταμάχητος, -ον   (LXX+) *unconquerable* Wsd 5:19.*

ἀκαταπάτητος, -ον   (h.l.) *not to be stepped on* Job 20:18VL.*

ἀκατάποτος, -ον   (h.l.) *not to be swallowed* Job 20:18.*

ἀκατασκεύαστος, -ον   (Theophr) *unformed* Gen 1:2.*

ἀκατέργαστος, -ον   (Aristot+) *unfinished, uncultivated*; (neut subst) *incompletion, lack of form or structure* (no //) Ps 138:16.*

ἄκαυστος, -ον   (X+) *unquenchable* (no //) Job 20:26.*

ἀκέραιος, -ον   (Hdt+) *blameless, guileless* Esth 8:12f.*‡

ἀκηδία   2. *exhaustion, weariness, anguish* Ps 118:28; Is 61:3.‡

ἀκηδιάω   (LXX+) 1. *be exhausted* Ps 60:3; 101:1; Sir 22:13. 2. *be in anguish* Ps 142:4; Bar 3:1; Da 7:15L.*

ἀκηλίδωτος, -ον   (LXX+) *spotless* Wsd 4:9; 7:26.*

ἀκιδωτός, -ή, -όν   (LXX+) *pointed* Pr 25:18.*

ἀκινάκης, -ου, ὁ   (Hdt+) *short sword* (Pers loanword) Jdth 13:6; 16:9.*

ἀκίς, -ίδος, ἡ   (Hippocr, Aristoph+) *needle* Job 16:10.*

ἀκλεής, -ές   (Hom+) *inglorious* 3 Macc 4:12; (adv) 6:34.*

ἀκληρέω   (Polyb+) *be unlucky, have misfortune* 2 Macc 14:8.*

ἄκλητος, -ον   (Aeschyl+) *unsummoned, unbidden* Esth 4:11.*

ἀκμαῖος, -α, -ον   (Aeschyl+) *ripe, vigorous, in full bloom* 3 Macc 4:8; (adv) 6:34VL.*

ἀκμή, -ῆς, ἡ   (Pind, Aeschyl+) *point, edge* 2 Macc 12:22; *culmination* 1:7; *fullest or highest expression* Esth 5:1b, d, 2 Macc 4:13; (of time) *best, most fulfilling* 4 Macc 18:9.*

ἀκοή 2 Km 23:23 mistrans of משמעה *bodyguard ("those always within hearing")* fr שמע *to hear;* cf. πατριά.‡

ἀκοινώνητος, -ον (Eur+) *not shared, incommunicable* Wsd 14:21.*

ἀκολασία, -ας, ἡ (HecataeusMil, Thu+) *intemperance* 4 Macc 13:7.*

ἀκόλαστος, -ον (Hdt+) *undisciplined, licentious* Pr 21:11; (subst) 19:29; *conducive to licentiousness* (of wine, no //) 20:1.*

ἀκολουθία, -ας, ἡ (Soph, Pla+) *consequence* (moral, no //) 4 Macc 1:21.*

ἀκονάω aor ἠκόνησα pf pass ptc ἠκονημένος (Aristoph+) *sharpen* Ps 44:6; 51:4; 63:4; 119:4; 139:4; Pr 5:4.*

ἀκοντίζω (Hom+) *hurl, shoot* 1 Km 20:20ff.*‡

ἀκοντιστής, -οῦ, ὁ (Hom+: *javelin thrower*) *archer* (no //) 1 Km 31:3.*

ἀκοπιά(σ)τως (Aristot+: *unwearying*) *without labor* (no //) Wsd 16:20.*

ἄκοσμος, -ον (Hom+) *disordered, inappropriate* Pr 25:26; (adv) *in disorderly fashion* 2 Macc 9:1.*

ἀκουσιάζομαι (h.l.) *sin inadvertently or through ignorance* Num 15:28.*

ἀκούσιος, -ον (20x, Hdt+) *constrained, involuntary;* (subst, masc or neut) *involuntary or inadvertent offense* Num 15:25f; 4 Macc 8:25; Eccl 10:5; (adv) *inadvertently, involuntarily* Lev 4:2ff; Josh 20:3; Job 31:33.

ἀκουστής, -οῦ, ὁ (Menand) *auditor, hearer* Wsd 1:6.*

ἀκούω 8. almost as pass of λέγω *be spoken of (as), be reputed* (Hom, Hdt+); καλῶς ἀκούων *"being well spoken of, being of good repute"* 2 Macc 14:37.‡

ἄκρα see ἄκρος

ἀκριβάζω (LXX+) *thoroughly know or investigate;* (pass) *be truly known or tested* Sir 46:15.*

ἀκριβασμός, -οῦ, ὁ (LXX) **1.** *testing, examination* Judg 5:15A (perhaps reading חקר *search* for MT חקק; cf. BHS note ad loc, ἐξικνέομαι). **2.** (s.t. based on Judg 5:15A?) *precise limit* Pr 8:29VL, *precise requirement* 3 Km 11:34VL.*

ἀκρίς Hos 13:3 mistrans of אֲרֻבָּה *smoke hole, chimney* (cf. VL καπνοδοχη) as if אַרְבֶּה *locust.*‡

ἄκριτος, -ον (Hom+) *unjudged, without trial;* (adv) *unjustly* 1 Macc 2:37; 15:33.*

ἀκρόαμα, -ατος, τό (X+) *performance, recital* Sir 32:4.*

ἀκροάομαι aor inf ἀκρόασαι (Aristoph+) *listen intently* Wsd 1:10; Sir 6:35; 14:23; 21:24; Is 21:7.*

ἀκρόασις, -εως, ἡ (Thu+) **1.** *the act of paying attention, listening* Eccl 1:8; Sir 5:11. **2.** *sound, response* 3 Km 18:26; 4 Km 4:31; Is 21:7.*

ἀκρόδρυα, -ων τά (Pla+) *fruit trees* Tob 1:7; 1 Macc 11:34; SSol 4:13, 16; 7:14.*

ἀκρόπολις, -εως, ἡ (Hom+) *citadel, acropolis* 2 Macc 4:12, 28; 5:5.*

ἄκρος, -α, -ον (128x, Hom+) **1.** *uttermost, farthest* 4 Macc 10:7. **2.** (39; fem subst) *citadel* Dt 3:11; 2 Km 5:9; 1 Macc 1:33; Is 22:9. **3.** (84; neut subst, = BDAG) *highest point, tip, extremity* Gen 28:18; Ex 29:20; Judg 1:6, 7; 1 Ch 14:15; 1 Macc 1:3; Ps 18:7; Pr 1:21; Mi 5:3; Is 2:2.‡

ἀκρότομος, -ον (Polyb+) **1.** *sharp-edged* (of flinty rock) Dt 8:15; Josh 5:2f; Ps 135:16; Wsd 11:4; (fem subst, SCIL γή) *flinty ground* Ps 113:8; Job 28:9; Sir 48:17; *precipitous* (of mountain) Job 40:20. **2.** *sawn, rough-quarried* (of building stone) 3 Km 6:7.*

ἀκροφύλαξ, -ακος, ὁ (Polyb, ins) *commander of the citadel;* (pl) *citadel guards* (no //) 4 Macc 3:13.*

ἀκρωτηριάζω (Hdt+) *mutilate, cut off* (members) 2 Macc 7:4; (pass) *suffer dismemberment* 4 Macc 10:20.*

ἀκρωτήριον, -ου, τό (Pind, Hdt+) *projecting part* 1 Km 14:4; *farthest place* Job 37:9; *prominence or eminence* Ezk 25:9, > (pl) *extremities, (bodily) members* Lev 4:11.*

ἀκύμα(ν)τος, -ον (Eur+) *without waves;* (fig) *calm, untroubled* Esth 3:13b.*

ἀκώλυτος, -ον (adv: cf. BDAG) *unhindered* Wsd 7:23.

αλαιμωθ translit of עלמות, unexpl mus term 1 Ch 15:20.*

ἀλάλαγμα, -ατος, τό (Callim+) *shout* Ps 43:13*vl*, PsSol 17:6cj.*

ἀλαλαγμός, -οῦ, ὁ (9x, Hdt+) *shout, loud cry* Josh 6:20; 3 Macc 4:1; Ps 26:6; Jer 20:16; Ps 150:5.

ἀλαλάζω 3. *shout* (in praise or confidence) Josh 6:20; Jdth 14:9; Ps 46:2; 80:2.‡

ἀλάστωρ, -ορος, ὁ (Aeschyl, Soph+) *avenging spirit, scourge;* > *demon, fiend* 2 Macc 7:9; 4 Macc 9:24; 11:23; 18:22.*

ἀλγηδών, -ονις, ἡ (16x, Hdt+) *suffering, pain, anguish* 2 Macc 6:30; 4 Macc 3:18; Ps 37:18.

ἄλγημα, -ατος, τό (Hippocr, Soph+) *pain* Ps 38:3; Eccl 1:18; 2:23.*

ἀλγηρός, -ά, -όν (LXX) *painful* Jer 10:19; 37:12f.*

ἄλγος, -εος, τό (Hom+) *pain, anguish* 2 Macc 3:17; Ps 68:27; Sir 26:6; La 1:12, 18.*

ἄλειμμα, -ατος, τό (Pla, Aristot+) *ointment* Ex 30:31; Is 61:3; Da 10:3Θ.*

ἀλείφω 3. *daub, plaster* (Hom+; Heb טוח *plaster, coat*) Ezk 13:10ff.‡

ἀλεῖται, ἀλοῦνται fut of BDAG: ἅλλομαι.

ἄλεκτος, -ον (not in HR; Pherecr, Polyb+) *not to be told, unspeakable* 3 Macc 4:2G.*

ἀλέω aor impv ἄλεσον (Hom+) *grind, mill* Is 47:2; Job 31:10cj (*RECTE*; Heb מחן *grind, mill*).*

ἀλήθεια 2 Ch 32:1 s.t. of אֱמֶת *faithfulness* as if *truth.*‡

ἀληθεύω 2. *render true, show to be true* Is 44:26.‡

ἄληκτος, -ον (ins+) *unending, unceasing* 3 Macc 4:2R.*

ἀλιαίετος, -ου, ὁ Gött ἀλιάετος (Eur, Aristot+) *osprey* Lev 11:13 = Dt 14:12.*

ἄλιμος, -ον (LXX+) 1. (neut subst) *salty plant, sea orache* Job 30:4. 2. *related to the sea;* (pl subst) *salty places* (no //) Jer 17:6.*

ἀλισγέω aor pass ἠλισγήθην pf pass ptc ἠλισγημένος (LXX) *make impure, pollute* Sir 40:29; Mal 1:7, 12; Da 1:8.*‡

ἁλίσκομαι fut mid ἁλώσομαι aor ἑάλων 3rd sg aor subj ἁλῷ ptc ἁλούς mid inf ἁλῶναι pass ἁλωθήναι pf ἑάλωκεν ptc ἑαλωκῶν (35; Hom+) *be caught, be captured* Ex 22:8; Dt 24:7; Pr 6:2; Sir 9:4; Zech 14:2; Is 8:15; Jer 2:26; Ezk 17:20.

ἀλιτήριος, -ον (Aristoph, Thu+) *guilty, disgraceful;* (subst) *wretch, mean person* 2 Macc 12:23; 13:4; 14:42; 3 Macc 3:16.*

ἀλκή, -ῆς, ἡ (Hom+) *power, force, strength* 2 Macc 12:28R (q.l.); 3 Macc 3:18; 6:12; Sir 29:13*vl* (q.l. // κρατους); Da 11:4L.*

ἄλλαγμα, -ατος, τό (11x, Hippocr+) 1. *thing exchanged* Lev 27:10. 2. *price, exchange, compensation* Dt 23:19; 2 Km 24:24; Ps 43:13; Job 28:17; Am 5:12; Is 43:3. 3. *change, alteration* (no //) Sir 2:4. PsSol 17:6 rd ἀλάλαγμα (mss).

ἀλλάσσω 2 aor pass ἠλλάγην 3. *gain, take in return* Is 40:33. 4. (ptc) ἀλλασσόμενος *change* (of clothes, no //) Judg 14:13B; 4 Km 5:5.‡

ἀλλαχῇ (Aristoph+) *in another direction;* ἄλλος ἀλλαχῇ *now here now there, in several directions* 2 Macc 12:22; Wsd 18:18.*

ἀλλόγλωσσος, -ον (Hdt, ins) *speaking a foreign language* Bar 4:15; Ezk 3:6.*

ἀλλοεθνής, -ές (DiodS+) *foreign* 3 Macc 4:6.*

ἄλλοθεν (Hom+) *from elsewhere* Esth 4:14.*

ἀλλοιόω fut pass ptc ἀλλοιωθησόμενος Ps 108:24 mistrans of כחש *be deprived* as if *be estranged* (*VEL SIM*); (subst of fut pass ptc) *those who will be changed, made different;* mistrans of שושנים, שושן *lilies* as if ששנים (fr שנה *change*) Ps 44:1; 59:1.*‡

ἀλλοίωσις, -εως, ἡ (Pla+) *change, alteration* Sir 37:17; 43:8. Ps 76:11 mistrans of שנות *years* as if fr שנה *change.*

ἄλλοτε (Hom+) *at another time;* εἰ πότε καὶ ἄλλοτε, καὶ νῦν *"if ever, then now"* 2 Macc 13:10.*

ἀλλοτριότης, -ητος, ἡ (Aristot+) *hostility* PsSol 17:13.*

ἀλλοτριόω (Hdt+) *estrange, alienate, make hostile;* (mid) *treat as a stranger, hold oneself aloof* Gen 42:7; (pass) *be treated as a stranger*

1 Esdr 9:4; *treat as an enemy* 1 Macc 6:24; 11:53; 15:27.*

ἀλλοτρίωσις, -εως, ἡ (Thu+) *foreignness* 2 Esdr 23:30; *estrangement* Jer 17:17.*

ἀλλοφυλέω (h.l.) *become foreign, accept foreign customs* 4 Macc 18:5.*

ἀλλοφυλισμός, -οῦ, ὁ (LXX) *adoption of foreign customs, assimilation to foreign ways* 2 Macc 4:13; 6:24.*

ἀλλόφωνος, -ον (h.l.) *speaking a foreign language* Ezk 3:6.*

ἅλμα, -ατος, τό (Hom+) *leap, jump* Job 39:25.*

ἅλμη, -ης, ἡ (Hom+) **1.** *brine, salt water* Sir 39:23. **2.** *saltiness, salty soil* Ps 106:34.*

ἁλμυρίς, -ίδος, ἡ (Hippocr, Aristoph+) *salty soil or land* Job 39:6.*

ἁλμυρός, -ά, -όν (Hom+) *salty* Jer 17:6.*

ἀλογέω (Hom+) *reckon as worthless;* (pass) *be of no account;* (of lives) *become worthless or forfeit* (no //) 2 Macc 12:24.*

ἀλογιστία, -ας, ἡ (Democr, Polyb+) *foolishness, recklessness* 2 Macc 14:8; 3 Macc 5:42.*

ἀλόγιστος, -ον (6x, Thu+) *mindless, unreasonable* 3 Macc 6:12; 4 Macc 3:11; Wsd 12:25; (adv) 4 Macc 6:14.

ἄλογος **3.** *inexpressive, not eloquent* Ex 6:12. **4.** *unsuitable, not to be reckoned or counted* (toward fulfillment of vow) Num 6:12.‡

ἁλοητός, -οῦ, ὁ (pap) *threshing season* Lev 26:5; Am 9:13.*

ἀλοιφή, -ῆς, ἡ (Hom+) **1.** *wiping out, erasure* Ex 17:14; *whitewashing or painting* Mi 7:11. **2.** *paint, whitewash* Job 33:24; Ezk 13:12.*

ἀλοῦνται see ἀλεῖται

ἄλσος, -εως, τό (43x, Hom+) *sacred grove* Ex 34:13; Judg 3:7; Jdth 3:8; Mi 3:12; Jer 4:29. In Gen oft for אשרה *cultic post,* but also (sg) N DEI; 4 Km 21:17; 23:4ff mistrans of N DEI *Asherah.*

ἀλσώδης, -ες (7x, Eur+) *growing in a wood or grove* 4 Km 16:4 = 2 Ch 28:4; Jer 3:6; *in the woods* Ezk 27:6.

ἁλυσιδωτός, -ή, -όν (Polyb+) *chain-fashion;* (subst) *chainwork* Ex 28:22, 29a; specif *chainmail* 1 Km 17:5; 1 Macc 6:35.*

ἄλφιτον, -ου, τό (Hom+) *barley* (grains or meal) Ruth 2:14; 1 Km 25:18; 2 Km 17:28; Jdth 10:5.*

ἀλφός, -οῦ, ὁ (Hes, Hippocr, Pla+) *pallor, leukoderma* (c. LSJ) Lev 13:39.*

ἀλω- see ἁλίσκομαι.

αλωθ translit of אהלות *aloes* (cf. BDAG: ἀλόη) SSol 4:14.*

αλωμων (dub; not in HR or LSJ) 2 Km 6:6vL. unexpl.*

ἅλων, -ωνος, ἡ or ὁ Dt 16:13; Ruth 3:2; cf. 1 Ch 21:21, 28.‡

ἀλώπηξ 3 Km 21:10 mistrans of שְׁעָלִים *handsful,* as if שֻׁעָלִים, *foxes.*‡

αμαδαρωθ see αμμαδαρωθ

ἀμαθία, -ας, ἡ (Heraclitus, Soph+) *ignorance* PsSol 18:4.*

ἀμαρία Dt 23:22R misprint for BDAG: ἁμαρτία.

ἁμαρτάνω **2.** *go awry, go astray* (without moral content, Hom+) Job 5:24. **3.** (caus, no //) *bring guilt upon* (τινά) Lev 4:3.‡

ἁμάρτημα **2.** (s.t. of חטאת *sin, offering for sin*) *offering for sin* (no //; cf. πλημμέλημα) Lev 4:29; Num 18:23.‡

ἁμαρτία **4.** (s.t. of חטאת *sin, offering for sin* or עון *sin, penalty for sin;* cf. πλημμέλημα) *offering for sin* (no //) Ex 29:14 Lev 4:21; Num 18:1; *penalty for sin* (no //) Lev 20:17.‡

αμασενιθ translit of השמנית, unexpl mus t.t. 1 Ch 15:21.*

ἀμάσητος, -ον (LXX+) *unchewed* Job 20:18.*

αματταρι translit of המטרה *the target* 1 Km 20:20.*

ἀμαυρός, -ά, -όν (Hom+) *dim, faint* Lev 13:4ff.*

ἀμαυρόω (Hes, Hdt+) *darken* (of eyes) Dt 34:7; Sir 43:4; *make dim* Wsd 4:12; (pass) *be dimmed, become dim* La 4:1.*

αμαφεθ translit of המפתן *the threshold* 1 Km 5:4.*

ἀμάω fut ἀμήσω, ἀμήσομαι; aor subj ἀμήσῃς (Hom+) *mow, harvest* Lev 25:11; Dt 24:19; Mi 6:15; Is 17:5; 37:30.*‡

ἀμβλάκημα, -ατος, τό (Aeschyl+) *failing, falling short* Da 6:5Θ.*

ἀμβλακία, -ας, ἡ   (Aeschyl+) *failing, falling short* 3 Macc 2:19.*

ἀμβλύνω   aor pass ἠμβλύνθησαν (Aeschyl+) *blunt, make dull;* (pass) *become dull;* (of eyes, no //, but cf. BDAG: ἀμβλυωπέω) *become blind* Gen 27:1.*‡

ἀμβρόσιος, -ον   (Hom+) *belonging to the divine* Wsd 19:21.*

ἀμείδητος, -ον   (h.l.) *unsmiling, grim* Wsd 17:4.*

ἀμειξία, -ας, ἡ   (so Ra; Gött, HR, LSJ ἀμιξία) (Hdt+) *conflict, persecution* (cf. ἐπιμ-) 2 Macc 14:3, 38.*

ἀμέλγω   (Hom+, usu of milk or milking animals) *squeeze out, press out* Pr 30:33; Job 10:10.*

ἄμελξις, -εως, ἡ   (Pind) *milking* Job 20:17.*

ἀμερής, -ές   (Hippocr, Pla+) *indivisible; instant* (of time, no //) 3 Macc 5:25; 6:29.*

ἀμεσσαῖος   (spur, not in LSJ) corrup of ὁ μεσαῖος (q.v.) 1 Km 17:23VL.*

ἀμέτρητος, -ον   (7x, Hom+) *immeasurable* 3 Macc 2:4; Odes 12:6; Sir 16:17; Is 22:18; Bar 3:25.*

ἄμηνις, gen -ιος   (not in HR; Joseph *AJ* 19.272) as adj, *not angry or vengeful* Sir 19:17VL.*

ἀμητός, οῦ, ὁ   or ἄμητος, -ου (Hom+) *harvest; grain to be harvested* (ἀμητός 12x) Dt 16:9; Ruth 2:21; 4 Macc 2:9; Pr 6:11a; Is 17:5; Jer 28:33G (W); *time of harvest* (ἄμητος 11x) Gen 45:6; 4 Km 19:29; Pr 6:8; Mi 7:1; Is 9:2; Jer 28:33R (RECTE).

ἀμήχανος, -ον   (Hom+) *impossible* 2 Macc 3:12.*

ἀμίνον   Esth 8:12c VL. itac misspelling of BDAG: ἀμείνον.

ἀμιξία   see ἀμειξία.

ἀμισθί   (adv of ἀμισθός, ArchilochusLyr, Eur+) *without wage or reward* Job 24:6.*

αμ(μ)αδαρωθ   translit of מִדַּהֲרוֹת *from galloping* Judg 5:22A.*

αμμαζειβη, αμμασβη   translit of הַמִּזְבֵּחַ *the altar* 4 Km 12:10VVLL*

ἀμμώδης, -ες   (Hippocr, Aristot+) *sandy* Sir 25:20.*

ἀμνάς, -άδος, ἡ   (24x, LXX) *lamb* Gen 21:28ff; Lev 5:6; Josh 24:32; Job 42:11.‡

ἀμνημονέω   (Aeschyl+) *be unmindful* Sir 37:6.*

ἀμνησία, -ας, ἡ   (LXX+) *unmindfulness, forgetfulness* Sir 11:25.*

ἀμνησικακία, -ας, ἡ   (h.l.) *not vengeful, not recalling injury* 3 Macc 3:21.*

ἀμνήστευτος, -ον   (Eur) *unbetrothed, uncourted* Ex 22:15.*

ἀμνηστία, -ας, ἡ   (Heraclitus, Pla+) *forgetfulness, neglect* Wsd 14:26; 19:4.*

ἀμοιρέω   (not in HR, Philod+) *have no share* (of τινός), *lack* Sir 3:25G.*

ἄμοιρος, -ον   (Aeschyl, Pla+) *left out of, deprived of* (τινός) Wsd 2:9.*

ἀμόλυντος, -ον   (LXX+) *undefiled* Wsd 7:22.*

ἀμόρα, -ης, ἡ   (not in HR; Philetus [III BCE], as cited in Athen) *sweet cake* SSol 2:5.*

ἀμορίτης, -ες   (h.l.) *sweetened* 1 Ch 16:3.*

ἄμορφος   2. *unshaped, formless* Wsd 11:17.*‡

ἀμπλάκημα   (or -κία) VVLL of ἀμβλ-.

ἀμύγδαλον, -ου, τό   (Hippocr, Aristot+) *almond tree* Eccl 12:5.*

ἀμύθητος, -ον   (Demosth+) *untold, unnumbered, unspeakably great* 2 Macc 3:6; 12:16; Job 8:7; 36:28; 41:22.*

ἄμυνα, -ας, ἡ   (TheopompCom [V BCE]) *defense, protection* (from τινός) Wsd 5:17.*

ἀμύνομαι   1.b. (trans) *avenge oneself against* (τινά) 2 Macc 10:17.‡

ἀμφιάζω   (mid) *be clothed (in), wear* Job 29:14 (act *clothe,* = BDAG, 31:19).*‡

ἀμφίασις, -εως, ἡ   (LXX) *garment, covering* Job 22:6; 24:7; 38:9.*

ἀμφιβολεύς, -έως, ὁ   (h.l.) *net caster, fisherman* Is 19:8.*

ἀμφιέννυμι   2. (mid) *be clothed (in), wear* Job 40:10. 4 Km 17:9 mistrans of אפא *attribute* (words to God, h.l.) as if חפה *veil, cover.*‡

ἀμφιλαφής, -ές   (Hdt+) *wide-spreading, full-branched* Wsd 17:17.*

ἀμφίταπος, -ου, ὁ   (pap+) *double-sided rug* 2 Km 17:28; Pr 7:16.*

ἀμφοτεροδέξιος, -ον   (LXX+) *ambidextrous* Judg 3:15; 20:16.*

ἀμφότεροι 1.b. (neut as adv) *in two respects, on both accounts* Wsd 14:30.‡

ἀνά 1.b.β. ἀνὰ μέσον . . . καὶ ἀνὰ μ. *between . . . and (between)*, repeated (no //) as in Hebrew Gen 1:4; Judg 1:5; Ezk 34:20 (but cf. 17), etc; three times 4 Km 11:17.‡

ἀναβαθμίς, -ίδος, ἡ (h.l.) *step* Ex 20:26.*

ἀναβάλλω 2. *lay, place, toss* 4 Macc 9:12; Tob 6:4BA. 3. (mid/pass) *be clothed, clothe oneself* 1 Km 28:14; Ps 103:2. Ps 77:21; 88:39 mistrans of עבר² *be angry* as if עבר¹ *let go by*.‡

ἀνάβασις, -εως, ἡ (42x, Hdt+) *ascent, upward way* Num 34:4; Josh 10:10; Jdth 4:7; 1 Macc 3:16; Hos 2:17; Is 15:5; (fig) Ps 83:6; Sir 25:20. Ezk 47:12 mistrans of עָלֶה *leaf, foliage* as if עָלָה *go up*.

ἀναβαστάζω (LXX+) *pick up* Judg 16:3.*

ἀναβιβάζω Att fut -βιβῶ 2. *cause to go up, send up* Ex 32:6; (fig) *send up as an offering, offer* (sacrifice, no //; Polyb *present* [on stage], *offer* [a drama]) Josh 22:23.‡

ἀναβίωσις, -εως, ἡ (LXX+) *coming back to life, renewed life* 2 Macc 7:9.*

ἀναβλαστάνω (Hdt+) *spring up* Job 5:6; 8:19.*

ἀναβολή 2. *mantle, cloak* 2 Esdr 15:13; Ezk 5:3. 1 Ch 19:4 renders מפשעה *hip, buttock*, perh (euphem?) *mound*.‡

ἀναβράσσω (Aristoph+) *heave up* (trans) Wsd 10:19; *cast* (stick, for divination) Ezk 21:26; (intr) *heave, surge* Na 3:2.*

ἀνάγλυφος, -ον (Ps-Callisth) *carved in relief* 1 Km 6:18.*

ἀναγνεία, -ας, ἡ (h.l.) *impurity, impiety* 2 Macc 4:13.*

ἀναγνώστης, -ου, ὁ (ins+) *trained reader,* > *scholar* (no //) 1 Esdr 8:8ff; 9:39ff.*

ἀναγορεύω (Aristot, Polyb+) *proclaim publicly* Esth 8:12l.*

ἀνάγωγος, -ον (Timon, DiodS+) *crude, proud;* (neut comp as adv) *insolently* 2 Macc 12:14.*

ἀναδενδράς, -άδις, ἡ (Demosth+) *vine growing up a tree* Ps 79:11; Ezk 17:6.*

ἀναδέω (Hdt+) *bind up;* (mid: specif of hair, Pind Νεμ 11.28) *bind or plait in a knot* Jdth 16:8vl.*

ἀναδίδωμι 1.b. *distribute, circulate* 2 Macc 13:15. 2. (intr) *burst forth* (Hdt 7.26.3) Sir 1:23.‡

ἀνάδυσις, -εως, ἡ (Pla+) *arising* Wsd 19:7.*

ἀναδύω (Hom+) *go, withdraw* 3 Macc 2:24vl.*

ἀναζεύγνυμι impf ἀνεζεύγνυσα aor ἀνέζευξα (17; Hdt+) *break camp, prepare to march* Ex 14:15; 40:36f; *march out* 1 Esdr 2:25; 8:60; Jdth 7:1; 1 Macc 11:22; 2 Macc 5:11.

ἀναζυγή, -ῆς, ἡ (Polyb 3.44.13) 1. *breaking camp, marching out* Ex 40:38. 2. *retreat, homeward march* 2 Macc 9:2; 13:26.*

ἀναθεματίζω pf pass ptc ἀνατεθεματισμένος 2. *put under sacral ban, destroy, obliterate* Num 21:2; Dt 20:17; Josh 6:21; 1 Ch 4:41; Da 11:44Θ; subj pagan king 4 Km 19:11.‡

ἀνακαίω (Hom+) *kindle, light* Jdth 7:5; 1 Macc 12:28; Sir 9:8; Hos 7:6; Ezk 5:2; 24:10.*

ἀνακαλέω (7x, Aeschyl, Hdt+) *summon, call up* Ex 31:2; Lev 1:1; Josh 4:4; 4 Macc 14:17.

ἀνακηρύσσω (Hdt+) *proclaim, extol* 4 Macc 17:23.*

ἀνακλάω pres pass ptc ἀνακλώμενος (Hippocr, Eur+) *bend back* 4 Macc 11:10.*

ἀνάκλισις, -εως, ἡ (Hippocr, Aristot+) *couch, seat* SSol 1:12.*

ἀνάκλιτον, -ου, τό (Hippocr+) *back* (of a couch or seat) SSol 3:10.*

ἀνακομίζω (Hdt+) *carry up;* (mid trans) *recover, take back* 2 Macc 2:22; 12:39; (pass intr) *come back* 3 Macc 1:1.*

ἀνακρούω (Hdt+) *strike up;* (mid, of music [Theocr 4.31 ἀγκρούομαι, =]) *play* (an instrument) or *sing* Judg 5:11; 2 Km 6:14, 16; 1 Ch 25:3, 5; Ezk 23:42.*

ἀναλαμβάνω 6. *take up again,* (intr) *resume* (cf. 13:30) Num 14:1; Da 3:51L. 7. *lift up, raise* (wings, no //) Ezk 10:19.*‡

ἀναλάμπω (X+) 1. *flame up* Wsd 3:7; Am 5:6. 2. *shine out* 2 Macc 1:22; Job 11:15; Is 42:4.*

ἀνάλγητος, -ον (Soph+) *without pain;* (subst) *comfortable person* Pr 14:23.*

ἀναλέγω (Hom, Hdt+) *gather, pick up; recover, return* (τι) 1 Km 20:38; *note, seize upon* (λόγον) 3 Km 21:33; (mid) *recover* (from disease) 3 Macc 2:24.*

ἀνάλημμα, -ατος, τό (Hippocr, ins+) *enclosing or retaining wall* 2 Ch 32:5; Sir 50:2.*

ἀναλημπτέον (Pla+) *it must be taken up* (i.e., confiscated, no // [but ἀναλαμβάνω (ins, pap) can mean *confiscate*]) 2 Macc 3:13.*

ἀναλημπτήρ, -ῆρος, ὁ (VL. -τωρ; dub, not in LSJ; Joseph AJ 8.88; //) *ladle* 2 Ch 4:16.*

ἀναλόγως (Hippocr, Pla+) *proportionally, by analogy* Wsd 13:5.*

ἀναλύω **1.b.** (fig) *undo, nullify, cancel* (commands) 3 Macc 5:40.‡

ἀνάλωσις, -εως, ἡ (Hippocr, Thu+) *consumption* Dt 28:20; Ezk 15:4, 6; > *destruction* 16:20.*

ἀναμ(ε)ίγνυμι pf pass inf ἀναμεμ(ε)ῖχθαι, ptc ἀναμεμειγμένος (7x, Hom, Hdt+) *mix* Esth 3:13d; Ezk 22:18; 46:14; Da 2:41, 43.*

ἀνάμειξις, -εως, ἡ (Theophr+: -μιξ-) *intermixing, interbreeding* PsSol 2:13.*

ἀναμιμνήσκω **2.** *call to mind,* > *make evident* (no //) Num 5:15. 2 Km 20:24; 4 Km 18:18 pres ptc s.t. of מזכיר *secretary, chronicler* fr זכר hiph *to remind* (cf. ὑπομιμ-).‡

ἀναμοχλεύω (Eur+) *pry loose, dislocate* 4 Macc 10:5.*

ἀναμφισβητήτως (AntiphoOr, Pla; adj Thu+) *without controversy or dispute* 1 Esdr 6:29.*

ἄνανδρος, -ον (Hdt+) *unmanly, cowardly, weak* 4 Macc 5:31; 6:21; 8:16.*

ἀνανεάζω (Aristoph+) *become young again* 4 Macc 7:13.*

ἀνάνευσις, -εως, ἡ (LXX+) *refusal* (lit *turning the head,* fr ἀνανεύω [c. LSJ], cf. Vulg RESPECTUS, *looking back or away*) Ps 72:4.*

ἀνανεύω (Hom+) *refuse* Ex 22:16; 2 Esdr 19:17; *disclaim* Num 30:6ff; Odes 12:11.*

ἀναντλέω (pap, Strabo+) *draw up, draw off;* (fig) *bring upon oneself* Pr 9:12. Job 19:26 (DionysHal etc, see BDAG) appar *endure* (as quoted freely in I Cl 26.3), so Gött, but Ra emends to ἀνέτλην, q.v.*‡

ἀναξηραίνω (Hom+) *dry up* (τι) Sir 14:9; 43:3; Hos 13:15; Jer 27:27.*

ἄναξις, -εως, ἡ (h.l.) *elevation, restoration* PsSol 18:6.*

ἀνάπαλιν (Hippocr, Pla+) *in reverse or contrary fashion* Wsd 19:21.*

ἀνάπαυλα, -ης, ἡ (not in HR; Soph, Thu+) *rest, relief* 2 Macc 4:6VL.*

ἀνάπαυμα, -ατος, τό (Hes+) *repose* Job 3:23; Is 28:12.*

ἀναπείρω (Hom, Hdt+) *pierce through, impale* 2 Macc 12:22.*

ἀναπετάννυμι pf pass ptc ἀναπεπταμένος (Hom, Hdt+) *spread out* Job 39:26; ptc subst *wide-open place* 2 Esdr 14:7VL.*‡

ἀναπηδύω (Theophr, Plu: -πιδύω, =) *well up* Pr 18:4.*

ἀναπλήρωσις, -εως, ἡ (Aristot+) *fulfillment, completion* 1 Esdr 1:54; Da 9:2L; 12:13.*

ἀναπνέω aor inf ἀναπνεῦσαι (Hom+) *draw breath, recover breath* Job 9:18.*‡

ἀναπνοή, -ῆς, ἡ (Pind+) *breath, respiration* Is 2:21VL.

ἀναποδίζω (Hdt+) *step back, pull back* 2 Macc 14:44; *move back, make a retrograde motion* (astronomical t.t.) Sir 48:23.*

ἀναποδισμός, -οῦ, ὁ (LXX+) *recovery, return* Wsd 2:5.*

ἀναποιέω (24x, Hippocr+) *mix, prepare* Lev 7:10; Num 7:13ff; Is 30:24 (renders בליל, not חמיץ [c. HR]).

ἀναπτερόω (Hdt+) *stir up, excite* (cf. Eng *ruffle one's feathers*) Pr 7:11; SSol 6:5; Sir 34:1.*

ἀναπτέρωσις, -εως, ἡ (h.l.) *agitation, disturbance* PsSol 4:12.*

ἀναπτύσσω **2.** *open up, unfold* (garment) Judg 8:25. Ezk 40:16 mistrans of מכוסות *covering* (?), *paneling* (?); 40:21 of מזוזות *doorposts,* both unexpl.‡

ἀναρπάζω (Hom, Hdt+) *ravage, carry off* Judg 9:25A.*‡

ἀναρρήγνυμι (Hom+) *tear open* 4 Km 8:12; 15:16; *tear apart* 2:24.*

ἀνασεσωμένοι Jer 51:14VL Ra not in Gött txt or app; mere error.

ἀνασκάπτω   pf pass ptc ἀνεσκαμμένη (Theophr+) *dig up* Ps 7:16; 79:17.*‡

ἀναστέλλω   aor pass ἀνεστάλη (Thu+) *push up, push back;* (pass) *be pushed up or convulsed* Na 1:5; *be put off or prevented* 1 Macc 7:24.*

ἀνάστημα, -ατος, τό   (Theophr+) *height;* **1.** *majesty, honor* Jdth 9:10 (-στεμα) 12:8. **2.** *structure, construction* Gen 7:23; 1 Km 10:5; Zech 9:8. Zeph 2:14 unexpl.*

ἀναστρατοπεδεύω   (Polyb+) *march off, move one's camp* 2 Macc 3:35.*

ἀναστρέφω   **1.b.** *turn away* (trans) Jdth 1:11; but 1:13 *overthrow*.‡

ἀνασύρω   (Hdt+) *expose* (by lifting one's garment) Is 47:2.*

ἀνασχίζω   (Hdt+) *rip open* Tob 6:4S, 5S; Am 1:13.*

ἀνασῴζω   **2.** (pass) *rescue oneself, escape* Gen 14:13.‡

ἀνατείνω   (Pind, Hdt+) *stretch out or up* 2 Macc 15:21; *lift up* (eyes) 4 Macc 6:6, 26.*

ἀνατέλλω   **2.b.** *grow* (of hair, Aeschyl Sept 535) 2 Km 10:5 = 1 Ch 19:5; Ezk 16:7.‡

ἀνατέμνω   (Hdt+) *cut open* Tob 6:4BA.*

ἀνατίθημι   **3.** *present* (as an offering; cf. BDAG: ἀνάθεμα, -θημα) Lev 27:28; 1 Km 31:10; Jdth 16:19; 2 Macc 5:16; Mi 4:13.‡

ἀνατίκτω   (Aelian) *bear again* 4 Macc 16:13.*

ἀνατιναγμός, -οῦ, ὁ   (h.l.) *violent shaking* Na 2:11.*

ἀνατλάω (ἀνατλέω)   see ἀνέτλην.

ἀνατλῶν   see ἀνέτλην.

ἀνατολή   Ezk 16:7 mistrans of צמח *sprout, shoot* as if (collective) *new growth*.‡

ἀνατρέπω   aor pass subj ἀνατραπῇ Eccl 12:6 corresp to MT רתק niph *be removed or destroyed;* qal רתק *be bound or fettered;* cj נתק niph *be snapped or severed* (cf. Judg 16:9; Is 5:27).‡

ἀνατρέχω   **2.** *jump up and run (up)* 2 Macc 14:43.‡

ἀνατροπή, -ῆς, ἡ   (Aeschyl+) *overturning; undoing* 3 Macc 4:5; *outpouring* Hab 2:15.*

ἀνατροφή, -ῆς, ἡ   (LXX+) *nurture, upbringing* 4 Macc 16:8.*

ἀνατυπόω   (LXX+) *form an image* Wsd 14:17.*

ἀναφαίνω   (pas) SSol 6:5 renders גלש *snip* (?), *come down* (?), unexpl. Cf. ἀποκαλύπτω.‡

ἀναφαιρέω   (dub; not in LSJ) *take away, remove* (?) 2 Km 4:7vl.*

ἀναφάλαντος, -ον   (pap) *w. receding hairline, w. bare forehead* Lev 13:41.*

ἀναφαλάντωμα, -ατος, τό   (LXX) *baldness of the forehead* Lev 13:42f.*

ἀναφθη-   see BDAG: ἀνάπτω.

ἀναφορά, -ῆς, ἡ   (Eur, Aristot+) **1.** *sacrificial offering* Ps 50:21. **2.** *particular burden, responsibility for carrying* (no //) Num 4:19.*

ἀναφορεύς, -έως, ὁ   (18x, LXX) *carrying pole* Ex 25:13ff; Num 4:6ff; 1 Ch 15:15; 2 Ch 5:8f.

ἀναφράσσω   (LXX+) *rebarricade, block up* 2 Esdr 14:1.*

ἀναφυράω   (Hippocr, Theophr+) *mix well* Num 15:6vl., 9vl.*

ἀναφύω   aor pass ἀνεφύην (Hdt+) *grow up* (act) Is 34:13; (mid/pass) *grow up* Gen 41:6, 23; Da 7:8L; 8:9L; *be produced* 1 Km 5:6; *grow again* Ezk 37:8vl.*

ἀναχαίνω   aor ptc ἀναχανών (Hippocr, Aristot+) *open the mouth wide* 2 Macc 6:18.*

ἀναχέω   (not in HR) see ἀνέχυσε.

ἀναψυχή, -ῆς, ἡ   (Eur, Pla+) *relief, refreshment* Ps 65:12; Hos 12:9; Jer 30:26.*

ἀνδραγαθέω   (Polyb+) *act heroically* 1 Macc 5:61, 67; 16:23; 2 Macc 2:21.*

ἀνδραγάθησις, -εως, ἡ   (spur; h.l.) = seq; 1 Macc 5:56vl.*

ἀνδραγαθία, -ας, ἡ   (8x, Hdt+) *heroism* Esth 10:2; 2 Macc 14:18; (pl) *heroic acts* 1 Macc 5:56.

ἀνδράποδον, -ου, τό   (Hdt+) *captive, slave* 3 Macc 7:5.*

ἀνδρεία, -ας, ἡ   (14x, Hdt+) *manliness, heroism, self sufficiency* 1 Macc 9:10; 4 Macc 1:4; Ps 67:7; Pr 21:30; EpJer 58.

ἀνδρειόω   (LXX+) *give manly or heroic strength* 4 Macc 15:23.*

ἀνδριοῦμαι   fut of BDAG: ἀνδρίζομαι Jer 2:25.‡

ἀνδρογύναιος, -ον   (h.l.) *androgynous;* (subst) *effeminate man* Pr 19:15.*

ἀνδρόγυνος, -ου, ὁ   (Hdt+) *effeminate man* Pr 18:8.*

ἀνδρολογία, -ας, ἡ   (dub; h.l. Gött κατ' ανδρα λογειαν) *per-man assessment* (?), *census reckoning* (?) 2 Macc 12:43R.*

ἀνδροφονέω   (Hippocr, Strabo+) *commit murder* 4 Macc 9:15.*

ἀνδρόω   (Hdt+) *make into a man;* (pass) *reach manhood* Job 27:14; 33:25.*

ἀνδρωδῶς   (adj since Empedocles [V BCE], X+) *in manly fashion* 1 Macc 6:31; 2 Macc 14:43.*

ἀνεγείρω   (Hom+) *raise up, (re)build* Sir 49:13.*

ἀνείκαστος, -ον   (LXX) *incomparable, immense* 3 Macc 1:28.*

ἀνειλέω   (Thu+) *unroll* Ezk 2:10.*

ἀνειμένος   see ἀνίημι.

ἄνειμι   ptc ἀνιών (Hom, Hdt+) *come up, approach* 4 Macc 4:10.*

ἀνεκλιπής, -ές   (LXX) = BDAG: ἀνέκλειπος *limitless, unfailing* Wsd 7:14; 8:18.*

ἀνελεημόνως   (AntiphoOr) *unmercifully* Job 6:21; 30:21.*

ἀνέλπιστος, -ον   (Heraclitus, Aeschyl+) *without hope* Is 18:2; (adv) *in unhoped-for fashion* Wsd 11:7.*

ἀνεμοφθορία, -ας, ἡ   (ins) *desiccation, blight* (from wind) Dt 28:22; 2 Ch 6:28; Hg 2:17.*

ἀνεμόφθορος, -ον   (LXX+) *wind-blasted, blighted* Gen 41:6ff; Hos 8:7; Is 19:7; (subst) Hos 8:7; (fig, of person) Pr 10:5.*

ἀνενήνοχα   pf of ἀναφέρω.

ἀνεξέλεγκτος, -ον   (Thu+) *impossible to refute or criticize* Pr 10:17; 25:3.*

ἀνεξικακία, -ας, ἡ   (LXX+) *endurance, forbearance* Wsd 2:19.*

ἀνεπίγραφος, -ον   (not in HR; Polyb+) *without title or inscription* Ps 2:1VL., etc.

ἀνεπιεικής, -ές   (Thu+) *unreasonable, inconsiderate* Pr 12:26.*

ἀνεπιστρέπτως   (LXX+) *heedlessly, indifferently* 3 Macc 1:20.*

ἀνεργεία, -ας, ἡ   (Joseph BJ 4.582) *cessation from work* 2 Macc 3:29VL.*

ἀνερευνάω   (Pla+) *search throughout* (mid) 4 Macc 3:13.*

ἄνεσις   2 Ch 23:15 mistrans of ידים *hands* (Heb they laid hands on her/seized her, unexpl).‡

ἀνέστραπται   = ἀνεστράφη.

ἀνέτλην   ptc ἀνατλῶν (aor without pres; Hom+, not in HR) *endure* Job 19:26R (Gött ἀναντλέω).

ἀνετράπην   2 aor pass of ἀνατρέπω.

ἀνέφικτος, -ον   (LXX+) *unapproachable* 3 Macc 2:15.*

ἀνέχυσε   f.l. (X for Λ) perh felt as related to ἀναχέω/-χύνω *spread out* (but act aor in -χυ- would have no //) 2 Macc 12:7VL.*

ἀνέχω   4. *restrain, hold back* 4 Macc 1:35; Am 4:7; Hg 1:10; *close off* Sir 48:3; (intr) *hold (oneself) back* Is 64:11; *refrain from* (+ inf) 3 Km 12:24z; PsSol 17:18.‡

ἄνηβος, -ον   (Heraclitus+) *not grown, not mature;* (subst) *youth* 2 Macc 5:13.*

ἀνήκεστος, -ον   (Hom, Hdt+) *fatal, incurable, inescapable* Esth 8:12e; 2 Macc 9:5; 3 Macc 3:25.*

ἀνήκοος, -ον   (Pla+) *unhearing,* > *willfully ignorant or disobedient* Num 17:25; Pr 13:1; Job 36:12; Jer 5:23; 6:28.*

ἀνήλατος, -ον   (Anacr, Aristot) *not malleable* Job 41:16.*

ἀνηλεής, -ές   (Menand+) *pitiless* 3 Macc 5:10.*

ἀνηνεγμένος   (better: ἀνενηνεγ-) pf pass ptc of BDAG: ἀναφέρω.

ἀνήνυτος, -ον   (Soph+) *incomplete, unattained* 3 Macc 4:15.*

ἀνήρ   2.b. (s.t., rendering איש *man, person, every*) *each one* (cf. ἄνθρωπος) Judg 2:6B; 1 Km 4:2; 2 Ch 23:7; 1 Macc 2:40; Job 41:9; ανηρ ανηρ *each and every man* Lev 15:2; (gen) Num 5:12. 4 Km 12:10 οἴκῳ ἀνδρός mistrans of בבוא איש *as one would go in* as if בב(י)ת איש *in the house of a man.*‡

ἀνῃρημένος   pf pass ptc of ἀναιρέω; (subst) *the slain* Is 10:4VL.

ἀνθαιρέομαι   (Thu, Eur+) *choose instead, prefer* (τι rather than τινός) Pr 8:10.*

ἀνθέμιον, -ου, τό   (X+) *flower pattern* (esp on Ionic column [ins]); Eccl 12:6 mistrans of גלה *bowl* as if *projection* (on a column).*

ἄνθημα, -ατος, τό (ins) alt spelling of BDAG: ἀνάθεμα *offering* 3 Macc 3:17VL.*
ἀνθῆσαι aor opt of BDAG: ἀνθέω Ps 89:6
ἄνθινος, -η, -ον (Hom+) *like flowers;* (subst) *artificial flower* Ex 28:34.*
ἀνθομολογέομαι 2. *confess, admit* (fault) 1 Esdr 8:88; Sir 20:3.*‡
ἀνθομολόγησις, -εως, ἡ (Polyb+) *praise* (no //) 2 Esdr 3:11; Sir 17:27.*
ἀνθράκινος, -ον (pap) *made of ruby* (no //, but cf. ἄνθραξ) Esth 1:7.*
ἀνθράκιον, -ου, τό (Theophr+) *small ruby or garnet* Esth 1:7VL.*
ἄνθραξ 2. *garnet* Gen 2:12; Tob 13:17BA, Sir 32:5; Is 54:11; (but 54:16 *coal*); Ezk 10:9.‡
ἄνθρωπος (s.t., rendering אִישׁ *man, person, every*) *each* Lev 13:3 etc; doubled (*each and every one*) Num 9:10; Ezk 14:4; ἄνθρωπος ἀνθρώπῳ *each to the other* Sir 25:3. Jer 48:4 s.t. of אִישׁ *anyone*.‡
ἀνθρωπότης, -ητος, ἡ (Philo [DET 76]+) *humanity* 4 Macc 13:19VL.*
ἀνθυφαιρέω (ins, pap+) *reduce or take away in compensation* Lev 27:18.*
ἀνιερόω (Aristot+) *dedicate; commemorate* (days of thanksgiving) 3 Macc 7:20; (pass) *be offered as a sacrifice* 1 Esdr 9:4.*
ἀνίημι fut ἀνήσω impf mid ἀνίεντο 1 aor ἀνῆκε 2 aor subj ἀνῇ, ἀνῶμεν, impv ἄνες, pass ἀνέθη, pf pass ἀνεῖται, ptc ἀνειμένος (41; Hom+) 1. *leave alone* Ex 23:11; 1 Km 11:3; *let go free* Ps 38:14; Mal 3:20; *spare, pass by* (pers or place) Gen 18:24; 4 Macc 12:12; Odes 12:13; Is 2:9; *overlook, forgive* (sins) Josh 24:19; Is 1:14. 2. *abandon, forsake* Dt 31:6; 1 Ch 28:20; Is 2:6; *neglect* 1 Km 12:23; (pass) *be neglected* Sir 30:8. 3. *slacken, let go limp* Judg 8:3; (trans, obj "hand") 2 Km 24:16 = 1 Ch 21:15; Sir 33:26; Is 25:11; *give up on, lose concern about* 1 Km 9:5; (mid) *relax, be generous* (opp ἐπιτείνω) Wsd 16:24; *cease, be quiet* 1 Km 15:16; 2 Esdr 20:32; Is 62:1; *give up* Is 42:2.‡
ἀνίκητος, -ον (Hes, Soph+) *invincible* 2 Macc 11:13; 3 Macc 4:21; 6:13; 4 Macc 9:18; 11:21, 27.*

ἀνίσχυς, -υ (SEG 35[1985] 216.18) *weak, without strength* Is 40:30.*
ἀνιών see ἄνειμι.
ἄνοδος, -ου, ἡ (not in HR; Hdt, Pla+) *way up, journey inland* 3 Macc 7:10VL.*
ἀνοέω (dub; not in LSJ) *act foolishly or wantonly* Da 12:10ΘVL.*
ἄνοιγμα, -ατος, τό (ins+) *opening, doorway* 3 Km 14:6(VL).*
ἀνοίκητος, -ον (Hdt+) *uninhabited* 1 Macc 3:45VL.*
ἄνοικτος, -ον (Eur+) *pitiless* 3 Macc 4:4.*
ἀνοίσω irreg fut of BDAG: ἀναφέρω.
ἀνομβρέω (Philo) *gush,* (trans) *pour out* Sir 18:29; 39:6; 50:27.*
ἀνομέω 2. (trans/caus, no //) *cause to sin, involve in sin* Ezk 22:11.‡
ἀνορύσσω (Hdt+) *dig up* Job 3:21; 39:21.*
ἄνους, -ουν (Hom+) *mindless, silly* 2 Macc 11:13; Ps 48:11; Pr 13:14; Hos 7:11.*
ἀνταγωνιστής, -οῦ, ὁ (Eur+) *antagonist, opponent* 4 Macc 3:5.*
ἀνταίρω (Thu+) *raise* (τι) *against* Mi 4:3.*
ἀντάλλαγμα Ps 88:52 mistrans of עֲקֵבוֹת *footsteps* (sg *heel*) as if עֵקֶב *result, reward*.‡
ἀνταλλάσσω (Aeschyl+) *change* Job 37:4; (mid) *exchange* (τι for τινός) Pr 6:35.*
ἀντάμειψις, -εως, ἡ (h.l.) *repayment, requital* Ps 118:112.*
ἀντανακλάω (LXX+) *reflect, send back;* (pass ptc) *reflected, echoed* Wsd 17:18.*
ἀντανίστημι (Soph+) *rise up instead* (no //) Bar 3:19.*
ἀνταποθνήσκω (AntiphoOr+) *put to death in turn* (as penalty) Ex 22:2.*
ἀνταπόκρισις, -εως, ἡ (LXX+) *reply, response* (no //) Job 13:22; 34:36.*
ἀνταποστέλλω (Polyb+) *send in response* 3 Km 21:10.*
ἀνταποτίνω fut -τείσω (AnthPal) *repay* 1 Km 24:20.*
ἀντερείδω (Hippocr, Pind+) *offer resistance;* (mid) *compete, contend* (with τινί) Wsd 15:9.*
ἀντερῶ fut of BDAG: ἀντιλέγω.
ἀντέχω 3. (intr abs) *hold out, stand firm* Sir 1:23; *stand by* (in support) 2 Esdr 14:10.‡

ἀντηχέω (Hippocr, Eur+) *sound in opposition* Wsd 18:10.*

ἀντί **2.** (w. attraction to the relative) ἀνθ' οὗ Ezk 26:2VL, 28:1VL, 36:2VL (Gött, P967, Ra all have ἀνθ' ὧν); ἀνθ' οὗ ὅσον *because of how* 3 Km 14:15VL. ἀνθ' ὧν *because* (55x, = BDAG) Gen 22:18; Judg 11:36A; Esth 4:17m; Ps 108:16; Pr 1:32; Hos 8:1; Is 3:16; Da 11:30L; *because of which, therefore* (= BDAG) Jdth 9:3; 4 Macc 12:12; 18:3; Wsd 18:3; *just as* 1 Macc 10:27; *corresponding to* (τινός) Ps 89:15; (τί) Wsd 16:20; (contrastive) *although, even though* Josh 24:20; Zech 12:10. ἀνθ' ὧν ὅτι *because* 2 Km 12:6; 4 Km 18:12; 2 Ch 1:22; Ezk 36:34; (contrastive) *even though* Dt 28:62. ἀνθ' ὧν ὅσα *because of* Judg 2:20; *because* 4 Km 10:30.‡

ἀντιβάλλω (Thu, Polyb, NT+) *throw against;* > *collate*, (Strabo 13.1.54) *compare;* (πρὸς εαυτον) *assess for oneself* (no //) 2 Macc 11:13.*‡

ἀντιγράφω (Lysias+) **1.** *write back, write in reply* 1 Esdr 2:19; 1 Macc 12:23. **2.** *copy, transcribe* 1 Macc 8:22.*‡

ἀντιδίδωμι (Hdt+) *give in return* Ezk 27:15; *give instead* Da 1:16L.*

ἀντιδικέω (X+) *challenge, oppose* Judg 6:31A; 12:2A.*

ἀντιδοκέω (dub; *h.l.*) *suppose instead* 2 Macc 9:8VL.*

ἀντιδοξέω (Polyb+) *disagree w., think differently from* Esth 4:17b.*

ἀντίθετος, -ον (Aristoph, Aristot+) *contrary or opposed to* (τινί) Esth 3:13d; (subst) *antithesis, refutation* Job 32:3.*

ἀντικαθίζω (Hdt+) *settle in place of another* (no //) 4 Km 17:26.*

ἀντικαθίστημι **2.** (trans) *put in place instead of, substitute* Josh 5:7.‡

ἀντικαταλλάσσομαι (Isocr, Aristot+) *exchange* 3 Macc 2:32; Sir 46:12.*

ἀντικρίνομαι (LXX+) *answer back, argue* Job 9:32; 11:3.*

ἀντιλαμβάνω **1.** (τινί) 1 Ch 22:17. **5.** (mid) *lay claim to, take hold of* (τινός) 2 Ch 7:22; 1 Macc 2:48.‡

ἀντιλάμπω (Sappho, Aeschyl+) *shine back, light up in turn* 2 Macc 1:32.*

ἀντίλημψις, -εως, ἡ (Thu+) *help; assistance* Sir 11:12; pl (= BDAG) *helpful acts* 2 Macc 8:19; 3 Macc 5:50; *support* 1 Esdr 8:27; *protection* Ps 21:1, 20; PsSol 16title, *defense (legal or military)* 2 Macc 11:26. Ps 107:9 mistrans of מעון *fortress* as if מעין *help* (Heb מעון ראשי means *my chief fortress* or *my highest stronghold*).‡

ἀντιμαρτυρέω (Aristoph+) *testify against* 2 Macc 7:6.*

ἀντίον, -ου, τό (Aristoph+) *beam (of a loom;* cf. μέσακλον) 2 Km 21:19; 1 Ch 11:23; 20:5.*

ἀντίπαλος, -ου, ὁ (Aeschyl, Hdt+) *adversary* 2 Macc 14:17; 3 Macc 1:5.*

ἀντιπαραβάλλω (not in HR; Pla+) *set against for comparison, measure against* (τινί) Sir 23:12.*

ἀντιπαράγω (X+) *march parallel to or along with* (τινί) 1 Macc 13:20.*

ἀντιπαραγωγή, -ῆς, ἡ (Polyb+) *subversion, hostility* Esth 3:13e.*

ἀντιπαρατάσσω (Thu+) *array or take the field against* 1 Esdr 2:21.*

ἀντιπεριβάλλω (Hippocr+) *wrap around;* (pass) *be embraced or entangled in* (τινί) Sir 23:12VL.*

ἀντιπίπτω **2.** *be opposite (of curtain hooks)* Ex 26:5, 17.‡

ἀντιποιέω (Thu+) *do in return;* (pass) *be done in return* Lev 24:19; (mid) *exert oneself, strive for* (τινός) 1 Macc 15:3; *strive with or against* (τινί) Da 4:35Θ.*

ἀντιπολεμέω (Thu+) *fight or war against* Is 41:12.*

ἀντιπολιτεύομαι (Aristot+) *mount political opposition* 4 Macc 4:1.*

ἀντιπράττω (Hdt+) *oppose, act in opposition* (to τινί) 2 Macc 14:29.*

ἀντιπρόσωπος, -ον (X+) *facing toward one another, facing in the direction of* (τινί) Gen 15:10; Ex 26:5; Ezk 42:8; (abs) 1 Ch 19:10; Ezk 42:3; (subst) *mirror image, corresponding order* 2 Km 10:9.*

ἀντίπτωμα, -ατος, τό (LXX+) *occasion or means for stumbling and falling* Sir 31:29; 32:20.*

ἀντίρρησις, -εως, ἡ (Polyb+) *counterstatement, refutation, repudiation* Eccl 8:11.*

ἀντιρρητορεύω (MaximusTyr) *speak in opposition or refutation* 4 Macc 6:1.*

ἀντιστήριγμα, -ατος, τό (Hippocr) *support* Ps 17:19; Ezk 30:6.*

ἀντιστηρίζω (Hippocr+: *press against*) *support, restore to strength* (no //) Ps 36:24; (pass) Is 48:2; 50:10.*

ἀντισχύω (CassDio) *prevail in opposition* Wsd 7:30VL.*

ἀντιτίθημι (Hdt+) *replace, place instead* Lev 14:42; 4 Macc 3:16.*

ἀντιφιλοσοφέω (Lucian) *reason against* (τινί) 4 Macc 8:15.*

ἀντιφωνέω (Aeschyl+) *answer back, respond* (by letter, Polyb+) 1 Macc 12:18.*

ἀντίψυχος, -ον (LXX+) *instead of a life* 4 Macc 6:29; (subst) *payment for a life* 17:21.*‡

ἄντρον, -ου, τό (Hom+: *cave*) *inner room* (no //) 3 Km 16:18.*

ἀντρώδης, -ες (X+) *cavelike* 2 Macc 2:5.*

ἀνυπερθέτως (ins+) *without delay* 3 Macc 5:20, 42.*

ἀνυπόδετος, -ον (Epicharmus, Aristoph, Pla+: -δητος) *unshod, barefoot* 2 Km 15:30; Mi 1:8; Is 20:2ff.*

ἀνυπομόνητος, -ον (Aristot+) *unbearable* Ex 18:18.*

ἀνυπονόητος, -ον (Demosth, Polyb+) *unsuspected* Sir 11:5.*

ἀνυπόστατος, -ον (X+) *irresistible* 2 Macc 1:13; 8:5; Ps 123:5; Odes 12:5.*

ἀνυψόω (29x, LXX+) **1**. *raise up* 1 Km 2:7; *erect* Sir 49:12; (pass) *be raised up* Da 4:22L, *be made proud* 5:2G; *become high, tall* Sir 24:13. **2**. *lift up, exalt* Ps 112:7; Sir 1:19; (obj "voice") 21:20. **3**. *enlarge, make great* Sir 20:28. **4**. *set in place, establish* 2 Esdr 4:12.

ἀνύω (Hom, Hdt+) *accomplish* 4 Macc 9:12.*

ἀνώνυμος, -ον (Hom, Hdt+) *nameless, unspeakable* Wsd 14:27.*

ἀνώτατος, -ον (Hdt+; superl fr ἄνω, cf. BDAG: ἀνώτερος) *highest, farthest* Tob 8:3.*

ἀξία, -ας, ἡ (Hdt+) *merit, worth* Sir 10:28; 38:17.*

ἀξίωμα, -ατος, τό (Soph+) **1**. *suitability, self-evident principle* Ex 21:22. **2**. *worthy quality* 1 Esdr 8:4. **3**. *prestige, noble rank* 2 Macc 4:31. **4**. *request, petition* Esth 5:3ff; 7:2f; Ps 118:170; Da 6:6ffL.*

ἄξων, -ονος, ὁ (Hom+) *axle* Ex 14:25; 4 Macc 9:20; Sir 33:5; *path, course* (no //; Heb *wheel*, > *track*) Pr 2:9, 18; 9:12b (not in MT, but Heb idiom required for parallelism w. ὁδός).*

ἀοίδιμος, -ον (Hom, Hdt+) *to be praised in song* 4 Macc 10:1.*

ἄοκνος, -ον (Hes, Soph+) *unshrinking, resolute* Pr 6:11a.*‡

ἀορασία, -ας, ἡ (Polyb, ins) *blindness* Gen 19:11; Dt 28:28; 4 Km 6:18; 2 Macc 10:30; Wsd 19:17.*

ἀπαγγελία, -ας, ἡ (Thu+) *message, report* Ruth 2:11.*

ἀπαγγέλλω **3**. *interpret, explain* (no //) Gen 41:8.‡

ἀπαγορεύω pf pass ptc ἀηγορευμένος (Hdt+) *forbid* 4 Macc 1:34 (aor supplied by ἀπεῖπον, q.v.; cf. 1:33).*

ἀπαγωγή, -ῆς, ἡ (Hdt, Demosth+) *summary arrest and imprisonment* 1 Esdr 8:24.*

ἀπαδικέω (pap) *wrongfully withhold* Dt 24:14.*

ἀπαιδευσία, -ας, ἡ (Thu+) *ignorance, lack of education or (self)-discipline* Sir 4:25; 21:24; 23:13; Hos 7:16.*

ἀπαίρω aor ἀπῆραν aor ptc ἀπάραντες **2**. *leave, depart* Gen 12:9; Dt 1:7; Josh 3:1; 1 Macc 3:37; Sir 48:18; Ezk 10:4. **3**. *bring out* (wind) Ps 77:26 (no //).‡

ἀπαίτησις, -εως, ἡ (Hdt+) *requesting, demanding* (usu for [re]payment) 2 Esdr 15:10; 20:32; 2 Macc 4:28; Sir 31:31; Zeph 3:5.*

ἀπαλείφω (Demosth+) *expunge, wipe out* Gen 6:7; 4 Km 21:13; 3 Macc 2:19; Is 44:22; Da 9:24; pf pass ptc ἀπηλειμμένων Is 5:17RH (= BHS cj).*

ἀπαλλάσσω pf ἀπήλλαχα **1.c**. *do away with, repudiate* Job 27:5; 34:5; *remove* Jer 39:31.‡

ἀπαλλοτρίωσις, -εως, ἡ (Aristot+) *alienation, estrangement* Jer 13:27; *exclusion* Job 31:3.*

ἀπαλότης, -ητος, ἡ (Hippocr, X+) *softness, tenderness* Dt 28:56; *tender shoot* (no //) Ezk 17:4. 17:9 mistrans of יִנָּתֵק *he shall tear up* as if יִנִּיקָה (17:4) or יוֹנֶקֶת (17:22) *tender shoot.**

ἀπαλύνω (Hippocr, X+) *soften, make soft or smooth* Job 33:25; (pass) *be made soft or gentle* 4 Km 22:19; Ps 54:22.*

ἀπαμαυρόω (ins, Agatharchides [II BCE]) *lose ability* Is 44:18.*

ἀπαμύνω (Hom, Hdt+) *defend against, ward off* 4 Macc 14:19.*

ἀπαναισχυντέω (Pla+) *act shamelessly* Jer 3:3.*

ἀπανίστημι (Hdt+) *leave behind, depart (from, ἀπό)* Wsd 1:5.*

ἀπαντάω 1.b. *confront; face* Judg 8:21A; *oppose* Jer 34:18. 2. *plead with, entreat* Ruth 1:16 (cf. class *appear in court to plead a case*). 2 Macc 7:39 *attack, fall upon* (no //, but cf. 1 Km 22:17f; 2 Km 1:15 s.t. of פגע *attack, fall upon* as if *encounter, meet*).‡

ἀπαντή, -ῆς, ἡ (26x, LXX) *meeting, encounter* Judg 4:22A; 2 Km 10:5; 19:16ff; 3 Km 2:8; 4 Km 4:26.

ἀπάντημα, -ατος, τό (Eur [OR 514]) *encounter, confrontation* 3 Km 5:18; Tob 6:8S; > *opportunity, chance* (no //) Eccl 9:11.*

ἀπάντησις 2. *response* Esth 8:12i.‡

ἀπάνωθεν (LXX) 1. (adv) *from above* Job 31:2. 2. (prep w. gen) *from upon* Judg 16:20B; 2 Km 11:20, 24; 20:21; 3 Km 1:53.*

ἅπαξ 1.b. ἅπαξ καὶ ἅπαξ *"one time and another," from time to time* (no //) Judg 16:20; 1 Km 3:10. 2.b. εἰς ἅπαξ (one word in HR, LSJ; Aeschyl, Hdt+) *all at once* Num 16:21; Josh 10:42; PsSol 2:8; 11:2; Is 66:8; Da 2:35Θ; 3:46G.‡

ἀπαραίτητος, -ον (Thu [adv]; Lysias+) *merciless, inexorable* Wsd 16:4, 16.*

ἀπαραλλάκτως (DiodS+) *unchangeably* Esth 3:13c.*

ἀπαραπόδιστος, -ον (ins+) *unimpeded, unhindered* 3 Macc 6:28.*

ἀπαρασήμαντος, -ον (ins) *unobserved* 2 Macc 15:36.*

ἀπαρέσκω aor ἀπήρεσα (Hom+) *displease* (τινί) Sir 21:15.*

ἄπαρσις, -εως, ἡ (LXX+) *departure* Num 33:2.*

ἀπαρτία, -ας, ἡ (9x, Hipponax+) *property, moveable goods* Ex 40:36; Num 10:12; Jdth 2:17; Ezk 25:4.

ἀπάρχομαι (Hom, Hdt+) *offer in sacrifice* 2 Ch 30:24; 35:7ff; Pr 3:9.*

ἀπατάω 1.b. (act trans) *distract, beguile* Sir 14:16; 30:23. Jer 30:2 (Gött 29:9) mistrans of נוס *flee* as if נשׁא *deceive*.‡

ἀπατηλός, -ή, -όν (Hom+) *beguiling, deceiving* 4 Macc 18:8VL.*‡

ἀπάτησις, -εως, ἡ (LXX+) *beguilement, deception* Jdth 10:4.*

ἀπατητής, -οῦ, ὁ (not in HR, *h.l.*) *deceiver* 4 Macc 18:8VL.*

ἀπαύγασμα (c. BDAG) *reflection* (so NRSV; cf. ἔσοπτρον and εἰκών in // lines) Wsd 7:26.*‡

ἀπαυτομολέω (Thu+) *desert, go away from* (τινός) 4 Macc 12:16; Pr 6:11a.*

ἀπέδρασα fr ἀποτρέχω (1 aor ending).

ἀπειθέω 2. *be unpersuaded, refuse to comply* 4 Km 5:16.‡

ἀπεικάζω (Eur, X+) *make a representation or likeness* Wsd 13:13.*

ἀπείκασμα, -ατος, τό (Pla+) *representation, likeness* Wsd 13:10.*

ἀπειλή Zech 9:14 mistrans of תֵּימָן *south* as if related to אֵימָה *dread* (cf. Pr 20:2).‡

ἄπειμι² ptc ἀπιών (Hom, Hdt+) *leave, go away* Ex 33:8; 2 Macc 12:1; 13:22; 4 Macc 4:8.*‡

ἀπεῖπον (Hom, Hdt+) 1. (act or mid) *renounce, disown* (= BDAG) Job 6:14; 10:3; 19:18; Wsd 11:14; Zech 11:12. 2. (act) *declare forbidden* 3 Km 11:2; (pf pass ptc) *forbidden* 4 Macc 1:33. (Pres supplied by ἀπαγορεύω, q.v.; cf. 1:34).*‡

ἀπειράγαθος, -ον (adv DiodS 15.40.1) *unacquainted w. goodness* Esth 8:12d.*

ἀπείργω (Hom, Hdt+) *debar, demand rejection of* 2 Macc 12:40.*

ἀπεκδίδωμι (ins) *give away in marriage* (no //) Tob 3:8S.

ἀπέκταγκα late (Aristot, Menand+) pf of BDAG: ἀποκτείνω Num 17:6; 1 Km 24:12; ἀπεκταμμένος pf pass ptc 1 Macc 5:51.

ἀπέκτασις, -εως, ἡ (LXX+) *expansion, spreading out* Job 36:29.*
ἀπεκχέω (dub; not in LSJ) *pour out* Jdth 15:4VL.*
ἀπελάσω fut of BDAG: ἀπελαύνω.
ἀπελέγχω (AntiphoOr+) *expose, convict* 2 Macc 4:33; 4 Macc 2:11.*
ἀπελέκητος, -ον (LXX+) *unhewn* 3 Km 6:1a, 36; 7:48f; 10:11f πελ-, q.v.*
ἀπελευθερόω (Pla+) *emancipate, set free* Lev 19:20.*
ἀπεναντίον = BDAG: ἀπέναντι.
ἀπένειμα aor of ἀπονέμω.
ἀπενεόομαι aor pass ἀπηνεώθην (h.l.) *become mute* Da 4:19Θ.*
ἀπενηνεγμένος pf pass ptc of BDAG: ἀποφέρω, *having won or attained* Esth 3:13c.
ἀπένθητος, -ον (Aeschyl, ins) *unmourned, unlamented* 2 Macc 5:10.*
ἀπερείδω aor ἀπηρείσω (9x, X+) **1.** *deposit, place, lay* Judg 6:37A; 3 Km 14:28; 1 Esdr 1:39; Da 1:2L. **2.** *rest, lean* Am 5:19. **3.** *set upon, besiege* (no //) Ezk 24:2.
ἀπερικάθαρτος, -ον (Philo PLANT 113; =) *impure, unable to be purified* Lev 19:23.*
ἀπευθανατίζω (h.l.) *die a good death* 2 Macc 6:28.*
ἀπεχθάνομαι (Hom, Hdt+) *be hateful* 3 Macc 2:30.*
ἀπέχθεια, -ας, ἡ (Aeschyl, X+) *hatred* 3 Macc 4:1.*
ἀπεχθής, -ές (Soph+) *hateful* 2 Macc 5:23; 3 Macc 3:4; (adv) 3 Macc 5:3; Wsd 19:15.*
ἄπεω see ἀπωθέω.
ἀπῆκτο pf pass of ἀπάγω, ptc ἀπηγμένος.
ἀπηλιώτης, -ου, ὁ (Hdt+: *east wind*) *east, eastern direction* (no //) Ex 27:11; Jdth 7:18; 1 Macc 12:37; Jer 32:26; Ezk 21:3, 9.*
ἀπήλλαχα pf of ἀπαλλάσσω 1 Km 14:29.
ἀπήμαντος, -ον (Hom+) **1.** *unharmed* 2 Macc 12:25; 3 Macc 6:6, 8. **2.** *harmless* Wsd 7:22.*
ἀπηνήνατο aor of BDAG: ἀπαναίνομαι Ps 76:3.
ἀπηνής, -ές (Hom+) *rough, wild, hard* Wsd 17:17; (superl) 18.*

ἄπιος, -ου, ἡ (Aristot+) *pear tree* 1 Ch 14:14f.*
Ἄπις, -ιδος, ὁ (Hdt+) *Egyptian bull god* (renders אביר *bull*) Jer 26:15.*
ἄπλαστος, -ον (Aristot+) *unformed, > unaffected, natural, sincere* Gen 25:27.*
ἄπλατος or ἄπλετος, -ον (Hdt+) *immense* 3 Macc 4:11.*
ἀπληστεύομαι (LXX+) *be insatiable* Sir 31:17; 37:29.*
ἀπληστία, -ας, ἡ (Lysias, Pla+) *insatiability* Sir 37:30f.*
ἄπληστος, -ον (Theognis, Hdt+) *insatiable, greedy* Ps 100:5; Pr 27:20; 28:25; Sir 31:20; (comp) Pr 23:3.*
ἁπλοσύνη, -ης, ἡ (h.l.) *soundness, simplicity* Job 21:23.*
ἁπλόω **2.** *make straight* (no //) Job 22:3.‡
ἁπλῶς (Aeschyl+) *simply* 2 Macc 6:6; Wsd 16:27; *straightforwardly* Pr 10:9.*‡
ἄπνους, -ουν (Hippocr [ἄπνοος], Aristot+) *lifeless, without breath* Wsd 15:5.*
ἀπό **2.b.γ.** (ἀφότε) *from the time, when* 2 Esdr 5:12 (cf. 5:16b, ἀπὸ τότε [BDAG: under τότε 1.a.] *since then*). **4.b.** *(extending) from* (cf. mathematicians, of geometric figures) Judg 7:1². **5.f.** also to indicate weight (Polyb) or value (DIALEKT-INSCHR 3707); *of a value of, worth* Esth 1:7.‡
ἀποβαίη f.l. for -βαίνη 2 Macc 9:24VL.*
ἀποβαίνω **2.b.** *prove to be* Job 8:14; 9:20. **c.** *issue or result (from)* 2 Macc 9:24; Job 18:5.‡
ἀποβάπτω (Hdt+) *dip out* (no //) 2 Macc 1:20.*
ἀποβιάζομαι (X+) *repulse, treat w. violence* Pr 22:22; q.l. also (Heb =) 28:24.*
ἀποβλέπω SSol 6:1 mistrans of פנה *turn away* as if *face, concern oneself w.* Mal 3:9 mistrans of ארר *curse* as if ראה *look*.‡
ἀπόβλημα, -ατος, τό (LXX+) *piece of refuse, casting* Wsd 13:12f.*
ἀπογαλακτίζω (8x, LXX+) *wean* Gen 21:8; 1 Km 1:22; Ps 130:2; Hos 1:8; Is 28:9.
ἀπογεύομαι (Hippocr, X+) *taste, take a taste of* (τινός) 4 Macc 4:26; 5:2, 6; 6:15; 10:1.*
ἀπόγονος, -ον (Hdt+) *born from;* (subst) *offspring, descendant* 1 Km 21:11, 22; 1 Ch 20:6; Jdth 5:6; 4 Macc 18:1; Wsd 7:1.*

ἀπογραφή   2. *record, deposition* 2 Macc 2:1; Da 10:21L (practically = *"Scripture"*).‡

ἀποδειροτομέω   (Hom+) *behead* 4 Macc 15:20.*

ἀποδεκατίζω   (h.l.) *set aside the tithe* (w. cogn acc) Tob 1:7S.*

ἀποδεσμεύω   (Hippiatr) *bind* Pr 26:8.*

ἀπόδεσμος, -ου, ὁ   (Aristoph+) *bundle, sachet* SSol 1:13.*

ἀποδέω   aor ἀπέδησα (Pla+) *bind* Josh 9:4; Pr 6:27.*

ἀποδιαστέλλω   (pap) *divide* Josh 1:6; (pf pass ptc) *separated off, classified (as)* 2 Macc 6:5.*

ἀποδίδωμι   Da 8:25L mistrans of שׁבר *break, crush* as if שׁוב *return*.‡

ἀποδιώκω   (Thu+) *chase away, expel* La 3:43.*

ἀπόδομα, -ατος, τό   (LXX) *return, gift in return* Num 8:11ff.*

ἀπόδοσις, -εως, ἡ   (Hdt+) *return, restitution* Dt 24:13; Sir 29:5.*

ἀποδοχεῖον, -ου, τό   (pap+) *cistern, reservoir* Sir 39:17; 50:3; *wine vat* 1:17.*

ἀποδρᾶ   2 aor subj of BDAG: ἀποδιδράσκω Sir 33:33; ἀπόδραθι pass impv Gen 27:43.

ἀποδύρομαι   (Hdt+) *lament, bewail* 3 Macc 4:12.*

ἀποθαυμάζω   (Hom, Hdt+) *be astonished* Sir 11:13; 40:7; Da 4:19L; *wonder at, admire* Sir 47:17.*‡

ἀποθερίζω   (ArchilochusLyr, Eur+) *cut off* Hos 6:5.*

ἀποθήκη   2. *treasure, whatever is stored* (Hdt+) 1 Esdr 1:51.‡

ἀποικεσία, -ας, ἡ   (LXX) *exile, captivity* 4 Km 19:25; 24:15; 25:27; 2 Esdr 6:16ff.*

ἀποικία, -ας, ἡ   (32x, Pind, Hdt+: *colony; colonizing expedition* DiodS 20.41.1) *exile* (no //) Judg 18:30B; 3 Macc 6:10; Jer 13:19; *community of exiles* 2 Esdr 1:11; 2:1; Wsd 12:7; Jer 35:4; (pl) 39:44.

ἀποικίζω   fut ἀποικιῶ aor ἀπῴκισα aor pass ἀπῳκίσθην pf pass ἀπῴκισμαι (33; Aeschyl, Hdt+) *remove to a distant country, banish, exile* 1 Km 4:22; 4 Km 15:29; 1 Ch 9:1; 2 Esdr 2:1; Sir 29:18; Jer 13:19; Bar 1:9; pass ptc (subst) *exile(s)* Jer 24:5.

ἀποικισμός, -οῦ, ὁ   (X+: *settlement of a colony*) *exile* (no //) Jer 26:19; 31:11; 50:11; Bar 2:30, 32.*

ἀποίσω   fut of BDAG: ἀποφέρω Lev 20:19; (mid) 2 Km 13:13; Eccl 10:20.

ἀποίχομαι   aor ἀπῳχοντο (6x, Hom+) *go away, depart* Gen 14:12; Jdth 6:13; Hos 11:2.

ἀποκαθαίρω   aor mid subj ἀποκαθάρωμαι pass ptc ἀποκαθαρθέν (Aristoph+) *clear away, sweep away* Tob 12:9S; Pr 15:27a; Job 7:9; 9:30.*

ἀποκαθαρίζω   fut -ριῶ aor opt -ρίσαι (LXX) *purify, atone for* Tob 12:9BA, Job 25:4.*

ἀποκάθημαι   (8x, Hdt+) only fem ptc ἀποκαθημένη *(woman) sitting aside*, i.e., *menstruating and ritually unclean* (no //) Lev 15:33; Is 30:22; La 1:17; Ezk 22:10.

ἀποκαθίστημι   3. *hand over, give in return* Gen 23:16. 4. *replace, roll back into place* Gen 29:3. 5. *remove, dethrone* (no //; rd ἀφίστημι) 1 Esdr 1:33.‡

ἀποκαίω   (Hom+) *burn off, burn away* 4 Macc 15:20.*

ἀποκακέω   (h.l.) *despair, succumb to misfortune* Jer 15:9.*

ἀποκάλυμα, -ατος, τό   (h.l.) *revelation, thing discovered* Judg 5:2B.*

ἀποκαλύπτω   5. *remove, open up* (no //) Gen 8:13. SSol 4:1 renders גלשׁ *skip* (?), *come down* (?), unexpl; cf. ἀναφαίνω.‡

ἀποκενόω   (Hippocr, Aristot+) *empty out, drain* Judg 3:24B; Sir 13:5, 7.*

ἀποκεντέω   (Hippocr, DiogL) *pierce through, run through* Num 25:8; 1 Km 31:4; Ezk 21:16. Zeph 1:10 mistrans of הַדָּגִים *the fish* as if הֲרֻגִים *those who were killed*.

ἀποκέντησις, -εως, ἡ   (h.l.) *piercing* Hos 9:13.*

ἀποκιδαρόω   (LXX) *remove priest's headdress* Lev 10:6; 21:10.*

ἀποκλαίω   fut ἀποκλαύσομαι (Hdt+) *weep aloud, bewail* (in our lit, only mid) Pr 26:24; Jer 31:32; 38:15.*

ἀπόκλεισμα, -ατος, τό   (h.l.) *guardhouse, gate room* Jer 36:26.*

ἀπόκλειστος, -ον   (h.l.) *closed off.* 3 Km 6:12(vl) mistrans of סגור *gold leaf* as if fr סגר *close.**

ἀποκλείω   Jdth 13:1R (Gött ἀπολύω) read ἀπέκλισεν (w. Aq) fr ἀποκλίνω (cf. 2 Km 6:10); Judg 20:48A also emend to ἀπέκλισεν (ἀποκλίνω) mistrans, of שבה take captive as if שוב turn back (note that 20:48B ἐπιστρέφω makes same error).‡

ἀποκλίνω   (Hom+) turn aside; (trans) send away 2 Km 6:10; (intr) veer off 1 Macc 5:35.*

ἀποκλύζω   (Aristot+) wash off 2 Ch 4:6.*

ἀποκνίζω   fut -νιῶ or -νίσω (Hippocr, Aristoph+) pluck, pluck off Lev 1:15; 5:8; 1 Km 9:24; 4 Km 6:6; 4 Macc 1:29; Ezk 17:4, 22.*

ἀποκοσμέω   (Hom+) clear away, > kill (no //) 2 Macc 4:38.*

ἀπόκρημνος, -ον   (Hdt+) precipitous, steeply inclined 2 Macc 13:5.*

ἀποκρίνω   3. (act) condemn (dub, no //) Sus 50G (Ra cj). Zeph 2:3 mistrans of ענוה humility as if related to ענה answer.‡

ἀποκρυβή, -ῆς, ἡ   (LXX+) concealment Job 24:15.*

ἀποκρυφή, -ῆς, ἡ   (LXX) place of concealment 2 Km 22:12 = Ps 17:12; Jb 22:14.*

ἀπόκρυφος   2. (subst) hiding place Is 4:6.‡

ἀποκωλύω   (11x, Hdt+) withhold, restrain, hinder 1 Km 6:10; 1 Esdr 2:23; Sir 7:33.

ἀποκωφόομαι   (LXX+) be or become deaf Mi 7:16; Ezk 3:26; 24:27.*

ἀπολαύω   (Hdt+) enjoy, derive pleasure from (τινός) 4 Macc 5:9; 8:5; 16:18; Pr 7:18; Wsd 2:6.*

ἀπολέγω   (Hdt+) 1. choose, select out Jdth 10:17vL. 2. reject, refuse Jon 4:8.*

ἀπολείπω   5. fail to accomplish, leave undone (τι) Ex 5:19.‡

ἀπολεπίζω   (LSJ cites only GEOPONICA 10:58) peel away (trans; obj λευκώματα) Tob 11:8S, 12S.*

ἀπολήγω   (Hom+) cease, fall or die away Da 5:26L.*

ἀπολιθόω   (Aristot+) turn to stone; (pass) be petrified Ex 15:16.*

ἀπόλλω   (h.l.) = BDAG: ἀπόλλυμι 4 Macc 6:14.*

ἀπολόγημα, -ατος, τό   (Pla, Plu) plea in defense Jer 20:12.*

ἀπόλοιπος, -ον   (ins) left over; (subst) area left over or left free Ezk 41:9ff; 42:1, 10.*

ἀπολυτρόω   (Pla+) release Ex 21:8; Zeph 3:1.*

ἀπομαίνομαι   (Lucian) go insane Da 12:4L.*

ἀπομαρτυρέω   (ins, Polyb+) testify, bear witness 2 Macc 12:30.*

ἀπομάχομαι   (Thu+) fight (at the walls) 2 Macc 12:27.*

ἀπομέμφομαι   (Eur+) rebuke Job 33:27.*

ἀπομερίζω   (Pla+) separate off; distinguish, honor 2 Macc 15:2; apportion, distribute (no //) Da 11:39L.*

ἀπόμοιρα, -ας, ἡ   (ins, pap) portion (for the god) Ezk 45:20.*

ἀπονοέομαι   (Thu+) lose one's senses; act desperately 1 Esdr 4:26; revolt (no //) 2 Macc 13:23.*

ἄπονος, -ον   (Simonid, Aeschyl+) easy, painless 4 Macc 11:26.*

ἀποξαίνω   (LXX+) tear or cut away; (mid) endure the tearing away (of τι) 4 Macc 6:6.*

ἀποξενόω   (Soph+) banish, drive into exile 2 Macc 5:9; (mid/pass) be banished, become an exile Pr 27:8; > make oneself a stranger, pretend not to be oneself (no //) 3 Km 14:5(vL), 6(vL).*

ἀποξέω   (Hom+) strip off, scrape off Job 2:8vL.*

ἀποξηραίνω   (Hdt+) dry up Josh 4:23; 5:1; (pass) be dried up, wither away Ps 36:2; Jon 4:7.*

ἀποξύω   (Hom+) scrape off Lev 14:41ff.*

ἀποπαρθενόω   (h.l.) deflower, render non-virginal Sir 20:4.*

ἀποπειράομαι   (Hdt+) put to the test, make a trial of (τινός) Pr 16:29.*

ἀποπεμπτόω   (LXX) set aside one-fifth Gen 41:34; 47:26.*

ἀποπηδάω   (Hippocr, X+) stalk off, go away Pr 9:18a; Hos 7:13; Na 3:7R; Ezk 19:3.*

ἀποπιάζω   (LXX+; Hippocr, Aristot+: -πιέζω) squeeze out Judg 6:38A.*

ἀποπλάνησις, -εως, ἡ   (Pla+: digression) wandering, > (self-)deception (no //) Dt 29:18; Sir 34:11.*

ἀποπνέω   (Hom+) breathe out, > breathe one's last, die 4 Macc 15:18.*

ἀποποιέω (LXX+) (mid) *do away w.; reject, disclaim* Job 8:20 = 36:5; 14:15; 15:4; 19:18; 40:8.*

ἀποπομπαῖος, -α, -ον (LXX+) *cast out, abominable;* (subst) Lev 16:8, 10.*

ἀποπομπή, -ῆς, ἡ (Isocr+) *act* (or *place?* no //) *of averting or sending away* Lev 16:10.*

ἀποπρατίζομαι (h.l.) *sell, convert into cash* Tob 1:7BA.*

ἀποπτύω (Hom+) *spit out*, (fig) *spurn* 4 Macc 3:18.*

ἀπόπτωμα, -ατος, τό (Polyb+) *error, falling away* Judg 20:6B, 10B.*

ἀποργίζομαι (Menand) *be angry* 2 Macc 5:17.*

ἀπορείψω see ἀπορρίπτω.

ἀπορέω aor pass ptc ἀπορηθείς fut pass ἀπορηθήσομαι 2. *be at a loss for, lack* (τινός) Sir 10:27; (abs) *be without resources* Lev 25:47.‡

ἀπορία 2. *difficulty, constrainment by circumstance* Is 8:22.‡

ἀπορρέω aor ἀπερρύην 2. *fall away, desert* (Polyb) 1 Macc 9:7.‡

ἀπορρήγνυμι fut pass ἀπορραγήσομαι (Hom, Hdt+) *tear away* Lev 13:56; *separate, tear in two* Eccl 4:12; (fig) *detach, release* 4 Macc 9:25; Job 39:4.*‡

ἀπόρρητος, -ον (Hdt+) *unspoken,* > *secret, arcane* Sir 13:22.*

ἀπορρίπτω fut ἀπο(ρ)ρίψω (-ρείψω) itac Job 27:22VL; pf pass ptc ἀπερριμμένος.‡

ἀπόρροια, -ας, ἡ (X+) *emanation* Wsd 7:25.*‡

ἀπόρρωξ, gen -ῶγος (Hom+) *broken off;* > *sheer, precipitous;* (subst) *cliff, precipice* 2 Macc 14:45; 4 Macc 14:16; > *shooting off;* (subst) *offshoot, branch* (Heb רב *shoot*) Ezk 17:6cj.*

ἀποσάσσω (HR; LSJ -σάττω) aor ἀπέσαξεν (LXX+) *unsaddle, unload* Gen 24:32.*

ἀποσβέννυμι (Heraclitus, Hippocr, X+) *extinguish* Sir 3:30; 43:21; (pass) *be extinguished* Pr 31:18; Is 10:18.*

ἀποσείω (Hdt+) *shake off* Is 33:15.*

ἀποσημαίνω (Hdt+) *give a sign or signal* 1 Esdr 6:6G.*

ἀποσιωπάω (Isocr+) *remain silent* Jer 45:27.*

ἀποσκαρίζω (Aristoph+) *be convulsed* Judg 4:21A.*

ἀποσκεδάννυμι (Hom, Hdt+) *scatter, dispel* 4 Macc 5:11.*

ἀποσκευή, -ῆς, ἡ (30x, Polyb+) *household* (people and/or property) Gen 14:12; Ex 10:10; 1 Macc 5:13; *stock, provision, equipment* Ex 39:22R (Gött παρα-); *property* 2 Ch 32:29; *baggage* Jdth 7:2; *livestock and people* 1 Ch 5:21.

ἀποσκηνόω (LXX+) *move one's camp* Gen 13:18; (fig) *move away* (ἀπό τινος), *leave behind* PsSol 7:1*

ἀποσκληρύνω (Hippocr, Aristot+) *treat harshly* (no //) Job 39:16.*

ἀποσκοπεύω (LXX) *observe closely, watch, look out for* Jdth 10:10; PsSol 3:5; Hab 2:1; La 4:17.*

ἀποσκοπέω (Soph+) *keep watch* 1 Ch 12:30.*

ἀποσκορακίζω (LXX+) *cast off, reject* 1 Macc 11:55; Ps 26:9; Is 17:13.*

ἀποσκορακισμός, -οῦ, ὁ (LXX+) *casting out, damnation* Is 66:15.*

ἀποσκυθίζω (Eur+) *scalp in Scythian fashion* 4 Macc 10:7.*

ἀποσοβέω (Aristoph+) *frighten away, chase off* Dt 28:26; Sir 22:20; Jer 7:33.*

ἀπόσπασμα, -ατος, τό (Pla+) *shred, piece torn off.* Jer 26:20 mistrans of קרץ *biting or stinging insect* as if fr קרע *tear* (Aram קרץ *piece* Da 3:8; 6:25). La 4:7 renders גזרה (unknown) as if fr גזר *cut off.**

ἀποσπάω pf pass ptc ἀπεσπασμένος 2.b. (abs) *withdraw* (troops or military force implied obj; X ANAB 7.2.11) 2 Macc 12:10, 17. Lev 22:24 mistrans of כרת niph *be cut or mutilated* as if *be cut off or separated.*‡

ἀποστάζω (Aeschyl+) *drip, trickle* Pr 5:3; 10:31f; SSol 4:11.*

ἀποσταλάζω (LXX+) *drip, trickle* Am 9:13 = Joel 4:18.*

ἀπόστασις, -εως, ἡ (Hdt+) 1. *rebellion, desertion* 2 Ch 28:19; 33:19; 1 Esdr 2:21; 2 Esdr 4:19. 2. *emanation* Wsd 16:21VL (misspelled -σταξις).*‡

ἀποστατέω (Aeschyl+) **1.** *stand aloof, fall away (from)* Ps 118:118. **2.** *rebel* (no //, but cf. -στασις and -στάτης) 2 Esdr 12:19; 16:6; 1 Macc 11:14; 13:16; 2 Macc 5:11.*

ἀποστάτης **2.** *traitor, (political) subversive* 3 Macc 7:3.‡

ἀποστάτις, -ιδος, ἡ (Joseph *AJ* 11.22; =) *rebel, apostate* (fem of ἀποστάτης) 1 Esdr 2:14, 17; 2 Esdr 4:12, 15.*

ἀποστενόω (Theophr+) (pass) *be contracted or constricted* Esth 5:1b.*

ἀποστέργω (Aeschyl+) *deprive of love* Dt 15:7.*

ἀποστερέω (Aeschyl, Hdt, X+) **1.b.** *deprive* (ἑαυτόν of/from τινος) 4 Macc 8:23.‡

ἀποστολή **2.** *payment, civic or diplomatic gift* 3 Km 5:14b; 1 Esdr 9:51, 54; 1 Macc 2:18; SSol 4:13; (hostile or ironic) Ps 77:49; Jer 39:36. **3.a.** *sending away* Dt 22:7; *exile* Jer 39:36; Bar 2:25. **b.** *dismissal* (from military service, no //) Eccl 8:8.*‡

ἀποστρεβλόω (h.l.) *torture, wrench out of place* (pass) 2 Macc 9:7.*

ἀποστρέφω aor pass ἀπεστράφην 4 Km 23:26; ἀπεστρεψάμην Hos 8:3; pf ἀπέστροφα 1 Km 6:21; ἀπέστραμμαι Job 9:13. **4.b.** *bring back* Jer 40:11.‡

ἀποστροφή **2.** *recourse, refuge* Gen 3:16 (reading תשובה for תשוקה?). **3.** *turning away, apostasy* 3 Macc 2:10; Jer 5:6; *aversion, rejection* Sir 41:22.‡

ἀποστύφω (Aristot+) *contract, draw together* Tob 11:8S.*

ἀποσυμμείγνυμι (dub; *h.l.*) *join forces* Da 11:6Θvl.*

ἀποσυνάγω (LXX) *lead away, rescue, heal* (Heb אסף *gather in* or *withdraw*) 4 Km 5:3ff.*

ἀποσυρίζω (HomHymns+) *whistle* Is 30:14R (Gött -σύρω, = Heb).*

ἀποσύρω (Thu+) *tear away* 4 Macc 9:28; (Heb חשף *peel off*), > *skim* Is 30:14G.*‡

ἀποσφάζω (Hdt+) *cut the throat, slaughter* 4 Macc 2:19.*

ἀποσφενδονάω (DiodS+) *sling, hurl as from a sling* 4 Macc 16:21.*

ἀποσφράγισμα, -ατος, τό (pap, ins+) *seal, signet* Jer 22:24; Ezk 28:12.*

ἀποσχίζω (Hom, Hdt+) *cut off, detach;* (pass) *detach oneself, be separated* Num 16:21, 26; 2 Ch 26:21 Da 2:34Θ.*

ἀποτάσσω **3.** *appoint, leave in place* 1 Macc 4:61; 11:3; (pass ptc) *appointee* 1 Esdr 6:26. Jer 20:2 οἴκου ἀποτεταγμένου *house of the rejected one* renders בנימין *Benjamin* perh as if בת־מני (so BHS; for מני cf. Is 65:11; rendered τυχή).‡

ἀποτείνω (X+) *extend, strain* Ex 8:24.*

ἀποτέμνω (Hom, Hdt+) *sever, cut off* 2 Macc 15:30; 4 Macc 15:20; Sir 25:26; Jer 43:23; *decapitate* Judg 5:26A.*

ἀποτηγανίζω (Pherecr+) *roast, broil* ("*off the skillet*") Jer 36:22.*

ἀποτίναγμα, -ατος, τό (Sym) *tow, fiber* Judg 16:9A.*

ἀποτιννύω (-τειν-? W, p.31f) fut ἀποτείσω (HR -τίσ-), aor ἀπέτεισα; = BDAG: ἀποτίνω (cf. W, BDF 23).

ἀποτίνω 2 Km 15:7 s.t. of שלם *fulfill* (a vow) as if *repay, make compensation*.‡

ἀποτομή, -ῆς, ἡ (X+) *piece, segment.* Judg 5:26A mistrans of *h.l.* הלמות *hammer* as if pl noun fr הלם *beat* (to pieces).*

ἀποτρέμω (dub; not in LSJ) *frighten off* (?) Sir 20:29vl.*

ἀποτρέχω **2.** (fig) *run off (along), depart (by)* τὴν ὁδόν = *die* Josh 23:14.‡

ἀποτρίβω (Hom+) **1.** *wear out, rub away,* > (ins, Plu) *dismiss, reject* Hos 8:5. **2.** *crush* (no //, cf. BDAG: συντρίβω) Judg 5:26A; Mi 7:11mistrans of רחק *extend* as if מחק *crush*.*

ἀποτροπιάζομαι (LXX+) *avert evil* (by ritual or sacrifice) Ezk 16:21.*

ἀποτρυγάω (LXX+) *pluck or pick* Am 6:1.*

ἀποτυμπανίζω (Lysias+) *torture and kill, destroy* (cf. τύμπανον 2.) 3 Macc 3:27; Da 7:11L.*

ἀποτύφλωσις, -εως, ἡ (LXX+) *blindness* Zech 12:4.*

ἀποφαίνω aor ἀπέφηνα *declare* Job 27:5; 32:2; (mid) *declare oneself* 2 Macc 6:23; *declare* (= act) 15:4.*‡

ἀποφέρω fut ἀποίσω **1.b.** *bear, endure* (no //) 2 Km 13:13.‡

ἀποφθέγγομαι   2. *chant, sing* (no //; renders
נבא piel *declare as a prophet*) 1 Ch 25:1.‡

ἀπόφθεγμα, -ατος, τό   (X, Aristot+) *apo-
phthegm, pointed saying, declaration* Dt 32:2;
Ezk 13:19.*‡

ἀποφορίζω   (dub; not in LSJ) *levy, contribute
from taxes* 4 Macc 3:20VL.*

ἀποφράσσω   aor pass ἀπεφράγην (Hippocr,
Thu+) *block up, close off* La 3:8; (pass) 1 Macc
9:55.*

ἀποφυσάω   (Aristoph+) *blow away* Hos 13:3.*

ἀποχέω or ἀποχύννω   (Hom+) *pour out*
3 Km 22:35; 4 Km 4:4; La 4:21.*

ἀποχώρησις, -εως, ἡ   (Hdt+) *act of voiding*
Judg 3:24A.*

ἄπρακτος, -ον   (Hom+) *unsuccessful, without
accomplishment* Jdth 11:11; 2 Macc 12:18;
impotent, helpless 3 Macc 2:22.*

ἀπρονοήτως   (X+) *without forethought, carelessly* 3 Macc 1:14.*

ἀπρόπτωτος, -ον   (Chrysipp+) *deliberate, not
hasty* 3 Macc 3:14.*

ἀπτόητος, -ον   (LXX+) *undaunted, unintimi-
dated* Jer 27:2.*

ἄπυρος, -ον   (Hom, Hdt+) *unsmelted* Is
13:12.*

ἀπωθέω   fut ἀπώσομαι or ἀπεώσομαι
(4 Km 21:14VL) pass ἀπωσθήσομαι aor
pass subj ἀπωσθῇς aor mid inf ἀπώσασθαι
or ἀπεώσασθαι (4 Km 4:27VL) pf mid
ἀπῶσμαι Jon 2:5.‡

ἀπώλεια   3. *loss, > lost object or animal* (no //)
Ex 22:8; Lev 5:22f; Dt 22:3.‡

ἀπῶρυξ, -υγος, ἡ   (LXX+) *layer* (?); so LSJ,
NETS, but better cj ἀπορρώξ (qv, [Heb בד
shoot]) Ezk 17:6.*

ἀπωσμός, -οῦ, ὁ   (h.l.) *expulsion* La 1:7.*

ἀπωτέρω   (Soph+) *farther away* Da 9:7L.*

αρ   translit of הר *mountain* 2 Macc 6:2VL.*

αραaβ   (HR N PERS?) translit of הראב (? mean-
ing?) MT הראש *the head* (cf. L. C. Allen, *The
Greek Chronicles*, VTSup 25, 27 [Leiden:
Brill, 1974]) 1 Ch 24:31.*

αραβωθ   2 Km 15:28 (Qere, not Kethib);
17:16 translit of ערבות *waterless regions,
steppes*.*

ἀράομαι   aor ἠρασάμην (10x, Hom, Hdt+)
curse Num 22:6; Josh 24:9; 3 Km 8:31 = 2 Ch
6:22.‡

ἀραρότως   (Aeschyl+) *closely, vigorously*
3 Macc 5:4.*

αραφωθ   (VL αραβωθωθ) translit of הרפות *the
leavings, straw* 2 Km 17:19.*

ἀράχνη, -ης, ἡ   (Aeschyl+) 1. *spider web* Ps
38:12; 89:9; Job 8:14. 2. *spider* Job 27:18; (or
σῆτες = PUPAE? [no //]); Is 59:5.*

ἀργία, -ας, ἡ   (Soph+) 1. *idleness, inactivity*
Ex 21:19; Eccl 10:18; Sir 33:28. 2. *rest, leisure*
Wsd 13:13; Is 1:13.*

ἀργός   4. *unworked* 3 Km 6:7.‡

ἀργυρικός, -η, -ον   (ins, DiodS+) *monetary*
1 Esdr 8:24.*

ἀργύριον   2 Esdr 8:17 mistrans of Casiphia (N
LOC) as if כסף *silver*.‡

ἀργυροκοπέω   (h.l.) *refine or smelt silver* Jer
6:29.*

ἀργυρολόγητος, -ον   (h.l.) *subject to tribute*
2 Macc 11:3.*

ἀργυροχόος, -ου, ὁ   (h.l. but cf. χρυσοχόος)
silversmith Wsd 15:9.*

ἀργύρωμα, -ατος, τό   (Lysias, Menand+)
silver cup, (coll) *silver plate ware* Jdth 12:1;
15:11; 1 Macc 15:32.*

ἀργυρώνητος, -ον   (Hdt+) *bought for silver,
purchased* (alw of slave) Gen 17:12ff; Ex
12:44; Jdth 4:10.*

ἀρδαλόω   pf pass ptc ἠρδαλωμένος (Hippocr, PhilemonCom) *smear;* (pass ptc)
smeared Sir 22:1.*

ἄρδην   (Aeschyl+) *wholly, completely* 3 Km
7:31; Mal 3:23.*

ἀρεταλογία, -ας, ἡ   (LXX+ [Strabo 17.1.17VL])
recitation of divine excellence Sir 36:13.*

ἀρεταλόγιον, -ου, τό   (dub; not in LSJ) *recitation of divine excellence* Sir 36:13VL.*

ἀρήγω   (Hom+) *aid, help, succor* 3 Macc 4:16.*

ἀρήν   (HR ἀρνός, wrongly) acc sg ἄρνα,
dat pl ἀρνάσι Mi 5:6 mistrans of כרבבים *like
showers* as if ככרים *like young rams;* Heb perh
orig כרבים *like showers,* cf. Ugar RB(B) *rain.* Is
5:17 renders גרים *aliens, sojourners;* BHS cj
גרים *kids,* or rd כרים (masc?) *young rams.*‡

ἀρθρέμβολον, -ου, τό (Galen) *instrument of torture, for dislocating limbs* 4 Macc 8:13.*

ἀρθρέμβολος, -ον (not in LSJ) *dislocating, torturing* 4 Macc 10:5.*

ἄρθρον, -ου, τό (Hippocr, Hdt+) *joint* Job 17:11; 4 Macc 9:17.*

αριηλ translit of אר(י)ה(י)ל *warrior* 2 Km 23:20 = 1 Ch 11:22; or הראל N LOC (*Mountain of God*, of Jerusalem or its place of sacrifice, so MT) or אריאל *altar hearth* (cf. Is 29:2b) Ezk 43:15f.*

ἀριθμητός, -ή, -όν (CratinusCom, Aristot+) *numbered; counted, reckoned* Job 36:27; > *easily counted, few* 14:5; 15:20; 16:22.*

ἀριστεία, -ας, ἡ (Hdt+) *example of valor* 4 Macc 12:16.*

ἀριστερός 2. *north* (Heb, no //; opp δεξιός, q.v.) Gen 14:15; Jdth 2:21; Is 54:3.‡

ἀριστεύω (Hom, Hdt+) *gain the prize for valor, prevail* 4 Macc 2:18.*

ἄριστος see BDAG: ἀγαθός.

αριωθ translit of אורות *mallow* 4 Km 4:39.*

ἀρκεύθινος, -η, -ον (LXX+) *of cedar* 3 Km 6:31, 33; 2 Ch 2:7.*

ἄρκευθος, -ου, ἡ (Hippocr, Theophr+) *cedar, juniper* Hos 14:9.*

ἁρματηλάτης, -ου, ὁ (Pind, Soph+) *driver* (of chariot) 2 Macc 9:4.*

ἁρμονία, -ας, ἡ (Hom+) 1. *music* Ezk 23:42. 2. *joint, point of union* 37:7.*

ἁρμόνιος, -ον (LXX+) *suitable, fitting* Wsd 16:20.*

ἀροτήρ, -ῆρος, ὁ (Hom, Hdt+) *plowman* Is 61:5.*

ἀροτρίασις, -εως, ἡ (LXX+) *plowing* Gen 45:6.*

ἀροτριάω Sir 7:12 mistrans of חרש *prepare* as if *plow.*‡

ἀροτρόπους, -ποδος, ὁ (h.l.) *ploughshare* (Heb *ox goad*) Judg 3:31B.*

ἄρουρα, -ας, ἡ (Hom+) *field, section of land* (mistrans of אשל *tamarisk,* cf. Vulg NEMUS, *grove*) Gen 21:33; 1 Km 22:6; 31:13.*

ἅρπαγμα, -ατος, τό (17x, Lycophron) 1. *booty, prey* Lev 5:23; Job 29:17; Mal 1:13; Is 42:22; Ezk 18:7. 2. (*act of*) *robbery* Ps 61:11; Sir 16:13; Is 61:8.

ἁρπάζω dep fut ἁρπῶμαι (contr fr ἁρπάσομαι), 2 sg ἁρπᾷ (Lev 19:13VL), pf ἥρπακα.‡

ἀρρενωδῶς (h.l.) *bravely, in manly fashion* 2 Macc 10:35.*

ἄρρηκτος, -ον (Hom, Hdt+) *unbreakable* 3 Macc 4:9.*

ἄρριζος, -ον (Aristot+) *rootless* Job 31:8.*

ἀρρώστημα, -ατος, τό (Hippocr, Demosth+) *disease, illness* Sir 10:10; 30:17; 31:2, 22; 38:9.*

ἀρρωστία, -ας, ἡ (14x, Hippocr+) *fever, illness* 3 Km 12:24g; 1 Macc 6:8; Ps 40:4; Sir 18:19; *malady, affliction* Eccl 5:12ff.

ἄρσις, -εως, ἡ (Aristot+: *raising, lifting;* fr αἰρέω; in our lit, alw s.t. of נשא or סבל and deriv) 1. *portion, gift, presentation* (no //) 2 Km 11:8; 19:43. 2. *load, burden* (no //) 4 Km 8:9; Ps 80:7. 3. *levy, forced labor* (no //) 3 Km 2:46h; 5:29; 11:28; 12:24b.*

ἀρτάβη, -ης, ἡ (Hdt, pap, ins) *dry measure* (Persian or Egyptian, ca. 50*l*) Is 5:10; Bel 3.*

ἀρτήρ, -ῆρος, ὁ (Pherecr) *"shoe"; hod or other carrying tool* 2 Esdr 14:11.*

ἀρτίως (Hom, Soph+) *right now, just now* 2 Km 15:34.*

ἀρτοκοπικός, -ή, -όν (LXX+) *for baking, baked* 1 Ch 16:3.*

ἀρτός, -ή, -όν (not in LSJ) *arranged;* (neut pl subst) *things accomplished* (?) Num 4:27.*

ἀρχή 3.b. *source* (of river) Gen 2:10; (of road) 1 Km 13:17f; La 4:1 (no //; Heb ראש = Vulg CAPUT, *source,* as in class Lat from Plautus to Pliny). 6.b. *term of office,* > *reign* (no //, but Heb ראשית ממלכת *beginning of the reign* rather than *reign/authority of the king*) Jer 33:1 (emend βασιλέως to βασιλείας?). c. *column* ("command") *of troops* (no //) 1 Km 11:11; 1 Macc 5:33; > *sum total, census* (no //; cf. κεφαλαιον) Num 1:2; 4:22. 2 Esdr 19:17 mistrans of ראש *head* (נתן ראש *take it into one's head, start to plan*) as if (*make a*) *beginning.* SSol 4:8 see πίστις.‡

ἀρχηγενέτης, -ου, ὁ (dub; not in LSJ) *author, originator* 2 Macc 2:30VL.*

ἀρχηγέτης, -ου, ὁ (Hdt+) *author, originator* 2 Macc 2:30.*

ἀρχῆθεν   (Hdt+) *from the beginning* 3 Macc 3:21.*

ἀρχιδεσμοφύλαξ, -ακις, ὁ   (LXX+) *chief prison guard* Gen 39:21ff.*

ἀρχιδεσμώτης, -ου, ὁ   (h.l.) = prec Gen 40:4.*

ἀρχιεράομαι   (ins, Joseph) *be high priest* 4 Macc 4:18.*

ἀρχιερατεύω   (ins, pap) *be high priest* 1 Macc 14:47.*

ἀρχιερωσύνη, -ης, ἡ   (13x, ins, Plu) *status or office of high priest* 1 Macc 7:21; 11:27; 2 Macc 4:7ff; 4 Macc 4:1.

ἀρχιευνοῦχος, -ου, ὁ   (LXX+) *chief eunuch* Da 1:3ff.*

ἀρχιμάγειρος, -ου, ὁ   (24x, LXX+) *chief cook* Gen 37:36; *palace steward* 4 Km 25:8ff; Jer 47:1ff; Da 2:14.

ἀρχιοινοχοΐα, -ας, ἡ   (LSJ: -χοεία, h.l.) *office of chief cupbearer* Gen 40:13.*

ἀρχιοινοχόος, -ου, ὁ   (9x, LXX+) *chief cupbearer* Gen 40:1ff; Tob 1:22S.

ἀρχιπατριώτης, -ου, ὁ   (LXX) *head of clan* Josh 21:1; Da 3:94L.*

ἀρχισιτοποιός, -οῦ, ὁ   (7x, LXX+) *chief baker* Gen 40:1ff.

ἀρχιστράτηγος, -ου, ὁ   (21x, LXX+) *general, commander-in-chief* Gen 21:22; Josh 5:14; 1 Km 12:9; 1 Ch 19:16; Jdth 2:4; Da 8:11.‡

ἀρχισωματοφύλαξ, -ακις, ὁ   (ins, pap) *chief bodyguard* 1 Km 28:2; Esth 2:21.*

ἀρχιτεκτονέω   (Aristoph+) *be master builder, supervise construction* Ex 31:4; 35:32; 37:21.*

ἀρχιτεκτονία, -ας, ἡ   (Bito [III BCE]) *process of construction* Ex 35:32, 35.*

ἀρχίφυλος, -ου, ὁ   (LXX) *tribal chief* Dt 29:9; Josh 21:1; 1 Esdr 2:5.*

ἄρχω   Zech 6:10 renders חלדי (N PERS) as if fr חלל hiph *begin*. 2 Km 18:14 mistrans of אחילה *remain lingering, tarry* as if fr חלל hiph *begin* (οὕτως μενῶ is doublet).‡

ἄρχων   1.a.β. (fem) *princess, royal wife* (no //) 3 Km 11:1.‡

ἀρωδιός, -οῦ, ὁ   (cf. ἐρωδ-) *heron* Lev 11:19VL.*

ἀσάλευτος   3. (subst) *immovable object* (alw as rendering of טוטאפות *phylactery*) Ex 13:16; Dt 6:8; 11:18.*.‡

ασαραμελ or σαραμελ   1 Macc 14:27 either translit of חצר עם אל *court of God's people* (hence N LOC); or (more likely, so Syriac) translit of שר עם אל *prince of God's people,* title of Simon.

ασαρημωθ   translit of השרמות unexpl (Vulg TORRENTEM); rd (w. Qere) השדמות *the terraces* Jer 38:40.*

ἀσεβέω   2. *sin against* (τι; Aeschyl+) Pr 8:36; Zeph 3:4.‡

ἀσέβημα, -ατος, τό   (Thu+) *sacrilege, impious act* Lev 18:17; Dt 9:27; La 1:14; 4:22.*

ασεδεκ   appar translit of הצדק *the righteous;* VL ασεδ appar translit of הצד *the demon* (Heb הַ הֶרֶם as if fr הרם *demolish,* but cj הַ חֶרֶם *the sun* [Job 9:7], i.e., *Heliopolis* [so Sym]) Is 19:18.*

ασελισι   (Gött ασελισηλ) translit of השלישי *the third (in rank)* Jer 45:14.*

ασηρωθ   translit of צשרות *villages* Dt 2:23R (Gött N LOC; cf. Num 11:35; 1 Ch 6:56).*

ἀσθενέω   2.b. *weaken* (caus, no //) Mal 2:8. Hos 11:6 mistrans of חול *dance, whirl* as if חלה *be sick.*‡

ἀσθενόψυχος, -ον   (h.l.) *weak-spirited* 4 Macc 15:5.*

ἆσθμα, -ατος, τό   (Hom+) *gasp, gust* (of breath) Wsd 11:18.*

ἀσθμαίνω   (Hom+) *pant, gasp* Sir 31:19.*

ασιδα   translit of חסידה *stork, heron* Job 39:13; Jer 8:7.*

ἀσίδηρος, -ον   (Eur+) *not made of iron* Wsd 17:15.*

ἀσινής, -ές   (Hom, Hdt+) *unharmed* 3 Macc 6:7; 7:20.*

ασιρ   translit of אס(מ)ר *captive, prisoner* as if part of N PERS 1 Ch 3:17.*

ἀσιτέω   (Eur+) *abstain from food, fast* Esth 4:16; 1 Macc 3:17.*

ἀσιτί   (adv; h.l. but cf. ἀμισθί) *without food, lacking provisions* Job 24:6.*

ἀσκητής, -οῦ, ὁ   (Aristoph, X+) *practitioner* 4 Macc 12:11.*

ἀσκοπυτίνη, -ης, ἡ   (AntiphoOr, Menand+) *leather canteen, small wineskin* Jdth 10:5.*

ᾆσμα, -ατος το   (16x, Pla+) *song, hymn* Num 21:17; Ps 32:3; Eccl 7:5; Is 5:1.‡

ἀσμενίζω (Polyb+) *be glad, take pleasure (in)* 1 Km 6:19.*

ἄσμενος, -ον (Hom+) *glad, pleased* 2 Macc 10:33.*

ἀσπάζομαι **3.** *say farewell, take leave (of)* Tob 10:11S.‡

ἀσπάλαθος, -ου, ἡ (Aristot+) *camel thorn* Sir 24:15.*

ἀσπάλαξ, -ακος, ὁ (Aristot+) *mole* Lev 11:30.*

ἀσπιδίσκη, -ης, ἡ (6x, ins+) *small shield, > disk, boss* Ex 28:13ff; 1 Macc 4:57.

ἀσπίς², -ίδος, ἡ (18x, Hom+) *shield* 1 Km 17:6; 2 Ch 9:16; 1 Macc 6:39; Job 15:26; Jer 26:3.‡

ἀσταθής, -ές (LXX+) *unstable* 3 Macc 5:39.*

ἄστεγος, -ον (LXX+) *unroofed;* **1.** *open, exposed* Pr 10:8; 26:28. **2.** *homeless* Is 58:7.*‡

ἀστείως (adv is h.l.; cf. BDAG: ἀστεῖος) *honorably, nobly* 2Macc 12:43.*

ἄστεκτος, -ον (not in HR; Diosc+) *unendurable* Odes 12:5.*

ἀστραγάλος, -ου, ὁ (Hom, Hdt+) *ankle joint* Zech 11:16; *knuckle, joint* Da 5:5Θ, 24 Θ.*

ἀστραπή Job 20:25 mistrans of ברק (fig) *shiny point (of arrow) as if lightning.*‡

ἀστράπτω **2.** *send lightning, make to flash* (w. cogn acc) Ps 143:6.‡

ἀστρολόγος, -ου, ὁ (X+) *astrologer* Is 47:13.*

ἀστυγείτων, -ον, gen -ονος (Aeschyl, Hdt+) *bordering, neighboring* 2 Macc 6:8.*

ἀστυγής, -ές (dub; not in LSJ) *near or relating to the city* (?) 2 Macc 6:8vL.*

ἀσυλία, -ας, ἡ (Aeschyl+) *inviolability, right of sanctuary* 2 Macc 3:12.*

ἄσυλος, -ον (Parmenides, Eur+) *inviolable* 2 Macc 4:33f; Pr 22:23.*

ἀσυνετέω (Hippocr) *be ignorant* Ps 118:158vL.*

ἀσυνθεσία, -ας, ἡ (LXX) *faithlessness, violation of covenant* 2 Esdr 9:2, 4; 10:6; Jer 3:7.*

ἀσυνθετέω pf ἠσυνθέτηκα (7x, LXX) *violate covenant* 2 Esdr 10:2; Ps 72:15.

ἀσυρής, -ές (Polyb; adv Philod) *obscene, lewd* Sir 23:13.*

ἀσφαλίζω **3.** *fortify, make secure* 2 Esdr 13:15vL.‡

ἀσφαλτόπισσα, -ης, ἡ (h.l.) *blend of asphalt and pitch* Ex 2:3.*

ἄσφαλτος, -ου, ἡ (Hdt+) *pitch, tar* Gen 6:14; 11:3; 14:10.*

ἀσφαλτόω (h.l.) *cover with tar* Gen 6:14.*

ἀσφαλῶς **3.** *steadfastly, unshaken in purpose* Gen 34:25.‡

ἀσχήμων *dishonorable;* **2.** *disorderly* 2 Macc 9:2; *disgraceful* Wsd 2:20.‡

ἀσχολέω (Aristot+) *engage;* (pass) *be engaged or occupied, occupy oneself* Sir 39:1.*

ἀσχολία, -ας, ἡ (Pind, Thu+) *occupation, engagement* 3 Macc 5:34; *lack of leisure* Sir 40:1.*

ᾄσω, ᾄσομαι fut of ᾄδω.

ἀταξία, -ας, ἡ (Hdt+) *disorder* Wsd 14:26.*

ἀτάρ (Hom, Hdt+) *nevertheless* (strongly adversative) Job 6:21; 7:11.*

ἀταραξία, -ας, ἡ (Hippocr, Epicurus+) *calm, imperturbability* 4 Macc 8:26.*

ἄταφος, -ον (Hdt+) *unburied* 2 Macc 5:10.*

ἅτε (fr ὅστε; Hdt+) *inasmuch as* 3 Macc 1:29.*

ἀτείχιστος, -ον (Thu+) *unwalled* Num 13:19; Pr 25:28.*

ἀτεκνία, -ας, ἡ (Aristot+) *childlessness* 4 Macc 18:9; Wsd 4:1; Is 47:9; (fig) *barrenness, futility* Ps 34:12.*‡

ἀτεκνόω (20x, LXX) **1.** *make childless, deprive of children* Gen 42:36; 1 Km 15:33; La 1:20; Ezk 36:14; (pass) *be made childless* Gen 27:45; Hos 9:12; Jer 15:7; Ezk 36:12; (pf pass ptc) *separated from or deprived of children* 2 Km 17:8; Ezk 36:13. **2.** *be (made) barren* Gen 31:38; SSol 4:2; Hos 9:14; (fig, of earth) 4 Km 2:19.

ἀτέλεια, -ας, ἡ (Hdt+) *exemption, immunity* 1 Macc 10:34.*

ἀτέλεστος, -ον (Hom+) *unfulfilled, truncated;* (of offspring) *unable to reach maturity* (no //) Wsd 3:16; 4:5.*

ἀτελής, -ές (Hom+) **1.** *ineffectual* 3 Macc 5:42; (superl) Wsd 10:7. **2.** *exempt, immune* 1 Macc 10:34vL.*

ἀτιμασμός, -οῦ, ὁ (EpArist) *dishonor* 1 Macc 1:40vL.*

ἀτίμητος, -ον (Hom+: *worthless*) *priceless* (no //) 3 Macc 3:23; Wsd 7:9.*

ἀτιμώρητος, -ον (Hdt+) *unpunished* Pr 11:21; 19:5, 9; 28:20.*

ἀτμός, -οῦ, ὁ (Aeschyl+) *mist, vapor* Eccl 9:9VL.*

ἀτονέω (Aristot+) *be slack or weak* 2 Macc 2:28VL.*

ἀτοπία, -ας, ἡ (Aristoph+) *something out of place and wrong; sacrilege* Jdth 11:11.*

ἄτρακτος, -ου, ὁ (Hdt+) *spindle* Pr 31:19.*

ἀτράπελος, -ον (Schol Soph) *intractable* Job 39:9VL.*

ἀτραπός, οῦ, ἡ (Hom+) *path* Judg 5:6B; Job 6:19; 24:13; Wsd 5:10; Sir 5:9.*

ἀτρύγητος, -ον (Aristot+) *unharvested, ungathered* Ex 27:20VL.*

ἄτρυγος, -ον (Aristot) *without sediment, filtered* Ex 27:20.*

ἄτρωτος, -ον (Aeschyl+) *invulnerable* 2 Macc 8:36; 10:30; 3 Macc 5:47.*

ἀττάκης, -ου, ὁ (h.l.) *type of locust* Lev 11:22.*

ἀττέλεβος, -ου, ὁ (Hdt+) *locust* Na 3:17.*

ἀτυχέω (Hdt+) *fail, be unfortunate* Pr 27:10.*

ἀτυχία, -ας, ἡ (Hippocr, AntiphoOr) *defeat, failure* 2 Macc 12:30; 14:14.*

αὐγάζω 3. *become manifestly white* (no //) Lev 13:24ff; 14:56.*‡

αὔγασμα, -ατος, τό (LXX) *whiteness* Lev 13:38f; *brightness* Sir 43:11.*

αὐγέω (h.l.) *shine* Job 29:3.*

αὐγή 2. (pl) *rays, gleam* (of fire; πυρος αυγη Hom OD 6.305) 2 Macc 12:9.‡

αὐθέντης 2. *murderer* (Hdt+) Wsd 12:6.*‡

αὐθεντία, -ας, ἡ (LXX+) *standing, status* (no //) 3 Macc 2:29.*

αὐθημερινός, -ή, -όν (CratinusCom) *ephemeral, day-by-day* Job 7:1.*

αὐθημερόν (Aeschyl, Hdt+) *on the same day* Dt 24:15; Pr 12:16.*

αὐθωρί (LXX+) *immediately* 3 Macc 3:25; Da 3:15L.*

αὐλαία, -ας, ἡ (20x, Theophr, ins) *curtain, screen* Ex 26:1ff; 37:1ff; 40:19; Jdth 14:14; Is 54:2.*

αὐλαῖος, -α, -ον (h.l. [Hom+: αὔλειος]) *pertaining to the courtyard* 2 Macc 14:41.*

αὖλαξ, -ακος, ὁ or ἡ (Hom+) *furrow* Ps 64:11; Job 31:38; 39:10; Sir 7:3; (fig) 38:26; *track, path* (no //; Gött αὐ. τῶν ἀμπελώνων) Num 22:24R.*

αὐλάρχης, -ου, ὁ (h.l.) *palace steward, major domo* 2 Km 8:18.*

αὐλαρχία, -ας, ἡ (h.l.) *stewardship of the palace* 3 Km 2:46h.*

αὐλή Jer 30:23, 25 mistrans of חצור *Hazor* (N GENT/LOC) as if חצר *courtyard.* Ezk 47:16f mistrans of (part of) N LOC חצר *Hazor* as if חצר *courtyard.*‡

αὐλίζω [BDAG: -ομαι; 48x in LXX] (act used as caus, no //) *cause to dwell* Jer 38:9.*‡

αὐλών, -ῶνος, ὁ (12x, Hdt+) *valley, defile* 1 Km 17:3; 1 Ch 10:7; Jdth 4:4; Jer 31:8.

αυνανειν f.l. (not in LSJ) for δυναμιν (ΔΥΝΑΜ-, > ΑΥΝΑΝ-) 1 Km 14:48VL.

αὖρα 2. (fig) *"air," aura (radiance of), appearance* (no //, but cf. Lat e.g., Virg AEN 6.204) Ezk 8:2VL.*‡

αὔριον 3 Km 19:11 mistrans of בהר *on the mountain* as if מחר *tomorrow.*‡

αὐστηρία, -ας, ἡ (Theophr+) *harshness, severity* 2 Macc 14:30.*

αὐστότηρον neut comp of BDAG: αὐστηρός, as adv 2 Macc 14:30.

αὐταρκέω (Aristot+: *be sufficient*) caus *provide for* (no //) Dt 32:10 = Odes 2:10.*

αὐτάρκης 2. (of object) *sufficient* Sir 31:28; neut pl subst *necessary things* Pr 30:8.‡

αὐτίκα (Hom, Hdt+) *momentarily, at once* 4 Macc 1:12; 2:8.*

αὐτοδέσποτος, -ον (LXX+) *completely sovereign* 4 Macc 1:1, 30; 13:1.*

αὐτόθεν (Hom+) *from this place* Tob 8:21S.*

αὐτόθι (8x, Hom+) *there, at that very place* Josh 5:8; 1 Esdr 8:41; Tob 2:3S, 2 Macc 3:24.

αὐτοκράτωρ, -ορος, ὁ (Aristoph+) *absolute sovereign, complete master* 4 Macc 1:7ff; 8:28; 16:1.*

αὐτομολέω 1.b. *change sides* (DiodS 2.26.7), *come over or join* (μετά τινος) 2 Km 10:19.‡

αὐτοσχεδίως (adj since Hom) *randomly, by chance* Wsd 2:2.*

αὐτόχθων, -ον (14x, Hdt+) *native-born, indigenous* (alw subst) Ex 12:9; Lev 16:29; Josh 9:2d, Jer 14:8.

αὐχήν, -ένος, ὁ (Hom+) *neck* Josh 7:8, 12 (= *"turn their backs"*); 3 Macc 4:8; Ps 128:4; architectural or mechanical term 3 Km 7:19*VL*; δίδωμι αὐχένα (cf. Heb) *"turn one's back"* 2 Ch 29:6.*

αὐχμός, -οῦ, ὁ (Hdt+) *drought* (explanation of N LOC?) Jer 31:31.*

αὐχμώδης, -ες (Hdt+) *dry* 1 Km 23:14ff; (SCIL γῆς) 26:1. Mi 4:8 mistrans of (N LOC?) עפל *hill* as if עפר *dry dust*.

ἀφαγνίζω fut αφαγνιῶ pass αφαγνισθήσομαι (10; Eur+) *cleanse* Lev 14:49; (pass) *be cleansed* Num 19:12ff; *be consecrated* Num 6:2.

ἀφαίρεμα, -ατος, τό (38x, Joseph) *separated share or portion* (for sacrifice or consecration) Ex 29:27; Lev 7:14; Num 6:20; Ezk 44:30.

ἀφαίρεσις, -εως, ἡ (Pla+) *removal, theft* Sir 41:23; *seizure, capture* (no //) 3 Macc 1:1.*

ἀφαιρέω 3.b. (mid abs) *capture and take away* (pers or thing implied) PsSol 17:5.‡

ἀφάλλομαι aor ἀφηλάμην (Aeschyl+) *bound away* Sir 36:26; Na 3:17; Ezk 44:10.*

ἀφάπτω fut ἀφάψω pf mid ἀφῆπται (Hdt+) 1. *fasten from, hang from* (trans) Dt 6:8; 11:18; (mid) *let hang* Pr 3:3; 6:21. 2. (mid) *take hold of* (τινός) Judg 20:34A.*

ἀφασία, -ας, ἡ (Eur+) *speechlessness, > terror, consternation* 2 Macc 14:17.*

ἀφεγγής, -ές (Soph+) *without light* Wsd 17:3.*

ἄφεδρος, -ου, ὁ (Theophr+) *flow, secretion*; (specif) *menstruation* Lev 12:2, 5; 15:19ff; PsSol 8:12; Ezk 18:6.*‡

ἀφειδῶς (Hdt+) *unsparingly; generously* Pr 21:26; *mercilessly* 2 Macc 5:6, 12.*

ἄφεμα, -ατος, τό (pap) *remission, cancellation* (of tax or tribute; alw as cogn acc) 1 Macc 10:28; 13:37; 15:5.*

ἄφεσις 1.b. *release, stream* La 3:48, > *sluice, channel* 2 Km 22:16; Joel 1:20; 4:18. Ezk 47:3 cj αφεσιμ translit of (*h.l.*) אפסים (*up to the*) *ankles*, q.l.‡

ἀφέστιος, -ον (dub; *h.l.*) *far from home* Sir 37:11*VL*.*

ἀφεύκτως (not in LSJ) *inescapably, unavoidably* 3 Macc 7:9.*

ἁφή 2. *touch, > blow, affliction* (71x, 64x in Lev; alw transl נגע [except Jer]) of disease (no //) Lev 13:2ff; 14:3ff; Dt 24:8; 2 Ch 6:29; of human struggle or contest (no //, but class *grip* of wrestlers) Dt 17:8; 2 Km 7:14; Jer 31:9.‡

ἀφηγέομαι (33x, 23 in Ezk; Hdt: *tell*, X+) *go out in front, lead* Ex 11:8; Judg 1:1; 2 Macc 14:6; PsSol 17:26; (ptc subst) *leader* 1 Esdr 6:11; Ezk 11:1; 12:10.

ἀφήγημα, -ατος, τό (Hdt: *narrative*) *guidance* (no //) 4 Macc 14:6.*

ἀφήλαντο see ἀφάλλομαι.

ἀφῄρηκα pf of BDAG: ἀφαιρέω.

ἄφθονος, -ον (Aeschyl, Hdt+) *without envy, > ungrudging, overflowing* 3 Macc 5:2; 4 Macc 3:10; (adv) *ungrudgingly* Wsd 7:13.*

ἄφθορος, -ον (DiodS) *uncorrupted, pure* Esth 2:2.*

ἀφιερόω (Aeschyl, DiodS+) *consecrate* 4 Macc 13:13.*‡

αφιλ- Job 38:15*VVLL* itac misspellings of αφελ- 2 aor of BDAG: ἀφαιρέω.

ἀφίξομαι fut of BDAG: ἀφικνέομαι Jdth 8:32.

ἀφίστημι 1.b. *take away, remove* Dt 1:28; 4 Km 1:18c; 1 Esdr 1:33*VL* (q.l.); Ps 65:20; *cause to leave* Sir 47:24; *keep away, ward off* Sir 27:22R; 42:9.‡

αφιτω Eccl 11:6*VL* itac misspelling of αφέτω (txt).

ἄφοβος, -ον (Aeschyl+) *fearless* Pr 3:24; Wsd 17:4; *overconfident* Sir 5:5; *reckless, irreverent* Pr 19:23.*

ἀφόδευμα, -ατος, τό (LXX+) *excrement* Tob 2:10S.*

ἀφοδεύω (Hippocr+) *void excrement* Tob 2:10BA.*

ἄφοδος, -ου, ἡ (Hdt+) *journey away* 3 Macc 7:10.*

ἀφόμοιος, -ον (LXX+) *comparable, similar*; (subst) *copy* Sir prol 29.*

ἀφόρητος, -ον (Hdt+) *unbearable* 2 Macc 9:10.*

ἀφορία, -ας, ἡ (Pla+) *sterility, barrenness* Hg 2:17.*

ἀφορίζω   2 Km 8:1 pf pass ptc, MT מתג־מאמה
   (N LOC?) unexpl (McCarter AB emends
   to מגרש *common land*, but nowhere does
   ἀφορίζω render that root).‡

ἀφόρισμα, -ατος, τό   (12x, LXX) *what is set
   apart* (land) Num 35:3; (specif) *consecrated*
   Ex 29:24ff; Num 15:19; Ezk 44:29.

ἀφορισμός, -οῦ, ὁ   (Aristot+) *setting aside;
   > what is set aside, offering* (no //) Ezk 20:31,
   40; 48:8.*

ἀφορμή   Ezk 5:7 renders המון *uproar*; perh
   repulsion (Stoic usage) or *pomp, wealth*.‡

ἀφορολόγητος, -ον   (Polyb, ins, Plu) *exempt
   from tribute* 1 Esdr 4:50; 1 Macc 11:28.*

ἀφρονέστατος, -η, -ον   superl of BDAG:
   ἄφρων Pr 10:18; 30:2.

ἀφρονεύομαι   (Sym) *be foolish, act foolishly*
   Jer 10:21.*

αφφουσωθ   translit of החפשית (שות-?) *isolation*
   4 Km 15:5 = 2 Ch 26:21.*

αφφω   **1.** translit of אף־הוא *he himself* 4 Km
   2:14. **2.** translit of אפוא *then* 4 Km 10:10.*

ἀχανής, -ές   (Aristot+) *yawning, gaping* Wsd
   19:17.*

ἄχαρις, -ι, gen -ιτος   (Sappho, Hdt+) *grace-
   less, unpleasant* Sir 20:19.*

ἀχαρίστως   (X+) *gracelessly, disagreeably* Sir
   18:18.*

ἀχάτης, -ου, ὁ   (Theophr+) *agate* Ex 28:19 =
   36:19; Ezk 28:13.*

ἀχθοφόρος, -ον   (not in HR; Hdt+) *burden-
   bearing*; (subst) *porter* 2 Esdr 14:4 (q.l. c. Ra;
   MT הַסַּבָּל *the [group of] porters*).

ἄχι, ἄχει   ([indecl] pap) *reeds* Gen 41:2, 18;
   Sir 40:16; Is 19:7 (Egyptian? Heb אָחוּ).*

αχουχ   translit of (ה)חוח *the thornbush* 2 Ch 25:18.*

ἀχρειότης, -ητις, ἡ   (LXX) *worthlessness* Tob
   4:13².*

ἀχρειόω   **3.** *destroy* Da 6:21L.‡

ἄψομαι   fut mid of BDAG: ἅπτω.

ἀωρία, -ας, ἡ   (Aristoph+) *late at night*
   1 Esdr 1:14; *midnight* Ps 118:147; *darkness*
   Zeph 1:15; Is 59:9.*

ἄωρος   **2.** *out of season; unripe, immature* Pr
   11:30; Wsd 4:5.‡

B

βααλταμ   translit of בעל טעם *chief advisor*
   2 Esdr 4:8, 9, 17.*

βαδδιν   translit of בדין/בדים *linen* (cf. βαρ) Da
   10:5Θ; 12:6fΘ.*

βαδίζω   (68x) **2.** (of a ship) *travel* Jon 1:3.‡

βάδος, gen pl βάδων   (LXX; = BDAG: βάτος,
   cf. also βεθ) *liquid measure* (Heb בת; ca. 35*l*)
   2 Esdr 7:22.*‡

βαθύγλωσσος, -ον   (h.l.) *incomprehensible in
   speech* Ezk 3:5VL.*

βαθύφωνος, -ον   (h.l.) *incomprehensible in
   speech* Is 33:19.*

βαθύχειλος, -ον   (h.l.) *incomprehensible in
   speech* Ezk 3:5.*

βαΐνη, -ης, ἡ   (dub, h.l.; cf. BDF 6) *palm rod*
   (?) 1 Macc 13:37R.*

βαίνω   pf βέβηκα unaugm plpf βεβήκη
   (Hom+) *walk* Dt 28:56; (pf) *stand poised*
   3 Macc 6:31; Wsd 4:4; 18:16.*.‡

βάϊς, acc βάϊν, gen pl βαΐων, ἡ   (accent: cf.
   BDF 6) (pap+; Coptic loanword) *palm frond*
   1 Macc 13:37G, 51.*

βακελ(λ)εθ   translit (?) unexpl, corresp to MT
   בץ קלנו N LOC 4 Km 4:42VL.*

βακτηρία, -ης, ἡ   (10x, Aristoph+) *staff, rod*
   Ex 12:11; 1 Km 17:40; Ps 22:4; Pr 13:24; Jer
   1:11.

βακχούριον, -ου, τό   (h.l. VL -ρον) *firstfruits*;
   translit/loanword (decl) fr בכורים *firstfruits*
   2 Esdr 23:31.*

βάλανος, -ου, ἡ   (Hom+) **1.** *acorn* Is 2:13;
   6:13. **2.** *oak tree* Gen 35:8; Judg 9:6. **3.** *fastening, iron bolt* Jer 30:26.*

βάλλω   **1.a.β.** (γῆν) ἐν κλήρῳ *distribute
   (land) by lot* (no //) Ezk 47:22; 48:29.‡

βαμα   translit of במה *high place* 2 Ch 1:13
   (also N LOC; cf. 1 Km 9:12; 10:5; 1 Ch 16:39;
   21:29).*

βάμμα, -ατος, τό (Pla+) substance into which something is dipped (BDAG: βάπτω), dye; > dyed stuff, dyed cloth (no //) Judg 5:30.*
βαπτίζω 4. flood, sink, overwhelm Is 21:4.‡
βαπτός, -ή, -όν (Eur, Aristoph+) dipped, dyed; brightly colored Ezk 23:15.*
βαρ mistranslit of בד linen 1 Km 2:18.*
βάραθρον, -ου, τό (Hdt+) pit Is 14:23.*
βαρακηνιμ translit of ברקנים thornbushes (cf. αβαρκηνιν, βαρκοννιμ) Judg 8:16.*
βαρβαρόομαι (Soph+) become barbarous 2 Macc 13:9.*
βαρέως β. φέρειν bear w. difficulty, be displeased 2 Macc 14:27.‡
βάρις, -εως, ἡ (10x, Hdt+: boat; Egyptian loanword?) in our lit alw tower, citadel 2 Ch 36:19; 1 Esdr 6:23; Ps 44:9; La 2:5; Da 8:2Θ.
βαρκοννιμ translit of ברקנים thornbushes (cf. αβαρκηνιν) Judg 8:7A.
βαρουχ translit of ברוך blessed 1 Km 25:32vL.*
βαρύγλωσσος, -ον (h.l.) heavy-tongued, difficult to understand Ezk 3:5.*
βαρυηχής, -ές (Orphica, DiodS+) deep-sounding, deep-rumbling 3 Macc 5:48.*
βαρυθυμέω (DiodS [20.41.3]+) be despondent and resentful Num 16:15; 3 Km 11:22; PsSol 2:9.*
βαρύθυμος, -ον (Eur+) resentful, sullen 3 Macc 6:20.*
βαρυκάρδιος, -ον (h.l.) heavy or slow of heart Ps 4:3.*
βαρύνω 2. make heavy or burdensome (no //) Ex 8:28; 3 Km 12:10 = 2 Ch 10:10; 1 Macc 8:31; Job 35:16; Mal 3:13; Is 47:6; La 3:7; (pass) become heavy, press severely 1Rg 31:3 = 1 Ch 10:3.‡
βαρυωπέω (h.l.) lose vision, be dimmed Gen 48:10.*
βαρχαβωθ (not in HR or LSJ) 1 Km 4:21 χαβωθ translit of כבוד glory; βαρ reflects nothing in MT, is missing in Orig, and may reflect βάρος as transl (in conflated doublet) of כבוד weight, glory.*
βασανιστήριον, -ου (Theopomp, Plu+) test; (pl) instruments of torture 4 Macc 6:1; 8:1ff.*

βασιλεία 1.a.β. (temporal) reign Gen 14:1; 4 Km 25:1; 2 Ch 16:13; 2 Esdr 8:1; Is 1:1; Da 2:1. 1.a.γ. dynasty 4 Km 11:1.‡
βασίλειος, -ον 2. (ins) diadem, crown 2 Km 1:10; 2 Ch 23:11; Wsd 5:16.‡
βασιλεύω 3. (trans/caus) appoint or install a(s) king (no //) Judg 9:6; 1 Km 8:22; 3 Km 12:20; 1 Ch 11:10; 1 Macc 8:13; Hos 8:4; Is 7:6; Jer 44:1(2).‡
βασιλικός 2. (neut subst) royal treasury Tob 1:20S; Da 2:5L.‡
βασιλίσκος², -ου, ὁ (Hippocr+) basilisk, serpent Ps 90:13; Is 59:5.*‡
βάσις 2. base, pedestal Ex 26:19; 4 Km 16:17; Wsd 4:3; Ezk 41:22; platform 16:31.‡
βάσταγμα, -ατος, τό (7x, Eur+) burden, load 2 Esdr 23:15, 19; Jer 17:21ff; (fig) 2 Km 15:33.*
βαφή, -ῆς, ἡ (Aeschyl, Aristot+) 1. tempering (metal, by dipping in water) Sir 31:26. 2. dying, > dyed stuff Judg 5:30A.*
βδέλλα, -ης, ἡ (Hdt+) leech Pr 30:15.*
βδελυγμός, -οῦ, ὁ (LXX) abomination 1 Km 25:31; Na 3:6.*
βδελυρός, -ά, -όν (Aristoph+) disgusting, abominable Sir 41:5.*
βδελύσσομαι 2. (caus act) make abominable (no //) Ex 5:21; 1 Macc 1:48.‡
βεβαίωσις 2. permanence; εἰς βεβ. in perpetuity, permanently (no //) Lev 25:23.‡
βεβήλωσις, -εως, ἡ (8x, LXX+) desecration Lev 21:4; Jdth 4:3; 1 Macc 1:48; 3 Macc 1:29; PsSol 8:21.
βεβοήθηται pf pass of βοηθέω.
βεβρωμένος pf pass ptc of BDAG: βιβρώσκω Josh 9:5.
βεδεκ translit of בדק crack, chink, flaw 4 Km 12:6ff; 22:5f.*
βεζεκ Ezk 1:14vL translit of בָּזָק (otherwise unattested; prob error for ברק lightning—Vulg FULGURIS CORUSCANTIS, flash of glittering (lightning).
βεθ translit of בת (Heb measure) 3 Km 5:25.*
βελοστασία, -ας, ἡ (AthenaeusMech [no date]) battery (of catapults, etc) 1 Macc 6:20vL, 51vL.*

βελόστασις, -εως, ἡ   (Polyb+) = prec 1 Macc 6:20, 51; Jer 28:27; Ezk 4:2; 17:17; 21:27.*

βέλτιστος, -η, -ον   irreg superl of ἀγαθός.

βερ(σ)εχθαν   mistranslit of בארגז in Ergaz (cf. εργαβ vs 11) 1 Km 6:8.*

βῆμα   1.b. (pl) gait Sir 19:30.‡

βηρύλλιον, ου, τό   (= BDAG: βήρυλλος) Ex 28:20; 36:20; Ezk 28:13.*

βία   2 Esdr 15:14f renders לחם הפחה the bread of the governor; perh something extorted (so LEH, but no //). Ezk 44:18R see βιζα.‡

βιάζω   1.b. restrain, hinder (from departing) Judg 13:15A; constrain, urge forcefully 2 Km 13:25, 27.‡

βιβάζω   (Soph+) cause to mount; (pass) be bred, have sex (Aristot+) Lev 18:23; 20:16.*

βιβλιαφόρος, -ου, ὁ   (pap, Polyb, DiodS) letter carrier Esth 3:13; 8:10.*

βιβλιοθήκη, -ης, ἡ   (CratinusJun, Polyb+) library, archive 2 Esdr 6:1; Esth 2:23; 2 Macc 2:13.*

βιβλιοφυλάκιον, -ου, τό   (pap [II CE]) archive 1 Esdr 6:20, 22.*

βίβλος   3. public reading (? no //) Bar 1:3.‡

βιζα   (not in HR) translit of ביז in (any fabric inducing) sweat Ezk 44:18G.*

βῖκος, -ου, ὁ   (Hdt+) jar Jer 19:1, 10.*

βιοτεύω   (Pind, Eur+) live Sir prol 36.*

βιότης, -ητος, ἡ   (HomHymns, ins) sustenance, means of life Pr 5:23.*

βιρα   translit of בירה citadel 2 Esdr 17:2.*

βλάστημα, -ατος, τό   (Aeschyl+) offshoot Sir 50:12.*

βλέπω   pres ptc ὁ βλέπων the seer (Heb; no //; cf. ὁράω) 1 Km 9:9; 1 Ch 9:22.‡

βοάω   1.d. call out, summon Judg 4:10B.‡

βοηθέω   1.b. (pass) be helped, derive benefit Pr 28:18.‡

βοήθημα, -ατος, τό   (Aristot+) aid, resource 2 Macc 15:8; Wsd 17:11.*

βόθρος   Am 9:7 mistrans of N LOC קיר as if fr קור dig; cf. 1:5; where קירה to Qir is rendered ἐπίκλητος as if fr קרא call.‡

βοΐδιον, -ου, τό   (Aristoph+) calf, young cow (dim of BDAG: βοῦς) Jer 27:11.*

βόλβιτον, -ου, τό   (Theophr+) dung Sir 22:2; Zeph 1:17; Ezk 4:12, 15.*

βολή   2. > ray, beam (ἡλίου; Soph AJ 877; Eur ION 1134) 3 Macc 5:25.*‡

βομβέω   (Hom+) roar, rumble, crash (of the sea) 1 Ch 16:32 (VL βοββ-, =); hum, sound (of flutes) Jer 31:36; cause to roar (no //) Jer 38:36.*

βόμβησις, -εως, ἡ   (h.l.) buzzing or tumultuous crowd Bar 2:29.*

βοοζύγιον, -ου, τό   (h.l.) ox yoke Sir 26:7.*

βορέας or -ης, gen -ου, ὁ   (Sir 43:17; 43:20) (Hom, Hdt+) = BDAG: βορρᾶς.

βόσκημα, -ατος, τό   (7x, Soph+) 1. cattle 2 Ch 7:5; 2 Macc 12:11. 2. pasture (no //) Is 7:25; 27:10; Jer 32:36.

βόστρυχος, -ου, ὁ   (ArchilochusLyr, Aeschyl+) lock, curl (of hair) Judg 16:14A, 19A; SSol 5:2, 11.*

βοτρύδιον, -ου, τό   (LXX+) small cluster of grapes Is 18:5.*

βότρυς   2. cluster of other fruit (cypress? henna? no //) SSol 1:14; (palm) 7:8.‡

βούβαλος, -ου, ὁ   (Aristot+) antelope Dt 14:5.*

βούκεντρον, -ου, τό   (h.l. except for Lucianic VL at 1 Km 13:21) ox goad Eccl 12:11.*

βουκόλιον, -ου, τό   (21x, Hdt+) herd, flock Ex 13:12; 1 Km 8:16; Jdth 2:27; Eccl 2:7; Am 6:4; Is 65:10.

βουλευτήριον, -ου, ὁ   (Hdt+) council chamber (fig) 4 Macc 15:25. > council itself; (specif) Senate (of Rome) 1 Macc 8:15, 19; 12:3.*

βουλευτικός, -ή, -όν   (X, Pla+) able to deliberate or take counsel Pr 24:6.*

βουλεύω   so rd for βούλομαι 2 Ch 25:16; Pr 12:10 c. Ra (W, p.242; renders יעץ counsel).‡

βουνίζω   (LXX) pile up Ruth 2:14; (pass ptc) 2:16.*

βουνός   2. mound, heap Gen 31:46; 4 Km 10:8. 3. "high place," (illegitimate) place for sacrifice Ps 77:58 (cf. βωμός).‡

βούτομον, -ου, τό   (Aristoph+) sedge Job 8:11; 40:21.*

βούτυρον, -ου, τό   (8x, Hippocr+) butter Gen 18:8; Judg 5:25; Pr 30:33; Is 7:15.

βραγχιάω (Aristot) *be sore* (of throat) Ps 68:4.*
βραγχνιάω (dub; not in LSJ) = prec, Ps 68:4VL.*
βραχέως (adv of BDAG: βραχύς; Soph, Thu+) *briefly, for a short time* 2 Macc 5:17; 7:33; 14:17VL (q.l. w. AB, NRSV); *just recently* 13:11.*
βραχήσομαι fut pass ("*be wetted or soaked*") of BDAG: βρέχω Is 34:3.
βραχίων 2. *shoulder* (of animal, the priests' portion) Ex 29:22; Dt 18:3; Sir 7:31.‡
βραχυτελής, -ές (h.l.) *soon-ending, brief* Wsd 15:9.*
βρίθω (Hom+) *weigh down, burden* Wsd 9:15 (dbl acc, *load the mind w. much care* or *load much care on the mind*).*
βρόμος, -ου, ὁ (Hom+) *loud noise, crash* Wsd 11:18; > *stink, stench* (c. LSJ; cf. W) Job 6:7; 17:11; Joel 2:20.*
βροντάω (9x, Hom+) *thunder* 1 Km 2:10; 2 Km 22:14 = Ps 17:14; Job 37:4; Sir 46:17.
βροῦχος, -ου, ὁ (10x, Theophr+) 1. *locust* Lev 11:22; 3 Km 8:37. 2. (wingless) *larva of locust* 2 Ch 6:28; Ps 104:34; Am 7:1.

βρῶμα EpJer 10 prob mistrans of some deriv of אכל *consumption, decay* as if *food*.‡
βύβλινος, -η, -ον (Hom, Hdt+) *of papyrus* Is 18:2.*
βύβλος = BDAG: βίβλος.
βυθίζω (Soph, Polyb+) *sink*, (trans) *drown* 2 Macc 12:4.*‡
βυθοτρεφής, -ές (h.l.) *sustained in the deep* 3 Macc 6:8.*
βύρσα, -ης, ἡ (Hdt+) *hide, skin* Lev 8:17; 9:11; Job 16:15; 40:31.*
βῶλαξ, -ακος, ἡ (Theocr, Pind, Apollon-Rhod) *lump, clump* Job 7:5.*
βῶλος, -ου, ἡ (Hom+) *lump, clump* Job 38:28; Sir 22:15; Ezk 17:7, 10.*
βωμός LXX (47x) oft of במה (pagan) *altar, high place* in the prophets (Hos 10:8; Is 15:2; Jer 7:21) otherwise renders מזבח *altar* when pagan (Ex 34:13; Num 23:1ff; 2 Ch 31:1), cf. 1 Macc 1:46ff; but 2 Macc 2:19 *altar* of God in Jerusalem; Josh 22:10ff reflects ambiguity of story (true or false altar?).‡

Γ

γαβης 1 Ch 4:9 translit of עבץ N PERS (except for this name, unknown in MT. But cf. Ugar עבץ = Aram עבק *swift*).*
γαβιν 4 Km 25:12 appar translit of גבים *backs, arches* (cf. BHS note; prob error for MT יגבים *farmers*, so LXX L mss)*.
γαβις translit of גביש *crystal* Job 28:18.*
γαζαρηνός, -οῦ, ὁ (LXX [LSJSup]; loanword, Aram גזרין *astrologers*) *astrologer* Da 2:27; 4:7Θ; 5:7ff.*
γαζοφύλαξ, -ακις, ὁ (Phylarchus [III BCE], Strabo+) *treasurer* 1 Ch 28:1; 1 Esdr 2:8; 8:19, 45.*
γαι Ezk 39:11, 15 translit of גיא *valley*.*
γαῖα, -ας, ἡ (7x, Hom+) *land, country* 4 Km 18:35; 2 Esdr 3:3; Ps 48:12; Ezk 36:24.
γαῖσος, -ου, ὁ (Polyb, pap+) *type of javelin* Josh 8:18; Jdth 9:7.*

γαλαθηνός, -ή, -όν (Hom, Hdt+) *nursing, very young* 1 Km 7:9; Sir 46:16; Am 6:4.*
γαλακτοποτέω (Hippocr, Theophr+) *drink milk* (VL -τοτροφέω *nourish w. milk* only Philo) 4 Macc 13:21.*
γαλακτοτροφία, -ας, ἡ (LXX+) *act of nourishing w. milk*; > *nursing* 4 Macc 16:7.*
γαλέαγρα, -ας, ἡ (Hyperid+) *weasel cage*; > *animal cage* (Strabo 6.2.6) Ezk 19:9.*
γαληνός, -όν (Eur+) *calm* 4 Macc 13:6.*
γαμβρεύω (LXX) *marry, unite in marriage* Gen 38:8; Dt 7:3.*
γαμβρός, -οῦ, ὁ (28x, Hom+) 1. *son-in-law* Gen 19:12ff; Judg 19:5A; 2 Esdr 16:18; 1 Macc 16:12. 2. *father-in-law* (= πενθερός) Ex 3:1; Num 10:29; Judg 19:7.
γαμικός, -ή, -όν (Pla+) *marital* 3 Macc 4:6.*

γαρεμ 4 Km 9:13 translit of גרם *bone* ("framework"?, of staircase).*

γασβαρηνός, -οῦ, ὁ (not in LSJ; Vulg N PERS "Gazabar" [Caspar], Pers loanword in Akk, Aram, post-Bib Heb; *h.l.* [גובר] here in MT) *treasurer* (declined, should be accented) 2 Esdr 1:8.*

γαστριμαργία, -ας, ἡ (Hippocr, Pla+) *gluttony* 4 Macc 1:3.*

γαστρίμαργος, -ον (Pind, Aristot+) *gluttonous* 4 Macc 2:7.*

γαυρίαμα, -ατος, τό (LXX+) *exaltation, glory* Jdth 10:8; 15:9; Job 4:10; Sir 43:1; 47:4.*

γαυριόομαι (not in LSJ) *exult* Num 23:24.*

γεδδουρ, ὁ or **τό** (5x) mistranslit of גדוד *band of raiders or robbers* 1 Km 30:8f; 1 Ch 12:22.*

γεδωρ translit of גדור (N LOC? N PERS?) 1 Ch 12:8.*

γεῖσος, -ους, τό (ins) or **γεῖσον, -ους, τό** (Eur+) *projecting edge* Ezk 40:43; 43:13, 17; (specif) *cornice* (of roof) 3 Km 7:46; *capital* (of pillar) Jer 52:22.*

γειτνιάω (Soph+) *adjoin, be next to* (τινί) 2 Macc 9:25; Sus 4.*

γειώρας, -ου, ὁ (Philo) *resident alien, sojourner* (Heb גר) Ex 12:19; Is 14:1 (γιωρας).*

γελοιάζω (LXX+) *jest, joke* Gen 19:14.*

γελοιασμός, -οῦ, ὁ (h.l.) *jest, jesting* Jer 31:27.*

γελοιαστής, -οῦ, ὁ (LXX+) *jester* Job 31:5.*

γελοῖος, -α, -ον (Hom+) *absurd, ludicrous* 4 Macc 1:5; 3:1; 6:34.*

γέλως 2. (Soph, Thu+) *object of laughter or derision* Jer 31:39.‡

γένειον, -ου, τό (Hom+) *chin, beard* (sg or pl) 4 Macc 9:28; 15:15.*

γενεσιάρχης, -ου, ὁ (LXX+) *originator, author* Wsd 13:3.*

γενεσιουργός, -οῦ, ὁ (LXX+) *originator, first maker* Wsd 13:5.*

γένεσις 5. *generative factor or process* (pl, cf. Pla *PHAEDO* 71e) Wsd 1:14.‡

γενέτις, -εως, ἡ (fem LXX+) *parent, author* Wsd 7:12.*

γένημα 2. (fig) of people: *"fruits," offspring* (of a city, no //) 1 Macc 1:38; cf. 3:45—mistrans?‡

γενικός, -ή, -όν (Aristot+) *belonging to the clan or nation* 1 Esdr 5:39.*

γεννήτωρ, -ορος, ὁ (Aeschyl+) *begetter, father* Sir 22:7VL.*

γεραιός, -ά, -όν (7x, Hom+) *old, venerable* 4 Macc 8:3; (subst) *old person* 6:2; 3 Macc 1:23.

γεραίρω (Hom, Hdt+) *celebrate* (mid abs) 3 Macc 5:17.*‡

γεῦμα, -ατος, τό (Hippocr, Aristoph+) *taste, flavor* Ex 16:31; Num 11:8; Job 6:6; Jer 31:11; (fig) *sample, indication* 2 Macc 13:18.*

γεύω (BDAG: γεύομαι) (act: Hdt+) *give a taste* Gen 25:30.‡

γέφυρα, -ας, ἡ (Hom, Hdt+) *dike, embankment* 2 Macc 12:13R; Is 37:25.*

γεφυρόω (Hom, Hdt+) *build a dike* 2 Macc 12:13G.*

γεώδης, -ες (X+) *earthy* Wsd 9:15; 15:13.*

γεωμετρία, -ας, ἡ (Hdt+) *measuring of land* (pap) Is 34:11.*

γεωμετρικός, -ή, -όν (Pla+: *for geometry*) *for measuring land* (no //) Zech 2:5.*

γεωργία, -ας, ἡ (Thu+) *agriculture, farming* 2 Macc 12:1; Wsd 7:15.*

γῆμαι aor inf of BDAG: γαμέω.

γηράσκω fut γηράσω.‡

γηροβοσκέω (Aristoph+) *tend and care for elderly* (esp one's parents) Tob 14:13S.*

γίγαρτον, -ου, τό (Simonid, Aristoph+) *grape seed* Num 6:4.*

γίγας, -αντος (40x, Hom+) *giant, hero, strong man* Gen 6:4; Dt 1:28; 2 Km 21:11; 1 Macc 3:3; Ps 18:6; Wsd 14:6; Is 3:2. Pr 21:16 mistrans of רפאים[1] *ghosts, shades* as if רפאים[2] *giants.*

γίνομαι 2 Esdr 13:16 s.t. of עשויה (niph ptc of עשה) *do, make, made, constructed,* > *man-made, artificial.*‡

γιώρας see γει-.

γλαύξ, γλαυκός, ἡ (Epicharmus, Aristot+) *owl* Lev 11:16, 19R; Dt 14:15.*

γλυκάζω (LXX+) *taste sweet* Ezk 3:3.*

γλυκαίνω (13x, Hippocr, Aristot+) *make sweet, sweeten* Ps 54:15; Sir 47:9; *become sweet* (intr) Sir 12:16; (pass) Ex 15:25; Pr 24:13; Job 20:12; Sir 38:5.

γλύκασμα, -ατος, τό (LXX) *sweet thing* 1 Esdr 9:51 = 2 Esdr 18:10; Sir 11:3; *sweetness* Pr 16:24.*

γλυκασμός, -οῦ, ὁ (LXX+) *sweetness* SSol 5:16; Am 9:13 = Joel 4:18.*

γλύκειος, -α, -ον (ins) *sweet* Ps 118:103VL.*

γλυκερός, -ά, -όν (Hom+) *sweet* Pr 9:17.*

γλύμμα, -ατος, τό (EupolisCom+) *carved figure* Ex 28:11; Sir 22:17G; 38:27; 45:11; Is 45:20; 60:18.*

γλυφή, -ῆς, ἡ (9x, DiodS+) *carving* Ex 25:7; 3 Km 7:27; 2 Ch 2:6; Wsd 18:24; Ezk 41:25.

γλύφω fut γλύψω aor ἔγλυψα pass ἐγλύφην pf pass ptc γεγλυμμένος (13; Hdt+) *carve out, engrave* Ex 28:9; 2 Ch 2:6; Wsd 7:1; Hab 2:18; Is 44:9.

γλῶσσα 4. *bar* (of gold, no //, Heb) Josh 7:21.‡

γλωσσότμητος, -ον (h.l.) *w. tongue cut out* Lev 22:22.*

γλωσσοτομέω (or γλωττ-; LXX+) *cut out the tongue* 2 Macc 7:4; 4 Macc 10:19; 12:13.*

γλωσσοχαριτέω (h.l.) *flatter*; (ptc subst) *flatterer* Pr 28:23.*

γνάθος, -ου, ὁ (Hom: γναθμός; Aeschyl, Hdt+) *jaw, cheek* Judg 4:21Af; 5:26A.*

γνοφερός, -ά, -όν (h.l. [LSJSup], Hom+: δνοφ-) *gloomy, dark* Job 10:21.*

γνοφόω (h.l.) *darken* La 2:1.*

γνοφώδης, -ές (LXX+; Eur+: δνοφ-) *dark* Ex 19:16; Pr 7:9.*

γνώριμος 2. *well-known, evident* EpJer 14. Ruth 2:1; 3:2 mistrans of מ(וֹ)דע(ת) (*distant*) *relative* as if *acquaintance* (ידע *to know*).‡

γνωριστής, -οῦ, ὁ (AntiphoOr) *one who knows*; 4 Km 23:24 mistrans of ידעני *necromancer*, fr ידע *know*; cf. γνωστής.

γνωστέον (Pla+) *it must be known* EpJer 51.*

γνώστης 1 Km 28:3, 9; 4 Km 21:6; 2 Ch 35:19a mistrans of ידעני *necromancer* fr ידע *know*; cf. γνωριστής.*‡

γνωστῶς (Aristot+) *recognizably, so as to be known* Ex 33:13; Pr 27:23.*

γλωττ- see γλωσσ-

γόγγυσις, -εως, ἡ (h.l.) *grumbling, complaining* Num 14:27.*

γοερός, -ά, -όν (Aeschyl+) *mournful* 3 Macc 5:25.*

γοητεία, -ας, ἡ (Gorgias of Leontini, Pla+) *sorcery,* > *guile, trickery* 2 Macc 12:24.*

γομορ (15x) translit of חֹמֶר *dry measure* of 400l (Hos 3:2; Ezk 45:11ff; so also of 1 Km 25:18 [though not in MT]; 1 Km 16:20 mistrans of חמור *donkey(-load)* as if חמר. Ex 16:16ff translit of עֹמֶר *dry measure* of ca 4l (contra NETS; cf. Ex 16:36).

γόμος, -ου, ὁ (Hdt+) *cargo, load* Ex 23:5; 4 Km 5:17.*‡

γομφιάζω (LXX) *gnash, grind* Sir 30:10; Ezk 18:2.*

γομφιασμός, -οῦ, ὁ (h.l.; Hdt 9.83.2 γόμφιοι *grinding teeth, molars*) *grinding or gnashing of teeth* Am 4:6.*

γονορρυέω (h.l.) *be subject to genital flow* Lev 22:4VL.*

γονορρυής, -ές (14x, Philo Leg 3.7) *subject to genital emission or flow* Lev 15:4ff; Num 5:2; 2 Km 3:29.*

γόνος, -ου, ὁ (Hom, Hdt+) *semen* Lev 15:3; *offspring* 3 Macc 5:31.*

γόος, -ου, ὁ (Hom, Aeschyl+) *wailing* 3 Macc 1:18; 4:3, 6; 5:49.*

γραμματεία, -ας, ἡ (pap+) *learning, scholarship* (no //) Ps 70:15; Sir 44:4.*

γραμματεύω (Thu, ins) *be secretary or scribe* 1 Ch 26:29; Jer 52:25.*

γραμματικός, -ή, -όν (X+) *educated, learned* (person) Da 1:4L; (subst) *scholar* Is 33:18; *learned* (skill, no //) Da 1:17L; (fem subst) *grammar* (Pla+) 1:17Θ.*

γραμματοεισαγωγεύς, -έως, ὁ (LXX) *interpreter, teacher of the text* Dt 1:15; 16:18; 29:9; 31:28.*

γραπτός 2. (neut subst) *something written, document* 2 Ch 36:22; 2 Macc 11:15.‡

γραφή 1.b. *enrollment, genealogical list* 1 Esdr 8:30. 1.c. *record, accounting* 2 Esdr 7:22.‡

γραφικός, -ή, -όν (Hippocr, Pla+) *for writing* 3 Macc 4:20.*

γραφίς, -ίδος, ἡ (Pla+) 1. *stylus* (for writing) Is 8:1; *chisel* (sculpting or engraving tool) Ex 32:4; 3 Km 6:29. 2. *paintbrush* Ezk 23:14.*

γράφω 3. *enroll, record* 1 Macc 10:65. **4.** *draw or paint* (a picture) 3 Km 6:29. Is 22:16 mistrans of חקק *carve, hew* as if *mark out*.‡

γρηγόρησις, -εως, ἡ (LXX) *alertness, awareness* PsSol 3:2; 16:4; Da 5:11Θ, 14Θ.*

γρύψ, γρυπός, ὁ (Aeschyl, Hdt+) *griffin* Lev 11:13; Dt 14:12.*

γυμνάζω (Aeschyl, Hdt+) *harass* 2 Macc 10:15.*‡

γυμνάσιον, -ου, τό (Hdt+) *gymnasium* (center for schooling in athletics and Greek culture) 1 Macc 1:14; 2 Macc 4:9, 12; 4 Macc 4:20.*

γύμνωσις, -εως, ἡ (Thu: *exposed* or *vulnerable side*) *nakedness, exposure* (no //) Gen 9:22, 23.*

γυναικίος = BDAG: γυναικεῖος Gen 31:35vL.‡

γυναικών, -ῶνος, ὁ (X *Cyr* 5.5.2) *harem* (residence of the women) Esth 2:3ff.*

γύναιον, -ου, τό (adj Hom+; neut subst Aristoph+) *woman* (but Heb *widow*, vL ἀγύναιος, q.l.) Job 24:21.*

γῦρος, -ου, ὁ (Theophr+ [adj since Hom]) *circle* (of the horizon) Job 22:14; Sir 24:5; Is 40:22.*

γυρόω (Arat+) *inscribe a circle* (no //) Job 26:10; Sir 43:12.*

γύψ, γυπός, ὁ (Hom+) *vulture* Lev 11:14 = Dt 14:13; Job 5:7; 15:23; 28:7; 39:28.*

γωλαθ 2 Ch 4:12f translit of גלות *bowls* (archit t.t. for extrusions from pillars? 3 Km 7:27// στρέπτα *braid work*).*

γωληλα 2 Esdr 12:13 mistranslit of גיא לילה *Valley (Gate) by night* as if N LOC.*

γωνιαῖος, -α, -ον (PlaCom: *angular*; ins+) *at the angle or corner* Job 38:6.*

Δ

δαβιρ (14x) translit of דביר *(inner) room*, esp the holy of holies 3 Km 6:5; 2 Ch 3:16. 3 Km 6:16 arises fr gloss "holy of holies" in MT; translator failed to render as mere repetition.

δαδουχία, -ας, ἡ (LXX+) *act of carrying a torch* 2 Macc 4:22.*

δακτυλήθρα, -ας, ἡ (X+) *thumbscrew* (no //) 4 Macc 8:13.*

δάκτυλος **2.** (τῶν ποδῶν) *toe* (X *Anab* 4.5.12) 2 Km 21:20; Da 2:41f.‡

δαλός, -οῦ, ὁ (Hom+) *firebrand* Am 4:11; Zech 3:2; 12:6; Is 7:4; Ezk 24:9.*

δανεισμός, -οῦ, ὁ (Eur+) *borrowing money* Sir 18:33.*

δάνος, -εος, τό (Callim *Ep* 48) *loan* Sir 29:4.*

δαπάνημα, -ατος, τό (X+) **1.** *expense, cost* 1 Esdr 6:24; 2 Macc 3:3. **2.** (pl) *supplies,* > *food* (Polyb 9.42.4) 2 Macc 11:31.*

δάσος, -εος, τό (Menand+) *thicket* 2 Km 18:9; Is 9:17.*

δασύς, -εῖα, -ύ (11x, Hom+) **1.** *hairy, shaggy* Gen 25:25; 4 Km 1:8. **2.** *leafy* Lev 23:40; 2 Esdr 18:15; Sir 14:18; Hab 3:3; Is 57:5.

δαψιλεύομαι (LXX+, ins) *abound* (in concern? no //) 1 Km 10:2; dub, since same Heb word (דאג) is correctly rendered (φροντίζω) 9:5.

δαψιλής, -ές (Hdt+) *abundant, profuse, lavish* 1 Macc 3:30; 3 Macc 5:2, 31; Wsd 11:7.*

-δε (Hom+; directional suffix w. acc of motion) *toward* (w. N LOC) Κυρηνηνδε *toward Cyrene* 4 Km 16:9vL, ωφιρδε *toward Ophir* 3 Km 22:49(vL).*

δεβραθα mistranslit of כִּבְרַת *some distance* as if N LOC 4 Km 5:19 (cf. χαβραθα).*

δεδίδαχα, δεδιδαγμένος see διδάσκω.

δέδοικα pf of δείδω.

δεδομένος pf pass ptc of BDAG: δίδωμι.

δεῖ fut δεήσει Josh 18:4; pres ptc δέον Sir prol 10vL; (pl subst) *necessities, provisions* Ex 16:22; 3 Km 5:2; Tob 5:15; Pr 30:8; Da 1:26Θ.‡

δείδω pf (w. pres meaning) δέδοικα ptc δεδοικώς 3rd sg plpf ἐδεδοίκειν (8x, Hom, Hdt+) *fear, dread* Job 3:19, 25; 7:2; Is 60:14. Job 26:13 mistrans of שפר *stretch out* (?, so

Habel OTL ad loc) unexpl; 38:40 mistrans of שחח *crouch, lie down*, unexpl.

δείλαιος, -αία, -αιον (Aeschyl+) *wretched, pitiful* Hos 7:13; Na 3:7; Bar 4:31f. = δήλαιος Ezk 5:15vl, superl δηλαϊστός txt.*

δειλανδρέω (LXX) *be(come) a coward* 2 Macc 8:13; 4 Macc 10:14; 13:10.*

δείλη, -ης, ἡ (13x, Hom+) *evening, (late) afternoon* Gen 24:63; 1 Km 20:5; 2 Ch 2:3; 1 Macc 10:80; Zeph 2:7; Jer 31:33.

δειλία Ps 88:41 mistrans of מחתה *destruction* as if *terror*.‡

δ(ε)ιλιάζω (dub; not in LSJ) *be frightened* 2 Macc 13:25vl.*

δειλιαίνω aor subj δειλιάνω (h.l.) *make fearful or cowardly* Dt 20:8.*

δειλός 2. *wretched, worthless* Wsd 9:14.‡

δειλόψυχος, -ον (LXX) *cowardly in spirit* 4 Macc 8:16; 16:5.*

δεῖμα, -ατος, τό (Hom+) *terror, dread* Wsd 17:8.*

δεινάζω (LXX) *be distressed* 2 Macc 4:35; 13:25.*

δεκάδαρχος, -ου, ὁ (X+) *commander of ten* Ex 18:21, 25; Dt 1:15; 1 Macc 3:55.*

δεκαμηνιαῖος, -α, -ον (LXX+) *relating to the tenth month* Wsd 7:2.*

δεκάμηνος, -ον (Hdt, X, ins+) *of ten months* 4 Macc 16:7.*

δεκάπηχυς, -υ (Hdt, Polyb+) *ten cubits long* 3 Km 7:47.*

δεκαπλασιάζω (aor pass ptc Philo Migr 169) *increase tenfold* Bar 4:28.*

δεκαπλασίων, -ον (Schol Iliad) *ten times greater* Da 1:20Θ.*

δεκαπλασίως (Hippocr) *ten times over* Da 1:20L.*

δεκάς, -άδος, ἡ (Hom+: *company or group of ten*) *tithe, tenth* (no //, but cf. Hesychius, [so LSJ]) 2 Esdr 20:39vl.*

δεκάχορδος, -ον (Ion of Chios) *ten-stringed* (alw w. ψαλτήριον) Ps 32:2; 91:4; 143:9.*

δεκτέον (Strabo+) *it must be accepted or understood* EpJer 56vl.*

δέλτος, -ου, ὁ (Hdt+) *writing tablet* 1 Macc 8:22; 14:18ff.*

δένδρος, -εος, τό (Hdt+) = BDAG: δένδρον Dt 22:6.*

δενδροτομέω (Thu, Aristot+) *cut down trees,* > *deforest, lay waste a territory* 4 Macc 2:14.*

δεξαμενή, -ῆς, ἡ (Hdt+) *receptacle, cistern* Ex 2:16.*

δεξιάζω (pap [IV bce]) *offer* or (pass) *receive right hand* (of friendship) 2 Macc 4:34.*

δεξιός 2.c. *south* (s.t.; Heb ימין *right* = *south* when facing rising sun; cf. ἀρίστερος, εὐώνυμος) 1 Km 23:19; Ezk 16:46.‡

δέομαι pres inf δέεσθαι, δεῖσθαι, fut δεηθήσομαι. 2. *be in need* Sir 26:5R; (ptc) *needy person* 4 Macc 2:8.‡

δέρρις, -εως, ἡ (26x; Thu+) *mat, curtain* (of hair fabric; DiodS 20.9.1; ins) Ex 26:7ff; 1 Ch 17:1; Ps 103:2; SSol 1:5; Zech 13:4; Jer 4:20.‡

δέσις, -εως, ἡ (Pla+) *binding; setting* (for stones) Sir 45:11.*

δεσμεύω 1 Km 14:12 mistrans of צדה *hunt down* as if צרר *tie, bind* (cf. 25:29).‡

δεσμός 3. *(tightly wound) bundle* (no //) Gen 42:35; 1 Km 25:29; Hg 1:6.‡

δεσμώτης, -ου, ὁ (Aeschyl, Hdt+) *prisoner* Gen 39:20. Jer 24:1 (also Bar 1:9; //); 36:2 mistrans of מסגר² *smith, metalworker* as if related to מסגר¹ *dungeon*.*‡

δεσποτεία, -ας, ἡ (Pla+) *sovereignty, absolute authority* Ps 102:22; 144:13.*

δεσποτεύω (ins, LXX+) *rule absolutely* 3 Macc 5:28.*

δευτερεύω (Polyb+; cf. BDAG: πρωτεύω) *be or rank second* (to τινί) 1 Ch 16:5; 2 Ch 35:24; Esth 4:8; Jer 52:24.*

δευτέριος, -α, -ον (LXX+) *second, lesser* (W -είος) 1 Esdr 1:29.*

δευτέρας, ἐκ (= BDAG: ἐκ δευτέρου) Tob 1:22.

δευτερολογέω (h.l.) *negotiate a second time* 2 Macc 13:22.*

δευτερονόμιον, -ου, τό (LXX+) *recapitulation of the Torah* Dt 17:18; Josh 9:2.*

δευτερόω (12x, LXX) *do or act again* 1 Km 26:8; 3 Km 21:20; 2 Esdr 23:21; Sir 7:14; (impers) *happen again, be repeated* Gen 41:32; PsSol 5:13. Jer 2:36 mistrans of שנה *change* as if *repeat*.‡

δευτέρωσις, -εως, ἡ (Justinian [VI CE] w. reference to Judaism) *repetition* Sir 41:26; *second rank* 4 Km 23:4; 25:18.*

δέω (σύν)δεσμον 4 Km 12:21 mistrans of קשרו קשר *enter into a conspiracy* as if *bind a bond.*‡

δῆγμα, -ατος, τό (Aeschyl+) *sting* Wsd 16:5, 9. Mi 5:4 mistrans of נסיך *prince* as if fr נשך *bite.**

δήλαιος cf. δείλαιος.

δῆλος 2. (pl subst) *manifestation, sign, revelation* (no //) Num 27:21; Dt 33:8; 1 Km 14:41; Sir 33:3; Hos 3:4.

δήλωσις, -εως, ἡ (Thu+) *explanation, interpretation* Ps 118:130; Da 2:27L. Ex 28:30; Lev 8:8 render אורים *oracular instruments* (s.t.; ἀλήθεια *truth* for תומים), so also 1 Esdr 5:40.*

δημαγωγέω (Aristoph+) *manipulate the people* 1 Esdr 5:70VL.*

δημαγωγία, -ας, ἡ (Aristoph+) *demagoguery* (Polyb 2.21.8) 1 Esdr 5:70.*

δημεύω (Thu+) *make public property, confiscate* Da 3:96L.*

δημηγορέω (Aristoph, Pla+ w. neg connotations) *harangue the people* Pr 30:31; *address the public assembly* (no //) 4 Macc 5:15.*‡

δήμιος, -ον (Aeschyl+) *public*; (subst, euphem; SCIL δοῦλος) *executioner* (Pla REP 439e) 2 Macc 5:8; 7:29.*‡

δῆμος, -ου, ὁ (Hom, Hdt+; 220) 1. *assembly, crowd* (= BDAG) Jdth 6:1. 2. *people, nation* Jdth 4:8; 1 Macc 8:29. 3. *clan, tribe* (no //; renders משפחה) Num 1:20ff (100x); Josh 7:14ff (30x); Judg 17:7; 2 Esdr 14:7.

δημοτελής, -ές (Hdt, Polyb+) *at public expense* 3 Macc 4:1.*

δημότης, -ου, ὁ (Tyrtaeus [VII BCE], Hdt+) *ordinary citizen* Wsd 18:11.*

δήξομαι see δάκνω.

δήσουσιν fut of BDAG: δέω.

δηχθείς ptc fr ἐδήχθην, 2 aor pass of δάκνω.

διαβάθρα, -ας, ἡ (pap, Strabo+) *ladder or gangplank* 2 Km 23:21.*

διάβασις, -εως, ἡ (12x, Hdt+) 1. *ford* (of river) Gen 32:23; Josh 2:7; PsSol 6:3; Jer 28:32; *(place of) crossing* (of gulley or pass) 1 Km 14:4. 2. *(act of) crossing* Josh 4:8; Is 51:10; *of passing through* Wsd 5:10. 2 Km 19:19—lit rendering of corrupt txt: *the ford crossed over* for *they crossed over the ford* (VEL SIM); LSJ: *ferryboat* is absurd; LXX precedes with doublet *they performed the service*, mistrans of עבר *cross over* as if עבד *serve.*

διαβιάζομαι (Eur, Theophr, Polyb) *force one's way through, go forcefully* Num 14:44.*

διαβιβάζω (8x, Hdt+) *bring over, cause to cross over* Gen 32:24; Josh 7:7; Wsd 10:18.

διαβιόω (Pla, X+) *live through, survive* Ex 21:21.*

διαβοάω aor pass διεβοήθη (Aeschyl+) *announce, proclaim* Gen 45:16; Lev 25:10; Jdth 10:18.*

διαβολή 2. *enmity* (cf. ἐνδιαβάλλω) Num 22:32.‡

διάβολος 3. (subst) *menace, threat* 1 Macc 1:36.‡

διαβουλεύομαι (Thu+) *deliberate, decide*; (ptc) *counselor* Gen 49:23.*

διαβουλή, -ῆς, ἡ (dub; not in LSJ) *counsel* Sir 51:2VL.*

διαβούλιον, -ου, τό (11x, Polyb+) 1. *plot, trap, scheme* Ps 5:11 (c. LSJ, LEH). 2. *counsel, deliberation* (good) Sir 15:14; (bad) Wsd 1:9; Hos 4:9; Ezk 11:5.

διάγγελμα, -ατος, τό (h.l.) 3 Km 5:1 mistrans of הַקֹּרֵב *what arrives* as if הַקָּרֵא (niph inf) *to be announced.*

διαγίνομαι (Thu, Lysias, Aristoph+) *go through life, continue* 2 Macc 11:26.*‡

διαγινώσκω 2. *discern, know the difference* Dt 2:7.‡

διαγλύφω pf pass ptc διαγεγλυμμένος (DiodS+) *engrave, carve out* Ex 28:11; 2 Ch 4:5; Ezk 41:19f.*

διαγορεύω (Pla, pap+) *establish, prescribe* Sus 61G; (pass) 1 Esdr 5:48.*

διαγραφή, -ῆς, ἡ (Pla+) *delineation, plan* Ezk 43:12.*

διαγράφω (9x, Lysias, Eur+) 1. *inscribe* Ezk 4:1; 8:10. 2. *delineate, describe* Josh 18:4; Ezk 43:11. 3. *subscribe for, promise payment of* Esth 3:9; 4 Macc 4:9. SSol 8:9 mistrans of צור *enclose, barricade* as if Aram צור *delineate.*

διάγω   1.b. *spend time, celebrate* 3 Macc 6:35. 2. *bring through* Ps 77:13; 135:14; Wsd 10:18; *lead through* 4 Km 17:17; 2 Ch 28:3; Zech 13:9; *lead off or away* 3 Macc 1:3; Job 12:17; Ezk 20:37; (pass) *be led* Is 55:12G. 2 Km 12:31 renders MT העביר *cause to go through*, but emend (McCarter AB) to העביד *set to work* (trans).‡

διαγωγή, -ῆς, ἡ   (Pla+) *conduct, way of life* Esth 3:13e.*

διαδέχομαι   1.b. *relieve, take someone's place* 1 Ch 26:18. 2. *act as deputy* (cf. διάδοχος 2.) Esth 10:3; 2 Macc 4:31; (ptc subst) *deputy, assistant* 2 Ch 31:12 (but 2 Macc 9:23 *successor*).‡

διαδέω   (Hdt, Pla+) *bind tightly* 4 Macc 9:11.*

διάδηλος, -ον   (Thu+) *distinguishable, observable* Gen 41:21; *manifest, apparent* 3 Macc 2:5.*

διαδιδράσκω   (Hdt+) *escape, flee* Sir 11:10; (reflex) *take (oneself) off, flee* 2 Macc 8:13.*

διαδίδωμι   2. *put out, spread forth* Sir 23:25; (pass, of news) *be spread abroad* 2 Macc 4:39.‡

διάδοχος, -ου, ὁ   (Aeschyl, Hdt+) 1. *successor* Sir 46:1; 48:8. 2. *deputy* (LXX+) 1 Ch 18:17; 2 Ch 26:11; 28:7; 2 Macc 4:29; 14:26.*‡

διαδύνω   (Hdt+, act or mid deponent) *slip or pass through* 1 Km 17:49.*

διαζάω   (Hdt+) *live, sustain oneself* 2 Macc 5:27.ꞌ

διάζομαι   (NicophoCom [IV BCE] *prepare a loom*) *weave, plait* (no //) Judg 16:14A; Is 19:10.*

διαθερμαίνω   aor pass διεθερμάνθη *warm up* Ex 16:21; 1 Km 11:9, 11; 4 Km 4:34.*

διάθεσις, -εως, ἡ   (9x, Hippocr, Pla+) 1. *disposition, arrangement* Esth 8:12q; 3 Macc 2:28. 2. *propensity, inclination* 2 Macc 5:23; 4 Macc 1:25; Ps 72:7.

διαθρύπτω   aor pass διεθρύβην (Hom+) *break* (bread) Lev 2:6; Is 58:7; (pass) *be broken, crumble* Sir 43:15; Na 1:6; Odes 4:6 = Hab 3:6.*‡

διαίρεσις   1.b. *division, allotted or assigned group* (of people) 1 Ch 24:1; 2 Esdr 6:18.‡

διαιρέω   pf pass ptc διῃρημένος.‡

δίαιτα   Job 20:24 mistrans of מררה *gall bladder*, perh as if fr מרר *bitter herbs or fruit*.‡

διαιτάω   (Hdt+) *control, govern* 4 Macc 2:17; (mid) *live one's life* Job 30:7; Sir 26:27(VL; or read διαρτηθῆναι [Num 23:19]).*

διαιτέω   (h.l.) *cajole, persuade*, (pass) *be persuaded* Jdth 8:16.*

διακαθιζάνω   (LXX+) *sit down at a distance* Dt 23:14.*

διακαθίζω   (X) *take their position, deploy* (no //, but = διακάθημαι in Joseph) 2 Km 11:1.*

διακαίω   ((Hdt+) *burn through* 4 Macc 11:19.*

διακάμπτω   (h.l.) *bow down full-length* 4 Km 4:34.*

διακαρτερέω   (Hdt+) *hold out, endure* Jdth 7:30; 4 Macc 6:9.*

διακατέχω   2 aor inf διακατασχεῖν (DiodS+) *secure, occupy* Jdth 4:7.*

διάκειμαι   (Hes, Hdt+) *be (well) inclined or disposed* 3 Macc 3:23; *be situated* 4:10.*

διάκενος, -ον   (Thu+) *porous, thin* Num 21:5.*

διακινδυνεύω   (Thu+) *run (great) risk, make a desperate attempt* 2 Macc 11:7.*

διακινέω   (Hdt+) *put in motion* 3 Macc 5:23.*

διακλάω   (Hom+) *break* (bread, no // but cf. BDAG: κλάω) La 4:4.*

διακλείω   (Polyb+) *shut off* 1 Macc 5:5VL.*

διακλέπτω   (Hdt+) *survive by stealth*; (mid) *steal away* 2 Km 19:4.*

διακολυμβάω   (Polyb+) *swim across* 1 Macc 9:48.*

διακομίζω   aor pass διεκομίσθην (10; Hdt+) *carry across* Josh 4:3, 8; 3 Macc 2:7; (pass) *be carried* 1 Esdr 2:11; (of person) *have oneself conveyed, convey oneself* 2 Macc 4:5; 9:29; 3 Macc 1:2.

διακονία   2.b. also (coll) *utensils, instruments* (cf. our "*table service*") 1 Macc 11:58.*‡

διακοπή, -ῆς, ἡ   (13x, Hippocr+) *cleft, breach* Judg 21:15; 2 Km 6:8²; Mi 2:13; *narrow pass* 2 Km 5:20; *inlet, channel* Judg 5:17A; Job 28:4; *deep wound* 2 Km 6:8¹; Pr 6:15.

διακόπτω   aor διέκοψα, pass διεκόπη (17x, Anacr, Thu+) *cut through, cleave, slash* 2 Macc 10:36; Ps 28:7; Am 9:1;

διακοσμέω (pass) Gen 38:29; 2 Km 5:20(2); *break through* (enemy ranks X ANAB 1.8.10) 2 Km 5:20(1); 1 Ch 15:13; (pass) 2 Macc 10:30R (Gött διεξίπταμαι, q.l.); *breach* ([walls of] a city) 3 Km 2:35f; Jer 52:7.

διακοσμέω **2.** *array, adorn* 2 Macc 3:25.‡

διακρατέω (Phylarchus [III BCE]+) *control, hold securely* 1 Esdr 4:50; Jdth 6:12.*

διακριβάζομαι (not in LSJ) *prove oneself strict or precise* Sir 51:19.*

διακρίβεια, -ας, ἡ (h.l.) *precise observance* 3 Km 11:33VL.*

διακριβόω (X, Pla+) *examine precisely or minutely* 2 Macc 2:28; (mid) *prove oneself precise* Sir 51:19VL.*

διακρύπτω (DiogL, Pollux) *conceal* 1 Km 3:17VL, 2 Macc 14;30VL.*

διακύπτω (11x, Hdt+) *look out, look down* Judg 5:28A; 2 Km 6:16; 2 Macc 3:19G (Ra διεκκύπτω); Ps 13:2; La 3:50; Ezk 41:16.

διαλαμβάνω (Hdt+) *determine, apprehend* (intellectually) Esth 3:13e; Jdth 8:14, > *think, believe* 2 Macc 5:11; 6:29; 3 Macc 3:26.*

διαλανθάνω (Thu+) *escape or pass unnoticed* 2 Km 4:6.*

διαλείπω *leave an interval of time*; hence not only *stop, cease* (= BDAG) but also **2.** *wait, delay, hesitate* 1 Km 10:8; 2 Ch 29:11.‡

διάλευκος, -ον (Aristot+) *completely white* Gen 30:32ff; 31:10ff.*

διάλημψις, -εως, ἡ (Aristot, Polyb+) *opinion, apprehension* 2 Macc 3:32.*

διαλλαγή, -ῆς, ἡ (Hdt+) *reconciliation* Sir 22:22; 27:21.*

διαλλάσσω (10x, Aeschyl, Hdt+) **1.** *change, alter* Job 5:12; Wsd 19:18; (mid/pass, cf. BDAG: -άσσομαι) *differ, be different* Job 36:28b; Wsd 15:4. **2.** *exchange*; διαλλ. τὸν βίον *"die"* 2 Macc 6:27. **3.** *reconcile* (act) Judg 19:3; (mid/pass, = BDAG) *be reconciled* 1 Km 29:4; 1 Esdr 4:31.‡

διάλλομαι (X+) *leap over or across* SSol 2:8.*

διαλογή, -ῆς, ἡ (Aristot+) *enumeration, discourse* Ps 103:34.*

διάλογος, -ου, ὁ (Pla+) *dialogue, debate* Job 7:13VL.*

διαλοιδόρησις, -εως, ἡ (h.l.) *verbal abuse, railing* Sir 27:15.*

διαλυτός, -ή, -όν (Pla+) *capable of coming apart* Ex 36:30VL.*

διαλύω **4.** (abs) *grow slack, become dissolute* 2 Esdr 11:7; *become pliant, be reconciled* Pr 6:35.‡

διαμαρτυρέω pf mid διαμεμαρτύρημαι (Lysias+; in our lit only mid) *attest, affirm* Gen 43:3; Ex 19:23; 21:36; 1 Km 21:2.*

διαμαρτυρία, -ας, ἡ (Demosth+) *accusation, (legal) plea, testimony* Gen 43:3; 4 Macc 16:16.*

διαμαρτύρομαι **3.** *call as witnesses* Dt 8:19 = 30:19; w. cogn acc *provide witnesses* Jer 39:10, 44.‡

διαμασάομαι (Aristot+) *chew thoroughly*; (fig) *"chew your way through"* Sir 31:16.

διαμαχίζομαι pf διμεμάχισται (h.l.; LSJ-Sup) *exert oneself, contend fiercely* Sir 51:19.*

διαμελίζω (DiodS+) *dismember* Da 3:96L.*

διαμερισμός **2.** *division, separate part* Ezk 48:29.‡

διαμετρέω (37x, Hdt+) *measure out, apportion* 2 Km 8:2; Ps 59:8; Zech 2:6; Ezk 40:5ff.

διαμέτρησις, -εως, ἡ (ins+) *measurement* 2 Ch 3:3; Jer 38:39; Ezk 42:15; 45:3; *diameter* 2 Ch 4:2.*

διαναπαύω (Aristot+) *relieve, allow to rest* Gen 5:29.*

διαναφέρω (dub; not in LSJ) *bring as an offering* Lev 4:10VL.*

διανέμω aor διένειμα (Pind, Aristoph, X+) *apportion, assign* Dt 29:25.*‡

διανήθω pf pass ptc διανενησμένος *spun out* Ex 28:8, 33; 35:6; 36:10, 12, 15.*

διανθίζω (LXX+) *decorate w. flowers* (Luc) or *jewels* (Joseph) Esth 1:6.*

διανίστημι pres pass ptc διανιστάμενος (Thu+) *arise* Jdth 12:15; *rise from sleep* (2 aor and pass) Dt 6:7; 11:9.*

διανοέομαι **2.** *have in mind, intend* 2 Km 21:16.‡

διανόησις, -εως, ἡ (Pla+) *thought,* > *skill, technique* (no //) 2 Ch 2:13.*

διαξαίνω aor διέξανα (Aristoph+) *card, comb* Jdth 10:3R (q.l.; Vulg DISCRIMINAVIT, *parted, combed*).*

διαπαρατηρέομαι (h.l.) *constantly lie in wait, persistently seek to ambush* 2 Km 3:30.*

διαπαρθενεύω (Hdt+) *have sex for the first time, deflower;* (pass) *lose one's virginity* Ezk 23:3, 8.*

διαπαύω (X+) *take away, omit, let cease* Lev 2:13; Hos 5:13.*

διαπειλέω (Hdt+) *threaten violently* 3 Macc 6:23; 7:6; Ezk 3:17.*

διαπειράζω (Joseph *AJ* 15.97 *attempt*) *test, try* (no //) 3 Macc 5:40.*‡

διαπείρω (Hom [tmesis], Eur+) *pierce, transfix* 4 Macc 11:19.*

διαπέμπω or **-ομαι** (Hdt+) **1.** *send on, send along* Jdth 14:12; 2 Macc 3:37; 3 Macc 1:8; (mid) *transmit, send* (a message) 1 Esdr 1:24; 2 Macc 11:26. **2.** *disperse* Pr 16:28.*‡

διαπετάννυμι aor διεπέτασα pf act ptc διαπεπετακότα pf pass ptc διαπεπετασμένος (23; Aristoph+) *extend and spread out* 2 Km 17:19; 3 Km 6:27ff; 1 Ch 28:18; Tob 3:11S; Ps 43:21; 87:10; La 1:13ff; Ezk 16:8. La 2:6R see διασπάω.

διαπέτομαι or **διίπταμαι** (Hom, Eur+) *fly through* Wsd 5:11.*

διάπηγον, -ου, τό (h.l.) *side? frame?* 3 Km 7:17vl.*

διαπίπτω aor διέπεσεν pf ptc διαπεπτωκώς (18; Aristoph+) **1.** *fall away* Num 5:21ff; 2 Macc 2:14; *decay* (flesh) 9:9. **2.** *crumble, fall to pieces* Job 14:18; Na 2:7; Jer 18:4. **3.** *fall down (and die)* Dt 2:14ff; (of people) *break down, collapse* 2 Esdr 18:10. **4.** *fail, prove false* Josh 21:45; Jdth 6:9.

διαπλατύνω (X+) *widen, expand* Ezk 41:7.*

διαπληκτίζομαι (LXX+) *spar, dispute* Ex 2:13.*

διαπνέω aor διέπνευσα (X+) *blow* (air or breath) *through, breathe* SSol 2:17; 4:6, 16.*

διαπονέω **1.b.** *be worn out* (by toil) Eccl 10:9. **2.** (act) *work through, struggle through* 2 Macc 2:28.*‡

διάπρασις, -εως, ἡ (pap+) *sale* Lev 25:33.*

διαπράσσω (Hom, Hdt+) *go through;* (mid) *perform, accomplish* 2 Macc 8:29; 10:38.*

διαπρεπής, -ές (Pind, Thu+) *distinguished, magnificent* 2 Macc 3:26; 10:29.*

διαπρέπω (Aeschyl, Pla+) *be eminent or conspicuous* PsSol 10:3vl.*

διάπτωσις, -εως, ἡ (LXX+) *fall, failure, breaking to pieces* Jer 19:14R (Gött N LOC).*

διάπυρος, -ον (Anaxagoras, Eur+) *red-hot* 3 Macc 6:6; Da 3:46L.*

διαπυρόω (Eur+) *set on fire;* (pass, fig) *be inflamed* (w. thirst) 4 Macc 3:15.*

διαραντός, -ή, -όν (h.l. not in LSJ) *thoroughly spotted* Gen 30:32vl.*

διαριθμέω (Eur+) *reckon, take into account* 3 Macc 3:6.*

διαρκέω (Aeschyl+) *suffice;* (pass) *find sufficient, be content* (no //) 3 Macc 2:26.*

διαρπαγή, -ῆς, ἡ (20x, Hdt+) **1.** *(act of) plundering* 2 Esdr 9:7; Esth 7:4; Jdth 8:19; Hab 2:7; Is 5:5. **2.** *booty, plunder* Num 14:3; 4 Km 21:24; Jdth 2:7; Mal 3:10.

διαρραίνω pf διέρραγκα (Soph, Aristot+) *sprinkle* Pr 7:17.*

διαρρέω aor (pass in form) διαρρυῆναι (Hdt, Soph+) *flow through;* (fig) *slip through, slip away* 2 Macc 10:20.*

διαρρήγνυμι or **-ρήσσω** 2 pf διερρηγώς or -ρωγώς (pass sense) **1.c.** *burst through, break through* (enemy fortifications Hom *Il* 12.308) 2 Km 23:16 = 1 Ch 11:18. 2 Esdr 19:21 mistrans of בצק *swell* (Dt 8:4 τυλόω "become calloused") as if Aram בזע *rend, tear.*‡

διαρρίπτω or **-ριπτέω** (Hom+) *throw about, disperse* Job 41:11; Is 62:10.*

διαρρυῆναι see διαρρέω.

διαρρυθμίζω (ins) *arrange, set in order* 2 Macc 7:22.*

διαρτάω (Menand, Polyb+) *mislead, deceive;* (pass) *be misled* Num 23:19; Sir 26:27cj.*

διαρτίζω (LXX) *mold, shape;* (pass) *be shaped* Job 33:6.*

διασαλεύω (Polyb+) *shake violently;* (pass) *be violently shaken* Hab 2:16.*

διασαφηνίζω (X+) = BDAG: διασαφέω 2 Macc 3:9vl.*

διασάφησις, -εως, ἡ (LXX) **1.** *interpretation, explanation* Gen 40:8. **2.** *report, clear presentation* 2 Esdr 5:6; 7:11.*

διασαφίζω (h.l.) = BDAG: διασαφέω 2 Macc 1:20VL.*

διασκάπτω (Lysias, ins+) *dig through, breach* Jdth 2:24VL.*

διασκεδάζω or **-άννυμι** aor διεσκέδασα (46; Hom+) **1.** *scatter, disperse* Ex 32:25; 2 Ch 16:3; Eccl 12:5; Job 38:24; Is 9:10. **2.** (no //) *dissolve, disobey* (διαθήκην, ἐντολήν) Gen 17:14; Judg 2:1; 1 Macc 2:31; Ps 118:126; Jer 11:10; *dissolve, render void* (διαθήκην, subj God) Da 3:34 = Odes 7:34; *subvert* (βουλήν, κτλ) 2 Km 15:31; 2 Esdr 4:5; 3 Macc 5:30; Ps 32:10; Is 8:10; *render void or meaningless* (ἐλεός) Ps 88:34; (εὐλογίαν) Mal 2:2; (pass) *be subverted or voided* Hab 1:4.

διασκευάζω (X, Polyb+) *get ready, equip;* (pass) *be readied* (for battle) Josh 4:12; 1 Macc 6:33.*

διασκευή, -ῆς, ἡ (Polyb+) **1.** *equipment* Ex 31:7. **2.** *readiness* (for battle, no //) 2 Macc 11:10.*

διασκιρτάω (LXX+) *leap or skip about* Wsd 19:9.*

διασκορπισμός, -οῦ, ὁ (pap) *dispersal* Jer 24:9; Ezk 6:8; *scattering, confusion* Da 12:7Θ. Ezk 13:20 mistrans of לְפֹרְחֹת unexpl, as if fr Aram פרח *to fly* (cf. Vulg AD VOLANDUM).*

δίασμα, -ατος, τό (Callim+) *warp* (of loom) Judg 16:13B, 14.*

διασπασμός, -οῦ, ὁ (Philod+) *rending, tearing apart* Jer 15:3.*

διασπάω *tear up, tear apart* La 2:6G cj (L, al ἐκσπάω).‡

διάσταλσις, -εως, ἡ (h.l.) *condition, provision* (of treaty or compact) 2 Macc 13:25.*

διάστασις, -εως, ἡ (Hdt+) *difference, contrast* 3 Macc 3:7.*

διαστέλλω fut διαστελῶ pass διασταλήσομαι aor διέστειλα pass διεστάλη pf pass ptc διεσταλμένος (57; Pla+) **1.a.** *intrude, come between* Judg 1:19; Ruth 1:17; 4 Km 2:11; *separate out* Mi 5:7; (pass) *be separated or set off* 2 Esdr 10:8; Jer 22:14. **1.b.** *distinguish, set aside* Gen 30:35; Num 8:14; 3 Km 8:53; 2 Esdr 8:24; *draw aside* (a curtain) Jdth 14:15; (pass) *become distinct, be divided* Gen 25:23; *be set aside* Lev 16:26; > *disappear, be destroyed* (no //) Na 1:12. **2.a.** *define, make distinct* Gen 30:28; 2 Esdr 18:8; pf pass ptc pl subst *(matters) defined (previously), conditions, stipulations, agreements* 2 Macc 14:28; *make distinction(s)* PsSol 2:34; Ezk 22:26; 24:14; 42:20; (ptc) *distinct* 1 Km 3:1. **2.b.** *declare, announce* Lev 5:4; Ps 65:14; *address, speak to* Sus 48G. **2.c.** *assign, appoint* Sir 16:26; Ezk 39:14; (mid; only meaning in BDAG) *give a command* Jdth 11:12; 2 Macc 14:28. Ps 67:15 mistrans of פרש *scatter* as if פרש *inform, explain.*‡

διάστημα **2.** *extension* (of space) 3 Km 6:6; 7:46; Ezk 41:6ff; *opening, open space* 2 Macc 14:44.‡

διαστηρίζω (Hippocr+) *strengthen, make firm* Sir 28:1VL.*

διαστολή **2.** *boundary, separation* Ex 8:19; 1 Macc 8:7. **3.** *dilation, opening* (χειλέων *of the lips,* to speak) Num 30:7. **4.** *specific injunction, contractual article* Num 19:2.*‡

διαστράπτω (h.l.) *flash as lightning* Wsd 16:22.*

διαστροφή, -ῆς, ἡ (Hippocr, Aristot+) *perversion, distortion* Pr 2:14.*

διαστρώννυμι (HR διαστορέννυμι; Phylarch) *spread out bedding* 1 Km 9:25.*

διασυρίζω (h.l.) *whistle through* Da 3:50.*

διασφαγή, -ῆς, ἡ (pap) *gap* 2 Esdr 14:1.*

διασφάλλω (Aeschin, Polyb+) *overturn;* (pass) *be disappointed, fail* (w. respect to τινός) 3 Macc 5:12.*

διασφραγίζομαι (h.l.) *seal up* Jer 39:10VL.*

διασχίζω (Hom+) *sever, cut in two* Ps 34:15; Wsd 18:23.*

διασῴζω Josh 6:26 (aor pass ptc) mistrans of (N PERS) שׂגב *exalted* as if *made safe;* cf. 3 Km 16:34.‡

διάταξις **2.** (Hdt+) *arrangement, disposition* Ezk 42:15, 20; *deployment* (of troops) Jdth 1:4.‡

διατάσσω **3.** *put in order, arrange* Jdth 10:3G; (cf. διαξαίνω) Ezk 42:20; (pf pass ptc) *in (battle) order* (Hdt, Thu); (subst) *those stationed there, guards* (no //) Judg 3:23B.‡

διατείνω fut διατενῶ pf pass ptc διατεταμένος (Hdt+) **1.** *stretch out* Ps 139:6; Is 40:22; (pass ptc) *stretched, fully drawn* (arrow) Is 21:15. **2.** (intr) *extend, reach* Wsd 8:1. **3.** *extend, maintain* (trans, no //) Ps 84:6.*

διατήκω 2 aor pass διετάκην (Aristoph+) *melt*; (pass) *melt away* Odes 4:6 = Hab 3:6.*

διατήρησις, -εως, ἡ (DiodS+) *preserving, preservation* Ex 16:33f; Num 17:25; 18:8; 19:9.*

διατίθημι **1.** (c. BDAG) *settle or arrange together*; (w. cogn acc διαθήκη) *enter into a mutual agreement* (Aristoph *Av* 440) Gen 9:17; Ex 24:8; Josh 9:6; 4 Km 23:3; Hos 12:2; Jer 38:31; (of the nations, against God) Ps 82:6; (mid abs) *submit (oneself) to a treaty relationship* 1 Ch 19:19; (God as subj) PsSol 9:10. **4.** *arrange* (Hdt+) Ps 83:6; *distribute* (as property), *dispose of* (τινί) Is 57:8vL.‡

διατίλλω aor διέτιλε(ν) (Soph *FR* 659.7) *pluck* Job 16:12.*

διατόνιον, -ου, τό (CallixenusHist, pap: -τόναιον *joist, curtain rod*) *post or rod* (for curtains) Ex 35:11.*

διατόρευμα, -ατος, τό (h.l.) *engraved work* 3 Km 7:17vL.*

διατρεπής, -ές (dub; not in HR or LSJ) *deterring, perplexing* 2 Macc 3:26vL.*

διατρέπω aor pass διετράπην pf pass ptc διατετραμμένος (Hippocr, Demosth, Polyb+) *overturn, pervert* Judg 18:7; (pass) *be contorted* Esth 7:8; *be disfigured* Da 1:10L, 13G, *be afraid of, refuse to face* (τινά) Job 31:34.*

διατρέφω fut διαθρέψει aor διέθρεψα, pass διετράφη (17; Thu+) *feed* 3 Km 17:4; > *care for, preserve* Gen 7:3; Ruth 4:15; 2 Km 19:33; 2 Esdr 19:21; Ps 30:4; (pass) *be preserved* Gen 50:20; Jdth 5:10; Pr 22:9.

διατρέχω fut διαδραμοῦμαι aor διέδραμον (Hom+) *run through or around* Ex 9:23; 3 Km 18:26; Wsd 3:7; Na 2:5; *run to or up to* 1 Km 17:17(vL).*

διατριβή, -ῆς, ἡ (Aristoph, Pla+) *place to spend time, haunt* Lev 13:46; Pr 12:11a; 14:24; 31:27; Jer 30:28.*

διατροπόω (not in LSJ) *thoroughly rout* 1 Macc 10:72vL.*

διατυπόω (Aristot+) *shape, arrange* Wsd 19:6.*

διαφαίνω (Hom, Hdt+) *shine through* Wsd 17:6; (itac -φεν-) 18:10vL.*‡

διαφαύσκω (Ionic διαφώσκω Judg 19:26B) aor διέφαυσα (Hdt+) *dawn, become light* Gen 44:3; Judg 16:2B; 19:26; 1 Km 14:36; 2 Km 2:32; Jdth 14:2.*

διαφείδομαι (spur; not in HR, LSJ, Gött app) 2 Macc 1:18vLR.*

διαφέρω pf pass ptc διενηνεγμένος **2.b.** *carry off (to different places)* 2 Macc 4:39. **3.b.** *separate, move apart*; (pass) *be separated* Wsd 18:2; (fig) *disagree, quarrel* (w. τινί) 2 Macc 3:4.‡

διαφθείρω Judg 16:7B mistrans of חֹרֶב *dried as if ruined.*‡

διαφλέγω (LXX+) *burn through, burn up* Ps 82:15.*

διαφοβέω (spur; not in HR or LSJ) *fear; f.l.* for -φορ- Jer 37:16vL.*

διαφόβημα, -ατος, τό (spur; not in HR or LSJ) *fearful thing; f.l.* for -φορ- Jer 37:16vL.*

διαφορέω (Hom, Hdt+) *plunder* Jer 37:16.*

διαφόρημα, -ατος, τό (h.l.) *plunder, booty* Jer 37:16.*

διάφορος **3.** (neut subst) *money, cash* (ins, pap, Polyb) 2 Macc 3:6; 4:28; Sir 7:18; 27:1; (adv) *differently* Da 7:7G.‡

διαφρύγω (LXX+) *bake* 4 Macc 3:11vL.*

διαφυλάσσω (Att -λάττω 2 Macc 6:6; Wsd 17:4) **2.** *keep up, observe* 2 Macc 6:6.‡

διαφωνέω pf διαπεφώνηκεν (Pla+: *strike a false note*) **1.** *be lost, perish* (ins) Ex 24:11; Num 31:49; 1 Km 30:19; Jdth 10:13; Ezk 37:11. **2.** *fail* (of promises) Josh 23:14; 3 Km 8:56.*

διαφώσκω see διαφαύσκω.

διαφωτίζω (LXX+) *shed light* 2 Esdr 18:3.*

διαχέω impf mid/pass διεχεῖτο aor διέχεα pass διεχύθην pf pass διακέχυμαι (25; Hom+) *be dispersed* 1 Km 30:16; 2 Macc 8:7G; Wsd 2:3; Da 3:47; *be poured out* Job 21:24; Ezk 30:16; *be dissolved* Jer 2:20; *spread* (of disease) Lev 13:22ff; (of dawn) 2 Macc 10:28.

Zech 1:17 mistrans of פוץ *overflow* as if *scatter, disperse.*

διαχρίω (Hippocr, Aristot+) *thoroughly smear* Lev 2:4; 7:12.*

διάχρυσος, -ον (Polyb+) *interwoven w. gold* 2 Macc 5:2; Ps 44:10.*

διάχυσις, -εως, ἡ (Hippocr, Pla+) *expansion, spread* (of disease) Lev 13:22G, 27, 35; 14:48.*

διαχωρίζω Num 32:12 pf pass ptc *who separated himself* renders הקיני *the Kenite;* Judg 13:19B mistrans of Heb מפל(י)א *doing wonders* as if fr Aram פלא *depart.*‡

διάψαλμα, -ατος, τό (92x, LXX; alw for Heb סלה unexpl) *musical interlude* Ps 2:2; 3:3, 5, etc; PsSol 17:29; 18:9.

διαψεύδω pf pass ptc διεψευσμένος (Pla+) *deceive, cheat* 4 Km 4:16; 1 Macc 13:19; (pass) *be cheated out of* (τινός), *fail in* 3 Macc 5:12.*

διαψιθυρίζω (Theophr+) *whisper* Sir 12:18.*

διγομία, -ας, ἡ (h.l.) *double load* (cf. γόμος), renders משפתים *saddlebags* Judg 5:16B.*

διδάσκω pf δεδίδαχα pass ptc δεδιδαγμένος. Is 55:12R scribal error for διάγω (so Gött; MT תובלון, fr יבל *bring, lead*). Da 11:4L mistrans of מלבד *apart from* as if מלמד *teaching.*‡

διδυμεύω (LXX) *bear twins* SSol 4:2; 6:6.*

δίδυμος, -ον (Hom+) *double, twin* (tree) Josh 8:29; (fawns) SSol 4:5; 7:4; (children, neut, sc τέκνα) Gen 25:24; 38:27; (abs) *testicles* (no //) Dt 25:11.*

δίδωμι pf pass ptc δεδομένος δ. εἰς καρδίαν *lay it to heart, keep in mind* Eccl 7:2. 1 Ch 9:2 renders נתינים *hierodules* (lit *donated* or *appointed,* fr נתן *give*).‡

διεγγυάω (Thu+) *pledge property as security* 2 Esdr 15:3.*

διεγείρω 2. (Joseph *BJ* 6.5.156) *raise, construct;* (pf pass ptc) *raised, built* Jdth 1:4.‡

διείς see διίημι.

διεκβάλλω (9x, Polyb+) *pass through, extend through* Josh 15:4ff; 16:7.*

διεκβολή, -ῆς, ἡ (Polyb+) *way through or out; mountain pass* Ob 14; Jer 12:12; *watercourse* Zech 9:10; Ezk 47:8, 11; *city gate* 48:30.*

διεκκύπτω (LXX+) *lean out* 2 Macc 3:19R (Gött διακύπτω).*

διελαύνω aor διήλασα (Hom+) *drive* (τι) *through* Judg 4:21A; 5:26A.*‡

διελέγχω 1.b. (pass) *argue a case* Mi 6:2.‡

διεμβάλλω (LXX+) *insert, implant* Ex 40:18; Num 4:6ff.*

διεμπίμπλημι pf pass ptc διεμπιπλαμένος (h.l.) *fill completely* 2 Macc 4:40.*

διενηνεγμένος see διαφέρω.

διεξάγω (Chrysipp, Polyb+) *conduct, accomplish* 2 Macc 10:12; 14:30; Sir 3:17; (pass) Hab 1:4; (abs) *conduct oneself, act* Esth 3:13b.*

διέξειμι 3rd pl aor διεξήεσαν (Hdt+) *go throughout* 4 Macc 3:13.*

διεξέρχομαι 2. *go completely through* Job 20:25.*‡

διεξίπταμαι (h.l.; not in HR or LSJ, cf. ἐξίπταμαι Pr 7:10) *fly off;* (fig) *flee* (ἀορασίᾳ *blindly*) *in all directions* 2 Macc 10:30G (q.l.).*

διεξοδεύω (Hippocr, Joseph+) *find a way out, come out* Da 3:48L.*

διέξοδος 2. *way out,* > *boundary* (no //) Num 34:4ff; Josh 15:4ff.‡

διερεθίζω (Aristot+) *stimulate, provoke; fan* (flames) 4 Macc 9:19.*

διερευνάω (Pla+) *investigate* Wsd 6:3; 13:7.*

διέρραγκα see διαρραίνω.

διέρρηχα pf of BDAG: διαρρήγνυμι; ptc διερρηχώς 2 Km 14:30; pf ptc intr, pass sense διερρηγώς 1 Km 4:12; -ρρωγώς 2 Km 1:2; EpJer 30; pf pass ptc διερρηγμένος 1 Esdr 8:70.

διέρχομαι 1.c. (of time) *pass, go by* Ex 14:20; Tob 1:21; 2 Macc 1:20.‡

δίεσις, -εως, ἡ (Hippocr, Aristot+) *dismissal, release* (of offenders) Wsd 12:20.*

διεστραμμένως (Heliod [2.19]) adv fr pf pass ptc of BDAG: διαστρέφω; *in misleading or distorted fashion* Sir 4:17.*

διετηρίς, -ίδος, ἡ (ins) *two-year interval* 2 Km 13:23.*

διευλαβέομαι (Pla+) *fear, guard against, be wary of* Dt 28:60; 2 Macc 9:29; Job 6:16.*

διηγέομαι 2. *be a leader, set an example* (w. respect to his ἀγωγή; no //, as if = ἡγέομαι) Esth 10:3.‡

διήγημα, -ατος, τό (Phoenicides, Polyb+) 1. *narrative* 2 Macc 2:24; Ezk 17:2. 2. *maxim, byword* (no //) Dt 28:37; 2 Ch 7:20; Sir 8:8f.*‡

διήγησις 2. *speech, recitation* (no //) Sir 9:15; 27:11, 13; 38:25.‡

διηθέω (Hdt+) *filter, strain, cleanse* Job 28:1.*

διήκω (Aeschyl, Hdt+) *pervade* Wsd 7:24.*

διήλασα aor of διελαύνω.

διηλόω (Julian) *drive* (τι) *through, nail down* Judg 5:26B.*

διῃρημένος pf pass ptc of BDAG: διαιρέω.

διηρπασμένος pf pass ptc of BDAG: διαρπάζω Jer 21:12.

διηχέω (LXX+) *resound;* (pass) *be widely proclaimed* 2 Macc 8:7R (Gött διαχέω).*

δίθυμος, -ον (h.l.) *dissenting;* (subst) *dissenter, contentious person* Pr 26:20.*

δίημι pres ptc διείς (Hom+) *push through, allow to pass through* Dt 32:11 = Odes 2:11.*

διίπταμαι or διίπτομαι see διαπέτομαι

διΐστημι 2.b. *set aside; separate* Tob 7:11S, *provide (for)* 2 Macc 8:10.‡

δικάζω 2. (mid) *go to court, plead a case* Judg 6:31; Sir 8:14.‡

δικαιοκρίτης, -ου, ὁ (pap [II CE]) *just judge* 2 Macc 12:41.*

δικαιολογία, -ας, ἡ (Aristot+) *court speech* 2 Macc 4:44.*

δίκαιος 2.b. (pl subst) *legal or civil rights* Wsd 19:16.‡

δικαίωμα 1 Km 27:11; 4 Km 17:8 s.t. of משפט *habit, pattern* as if *legal decision or standard.*‡

δικαστήριον, -ου, τό (Hdt+) *court, place of judgment* Judg 6:32A.*

δίκη 3. δίκην (acc as adv) *in the manner of, like* (τινός) Wsd 12:24.‡

δίκτυον 2. *lattice, lattice work* (ins) SSol 2:9.‡

δικτυόω (Babrius) *enmesh;* (pass) *be latticed or covered w. netting* 3 Km 7:6.*

δικτυωτός, -ή, -όν (Polyb+) *net-like; latticed* Ex 27:4; 38:24; in appos to θυρίς Judg 5:28A, cf. Ezk 41:16; (subst) *latticed doorway* 4 Km 1:2.*

διμαφουν f.l. (not in HR or LSJ) 3 Macc 5:27VL.*

διμερής, -ές (Aristot+) *bipartite, divided* Da 2:41L.*

δίμετρον, -ου, τό (LXX) *double measure* 4 Km 7:1, 16, 18.*

δίνη, -ης, ἡ (Hom, Hdt+) *whirlpool* Job 28:10; *whirlwind* (Eur+) 37:9.*

δίοδος, -ου, ἡ (11x, Hom+) *way through, way in or out* Dt 13:17; Jdth 5:1; 1 Macc 11:46; Pr 7:8; Is 11:16.

διοικέω (Thu+) *administer, govern* Wsd 8:1, 14; 12:18; 15:1; Da 3:1L.*

διοικητής, -οῦ, ὁ (Menand+) *administrator, steward* 2 Esdr 8:36; Tob 1:22; Da 3:2L.*

διοικοδομέω (Thu, Pla, DiodS) *block off, build (as) a barricade* 2 Esdr 12:17.*

διόλλυμι (Soph+) *completely destroy* Wsd 11:19; 17:9.*

διόλου = BDAG: δι' ὅλου (ὅλος 2.) Bel 12Θ.

διοράω (X, Pla+) *see through, perceive* Job 6:19.*

διοργίζομαι (Polyb+) *be angry* 3 Macc 3:1; 4:13.*

διορθρίζω (h.l.) *rise early* 1 Km 29:10VL.*

διορθωτής, -οῦ, ὁ (LXX+) *corrector, reformer* Wsd 7:15.*

διορίζω 2. *mark off, separate, make distinct* (τινά) Lev 20:24; Job 35:11. 3. *branch off* (of river, cf. Polyb 4.43.7) 2 Ch 32:4.‡

διόρυγμα, -ατος, τό (Thu: *canal*) *breach, hole* (in a wall) Ex 22:1; Zeph 2:14; Jer 2:34.*

δίπηχυς, -υ (Hdt+) *two cubits* (ca. 1m) *deep* Num 11:31.*

διπλασιάζω (Pla+) *double, (re)double* (in size, extent, or number) Ezk 21:19; 43:2.*

διπλασιασμός, -οῦ, ὁ (AntiphoSoph, Pla+) *doubling* Job 42:10.*

διπλάσιος, -α, -ον (Hdt+) *doubled, two-fold* Sir 12:5; 26:1.*

διπλοΐς, -ΐδος, ἡ (9x, LXX+) *double cloak* 1 Km 2:19; Job 29:14; Ps 108:29; Bar 5:2.

δίσκος, -ου, ὁ (Hom+) *discus* 2 Macc 4:14.*

δισμύριοι, -αι, -α (Hdt+) *20,000* 2 Macc 5:24; 8:9, 30; 10:17, 23, 31.*

δισχιλιάς, -άδος, ἡ   (dub; h.l.) *number of 20,000* 1 Macc 9:4VL.*

διτάλαντος, -ον   (Hdt+) *weighing two talents;* (neut subst) *mass of two talents* 4 Km 5:23.*

διυφαίνω   (LXX+) *weave completely* Ex 36:30.*

διφθέρα, -ας, ἡ   (Hdt+) *piece of leather* Ex 39:20.*

δίφορος, -ον   (Aristot, Theophr+: *bearing fruit twice a year*) *bearing two kinds of fruit* (Philo SPEC 4:203, 208; =) Dt 22:9VL (q.l. so also Lev 19:19; cf. MT כלאים *of two kinds*).*

δίφραξ, -ακος, ἡ   (Theocr 14.41 *seat, chair*) *chariot* (no //, but cf. δίφρος, which can also mean *chariot* or *chair*) 2 Macc 14:21.*

διφρεύω   (Eur+: *drive a chariot*) *sit on a chair, sit apart* (no //) EpJer 30.*

δίφρος, -ου, ὁ   (12x, Hom+) *seat, throne* Dt 17:18G; 1 Km 1:9; Jdth 11:19; 2 Macc 14:21; Job 29:7; Sir 38:33; *night stool, latrine seat* Judg 3:24A.

δίχα   2. (adv) *at variance, in opposition* Sir 47:21.*‡

διχηλεύω   (dub; h.l.) *have a divided hoof* Dt 14:6VL.*

διχομηνία, -ας, ἡ   (ins, pap) *full moon* Sir 39:12.*

διχοτόμημα, -ατος, τό   (LXX+) *cut-up piece* (of something cut in two or dismembered) Gen 15:11, 17; Ex 29:17; Lev 1:8; Ezk 24:4.*

δίψα, -ης, ἡ   (16x, Hom+) *thirst* Dt 8:15; 2 Ch 32:11; Jdth 7:13ff; 4 Macc 3:6ff; Ps 68:22; Wsd 11:4; Am 8:11; (τινός *for something*), Is 5:13.

διψάω   Job 18:9 mistrans of צמים *snare* (?) as if fr אמצ *be thirsty*.‡

διψώδης, -ες   (Hippocr, Plu) *making thirsty* Pr 9:12c.*

διωγμός   2. *pursuit* 2 Macc 12:23.‡

διωθέω   (Hom+) *push away* Ezk 34:21; (abs) *refuse* 1 Macc 4:8VL.*

διώροφος, -ον   (LXX+) *of two stories;* (neut pl) *second-story rooms* Gen 6:16.*

διῶρυξ, -υγος, ἡ   (8x, Hdt+) *channel, trench* Ex 7:19; Sir 24:30f; Is 19:6; Jer 38:9.

διωστήρ, -ῆρος, ὁ   (LXX+) *pole* Ex 38:4ff; 39:14; 40:20.*

δοκιμαστής, -οῦ, ὁ   (c. HR; Lysias, Pla+) *tester, examiner* Jer 6:27.*

δοκιμῶ   alt fut of BDAG: δοκιμάζω.

δόκωσις, -εως, ἡ   (Plu+) *roofing, structure of rafters* Eccl 10:18.*

δόμος, -ου, ὁ   (Hom+: *house, chamber*) *course* (of masonry, Hdt+) 1 Esdr 6:24; 2 Esdr 6:4.*

δόξα   5. *appearance, seeming* Is 11:3.‡

δόξασμα, -ατος, τό   (Thu+: *notion, idea*) *glorious thing, (manifestation of) glory* (no //) Is 46:13; La 2:1.*

δοξαστός, -ή, -όν   (Pla+: *matter of conjecture or opinion*) *glorious, honored* (no //) Dt 26:19.*

δοξικός, -ή, -όν   (not in LSJ) *splendid, magnificent* 2 Macc 8:35.*

δοξολογέω   (not in HR or LSJ) *praise* Odes 14:7.*

δορά, -ᾶς, ἡ   (Hdt+) *skin, hide* Gen 25:25; 4 Macc 9:28; Mi 2:8.*

δορατοφόρος, -ον   (LXX+) *spear-carrying* 1 Ch 12:25.*

δοριάλωτος, -ον   (Hdt+) *captured at spearpoint;* (of pers) *taken captive* 3 Macc 1:5; (of place) *taken by storm* 2 Macc 5:11; 10:24.*

δορκάδιον, -ου, τό   (ins: *small statue of gazelle*) *little gazelle* Is 13:14.*

δόρκων, -ωνος, ὁ   (LXX+) *male deer* (cf. BDAG: Δορκάς) *or gazelle* SSol 2:17.*

δορυφορία, -ας, ἡ   (X+) *detachment of bodyguards* (no //) 2 Macc 3:28.*

δορυφόρος, -ον   (11x, Aeschyl+) *spearbearing;* (subst) *spear bearer, bodyguard* 2 Macc 3:24; 4 Macc 5:2.

δοτός, -ή, -όν   (LXX+) *granted, given* (subst) 1 Km 1:11.*

δουλεία   3. *service, labor* (no //, s.t. of עבד *be a slave, serve* and cogn); *indentured* Gen 30:26; *for hire or wage* 3 Km 5:20; *in the cult* 2 Esdr 6:18; *any kind of work* Ps 103:14. 1 Km 14:40 mistrans of עבר *(opposite) side* (cf. L μέρος) as if עבד *slave*.‡

δοῦλος, -η, -ον   (Hdt+) *serving* Wsd 15:7; (neut subst) Ps 118:91.*‡

δράγμα, -ατος, τό   (18x, Hom+) *sheaf* (of grain) Gen 37:7; Ruth 2:7; Jdth 8:3; Ps 125:6; Hos 8:7.

δράκος (dub; *h.l.*) prob *f.l.* for δράξι (see δράξ 2.) 3 Macc 5:2 (W, p. 290; n. 59).*

δρᾶμα, -ατος, τό (Aeschyl, Pla+) *production, drama*; (fig) *"staged" action, (false) role* 4 Macc 6:17.*

δραμῶ fut of τρέχω SSol 1:4; (mid) 4 Km 5:20; Ps 147:4.

δράξ **2.** *handful* Lev 2:2; 3 Km 17:12; 3 Macc 5:2 (q.l. cf. δράκος) Eccl 4:6; Ezk 10:2.‡

δραπέτης, -ου, ὁ (Hdt+) *runaway, fugitive* 2 Macc 8:35.*

δρεπανηφόρος, -ον (X+) *wielding a scythe* (of chariot: X ANAB 1.7.10) 2 Macc 13:2.*

δρομεύς, -έως, ὁ (Eur+) *runner* Pr 6:11, 11a; 24:34; Job 9:25; Am 2:14.*

δρόμος **1.b.** *footrace, contest* Eccl 9:11; δρόμῳ *at a run, at full speed* 2 Macc 14:45.‡

δροσίζω **2.** *make like dew* (no //) 3 Macc 6:6.*‡

δρόσος, -ου, ἡ (43x, Aeschyl+) *dew, moisture* Gen 27:28; Judg 5:4; Ps 132:3; Pr 3:20; Wsd 11:22; Hos 6:4; Is 18:4; Da 3:50.

δρυμός, -οῦ, ὁ (65x, Hom+) *woodland, copse, thicket* Dt 19:5; Josh 17:15; 1 Ch 16:33; 1 Macc 4:38; Ps 28:9; Eccl 2:6; Hos 13:8; Is 7:2. 3 Km 10:17, 21 = 2 Ch 9:16, 20 almost N LOC for peristyle hall w. cedar columns *(House of) the Forest (of Lebanon)*.

δρῦς, δρυός, ἡ (22x, Hom+) *oak tree* Gen 12:6; Dt 11:30; 1 Km 10:3; Hos 4:13; Jer 2:34.

δυεῖν gen & dat of BDAG: δύο; 4 Macc 1:28; (VL δυοῖν, =) 15:2; Job 13:20.*

δύναμαι **2.** *prevail, be strong* Num 13:30; Ob 7; *overcome* (πρός τινα) Gen 32:26; Judg 16:5A; Jer 1:19; (τινί) 20:10; Judg 16:5B.‡

δύναμις SSol 2:7; 3:5 etc mistrans of צבאה *gazelle* as if צבא *army, (military) force*. Da 8:9L mistrans of צבי *glorious* (city, i.e., Jerusalem) as if צבא *army, military force* (G βορρᾶν as if צפון *North*).‡

δυναστεία, -ας, ἡ (60x, Soph+) **1.** *dominion, authority* Ex 6:6; Ps 65:7 Wsd 6:3; Sir 3:20; Jer 25:15. **2.** *power, might* Judg 5:31A; Jdth 9:11; 2 Macc 3:28; Ps 64:7 Sir 34:16; Mi 3:8; Ezk 22:25; Da 3:44. **3.** *mighty work* (no //) 3 Km 15:23; (pl) 16:5; Ps 19:7; Am 2:16.

δυνάστευμα, -ατος, τό (*h.l.*) *resource* 3 Km 2:46c.*

δυναστεύω (Hdt+) **1.** (trans) *rule over, command* (τι) Esth 8:12t; Da 11:4L; (τινός) 3 Macc 2:7; 5:7; (εἰς τινά) Da 9:27L; *overpower, dominate* 1 Ch 16:21; Sir 5:3; 12:5. **2.** (abs) *hold or exercise power or authority* Esth 8:12g; Pr 19:10; Da 11:5L; (ptc subst) *noble, official* Jer 13:18; (fem) *the Lady* (i.e., queen mother, of Jezebel) 4 Km 10:13.*

δύνω **2.** (trans) *cause to sink* (Hom, Theophr) Joel 2:10; 4:15; (intr) *enter into, sink into* Pr 11:8VL.‡

δυσάθλιος, -α, -ον (Soph OEDCOL 330) *most wretched, very miserable* 3 Macc 4:4.*

δυσαίακτος, -ον (*h.l.*) *most lamentable* 3 Macc 6:31.*

δυσάλυκτος, -ον (Nicander) *difficult to escape* Wsd 17:16.*

δυσγένεια, -ας, ἡ (not in HR; Soph+) *low or mean birth* Sir 22:7VL.*

δυσδιήγητος, -ον (*h.l.*) *hard to explain or describe* Wsd 17:1.*

δυσημερία, -ας, ἡ (Aeschyl+) *unlucky day; misfortune, misery* 2 Macc 5:6.*

δυσκατάπαυστος, -ον (Aeschyl+) *difficult to stop or check* 3 Macc 5:7.*

δυσκλεής, -ές (Hom+) *shameful, inglorious* 3 Macc 3:25; (superl) δυσκλεέστατος 3:23.*

δυσκολία, -ας, ἡ (Aristoph, Pla+) *discontent, fretfulness* Job 34:30.*

δύσκωφος, -ον (Hippocr, Aristot+) *hard of hearing* Ex 4:11.*

δυσμένεια, -ας, ἡ (Soph+) *ill will, malice* 2 Macc 6:29; 12:3; 14:39; 3 Macc 3:19; 7:4.*

δυσμενής, -ές (Hom, Hdt+) *hostile, malicious* Esth 3:13d, g; 3 Macc 3:2ff; (adv) 2 Macc 14:11.*

δυσμή Ezk 27:9 mistrans of ערב מערב (both fr ערב[1] *pledge, barter*) *barter for trade goods* as if (both fr ערב[4] *become evening*) *evening of the sunset*.‡

δυσνοέω (LXX, Plu) *think badly of, be ill-disposed toward* (τινί) Esth 3:13e; (VL δυσνοής [?] spur) 3 Macc 3:24.*

δυσπέτημα, -ατος, τό   (h.l.) bad consequence, misfortune 2 Macc 5:20.*

δυσπολιόρκητος, -ον   (X, Polyb+) resistant to siege, hard to capture 2 Macc 12:21.*

δυσπρόσιτος, -ον   (Eur+) hard to approach or attack 2 Macc 12:21.*

δυσσέβεια, -ας, ἡ   (trag) impiety 1 Esdr 1:40; 2 Macc 8:33.*

δυσσεβέω   (trag) act impiously 2 Macc 6:13.*

δυσσέβημα, -ατος, τό   (LXX+) impiety, impious act 1 Esdr 1:49; 2 Macc 12:3.*

δυσσεβής, -ές   (7x, trag) impious 2 Macc 3:11; 3 Macc 5:47; (subst) 2 Macc 9:9; 3 Macc 3:1.

δυστοκέω   (Hippocr+) struggle or suffer in labor Gen 35:16.*

δύσφημος, -ον   (Hes, Pind+) cursing, blasphemous 2 Macc 13:11; 15:32.*

δυσφορέω   (Hdt+) be displeased or indignant 2 Macc 4:35; 13:25.*

δύσφορος, -ον   (Aeschyl+) hard or grievous to bear; (adv) in troubled or grieving fashion 2 Macc 14:28; 3 Macc 3:8.*

δυσχέρεια, -ας, ἡ   (Soph, Pla+) difficulty 2 Macc 2:24; vexation, unpleasantness 9:21.*

δυσχερής, -ές   (Aeschyl, Pla+) hard to manage (opp BDAG: εὐχερής, lit well in hand), difficult; unpleasant 2 Macc 9:24; severe 9:7; 14:45; odious 6:3.*

δυσώδης, -ες   (Hdt, Soph+) foul-smelling, stinking 4 Macc 6:25.*

δωδεκάμηνος, -ον   (Hes, Pind+) of twelve months; (neut subst) year Da 4:29Θ.*

δωροδέκτης, -οῦ, ὁ   (h.l.) taker of bribes Job 15:34.*

δωροκοπέω   (LXX) bribe Sir 35:11; (pass) accept a bribe 3 Macc 4:19.*

δωρολήμπτης, -ου, ὁ   (h.l.) taker of bribes Pr 15:27.*

δῶρον   2. bribe Sir 40:12; Hos 8:9; Is 1:23.‡

E

ἑάλων   aor ἑάλωκα pf of ἁλίσκομαι.

ἔαρ, ἔαρος, τό   (Hom+) season of spring Gen 8:22; Num 13:20; Ps 73:17; Wsd 2:7; Zech 14:8.*

ἐάω   pf pass ἔαμαι, inf ἐᾶσθαι.‡

ἐβάφην   aor pass of βάπτω.

ἑβδομηκοστός, -ή, -όν   (7x, Hippocr) seventieth 1 Macc 13:41; 14:1; Zech 1:12.

ἐβλάβην   2 aor pass of BDAG: βλάπτω.

ἐβρώθην   cf. BDAG: βιβρώσκω.

ἐγγαστρίμυθος, -ον   (15x, Hippocr, Philochorus+) capable of ventriloquism and/or imparting oracles 1 Km 28:7; (subst) ventriloquist or oracular person Lev 19:31; 1 Km 28:3, 9; 1 Ch 10:13; Is 8:19; (neut?) oracle, oracular power (no //) 1 Km 28:8.

ἐγγελάω   (Soph+) laugh at, mock 4 Macc 5:27VL.*

ἐγγεννάω   see ἐνγ-.‡

ἐγγίζω   1.c. be nearly related Lev 25:25R. 3. (trans) bring near, bring up to (Polyb+) Gen 48:10; 4 Km 4:6; Ezk 22:4.‡

ἐγγίνομαι   (Hom+) spring up, appear Hos 7:6VL.*

ἐγγίων, -ον   comp adj fr BDAG: ἐγγύς Ruth 3:12; superl ἐγγύτατος, -η, -ον Job 6:15.

ἐγγλύφω   pf pass ptc ἐγγεγλυμμένος (Hdt+) engrave, carve 1 Macc 13:29; Job 19:24.*

ἔγγονος, -η, -ον   (Pla+) descended from; (subst) grandchild, (neut pl) descendents, offspring Pr 23:18VL, Is 14:29VL.*

ἔγγραπτος, -ον   (Polyb+ [Strabo 6.1.8 of written laws]) written, prescribed Ps 149:9.*

ἐγγραφή, -ῆς, ἡ   (not in HR; Aristot+) engraving, written testimony 2 Ch 21:12.*

ἐγγυάω   aor (incorrectly) ἐνεγυήσω (8x, Hom+). 1. give in pledge; (mid) go surety (for) Pr 6:1, 3; Sir 8:13. 2. betroth (a daughter) Tob 6:12S.

ἐγγύη, -ης, ἡ   (Hom+) pledge, surety Pr 17:18; 22:26; Sir 29:17, 19.*

ἐγγύθεν   (Hom+) up close, nearby Josh 6:13; 9:16; Ezk 7:5.*

ἔγγυος   2. (subst, of pers) guarantor Sir 29:15f.‡

ἐγγύτατος   see ἐγγίων
ἔγερσις   2. *awaking, (act of) rising* Ps 138:2; *(act of) standing up* Judg 7:19A. 3. *raising up, restoring* (of temple) 1 Esdr 5:59.*‡
ἔγημα   see BDAG: γαμέω.
ἐγκάθετος, -ον   (homonym Polyb 13.5.1; Lk 20:20+; but LXX word [uniquely] derives fr ἐγκάθημαι [LSJ] rather than ἐγκαθίημι) *lying or crouching in wait or ambush* Job 19:12; 31:9.*‡
ἐγκάθημαι   2. (Polyb) *be positioned or stationed* (of military garrisons) 3 Km 11:16; *sit* EpJer 42, > *dwell, live* (no //, s.t. of ישב *sit, dwell, live*) Ex 23:31; Num 13:19; Judg 2:2; Is 8:14.‡
ἐγκαθίζω   (Pind, Hdt+) 1. *come to sit, sit* 1 Macc 10:52; *occupy a position, prepare an ambush* Josh 8:9; Ezk 35:5; (fig) Sir 8:11. 2. (trans) *seat, position* 3 Km 20:10. Ezk 35:5 mistrans of נגר *pour out* (cf. Jer 18:21) as if גור *attack.*
ἐγκαίνια   1.b. *dedication* (pagan) Da 3:2Θ.‡
ἐγκαινίζω   Is 16:11 mistrans of חֶרֶשׂ *fired clay* as if חדש (piel) *renew, restore.*‡
ἐγκαίνισις, -εως, ἡ   (h.l.) *dedication* Num 7:88G.*
ἐγκαινισμός, -οῦ, ὁ   (13x, LXX) *dedication* Num 7:10; 1 Macc 4:56; Ps 29:1; Da 3:2L, 3Θ.
ἐγκαίνωσις, -εως, ἡ   (h.l.) *dedication* Num 7:88R.*
ἐγκαίω   (ins+) *burn in;* > *paint w. pigment in wax* 2 Macc 2:29.*
ἐγκαλύπτω   (Aristoph, X+) *veil, cover up* Pr 26:26VL.*
ἐγκαρτερέω   (Thu, Eur+) *hold out, remain steadfast* 4 Macc 14:9.*
ἐγκατακρύπτω   (Lycophron) *hide* Am 9:3VL.*
ἐγκαταλείπω   3 Km 20:21 see συνέχω.‡
ἐγκαταλιμπάνω   (Hippocr+) *abandon, forsake* Ps 118:53.*
ἐγκαταλοχίζω   (h.l.) *enroll, register* 2 Ch 31:18VL (q.l. c. Ra; cf. MT).*
ἐγκαταπαίζω   (LXX) *laugh at;* (pass) *be laughed at* Job 40:19; 41:25.*
ἔγκατον, -ου, τό   (Hom+) *intestine, interior,* (pl) *entrails* Tob 6:4S; Ps 50:12; 108:18; Job 21:24; 41:7; Sir 21:14.*

ἔγκειμαι   (Hom, Hdt+) 1. *be devoted to* Gen 8:21; 34:19. 2. *press hard or weigh heavily upon* (τινί) Esth 9:3.*‡
ἐγκεντρισμός, -οῦ, ὁ   (Geopon, ins) *engrafting, injection* (fig) 3 Macc 5:29VL.*
ἐγκέχηνα   pf of ἐγχάσκω.
ἐγκηδεύω   pf pass ἐγκεκήδευμαι (LXX+) *bury;* (pass) *be buried* 4 Macc 17:9.*
ἐγκισσάω   (LXX) *be in heat, breed* Gen 30:38ff; 31:10.*
ἐγκλείω   (Hdt+) *confine, imprison* (mid) Ezk 3:24; (pass) 2 Macc 5:8.*‡
ἔγκληρος, -ον   (Soph+) *possessed as an inheritance* Dt 4:20.*
ἐγκλοιόομαι   (h.l.) *encircle as a collar* Pr 6:21.*
ἐγκοίλιος, -ον   (Theophr+) *within the belly;* (neut subst) *intestine* Lev 1:9, 13.*
ἔγκοιλος, -ον   (Hippocr, Pla+) *sunken, concave* Lev 13:30f.*
ἐγκολαπτός, -ή, -όν   (ins+) *engraved, carved* 3 Km 6:29, 32.*
ἐγκολάπτω   (Hdt+) *carve in stone* 3 Km 6:32, 35.*
ἐγκολλάω   (ins+) *glue or fasten together* Zech 14:5.*
ἔγκοπος, -ον   (LXX+) *weary, tired* Job 19:2; Is 43:23; *tiresome* Eccl 1:8.*
ἐγκοσμέω   (Hom+) *arrange, adorn;* (pass) *be arrayed or adorned* (fig) 4 Macc 6:2.*
ἐγκοτέω   (trag) *be vindictive, bear a grudge* Gen 27:41; Ps 54:4.*
ἐγκότημα, -ατος, τό   (h.l.) *object of hatred or vindictiveness* Jer 31:39.*
ἐγκρατέω   (LXX+) *control, hold power over* (τινός) Ex 9:2.*
ἐγκρατής   2. *in control of* (τινός) Tob 6:3S; 2 Macc 8:30; Sus 39Θ; *in possession of* (SCIL Wisdom) Wsd 8:21; *under the control of* Sir 27:30.‡
ἐγκρούω   (Aristoph+) *hammer in(to)* Judg 4:21A; 16:13.*
ἐγκρυφίας, -ου, ὁ   (8x, Hippocr+) *loaf* (in ashes for baking) Gen 18:6; 3 Km 17:12f; Hos 7:8; Ezk 4:12.
ἐγκτάομαι   (Hdt+) *acquire in a foreign land* Gen 34:10.*

ἔγκτημα, -ατος, τό (Demosth+) *land held by a foreigner* Num 31:9VL.*

ἔγκτησις, -εως, ἡ (X+) *right of tenure* (to land) Lev 25:13, 16G (Ra: κτησις).*

ἔγκτητος, -η, -ον (LXX+) *held or owned in a foreign country* Lev 14:34; 22:11; Num 31:9.*

ἐγκύκλιος, -ον (Eur, Isocr+) *circular,* > *general* (letter) Da 4:37bL.*

ἐγκυλίω (Hippocr, X+) *roll or wrap*; (pass) *be wrapped or embraced* Pr 7:18; Sir 23:12; *be involved, involve oneself* 37:3.*

ἐγκωμιάζω (Hdt+) *praise, extol* Pr 12:8; 27:2, 21; 28:4; 29:2.*

ἐγκώμιον, -ου, τό (Aristoph+) *word of praise, panegyric* Esth 2:23; Pr 10:7.*

ἐγρήγορος, -ον (LXX+) *wakeful, wide awake* Da 4:13ΘVL. La 4:14 mistrans of עור *blind* as if Aram עור *awake, keeping watch.*

ἐγχάσκω pf ἐγκέχηνα (Aristoph) *grin, gape, stare* 1 Esdr 4:19.*

ἐγχειρέω (Soph+) *take in hand* 2 Ch 23:18 (but cf. -ίζω); *undertake* Jer 18:22; 28:12; 30:10 (cf. -ίζω).*

ἐγχείρημα, -ατος, τό (Soph+) *undertaking, attempt* Jer 23:20; 37:24.*

ἐγχειρίδιος, -ον (Hdt+) *handheld*; (in our lit, only subst) 1. *weapon, dagger* Jer 27:42; EpJer 13; Ezk 21:8ff. 2. *hand tool, chisel* (no //) Ex 20:25.*

ἐγχειρίζω (Hdt+) *put into (someone's) hand*; > *entrust* 2 Ch 23:18VL (q.l.; Heb שׂים). Jer 30:10 (29:17G) rd -ίζω, (w. O, L al, VL Gött), mistrans of נשׁא² (hiph) *deceive* as if נשׁא¹ *lend,* > *entrust.*

ἐγχειρόω (dub; not in LSJ) *undertake* Jer 18:22VL.*

ἐγχέω aor ἐνέχεεν (Hom+) *pour, pour in* Ex 24:6; Judg 6:19A; 4 Km 4:40f; Jer 31:11; Ezk 24:3G.*

ἐγχρονίζω (Hippocr, Thu, Pla+) *spend time, linger* Pr 9:18a; 10:28; 23:30.*

ἐγχρυσόω (not in HR; Tzetzes [XII CE]) *gild* 2 Ch 3:9VL.*

ἔγωγε (Hom, Pla, X+) *emphatic form of* BDAG: ἐγώ; *even I, I for my part* 4 Macc 8:10; 16:6.

ἐδεδοίκειν see δείδω.

ἔδεσθε aor pass impv of ἐσθίω; 1 Macc 4:8VL rd αἴδεσθε (itac).

ἐδήχθην aor pass of BDAG: δάκνω.

ἐδιλίαζον itac impf of δειλιάζω.

ἕδρα, -ας, ἡ (Hom+) *seat, rump* 1 Km 5:3, 9¹, 12; > *hemorrhoid* (no //) Dt 28:7; 1 Km 5:9²; 6:4ff.*

ἑδρασθῆναι aor pass inf of BDAG: ἑδράζω.

ἕδρασμα, -ατος, τό (Eur+) *seat, residence; sanctuary* (of a god) 3 Km 8:13(VL).*

ἐζωσμένος pf pass ptc of BDAG: ζώννυμι.

ἐθελοκωφέω (not in HR; cf. BDAG: ἐθελο-) *feign deafness* Sir 19:27.*

ἐθερμάνθη aor pass of θερμαίνω Ps 38:4.

ἐθισμός, -οῦ, ὁ (Aristot+) *habit, usage, custom, manner of life* Gen 31:35; 3 Km 18:28; Jdth 13:10; 2 Macc 4:11; 12:38; Sir 23:14.*

ἐθνηδόν (h.l.) *nation-wide, including a whole people* 4 Macc 2:19.*

ἐθνοπάτωρ, -τορος, ὁ (not in LSJ; h.l.) *national ancestor* 4 Macc 16:20.*

ἐθνόπληθος, -ους, τό (not in LSJ; h.l.) *whole body or entire mass of the people* 4 Macc 7:11.*

ἔθνος 1.b. ἔθν. ἔθν. (sg or pl) *each of the nations* (Heb idiom; cf. ἀνήρ, ἄνθρωπος) 4 Km 17:29, 32.‡

εἰ μή 6.i.α.ב. *surely* (לָךְ) Ezk 5:11.‡

εἰδέχθεια, -ας, ἡ (h.l. [adj Theophr+]) *hateful appearance, ugliness* Wsd 16:3.*

εἰδήσαι, εἰδήσαν false 1 aor of εἶδον, Dt 4:35 etc, cf. W, pp. 335f.

εἴδησις, -εως, ἡ (Aristot+) *understanding, knowledge* Sir 42:18.*

εἴην opt of BDAG: εἰμί.

εἶθ᾽ (followed by rough breathing) = BDAG: εἶτα 2 Macc 4:22; Wsd 17:15.

εἴθε (Hom+) *would that, if only* (w. wishes) Job 9:33.*

εἰκάς, -άδος, ἡ (27x; Hes, Aristoph+) *20th day of the month* Gen 7:11; 4 Km 25:27; 1 Esdr 7:5; Zech 1:7; Jer 52:31.

εἰκοσαετής, -ές (33x, Hdt+) *of twenty years, twenty years old* Ex 30:14; Lev 27:3; 1 Ch 27:23.

εἰκοστός, -ή, -όν (26x; Hom, Thu+) *twentieth* 3 Km 15:8f; 1 Ch 24:16ff; Jer 52:1; Dn 10:4Θ.

εἰκότως (adv of pf ptc εἰκώς fr ἔοικα, q.v.; Aeschyl+, X Anab 2.2.3) *seemingly, evidently* 4 Macc 9:2.*

εἰλημένος pf pass ptc of BDAG: εἰλέω.

εἰλημμένος pf pass ptc of BDAG: λαμβάνω.

εἴλου 2 aor impv of αἱρέω Dt 26:17.

εἶπον PsSol 2:25 prob mistrans of (I) דבר¹ *drive away* as if דבר² *speak*.‡

εἴργω aor εἶρξα pass εἴρχθην (Hom, Hdt+) 1. *shut out, exclude* 3 Macc 3:18. 2. *hinder, prevent* 1 Esdr 5:69, 71.*

εἰρήνη 2 Esdr 4:7 ἐν εἰρήνῃ mistrans of בִּשְׁלָם N pers (?) as if בְּשָׁל(וֹ)ם *in peace,* also misconstruing next N pers as gentilic.‡

εἰρηνικός 2. (fem subst) *peace offering* (no //) 1 Km 11:15; 2 Km 6:17.‡

εἱρκτή, -ῆς, ἡ (Hdt+) *prison, enclosure* Wsd 17:15.*

εἰσάγω 2. *put into, insert* (τι) Ex 25:14; 26:29.‡

εἰσαγωγή, -ῆς, ἡ (Pla+) *entrance, introduction* Sir 21:9vl.*

εἰσβάλλω (Hdt+) *throw in, send in* (army) 2 Macc 13:13; (intr) *rush in* 14:43.*

εἰσβλέπω (Hdt+) *look at or into* Job 6:28; 21:5; Is 37:17.*

εἰσδύνω aor εἰσέδυ(σαν) (Hom+) *crawl (under, into), enter* 1 Macc 6:46; Jer 4:29.*

εἰσηγέομαι ptc εἰσηγούμενος (Hdt+) *lead in,* > *advise, instruct* 2 Km 5:2vl.*‡

εἰσηγορέομαι (dub; not in LSJ) *address, initiate conversation* Sir 13:11vl.*

εἰσκολάπτω (h.l.) *carve on or into* 3 Km 6:35vl.*

εἰσκυκλέω (Aristoph+) *wheel or roll (into);* (pass, fig) *be drawn into* (τινί) 2 Macc 2:24.*

εἰσκύπτω (lxx+) lit *peep into* (cf. ἐκκύπτω); *overlook* 1 Km 13:18.*

εἰσοδιάζω (lxx, ins+) *collect* (revenue); (pass) *be paid* 4 Km 12:5; 2 Ch 34:14.*

εἰσόδιον, -ου, τό (pap) *income* Da 11:13Θ.*

εἰσοίσει fut of BDAG: εἰσφέρω.

εἰσοράω aor εἰσεῖδον (Hom, Hdt+) *attend to, look into or upon* Jdth 4:13.*

εἰσπέμπω (Soph, Thu+) *send in* 2 Macc 13:20.*

εἰσπλέω (Hdt, Soph+) *sail in(to)* 2 Macc 14:1; 4 Macc 13:6.*

εἰσσπάομαι (h.l.) *draw in* Gen 19:10.*

εἰσφορά, -ᾶς, ἡ (Thu+) *levy, tax* Ex 30:13ff.*

εἴτοι ... εἴτοι *whether ... or* (cf. BDAG: εἰ, τοί) Ruth 3:10.‡

ἐκ 1.e. ἐξ ἑαυτῆς *beside herself, ecstatic* 3 Km 10:5 = 2 Ch9:4.‡

ἐκάησαν 2 aor pass of BDAG: καίω.

εκαθιοαν (spur) 1 Macc 2:7vl (Ra) rd εκαθισαν (= Gött txt).

ἑκατέρωθεν (Hdt+) *on each side* 4 Macc 6:3; 9:11.*

ἑκατοντάς, -άδος, ἡ (Hdt+) *group or unit of 100* 1 Km 29:2; 2 Km 18:4; 1 Ch 28:1.*

ἑκατοστεύω (h.l.) *bear a hundredfold* Gen 26:12.*

ἑκατοστός, -ή, -όν (27x, Hdt+) *hundredth* 1 Macc 1:10; 2 Macc 1:7.

ἐκβαίνω 2. *turn out* Sir 30:8; *happen, occur* 1 Macc 4:27.‡

ἐκβάλλω 2.b. *divorce* (DiodS 12.18.1) Pr 18:22a; Sir 7:26; pf pass ptc *divorced (woman)* Lev 21:7; Ezk 44:22.‡

ἐκβασσεύω (dub, not in LSJ) *march out* (?) 1 Macc 15:40vl.*

ἐκβεβηλόω (h.l.) *defile, profane* Lev 21:9vl.*

ἐκβιάζω (Soph+) 1. *expel, drive out* (act) Judg 14:15B; (mid) Pr 16:26. 2. *act violently* Ps 37:13; *seize by force* Sus 19G; *compel, wrench* (by an artistic tour de force; cf. Plu Tim 36) Wsd 14:19.*

ἐκβλαστάνω (Hippocr, Pla, Theophr+) 1. *sprout, grow* Num 17:20, Is 55:10. 2. *cause to grow* Job 38:27.*‡

ἐκβλύζω (Orphica, Plu) *gush out* Pr 3:10.*

ἐκβοάω (X, Pla+) *call out* 4 Km 4:36.*

ἐκβράζω (Hdt+) *drive out* 2 Esdr 23:28; 2 Macc 1:12; 5:8.*

ἐκβρασμός, -οῦ, ὁ (h.l.) *upheaval, expulsion* Na 2:11.*

ἐκγελάω dep fut -άσομαι (6x; Hom+) *laugh aloud at* 2 Esdr 12:19; Ps 2:4; Wsd 4:18.

ἐκγεννάω aor ἐξεγέννησα (EupolisCom) *bring forth, bring to birth* Ps 109:3.*

ἐκγράφω (Aristoph, ins+) *copy out, write out* Pr 25:1.*

ἐκδανείζω (Aristot+) *lend out at interest* Ex 22:24; Dt 23:20.*

ἐκδειματόω (Pla+) *terrify* Wsd 17:6.*

ἐκδεκτέον (LXX+) *it must be accepted or admitted* EpJer 56.*

ἐκδέρω aor ἐξέδειρα (Hom+) *skin, remove hide* Lev 1:6; 2 Ch 35:11; Mi 2:8; 3:3.*

ἐκδέχομαι **2.** *receive in trust* Gen 43:9. **3.** *take in, accept* (τῃ καρδίᾳ *"take to heart"*) Is 57:1.‡

ἐκδέω (Hom+) *tie* (so as to hang out or down) Josh 2:18; 2 Macc 15:35.*

ἐκδημία, -ας, ἡ (Eur, Pla+) *journey away* 3 Macc 4:11.*

ἐκδιαιτάω (Aristot+) *change one's way of life* 4 Macc 4:19; 18:5.*

ἐκδιδάσκω (Sappho, Hdt+) *instruct, teach* 4 Macc 5:23f; Wsd 8:7.*

ἐκδιδύσκω (Joseph) **1.** *plunder* 1Km 31:8; 2 Km 23:10; Hos 7:1. **2.** (mid) *strip off, remove* (one's own garment) 2 Esdr 14:17.*

ἐκδίδωμι 3rd pl aor act ἐξέδοσαν pass ἐξεδόθη **1.b.** (act) *pay out* (to hired workers) 4 Km 12:12. **2.** *give in marriage* (Hdt+) Ex 2:21; Tob 3:8S; 1 Macc 10:58; Sir 7:25. **3.** *hand oneself over, surrender* Jdth 2:10; (pass) *be handed over* Da 2:18L. **4.** *distribute* (of books); *publish* Sir prol 33; (pass) *be handed down, become a custom* (no //) 1 Esdr 1:30; *be promulgated* 8:3.‡

ἐκδικάζω dep fut ἐκδικῶμαι (Eur+) in our lit only mid/pass *find vindication, be avenged* Lev 19:18; Dt 32:43; *suffer vengeance, be punished* Jdth 11:10. Act impf ἐξεδίκα and aor subj ἐκδικᾷ fr ἐκδικάω (LXX) *take vengeance on* (τινα) 1 Macc 9:26; 2 Macc 6:15.*

ἐκδικάω impf mid/pass ἐξεδίκα (h.l.) *take vengeance* (on τινά) 1 Macc 9:26.

ἐκδικέω **2.b.** *punish, condemn* Jer 25:12; Ezk 7:7.‡

ἐκδικητής, -οῦ, ὁ (LXX+) *avenger* Ps 8:3.*

ἐκδύνω or (BDAG) ἐκδύω (Hom+) **1.b.** *strip, lay bare* (one's breasts) La 4:3. Pr 11:8 stereot trans of niph צלה *be rescued* as if qal *be stripped away.*

ἐκζέω (Hdt+) **1.** *boil over* Gen 49:4; (fig) Job 30:27. **2.** *erupt, break out* (of disease); **a.** (trans) *breed* (parasites) Ex 16:20; 1 Km 6:1 **b.** *make ill, afflict with plague* (τινί) 1 Km 5:6. **3.** *swarm, teem* (no //) Ezk 47:9.*

ἐκζητητής, -οῦ, ὁ (h.l.) *seeker* Bar 3:23.*

ἔκθεμα, -ατος, τό (pap, ins, Polyb) *proclamation, public notice* Esth 8:17; Ezk 16:24.*

ἐκθερίζω (Demosth, pap+) *reap or harvest thoroughly* Lev 19:9; 25:5.*

ἔκθεσις, -εως, ἡ (Hdt+) **1.** *exposure, casting out* (of a child) Wsd 11:14. **2.** *prescription, (of diet) ration* (no //) Da 1:5L.*

ἔκθεσμος, -ον (Philo+) *unlawful* 4 Macc 5:14.*

ἐκθηλάζω (Hippocr, Aristot+) *suck out* Is 66:11.*

ἐκθλιβή, -ῆς, ἡ (h.l.) *oppression* Mi 7:2.*

ἐκθλίβω aor ἐξέθλιψα pf pass ptc ἐκτεθλιμμένος (25; Aristot+) **1.** *squeeze out* Gen 40:11; *crush* Lev 22:24. **2.** (fig) *oppress, harass* Judg 1:34; 4 Km 13:22; Ps 34:5; Sir 16:28; Am 6:14; Ezk 34:21; *crush, defeat* Josh 19:47a; Ps 17:39; Is 29:2.

ἔκθλιψις, -εως, ἡ (Hippocr, Aristot+: squeezing out) *oppression, affliction* (fig, no //) 2 Esdr 13:21vl, Ezk 12:18vl.*

ἔκθυμος, -ον (Plu: spirited) *enraged, having lost one's temper* (no //) 2 Macc 7:3, 39; 14:27.*

ἐκκαθαρίζω (LXX) *clean out* Dt 32:43; Judg 20:13B; Is 4:4; *clear* (land) Josh 17:18.*

ἐκκαίδεκα (8x, Hdt+) *sixteen* Num 31:40; 3 Km 12:24a; 4 Km 13:10; 1 Ch 4:27.

ἐκκαιδέκατος, -η, -ον (Hdt+) *sixteenth* 1 Ch 24:14; 25:23; 2 Ch 29:17.*

ἐκκαλέω (Hom+) (mid) *call out to, address* (τινά) Gen 19:5; Dt 20:10.*

ἐκκαλύπτω (Aeschyl, Hdt+) *uncover* Pr 26:26.*

ἐκκενόω aor pass ἐξεκενώθη (14; Aeschyl+) *empty out* Gen 24:20; Judg 20:31B; 2 Ch 24:11; Ps 74:9; SSol 1:3; Is 51:17; *leave desolate* Ps 136:7. Ezk 5:2 etc (Heb idiom) *draw* (a sword, no //—cf. ἐκχέω). Da 9:25Θ corresp to בצוק (txt?) *in oppression or distress,* unexpl.

ἐκκεντέω (9x, Aristot, Polyb+) *stab, kill by stabbing* Num 22:29; Josh 16:10; 2 Macc 12:6; Is 14:9; (pf pass ptc) *stabbed, killed* PsSol 2:26.‡

ἐκκήρυκτος, -ον (h.l.) *banished by proclamation* Jer 22:30.*

ἐκκινέω (Soph+) *move out*; (pass, fig) *be put out, be frustrated or distressed* 4 Km 6:11.

ἐκκλεῖναι Pr 4:5vl, Sir 46:2vl itac misspelling of ἐκκλῖναι.

ἐκκλησιάζω (Aristoph+; cf. ἐξεκκλ-) *summon to assemble, convene* Lev 8:3; Num 20:8; Dt 4:10; 31:12, 28; 1 Ch 13:5; Esth 4:16.*‡

ἐκκλησιαστής, -οῦ, ὁ (Pla+: *member of the assembly*) *speaker or summoner of the assembly* (Heb, no //) Eccl 1:1ff; 7:27; 12:8ff.*

ἔκκλητος, -ον (X+) *summoned* (to court or council) Sir 42:11.*

ἐκκλίνω 3. *turn aside* (toward) Gen 18:5; Pr 9:4. 4. (trans) *turn* (τὴν ὁδόν *one's course*) Gen 38:16; *deflect, tilt* (τι) 1 Ch 13:9; *mislead, turn aside* 2 Esdr 23:26; *pervert* (no //) 1 Km 8:3².‡

εκκλιο- itac misspelling of εκκλειο-.

ἐκκλύζω (Hippocr, Pla+) *wash or rinse out* Lev 6:21.*

ἐκκόλαμμα, -ατος, τό (h.l. not in LSJ) *inscription, something carved out* Ex 36:13.*

ἐκκολαπτός, -ή, -όν (dub; not in LSJ) *carved out* 3 Km 6:29vl.*

ἐκκομιδή, -ῆς, ἡ (Hdt, ins+) *removal* 2 Macc 3:7.*

ἐκκοσμέω (Aristides [II CE]) *deck out, adorn* 4 Macc 6:2vl.*

ἐκκρεμάννυμι (Eur, Thu+) *hang from*; (fig) *be devoted to or dependent on* Gen 44:30.*‡

ἐκκρούω (Aristoph, Thu+) *knock off, push away*; (pass) *come off* (τινί) Dt 19:5.*

ἐκκύπτω pf ἐκκέκυφεν (Aristoph+) 1. *peep out, look out* 1 Macc 4:19; Ps 101:20; SSol 2:9; 6:10. 2. *pop out, burst forth* 1 Macc 9:23; Jer 6:1.*

ἐκλαμβάνω (Hdt+) 1. *seize and carry away* Job 3:5; 22:22; Jer 23:3G (RECTE; MT לקח—cf. περιλαμβάνω as well as Job 22:22; 31:39). 2. *receive, accept* Jer 39:33G.*

ἔκλαμπρος, -ον (LXX+) *bright* Wsd 17:5.*

ἔκλαμψις, -εως, ἡ (Hippocr+) *brightness* 2 Macc 5:3.*

ἐκλατομέω (Strabo+) *hew out* Num 21:18; Dt 6:11.*

ἐκλεγείσης 2 aor pass ptc of ἐκλέγω Tob 1:4.

ἐκλείπω pf ἐκλέλοιπα 4. (trans) *use up, exhaust* Jdth 7:20; *fail, forsake* Job 21:19; *leave off, lose* 2 Macc 10:13; Sir 17:24.‡

ἐκλείχω (Hippocr+) *lick up* 3 Km 22:38; > *consume* (no //; s.t./pun (similar sound) on לחך *lick up, consume*; cf. Philo MIGR 143; CONGR 55) Num 22:4; 3 Km 18:38; Jdth 7:4; EpJer 19.*

ἔκλειψις, -εως, ἡ (Hdt+) *end* 2 Esdr 13:21; *passing away, giving out* Dt 28:48; Is 17:4; *extinction* (of a people, Strabo 9.5.12) Pr 14:28; Zeph 1:2; Ezk 5:16R (Gött εξαλ-).*

ἐκλεκτέον (Pla, Aristot+) *one must select* EpJer 63vl (error for εκδεκ-, Δ, > Λ).

ἐκλευκαίνω (Eur, Theophr) *become white* (pass) Da 12:10Θ.*

ἔκλευκος, -ον (Hippocr, Aristot, pap) *white, whitened out* Lev 13:24.*

ἐκλικμάω (LXX) *sift, winnow out* Wsd 5:23; (fig) *thresh and crush utterly* (cf. BDAG: λικμάω) Jdth 2:27.*

ἐκλιμία, -ας, ἡ (h.l.) *great hunger* Dt 28:20.*

ἐκλιμπάνω (Eur+) *fail, die* Zech 11:16.*

ἐκλογίζομαι (Hdt, Eur+) *consider; reckon, compute* (money), > *audit* (τινά) 4 Km 12:16; 22:7.*

ἐκλογιστής, -οῦ, ὁ (pap, ins) *accountant* Tob 1:22.*

ἐκλογιστία, -ας, ἡ (h.l.) *account, official record* Tob 1:21.*

ἐκλοχίζω (h.l.) *pick out of a band* (λόχος) *of troops*; (pass ptc) *picked, selected* SSol 5:10.*

ἔκλυσις, -εως, ἡ (Theognis, Aeschyl+) 1. *feebleness, fainting* Esth 5:1d, 2b, 2 Macc 3:24; Ezk 23:33. 2. *deliverance* Is 21:3; Jer 29:3.*

ἐκλύτρωσις, -εως, ἡ (h.l.) *redemption* Num 3:49.*

ἐκλύω pf pass ptc ἐκλελυκώς 2. (act) *unloose; let down* Jer 12:5; *undo* Gen 27:40; *release* Josh 10:6; Job 19:25; *weaken* 2 Esdr 4:4; Jer 45:4. 3. *depart, remove oneself* (no //) 2 Macc 12:18; 13:16.‡

ἐκμαρτυρέω (Aeschyl+) *testify, bear witness* 2 Macc 3:36.*

ἐκμελετάω (AntiphoOr, Ps-Pla+) *learn perfectly*; (pass ptc) *utterly learned* (in τι), *having perfectly learned* 2 Macc 15:12.*

ἐκμελίζω (LXX) *put out of joint, dislocate* 4 Macc 10:5, 8; 11:10.*

ἐκμελῶς (Pollux) *in discordant or unruly fashion* 4 Macc 11:18VL.*

ἐκμεμαχώς pf ptc of BDAG: ἐκμάσσω.

ἐκμετρέω (Soph+) *measure out* (distance) Dt 21:2; (volume, dry measure) Hos 2:1.*

ἐκμιαίνω (Hippocr, Aristoph+) *defile*; (pass) *become defiled* Lev 18:20, 23; 19:31.*

ἐκμυελίζω (h.l.) *suck out the marrow*; (fig) *debilitate* Num 24:8.*

ἐκνεύω Mi 6:14 Heb orig prob נשׂא *overtake*, mistrans as if שׁגה *go astray*.‡

ἐκνήφω Sir 31:2 unexpl (Vulg cj ANIMAM for ὕπνον: *sobers* [act trans, no //] *the mind*; AB cj [w. Grotius] ἐκνίπτω *wash away*).‡

ἔκνηψις, -εως, ἡ (LXX) *recovery of senses* La 2:18; > *self-possession, calm* 3:49.*

ἑκουσιάζομαι (LXX) *offer oneself freely* Judg 5:2B, 9B; 2 Esdr 2:68; 7:13; 21:2; 1 Macc 2:42; (trans) *freely or willingly offer* 2 Esdr 3:5; 7:15; (abs) *make a freewill offering* 2 Esdr 7:16.*

ἑκουσιασμός, -οῦ, ὁ (h.l.) *freewill offering* 2 Esdr 7:16.*

ἑκούσιος 2. (neut subst) *freewill offering* (no //) Lev 7:16; Dt 12:6; 2 Esdr 3:5; Jdth 16:18.‡

ἐκπαιδεύω (Eur, Pla+) *train, teach* Da 1:5L.*

ἐκπαίζω (LXX+) *mock, scorn* 1 Esdr 1:49.*

ἐκπεράω (Hom+: *come through or out, pierce*) *bring out* (no //) Num 11:31.*

ἐκπεριπορεύομαι (LXX+) *go out around* Josh 15:3.*

ἐκπετάννυμι (2 Esdr 9:5; Job 26:9 ἐκπετάζω) fut ἐκπετάσω aor pass ἐξεπετάσθη 2. *spread out, open* (a book, no //) 1 Macc 3:48; (curtains) 4:51; (net) Ezk 17:20; (fig) *open up,* > *invite* (trouble) Pr 13:16. 3. (aor pass) *fly away* (no //, but cf. πετάννυμι) Job 20:8; PsSol 17:16; Hos 9:11; (fut) Na 3:16.‡

ἐκπιέζω or -άζω aor εξεπίεσε, -ασε (Hippocr, Aristot+) *wring out, squeeze out* Judg 6:38B; 18:7B; Pr 30:33; (fig) *oppress* 1 Km 12:3; Zeph 3:19; Ezk 22:29.*

ἐκπικραίνω (LXX+) *embitter, provoke to anger* Dt 32:16 = Odes 2:16.*

ἐκπίνω (Hom, Hdt+) *drink off, drain* Job 6:4; Zech 9:15; Is 51:17; Bel 15.*

ἐκπίπτω 5. (act, of a decree or proclamation, Polyb 30.32.10) *be published or issued* 2 Macc 6:8.‡

ἐκπλύνω (Hdt+) *wash out* Is 4:4.*

ἐκποιέω (Hdt+) *furnish, provide* Ezk 46:7, 11; *provide for, suffice* 3 Km 21:10; 2 Ch 7:7; Sir 39:11; *permit* Sir 18:4; (impers) *be permitted or possible* 42:17.*

ἐκπολεμέω (14x, Thu, X: *provoke to war*) *fight* (against, no //) Ex 1:10; Josh 9:2; Jdth 5:20; 1 Macc 4:28.

ἐκπολιορκέω (Thu+) *besiege and capture* Josh 7:3; 10:5, 34.*

ἐκπολιτεύω (h.l.) *alter or distort the form of government or community* 4 Macc 4:19.*

ἐκπορθέω (Soph+) *pillage, lay waste* 4 Macc 17:24; 18:4; (pass) *be pillaged* Job 12:5.*

ἐκπορνεύω 1.b. (fig, of idolatry; no //) Ex 34:15; Judg 2:17; Ezk 6:9. 2. (act trans, no //) *defile, prostitute* Lev 19:29¹; 20:5; *cause to be defiled* (through idolatry) 2 Ch 21:11, 13.‡

ἔκπρακτος, -ον (not in HR or LSJ) *undone, destroyed* Sir 10:8G.*

ἐκπρίαμαι (AntiphoOr+) *buy off, redeem* Pr 24:11.*

ἐκπρίω (Hippocr, Thu+) *cut off* Wsd 13:11.*

ἐκπυρόω (Eur, Aristot+) *heat up, make red-hot* 2 Macc 7:3f.*‡

ἐκρέω dep fut ἐκρυήσεται aor ἐξερρύησαν = dep ἐξερρύημεν (Hom+) *fall off* Dt 28:40 (Vulg DEFLUENT ET PERIBUNT, *fall away and perish*; DEFLUO precisely parallels whole semantic range of ἐκρέω [// etymology]; PERIBUNT no source in MT unless somehow misreading ויתיך) Is 64:6; (fig) *fall away, desert* (of troops; no //, but cf. ἀπορέω) 1 Macc 9:6.*

ἔκρηγμα, -ατος, τό (Hippocr, Theophr+) *breach* Ezk 30:16.*

ἐκρήγνυμι aor pass ἐξεράγην (Hom, Hdt+) *tear off*; (pass) *be torn away* Job 18:14.*

εκρημα f.l. (not in Gött app, LSJSup only here) for ἔκρηγμα (= MT) Ezk 30:16VL.*

ἐκριζωτής, -οῦ, ὁ (h.l.) *uprooter, destroyer* 4 Macc 3:5.*

ἐκρίθην   aor pass of BDAG: κρίνω.
ἐκρίπτω   aor pass ἐξερ(ρ)ίφην pf pass ptc ἐκρεριμμένος (Judg 15:15B) or ἐξερριμμένος (Bar 2:25). **3.** *throw or cast out* 2 Macc 5:10. Ps 1:4 ἐκρίπτει (pres, q.l. c. Ra) as in BDAG. Judg 15:9 mistrans of נטש niph *spread themselves out* as if *be cut off, be abandoned*.‡
ἐκσαρκίζω   (h.l.) *cut or strip meat* (from bones) Ezk 24:4.*
ἐκσιφωνίζω   (h.l.) *siphon or drain away* Job 5:5.*
ἐκσοβέω   (Menand+) *utterly terrify* Wsd 17:9.*
ἐκσπάω   (22x, Hom+) *draw out, pull out or up* Judg 3:22; 1 Km 17:35; Ps 21:10; Job 29:17; Am 3:12; Ezk 11:19; *pull off* Jer 22:24.
ἐκσπερματίζω   (h.l.) *produce* (seed), *be fertile w.* Num 5:28.*
ἐκσπονδυλίζω   (vl -σφον-, = ; h.l.) *break the back or vertebrae* 4 Macc 11:18.*
ἔκστασις   4 Km 4:13 see ἐξίστημι.‡
ἐκστραγγίζω   (Diosc?) *squeeze out* Ezk 23:34vL.*
ἐκστρατεύω   (Hdt+) *march out* Pr 30:27.*
ἐκστρέφω   **2.** *turn out, bend out* Zech 11:16.‡
ἐκσυρίζω   (Demosth+) *hiss loudly* Sir 22:1.*
ἐκσύρω   (AnthPal) *sweep away* Judg 5:21B.*
ἔκταξις, -εως, ἡ   (Polyb+) *distribution* (of food; Joseph *AJ* 15.309) 4 Km 4:13vL.*
ἔκτασις, -εως, ἡ   (Hippocr, Pla+) *stretching; tension* Judg 16:14A; Jer 5:30vL; *extension* Ezk 17:3.*
ἐκτάσσω   aor pass ἐξετάγη (ἐξετάχθη) pf pass ptc ἐκτεταγμένος (X+) **1.** *muster, deploy* (troops) Num 32:27; 4 Km 25:19; 2 Macc 15:20; also 1 Macc 6:40 cj—cf. AB; read ἐξετάχθη, cf. end of verse). **2.** (= τάσσω) *prescribe, order* (food) Da 1:10.*
ἐκτείνω   aor pass ἐξετάθην fut pass ἐκταθήσομαι Zech 1:16 pf pass ptc ἐκτεταμμένος **1.b.** *extend a line* (of troops), *deploy* Judg 9:33, 44. 1 Macc 6:40 cj ἐξετάχθη (ἐκτάσσω: *deploy, muster* in Polyb, DiodS, but cf. Judg 9:33, 44); 7:47[2] rd ἐξέθεσαν (ἐκτίθημι: *put on public display* [pap, ins III BCE]).‡

ἐκτείσω   fut of ἐκτίνω.
ἐκτελέω   **2.** *accomplish, fulfill* Da 3:40Θ = Odes 7:40.*‡
ἐκτέμνω   aor ἐξέτεμε(ν) (Hom+) *cut out, cut off* Tob 2:12S; 2 Macc 15:33; 4 Macc 10:17, 21; 18:21; Is 38:12 = Odes 11:12.*
ἐκτενία, -ας, ἡ   2 Macc 14:38R; 3 Macc 6:41R better (so Gött, W), BDAG: ἐκτένεια.
ἐκτεταμένος   pf pass ptc of ἐκτείνω 1 Ch 21:16; Sir 4:31; Jer 21:5; Ezk 1:11
ἐκτήκω   aor ἐξέτηξεν (Aeschyl+) **1.** *cause to fail, melt or waste away* Ps 38:12; 118:139; Job 31:16; Sir 18:18; 31:1; (mid/pass) *melt or waste away* Ps 118:158; 138:21. **2.** *melt out* (act intr, no //) Lev 26:16.*
ἐκτίκτω   (Pla+) *bring forth or produce* (living things) Is 55:10.*
ἐκτιλῶ   fut, ἐκτιλήσομαι fut mid of BDAG: ἐκτίλλω.
ἐκτιναγμός, -οῦ, ὁ   (LXX+) *shaking out, winnowing* Na 2:11.*
ἐκτινάσσω   pf pass ptc ἐκτετιναγμένος **3.** (ins) *search out* 2 Km 22:33. **4.** *launch, propel* (no //) 1 Macc 10:80. 3 Km 3:25 mistrans of נפץ[1] *break up* as if נפץ/פוץ[2] *scatter*. 2 Esdr 14:10 mistrans of נערי *my lads* (Nehemiah's personal retinue), 15:15 mistrans of נעריהם *their servants*, Ps 126:4 mistrans of נעורים *youth* (time of life), all as if fr נער *shake out*.‡
ἐκτίνω   fut ἐκτείσω (Aeschyl, Hdt+) *pay in full* Job 2:4.*
ἐκτοκίζω   (ins) *charge interest* Dt 23:20f.*
ἐκτομίας, -ου, ὁ   (Hdt+) *castrated person, eunuch* Lev 22:24.*
ἐκτομίς, -ίδος, ἡ   (AnthPal+) *something cut or mutilated* Lev 22:24vL.*
ἐκτοπίζω   (Aristot, pap, Polyb+) *depart, take (oneself) off, go elsewhere* 2 Macc 8:13.*
ἐκτός   **3.b.** *apart from, besides* Judg 3:31A; 1 Ch 29:3. SSol 4:1, 3; 6:7 cf. σιώπησις.‡
ἕκτος   **2.** *sixth part, one sixth* Ezk 4:11; 45:13; 46:14.‡
ἐκτρεπής, -ές   (dub; not in HR or LSJ) *diverting, turning away* (?) 2 Macc 3:26vL.*
ἐκτρέχω   (Hom+) *run off, run out* Judg 13:10A; 3 Km 18:16.*

ἐκτριβή, -ῆς, ἡ (h.l.) destruction Dt 4:26.*
ἐκτρίβω aor pass subj ἐκτριβῇς 3. rub out, scour, polish Lev 6:21.‡
ἔκτριψις, -εως, ἡ (LXX+) ruin, destruction (no //; cogn dat w. ἐκτρίβω) Num 15:31.*
ἐκτρυγάω (pap) gather Lev 25:5.*
ἐκτρώγω (Aristoph+) eat up, consume Mi 7:4.*
ἐκτύπωμα, -ατος, τό (Pla+) figure in relief Ex 28:36; Sir 45:12.*
ἐκτύπωσις, -εως, ἡ (LXX+) relief work, figure work 3 Km 6:35.*
ἐκτυφλόω (Hdt+) render blind Ex 21:26; 23:8; Dt 16:19; 4 Km 25:7 = Jer 52:11; Tob 2:10S; Zech 11:17; Is 56:10.*
ἐκφαίνω aor pass ἐξεφάνθη (14; Hom, Hdt+) reveal, disclose 3 Macc 4:1; Sir 8:19; Da 2:19L.
ἐκφαυλίζω (LXX+) despise, disdain Jdth 14:5.*
ἐκφλέγω (Aristoph+) set on fire; (pass ptc) ignited, burning 4 Macc 16:3.*
ἐκφορά, -ᾶς, ἡ (Aeschyl, Thu+) carrying out (of corpse, for burial), funeral procession 2 Ch 16:14; 21:19.*
ἐκφόριον, -ου, τό (Hdt+) produce, output Lev 25:19; Dt 28:33; Judg 6:4A; Hg 1:10; Mal 3:10.*
ἐκφυγή, -ῆς, ἡ (h.l.) escape 3 Macc 4:19.*
ἐκφύρω aor pass ἐξεφύρθην (h.l.) mix, defile; (pass) be defiled Jer 3:2.*
ἐκφυσάω aor ἐξεφύσησα (Aeschyl+) 1. fan (a fire) 4 Macc 5:32; Ezk 22:20f. 2. blow out (smoke and fire) Sir 43:4; (fig) scorn, snort in contempt over Mal 1:13. 3. scatter with wind Hg 1:9.*
ἐκφύσημα, -ατος, τό (DiodS) eruption Ezk 22:21VL.*
ἐκχέω 4. draw (sword, no //; Heb, cf. ἐκκενόω) Ps 34:3.*‡
ἐκχολάω (h.l.) be enraged 3 Macc 3:1R.*
ἐκχωρίζω (Aristot+) set apart 1 Esdr 4:44, 57.*
ἐλαιαλογέω (h.l.; better, w. Gött, Philo [VIRT 91; =] ἐλαιο-, =) pick olives Dt 24:20R.*
ἐλάϊνος, -η, -ον (Hom+) of the olive Lev 24:2.*

ἔλασμα, -ατος, τό (DiodS+) object of beaten metal Hab 2:19.*
ἐλασσονέω = BDAG: ἐλαττονέω.
ἐλασσονόω see ἐλαττονόω
ἐλασσόω = BDAG: ἐλαττόω.
ἐλάσω fut of ἐλαύνω.
ἐλάτη, -ης, ἡ (Hom+) fir tree Gen 21:15; SSol 5:11; Ezk 31:8.*
ἐλάτινος, -η, -ον (Hom+) made of fir Ezk 27:5.*
ἐλατός, -ή, -όν (Aristot+) of beaten metal Num 10:2; 17:3; 3 Km 10:16f; 2 Ch 9:15f; Ps 97:6; Sir 50:16.*
ἐλαττονόω or ἐλασσο- Pr 14:34 (10; LXX) diminish; (trans) reduce Lev 25:16; Pr 14:34; (mid/pass) become less Gen 8:3; 3 Km 17:16; (pass) be taken away Tob 14:4S, be defeated 2 Macc 12:11.
ἐλαττόω 1.b. make fewer or less Sir 30:24; diminish, reduce (trans) 39:18.‡
ἐλάττωσις, -εως, ἡ (7x, Aristot+) loss, diminishment Tob 4:13BA, Sir 20:2ff; 22:3.
ἐλαύνω 2. strike; (specif) forge (metal) Ex 25:12.‡
ἔλαφος, -ου, ὁ or ἡ (masc Is 35:6; fem Dt 12:22, 20x, Hom+) deer Dt 12:15; 2 Km 22:34 = Ps 17:34; SSol 2:9; Is 34:15.
ἔλεγξις 2. refuting, vindication Job 21:4; 23:2.*‡
ἐλέγχω 4. (pass) be disgraced by, be ashamed of (τινός) Wsd 1:5 (no //).‡
ἐλεέω Job 41:4 renders יִן (h.l. unexpl) as if fr חנן be gracious.‡
ἐλεημοποιός, -όν (h.l.) doing charity, giving alms Tob 9:6S.*
ἐλεημοσύνη 3. (Heb) צדקה mercy, generous treatment Ps 23:5; PsSol 15:13; source of mercy Dt 6:25.‡
ἐλεόπολις see ἑλέπολις
ἔλεος 2. plea for mercy (no //, but cf. Eur OR 832 piteous thing) Jer 43:7; 44:20; 45:26; 49:2; Da 9:20Θ (s.t. of תחנה plea for mercy, supplication; mercy, pardon).‡
ἑλέπολις, -εως, ἡ (Ra: ἐλεόπολις; DiodS, adj [city-destroying] since Aeschyl) siege engine 1 Macc 13:43f.*

ἕλεσθε   2 aor impv of BDAG: αἱρέω Josh 24:15.
ἐλευστέον   (h.l.) *one must go on* 2 Macc 6:17.*
ἐλεφαντάρχης, -ου, ὁ   (Phylarchus, Plu+) *commander of troop of elephants* (c. LSJ, in our texts a large number—e.g., 500) 2 Macc 14:12; 3 Macc 5:4, 45.
ἐλέφας, -αντος, ὁ   (17x, Hom+) **1.** *elephant* 1 Macc 1:17; 2 Macc 11:4; 3 Macc 5:1ff. **2.** *ivory* Ezk 27:6.
ἔληξα   see λήγω.
ἐλήσθην   aor pass of λανθάνω, (ἐπ-) Ps 34:3.
ἐλιγήσομαι   (2 aor) fut pass of BDAG: ἑλίσσω Is 34:4.
ἑλικτός, -ή -όν   (HomHymns, Soph+) *twisted, rolled* (bread) Lev 6:14; *winding* (staircase) 3 Km 6:8.*
ἕλιξ, -ικος, ἡ   (Hom+) *spiral;* (specif) *grapevine* Gen 49:11.*
ἕλκω   **4.** (trans) *draw off* (an army, for redeployment, no //) 1 Macc 10:82. **5.** *plow* (obj furrow, no // but Hom *Il* 10.353 *draw a plow*) Job 39:10. Job 28:18 mistrans of מֶשֶׁךְ *pouch* as if מֶשַׁךְ *pull or drag.* 2 Esdr 19:30 mistrans of משׁך *extend* (oneself), > *be patient* as if *pull, drag.* Eccl 2:3 = MT למשך *to draw or drag,* but cj לשׂמך *to delight.*‡
Ελλην   (c. HR; = BDAG) *Greek;* > *heathen, pagan* 4 Km 21:6VL.*
ἐλλιπής, -ές   (Thu+) *lacking, having in short supply* Sir 14:10; PsSol 4:17.◊
ελλουλιμ   translit of הלולים *cultic procession or celebration* Judg 9:27B.*
ελμωνι   translit of אלמני *particular, designated* 4 Km 6:8.*
ἕλος, -εος, τό   (12x, Hom+) *marsh, marshy ground* Ex 2:3; 1 Macc 9:42; Is 19:6.
ἐλπίζω   Gen 4:26 mistrans of חלל *begin* as if יחל *wait for, expect.*‡
ἐλπίς   Ps 59:10 = 107:10 mistrans of רחץ *washing* as if Aram *rely on, trust.* Is 28:17 mistrans of קו *line, cord* as if fr קוה *wait hopefully.*‡
ἐλυμηνάμην   aor mid of BDAG: λυμαίνω.
ἑλῶ   2 fut of αἱρέω.
ελωαι   translit of אלהי *my God* 1 Km 1:11.*
ἐμβάλλω   **2.** *set upon, attack* Pr 7:5.‡

ἐμβίωσις, -εως, ἡ   (LXX+) *means of life* Sir 34:22; 38:14; *manner of life* 3 Macc 3:23.*
ἐμβολή, -ῆς, ἡ   (Aeschyl, Thu+) *embarkation, loading* (of a ship) 3 Macc 4:7.*
ἐμβρίμημα, -ατος, τό   (h.l.) *indignation, anger* La 2:6.*
ἐμέθυσα   aor of μεθύσκω 2 Km 11:13.
εμεισουν   itac error for εμισουν Ezk 23:38VL.
ἔμετος, -ου, ὁ   (Hippocr, Hdt+) *vomit* Pr 26:11.*
ἐμμανής, -ές   (Hdt+) *insane, raving* Wsd 14:23.*
ἐμμελέτημα, -ατος, τό   (LXX+) *instrument* (for practice of a craft) Wsd 13:10.*
ἐμμέσῳ   = ἐν μέσῳ Num 19:10VL, Ezk 28:16VL.*‡
ἐμμολύνομαι   (h.l.) *be polluting* (to τινί) Pr 24:9.*
ἔμμονος, -ον   (X+) *lasting, chronic* Lev 13:51f; 14:44; Sir 30:17.*
ἔμπαιγμα, -ατος, τό   (LXX) *delusion* Wsd 17:7; Is 66:4.*
ἐμπαίζω   **3.** *play, sport* Ps 103:26; Na 2:4; Bar 3:17.‡
ἐμπαραγίνομαι   (h.l.) *come in upon* (τινί) Pr 6:11.*
ἐμπαρρησιάζω   (so HR, mss ἐνπ-; dub, not in LSJ) *be confident* Job 22:26VL.*
ἐμπάσσω   aor impv ἔμπασον (Hom+) *sprinkle* Tob 11:8SGött (not in HR or Ra, who both read ἔμπλασον).*
ἐμπειρέω   (Polyb+) *be experienced in, know by experience* Tob 5:4S, 6.*
ἐμπειρία, -ας, ἡ   (Thu+) *experience, knowledge gained from experience or practice* Wsd 13:13.*
ἔμπειρος, -ον   (Aeschyl, Hdt+) *informed, experienced* Tob 5:5BA, PsSol 15:9.*
ἐμπήγνυμι   aor ἐνέπηξεν aor pass ἐνεπάγην pf pass ptc ἐμπεπηγός (9x, Pind+) *thrust, stick* Judg 3:21; 2 Km 18:14; (pass) *be thrust, pushed* 1 Km 26:7; La 2:9; (intr) *stick, be stuck* Ps 9:16; 37:3. Ps 31:4 mistrans of קיץ בחרבני *in heat of summer* as if קוץ *thorns* and vb חרב related to *sword.*
ἐμπηδάω   (Hdt+) *leap, jump* 1 Macc 9:48.*

ἐμπι(μ)πλάω = BDAG: -πλημι impf mid/pass ἐμπιπλάμην pf pass ptc ἐμπιμπλαμένος 4. εμπ. τας χειρας (την χειρα) "fill the hands," ordination formula for priesthood (Heb) Ex 28:37; (cf. πληρόω). 1 Km 20:3 mistrans of orig כי נשבע for he has sworn (McCarter AB; MT כפשע but a step?) as if נשבע he is sated or filled.‡

ἐμπίπτω 2.b. ἐμπ. πρός τινα "fall in w. someone," join someone 1 Km 29:3; (abs) meet, encounter 2 Macc 5:12.‡

ἐμπιστεύω (22x, DiodS+) 1. trust (w. ἐν or dat) Dt 1:32; 2 Ch 20:20¹,³; Sir 2:10; Jon 3:5; prove trustworthy Sir 50:24; (pass) be (found) faithful 2 Ch 20:20²; 1 Macc 1:30; Sir 1:15. 2. (trans) entrust (τι) 2 Macc 7:24; (pass ptc) 10:13.

ἐμπλάσσω aor impv ἔμπλασον (Hdt+) plaster, apply Tob 11:8SR (Gött ἐμπάσσω, q.v.).*

ἐμπλατύνω (Strabo 8.7.3) expand, extend Ex 23:18; Dt 12:20; 19:8; 33:20; Am 1:13; (fig) Pr 18:16; Mi 1:16.*

ἐμπλέκω 2.b. "mix it up," be involved in fighting 2 Macc 15:17.‡

ἐμπληθύνω (h.l.) fill; (pass) be filled 3 Macc 5:42.*

ἐμπλήσω fut of ἐμπί(μ)πλημι Ex 15:9; Ps 90:16; Is 11:3.

ἐμπλόκιον, -ου, τό (7x, pap+) braided (gold) cord or chain (no //) Ex 35:22; Is 3:18.

ἔμπνευσις, -εως, ἡ (h.l.) breathing or blowing Ps 17:16.*

ἔμπνους, -ουν (Hdt, Eur+) still breathing, still alive 2 Macc 7:5; 14:45.*

ἐμποδιστικός, -ή, -ον (Aristot+) hindering, impeding 4 Macc 1:4.*

ἐμποδοστατέω (h.l.) catch in a trap (VL εμπεποδεστατη is scribal error conflating this and seq) Judg 11:35.*

ἐμποδοστάτης, -ου, ὁ (h.l.) hindrance 1 Ch 2:7.*

ἐμποιέω (Hom+) cause, bring about; (mid) lay claim to (τινός) Ex 9:17 1 Esdr 5:38.*

ἐμπολάω (Hom, Hdt+) deal, engage in commerce Am 8:5.*

ἐμπολιορκέω (Strabo) besiege Josh 7:3VL, Sir 50:4VL.*

ἔμπονος, -ον (Hippocr+) labored 3 Macc 1:28.*

ἐμπορπάω (Hdt+) fasten with pin or brooch; pass ptc (fig) having fastened on, > girded or clothed w. 3 Macc 7:5 (VL ἐμπεπηρμενοι is scribal error). -πόω (h.l. =) mid, with cogn acc 1 Macc 14:44.*

ἔμπροσθεν 2.g. before (temp; Pla, pap), earlier Judg 1:10A; 2 Macc 14:38; earlier than 2 Ch 35:19b; Eccl 1:10, 16; Da 7:8Θ; οἱ ἐμπρ- those who were former or previous Zech 1:4; Ezk 36:11; cf. 4 Km 18:5.‡

ἐμπρόσθιος, -ον (Hdt+) to the fore, concerning the front or front side (cf. ὀπίσθιος) 2 Macc 3:25; (pl subst) front sides or parts Ex 28:14; 1 Km 5:4.*

ἔμπτυσμα, -ατος, τό (h.l.) spitting, spittle Is 50:6.*

ἐμπυρίζω fut ἐμπυρίω aor pass ἐνεπυρίσθη, pf pass ἐμπεπύρισται (55; Demosth, DiodS, pap) set on fire, burn up Lev 10:6; 1 Km 30:1; 1 Macc 1:56; Ps 9:23; Sir 8:10; Is 3:14; Da 3:48.

ἐμπυρισμός, -οῦ, ὁ (pap, Polyb+) burning, conflagration Lev 10:6; Josh 6:24; 3 Km 8:37; Da 3:95L.*

ἐμπυριστής, -ές (Eustath) setting on fire, causing to burn up 4 Macc 7:11.*

ἔμπυρος, -ον (Pind, Soph+) fiery, inflamed Am 4:2; (pl subst) sacrificial fires (Eur IA 59 sacrifices) Ezk 23:37.

ἐμφαίνω aor pass impv ἐμφάνθι (Pla+) display, make manifest 2 Macc 3:16; (pass) be manifest, be visible Ps 79:2.*

ἐμφανισμός, -οῦ, ὁ (Pla+) declaration, disclosure 2 Macc 3:9.*

ἐμφανῶς (Aeschyl, Hdt+; adv of BDAG: ἐμφανής) visibly, manifestly Ps 49:2; Pr 9:14; Zeph 1:9.*

ἔμφασις, -εως, ἡ (Aristot+) appearance, impression 2 Macc 3:8.*

ἐμφέρω (Hippocr, ins, AppolonRhod) bear in; (mid) rush in, attack (no //) 2 Macc 15:17.*

ἐμφραγμός, -οῦ, ὁ (LXX) stopping, shutting Sir 27:14; Mi 5:1G.*

ἐμφράσσω **1.b.** *hem in, block (passage)* La 3:9.‡

ἐμφυράω (pap967) or -φύρω (Aeschyl+) *mix up* Ezk 22:6VL.*

ἐμφυσιόω (X+) *instill, breathe life into* 1 Esdr 9:48; (pass) *be instructed and inspired* 9:55.*

ἐν **5.b.** also, ἐν ἐμοί, κύριε mistrans of בי אדני (an oath formula), understood as *(I swear) by my own self, my lord* Judg 6:13; 1 Km 1:26; 3 Km 3:17; Ezk 14:7 (but ἐν ἐμοὶ, ὁ θεός Ps 55:13 renders עלי אלהים *upon me, O God*). Judg 8:26 s.t. of prep ב *in, upon*.‡

ἐναγκάλισμα, -ατος, τό (LXX+) *embrace* 4 Macc 13:21.*

ἐναγωνίζομαι (Hdt+) *compete in athletic contest* 4Macc16:16.*

ἐναθλέω (DiodS+) *struggle (against), bear up* 4 Macc 17:13.*

ἐνακούω (Hippocr, Soph+) *hear, listen to* Na 1:12, > *obey* 1 Esdr 4:3, 10.*

ἐναλλαγή, -ῆς, ἡ (LXX+) *variation, perversion* Wsd 14:26.*

ἐνάλλομαι fut ἐναλοῦμαι **1.b.** *rush against, attack* 1 Macc 3:23; Job 16:4.‡

ἐναντιόομαι (8x, Aeschyl, Hdt+) *oppose, confront* (as enemies) 1 Esdr 1:25; 3 Macc 3:1; Pr 20:8; Wsd 2:12.‡

ἐναπερείδομαι (Polyb [22.13.2]+) *fix upon, direct against* (τι εἰς τινά) 2 Macc 9:4.*

ἐναποθνῄσκω (Hdt+) *die in* (of place) 1 Km 25:37; (of circumstance) 4 Macc 6:30; 11:1.*

ἐναποσφραγίζω (Zeno+) *impress upon* 4 Macc 15:4.*

ἔναρα, -ων, τό (Hom+) *booty, spoils* Josh 13:21VL.*

ἐναρίθμιος, -ον (Hom+) *reckoned, valued* Sir 38:29.*

ἐναρμόζω (Pind, Eur+) **1.** *play harmoniously* Jdth 16:2. **2.** *fit, adapt*; (mid) *fit oneself* 4 Macc 9:26.*

ἐνάρμοστος, -ον (LXX+) *harmonious, suited to each other* 4 Macc 14:3VL.*

ἐνάρχομαι 3rd sg plpf ἐνῆρκτο Num 17:12.‡

ἐνατενίζω (Crates+) *fix one's gaze, stare* 3 Macc 5:30.*

ἐνγεννάω (better ἐγγ-; Plu+) *generate, produce* Sir 22:4VL.*‡

ἔνδεια, -ας, ἡ (20x, Thu+) *lack, need, poverty* Dt 28:20; Tob 4:13BA, Pr 6:11; Job 30:3; Wsd 16:4; Am 4:6; Is 25:4.

ἐνδείκτης, -ου, ὁ (pap+) *informer* 2 Macc 4:1.*

ἐνδελεχέω (Stephanus) *make persistent or constant* Sir 30:1.*

ἐνδελεχής, -ές (13x, Critias, Pla+) *persistent, constant* 1 Esdr 6:23; Sir 17:19; (superl) ἐδελεχιστός Da 11:31ΘVL; (adv) *constantly* Ex 29:38; Sir 20:26; Da 6:17.

ἐνδελεχίζω (8x, Epicurus) *be constant(ly), persevere* Sir 9:4; 12:3; 41:6.

ἔνδεσμος, -ου, ὁ (ins+) *bond, joint* (of ceiling or floor? MT unexpl) 3 Km 6:10; (of wall) Ezk 13:11. **2.** *bundle* Pr 7:20.*

ἐνδέχομαι (Hdt, Eur+) **1.** *receive, accept* Ps 118:122. **2.** *be possible*; (ptc subst) *possible things, possibilities* 2 Macc 11:18; (adv of ptc) *as well as possible* 13:26.*‡

ἐνδέω¹ pf pass ptc ἐνδεδεμένος *bound up*, > *plated, covered* (no //) 2 Ch 9:18.‡

ἐνδιαβάλλω (Ctesius+) *slander* Ps 37:21; 70:13; 108:4ff. Num 22:22 mistrans of לְשָׂטָן as *an adversary* as if לִשְׂטֹם *to bear a grudge*.

ἐνδιαλλάσσω pf pass ptc ἐνδιηλλαγμένος (Aristot+) *alter*; pf pass ptc (*"altered one"*) renders קדש *male cult prostitute* 3 Km 22:47VL (fem Aq Gen 38:21).*

ἐνδιατρίβω (Aristoph, Thu+) *continue in, dwell upon* (τινί) Pr 23:16.*

ἐνδίδωμι (Hdt+) **1.** *give way* Gen 8:3; *yield, give in* Pr 10:30; Ezk 3:11. **2.** *lend, offer* (φωνήν) Num 14:1VL.*

ἐνδογενής, -ές (ins) *born in the (same) house* Lev 18:9.*

ἔνδον (11x, Hom+) *inside, within* Lev 11:33; Dt 21:12; 2 Macc 6:4; 9:5.

ἐνδόσθια, -ων τά (LXX; Aristot+: ἐντ-) *internal organs* Ex 12:9; 29:17; Lev 4:8; 7:3; 8:16; Sir 10:9.*

ἐνδυάζω Ps 140:4VL; LSJ: = ἐνδοιάζω *be in doubt* (some mss have συνδοιάζω, = , not in LSJ).

ἐνέγκαι, ἐνεγκεῖν aor infs of φέρω 2 Esdr 8:17, 30. ἐνέγκαισαν aor opt of φέρω (not in HR) Is 66:20.

ἔνεδρον   3 Km 21:40 renders משפט *judgment, decree*, unexpl.‡

ἔνεδρος, -ου, ὁ   (not in HR; Soph [PHIL 153]+) *indweller, inhabitant* Pr 14:33vL (q.l. renders תנוה *lives, dwells*).

ενεθυ / τειλατο   La 2:17vL appar partial correction of ἐνεθυμήθη to ἐνετείλατο.

ἐνεῖδον   (Soph+) *observe, notice* Gen 20:10.*

ἐνείρω   (Hdt+) *lace, intertwine* Job 10:11.*

ἐνεμπίμπλημι   (not in HR or LSJ; f.l.) *fill up* Pr 30:15vL.*

ἐνεμπορεύομαι   (h.l.) *engage in trade* Ezk 27:13vL.*

ἐνενηκονταετής, -ές   (LXX+) *ninety years old* 2 Macc 6:24.*

ἐνεξουσιάζω   (LXX+) *show independence*; (mid) *assert one's own authority* Sir 20:8; (pass) *become subject, yield independence* 47:19.*

ἐνεργάζομαι   (Hdt, X+) *effect, produce* (in τινί) 2 Macc 14:40.*

ἐνεργός, -όν   (Hdt, X+) *productive, for working* Ezk 46:1.*

ἐνευφραίνομαι   (Philo) *delight (in)* Pr 8:31.*

ἐνεχθείς   aor pass ptc, ἐνεχθήσομαι fut pass of BDAG: φέρω.

ἐνεχυράζω   (10x, Pla+) *take (as) a pledge, secure a loan* Ex 22:25; Job 22:6; Ezk 18:16; (fig) *secure as w. a pledge* Jdth 8:16.

ἐνεχύρασμα, -ατος, τό   (LXX+) *pledge, security* Ex 22:25; Ezk 33:15.*

ἐνεχυρασμός, -οῦ, ὁ   (Plu) *pledge, security* Ezk 18:7ff.*

ἐνέχυρον, -ου, τό   (Hdt+) *pledge* Dt 24:10ff.*

ἐνέχω   **2.b.** *be caught or entangled* (X ANAB 7.4.17) Ezk 14:4.‡

ἐνήλατο   aor of BDAG: ἐνάλλομαι Job 16:10

ἐνῆλιξ, -ικος, ἡ or ὁ   (ins, pap) *time or stage of maturity* 4 Macc 18:9.*

ἐνήνοχα   2 pf ἐνηνεγμένος pf pass ptc of BDAG: φέρω.

ἐνηχος, -ον   (Philostrat+) *resonant ("echoing within")* Sir prol 13vL.*

ἔνθεμα, -ατος, τό   (Theophr+: *thing put on*) *decoration, ornament* (no //) SSol 4:9.*

ἐνθέμιον, -ου, τό   (Pollux) *inset, socket* Ex 38:16.*

ἔνθεν   ἔνθεν... ἔνθεν... *on one side... on the other...* (X ANAB 3.5.7.) Ezk 47:7.‡

ἔνθεσμος, -ον   (LXX+) *lawful, valid* 3 Macc 2:21.*

ἐνθουσιάζω   (trag:-σιάω; Pla+) *be inspired or possessed* (by τινί) Sir 31:7.*

ἐνθρονίζω   (DiodS 33.13) *enthrone* 4 Macc 2:22.*

ἐνθρύπτω   (Hippocr+) *cook bread in liquid, make a sop* Bel 33.*

ἐνθυμέομαι   **2.** *be concerned or angry* Gen 6:6 (cf. ἐνθύμιος). **3.** *desire* (no //) Dt 21:11.‡

ἐνθύμημα, -ατος, τό   (27x, Soph+) **1.** *argument, reasoning* 1 Ch 28:9; Sir 27:6; Ezk 14:22; (ironic) *"bright idea," inclination* Ps 118:118; Sir 32:12; Mal 2:16; Jer 3:17; Ezk 24:14. **2.** *device, construction* Ezk 16:36.

ἐνθύμιος, -ον   (Hom+) *troubling the mind*; (subst) *deep concern* (distress or anger; cf. Aeschyl EUM 222 ἐνθυμέομαι) Ps 75:11.*

ἐνιαύσιος, -α, -ον   (51x, Hdt+) *year-old* Ex 12:5; Lev 9:3; Num 6:12; Mi 6:6; Ezk 46:13.

ἐνίημι   ptc ἐνιείς aor ἐνῆκα (Hom, Hdt+) *send in, cast or throw* 4 Macc 4:10; Bar 2:20.*

ἐνικός, -ή, -όν   (Chrysipp+) *single, individual* 4 Macc 18:9vL.*

ἐνισχύω   **1.b.** *prove strong, prevail* Gen 32:29.‡

ενκτησις   = ἔγκτ- 4 Km 4:13vL.*

ἐννακισχίλιοι, -αι, -α   (Hdt, Pla+) *nine thousand* 2 Macc 8:24; 10:18.*

ἐννακόσιοι, -αι, -α   (19x, Hdt, Thu+) *nine hundred* Gen 5:5ff; Judg 4:3; 1 Esdr 5:12.

ἐννεακαίδεκα   (Hom+) *nineteen* 2 Km 2:30.*

ἐννεακαιδέκατος, -η, -ον   (Hippocr, ins) *nineteenth* 4 Km 25:8 = Jer 52:12; 1 Ch 24:16; 25:26.*

ἐννέμω   (ins+) *pasture, > dwell* 3 Macc 3:25.*

ἔννευμα, -ατος, τό   (h.l.) *gesture, signal* Pr 6:13.*

ἐννόημα, -ατος, τό   (Aristot+) *notion, conception* Sir 21:11.*

ἐννοσσεύω   (Aristoph+) *nest* Ps 103:17; Jer 22:23.*

ἐννοσσοποιέομαι   (h.l.) *make nests for oneself* (*on* τι) 4 Macc 14:16.*

ἐνοικειόω (DiodS+) *introduce;* (mid) *be related* (no //) Esth 8:1.*

ἐνοικίζω (Aeschyl, Hdt+) *cause or allow to dwell, introduce as a tenant* (ins) Sir 11:34.*

ἔνοικος, -ου, ὁ (Aeschyl, Thu+) *inhabitant* Judg 5:23A; Jer 31:9; 51:2.*

ἐνοπλίζω (9x, Lycophron+) *arm oneself, prepare for war;* LXX only mid/pass ptc (aor or pf) *armed, ready for war* Num 31:5; 32:17ff; Dt 3:18; Josh 6:7; Jdth 15:13.*

ἐνοράω see ἐνεῖδον.‡

ἐνόρκιος, -ον (Pind) *bound by oath* Num 5:21.*

ἔνορκος, -ον (Soph+) *bound by oath* 2 Esdr 16:18; adv Tob 8:20BA.*

ἐνπροσθέσ(ε)ιος, -ον (spur; not in LSJ) *set before, set in front* 2 Macc 3:25VL.*

ἐνσείω (Hippocr, Soph+) **1.** (trans) *hurl or thrust* (τι at τινί) 2 Macc 3:25; 14:46; *hurl to their death* (against rocks? over cliffs? no //) 4 Km 8:12. **2.** (intr) *rush upon, attack* (DiodS+) 2 Macc 12:15, 37.*

ἐνσιτέομαι (h.l.) *feed on, eat* Job 40:30.*

ἐνσκολιεύομαι (h.l.) *ensnare* Job 40:24.*

ἐντάσσω **2.** *insert* Am 7:8. **3.** *arrange, present* Da 5:24Θ; 10:21Θ.‡

ἐνταφιαστής, -οῦ, ὁ (Strabo, pap+) *embalmer, undertaker* Gen 50:2.*

ἐντείνω pf pass ptc ἐντεταμένος (22; Hom+) *stretch tight; draw, aim* (a bow) 3 Km 22:34 = 2 Ch 18:33; Ps 7:12; (abs) 44:5; (fig) Jer 9:2; (pass ptc) *taut, aimed* Hos 7:16; Is 5:28.

ἐντέλλω 1 Km 25:15 mistrans of פקד niph *be missing* as if *order, appoint.*‡

ἐντεῦθεν **3.** (of time) *from now on* Tob 7:11S.‡

ἐντήκω 2 aor ἐνετάκην (Soph+) *melt in,* (pass) *be dissolved;* (fig) *melt away, waste away* (no //) Ezk 24:23; (fig) *melt into,* > *stir the emotions* 4 Macc 8:26.*

ἐντιμόομαι (LXX) *be honored, be treated w. respect* 4 Km 1:13f.*

ἔντιναγμα, -ατος, τό (LXX+) *shaking* (being shaken? Vulg INPACTU) Sir 22:13VL.*

ἐντιναγμός, -οῦ, ὁ (h.l.) *excitation, frenzy* Sir 22:13.*

ἐντινάσσω (LXX+) *hurl* 1 Macc 2:36; 2 Macc 4:41; 11:11.*

ἐντομίς, -ίδος, ἡ (LXX+) *incision* (no //) Lev 19:28; 21:5; Jer 16:6.*

ἐντότερος, -η, -ον (h.l. comp of ἐντός) *more interior* Esth 4:11VL.*

ἐντρεχής, -ές (Pla+) *skilled, prepared* Sir 31:22.*

ἔντριτος, -ον (h.l.) *three-ply* Eccl 4:12.*

ἐντρύφημα, -ατος, τό (Philo SOMN 2.242 *source of enjoyment*) *revel, party* (no //) Eccl 2:8.*

ἐντυχία, -ας, ἡ (pap+) *petition* 3 Macc 6:40.*

ἔνυδρος, -ον (Hes, Hdt+) *in water;* (subst) *fish, water creature* 4 Macc 1:34; Wsd 19:10, 19.*‡

ἐνυπνιαστής, -οῦ, ὁ (LXX+) *dreamer* Gen 37:19.*

ἐνυποκρίνομαι (h.l.) *be a hypocrite* Sir 33:2VL.*

ἐνυποτάσσω (h.l.) *enjoin;* (pass impers) *it will be enjoined* (by your example) Tob 14:7S.*

ἔνυστρον, -ου, τό (Aristoph, Aristot+: ἤν-; so Mal 2:3R) *fourth stomach* (of ruminants) Dt 18:3; Mal 2:3G.*

ἐνυψόω (dub; h.l.) *excite, make proud* Da 5:1LVL.*

ενφωθ (not in HR) translit of הנטפות *earrings* (prob doublet w. ὁρμίσκος) Judg 8:26A.*

ἐνώπιος, -ον (usu [= BDAG] neut sg as prep w. gen) **6.** (temp) *prior to, earlier than* (no //) Gen 11:28; 3 Km 15:3. **7.** (adv) *face to face, in person* Gen 16:13. **8.** (true adj) *visible, apparent* (no //) Lev 13:37; Pr 8:9; ἐνώπιος ἐνωπίῳ *face to face* Ex 33:11; ἄρτους ἐν- *bread of the Presence* Ex 25:30.‡

ἐνωτίζομαι (36x) aor ἐνωτισάμην or (incorrectly) ἤνωτ-.‡

ἐνώτιον, -ου, τό (17x, Aeschyl+) *earring* Gen 24:22; Judg 8:24; Jdth 10:4; Hos 2:15; = *nose ring* (no //) Pr 11:22; Ezk 16:12.

ἐξαγορεύω (13x, Hom+) *declare, make public* 3 Km 8:31; Bar 1:14; (specif) *confess* (sin) Lev 5:5; 2 Esdr 10:1; Ps 31:5 Job 31:34; Da 9:20Θ.

ἐξαγορία, -ας, ἡ (not in HR; Ptolem) *confession* (of sin) PsSol 9:6.*

ἐξαγριαίνω   aor pass ἐξηγριάνθη (Pla+; vl -ριόω Hdt, Pla+) *make wild or savage;* (pass) *become wild or savage* Da 8:7Θ.*

ἐξάδελφος, -ου, ὁ   (lxx+) *nephew* Tob 1:22; 11:19.*

ἔξαιμος, -ον   (Hippocr, DiodS 3.35.3) *drained of blood* 2 Macc 14:46.*

ἐξαίρω   aor pass ἐξήρθην La 1:6G **2.** (intr) *rise up, lift off* Ezk 1:4, 19; (trans) *lift, raise from the ground* Gen 29:1; Is 62:10; *lift up* (hands, in blessing) Lev 9:22; (wings) Ezk 11:22; (fig) *exalt, praise* Sir 37:7. **3.** *set out, depart* Gen 35:5; Ex 13:20; 2 Esdr 8:31.‡

ἐξαίσιος, -α, -ον   (9x, Aeschyl, Hdt+) *extraordinary, egregious* Job 4:12; 5:9.

ἐξακονάω   (lxx) *sharpen* Ezk 21:16.*

ἐξακοσιοστός, -ή, -όν   (lxx) *six hundredth* Gen 7:11; 8:13.*

ἐξάλειπτρον, -ου, τό   (Aristoph, ins+) *small pot for ointments* Job 41:23.*

ἐξάλειψις, -εως, ἡ   (ins) **1.** *painting, whitewashing* (w. play on 2.) Mi 7:11. **2.** *wiping out, destruction* (no //) Ezk 5:16G; 9:6.*

ἐξαλλάσσω   pf pass ptc ἐξηλαγμένος (Soph+) *change, vary;* (ptc subst) *change* obj suit (of clothes, no //) Gen 45:22; (pf pass ptc) *different, strange, unusual* Wsd 2:15.*

ἐξαλλοιόω   (Theophr+) *change drastically or utterly* 3 Macc 3:21.*

ἔξαλλος, -ον   (Polyb, ins+) *distinctive, special* 2 Km 6:14; *strange, unusual* Esth 3:8; 3 Macc 4:4; Wsd 14:23; > *shocking* Da 11:36L.*

ἐξαλλοτριόω   (Strabo, pap+) *alienate, estrange;* (pass) *be estranged* 1 Macc 12:10.*

ἐξαμαρτάνω   **2.** (trans) *cause to sin, draw into sin* 3 Km 15:26; 4 Km 1:18c; Eccl 5:5; Sir 47:24. **3.** (orig meaning) *miss the mark* Judg 20:16B.‡

ἐξάμηνος, -ον   (X+) *for half a year, lasting six months* 4 Km 15:8; 1 Ch 3:4.*‡

ἐξαναλίσκω   fut ἐξαναλώσω aor ἐξανήλωσα aor pass ἐξανηλώθη pf pass ἐξανήλωμαι (27; Aeschyl+) *destroy* (mountains & forests) EpJer 61; (crops) Dt 28:42; (animals) Lev 26:22; (people) Ex 32:12; Josh 24:20; 1 Macc 5:15; Jer 9:15; *consume* (food) Jdth 11:13; (pass) *perish* Num 17:27; 32:13; Ezk 35:15.

ἐξανάστασις   Gen 7:4 mistrans of יקום *that which subsists or lives* as if fr קום *arise.*‡

ἐξανατέλλω   **2.** (caus) *make to spring up* Ps 103:14; 146:8. **3.** *rise, come forth* (of sun or light) Ps 111:4.‡

ἐξανθέω   (22x, X+) **1.** *bloom, produce flowers* Ex 28:33; Ps 71:16; SSol 6:11; Sir 51:15G; Hos 14:8; Is 27:6. **2.** *erupt, break out* Lev 13:12ff; Hos 7:9.

ἐξαντλέω   (Eur+) *drain away, draw off* Pr 20:5; Hg 2:16.*

ἐξαπίνης   (Hom, Hdt+; older form of BDAG: ἐξάπινα) *suddenly, unexpectedly* Pr 6:15; 29:1; Is 47:11.*

ἐξαπόλλυμι   (Hom+) *utterly perish, die out* Wsd 10:6.*

ἐξαποστολή, -ῆς, ἡ   (PhiloMech, Polyb+) *expulsion* 3 Macc 4:4.*

ἔξαρθρος, -ον   (lxx+) *dislocated, out of joint* 4 Macc 9:13.*

ἐξαρθρόω   (Aristot+) *dislocate* 4 Macc 10:5.*

ἐξαρκέω   (Hdt+) *prove strong, be sufficient* Num 11:23.*

ἐξαρνέομαι   (Hdt, Eur+) *deny, repudiate* 4 Macc 5:35.*

ἔξαρσις, -εως, ἡ   (ins+) *removal; setting out* Num 10:6; *destruction* Jer 12:17.*

ἐξάρχω   (13x, Hom+) *start up, initiate; begin to sing* (no //) Ex 32:18; Num 21:17; 1 Km 18:7; Jdth 16:1; 3 Macc 4:6; Ps 146:7; Is 27:2; > *teach a song* (no //) Ex 15:21; Jdth 15:14.

ἐξασκέω   (Soph, X+) *train thoroughly* 4 Macc 5:23; 13:24.*

ἐξατιμόομαι   (h.l. but -μαζω Soph OedCol 1378) *be completely disgraced* Ezk 16:61.*

ἐξαφίημι   (Soph+) *let loose, set free* 2 Macc 12:24.*‡

ἐξαφίστημι   aor ἐξαπέστην (Soph+) *dispatch, remove* Jer 5:25vl.*

ἐξεγείρω   **1.b.** (fig) *arouse, stir up* 2 Ch 36:22. Judg 5:16A mistrans of עדרים *flocks* (by metonymy *shepherds;* cf. αγελη) as if fr עור *be awake, bestir oneself.*‡

ἐξέγερσις, -εως, ἡ   (Polyb+) *awakening, (act of) waking up* PsSol 4:15.*

ἐξεδο-   see ἐκδίδωμι.

ἐξέδρα, -ας, ἡ   (21x; Eur, ins+) *hall, room* (לשכה [41:11] צלע]) Ezk 40:44ff; 41:10f; 42:11f; 44:19; 46:19; *cubicle or bench* (טור, טירה) 46:23.*

ἐξεικονίζω   (LXX+) *make a likeness;* (pass) *be recognizably formed* Ex 21:22f.*

ἐξεζητημένος   pf pass ptc of ἐκζητέω.

ἐξεκκλησιάζω   (19x, Aristot+) *summon to assemble, convoke* Lev 8:4; (cf. 8:3 ἐκκλησ-), Num 20:10; Josh 18:1; 1 Ch 13:5; 1 Macc 6:19; Jer 33:9.

ἐξελαύνω   (Hom, Hdt+) *drive out, march out* (esp military forces) Zech 9:8; 10:4.*

ἐξελέγην   aor pass of BDAG: ἐκλέγω.

ἐξέλευσις, -εως, ἡ   (h.l.) *going out, departure* 3 Km 15:20.*

ἐξελίσσω   (Eur, X+) *unroll,* > (of military forces) *deploy, extend;* (pass ptc) *arranged, extended* (of building, no //) 3 Km 7:45.*‡

ἐξέλκω   2. *drag out* Gen 37:28; Pr 30:33.‡

ἐξεμέω   aor pass ἐξεμέ(σ)θην (Hom+) *vomit, disgorge* (act or mid) Pr 23:8; 25:16; Jer 32:16, 27; (pass) *be disgorged* Job 20:15.*

ἐξέπτησαν   see ἐκπέτομαι.

ἐξεργάζομαι   (Hdt+) *work out, compose* Esth 8:12r; *prepare* Ps 7:14; 30:20.*

ἐξεργαστικός, -ή, -όν   (X+) *able to accomplish;* (subst) *working out, full presentation* 2 Macc 2:31.ᴬ

ἐξερεύγομαι   aor ἐξηρεύξατο (Hdt+) *discharge, pour forth* Ex 7:28; Ps 44:2; 118:171; 144:7; Wsd 19:10; (intr) *empty out* Ps 143:13.*

ἐξερευνάω   (BDAG: -αυναω) aor pass ἐξηρευνήθη *search through* Zeph 1:12; (trans) *search out* Pr 2:4; PsSol 17:9; (pass) *be found out, be discovered* Ob 6; La 3:40.‡

ἐξερεύνησις, -εως, ἡ   (h.l.) *investigation* Ps 63:7.*

ἐξερημόω   (19x, Soph+) 1. *devastate, ruin* Lev 26:31; Judg 16:24A; PsSol 15:11; Hg 1:4; Is 37:26; Da 4:19L. 2. *dry up* 4 Km 19:24; Hos 13:15; Is 50:2.

ἐξέρπω   (Soph, X+) *creep out, crawl out;* (trans) *cause to creep out* (no //) Ps 104:30.*

ἐξετάθη   aor pass of ἐκτείνω 1 Macc 6:40.

ἐξέτασις, -εως, ἡ   (Thu+) 1. *investigation* 3 Macc 7:5. 2. *test, examination* Wsd 1:9.*

ἐξεταστέον   (Pla+) *it must be examined or investigated* 2 Macc 2:29.*

ἐξευμενίζω   (LXX+) *propitiate* (act or mid) 4 Macc 4:11.*

ἐξεύρεσις, -εως, ἡ   (Hdt+) *finding out, complete exploration* Is 40:28; Bar 3:18.*

ἐξευρίσκω   2 aor ἐξεῦρον (Hom+) *invent, discover* 2 Macc 7:23; Bar 3:32, 37.*

ἐξευφραίνομαι   (HermWr) *enjoy oneself, take pleasure* (c. LSJ; cf. ευφ-) Ezk 23:41vL.*

ἐξέχω   (pass ptc) *projection, convex surface* (act Pla+), renders שלמים *crossbars* 2 Km 7:15f.‡

ἐξηγητής, -οῦ, ὁ   (Hdt+) *interpreter, advisor* Gen 41:8, 24; Pr 29:18.*

ἐξηγορία, -ας, ἡ   (LXX) *pronouncement, utterance* Job 22:22; 33:26.*

ἐξηκονταετής, -ές   (Mimnermus, Hippocr+) *of sixty years, sixty years old* Lev 27:3, 7.*

ἐξηκοστός, -ή, -όν   (Hdt+) *sixtieth* 1 Macc 10:1ff; 11:19; 2 Macc 1:7.*

ἐξηλιάζω   (LXX) *expose to the sun* 2 Km 21:6, 9, 13.*

ἐξῆμαι   pf mid/pass, ἐξήφθην ἐξηψήθην alt aor passives of BDAG: ἐξάπτω.

ἐξημερόω   (Hdt, Eur+) *tame, subdue to cultivation* (fig) 4 Macc 1:29.*

ἐξικνέομαι   (Hom+) *reach, suffice* (renders חקק *limit, decree;* txt? meaning?) Judg 5:15B.*

ἐξίλασις, -εως, ἡ   (LXX+) *atonement, propitiation* Num 29:11; Hab 3:17 = Odes 4:17.*

ἐξιλάσκομαι   2. *offer in expiation* (obj αἷμα, no //) 2 Ch 29:24. 3. *cleanse, consecrate* (no //, obj altar) Ezk 43:20ff.‡

ἐξίλασμα, -ατος, τό   (LXX) *offering for atonement or propitiation* 1 Km 12:3; Ps 48:8.*

ἐξιλασμός, -οῦ, ὁ   (15x, LXX+) *atonement, propitiation* Ex 30:10; 1 Ch 28:11; 2 Macc 12:45; Wsd 18:21; Ezk 7:25.

ἐξιππάζομαι   (Joseph AJ 9.42) *ride out* Hab 1:8.*

ἐξίπταμαι   (Aristot+; later form of ἐκπέτομαι) *fly out* Pr 7:10.*

ἕξις 2. *condition, state* (of having or possessing, fr ἔχω) 1 Km 16:7; Odes 4:16 = Hab 3:16; *posture or condition* (of body) Da 1:15L. **3.** *interior* (no //, but ἔχω *hold, contain*) Da 7:15Θ. Judg 14:9A mistrans of גויה *corpse* as if fr Aram גו *interior*.‡

ἐξισάζω (Strabo+) *make equal;* (mid) *claim equality for oneself* Sir 32:9R.*

ἐξισόω (Hdt+) *make equal;* (pass ptc) *equal, of the same size* Ex 37:16; 38:15.*

ἐξίστημι 4 Km 4:13 mistrans of חרד (w. cogn acc) *put oneself out, go to the trouble* as if *tremble, be terrified*.‡

ἐξιχνεύω (Eur+) *track down, search out* Sir 6:27; 18:4; 42:18.*

ἐξιχνιάζω (15x, LXX+) *track down, search out, explore* Judg 18:2; Ps 138:3; Eccl 12:9; Sir 1:3.

ἐξιχνιασμός, -οῦ, ὁ (LXX, Aq) *exploration, (act of) tracking down* Judg 5:16A.

ἐξοδεύω (Polyb+) *march out* 2 Macc 12:19; (specif) *go out to raid or plunder* (no //) 1 Esdr 4:23; 1 Macc 15:41; (pass) *plundered or stripped* (no //) Judg 5:27B.*

ἐξοδία, -ας, ἡ (Hdt+) **1.** *expedition* 2 Km 3:22; 11:1. **2.** *departure* Dt 33:18; (specif) *Exodus* Dt 16:3; Mi 7:15.*

ἐξοδιάζω aor pass ἐξωδιάσθη (ins) *pay in full, discharge;* (pass) *be spent, be paid out* 4 Km 12:13.*

ἐξόδιος, -ον (CratinusCom) *relating to an exit or departure* (no //); *relating to the Exodus,* (subst) *holiday commemorating the Exodus* Lev 23:36; Num 29:35; Dt 16:8; 2 Ch 7:9; 2 Esdr 18:18; Ps 28:1.*

ἔξοδος **4.** *way out, exit* 2 Ch 9:28; Pr 1:20. **5.** *bodily discharge or emission* (e.g., semen or excrement [Heb], no //) Pr 30:12.‡

ἐξοικοδομέω (Hdt, Aristoph+) *build, finish building* 2 Esdr 13:15VL.*

ἔξοικος, -ον (h.l.) *homeless, living out of doors* Job 6:18.*

ἐξοκέλλω aor ἐξώκειλα (Aeschyl, Hdt+) *run aground,* (fig) *drive to ruin* Pr 7:21.*

ἐξολέθρευμα, -ατος, τό (h.l.) *that which is set aside for destruction* 1 Km 15:21.*

ἐξολέθρευσις, -εως, ἡ (LXX) *destruction* 1 Macc 7:7; Ps 108:13; Ezk 9:1.*

ἐξολλύω or -όλλυμι fut ἐξολῶ (Hom+) *destroy completely* Pr 11:17; 15:27; (mid/pass) *perish, be completely destroyed* Pr 10:31; Sir 5:7.*

ἐξομβρέω (LXX) *pour out, rain down* Sir 1:19; 10:13.*

ἐξόμνυμι (Soph, Demosth+) (mid) *swear in denial,* > *renounce by oath* 4 Macc 4:26; 5:34; 9:23; 10:3.*

ἐξομολόγησις **2.** *admission, confession* PsSol 9:6.‡

ἐξόπισθεν (7x, Pla+) *from behind* 1 Ch 19:10; (prep w. gen) *from following after* 3 Km 19:21; Ps 77:71; *behind* 1 Macc 5:33.

ἐξοπλησία, -ας, ἡ (LSJ: -πλάσια, -ίσια [so Gött], = ; X ANAB 1.7.10; Polyb+) *review, muster* (of troops under arms) 2 Macc 5:25.*

ἐξοπλίζω (Hdt+) *arm;* (mid) *arm oneself, prepare for battle* Num 31:3; (pf pass ptc) *fully armed* 32:20; 2 Macc 5:2.*

ἐξορίζω (Eur+) *banish* 1 Macc 1:11VL.*

ἐξορμάω (Aeschyl, Hdt+) *set out, march out* Judg 7:3A; 2 Macc 11:7; 3 Macc 1:1; 5:47; *rush out* 1:18.*

ἐξουδένημα = BDAG: ἐξουθ.

ἐξουδένωμα, -ατος, τό (h.l.) *object of scorn, despised thing;* Ps 89:5 mistrans of זְרַמְתָּם *you sweep them away* as if זְרְמָתָם (cf. Ezk 23:20) *their phalluses*.*

ἐξουδένωσις, -εως, ἡ (7x, LXX) *scorn, contempt* 1 Macc 1:39; Ps 30:19; SSol 8:7.

ἐξουσιάζω **2.** (trans, no //) *give authority or right* (τινί + inf w. gen) Eccl 6:2; *place* (τινά) *in authority* 5:18.‡

ἐξουσιαστής, -οῦ, ὁ (CatCodAstr+) *person in authority* Is 9:5VL.*

ἐξυβρίζω (Hdt+) **1.** *show arrogance, be insolent* Gen 49:4; 2 Macc 1:28; PsSol 1:6. **2.** *be excessive, be (too) abundant* (cf. Gen 49:4) Ezk 47:5.*

ἐξυμνέω (not in HR; Polyb [6.47.7]+) *sing praise* PsSol 6:4.*

ἐξυπνόω (LXX+) *awaken* 4 Macc 5:11*

ἐξυψόω (Diosc in AnthGr) *exalt, lift up* Sir 1:30; Da 3:51L.*

ἔξω superl ἐξώτατος 2.c. *apart from, besides, except* Josh 22:19; Job 39:3.‡

ἔξωθεν Jer 44:21 mistrans of מחוץ *from the street (of bakers, Baker Street)* as if *outside.*‡

ἐξωθέω fut ἐξώσω aor ἐξέωσα or ἔξωσα pass ἐξώσθην pf pass ptc ἐξ(ε)ωσμένος (28; Hdt+) **1.** *drive away, eject, remove* Dt 13:6; Is 41:2; *uproot* 2 Km 23:6; *displace* 4 Km 17:21. **2.** *expel, banish* 2 Km 14:13f; Ps 5:11; Pr 2:22; Mi 2:9; Jer 8:3; 16:15; Da 11:30L. 2 Km 15:14 mistrans of נדה² hiph *bring* as if fr נדה¹ *force out.*‡

ἔξωσμα, -ατος, τό (h.l.) *banishment, expulsion* La 2:14.*

ἐξώτατος, -η, -ον superl of ἔξω 3 Km 6:30; 2 Esdr 21:16vl.*

ἐξωτέρω (comp adv of ἔξω; Aeschyl+) *further outside* Job 18:17.*

ἔοικα (Hom, Hdt+; pf w. pres meaning) *be like, be similar;* ως εοικεν *as it seems, as is likely* Job 6:3, 25.‡

ἑόρτασμα, -ατος, τό (h.l.) *festival, celebration* Wsd 19:16.*

ἐπάγην 2 aor pass of πήγνυμι Ex 15:8; La 4:8.

ἐπάγω **2.** *march against, attack* (τινί) Is 10:12; *lead, conduct* (πολέμους; cf. Polyb) Sir 46:3.‡

ἐπαγωγή, -ῆς, ἡ (12x, Thu+) **1.** *introduction, bringing in, attack* PsSol 2:22. **2.** *enticement, temptation* Is 10:4 (but Heb = 3.) **3.** *distress, difficulty* (no //, but ἐπάγω *attack* Is 10:12) Dt 32:36; Sir 2:2; 3:28; Is 14:17.

ἐπαγωγός, -όν (Aeschyl, Hdt+) *tempting, alluring;* (neut subst) *tempting things* 4 Macc 8:15.*

ἐπαείδω aor inf ἐπᾶσαι (Aeschyl, Hdt+) *sing* (incantations) Dt 18:11R (contr ἐπάδω Gött), *charm* (snakes) Jer 8:17; (ptc subst) *snake charmer* Ps 57:6; Eccl 10:11.*

ἐπαινεστός, -ή, -όν (superl of ἐπαινός *praised* [Hom+, only fem, of goddesses]) *highly to be praised* Ezk 26:17.*

ἐπαινετός, -ή, -όν (Pla+) *praiseworthy* Ezk 26:17vl.*

ἐπαινέω **2.** *recite publicly* Ps 55:5. Ps 101:9 mistrans of הלל³ *mock* as if הלל² *praise.*‡

ἔπαιξα aor of παίζω.

ἐπαίρω pf pass ptc ἐπηρμένος *exalted* 2 Esdr 7:28 or *elated.* Judg 11:1 mistrans of גבור *hero* as if pass of גבר *rise, be superior.* Zeph 1:11 renders נטיל (h.l.) *weigher* as if pass ptc of נטל *lift up.* 4 Km 18:29; 19:10; Ob 3 mistrans of נשא² *mislead, give false hope* as if נשא *lift up, exalt* (same error possible in MT of 4 Km 14:10). Ps 72:18 mistrans of משואות (h.l.) *deceptions* as if fr נשא hoph *be exalted.* La 4:2 renders מְסֻלָּאִים pu'al ptc of h.l. סלע *paid? valued?*‡

ἔπαισα aor of παίω.

ἐπαίτησις, -εως, ἡ (LXX+) *begging, being a beggar* Sir 40:28, 30.*

ἐπαίτιος, -ον (Hom+) *blameworthy* Sir 37:11vl.*

ἐπακουστός, -όν (Empedocles) *heard, obeyed* 1 Esdr 4:12.*

ἐπακούω **1.b.** *answer, respond* 3 Km 18:24ff. Eccl 10:19 mistrans of ענה¹ *answer (for)* as if ענה² *bend down, submit* (cf. Vulg OBEDIENT, *obey*)‡

ἐπακρόασις, -εως, ἡ (h.l.) *heeding, obedience* 1 Km 15:22.*

ἐπαλγέστερος, -α, -ον (comp of ἐπαλγής, -ές [Strabo+] *painful*) *excruciating* 4 Macc 14:10.*

ἔπαλξις, -εως, ἡ (7x, Hom, Hdt+) *battlement* 3 Km 2:35f; Jdth 14:1; Sir 9:13; Is 54:12.

ἐπαμύνω (Hom, Hdt+) *come to help* 3 Macc 1:27; 4 Macc 14:19.*

ἐπαναγωγή, -ῆς, ἡ (Thu, Pla+) *approach; f.l.* for επανω πηγης Ezk 25:9vl.*

ἐπαναιρέω aor mid ptc ἐπανελόμενος (Pla, Polyb+) *take possession of,* > *capture and destroy* 2 Macc 14:2, 13.*

ἐπανακαινίζω (Philod) *renew* Job 10:17.*

ἐπανακαλέω (Aeschyl+) *invoke, summon* Sir 48:20vl.*

ἐπαναπαύω (BDAG: -ομαι) **1.b.** (act trans) *give rest, allow to rest* Judg 16:26A.‡

ἐπανάστασις, -εως, ἡ (Hdt+) **1.** *rebellion* 4 Km 3:4. **2.** *projection, protuberance* 3 Km 6:18vl.*

ἐπαναστρέφω (9x, Aristot+) *return, come back* Gen 18:10; Ex 14:28; Job 16:22.

ἐπανατρυγάω (LXX) *go back over* (the vineyard, after first harvest) Lev 19:10; Dt 24:21.*

ἐπανδρόω (h.l.) *make manly, cause to grow into manliness* 2 Macc 15:17.*

ἐπανθέω (Hdt+) *bloom* Job 14:7.*

ἐπανιστάνομαι = BDAG: ἐπανίστημι Jdth 16:17R.*‡

ἐπάνοδος, -ου, ὁ (Hippocr, Eur+) *way back, return* Sir 17:24; 22:21; 38:21.*

ἐπανορθόω (Pla+) *restore, reestablish* (no //) 2 Macc 2:22; 5:20.*

ἐπανόρθωσις, -εως, ἡ (Aristot+: *correction, improvement*) *supply, provision* (no //, but cf. Lysias επανορθοω *supply*) 1 Esdr 8:52; 1 Macc 14:34.*‡

ἐπάνω **1.b.** (adv of time) *later, afterwards* (no //) 1 Km 16:13.‡

ἐπάνωθεν (33x, Eur+) **1.** (adv) *outward, upward* Ex 25:20; Ezk 1:22; (fig) 1 Ch 29:25; (*from*) *up above* Job 18:16; Am 2:9; Ezk 40:43. **2.** (prep w. gen) **a.** *up from* Judg 13:20A, *up above* 4 Km 2:3. **b.** (no //) *out from* Judg 3:21B, *away from* 2 Km 13:9; *from on top of* 11:21.‡

ἐπαξονέω (h.l.) *tabulate, enroll* (on a tablet; cf. ἄξων *tablet*) Num 1:18.*

ἐπαοιδή, -ῆς, ἡ (Hom+) *incantation, charm* Dt 18:11; Is 47:9, 12.*

ἐπαποστέλλω (10x, Polyb+) *send* (upon or against, in judgment; God alw the agent) Ex 8:17; 3 Km 12:24k; Wsd 11:15; Jer 9:15; (pass ptc) *thing sent* Wsd 16:3.

ἐπάρδω (LXX+) *water generously* 4 Macc 1:29.*

ἐπαρήγω (Hom, dramatists, X) *come to help* (τινί) 2 Macc 13:17.*

ἐπαρκέω (Hom, Hdt+) **1.** *supply, provide* 1 Macc 8:26. **2.** *credit, grant* (remission of taxes, no //) 11:35.*‡

ἐπαρκῶς (adj Empedocles+) *helpfully* 1 Macc 11:35vL.*

ἔπαρμα, -ατος, τό (Hippocr, Sotades+) *height, elevation* 2 Esdr 6:3.*

ἔπαρξις (LSJ: "f.l.") Zech 12:7vL.*

ἔπαρσις, -εως, ἡ (Hippocr, Aristot+) *lifting up* Ps 140:2; *pride, sense of superiority* Zech 12:7; Ezk 24:25. 4 Km 9:25; La 3:47 mistrans of שאת *devastate* as if נשא *lift up.**

ἐπαρυστήρ, -ῆρος, ὁ (h.l.) *oil pitcher or pourer* Ex 25:38.*

ἐπαρυστρίς, -ίδος, ἡ (LXX) *oil pitcher or pourer* Ex 38:17; Num 4:9; 3 Km 7:35; Zech 4:2, 12.*

ἐπάρχω (X+) *rule over* Esth 3:13b.*

ἐπᾶσαι see ἐπαείδω.

ἐπασθμαίνω (PhilostratJun) *gasp for breath, breathe in labored fashion* 4 Macc 6:11.*

ἐπαύξω (X+) *enlarge, increase* 3 Macc 2:25.*

ἐπεγγελάω (Soph+) *laugh or exult over* (τινί, X *Anab* 2.4.27) 4 Macc 5:27.*

ἐπείγω (Hom, Hdt+) *press hard, urge* 2 Macc 10:19; Bel 30Θ; *drive on* Da 3:22L.*‡

ἐπεῖδον (cf. also ἐφοράω) **2.** *look upon in triumph* (cf. Hom *Il* 14:145) Ps 53:9; Mi 4:11; Ob 12.‡

ἔπειμι inf ἐπεῖναι (Hom, Hdt+) *be present, stand* Ex 8:18; 9:3; 3 Km 10:16 = 2 Ch 9:15; Sir 42:19; *remain, be at hand, fall (to)* 4 Macc 1:10.*‡

ἔπειμι inf ἐπιέναι ptc ἐπιών (Hom, Hdt+) *come (upon), overtake, approach;* (ptc) *approaching, succeeding* (period of time) Dt 32:29 = Odes 2:29; 1 Ch 20:1; Pr 3:28 = 27:1.*

ἐπεισφέρω (Eur: *bring in besides*) *reach beyond* (no //) Judg 3:22.*

ἐπέκεινα **2.** (temp) *from then on, afterward* (of future, no //) Lev 22:27; 1 Km 18:9; 1 Macc 10:30; Mi 4:5; Ezk 39:22; Sus 64Θ.‡

ἐπέκτασις, -εως, ἡ (Aristot+) *stretching, extension* Job 36:29vL.*

ἐπεκχέω (pap+) *pour out upon;* (pass, fig) *rush or fall upon* Jdth 15:4.*

ἐπελπίζω (Thu+) **1.** *inspire with hope* 4 Km 18:30; Ps 118:49. **2.** *hope (in)* Ps 51:9; 118:43, 74ff.*

ἐπενδύτης, -ου, ὁ (Soph+) *outer garment* 2 Km 13:18.*‡

ἐπεξέρχομαι (Hdt+) *proceed against, prosecute, punish* (τι) Wsd 14:31; *prevent* (τινί, no //) Jdth 13:20.*

ἐπερείδω (Hom+) *lean upon* (τινί) Esth 5:1a; Pr 3:18.*

ἐπερρώσθην   aor pass of ἐπιρρώνυμι.
ἐπερώτησις, -εως, ἡ   (Hdt+) *questioning* Gen 43:7.*
ἐπέσκεμμαι   pf of ἐπισκέπτομαι Ex 3:16; ἐπεσκέπησαν 2 aor pass *be cared for* Sir 49:15.
ἐπετάσθη   aor of BDAG: πέτομαι.
ἐπέτειος, -ον   VL -τιος, = (Hdt+) *yearly, for a year* (cf. ἐφέτειος) Sir 37:11G.*
ἐπευθυμέω   (h.l.) *rejoice over* (τινί) Wsd 18:6.*
ἐπευκτός, -ή, -όν   (LXX) *desired, longed for or celebrated* PsSol 8:16; Jer 20:14.*
ἐπευλαβέομαι   (h.l.) *hesitate to, be wary of* (+inf) 2 Macc 14:18VL.*
ἐπεύχομαι   (Hom+) *pray* Dt 10:8; 1 Ch 23:13.*
ἐπήκοος, -ον   (Aeschyl+) *listening, hearing* (as oft in ins of god hearing prayer) 2 Ch 6:40; 7:15. 1 Km 23:24VL mistrans of מעון N LOC as if fr ענה *answer*.
ἐπημμένος   see ἐφάπτω.
ἐπηρμένος   pf pass ptc of ἐπαίρω.
ἐπιβάθρα, -ας, ἡ   (Polyb+: *means of ascent*) *fare* (no //; = -θρον) 3 Macc 2:31.*
ἐπίβαθρον, -ου, τό   (Hom+) *fare, tariff* 3 Macc 2:31VL (q.l.; cf. ApollonRhod 1.421; sacrifice to Apollo as "fare" for safe voyage).*
ἐπιβαίνω   3. *set upon, assault* (X+) Pr 21:22; Job 30:21.‡
ἐπιβάλλω   1.c. *assess or impose* (fine or penalty, Hdt+) Ex 21:22, 30; (any obligation) Dt 24:5; (impers) *fall due, be payable* 2 Macc 3:3. **2.a.β.** (hostile) *set upon* (τινί DiodS 17.64.3 [c. Loeb]), *attack* 2 Macc 15:1.‡
ἐπίβασις, -εως, ἡ   (Hdt+) 1. *stepping in, entering, arrival* Wsd 5:11. 2. *stepping, standing* Wsd 15:15. 3. *cover, covering* Ps 103:3; SSol 3:10.*
ἐπιβάτης, -ου, ὁ   (Hdt+) *rider* (on chariot) 4 Km 7:14; (on horseback) 9:17ff; 2 Macc 3:25; Job 39:18; (on ship) Ezk 27:29.*
ἐπιβιβάζω   Att fut ἐπιβιβῶ (Hos 10:11) 2. *place* (of obj, no // but not unknown w. ἐπιβαίνω) 4 Km 13:16.‡
ἐπιβιόω   (Thu, Pla+) *survive* 4 Macc 6:20.*
ἐπιβοηθέω   (Hdt+) *help, assist* (τινί) 1 Macc 7:7; 2 Macc 8:8; 11:7; 13:10.*

ἐπιβόλαιον, -ου, τό   (Aristophanes of Byzantium [III BCE]+) *covering, wrap* Judg 4:18B; Ezk 13:18, 21.*
ἐπιβολή, -ῆς, ἡ   (Thu+) *imposition; assessment, levy* 1 Esdr 8:22; *attack, assault* 2 Macc 8:7.*
ἐπιβουλεύω   (Tyrtaeus, Hdt+) *plot against* (τινί) Esth 8:12u; Pr 17:26.*
ἐπίβουλος, -ον   (13x, Aeschyl+) *plotting, treacherous;* (subst) *conspirator, traitor* 1 Km 29:4; 2 Macc 3:38; Hab 2:7; Bel 31G.
ἐπιβρέχω   (LXX+) *rain down* Ps 10:6.*
ἐπιβρίθω   (Hom+) *press heavily, be weighty* Job 29:4.*
ἐπιγαμία, -ας, ἡ   (Hdt+) *intermarriage, marriage w. a foreigner* Josh 23:12.*
ἐπιγεμίζω   (h.l.) *load, set* (on an animal) 2 Esdr 23:15.*
ἐπιγίνομαι   2. *come after or later* EpJer 47.‡
ἐπιγινώσκω   Zech 6:10, 14 pf ptc renders יְדַעְיָה (N PERS) as if יְדֵעֶיהָ *those who knew her.*‡
ἐπιγλύφω   pf pass ptc ἐπιγεγλυμμένος (LXX+) *carve on;* (pass ptc) *carved* 1 Macc 13:29VL.*
ἐπιγνωμοσύνη, -ης, ἡ   (h.l.) *perceptiveness, understanding* Pr 16:23.*
ἐπιγνώμων, -ον, gen **-ονος**   (Lys, Pla+) *discerning, capable of sound judgment* Pr 12:26; 17:27; 29:7; (subst) *arbiter, critic, judge* 13:10.*
ἐπίγνωστος, -ον   (h.l.) *recognized, known* Job 18:19.*
ἐπιγονή, -ῆς, ἡ   (ins, pap+) *offspring, increase* 2 Ch 31:16, 18; Am 7:1.*
ἐπιδεής, -ές   (Pla+) *needy, destitute* Sir 4:1; 31:4.*
ἐπιδεήσω   fut of BDAG: ἐπιδέομαι *need* (τινός, τινί) Sir 33:32.
ἐπίδειξις, -εως, ἡ   (Hdt, Aristoph, Pla+) *demonstration* 4 Macc 13:10.*
ἐπιδέκατος, -ον   (19x, X+) *one tenth;* (neut subst) *tenth part, tithe* Num 18:21ff; 2 Ch 31:5ff; Am 4:4; Is 6:13.
ἐπιδέξιος, -ον   (Hom+) *dextrous, clever, elegant* 2 Esdr 5:8. Pr 27:16 renders ימין (?), vs very obscure; βορέας renders MT צפן *keep, store* as if צפן *north;* possibly orig Heb

involved play on "north" and "south" (cf. δέξιος).*

ἐπιδέομαι   fut act ἐπιδεήσεις 2. (act) *have need of* (τινί) 1Sir33:32.‡

ἐπιδέχομαι   pf pass ptc ἐπιδεδεγμένος 3. *take upon oneself, undertake to act* 1 Esdr 9:14; 2 Macc 2:26.‡

ἐπιδέω   aor ἐπέδησα (Hdt+) **1.** *tie or fasten on* Jer 28:63. **2.** *bind, tie up* (no //) Judg 16:21B; Tob 8:3S.*

ἐπίδηλος, -ον   (Theognis, Hdt, Aristoph+) *completely obvious* 2 Macc 15:35.*

ἐπιδιαιρέω   (Hdt+) *distribute* Gen 33:1.*

ἐπιδίδωμι   1 Km 14:13 mistrans of ממותת *deliver the death-blow* (fr מות) as if related to מתת *gift*.‡

ἐπιδιηγέομαι   (AelAristid) *recount* Esth 1:17VL.*

ἐπιδιπλόω   (LXX+) *fold double* Ex 26:9.*

ἐπιδιώκω   (Hdt+) *pursue, overtake* Gen 44:4; 3 Macc 2:7.*

ἐπίδοξος, -ον   (Hdt+) *impressive, notable* Pr 6:8b; Sir 3:19G; Da 2:11L; (adv) *conspicuously* 1 Esdr 9:45.*

ἐπιδύνω   = BDAG: ἐπιδύω‡

ἐπιεικεύομαι   (h.l.) *be gentle or forbearing* 2 Esdr 9:8.*

ἐπιεικέως   (Ionic for -κῶς adv of BDAG: ἐπιεικής) **1.** *gently, kindly* 1 Km 12:22. **2.** *perhaps* (Pla GORG 493c) 4 Km 6:3.*

ἐπιζάω   aor ἐπέζησεν (Hdt+) *survive, live* Gen 47:28; 4 Macc 18:9.*

ἐπιζεύγνυμι   (Aeschyl, Hdt+) *join, connect* 2 Macc 2:32.*

ἐπιζήμιον, -ου, τό   (adj *liable*, Thu, Pla+) *penalty, fine* (ins) Ex 21:22.*

ἐπιθαυμάζω   (Aristoph+) *honor, wonder at* Sir 47:17VL.*

ἐπίθεμα, -ατος, τό   (18x, Aristot+) *cover* Ex 25:17; (specif) *capital* (of column) 3 Km 7:4ff; Lev 7:34; Num 6:20 et al render תנופה *wave offering* as *what is placed before* (no //).

ἐπίθεσις, -εως, ἡ   (AntiphoOr, Pla, ins+) *onset, attack* (X ANAB 4.4.42; 7.4.23) 2 Ch 25:27; 2 Macc 4:41; 5:5; 14:15. Ezk 23:11 renders עגבה *sexual desire, lust*; euphem *onset, effort* (to seduce, no //).*‡

ἐπιθεωρέω   (Hippocr, Theophr+) *examine, consider* 4 Macc 1:30.*

ἐπιθύμημα, -ατος, τό   (20x, Hippocr, X+) *object of desire* 3 Km 21:6; Sir 1:17; Hos 9:16; Is 27:2; La 1:7; Da 11:38. Num 16:15 mistrans of חמור *donkey* as if חמוד *desired thing*; MT is correct—cf. 1 Km 12:3.

ἐπιθυμητός, -ή, -όν   (18x, Aristot+) *desirable, attractive* 2 Ch 20:25; 1 Macc 1:23; Ps 18:11; Pr 21:20; Wsd 8:5; Hos 13:15; Jer 12:10; Da 11:8Θ, (subst) 11:43Θ.

ἐπικάθημαι   (Hdt+) *sit* (upon τινί), *ride* 2 Km 16:2 (ptc subst) *rider* 2 Macc 3:25; Sir 33:6; (of birds) *perch* (ἐπί τινος) EpJer 70.*

ἐπικαινίζω   (h.l.) *renew*; (pass inf) *to be restored* 1 Macc 10:44.*

ἐπίκαιρος, -ον   (Soph, Thu+) *timely, opportune*, > (of places, Thu+) *strategic, key* 2 Macc 8:6, 31; 10:15; 14:22.*

ἐπικαλέω   2 Km 20:1 mistrans of קרה/קרא² niph *be present, appear on the scene* as if קרא¹ *call, summon*.‡

ἐπικαρπολογέομαι   (h.l.; VL -καρπόω dub, not in LSJ) *glean* 4 Macc 2:9.*

ἐπικαταλαμβάνω   (Thu+) *overtake* Num 11:23.*

ἐπικαταράομαι   (11x, LXX) *curse* Num 5:18ff; Ps 151:6; Mal 2:2.

ἐπικερδής, -ές   (Aesop, ins) *advantageous, profitable* Wsd 15:12.*

ἐπικίνδυνος, -ον   (Hdt, Pla+) *dangerous* (X ANAB 1.3.19) 2 Macc 5:33.*

ἐπικινέω   (Philod+) (pass) *be shaken or moved* 1 Esdr 8:69.*

ἐπικληρόω   (Demosth, Pla+) *assign by lot* Josh 21:9VL.*

ἐπίκλησις, -εως, ἡ   (Hom, Hdt+) **1.** *naming* 2 Macc 8:15. **2.** *invocation, prayer* (LXX+) 15:26.*

ἐπίκλητος, -ον   (Hdt+) *designated* Josh 20:9; *summoned* Am 1:5; (fem subst) *council* (cf. κλητός 2.) Num 28:18, 26; (masc pl) *counselors* Num 1:16; 26:9.*

ἐπικλίνω   (Hom+) *tilt, incline* Gen 24:14; 3 Km 8:58.*

ἐπικλύζω (Hom+) *overflow* Dt 11:4; Jdth 2:8; (trans) *flood, overwhelm, sweep away* 3 Macc 2:7; Is 66:12.*

ἐπικοιμάομαι (Hippocr, Pla+) *remain lying or sleeping* Dt 21:23; 3 Km 3:19; (fig) *impose upon, weigh down, hinder* (τινί) 1 Esdr 5:69G.*

ἐπικοινωνέω (Hippocr, Pla+) *be or come in touch* (w. τινί) Sir 26:6; *belong w.* (no //) 4 Macc 4:3.*

ἐπικοπή, -ῆς, ἡ (Theophr+) *cutting down* Dt 28:25.*

ἐπικοσμέω (Hdt: decorate) *perfect, set right* (no //, but cf. BDAG: κοσμέω, LSJ: ἐπικόσμησις); (pass) *be made right* Eccl 1:15.*

ἐπικουφίζω (Hdt, Soph+) *lighten, alleviate* 4 Macc 9:31.*

ἐπίκουφος, -ον (dub; not in LSJ) *light, easy* 4 Macc 4:5VL.*

ἐπικραταιόω (h.l.) (pass) *be defeated, be overcome* Eccl 4:12.*

ἐπικράτεια, -ας, ἡ (X+) *ruling power* 4 Macc 1:31, 34; 3:1, 18; 6:32.*

ἐπικρατέω (31x, Hom, Hdt+) 1. *overpower* (τινός) Gen 47:20; *rule over* (τινός) Esth 3:13b; (τινά) 8:12r; *take control of* (τινός) Jdth 7:12; PsSol 16:7; *conquer* (τινά) 4 Macc 17:20; (abs) *become powerful* Gen 7:18f; *seize power* 1 Macc 1:8; Jer 5:31G; (pres ptc) *ruler* Esth 8:12f. 2. *take hold of* (no //, + ἐπι) Ezk 29:7.

ἐπικράτησις, -εως, ἡ (Thu+) *dominion, empire* (no //) Esth 8:12o.*

ἐπικρεμάννυμι (Pind, Thu+) *hang upon*; (pass) *be hung* Hos 11:7; (fig) *be dependent* (upon τινί) Is 22:24.*

ἐπικροτέω (Hes+) *clap* (hands) Pr 17:18; Sir 12:18; Am 6:5; Is 55:12; Jer 5:31R (Gött ἐπικρατέω, RECTE, cf. Heb).*

ἐπικρούω (Aeschyl, Aristoph +: *beat, strike*) *slap, clap* (hand, no //) Jer 31:26; but mistrans of פסס² *vomit* as if ספק¹ *slap.*

ἐπικρύπτω (Aeschyl, Pla+) *conceal* 2 Km 19:5VL.*

ἐπίκτητος, -ον (Hdt+) *acquired* 2 Macc 6:23.*

ἐπικυλίω (X, Polyb+) *roll* (stones) Josh 10:27.*

ἐπικύπτω (Hippocr, Aristot+) *stoop over, lean upon* Esth 5:1d VL.*

ἐπίκυφος, -ον (h.l.) *bent over* 3 Macc 4:5.*

ἐπιλαμβάνομαι 1.b. *reach, touch* (τινός) 3 Km 6:6. 2. *accept, receive* Jer 39:33R cj; Gött ἐκλαμβ-, q.v.)‡

ἐπιλέγω 3 Km 14:10; 22:47(VL) mistrans of בער *sweep away, extirpate* as if בחר *choose.*‡

ἐπίλεκτος, -ον (16x, X+) 1. *chosen, selected* (esp of soldiers,"*picked troops*") Ex 15:4; Josh 17:16; 1 Macc 4:28; Ezk 23:6. 2. *select, choice* (subst) Joel 4:5; Ezk 17:3.

ἐπιλημπτεύομαι (HR, LSJ: -ληπ-; LXX) *rave insanely* 1 Km 21:16; Jer 30:19.*

ἐπίλημπτος, -ον (HR, LSJ: -ληπ-; Hippocr, Hdt+: *suffering from epilepsy*) *insane, raving* (no //, but cf. prec) 1 Km 21:15f; 4 Km 9:11.*

ἐπιλήσομαι fut of BDAG: ἐπιλανθάνω; fut pass ἐπιλησθήσομαι.

ἐπιλογίζομαι (Hdt, Pla+) *take into account, consider* 2 Macc 11:4; 4 Macc 3:6; 16:5.*

ἐπιλυπέω (LXX+) *aggrieve, offend* 2 Macc 8:32; 3 Macc 7:9; (pass) *be aggrieved* 2 Macc 4:37.*

ἐπιμαίνω (Hom, Aeschyl+) *drive insane, madden* (act/trans sense, no //) 4 Macc 7:5.*

ἐπιμαρτύρομαι (8x; Hdt, Aristoph+) *adjure, appeal to* 3 Km 2:42; 2 Esdr 19:29; Sir 46:19; Am 3:13; Jer 39:25.

ἐπιμ(ε)ίγνυμι aor ἐπεμ(ε)ίγην (for spelling, cf. LSJ, W; Pind, Thu+) *intermingle, intermix* 1 Esdr 8:67, 84; Pr 14:10; Ezk 16:37.*

ἐπίμ(ε)ικτος, -ον (for spelling see LSJ, W; Nicander+) *mixed*; (subst) *mob, hangers-on* Ex 12:38; Num 11:4; Jdth 2:20; *foreigner, person of mixed ancestry* (no //) 2 Esdr 23:3; Ezk 30:5.*

ἐπιμ(ε)ιξία, -ας, ἡ (Hdt+) 1. *mixing* Wsd 14:25VL. 2. *time of peace* (of social and commercial intercourse between peoples) 2 Macc 14:3VL.

ἐπίμ(ε)ιξις, -εως, ἡ (Theognis+) *mixture* Wsd 14:25VL.*

ἐπιμελέστερον comp of BDAG: ἐπιμελῶς 1 Esdr 7:2.‡

ἐπιμέλομαι = BDAG: -λέομαι.‡
ἐπιμερίζω (Strabo+) *distribute* Job 31:2vl.*
ἐπιμήκης, -ες (Democr, Aristot+) *long, > extensive, far-reaching* Bar 3:24.*
ἐπιμιγ- see -μειγ-.
ἐπιμιμνῄσκομαι (Hom+) *remember, consider* (τινός) 1 Macc 10:46.*
ἐπιμίξ (Hom) *in confusion, in mixed-up fashion* Wsd 14:25.*
επιμιξ- see -μειξ-.
ἐπιμονή, -ῆς, ἡ (Thu, Pla+) *persistence, abiding concern* Sir 38:27.*
ἐπίμοχθος, -ον (Hippocr+) *laborious*; neut as adv Wsd 15:7.*
ἐπιμύλιον, -ου, τό (LXX) *upper millstone* Dt 24:6; Judg 9:53B.*
ἐπινεφής, -ές (Aristot+) *clouded over* 2 Macc 1:22.*
ἐπινικάω (not in HR or LSJ) *triumph over*; 2 Esdr 3:8vl s.t. of לנצח *in perpetuity* (cf. νῖκος).
ἐπινίκιος, -ον (Pind, Aeschyl+) *triumphant*; (neut subst) *victory prize* 1 Esdr 3:5; *victory celebration* 2 Macc 8:33.*
ἐπινοέω (Hdt, Aristoph+) **1.** *conceive, contrive* 4 Macc 10:16; Wsd 14:2; (pass) *be planned* 14:14. **2.** *notice, detect* Job 4:18.*‡
ἐπινύσσω (AntyllusMed [II BCE]) *prick, stab* (?) 1 Macc 6:57vl.*
ἐπινυστάζω (Plu+) *fall asleep* Pr 6:4.*
ἐπιξενόομαι (Aeschyl, Isocr+) *come as a guest* Esth 8:12k; Sir 29:27. Pr 21:7 mistrans of גרר *drag out* as if גור *be a sojourner.*
ἐπιορκία, -ας, ἡ (X+) *breaking of oaths, perjury* Wsd 14:26.*
ἐπιπαραγίνομαι (Satyrus [III BCE], Polyb+) *come upon, arrive* Josh 10:9.*
ἐπιπαρέρχομαι (CassDio+) *go on by* Jer 40:13vl.*
ἐπιπείθω (Hom+, not in HR) = BDAG: πείθω 1 Macc 10:71vl.*
ἐπίπεμπτος, -ον (8x, X+) *plus 20%*; (subst) *an additional fifth* Lev 5:16; 22:14; Num 5:7.
ἐπιπέμπω (Hdt, Pind+) *send out* Pr 6:19; *send upon* (τινί) 3 Macc 6:6; Wsd 11:17.*
ἐπίπληξις, -εως, ἡ (Hippocr, Demosth+: *criticism*) *punishment* (ins) 2 Macc 7:33.*

ἐπιπληρόω (Thu+) *fill up* 2 Macc 6:4R (Gött πληρόω plpf [w. augm]).*
ἐπίποκος, -ον (ins?) *covered w. wool* 4 Km 3:4vl.*
ἐπιπολάζω (Hippocr, X+) *come to the surface* 4 Km 6:6.*
ἐπιπολαῖος, -ον (HR Supplement; Hippocr, X+) *on the surface, > obvious*; (adv) *obviously* 3 Macc 2:31.*
ἐπίπονος, -ον (Soph+) *painful, grievous* 3 Macc 5:47; *laborious* Sir 7:15.*
ἐπιπορεύομαι **2.** *come upon* (no //) Lev 26:33.‡
ἐπιπροστίθημι (LXX+) *add on, progress* Sir prol 14.*
ἐπιρραίνω (Aristot+) *sprinkle* 2 Macc 1:21.*
ἐπιρραντίζω (Hippiatr) *sprinkle*; (pass) *be sprinkled* Lev 6:20.*
ἐπιρρέω (Hom, Hdt+) *flow, keep on flowing* Job 22:16.*
ἐπιρ(ρ)ίπτω **1.b.** *apply, inflict* 2 Macc 3:26. **2.b.** *cast* (τι) *upon* (someone) *as a task, concern, or destiny* Josh 23:4 (aor pass w. act ending and meaning; τινί, cf. Aeschyl PROM 737–38); (ἐπὶ τινα) Jer 15:8, both rendering נפל hiph *cause to fall.*‡
ἐπιρρωγολογέομαι (h.l.) *glean* (grapes) 4 Macc 2:9.*
ἐπιρρώννυμι aor pass ἐπερρώσθην (Hdt, Soph+) *strengthen, encourage* (= BDAG); (pass) *be encouraged, recover strength* (Polyb 1.24.1) 2 Macc 11:9.*
ἐπίσαγμα, -ατος, τό (Soph: *burden*) *saddle* Lev 15:9.*
ἐπισάσσω aor ἐπέσαξα pf pass ptc ἐπισεσαγμένος (16; Hdt+) *load, saddle* Gen 22:3; Judg 19:10; 3 Km 2:40; Jer 26:4.
ἐπισημαίνω (Hippocr, Eur, Thu+) *mark, indicate* 2 Macc 2:6; *signify* Job 14:17.*
ἐπίσημον, -ου, τό (Hdt, ins+) *mark, sign* (of status or ownership) PsSol 2:6.*
ἐπίσημος **1.b.** *marked, having distinctive markings* (w. play on 1.) Gen 30:42.‡
ἐπισιτίζομαι (Hdt+) *provide oneself w. food* Josh 9:4.*
ἐπισκάζω (ApollonRhod) *limp upon* (τινί) Gen 32:32.*

ἐπισκεπάζω (LXX; both סכך cover, wrap) wrap, cover (oneself) La 3:43; wrap (τι around τινί) 3:44.*

ἐπισκέπτομαι 2 aor pass ἐπεσκέπην pf pass ptc ἐπεσκεμμένος 4. assess, poll, levy Ex 39:2; (pass) Num 1:47; Judg 20:15. 5. visit with retribution, punish, repay (no //; s.t. of פקד visit, > punish) Ps 88:33; (pass) Judg 21:3. 4 Km 10:19 mistrans of פקד niph'al be missing as if be visited or appointed.‡

ἐπισκευάζω 1. (act) repair (temple; X ANAB 5.3.13) 2 Ch 24:4, 12; 34:10; (doors) 29:3; (wall) 1 Macc 12:37. 2. (act) make ready, prepare Ex 30:8VL. (pass) be made ready 1 Km 3:3.*‡

ἐπίσκεψις, -εως, ἡ (59x, Hippocr, X, Pla+) visitation Num 16:29; Jer 11:23; 23:12; review, survey 2 Macc 14:20; oversight 3 Macc 7:12; inspection 2 Macc 3:14; (specif) census (no //) Ex 30:13f; Num 1:21ff; 2 Km 24:9 = 1 Ch 21:5. Num 3:36; 1 Ch 23:11; 24:3 s.t. of פקדה appointment, duty, work group as if visitation.

ἐπισκοπή 4. muster (enumerated and enrolled; no //, s.t. based on פקד survey, visit Ex 30:12 etc.‡

ἐπισκορακίζω (dub, not in HR or LSJ) dismiss, release from duty 1 Macc 11:55VL.*

ἔπισος (= ἐπ' ἴσος?) see ἔφισος 2 Macc 11:14VL.

ἐπίσπαστρον, -ου, τό (DiodS+) draw curtain Ex 26:36.*

ἐπισπεύδω (IIdt+) drive along; escort, conduct Esth 6:14; (intr) hurry along 1 Esdr 1:25; Pr 6:18.*

ἐπισπλαγχνίζομαι (h.l.) be compassionate Pr 17:5.*

ἐπισπουδάζω (LXX+) 2. hurry along, quicken Gen 19:15; (pass) arrive quickly Pr 13:11; 20:9b.*‡

ἐπισπουδαστής, -οῦ, ὁ (pap) one who is hasty or overzealous (no //) Is 14:4.*

ἐπιστατέω (Aeschyl, Hdt+) supervise, preside over (τινός) 1 Esdr 7:2.*

ἐπιστατός, -ή, -όν (Doric for -στητός, Pla, Aristot+) well or scientifically known; cj ἐπιστατά for Ra: ἐπίσταται (// in 14:8a) PsSol 14:8.*

ἐπιστήριγμα, -ατος, τό (h.l.) support, sure help 2 Km 22:19.*

ἐπιστηρίζω fut ἐπιστηριῶ fut mid ἐπιστηρίσομαι aor pass ἐπεστηρίχθην pf mid/pass -στήρικται plpf mid/pass -στήρικτο (Aristot; BDAG: strengthen) 1. (cause to) rest upon Ps 31:8; (hostile) 37:3; 87:8. 2. (mid or pass) lean on Judg 16:26ffA, 2 Km 1:6; SSol 8:5; Is 36:6; depend upon Jdth 8:24; Ps 70:6; (pass) be set firmly upon Gen 28:13; Judg 16:26ffB.*‡

ἐπιστοιβάζω (LXX) stack, arrange Lev 1:7ff; Sir 8:3.*

ἐπιστρατεία, -ας, ἡ (Hdt+) military expedition (X ANAB 2.4.1.) 3 Macc 3:14.*

ἐπιστρατεύω (Aeschyl, Hdt+) make war (επι upon, against) 2 Macc 12:27; 3 Macc 5:43; Zech 14:12; Is 29:7f; (επι on behalf of) Is 31:4.*

ἐπιστράτηγος, -ου, ὁ (ins, pap, Polyb) military governor 1 Macc 15:38.*

ἐπιστρατοπεδεύω (Polyb) camp near or over against Jdth 2:21.*

ἐπιστραφής, -ές (not in HR; AmmoniusGr) turning one's attention (more prob, misspelling for -στροφή) Sir 40:1VL.*

ἐπιστρέφω 1.α.β. change (name of person, no //) 4 Km 23:34. γ. restore, renew (no //; obj ψυχήν life) Ps 22:3; La 1:11, 16, 19. δ. deliver, bring (no //) 4 Km 3:4. Judg 20:48B mistrans of שבה take captive as if שוב turn back (cf. 20:48B cj ἀνοκλίνω, same error).‡

ἐπιστροφή, -ῆς, ἡ (Aeschyl, Thu+) 1. turning about Judg 8:9B; Ezk 42:11; 47:7; bend, winding (of river) 47:11; (fig) conversion Sir 18:21; 49:2. 2. attention (ἐπί τινα turned toward someone) SSol 7:11.*‡

ἐπισυνάγω 2. bring in, pull in Gen 38:29.‡

ἐπισυνέχω (h.l.) acquire, take to oneself 1 Esdr 9:17.*

ἐπισυνίημι (dub, not in LSJ) arrive, come together 1 Macc 11:55VL.*

ἐπισυνίστημι (10x, Strabo, ins) 1. (trans) raise up (επι against) Lev 26:16; Num 16:19. 2. (intr) rise up (επι against) Lev 19:16; Num 14:35; Ezk 2:6; (τινί) Sir 45:18; Jer 20:10.

ἐπισυντελέω (not in HR; pap) *finish* Josh 4:1VL.*

ἐπισυστρέφω (LXX+) *convene, assemble* Num 17:7; 1 Macc 14:44.*

ἐπίταγμα, -ατος, τό (Pla, ins+) *command* 4 Macc 8:6.*

ἐπιταράσσω (Hdt+) *further disquiet,* (pass) *be (further) troubled* 2 Macc 9:24.*

ἐπίτασις, -εως, ἡ (Hippocr, Pla+) *intensity* 2 Macc 6:3; Wsd 14:18.*

ἐπιταφή, -ῆς, ἡ (dub; not in LSJ) *burial* Sir 40:1VL.*

ἐπιτάφιος, -ον (Pla, Aristot+) *of or on a tomb;* (neut subst, no //) *tomb* 4 Macc 17:8.*

ἐπιτείνω pf pass ἐπετέτατο (Hom+) **1.** *stretch taut, stretch out* Da 7:6L, (fig) Wsd 17:20; *raise intensity* 4 Macc 13:25; *nerve or empower* 15:23; (mid) *exert or strain oneself* Wsd 16:24. **2.** *torment, strain* 4 Macc 3:11; (pass) 2 Macc 9:11.*

ἐπιτέλλω (Hes, Hippocr, Aristot+) *rise, dawn* 3 Macc 5:20G.*

ἐπιτέμνω fut inf ἐπιτεμεῖν (Hdt+) *abridge, cut short* 2 Macc 2:23, 32.*

ἐπιτερπής, -ές (HomHymns, Pla+) *pleasant, delightful* 2 Macc 15:39.*

ἐπιτεύξομαι dep fut of BDAG: ἐπιτυγχάνω.

ἐπιτήδευμα **2.** (pl) *practices, (customary) acts* Lev 18:3; 1 Km 2:3; 1 Ch 16:8; Ps 9:12; Job 14:16; Hos 9:15; Jer 4:4; Ezk 6:9.‡

ἐπιτηδεύω **2.** *involve oneself* (εἰς *in*), *pursue* Mal 2:11; *attempt* (+ inf) 3 Macc 2:14.‡

ἐπιτίθημι **1.b.β.** (mid) *assume, take for themselves* 1 Macc 1:9; *apply oneself, undertake* Gen 11:6; *be employed* 3 Km 16:28d; Ezk 23:5, 9; (ἐπί τινα) 7; (τινά) etc, *make use of, involve oneself w.* rendering עגב *desire sexually;* cf. ἐπίθεσις. **2.b.** *mount* (an attack, cogn acc) 2 Ch 25:27.‡

ἐπιτίμησις, -εως, ἡ (9x, Thu+) *rebuke, warning* 2 Km 22:16 = Ps 17:16; Job 26:11; Wsd 12:26.

ἐπιτίμιον, -ου, τό (Aeschyl, Hdt+) *penalty,* (pl) *damages, penalties* 2 Macc 6:13G; Sir 9:5.*

ἐπίτιμος, -ον (Aristoph+) **1.** *subject to penalty;* (neut subst) *penalty, punishment* 2 Macc 6:13R; Sir 8:5. **2.** *valuable* Tob 13:17VL.*

ἐπιτομή, -ῆς, ἡ (Aristot+) *abridgment, epitome* 2 Macc 2:26, 28.*

ἐπιτρέπω **3.** *entrust, commit* Gen 39:6.‡

ἐπιτρέχω (Hom+) *run up (to), approach* Gen 24:17; 1 Macc 6:45; 4 Macc 7:11; Sus 19Θ.*

ἐπιτρίβω (Hdt+, Aristoph+) *rub, wear away* Job 29:4VL.*

ἐπίτριψις, -εως, ἡ (perh in single pap [I CE]) *breaking, rolling* (of waves; Vulg FLUCTUS) Ps 92:3VL.*

ἐπιτυχία, -ας, ἡ (Hippocr, Democr) *undertaking, attainment* Wsd 13:19.*

ἐπιφανής superl -νέστατος. Pr 25:14 mistrans of אִין *not, non-existent,* unexpl.‡

ἐπιφαυλίζω (LXX) *debase, render worthless* La 1:22VL, 2:20VL.*

ἐπιφαύσκω = BDAG: -φώσκω Job 41:10.‡

ἐπιφέρω (17x, Hom+) **1.** *put upon, place upon* (+επι) Pr 26:15; (χεῖρα) *lay a hand on* (i.e., *assault*) Gen 37:22; 1 Km 22:17; Esth 8:7; Zech 2:13; (ρημα πονηρον) *speak ill of, accuse* Jdth 8:8. **2.** *bring upon* Sus 53G, (mid/pass) *rush upon, bear down upon* Gen 1:2; 2 Macc 12:35. **3.** *rest upon* (οφθαλμοι no //; in logic, *adduce*) Job 15:12; (pass) *be borne along, be lifted and carried* Gen 7:18.‡

ἐπιφημίζω (Hdt+) *announce, declare;* (mid) *declare to oneself* Dt 29:18; Wsd 2:12.*

ἐπιφυλλίζω (LXX) *glean grapes;* La 1:22; 2:20; 3:51 mistrans of עלל *harass, afflict* (cf. Engl *"work over"*) as if *pick over, glean* (Vulg 1:22; 2:20 VINDEMIO, *gather grapes,* 3:51 DEPRAEDOR *plunder, pillage*).

ἐπιφυλλίς, -ίδος, ἡ (Aristoph+) *small grapes* (left for gleaners), alw fig Judg 8:2; Mi 7:1; Ob 5; Zeph 3:7. La 1:22; 2:20 -φυλλίδα ποιεῖν mistrans of עלל *work over* (cf. επιφυλλιζω) as if *glean grapes.**

ἐπιφύω (Hdt+) *cleave to, cling to* (τινί) 2 Macc 4:50.*

ἐπιφυτεύω (Aristoph PAX 168) *implant, plant in place* (fig) 4 Macc 15:6.*

ἐπιχαίρω (20x, Soph+) (act or mid) *rejoice, exult (over)* 4 Macc 12:9; Ps 34:19; Sir 23:3; Hos 10:5; Bar 4:12; Ezk 25:3.

ἐπιχαρής, -ές (Aeschyl Prom 161) *gratifying, attractive* Na 3:4; *gratified, exultant* (no //) Job 31:29.*

ἐπίχαρις, -ι (Aeschyl+) *pleasing, attractive* Na 3:4vl.*

ἐπίχαρμα, -ατος, τό (Eur+) *object of* (enemy's) *exultation* Ex 32:25; Jdth 4:12; Sir 6:4; 18:31; 42:11.*

ἐπίχαρτος, -ον (Aeschyl, Thu+) *producing (malignant) delight* Pr 11:3.*

ἐπιχειρέω 2. (abs) *make an attempt or attack* 2 Esdr 7:23.‡

ἐπιχείρημα, -ατος, τό (Thu+) *attempt, ploy* Sir 9:4.*

ἐπίχειρον, -ου, τό (Aeschyl, Pla+) 1. *wage for manual labor,* > *compensation,* (fig) *punishment* (ironically *reward, due payment*) 2 Macc 15:33; Jer 29:11G (διὰ χεῖρα Ra). 2. *arm* (part of body, no //) Jer 31:25; 34:5.*

ἐπίχυσις, -εως, ἡ (Aristoph, Pla+) *influx, anointing;* Job 37:18 mistrans of יצק hoph ptc *molten, having been cast or smelted* as if *poured out* (cf. καταχυσις).*

ἐπιχωρέω (Soph, ins+) *consent* 2 Macc 12:12; (pass) *be permitted* 4:9R (Gött ἐπιχορηγέω).*‡

ἐπιχώρησις, -εως, ἡ (pap+) *provision, permission* 2 Esdr 3:7.*

ἐπιψάλλω (Soph+: *play on lyre*) *sing, lead in singing* (no //) 2 Macc 1:30.*

ἐπιψοφέω (Callim+: *rattle,* > *applaud*) *stamp* (feet, no //) Ezk 25:6.*

ἔπληξα aor of BDAG: πλήσσω (no // except in compounds) Jer 30:6 Gött (30:23R πλήσατε).

ἔποδος see ἐφ-.

ἐπόζω aor ἐπώζεσα (lxx+) *stink, smell* Ex 7:18, 21; 16:20, 24.*

ἐποίκιον, -ου, τό (pap, Strabo+) *settlement, hamlet* 1 Ch 27:25.*

ἐποικτείρω (Xenophanes, Aeschyl+) *have compassion* Job 24:21vl.*

ἕπομαι (Hom, Hdt+) *follow, accompany* 3 Macc 2:26.*

ἐπονείδιστος, -ον (Eur, X+) *insulted, treated w. contempt* 3 Macc 6:31; Pr 18:1; 19:26; 25:10a; *insulting, contemptuous* (no //, but adv in act sense Polyb 1.14.5) 27:11.*

ἐποξύνω (Hierocles) *stimulate,* > *hasten* 2 Macc 9:7.*

ἐποπτικός, -ή, -όν (Pla+) *watching over, overseeing* (no //) 4 Macc 5:13.*

ἐποργίζομαι (lxx) *be(come) angered* 2 Macc 7:33; *attack in anger* Da 11:40L.*

ἐποτρύνω (Hom, Hdt+) *incite, urge on* 4 Macc 5:14; 14:1.*

ἔποψ, -οπος, ὁ (Epicharmus, Aristoph, Aristot+) *hoopoe* Lev 11:19; Dt 14:17; Zech 5:9.*

ἑπταετής, -ές (class ἑπτετής; Aristoph+) *seven years old* Judg 6:25.*

ἑπταιχώς pf ptc of BDAG: πταίω.‡

ἑπτακαίδεκα, -η, -ον (Hdt+) *seventeen* 4 Km 13:1; 1 Ch 7:11; 2 Ch 12:13; 1 Esdr 4:52.*

ἑπτακαιδέκατος, -η, -ον (Hippocr, Thu+) *seventeenth* 3 Km 22:52; 4 Km 16:1; 1 Ch 24:15; 25:24; Jdth 1:13.*

ἑπτάκι = BDAG: -κις, 4 Km 5:14; Pr 24:16 etc.‡

ἑπτακόσιοι, -αι, -α (47x, Hdt+) *seven hundred* Gen 5:4; Judg 8:26A; 1 Esdr 1:9; 2 Macc 12:17.

ἑπτάμηνος, -ου, ἡ (ins+) *period of seven months* Ezk 39:12, 14.*

ἑπταμήτωρ, -ορος, ἡ (h.l.) *mother of seven children* 4 Macc 16:24.*

ἑπταπλάσιος, -ον (Pla+) *multiplied by seven, sevenfold* Is 30:26; (acc as adv) Pr 6:31; Sir 20:12; 35:10; 40:8.*

ἑπταπλοῦς, -οῦν (h.l.) *sevenfold* Sir 35:10vl.*

ἑπτάπυργος, -ον (Eur+) *seven-towered* (fig) 4 Macc 13:7.*

ἔπτην 2 aor of BDAG: πέτομαι Job 20:8.

ἐπωμίς, -ίδος, ἡ (30x, Hippocr, Eur+) 1. *tunic, ephod* Ex 25:7; 28:4ff; Sir 45:8; *shoulder strap* Ex 28:7; 36:11; Ex 28:8 mistrans of אפדה *band, strap* as if *ephod.* 2. *"shoulder"* of doorway (Heb, no //); *frame? span? panel?* Ezk 40:48; 41:2f.

ἐπώνυμος, -ον (Hom, Hdt+) *named for or after* (τινός) Esth 8:12u.*

ἐπωρύω (lxx+) *howl* Zech 11:8.*

ἐραστής, -οῦ, ὁ   (19x, Hdt+) *lover* Wsd 8:2; Hos 2:7; Jer 4:30; La 1:19; Ezk 16:33.

εργαβ   mistranslit of ארגז *pouch* 1 Km 6:11, 15; 20:19.*

ἐργαλεῖον, -ου, τό   (Hdt+) *instrument, tool* Ex 27:19; 39:9, 19, 21.*

ἐργασία   **1.b.** *work, labor* Gen 29:27; Ruth 2:12; 2 Ch 4:11; Ps 103:23; Sir 33:28; Is 1:31. **4.b.** *construct, product* Ezk 15:3.‡

ἐργάσιμος, -ον   (X+) *worked, made from* Lev 13:48f; *for working* 1 Km 20:19.*

ἐργατεία, -ας, ἡ   (LXX+) *craft, skilled trade* Wsd 7:16.*

ἐργατεύομαι   (DiodS 20:92.4; pap) *work, find employment* Tob 5:5S.*

ἐργάτις, -ιδος, ἡ   (fem of BDAG: ἐργάτης; ArchilochusLyr, Hdt+) *hard worker* Pr 6:8.*

ἐργοδιωκτέω   (h.l.) *oversee, be a taskmaster* 2 Ch 8:10.*

ἐργοδιώκτης, -ου, ὁ   (pap) *taskmaster, overseer* Ex 3:7; 5:6ff; 1 Ch 23:4; 2 Ch 2:17; 1 Esdr 5:56.*

ἐργολαβία, -ας, ἡ   (Isocr, DiodS+) *profit* Sir 29:19.*

ἐργῶμαι   fut of ἐργάζομαι Gen 4:12; Ezk 48:19; κατ- Dt 28:39.

ἐρεθίζω   **2.** *be rebellious or contentious* (Philo EBR 16 distinguishes this contentiousness from mere disobedience, discussing this passage) Dt 21:20.‡

ἐρεθισμός, -οῦ, ὁ   (Hippocr, Theophr+) *irritation,* (of disease) *inflammation* Dt 28:22; *rebelliousness* Dt 31:27; *contentiousness* Sir 31:29.*

ἐρεθιστής, -ές   (Philo EBR 14; =) *contentious, rebellious* Dt 21:18.*

ἐρείδω   **2.** (trans) *fix firmly, plant* Pr 3:26; 29:23; (mid/pass) *be firmly planted, be firm or secure* Pr 5:5; 11:16.‡

ἐρεῖσαι   aor inf of ἐρίζω.

ἔρεισμα, -ατος, τό   (Pind, Pla+) *prop, support* Pr 14:26.*

ἐρεοῦς, -ᾶ, -οῦν   (Pla, ins, pap+) *made of wool* Lev 13:47ff; Ezk 44:17.*

ἔρετης, -ου, ὁ   (Hom+) *rower* Sir 11:31vL? (dat pl should be -αις; ερετοις itac for αιρετοις)?

ἐρεύγομαι   (Hom, Pind+) **1.** *announce, proclaim* Ps 18:3. **2.** *pour forth* (no //, but cf. ἐξερ-) Lev 11:10. **3.** *roar, bellow* (diff word? LSJ contrasts Lat ERUGERE *disgorge* and RUGIRE *roar*) 1 Macc 3:4; Hos 11:10; Am 3:4, 8.*‡

ἔρευνα, -ας, ἡ   (Soph+) *examination* Wsd 6:8.*

ἐρευνάω   = BDAG: ἐραυ-.‡

ἐρημία   **2.** *desolation* (Eur, Thu+) Bar 4:33.‡

ἐρημικός, -ή, -όν   (LXX) *of the wilderness* Ps 101:7; 119:4.*

ἐρημίτης, -ου, ὁ   (h.l.) *one who lives in the wilderness* Job 11:12.*

ἐρημόω   **2.** *abandon;* (pass) *be abandoned or bereft* Jer 3:2. Judg 16:7A mistrans of חָרֵב *dried* as if *ruined*.‡

ἐριθεύομαι   (Aristot+: *seek political office*) *work for wages* (Heliod) Tob 2:11.*

ἔριθος, -ου, ὁ or ἡ   (Hom+) *hired worker* Is 38:12.*

ἐρικτός, -ή, -όν   (Hippocr+: -ρεικ-) *pounded, beaten* Lev 2:14.*

ἑρπετόν   **2.** *four-footed creature* Gen 9:3.‡

ἕρπω   (12x, Hom+) *move slowly, crawl* Gen 1:26; Lev 11:29; Ps 68:35; Ezk 38:20.

ἐρράγην   aor pass of BDAG: ῥήγνυμι.

ἐρράχθην   aor pass of BDAG: ῥασσω.

ἔρριπτο   plpf pass 2 Macc 3:29; ἐρρίφην aor pass of BDAG: ῥίπτω Ezk 19:12; ἐρίφθην Wsd 18:18vL*.

ἐρρύην   Att aor (pass in form) of BDAG: ῥέω Ps 77:20

ερ(σ)ουβα   (not in HR) translit of ערובה *pledge, token* (cf. BDAG: ἀρραβών) 1 Km 17:18(vL).*

ἐρυθαίνω   (Hom+) *redden* Wsd 13:14.*

ἐρύθημα, -ατος, τό   (Hippocr+) *redness* Is 63:1.*

ἐρυθριάω   (Pla+) *become red, blush* (in anger) Tob 2:14BA, (in beauty) Esth 5:1b.*

ἐρυθροδανόω   alw pf pass ptc ἠρυθροδανωμένος (LXX) *dye red;* (ptc) *dyed red* Ex 25:5; 26:14; 35:7, 23; 39:20.*

ἐρυμνός, -ή, -όν   (Hes, Thu+) *strong, easily defended* (whether naturally or by fortification; X ANAB 1.2.8) 2 Macc 11:5.*

ἐρυμνότης, -ητος, ἡ   (X, Aristot, Polyb) strength, (military) security 2 Macc 10:34; 12:14.*

ἐρυσίβη, -ης, ἡ   (Pla+) rust (on plants) Dt 28:42; 3 Km 8:37; Ps 77:46; Hos 5:7; Joel 1:4; 2:25.*

ἐρωδιός, -οῦ, ὁ   (Hom+; prop ἐρῳδ-) heron Lev 11:19; Dt 14:16; Ps 103:17.*

ἐρωμένος   pf pass ptc of BDAG: ἐράω, ἔραμαι 1 Esdr 4:24.

ἐρώτημα, -ατος, τό   (Thu+) question, (specif) leading question Sir 33:3.*

ἐσάπην   aor pass of BDAG: σήπω Ps 37:6.

εσεφιν   (vvll -φειν, -φ[ε]ιμ) translit of אספים what is gathered and stored; stores, supplies 1 Ch 26:15, 17.*

ἔσθησις, -εως, ἡ   (BDAG: dub; Strabo [3.3.7]+) only dat pl ἐσθήσεσι(ν) clothing (= BDAG: ἔσθης) 2 Macc 3:33; 3 Macc 1:16.*

ἐσπαρμένος   pf pass ptc of BDAG: σπείρω.

ἔσπεισα   aor of σπένδω 2 Km 23:16; Sir 50:15; Ezk 20:28.

ἑσπέρα   2. west (Hdt+) 2 Esdr 4:20.‡

ἐσπεσμένος   pf pass ptc of BDAG: σβέννυμι.

ἑστία, -ας, ἡ   (Hom+) hearth, > family, home Tob 2:12S*

ἑστιατορία, -ας, ἡ   (pap) feast, banquet 4 Km 25:30; Da 5:1G, 23L.*

ἔστρωμαι   aor pass of BDAG: στρώννυμι Job 26:12vl.

ἐσχάρα, -ας, ἡ   (14x, Hom+) 1. brazier Lev 2:7; Pr 26:21; Jer 43:22f. 2. hearth grate (for altar, no //) Ex 27:4f; 2 Ch 4:11; Sir 50:12.

ἐσχαρίς, -ίδος, ἡ   (ins+) brazier Ex 30:3vl.*

ἐσχαρίτης, -ου, ὁ   (Antidotus [IV bce]) bread baked over coals 2 Km 6:19.*

ἐσχατίζω   (lxx) arrive late Judg 5:28A, (ptc subst) stragglers, those coming last 1 Macc 5:53.*

ἐσχατογήρως, gen -ως   (Strabo, DiodS+) in extreme old age Sir 41:2; 42:8.*

ἐσώτατος, -η, -ον   superl of BDAG: ἔσω/ ἐσώτερος (7x, lxx+) innermost 3 Km 6:27, 30; 7:36. Job 28:18 mistrans of פנינים coral, pearls as if rel to פנימי innermost.

ἐτάζω   (12x, Pla+) 1. examine, test 1 Ch 28:9; Ps 7:10; Job 32:11; Wsd 6:6; Jer 17:10; La 3:40; put to the test Sus 51G. 2. put on trial and punish Esth 2:23; afflict Gen 12:17; Wsd 2:19.

ἑταίρα, -ας, ἡ   (Hom, Hdt+) courtesan Judg 11:2 (but Heb אחרת = ἕτερος); 2 Macc 6:4; Pr 19:13; Sir 41:22.*

ἑταιρίζω   (Hom+) associate with; (mid) be a courtesan Sir 9:3.*

ἐτάκην   2 aor pass of BDAG: τήκω Ps 74:4.

ἔτασις, -εως, ἡ   (lxx) 1. test, trial Job 31:14. 2. affliction Job 10:17; 12:6.*

ἐτασμός, -οῦ, ὁ   (lxx) 1. test, trial Jdth 8:27. 2. affliction Gen 12:17; 2 Macc 7:37.*

ἑτερόζυγος, -ον   (pap, Philo Spec 4.203; =) different in kind or species (c. BDAG) Lev 19:19.*

ἑτεροκλινῶς   (not in HR; lxx+) inclined (to one's own way), > dissentingly, rebelliously (no //, but cf. BDAG: ἑτεροκλινής) 1 Ch 12:34.*

ἑτεροκωφέω   (h.l.) be deaf in one ear Sir 19:27vl.*

ἑτέρωθεν   (Hom+) from the other side, on the opposite side 4 Macc 6:4.*

ἔτι   1.a.β. adv subst w. prep; ἀπὸ τοῦ ἔτι from the time, from of old (no //) Job 20:4.‡

ἑτοιμάζω   Ps 20:13 mistrans of כון polel shoot a bow as if be ready, prepare; 1 Km 13:13; 1 Ch 14:2; Pr 3:19; Hab 2:12; Ezk 4:3 etc mistrans of כון hiph establish, make immovable as if qal prepare (c. BDAG).‡

ἑτοιμασία   2 Esdr 2:68; 3:3; Ps 88:14; Zech 5:11; mistrans of מכון etc foundation etc, fr כון set in place, > prepare. So also Da 11:7Θff mistrans of כן position, station, fr כון.‡

ἕτοιμος   3 Km 8:39ff = 2 Ch 6:30ff mistrans of מכון place, fr כון set in place, > be ready.‡

ἐτράπην   2 aor pass (inf τραπῆναι) of BDAG: τρέπω.

ἐτράφην   2 aor pass of BDAG: τρέφω Esth 4:8; subj τραφῶ Wsd 16:23.

ἔτρησα   see τετραίνω.

ἔτρωσα   aor act of BDAG: τιτρώσκω.

εὐαγγελία, -ας, ἡ   (Joseph) good news, announcement of good 2 Km 18:20, 22, 27; 4 Km 7:9.*

εὐάλωτος, -ον   (X, Pla+) easily caught Pr 30:28.*

εὐανδρία, ας, ἡ   (Eur, X+) manliness (Eur El 367) 2 Macc 8:7; 15:17.*

εὐαπάντητος, -ον (ins) *courteous, gracious* 2 Macc 14:9.*

εὐάρμοστος, -ον (Eur, Pla+) *harmonious* 4 Macc 14:3; Ezk 33:32.*

εὖγε LXX (e.g., Ps 34:21; Ezk 6:11) oft ironic or malicious (no //).‡

εὐγένεια, -ας, ἡ (Aeschyl+) *nobility, excellence* 2 Macc 14:42; 4 Macc 8:4; Wsd 8:3; *noble birth* Sir 22:8vL.*

εὐγενίζω (PhilemonCom+) *ennoble* 2 Macc 10:13.*

ευγενναισας, -νασιας *f.ll.* (not in LSJ) 2 Macc 10:13 vvLL.*

εὐγενῶς (adj εὐγενής, BDAG; Eur+) *in well-bred or noble fashion* 2 Macc 14:42; 4 Macc 6:22, 30; 9:22; 12:14; 13:11.*

εὐγνωμοσύνη, -ης, ἡ (Aristot+) *good intention, prudence, counsel* Esth 8:12f.*

εὔγνωστος, -ον (Soph+) *well-known, easily known* Pr 3:15; 5:6; 26:26.*

εὐδοκέω Lev 26:41 mistrans of רצה² *make good, compensate for* as if רצה¹ *enjoy* (so also 26:34ff? Cf. προσδέχομαι).‡

εὐδοκιμέω (Theognis, Hdt+) *be esteemed, be held worthy* (act or pass) Gen 43:23; Sir 39:34; 40:25; 41:16.*

εὐδόκιμος, -ον (Aeschyl+) *esteemed, respected* 3 Macc 3:5.*

εὐδοξία, -ας, ἡ (Simonid, Pind+) *honor, excellence* Sir 1:27vL.*

εὐδράνεια, -ας, ἡ (*h.l.*) *strength, vigor* Wsd 13:19.*

εὐεκτέω (LXX+) *be wholesome, promote well-being* Pr 17:22.*

εὔελπις, gen -ιδος (Aeschyl, Thu+) *hopeful, confident* 3 Macc 2:33; Pr 19:18; Wsd 12:19.*

εὐεξία, -ας, ἡ (Hippocr, Eur+) *good physical condition, vigorous health* Sir 30:15.*

εὐεπίβατος, -ον (not in HR; PhiloMech, Strabo+) *easy to climb*; (subst) *easy-to-climb place* 2 Esdr 14:7vL.*

εὐεργέτημα, -ατος, τό (Hippocr, X+) *kind deed* 2 Macc 5:20.*

εὔζωνος, -ον (Hom+) *well-girded, well-armed or equipped* Josh 1:14; 4:13; Sir 36:26.*

εὐήθης, -ες (ArchilochusLyr, Hdt+) *guileless,* > *simple-minded, stupid* 2 Macc 2:32.*

εὐήκοος, -ον (Hippocr, Aristot+) *gladly or willingly listening* Pr 25:12; *responsive, obedient* PsSol 18:4; EpJer 59.*

εὐημερέω pf ptc ευημερηκώς (Soph+) *succeed, be victorious* 2 Macc 8:35; 12:11; 13:16.*

εὐημερία, -ας, ἡ (Pind, Eur+) *success, good fortune* 2 Macc 5:6; 8:8; 10:28; 14:14; 3 Macc 3:11.*

εὔηχος, -ον (Philod+) *pleasant-sounding, euphonious* Ps 150:5. Job 30:7 (cf. 4 ἠχέω) mistrans of שיח *bush* as if fr שיח *talk.**

εὐθαρσέως (dub; not in LSJ) *courageously* 2 Macc 7:10vL.*

εὐθαρσής, -ές (Aeschyl+) *confident, courageous* 1 Esdr 8:27; 2 Macc 8:21; 3 Macc 1:7; (adv) εὐθαρσῶς *courageously, boldly* 2 Macc 7:10.*

εὐθηνία 2. *plenty, abundance* (οινου) Ezk 16:49.‡

εὐθίκτως (LXX+; adj Aristot+) *cleverly, to the point* 2 Macc 15:38.*

εὔθραυστος, -ον (Aristot+) *easily broken* Wsd 15:13.*

εὔθυνα, -ης, ἡ (Aristoph+) *setting straight; punishment* 3 Macc 2:23; 3:28.*

εὐθύς 3. *level;* κατ' εὐθ- *"on the level (terrain)"* 3 Km 21:23, 25.‡

εὐιλατεύω (LXX) *be merciful to* (τινί) Dt 29:19; Jdth 16:15; *forgive* ([dat] *sins*) Ps 102:3.*

εὐίλατος, -ον (pap, ins) *most merciful* 1 Esdr 8:53; Ps 98:8.*

εὔκαιρος, -ον (Soph, Thu+) **1.** (temp; Soph OedCol 32) *timely, well-timed* 2 Macc 14:29; Ps 103:27. **2.** (spat) *favorable, well-situated* (superl also Polyb 4.38.1) 2 Macc 15:20; 3 Macc 4:11; 5:44. **3.** adv (Hippocr, Isocr+) *promptly* Sir 18:22.*‡

εὐκαταφρόνητος, -ον (X, Aristot+) *easily despised, quite contemptible* Jer 30:9; Da 11:21L.*

εὐκίνητος, -ον (Hippocr, Pla+) *moving easily, graceful* Wsd 7:22; *easy to move* 13:11.*

εὔκλεια, -ας, ἡ (Hom+) *reputation, honor, fame* 2 Macc 6:19; 3 Macc 2:31; Wsd 8:18.*

εὐκληματέω (LXX+) *put out many branches* Hos 10:1.*

εὔκληρος, -ον (pap+) *fortunate* Dt 4:20VL.*

εὔκολος, -ον (Aristoph, X+) *easy, simple* 2 Km 15:3.*

εὐκοπία, -ας, ἡ (DiodS [1.36.4], pap) *ease of labor* 2 Macc 2:25.*

εὐκοσμέω (h.l.) *rule well, administer effectively* 1 Macc 8:15.*

εὐκοσμία, -ας, ἡ (Eur+) *good administration, leadership* Sir 32:2; *adornment* (no //, but εὐκοσμός can mean *adorned*) 45:7.*

εὔκυκλος, -ον (Hom+) *well-rounded* Wsd 5:21.*

εὐλαβῶς adv of BDAG: εὐλαβής.‡

εὐλογέω 2 Km 6:20 prob mistrans of וַתְּבָרֶךְ *and she knelt* (not in MT) as if וַתְּבָרֶךְ *and she blessed*. 3 Km 20:10, 13 renders MT, a euphem TIQQUN SOPHERIM, which replaced *curse* w. *bless*.‡

ευλογιν itac misspelling of εὐλογεῖν 1 Ch 17:27VL.*

εὐλογιστία, -ας, ἡ (Pla+) *circumspection, > right thinking* 4 Macc 5:22; 8:15; 13:5, 7.*

εὐμαθῶς (Aeschin) *skillfully, in well-taught fashion* Wsd 13:11.

εὐμεγέθης, -ες (Aristoph, X+) *tall, large* 1 Km 9:2; Bar 3:26.*

εὐμελής, -ές (Aristot+) *melodious, graceful* Wsd 17:17; (adv) 4 Macc 11:18VL.*

εὐμένεια, -ας, ἡ (Hdt+) *good will, favorable attitude* 2 Macc 6:29.*

εὐμενής, -ές (Aeschyl, Hdt+) *favorably minded, well disposed* 2 Macc 12:31; 13:26; (adv) Wsd 6:16.*

εὐμετάβολος, -ον (Gorgias of Leontini, X, Pla+) *changeable, likely to change* Pr 17:20.*

εὐμήκης, -ες (Pla+) *tall* Dt 9:2.*

εὐμορφία, -ας, ἡ (Democr, Eur+) *beauty of bodily form* 4 Macc 8:10; Wsd 7:10.*

εὐνομία, -ας, ἡ (Hom, Hes+) *observance of traditional devotion* (Soph AJ 713) 4 Macc 3:20; 4:24; 7:9; 18:4.*

εὔνους, -ουν (Aeschyl, Hdt+) *thinking favorably of* (τινί) 4 Macc 4:3.*

εὐοδία, -ας, ἡ (7x, Aeschyl+) *good journey* 1 Esdr 8:6; (fig) *success* Tob 4:6; Pr 25:15; Sir 9:12G; 10:5; 11:22G.

εὔοδος, -ον (X+) *moving easily*, (fig) *prospering* Num 14:41; 1 Esdr 7:3; Pr 11:9; 13:13; (adv) 30:29.*

εὐοδόω aor εὐώδωσε pass εὐωδώθη (76; Hdt+) *help on the way, make travel easy* Gen 24:27; (w. cogn acc) Gen 24:21; Is 46:11; *send to help on the way* Judg 4:8; Tob 7:12BA, 13S; (fig) *cause to prosper* Josh 1:8; Wsd 11:1; (act or mid intr) *bring success* Gen 24:12; Ps 117:25; Is 54:17; *succeed* 1 Ch 22:11; 2 Ch 18:14; cf. // 3 Km 22:15; (pass, as in NT) *be made to prosper* 1 Ch 13:2; 1 Macc 3:6; Pr 17:8.‡

εὔοπτος, -ον (Hippocr, LXX+) *conspicuous, easy to see* EpJer 60.*

εὐπαθέω (Hdt+) *enjoy oneself, feel happy* Ps 91:15; Job 21:23.*

εὐπάρυφος, -ον (LXX+) *fine garment* (w. purple border) Ezk 23:12.*

εὐπείθεια, -ας, ἡ (Zeno the Stoic+) *willing obedience, compliance* 4 Macc 5:16; 9:2; 12:6; 15:9.*

εὐπειθέω (LXX+) *willingly obey, comply* 4 Macc 8:6.*

εὐπορέω 2. *cause to prosper* (no //) Wsd 10:10.‡

εὐπόρφυρος, -ον (h.l.) *fine purple* Ezk 23:12VL.*

εὐπραξία, -ας, ἡ (Hdt+) *good conduct* 3 Macc 3:5f.*

εὐπρεπής 1.a. neut pl subst *attractive things* (= Heb) Job 18:15; but could also be read as *pretences* (since Hdt: *seemly, > specious*).‡

εὐπροσήγορος, -ον (Eur+) *courteous, approachable*; (neut subst) *expression of courtesy* Sir 6:5.*

εὐπρόσωπος, -ον (Aristoph+) *fair-faced, attractive* Gen 12:11.*

εὕρεμα, -ατος, τό (BDAG: -ημα; Hdt+) **1.** *invention, discovery* (Eur BACH 59) Sir 35:9.

2. *lucky find, windfall* (X ΑΝΑΒ 7.3.13) Sir 20:9; 29:4, 6; Jer 45:2; 46:18; 51:35.*

εὕρεσις, -εως, ἡ (Pla+) *discovery* Wsd 14:12; *formulation* Sir 13:26.*

εὑρετής, -οῦ, ὁ (Pla, ins+) *inventor, contriver* 2 Macc 7:31; *discoverer* Pr 16:20.*

εὑρετός, -ή, -όν (Hippocr, X+) *discoverable; which can be found* Judg 9:6B.*

εὖρος, -ους, τό (57x, Hom+) *width* Ex 25:23; Dt 3:11; 2 Ch 3:3; Jdth 7:3; Job 11:9; Ezk 40:11ff; Da 3:1Θ.

εὔρυθμος, -ον (Aristoph+) *rhythmic, graceful, smooth-flowing* Esth 4:17s.*

ευρυμνοτης (not in HR, LSJ, Gött app) *f.l.* 2 Macc 12:15vLR.*

εὐρύς, -εῖα, -ύ (Hom, Hdt+) *wide* Ex 38:4, 10, 24.*

εὐρυχωρία, -ας, ἡ (Hdt+) *open space* Gen 26:22.*

εὔρωστος, -ον (X+) *strong, vigorous* Sir 30:15; (adv) 2 Macc 10:17; 12:27, 35; Wsd 8:1.*

εὐρωτιάω (Aristot, Theophr) *grow moldy* Josh 9:5.*

εὔσκιος, -ον (Pind, X+) *well-shaded* Jer 11:16.*

εὔσταθμος, -ον (pap? Justinian [VI CE]) *well-proportioned* Sir 26:18G.*

εὔστοχος, -ον (Eur, X+) *well-aimed* Wsd 5:21; (adv) 3 Km 22:34 = 2 Ch 18:33—here *hitting luckily* (Aristot+; cf. Heb) is also possible.*

εὐστροφία, -ας, ἡ (Chrysipp+) *versatility* Pr 14:35.*

εὐσυναλλάκτως (h.l.; adj Plu+) *bringing about peace and harmony* Pr 25:10a.*

εὐτακτέω (Thu, X+) *be in good order;* (trans) *pay* (τι) *regularly or in timely fashion* (ins, pap) 2 Macc 4:27.*

εὐτεκνία, -ας, ἡ (Eur, Aristot+) *blessing or happiness of having children* 4 Macc 18:9.*

εὐτελής, -ές (Hdt+) *simple, common* Wsd 10:4; *worthless, cheap* Wsd 11:15; 13:14; 15:10; (adv) *poorly, shabbily* 2 Macc 15:38.*

εὔτηκτος, -η, -ον (Aristot+) *highly meltable* Wsd 19:21.*

εὐτολμία, -ας, ἡ (Eur, Aristot+) *good courage, boldness* 2 Macc 13:18.*

εὐτονία, -ας, ἡ (Hippocr, PhiloMech+) *vigor or resilience* (of mind, Stoic term) Eccl 7:7.*

εὔτονος, -ον (Hippocr, Pla+) *vigorous* 2 Macc 12:23; 4 Macc 7:10.*

εὐτρεπίζω (Aeschyl+) *get ready, prepare* 4 Macc 5:32.*

εὐτρεπῶς (Demosth) *in well-prepared fashion* Wsd 13:11vL.*

εὐτυχία, -ας, ἡ (Pind, Hdt+) *good fortune* (f.l. for -ψυχ-) 4 Macc 6:11vL.*

εὐφημέω (Hom+) *shout praise* 1 Macc 5:64.*

εὔφθαρτος, -ον (Aristot+) *utterly mortal or perishable* Wsd 19:21.*

εὐφραίνω Ezk 23:41 mistrans of שמה *you placed* (שׂים, שׂום) as if fr שמח *rejoice.*‡

εὐφρονεύομαι (dub; not in LSJ) *be sensible* Jer 10:21vL.*

εὐφρόσυνος, -ον (Diosc, ins+) *cheerful, happy* Jdth 14:9; 3 Macc 6:36; 7:19.*

εὐφυής, -ές (Hom+) **1.** *favorable* (time) 2 Macc 4:32. **2.** *well-formed, well-developed* 1 Esdr 8:3; *gifted by nature* Wsd 8:19.*

εὐχαρής, -ές (MenandRhet) = seq Wsd 14:20vL.*

εὔχαρις, -ρι, gen εὐχάριτος (Eur, X+) *charming, gracious, urbane;* (neut subst) *sophistication* Wsd 14:20.*

εὐχαριστήριον, -ου, τό (Polyb, ins+) *thank offering* 2 Macc 12:45vL.*

εὐχή **2.b.** *votive offering* Dt 12:6.‡

εὔχομαι pf ptc ηὐγμένος **3.** *vow, take an oath* Gen 28:20; Dt 12:11; 1 Km 1:11; Jon 2:10.‡

εὐχρηστία, -ας, ἡ (Aristot+) *service, credit* 3 Macc 2:33.*

εὐψυχία, -ας, ἡ (Aeschyl, Thu+) *good courage, good spirit* 2 Macc 14:18; 4 Macc 6:11; 9:23.*

εὔψυχος, -ον (Aeschyl, Thu+) *stout-hearted, courageous* 1 Macc 9:14; Pr 30:31; (adv) *with good courage* 2 Macc 7:20; 3 Macc 7:18.*

εὐώδης, -ες (Hom, Hdt+) *fragrant* Ex 30:23; (superl) 3 Macc 5:45; 7:16.*

εὐωδιάζω (Strabo+) *give off fragrance, smell sweet* Sir 39:14; Zech 9:17.*

εὐώνυμος 2. *north* (s.t.; cf. δεξιός) Josh 13:3; Ezk 16:46.‡

εὐωχέω (Alcaeus, Hdt+) *give a banquet;* (mid/pass) *feast, be fed lavishly* Jdth 1:16; 3 Macc 6:40.*‡

εφαδανω translit of אפדנו *his palace* (h.l. Pers) Da 11:45Θ.*

ἐφαμαρτάνω (Trypho: *miss the mark*) *cause to sin* (no //) Jer 39:35.*

ἐφάπτω (Hom, Hdt+) *seize, treat violently* 2 Macc 7:1; (mid) *attain, partake of* Am 6:3; *approach* 9:5.*

ἐφαρμόζω (Hom+) *fit (onto)* 4 Macc 11:10.*

ἐφέλκω aor ἐφείλκυσα pass ptc ἐφελκυσθείς (Hom, Hdt+) *draw along, lead along;* (pass) *be led off* EpJer 43; *draw out, extend* (time) Josh 24:29; (pass) *be delayed, remain* Num 9:19; (mid) *draw to oneself, attract or compel attention* 4 Macc 15:21; (pass) *be attracted* Wsd 14:20.*

ἐφέξω fut of BDAG: ἐπέχω Sir 15:4.

ἐφέστιος, -ον (Hom, Hdt+) *by the hearth, > of the household* Sir 37:11vl.*

ἐφέτειος, -ον (ins, pap; cf. ἐπέτειος) *of one year, yearly* Dt 15:18G.

ἐφέτιος, -ον (not in LSJ; better -ειος or ἐπέτειος; cf. W) *of one year, yearly* Dt 15:18R; Sir 37:11R.*

ἐφηβεῖον, -ου, τό (Vitruvius [I BCE]) *courtyard for the youths in training* 2 Macc 4:9R.*

ἐφηβία, -ας, ἡ (so Gött; better -βεία, cf. W, p.40. ins+) *corps of* ἔφηβοι, or *process of training them* 2 Macc 4:9G.*

ἔφηβος, -ου, ὁ (X, Pla+) *adolescent, young man (16–18 yrs old)* 2 Macc 4:12.*

ἔφηλος, -ον (Callim+) *w. spotted or defective eye* Lev 21:20.*

ἔφθακεν pf of φθάνω.

ἑφθός, -ή, -όν (Hdt+) *boiled* Num 6:19; (subst) 1 Km 2:15.*

ἐφικτός, -ή, -όν (Empedocles, Aristot+) *accessible, achievable* 2 Macc 15:38.*

ἔφιππος, -ον (Soph, EupolisCom, Lysias+) *riding* (on horseback) 2 Macc 12:35; 4 Macc 4:10; (subst) *rider* 2 Macc 11:8.*‡

ἐφίπταμαι (Aristot+) = BDAG: ἐπιπέτομαι (aor ptc ἐπιπτάς) *light upon, fly upon* EpJer 21.*

ἔφισος, -ον (HR: επ-. LSJ: Polyb 3.115.1; but Loeb has ἐπ' ἴσος; LXX) *comparable, equal* Sir 9:10; 31:27*

ἐφίστημι 8. (act trans) *set up* 4 Km 4:38; 2 Km 8:3 = 1 Ch 18:3 (cf. χείρ); *cause to stand firm* Sir 40:25; *fix, cause to rest* Pr 9:18a; *appoint, institute* Is 1:26; 3:4; (obj "mind") *turn one's thoughts, attend* (to ἐπί) Ex 7:23; (πρός) 2 Esdr 18:13; *set* (one's face) *in opposition* Lev 20:3ff.‡

ἐφοδεύω aor ἐφώδευσα (X+) *inspect, explore* Jdth 7:7; 1 Macc 16:14; 2 Macc 3:8; (specif as a spy, no //) Dt 1:22.*

ἐφοδιάζω aor pass ἐφωδιάσθην (Hdt+) *equip, provide* (for a journey) Dt 15:14; (pass = mid) *provide for oneself* Josh 9:12.*

ἔφοδος¹, -ον (ins+) *on the road, accessible* (επ- for εφ-); 2 Macc 4:41vl.*

ἔφοδος², -ου, ἡ (9x, Aeschyl, Thu+) *approach, arrival* 1 Macc 11:44; 14:21; (fig) *approach, attempt, plan of attack* 1 Macc 9:68; 2 Macc 5:1.

ἐφοράω 2. *oversee, watch over* 2 Macc 15:2 (cf. BDAG: ἐπείδον).‡

ἐφορμάω (Hom, Hdt+) *rush against, attack* (f.l. for εφαρμοζω) 4 Macc 11:10vl.*

εφουδ, εφωδ, εφωθ (15x) translit of אֵפוֹד *ephod, priestly garment* Judg 17:5; 1 Km 2:18, *cult object* Judg 8:27; 1 Km 30:7.

εφραθ mistranslit (vl εβδαθ) of עֲבֹדַת *working* (in linen) as if part of N LOC 1 Ch 4:21.

ἐφύβριστος, -ον (LXX+) *contemptible* Wsd 17:7.*

ἐχθές Job 30:3 renders MT אֶמֶשׁ *yesterday, last evening*, prob emend to אֱנוּשׁ *disastrous, calamitous*.‡

ἔχθιστος, -ον (Hom+) superl of ἐχθρός; *most hateful* Esth 8:12x, Wsd 12:4; Da 3:32 = Odes 7:32.

ἐχθραίνω impf ἤχθρανα aor ἤχθρασα (12; X+) *attack, be hostile toward* (τινί) Num 25:17; 1 Macc 7:26; 11:38; Ps 3:8; (abs) *hate, feel enmity* Sir 28:6.

ἐχθρεύω (LXX+) *be hostile, show malice* Ex 23:22 = 2Macc10:26; Num 33:55.*

ἐχθρία, -ας, ἡ (*h.l.*) *enmity* Gen 26:21.*

ἐχθρός 2 Esdr 14:4 textual error for ἀχθοφόρος, q.v. Sir 49:9 mistrans of איוב *Job* as if אויב *enemy*.‡

ἐχῖνος, -ου, ὁ (ArchilochusLyr+) *hedgehog, porcupine* Zeph 2:14; Is 13:22; 14:23; 34:11, 15.*

ἔχις, -εως, ἡ (Pla+) *viper* Sir 39:30.*

ἔχω **3.c.** also "*hold back (from)*," *refrain from, refuse to* 2 Macc 6:11. **11.b.β.** (adv) ἐχομένως *immediately, right afterward* 2 Macc 7:15.‡

ἕψεμα, (-ημα), -ατος, τό (Hippocr, Pla+) *boiled food* Gen 25:29ff; 4 Km 4:38ff; Hg 2:12; Bel 33.*

ἕψω fut ἑψήσω aor ἥψησα pass ἡψήθην pf pass ptc ἡψημένον (28; Hdt+) *boil* Gen 25:29; 1 Km 2:13; 1 Esdr 1:12; Zech 14:21; Ezk 24:5; Bel 27.

ἑωθινός, -ή, -όν (8x, Hdt+) *early in the morning* Ex 14:24; 1 Macc 5:30; Ps 21:1; Sir 50:6; Jon 4:7.

ἕωλος, -ον (Hippocr, Aristot+) *stale, spoiled* Ezk 4:14.*

ἕως²; gen and acc ἕω, ἡ (Hom, Hdt+ [Ionic ἠώς]) *dawn* (X Anab 1.7.1) 3 Macc 5:45.*

ἔωσα aor of ὠθέω.

ἑωσφόρος, -ου, ὁ (7x, Hom+) "*bringer of morning*," *morning star* 1 Km 30:17; Ps 109:3; Job 3:9; Is 14:12.‡

Z

ζακχω mistranslit of גנזכיו *its treasures* 1 Ch 28:11.*

ζάω **5.** (trans/caus, no //) *bring to life, make alive* Ps 118:25, 37; 142:11; Ezk 13:22.‡

ζέα, -ας, ἡ (pap+) *type of wheat* Is 28:25.*

ζεμα (ζεμμα Ezk 24:13vL) translit of זִמָּה *infamy, outrage* Judg 20:6B.*

ζευγίζω (pap) *yoke*; (pass) *be joined to* (τινί) 1 Macc 1:15.*

ζεύγνυμι aor ἔζευξα **2.** *harness, hitch* Gen 46:29; 3 Km 18:44 (ptc, X Anab 1.2.5) *attached, connected* 2 Km 20:8.‡

ζήλωσις, -εως, ἡ (Thu+) **1.** *eagerness, zeal* Wsd 1:10. **2.** *jealousy* (no //) Num 5:14, 30.*

ζηλωτής **3.** (of God) *zealous* or *jealous one* Ex 20:5; 34:14.‡

ζηλωτός, -όν (Aeschyl+) *enviable, blessed* Gen 49:22; Ex 34:14.*

ζημία, -ας, ἡ (Hdt, ins+) *penalty* Pr 27:12; (monetary fine) 4 Km 23:33; 1 Esdr 8:24; (confiscation of property) 2 Esdr 7:26; (execution) 2 Macc 4:48.*‡

ζητι itac error for ζήτει (pres act impv) Jer 51:35vL.*

ζιβύνη, -ης, ἡ (pap, DiodS) *spear* Jdth 1:15; (σιβ-) Mi 4:3vL = Is 2:4; Jer 6:23.*

ζυγός (masc or neut; cf. BDAG) **3.** *thwart* (of ship; Hom, Hdt+) 3 Macc 4:9.‡

ζυγόω (Aeschyl+) *yoke, join together*; (pf pass ptc) *joined, bonded together* 3 Km 7:43; Ezk 41:26.*

ζῦθος, -ου, ὁ (Theophr+) *Egyptian beer* Is 19:10.*

ζυμίτης, -ες (CratinusCom+) *leavened* (ἄρτοι X Anab 7.3.21) Lev 7:13.*

ζυμωτός, -ή, -όν (LXX) *leavened* Ex 12:19f; 13:7; Lev 2:11.*

ζωγραφέω (Pla+) *paint, draw, represent in art* 2 Macc 2:29; 4 Macc 17:7; Is 49:16; Ezk 23:14.*

ζωγρεία, -ας, ἡ (Hdt, Polyb+) *taking or capturing alive* Num 21:35R; Dt 2:34R.*

ζωγρέω (Hom+) **1.** *capture alive* Num 31:15; Dt 20:16; 2 Ch 25:12. **2.** *preserve, keep alive* Num 31:18; Josh 2:13; 6:25; 9:20; 2 Km 8:2.*‡

ζωγρίας, -ου, ὁ (*recte* Ctesias+) *captive, one taken alive* Num 21:35; Dt 2:34; 2 Macc 12:35.*

ζωμός, -οῦ, ὁ (Aristoph+) *stew, sauce* Judg 6:19f; Is 65:4; Ezk 24:10.*

ζωοποίησις, -εως, ἡ (LXX) *vitalization, act of giving life* 2 Esdr 9:8, 9.*

ζωόω (Hippocr+) *bring to life, cause to live* Ps 79:19; 84:7.*

ζωπυρέω (Aeschyl, Hippocr+) *ignite*; (fig) *enkindle w. life* 4 Km 8:1, 5.*

ζώπυρον, -ου, τό (Pla, Aristot+) pl *bellows* (EphorusCumaeus) 4 Macc 8:13.*

ζῶσις, -εως, ἡ (h.l.) *girding on* Is 22:12.*

ζώσος aor ptc of ζάω (fr Ionic aor ἔζωσαν) Gen 1:20 & oft.

ζωτικός, -ή, -όν (X, Pla+) *life-giving, vital* Wsd 15:11.*

Η

ἡγέομαι Ps 103:17 mistrans of ברושים *junipers* as if בראשם *among their leaders*. Pr 5:19 *precede, go before*; mistrans of דדיה *her breasts* as of fr דדה *walk*. Ezk 21:2 renders MT השדה *the field* as if related to השר *the leader*.‡

ἥγημα, -ατος, τό (ins) *intention* (no //) Ezk 17:3.*

ἥγησις, -εως, ἡ (LXX) *leadership, command* Judg 5:14A; 1 Macc 9:31.*

ἡγητέον (X, Pla+) *to be considered or regarded, one must consider or regard* Pr 26:23.*

ἦγμαι 3rd sg ἦκται ptc ἡγμένος, all pf pass of ἄγω.

ἡγνέσθω error for γιγνέσθω (ΓΙΓ > ΗΓ) 1 Esdr 8:90vL.*

ἡδύνω aor ἥδυνα pass ἡδύνθην (10; Epicharmus, X+) *season, (add) spice*, > *delight, gratify* Pr 13:19; Sir 40:21; (act or pass) *be pleasing* (τινί) Ps 103:34; Job 24:5; Hos 9:4; Jer 6:20.

ἡδυπάθεια, -ας, ἡ (Hippocr, X+) *sexual desire or pleasure* 4 Macc 2:2, 4.*‡

ἥδυσμα, -ατος, τό (9x; Hippocr, Aristot+) *spice, aromatic* Ex 30:23; 3 Km 10:25 = 2 Ch 9:24; Esth 4:17k; Eccl 10:1; Ezk 27:22.

ἡδυσμός, -οῦ, ὁ (h.l.) *sweet aroma* Ex 30:34.*

ἡδύφωνος, -ον (Sappho+) *sweet-sounding, sweet-voiced* Ezk 33:32.*

ηδω (mis?)translit of אורו *his light* as if אדו *his (heavenly) current or stream* (cf. vs 27) Job 36:30.*

ἠθέληκα pf of BDAG: θέλω.

ἠθολογέω (Longinus [III CE]) *give characteristic expression to* (τι) 4 Macc 15:4.*

ἠκισμένος pf pass ptc of αἰκίζω.

ἠκονημένος see ἀκονάω.

ἤλεκτρος, -ου, ὁ or **ἡ** or **-ον, τό** (Hom+) *alloy of gold and silver* Ezk 1:4, 27; 8:2.*

ἡλιάζω (Aristot, Strabo, ins) *expose to or dry in the sun* 2 Km 21:14.*

ἡλικιώτης, -ου, ὁ (Hdt, Aristoph+) *one's equal in age, (suitable) companion* 4 Macc 11:14.*

ἡλισμένος pf pass ptc of BDAG: ἁλίζω.

ἧλος 3 Km 7:36; 4 Km 12:14 mistrans of מזמרת *snuffer, trimmer* as if מסמרות *nails*.‡

ἡμαρτηκώς pf ptc of BDAG: of ἁμαρτάνω.

ἡμίεφθος, -ον (Hippocr+) *half-boiled* Is 51:20.*

ἡμίθνητος, -ον (Lysias+: *semi-mortal*) *half-dead* (no //) Wsd 18:18.*

ἡμίονος, -ου, ὁ (25x, Hom+) *mule* Gen 12:16; 1 Km 21:8; 1 Esdr 5:42; Ps 31:9; Zech 14:15; Is 66:20.

ἡμίσευμα, -ατος, τό (pap+) *half, half-portion* Num 31:36ff.*

ἡμισεύω (LXX+) *halve, reduce by half* Ps 54:24.*

ἡμμένος pf pass ptc (mid sense: *touch*) of BDAG: ἅπτω Num 19:18.

ἠνειχόμην 3 Macc 1:22 fr BDAG: ἀνέχω (doubly augm; cf. BDF 69).

ἤνθηκα pf of BDAG: ἀνθέω Ezk 7:10.

ἡνία, -ας, ἡ (Pind, Aeschyl+) *reins* (pl) Na 2:4; τοὺς ἐπὶ τῶν ἡ. *cavalry commanders* 1 Macc 6:28.*

ἡνίοχος, -ου, ὁ (Hom+) *chariot driver* 3 Km 22:34 = 2 Ch 18:33.*

ἠνυπνια- false augm of BDAG: ἐνυπνιάζω.
ἤνυστρον see ἔν-.
ἠνωτισάμην see ἐνωτίζομαι.
ἧπαρ, -ατος, τό (21x, Hom+) *liver* Gen 49:6; Ex 29:13; Tob 6:4ff; Pr 7:23. 1 Km 19:13, 16 mistrans of כביר (h.l.) *cushion* (?) as if כבד *liver.*
ἡπατοσκοπέομαι (h.l.) *inspect liver* (for omens) Ezk 21:26.*
ἠπιότης, -ητος, ἡ (Epicurus+) *kindness* Esth 3:13b.*
ἧπται pf mid of BDAG: ἅπτω.
ἠράσω 2 sg aor mid of ἀράομαι Judg 17:2B.
ἦργμαι 3rd sg ἦρκται, pf pass of ἄρχω, in mid sense *I have begun* Num 17:11.
ηρδαλ- see αρδαλ-.
ἡρέθην aor pass of BDAG: αἱρέω.
ἠρεμάζω (LXX) *be motionless, be silent* 2 Esdr 9:3, 4.*
ἤροσαν irreg 3rd pl aor of BDAG: αἴρω Josh 3:14.

ἦσα aor of BDAG: ᾄδω.
ἠσεβηκώς pf ptc of ἀσεβέω.
ἠσθενηκώς pf ptc of BDAG: ἀσθενέω.
ἤσθοσαν Ezk 22:9 impf of BDAG: ἐσθίω/ἔσθω.
ἡστινοσοῦν see ὁστισοῦν.
ἡσυχῇ (Hdt+) *quietly, gently, stealthily* Judg 4:21A; Sir 21:20; Is 8:6.*
ἥσυχος, -ον (Hes+) *quiet, peaceful* Wsd 18:14; Sir 25:20.*
ἡττάω 2. (act: Polyb+; cf. BDAG: ἡττάομαι) *defeat, overcome* Is 54:17; Da 6:6L.‡
ἠχέω 2. (trans) *cause to resound* Is 51:15. 3. (of ears) *reverberate, feel shock* (no //) 4 Km 21:12. Job 30:4 mistrans of עלי שיח (*leaves of*) *shrub, bush* (cf. εὔηχος) as if על ישיח, fr שיח *talk.*‡
ἡψάμην see BDAG: ἅπτω.
ἡψήθη, ἥψησα see ἕψω.

Θ

θααλα (not in HR) translit of תעלה *trench* 3 Km 18:32ff.*
θαιηλαθα Ezk 40:7 MT תאים *guardrooms*; prob rd תא אל תא (*from*) *room to room* (LEH, ad loc).
θάλαμος, -ου, ὁ (Hom, Hdt+) *inner room, women's apartment* 3 Macc 1:18.*
θάλασσα 3. *west* (Heb) Josh 8:9, 12; 1 Ch 9:24.‡
θαλάσσιος, -α, -ον (Hom+) *from the sea, sea-colored* (describing both the source of the dye and the color tone; refers to ὑάκινθον as well as πορφύρον) 1 Macc 4:23.*
θαλλός, -οῦ, ὁ (Hom, Hdt+) *gift* (of branches; *cultic leafy branch or wreath* pap) 2 Macc 14:4.*
θαλπιωθ translit of תלפיות (h.l.) *stonework courses* SSol 4:4.*
θάμβος 2. *object of amazement or fear* SSol 6:4, 10.‡
θανατόω 1.b. *be fatal, cause death* (Philo Spec 1.237) Num 21:6; Eccl 10:1.‡

θανάτωσις, -εως, ἡ (Thu+) *act of putting to death* 1 Km 26:16.*
θανεῖν see θνήσκω.
θαννουριμ translit of תנורים *ovens* 2 Esdr 13:11 (cf. θενν-).*
θαραφιν see θερ-.
θαρραλέος, -α, -ον (Hom+) *daring, courageous* 4 Macc 13:13; adv 3 Macc 1:4, 23; 4 Macc 3:14.*
θαρρέω Att for BDAG: θαρσέω Pr 31:11vL, Bar 4:21vL.‡
θαρσις translit of תרשיש (*precious stone—chrysolite?*) SSol 5:14; Ezk 1:16; Da 10:6.*
θάρσος 2 Ch 16:8 renders רכב *chariotry*, unexpl; perh rel to רחב-לב θρασυκάρδιος Pr 21:4?‡
θαρσύνω (Hom, Hdt+) *encourage, make bold* Esth 4:17r.*
θαυμασμός, -οῦ, ὁ (Philod+) *wonder, (act of) wondering* 2 Macc 7:19; 4 Macc 6:13.*
θαυμαστόω (8x, Aristot+) 1. *treat wonderfully, deal marvelously with* (τινά) Ps 4:4;

(pass) 138:14. **2.** *make marvelous* (τι) Ps 15:3; (pass) *be marvelous* 2 Km 1:26; Ps 138:6.

θέα, -ας, ἡ (Hdt+) *sight, spectacle* Is 2:16; 27:11.*

θεε (13x) translit of תא (pl) תאות/תאים *guardroom* 3 Km 14:28; Ezk 40:7ff.*

θεεβουλαθω translit of תְחְבּוּלָתוֹ (MT pl) תְחְבּוּל(וֹ)ת(יו) *his piloting or guidance* Job 37:12.*

θειμ translit of תאים *guardrooms* Ezk 40:12, 14, 16.*

θεῖον, -ου, τό (8x, Hom+) *brimstone* Gen 19:24; 3 Macc 2:5; Ps 10:6; Jb 18:15; Is 30:33.‡

θεκελ translit of Aram תקל *enigmatic word on wall*, Da 5(preface)L; 5:25, 27Θ.*

θελητής, -οῦ, ὁ (LXX) *one who wills, desires or wishes* (τινός) 1 Macc 4:42; Mi 7:18. 4 Km 21:6; 23:24 mistrans of אוב *magician, wizard* as if fr אבה *desire.*

θελητός, -ή, -όν (LXX) *desired, wished for* 1 Km 15:22; Mal 3:12.*

θέμα **2.** *collection, pile* (of loaves, no //) Lev 24:6; Sir 30:18.‡

θεμελιόω 2 Esdr 7:9 mistrans of (c. MT) יסד piel (fig) *appoint, determine, initiate* as if (lit) *lay a foundation.*‡

θεμελίωσις, -εως, ἡ (ins) *laying of foundation* 2 Esdr 3:11f.*

θέμις, -ι(σ)τος, ἡ (Hom, Hdt+) *established custom, (divine) decree, (quality of) right* 2 Macc 6:20; 12:14.*

θεννουριμ translit of תנורים *ovens, furnaces* (cf. θανν-) 2 Esdr 22:38.*

θεόκτιστος, -ον (ins [II BCE]+) *created by God* 2 Macc 6:23.*

θεοτόκος, -ου ἡ (not in HR; post-NT Christian) *God-bearer, mother of God* Odes 9 superscr.*

θεράπαινα, -ης, ἡ (8x, Hdt+) *slave* Ex 11:5; Job 19:15; Is 24:2.

θεραφιν (θαρ- Judg 17:5B; 2 Ch 35:19a) translit of תרפים *figurines, idols* Judg 17:5; 18:14ff; 1 Km 15:23; 4 Km 23:24 = 2 Ch 35:19a.*

θερισμός Job 14:9; 18:16; 29:19 mistrans of קציר² *branch, bough* as if קציר¹ *harvest.*‡

θέριστρον, -ου, τό (pap) **1.** *light shawl or stole* Gen 24:65; 38:14, 19; SSol 5:7; Is 3:23. **2.** *scythe, harvest tool* (W: θεριστήριον) 1 Km 13:20.*

θεριῶ Att fut of BDAG: θερίζω.

θερμαίνω **2.** (pass) *be heated, be parched* Ps 38:4.‡

θερμασία, -ας, ἡ (Hippocr, X ANAB 5.8.15; Aristot+) *heat* Da 3:46L; (fig, no //) *passion* Jer 28:39.*

θερμαστρίς, -ίδος, ἡ (Aristot+) *pot for heating water* 3 Km 7:26, 31.*

θερμότης, -ητος, ἡ (Hippocr, Pla+) *heat* Wsd 2:4.*

θέσθαι, θέσθε 2 aor mid inf and impv of BDAG: τίθημι.

θέσις, -εως, ἡ (Pind, Aristoph, Pla+) **1.** *position, placement* 1 Esdr 1:3. **2.** (ἄστρων) *constellation* Wsd 7:19, 29. 3 Km 11:36 mistrans of ניר¹ *light, lamp* as if ניר² *plot of ground.*‡

θεσμός, -οῦ, ὁ (Hom+) *precept, custom, law* 3 Macc 6:36; 4 Macc 8:7; Pr 1:8 = 6:20; Wsd 14:23.*

θεωρητός, -ή, -όν (DiodS+) *visible* Da 8:5 Θ.*

θεωρός, -οῦ, ὁ (Soph, Pla+) *envoy, spectator* 2 Macc 4:19.*

θηλυμανής, -ές (Antimachus Colophonius [V-IV BCE], AnthPal+) *woman-crazy, obsessed w. women* Jer 5:8.*

θήρα **2.** mistrans of ציד *provisions, supplies* as if *hunting, game* Ps 131:15.‡

θήρευμα, -ατος, τό (Soph+) *prey, something hunted* Lev 17:13; Jer 37:17; *means of hunting, trap* (no //) Eccl 7:26.*

θηρευτής, -οῦ, ὁ (Hom+) *hunter* Ps 90:3; Sir 11:30; Jer 16:16.*

θηριάλωτος, -ον (9x, LXX+) *taken or killed by wild animals* Gen 31:39; Ex 22:12; Ezk 4:14.

θηριόβρωτος, -ον (DiodS 18.36.3) *eaten by wild animals* Gen 44:28.*

θηρίον **1.a.δ.** (specif) *elephant* (as used in war) 1 Macc 6:35ff; 11:56.‡

θηριόω pf pass ptc τεθηριωμένος (Pla+) *make into a beast;* (pass) *become brutal or beastly* 2 Macc 5:11.*

θηριώδης, -ες (Hdt, Pla+) *savage, brutal* 2 Macc 10:35; (superl) 4 Macc 12:13.

Adv -δῶς (Isocr, Polyb) *savagely, brutally* 2 Macc 12:15*

θησαύρισμα, -ατος, τό (Soph, Eur+) *treasure, store* Pr 21:6.*

θησαυροφύλαξ, -ακος, ὁ (pap, DiodS+) *treasurer, overseer of stores* 2 Esdr 5:14.*

θίασος, -ου, ὁ (Hdt+) *Bacchic revel or company* Wsd 12:5; Jer 16:5 (transl of מרזח *(pagan) cultic feast*; cf. Ugar [Gibson: CANAANITE MYTHS AND LEGENDS 152]).*

θῖβις, -εως, ἡ (pap) *papyrus basket* Ex 2:3, 5, 6.

θιγγάνω (rare) fut θίξω aor inf θιγεῖν (Aeschyl, X+) *touch* (τινός) Ex 12:22G (RECTE; καὶ θίξετε for καθ- mss, Ra); (τι) 19:12.*.‡

θιμωνία = BDAG: θημ- (q.l.; cf. W, Gött).

θίς, θινός, ὁ or ἡ (Hom+) *mound, hill* Gen 49:26; Dt 12:2; Job 15:7; Bar 5:7.*

θλαδίας, -ου, ὁ (Philo SPEC 1.325; =) *eunuch* Lev 22:24; Dt 23:2.*

θλάσμα, -ατος, τό (Aristot+) *bruise* Am 6:11.*

θλάω aor pass ἐθλάσθην pf pass ptc τεθλασμένος 1. *bruise, break* Sir 30:12; Is 42:3; Ezk 29:7. 2. *break, crush* Da 6:24L; (fig) *oppress* (no //) Judg 10:8; 2 Km 22:39.‡

θλίβεσθαι = θλιβῆναι 2 Km 22:7; Ps 106:6 (cf. 2 Ch 28:22).

θλιμμός, -οῦ, ὁ (LXX) *oppression* Ex 3:9; Dt 26:7.*

θνησιμαῖος, -ον (32x, LXX) *dead*; (neut subst) *carcass* (of animal; so alw in Pentateuch and Ezk) Lev 5:2; Dt 14:8; Ezk 4:14; *corpse* (of person) 3 Km 13:25; Ps 78:2; Is 5:25; Jer 41:20.

θνήσκω 2 aor inf θανεῖν.‡

θοβρος (spur; not in HR of LSJ) *f.l.* for βόθρος Ezk 32:21VL.*

θοῖνα, -ας, ἡ (Hes, Hdt+) *feast* 3 Macc 5:31; Wsd 12:5.*

θολερός, -ά, -όν (Aeschyl, Hdt+) *muddied, turbid*, > *passionate, raging* Hab 2:15.*

θραελ appar translit of תראל (t.t. meaning?), missing fr MT Ezk 41:8.*

θρασυκάρδιος, -ον (Hom+) *bold, reckless* Pr 14:14; 21:4.*

θρασύνω (Aeschyl+) *make bold or rash*; (mid/pass ptc) *emboldened* 3 Macc 1:22, 26.*

θρασύς, -εῖα, -ύ (11x, Hom+) 1. *bold* Num 13:28; Wsd 11:17. 2. *rash, arrogant* 3 Macc 2:6; Pr 9:13; Sir 4:29.

θραῦμα, -ατος, τό (Aeschyl+) = θραῦσμα Jdth 13:5VL.*

θραῦσις, -εως, ἡ (Aristot+) *shattering*; (fig, of people by war) *slaughter* 2 Km 17:9; 18:17; (fig, of people by disease) *plague* Num 17:12ff; 2 Km 24:15ff; Ps 105:23, 30; Wsd 18:20.*

θραῦσμα, -ατος, τό (Aristot+) 1. *breakage*, > *destruction* Jdth 7:9; 13:5. 2. *break, lesion* (in the skin) Lev 13:30ff; 14:54.*

θραυσμός, -οῦ, ὁ (h.l.) *breaking, weakening* Na 2:11.*

θραύω 3.b. *strike, enfeeble* 2 Km 12:15.‡

θρεπτός, -ή, -όν (Kysias+) *adopted, in one's care* Esth 2:7.*

θρέψει fut of τρέφω.

θρήνημα, -ατος, τό (Eur) *dirge, lament* Ezk 27:32.*

θρονίζω (pap) (pass) *be enthroned* Esth 1:2.*

θροῦς, -οῦ, ὁ (Hom, X+) *noise* (of music or crowd) 1 Macc 9:39; Wsd 1:10.*

θρυλέω (Eur+) *babble, repeat*; (pass) *become common talk or a byword* 3 Macc 3:6f; Job 31:30.*

θρύλημα, -ατος, τό (LXX) *common talk, byword* Job 17:6; 30:9.*

θυγάτηρ 4.b. (pl) *surrounding towns* (in neighborhood or sphere of influence of a city, s.t.) Judg 1:27; 11:26A; 1 Macc 5:8, 65; Ezk 5:14; 26:6 (Tyre).‡

θυΐα, -ας, ἡ (Aristoph+: θυεία, = Gött) *mortar* Num 11:8.*

θυΐσκη, -ης, ἡ (16x, LXX+) *censer* Ex 25:29; 3 Km 7:36; 1 Macc 1:22; Jer 52:19.

θυλάκιον, -ου, τό (Hdt+) *small sack* Tob 9:5BA.*

θύλακος, -ου, ὁ (Hdt+) *sack* 4 Km 5:23.*

θῦμα 2. *animals killed* (for food, not sacrifice; no //, but cf. BDAG: θύω) Gen 43:16; 1 Km 25:11.‡

θυμήρης, -ες comp -ρέστερος (Hom+) *very pleasing* Wsd 3:14.*

θυμιάζω (spur) Is 65:3vl; read θυσιάζω, = MT זבח *sacrifice*.

θυμώδης, -ες (8x, Aristot+) *fierce, angry* Pr 11:25; Sir 8:16; Jer 37:23.

θυρεοφόρος, -ον (Polyb+) *bearing oblong shield* 1 Ch 12:24.*

θυρόω (Aristoph, X+) *provide with doors* 1 Macc 4:57.*

θύρσος, -ου, ὁ (Eur [Bacch 80], ins+) *wand (for festal or cultic procession)* Jdth 15:12; 2 Macc 10:7.*

θύρωμα, -ατος, τό (25x, Hdt+) *doorway* 3 Km 6:31; 2 Macc 14:43; Sir 14:23; Ezk 40:38; 41:23; *door, door panel* 41:24¹,³; EpJer 17.

θυσία 2 Km 14:17 mistrans of לִמְנֻחָה *for a resting place*, > *final* as if לְמִנְחָה *for sacrifice*.‡

θυσιάζω (40x, DiodS, pap) *offer sacrifice* Ex 22:19; 2 Km 15:12; 1 Macc 1:51; Wsd 18:9; Hos 4:13; Is 65:3.

θυσίασμα, -ατος, τό (12x, LXX) *sacrifice, offering* Ex 23:18; Lev 2:13; 4 Km 5:17; 2 Esdr 6:3.

θωδαθα translit of תודות *hymns or songs of thanksgiving* 2 Esdr 22:27.*

θωρακίζω (Thu+) *arm w. breastplate*; pf pass ptc τεθωρακισμένος *armored, wearing a breastplate* 1 Macc 4:7; 6:35, 43.*

θωρακισμός, -όν (h.l.) *armored w. breastplate* 2 Macc 5:3.*

Ι

ιααρ (not in HR) translit of יער *forest* (doublet w. δρυμος) 1 Km 14:25.*

ιαμιβιν mistranslit of בימין *on the right* 4 Km 12:10.*

ιαμιν mistranslit of יעים *hearth shovels* 4 Km 25:14.*

ἰάομαι 2.c. *repair, rebuild* 3 Km 18:32.‡

ἰατής, -οῦ, ὁ (pap [IV CE]) *healer* Job 13:4.*

ἰατρεία, -ας, ἡ (Hippocr, Aristot+) *healing, recovery* 2 Ch 21:18; Jer 31:2.*

ἰατρεῖον, -ου, τό (Hippocr, Pla+) *medical care,* > *medical expense* Ex 21:19.*

ἰατρεύω (Hippocr, Pla+) *heal* Jer 37:17; 40:6; *treat medically* 28:9; (pass) *be healed, recover* 4 Km 9:15; 8:29 = 2 Ch 22:6; *be treated* Jer 37:13. 2 Ch 22:9 mistrans of חבא *hit be in hiding* as if חבש *bound, bandaged* (of wounds), or context?*

ἰατρός Ps 87:11; Is 26:14 mistrans of רפאים¹ *ghosts* as if fr רפא *heal*.*‡

ἶβις, ἴβεως, ἡ (Hdt+) *ibis* Lev 11:17; Dt 14:16; Is 34:11.*

ιγλααμ translit of הגלם (גלה) *deported them* (or N PERS?) 1 Ch 8:7.*

ἰγνύα, -ης, ἡ (Hom+) *ham, back of thigh* 3 Km 18:21.*

ἰδιόγραφος, -ον (LXX+) *separately written* (no //) Ps 151 superscr.

ἰδιοποιέω (Philod, DiodS+) *appropriate*; (mid) *win over (to oneself)* 2 Km 15:6.*

ἰδιότης, -ητος, ἡ (X+) *particular nature, individual character* 3 Macc 7:17; Wsd 2:23G (wrongly; cf. ἀϊδ-).*

ἱέραξ, -ακος, ὁ (Hom+) *falcon* Lev 11:16; Dt 14:17; Job 39:26.*

ἱερατικός, -ή, -όν (Pla, Aristot+) *priestly, sacerdotal* (in our lit, alw modifying στολή) 1 Esdr 4:54; 5:44; 2 Macc 3:15.*

ἱερεία, -ας, ἡ (ins) *cultic festival* (no //) 4 Km 10:20.*

ιερευμα (spur; not in HR, LSJ, Gött app) *f.l.* for ἱεράτευμα 2 Macc 2:17vl.*

ἱερόδουλος, -ου, ὁ (6x, pap, Strabo) *temple servant* 1 Esdr 1:3; 8:5.

ἱεροστάτης, -ου, ὁ (h.l.) *temple leader or governor* 1 Esdr 7:2.*

ἱεροσυλέω (Aristoph, Pla, ins+) *rob a temple* 2 Macc 9:2.*‡

ἱεροσύλημα, -ατος, τό (h.l.) *act of sacrilege* 2 Macc 4:39.*

ἱεροσυλία, -ας, ἡ (X, ins+) *sacrilege* 2 Macc 13:6.*

ἱερουργία, -ας, ἡ (Hdt, Pla, pap) *temple service or sacrifice* 4 Macc 3:20.*

ἱεροψάλτης, -ου, ὁ (6x, ins) *temple singer* 1 Esdr 1:15; 5:45.

ἱερόψυχος, -ον (h.l.) *having a holy soul* 4 Macc 17:4.*

ἱέρωμα, -ατος, τό (ins, Joseph+) *consecrated object or token* 2 Macc 12:40.*

ἴθι impv of BDAG: εἰμί.

ἱκανός 2.b. *"Competent One,"* N DEI (שדי *Shaddai* as if ש־די *what is sufficient*; E. Tov, *The Text-Critical Use of the Septuagint in Biblical Research* (Jerusalem: Simor, 1981), 49n; Ruth 1:20; sim μετα ικανου Job 40:2 renders אם־שדי with *Shaddai* (perh capitalize as N DEI). 4 Km 4:8 ἀφ᾽ ἱκανοῦ s.t. of מִדֵּי *from sufficiency or necessity,* > *from time to time, as often as needed.* Jer 31:30 mistrans of בד⁴ *vain speech, boast* as if fr די *sufficiency.*‡

ἱκανόω pres pass impv ἱκανούσθω (act) *let suffice, be satisfied* PsSol 2:22; (mid/pass) *satisfy, be enough, suffice* Dt 1:6; 1 Ch 21:15; SSol 7:10; Ezk 45:9; *be satisfied* Esth 4:17o; (past sense) *have been enough,* > *be over, come to an end* (no //) 3 Km 12:28 ("*Enough of going to Jerusalem!*"); Ezk 44:6.‡

ἱκετεία, -ας, ἡ (7x, Thu+) *supplication, entreaty* 2 Macc 3:18; 3 Macc 5:25; Sir 35:14.

ικετετον (spur; not in HR, LSJ, or Gött app) 2 Macc 11:6vLR.*

ἱκμάς 2. *humor, secretion;* Job 26:14 renders שֶׁמֶץ (occurs only here and 4:12; *whisper? exhalation?*).‡

ἴκτερος, -ου, ὁ (Hippocr) *jaundice* Lev 26:16; 2 Ch 6:28; Am 4:9; Jer 37:6.*

ἴκτηρ, -ερος, ὁ (dub; h.l.) *jaundice* Lev 26:16vL.*

ἱλαρόω (LXX+) *gladden, make cheerful* Sir 7:24; 35:8; 43:22.*

ἱλαρύνω (LXX+) *gladden, cheer* Ps 103:15; Sir 36:22.*

ἱλάσκομαι fut ἱλάσομαι 3. *be gracious* 2 Ch 6:30.‡

ἵλεως (τινί; cf. BDAG: Mt 16:22; BDF 128.5) *mercy* is clear meaning at Dt 21:8; 4 Macc 8:14; Am 7:2 (but note ἐσταί or γενοῦ). However, 2 Km 20:20 (εἰ + fut indic); and 2 Km 23:17 = 1 Ch 11:19 (τοῦ + inf); render חלילה (Holl "aversive negative interjection"); for 1 Macc 2:21 (inf following) the aversive sense is clear, and the underlying Heb must be as it is in 2 Km 23:17—hence these latter instances are closer to translit than to translation.‡

ἴλη, -ης, ἡ (Hdt, Soph+) *band, troop* (X ANAB 1.2.16) 2 Macc 5:3.*

ἰλύς, -ύος, ἡ (Hom+) *mud, slime* Ps 39:3; 68:3.*

ἱμάντωσις, -εως, ἡ (LXX+) *binder;* (specif) *cross-tie* (in masonry) Sir 22:16.*

ἱματιοφύλαξ, -ακος, ὁ (h.l.) *keeper of garments or wardrobe, chamberlain* 4 Km 22:14.*

ἱμείρομαι (Hom, Hdt+) = B: ὁμ- (cf. BDF 101).

ιν (21x) translit of הין (*liquid measure,* ca. 4*l*) Ex 29:40; Num 15:4ff; Ezk 4:11.

ἴνδαλμα, -ατος, τό (LXX, ins+) *phantom, hallucination* Wsd 17:3; Jer 27:39.*

ἰξευτής, -οῦ, ὁ (Lycophron+) *fowler, bird hunter* Am 3:5; 8:1, 2.*

ἰοβόλος, -ον (Aristot+) *venomous* Wsd 16:10.*

ἰόομαι (Aristot+) *corrode* Sir 12:10; 29:10.*

Ἰουδαϊστί (LXX) *in (the) Judean (language,* i.e., *Hebrew;* cf. BDAG: Εβραιστι etc) 4 Km 18:26 = Is 36:11, 13; 2 Ch 32:18; 2 Esdr 23:24.*

ἱππάζομαι (Hom, Hdt+) *ride a horse* Jer 27:42; Ezk 23:6, 12.*

ἱππάρχης, -ου, ὁ (ins, Polyb+) *master of horse, cavalry officer* 2 Km 1:6.*

ἵππαρχος, -ου, ὁ (Hdt+) *master of horse, cavalry officer* 2 Km 1:6vL.*

ἱππασία, -ας, ἡ (Aristoph, X+) *act of riding a horse* Hab 3:8 = Odes 4:8; *cavalry* Jer 8:16.*

ἱππεύω (Hdt+) *drive or ride horses* 4 Km 9:16; Ezk 23:23; (of horses) *run* (w. riders, X) Mi 1:13.*

ἱππικός, -ή, -όν (Aeschyl, Hdt+) *equestrian, mounted* (X ANAB 1.3.12) 1 Macc 15:38; 3 Macc 1:1.*‡

ἱππόδρομος, -ου, ὁ (Hom+) 1. *highway, chariot road* Gen 48:7. 2. *race course, hippodrome* 3 Macc 4:11; 5:46; 6:16.*

ἵππος, -ου, ἡ (Hdt+) *horses, cavalry* (coll sg) Gen 14:11ff; Dt 11:4.‡

ιρ (not in HR) translit of עיר *watcher, angel* Da 4:13Θ.*

ἶρις, ἴριδος or ἴρεως   2. *iris* (white or purple, Aristot+) Ex 30:24.*‡

ισανα   translit of ישנה *old* 2 Esdr 22:39 (N LOC 13:6).*

ἰσάστερος, -ον   (h.l.; HR -στηρ-) *like a star* 4 Macc 17:5.*

ἰσηγορέομαι   (h.l.; Hdt+ ἰσηγορία *equal right to speak, > political equality*) *speak as a peer* Sir 13:11.*

ἰσοδυναμέω   (Chrysipp, Polyb+) *be equivalent* Sir prol 21.*

ἰσοδύναμος, -ον   (LXX+) *equivalent* 4 Macc 3:15; 5:20.*

ἰσόθεος, -ον   (Hom, Aeschyl, Polyb+) *like a god;* (neut pl subst) *matters appropriate to God* 2 Macc 9:12R (RECTE; LECTIO DIFFICILIOR, cf. Vulg PARIA DEO).*

ἰσόμοιρος, -ον   (Soph, X+) *sharing equally* 2 Macc 8:30.*

ἰσονομέω   (Thu 6.38.5 [pass: *have equal rights, be equal*]) *deal impartially or fairly* (no //) 4 Macc 5:24.*

ἰσόπεδος, -ον   (Hom, Hdt+) *level, even; leveled to the ground* 2 Macc 8:3; 9:14; 3 Macc 5:43.*

ἰσοπολίτης, -ου, ὁ   (ins+) *one who has equal political rights* 3 Macc 2:30.*

ἰσοπολῖτις, -ίτιδος, ἡ   (LXX+) *sharing equal political rights* (of a city); > (ironic, of shared political punishments) 4 Macc 13:9.*

ἴσος   Job 41:4 mistrans of ערך *(legal) case, instance, example,* unexpl.‡

ἰσότης   Job 36:29; Zech 4:7 renders תשאות *shouts,* unexpl.*‡

ἰσόω   fut ἰσώσω pass ἰσωθήσομαι (Hom+) *be equal or equivalent,* > *compare* La 2:13G cj; *be compared* Ps 88:7; Job 28:17, 19; Is 40:25G.*

ἱστάνω   variant (Hdt+) of ἵστημι; inf ἱστῶν 2 Km 22:34 = Ps 17:34; 1 Macc 2:27; also ἱστάμενος = ἱστανομένος.‡

ἵστημι   pres opt ἱσταίην. 1 Km 28:20 ἑστηκώς renders מלא־קומתו *the fullness of his stature,* i.e., *full-length, stretched out.*‡

ἱστίον   2. *sheet, hanging* (no //) Ex 27:9ff.‡

ἱστορέω   2. (pass) *be recorded, set out, narrated* 1 Esdr 1:31; (pass ptc) 31, 40.*‡

ἱστορία, -ας, ἡ   (Hdt, Pla+) *history;* as event or process 2 Macc 2:24; 4 Macc 17:7; as narrative 2 Macc 2:30, 32; 4 Macc 3:19; as record or document Esth 8:12g.*‡

ἱστός, -οῦ, ὁ   (Hom, Hdt+) 1. *pole* Is 30:17; *mast* 33:23; Ezk 27:5. 2. *beam* (of loom); > *fabric* Tob 2:12S; Is 38:12 = Odes 11:12; (spider's) *web* Is 59:5f.*‡

ἰσχίον, -ου, τό   (Hom, Hdt+) *hip, hip joint* 2 Km 10:4.*

ἴσχυκα   pf of BDAG: ἰσχύω, ptc ἰσχυκώς Is 8:9

ἰσχύς   2. *military force, army* (X ANAB 1.8.22) 2 Km 24:2, 4. 3. *mighty deed* (no //; or ποιέω *show, manifest* [NRSV] no //, = Vulg FECIT VIRTUTEM) Jdth 13:11. SSol 2:7; 3:5 etc mistrans of אילה *doe* as if איל *strength.*‡

ἰταμία, -ας, ἡ   (LXX) *arrogance, effrontery* Jer 30:10, 20.*

ἰχθυηρός, -ά, -όν   (Aristoph+) *fishy;* (in N LOC) *Fish(-Gate)* 2 Esdr 13:3; 22:39.*

ἰχθυϊκός, -ή, -όν   (ins+) *fishy;* (in N LOC) *Fish(-Gate)* 2 Ch 33:14VL.*

ἰχνευτής, -οῦ, ὁ   (Hdt+) *tracker* Sir 14:22.*

ἰχνεύω   (Pind, Soph+) *track down, seek, follow* Pr 23:30; Sir 51:15.*

ἴχνος   3. *palm* (of hand, no //) 1 Km 5:4.‡

Κ

καδημιμ   (not in HR) translit of קדומים unknown, perh קִדְּמָם *confronted them* Judg 5:21A.*

καδησιμ   translit of קדשים traditionally *cult prostitutes* 4 Km 23:7.*

κάδιον, -ου, τό   (ins) *small container, pouch* 1 Km 17:40, 49.*

καθαγιάζω   pf pass ptc καθηγιασμένος (LXX+) *sanctify* Lev 8:9; 27:26; 1 Ch 26:20; 2 Macc 1:26; 2:8; 15:18.*

καθαρ(ε)ιότης, -ητος, ἡ (6x, Hdt+; for spelling cf. W) **1.** *purity, clarity* Ex 24:10; Sir 43:1. **2.** *cleanliness, innocence* 2 Km 22:21, 25 = Ps 17:21, 25.*

καθαριόω (pap?) *cleanse;* (pass) *be cleansed or purified* La 4:7.*

καθάρισις, -εως, ἡ (Aq, pap) *cleansing* Lev 12:4vL, 6vL.*

καθάρσιος, -ον (Aeschyl, Hdt+) *cleansing, purifying;* (subst) *expiation* 4 Macc 6:29.*

κάθαρσις, -εως, ἡ (Hdt+) *cleansing, purification* Lev 12:4, 6; Jer 32:29. Ezk 15:4 *pruning* (Theophr), mistrans of קצה *end* as if fr קצה piel *trim, prune* (reading שני *two* as if שנה *year*).*

καθεδοῦμαι fut of BDAG: καθέζομαι.

καθέδρα 2. *act or manner of sitting* Ps 138:2; *leisure, inactivity* is also possible. 4 Km 17:25; 19:27 mistrans of ישב *dwell* as if *sit*.‡

καθεισαι itac misspelling of καθίσαι Jer 16:8vL.

κάθεμα, -ατος, τό (AntiphanesCom) *necklace* Is 3:19; Ezk 16:11.*

καθέξω fut of BDAG: κατέχω Job 27:17; Da 7:18.

καθέστακα (Ra κατέστακα) pf of καθίστημι.

καθηγεμών, -όνος, ὁ (Hdt, ins+) *leader, guide* 2 Macc 10:28.*

καθηλόω (Polyb+) *nail down;* Ps 118:120 mistrans of סמר¹ *shudder, bristle* as if סמר² *nail in place* (later Heb; cf. מסמר *nail*).*‡

καθήλωμα, -ατος, τό (h.l.) *something nailed; panel? revetment?* 3 Km 6:21(vL).*

καθίγω (dub, not in LSJ) Ex 12:22 see θιγγάνω.

κάθιδρος, -ον (h.l.) *sweating profusely* Jer 8:6.*

καθιδρύω (Hom, Eur+) *dedicate, establish* 2 Macc 4:12; 3 Macc 7:20; EpJer 15.*

καθιεῖται fut mid of καθίζω Mal 3:3; Jer 39:5.

καθιζάνω (Sappho, Aeschyl+: *sit, perch*) *seat, cause to sit* (no //) Pr 18:16; Job 12:18.*

καθίζω 2 Esdr 23:27 mistrans of ישב hiph *establish in a household,* > *marry* as if *cause to dwell, settle*.‡

καθίομαι error for BDAG: καθιοῦμαι Judg 6:18B.

καθίπταμαι (h.l.) *fly down* (= καταπέτομαι) Sir 43:18.*

κάθισις, -εως, ἡ (vL -ησις dub, not in LSJ; lxx, Plu+) *sitting down, sitting position* Jer 30:2, 25.*

καθίστημι 3.b *seek to establish, declare* (w. ὡς) *falsely* (no //) 2 Macc 4:1. **4.** (2 aor) *come, (take a) stand, position oneself* 1 Km 1:9; 3:10; Jer 26:4. **5.** *set in order, restore* Is 49:8; *set in place* Jer 6:17. **6.** *become, prove to be* 2 Macc 4:50; 3 Macc 2:33. 2 Km 3:39 καθ- υπο βασιλεως mistrans of משוח מלך *anointed as king,* unexpl.‡

καθοδηγέω (Plu) *lead, guide* Jer 2:6; *lead down to destruction* Job 12:23; Ezk 39:2.*

κάθοδος, -ου, ἡ (Hdt+: *return*) **1.** *recurrence, regular occasion* (lxx+) 3 Km 9:25vL; *repetition, "over and over"* Eccl 6:6; 7:22. **2.** *way down* (Lucian+) 1 Esdr 2:18.*

καθομολογέω (Pla+) *promise,* (specif) *betroth* Ex 21:8f.*

καθοράω 2. *look down (upon)* Dt 26:15; Jdth 6:19; Job 39:26; Bar 2:16.‡

καθόρμιον, -ου, τό (pap) *necklace* Hos 2:15.*

καθυβρίζω (Hdt+) *treat w. disdain* 3 Macc 2:14; Pr 19:28; *afflict w. violence* Jer 28:2.*

καθυμνέω (Cleanthes, DiodS+) *sing a great deal, sing constantly* 2 Ch 30:21.*

καθύπερθε(ν) vL κατ-, f.l. (Hom, Hdt+) *down (from above)* 3 Macc 4:10.*

καθυπνόω (Hdt, X+) *fall asleep* Pr 24:33.*

καθυστερέω (Hippocr, Theophr+) **1.** *delay, hold back* (τι) Ex 22:28. **2.** *be kept waiting, be found wanting* 1 Ch 26:27; Sir 16:13; *lack, be in need of* (τινός) 37:20.*

καθυφαίνω pf pass ptc καθυφασμένος (lxx+) *weave through or into* Ex 28:17; Jdth 10:21.*

καινίζω (Aeschyl, ins+) **1.** (= BDAG) *make new* 1 Macc 10:10; Wsd 7:27; Zeph 3:17; Is 61:4. **2.** *innovate, introduce as new* 2 Macc 4:11.*‡

καινότης, -ητος, ἡ (Thu, Isocr+) *newness* 3 Km 8:53a; (of food) *freshness* Ezk 47:12.*‡

καινουργός, -οῦ, ὁ (Lucian: *novelty*) *initiator, contriver* (no //) 4 Macc 11:23.*

καίριος, -ον (Hom, Hdt+) *timely, seasonable* Pr 15:23.*

καίω 2 aor pass ἐκάην.‡

κακηγορέω (Pla+) *denounce, abuse, revile* 4 Macc 9:14.*

κακίζω (Hom, Hdt+) *denounce, revile;* (pass) *be denounced* (Thu 1.105.6) 4 Macc 12:2.*

κακόμοχθος, -ον (h.l.) *working evil* Wsd 15:8.*

κακοποίησις, -εως, ἡ (LXX+) *doing evil* 2 Esdr 4:22; 3 Macc 3:2.*

κακοπραγία, -ας, ἡ (Thu+) *doing wrong* Wsd 5:23.*

κακοτεχνέω (Hdt+) *plot evil* 3 Macc 7:9.*

κακότεχνος, -ον (Hom+) **1.** (of things) *craftily made, devised for evil* 4 Macc 6:25. **2.** (of people) *plotting evil, treacherous* Wsd 1:4; 15:4.*

κακότης, -ητος, ἡ (Hom, Hdt+) *badness* Pr 24:19vL.*

κακουργία, -ας, ἡ (Hom+) *treachery, acting harmfully, malice* 2 Macc 3:32; 14:22; Ps 34:17.*

κακοφροσύνη, -ης, ἡ (Oppian [H.3.363]) *recklessness, arrogance* Pr 16:18.*

κακόφρων, -ον (Pind, Aeschyl+) *reckless, imprudent* Pr 11:22; *malevolent, bad-tempered* 19:19.*

κακόω Num 29:7; 30:14; Da 10:12Θ s.t. of ענה piel *oppress,* > *humble (oneself);* cf. Lev 16:29; Da 10:12L ταπεινόω.‡

κάκωσις **2.** *distress* Wsd 3:2.‡

καλαβώτης, -ου, ὁ (pap; Aristoph+: ἀσκαλ-) *gecko, spotted lizard* Lev 11:30; Pr 30:28.*

κάλαθος, -ου, ὁ (Aristoph, Aristot+) *basket* Jer 24:1f.*

καλαμάομαι aor ἐκαλαμήσαντο inf καλαμήσασθαι (CratinusCom+) *pick up, gather, glean* (mid/pass) Dt 24:20; Sir 33:16; Is 24:13; Jer 6:9; (obj stragglers or captives) Judg 20:45; Is 3:12.*

καλάμινος, -η, -ον (Hdt+) *reed-like, straw-like* 4 Km 18:21 = Is 36:6; Ezk 29:6.*

καλαμίσκος, -ου, ὁ (Aristoph+) *tube* Ezk 25:31ff; 38:14f.*

κάλαμος SSol 4:14 mistrans of קנה *sweet cane* as if *reed, staff.*‡

καλέω Jer 41:8, 15 etc mistrans of קרא *declare, proclaim* as if *call, summon.*‡

καλλιόομαι (LXX) *be beautiful* SSol 4:10.*

καλλίπαις, gen **-αιδος** (Aeschyl, Pla+) *having beautiful children* 4 Macc 16:10.*

καλλίων, -ον comp of BDAG: καλός Jer 18:11.

κάλλος PsSol 17:12 prob mistrans of אפיו *(his) nostrils* (LXX oft θυμοῦ) as if יפיו *(his) beauty.*‡

κάλλυνθρον, -ου, τό (LXX+) *palm frond* Lev 23:40.*

καλλωπίζω (X+) *adorn, paint;* (mid) *apply cosmetics, beautify one's face* Gen 38:14; Jdth 10:4; (pass) *be adorned or decorated* Ps 143:12; Jer 10:4; 26:20.*‡

κάλος, -ου, ὁ (Hom, Hdt+) *rope, line* Num 3:37; 4:32.*

κάλπη, -ης, ἡ (Plu+) late form of κάλπις, -ιδος ἡ (Hom, Eur, Polyb+) *pitcher* 4 Macc 3:12.*

κάλυμμα **2.** *armor* (no //) 1 Macc 4:6.‡

κάλυξ, -υκις, ἡ (Hom+) *cup, pod;* ῥόδων καλ- *rosebud* Wsd 2:8.*

καλυπτήρ, -ῆρος, ὁ (Hippocr, Aristot+) *covering* Ex 27:3; Num 4:13f.*

κάλυψις, -εως, ἡ (not in HR; Schol Aristoph) *concealment* Sir 41:26R (Gött αποκαλ-).*

καλώδιον, -ου, τό (EupolisCom, Aristoph+) *cord* (dim of κάλος) Judg 15:13f; 16:11f.*

κάμαξ, -ακος, ἡ (Hom, Aeschyl+) *spear shaft* 2 Macc 5:3.*

κάματος, -ου, ὁ (Hom+) *toil, pain* 2 Macc 5:3vL.*

καμηλοπάρδαλις, -εως, ἡ (Agatharchides) lit *"camel-leopard"; giraffe* Dt 14:5.*

καμιναία, ας, ἡ (LXX) *furnace* Ex 9:8, 10.*

κάμινος Num 25:8 mistrans of (h.l.) קֻבָּה *tent, shrine,* unexpl.‡

καμπή, -ῆς, ἡ (Hdt+) *bend, turn* 2 Esdr 13:24, 31.*

κάμπη, -ης, ἡ (Hippocr, Aristot+) *caterpillar* Am 4:9; Joel 1:4; 2:25.*

καμπύλος, -η, -ον (Hom, Aeschyl+) *bent, curved* Pr 2:15.*

κἄν = καὶ ἄν, καὶ ἐάν, Is 8:14vL.‡

κάνθαρος, -ου, ὁ (Aristoph+) *beetle* (Heb *rafter*) Hab 2:11.*

κανθός, -οῦ, ὁ (Aristot+) *corner* (of the eye) Tob 11:13.*

κανοῦν, -οῦ, τό (15x, Hom+) *reed basket* Gen 40:16ff; Ex 29:3; Judg 6:19A.

κανών 4. *post, beam* Jdth 13:6.‡

κάπηλος, -ου, ὁ (Hdt+) *retailer, tavern keeper* (oft pejor—*huckster, cheat*) Sir 26:29; Is 1:22.*

καπνίζω (11x, Hom+) *give off smoke, smolder* (act, mid) Gen 15:17; Ps 103:32; Wsd 10:7; Is 7:4; (trans) *burn for smoke* (for fumigation) Tob 6:8.

καπνοδόχη, -ης, ἡ (Hdt+: -δοκ-) *smoke hole* (in roof; fr Θ, = MT) Hos 13:3vL (cf. ακρις).*

κάππαρις, -εως, ἡ (Hippocr, Aristot+) *caper-plant* Eccl 12:5.*

κάπτω (Aristoph, Aristot+) *gulp down, consume* Da 1:12L.*

καρασιμ appar translit of חרשים (Is 3:3) *magician* (though not in MT of 2K 23:24) 2 Ch 35:19a.*

καρδιόω (lexicog) *make bold or passionate* SSol 4:9.*

καρόω (Hippocr, AntiphoSoph+) *sink into deep sleep or stupor* Jer 28:39.*

καρπίζω (Eur+) *enjoy the fruit of* (τι) Josh 5:11; Pr 8:19.*

κάρπιμος, -ον (Aeschyl+) *fruitful, bearing fruit* Gen 1:11f.*

καρπόβρωτος, -ον (h.l.) *producing edible fruit* Dt 20:20.*

καρπός²; -οῦ, ὁ (Hom+) *wrist* 1 Km 5:4; Ps 127:2; Pr 31:20.*

καρπόω (Aeschyl+) *offer (as) sacrifice* (ins) Lev 2:11; Dt 26:14; 1 Esdr 4:52; Da 3:38.*

κάρπωμα, -ατος, τό (53x, Aeschyl SUPPL 1001 [dub, ed Oxford Classical Texts], Joseph: *fruit*; *thing sacrificed, offering* Ex 29:25ff; Lev 1:4ff; Josh 22:26ff.

κάρπωσις, -εως, ἡ (X, ins) *offering, sacrifice* Lev 4:10, 18; 22:22; Job 42:8; Sir 30:19; 45:16.*

καρπωτός, -ή, όν (LXX) *long-sleeved* (lit "reaching to the wrist") 2 Km 13:18f.*

κάρρον, -ου, τό (pap [II CE]+) *cart* (renders שמן *oil* [?]) 1 Esdr 5:53G.*

κάρταλλος, -ου, ὁ (pap) *basket* Dt 26:2, 4; 4 Km 10:7; Jer 6:9; (as birdcage) Sir 11:30.*

καρτερία, -ας, ἡ (6x, X, Pla+) *perseverance, endurance* 4 Macc 6:13; 8:26.

καρτερός, -ή, -όν (Hom, Hdt+) *strong; severe* 2 Macc 10:29; 12:11; 3 Macc 1:4; 4 Macc 15:32; *steadfast* 2 Macc 12:35; 4 Macc 3:12; (adv) 15:31.*

καρτεροψυχία, -ας, ἡ (h.l.) *steadfastness of spirit* 4 Macc 9:26.*

καρύα, -ης, ἡ (Soph+) *nut tree* SSol 6:11 (renders אגו *walnut tree*).*

καρύϊνος, -η, -ον (Aristoph+) *of or related to nuts;* (specif) *of walnut wood* (ins) Gen 30:17 (fr לח *almond*) Jer 1:11 (fr שקד *almond*).*

καρυΐσκος, -ου, ὁ (LXX) *almond (?) blossom* Ex 25:33f.*

κάρυον, -ου το (Aristoph+) *nut;* (perh specif) *almond* Gen 43:11; Num 17:23 (both שקד *almond*).*

καρυωτός, -ή, -όν (Strabo, ins) *embossed w. nut shapes* Ex 38:16.*

κασία, -ας, ἡ (Sappho, Hdt+) *cassia* (Sem loanword: קציעה) Ps 44:9; Ezk 27:17.*

κασσιτέρινος, -η, -ον (ins, Aristot+) *of tin* Zech 4:10.*

κασσίτερος, -ου, ὁ (Hom, Hdt+) *tin* Num 31:22; Sir 47:18; Ezk 22:18, 20; 27:12.*

κατά A.1.d. w. *respect to* ("having covered" [his head]) Esth 6:12.*‡

καταβαίνω 3 Km 6:32 mistrans of רדה hiph *subdue,* > *hammer out* as if ירד *go down*.‡

καταβάσιος, -ον (h.l.) *descending* Wsd 10:6.*

κατάβασις 3 Km 7:16 mistrans of מורד *hammered* (?, fr רדד) as if fr ירד *go down*.‡

καταβιάζω (Thu+) *urge strongly, constrain, press* Gen 19:3; Ex 12:33.*

καταβιβρώσκω aor pass κατεβρώθην (HomHymns, Hdt+) *devour;* (pass) *be*

καταβιόω

devoured or consumed 2 Esdr 12:3, 13; Sir 36:8; Ezk 39:4; Bel 32G, 42.*

καταβιόω (Pla+) *spend one's life* Am 7:12.*

καταβλάπτω (HomHymns, Pla, ins+) *inflict injury on, injure* (τινά) 3 Macc 7:8.*

καταβλέπω (LXX+) *look down* Gen 18:16.*

καταβόησις, -εως, ἡ (LXX+) *crying out, outcry* Sir 35:15.*

καταβόσκω (Theocr, ins+) *put a flock to graze* Ex 22:4¹, *graze* Ex 22:4²,³.*

καταβρωθ- see καταβιβρώσκω.

κατάβρωμα, -ατος, τό (10x, LXX) *source of food* Num 14:9; Jdth 10:12; Ezk 21:37.

κατάβρωσις, -εως, ἡ (LXX) **1.** *consumption, devouring* Gen 31:15. **2.** *food* (w. play on 1.?) Jdth 5:24.*

κατάγαιος, -ον (Hdt+) *on or under the ground;* (neut pl subst) *first-floor rooms* Gen 6:16; *underground chambers* PsSol 8:9.*

κατάγελως, -ωτος, ὁ (Aeschyl+) *laughing-stock, object of derision* Tob 8:10S; 1 Macc 10:70; Ps 43:14; PsSol 4:7; Mi 1:10G.*

καταγηράσκω (Hom, Hdt+) *grow old* Is 46:4.*

καταγίνομαι (Demosth+) *remain* Dt 9:9; *dwell* Ex 10:23; Num 5:3; Bel 21G.*‡

καταγογγύζω (h.l.) *complain against* 1 Macc 11:39.*

καταγράφω aor pass ptc καταγραφείς **2.** (pass) *be written or described* (ref to Mal 4:5, 6; rd ἕτοιμος [Gött] for ἐν ἐλεγμοῖς) Sir 48:10; *be enrolled or recorded* Num 11:26.‡

κατάγω 3 Km 6:35 unexpl; renders מישר *made even or smooth,* perh simply translator's guess by analogy w. καταβαίνω.‡

καταδαμάζω (Thu+) *subdue* Judg 14:18A.*

καταδαπανάω (X+) *squander;* (pass) *be consumed* Wsd 5:13.*

καταδείκνυμι (Hdt+) *invent, introduce* Gen 4:21; Is 40:26; 41:20; 43:15; 45:18.*

καταδέομαι aor κατεδεήθη (Pla [Apol 33e]) *plead with* (τινός) Gen 42:21; Is 57:10.*

καταδεσμεύω (LXX+) *bind* Sir 30:7, > *hold on to, repeat* 7:8.*

κατάδεσμος, -ου, ὁ (Pla+) *bandage* (no //) Is 1:6.*

καταδιαιρέω **2.** *divide up, distribute* Joel 4:2. **3.** *assess, analyze* (? renders פסג h.l. meaning?) Ps 47:14.‡

καταδιώκω **2.** *drive hard* (no //) Gen 33:13.‡

καταδολεσχέω (ins, Plu+) *chatter wearisomely* La 3:20.*

καταδρομή, -ῆς, ἡ (Thu, Pla+) *sortie, charge* 2 Macc 5:3.*

καταδυναστεία, -ας, ἡ (LXX) *oppression* Ex 6:7; Am 3:9; Jer 6:6; Ezk 22:12; 45:9.*

καταδύ(ν)ω aor κατέδυσα (Hom+) *go down, sink* Ex 15:5; Am 9:3; (trans) *cause to go down, sink* Jer 45:22G (q.l.; Heb טבע *sink*), > *forgive, dismiss* (fig) Mi 7:19; (mid/pass) *go down, be sunk* Jer 28:64.*

κατάδυσις, -εως, ἡ (Hipparchus [astronomer, II BCE]+) *descent;* 3 Km 15:13 mistrans of מגלצת *horrible thing, cause of shuddering,* unexpl.

καταθαρσέω (Polyb+) *take courage, become confident* 2 Ch 32:8.*

καταθλάω aor κατέθλασα (LXX) *crush utterly* Ps 41:11; Is 63:3.*

καταθύμιος, -ον (Hom, Hdt+) *of one's own mind, satisfactory;* (subst) *what one desires* Mi 7:3; Is 44:9.*

καταιδέομαι (Hdt, Soph+) *feel shame* (w. respect to τι) 4 Macc 3:12.*

καταικίζω (Hom, Eur, DiodS+: *mistreat* [inanimate objects, corpses]) *abuse, torment* (obj people, LXX+) 4 Macc 6:3; 7:2; 9:15; 11:1; 12:13; 13:27.*

κατακάλυμμα, -ατος, τό (12x, LXX) *covering* Ex 26:14; 38:19; Num 3:25; Is 14:11; *what is covered* 47:2.

κατακάμπτω (Eur, Pla+) *bend down;* (trans) *force down or back* 4 Macc 11:10; Ps 57:7; (pass) Ps 37:7; Odes 12:10.*

κατακάρπωσις, -εως, ἡ (LXX) *what is left from burning a sacrifice* (cf. καρπόω, κάρπωσις), *ashes* Lev 6:3, 4.*

κατάκαυμα, -ατος, τό (Hippocr, Theophr+) *burn* Ex 21:25; Lev 13:24ff; *burning* Hos 7:4; Jer 31:34; *place of burning* Num 19:6.*

κατακενόω (LXX+) *empty out* Gen 42:35; 2 Km 13:9.*

κατάκλειστος, -ον   (Callim+) **1.** *shut up, confined* 2 Macc 3:19; 3 Macc 1:18; Wsd 18:4. **2.** > *precious* Is 3:23VL.*

κατακληρονομέω   **2.** *obtain, take possession of* Dt 1:38; Ps 36:34; Sir 4:16. **3.** *dispossess, take away heritage of* (τινά) Dt 12:29. **4.** *cause to take possession, cause to inherit* 2 Km 7:1; Sir 46:1.‡

κατακληρόω   (pap, DiodS) *choose or assign by lot* 1 Km 14:42¹, 47; (pass) *be chosen* 10:20f; 14:42².*

κατάκλιστρος, -ον   (spur; not in LSJ) *f.l.* for -ιτος Is 3:23VL.*

κατάκλιτος, -ον   (h.l.) *for reclining* Is 3:23.*

κατακονδυλίζω   (Philo+) *oppress, treat badly* Am 5:11.*

κατακοντίζω   (Hdt+) *shoot down, strike down* Jdth 1:15; Job 30:14.*

κατακοπή, -ῆς, ἡ   (Theophr+) *cutting to pieces* Judg 5:26A (so HR; but cf. seq).*

κατάκοπος, -ον   (DiodS+) *very tired, exhausted* Judg 5:26A (so Ra); 2 Macc 12:36; Job 3:17; 16:7.*.

κατακόπτω   aor pass κατεκόπην pf pass ptc κατακεκομμένος Is 27:9. **3.** *cut down, massacre* Gen 14:5; Josh 10:10; Jdth 2:25; Am 1:5; Jer 20:4; (pass) *be cut down* 2 Macc 1:13.‡

κατακοσμέω   (Hom+) *adorn, decorate* Ex 39:5; 1 Macc 4:57; Is 61:10.*

κατακρατέω   (30x, Theophr+) **1.** *prevail, seize power* 3 Km 12:24u; *triumph over, take control of* (τινός) 1 Km 14:42; 2 Ch 12:4; 1 Macc 6:54; Sir 21:11; Mi 1:9; (pass) *be under control* 2 Ch 12:1; *be controlled or defeated* (by τινί) Jer 8:5 **2.** *rule* (τινά) 1 Esdr 4:2; 1 Macc 7:22; *hold, possess* (τινί) Jer 47:10; (τινός) Na 3:14¹; *retain mastery* (ὑπέρ τι) 3:14².

κατακρημνίζω   **2.** *throw down, overthrow* (city) 2 Macc 12:15.‡

κατακροτέω   (not in HR; h.l.) *applaud vigorously* Jer 27:15.*

κατακρούω   (Hippocr, Pla+) *pound, beat* Judg 16:14A.*

κατακρύπτω   (15x, Hom+) *conceal, hide* (act trans) Gen 35:4; 4 Km 7:8; 2 Macc 1:19; Ps 30:21; Is 2:18; Jer 13:4; (intr) *hide, conceal oneself* Ps 55:7; (pass, =) Josh 10:16; 2 Ch 18:24; Jer 43:19.

κατακτάομαι   aor inf κατακτήσεσθαι (Soph+) *win, gain for oneself* 2 Ch 28:10; 2 Macc 6:25.*

κατακτείνω   (Hom, Hdt+) *murder, kill* 4 Macc 11:3; 12:11.*

κατακυλίω   (Hdt+) *roll down* (trans) Jer 28:25; (pass) Judg 5:27B. 1 Km 14:8 mistrans of גלה niph *show oneself* as if גלל *roll.*

κατακύπτω   **2.** *look down* (Epict 2.16.22) 4 Km 9:32.‡

καταλαμβάνω   2 Ch 9:20 mistrans of סגור *hammered, refined* as if fr סגר *hand over, enclose.* 2 Macc 15:19 emend to καταλελειμμένοις (*left behind,* fr καταλείπω) or κατειλημμένοις, see κατειλέω.‡

καταλήγγω   *f.l.* for καταλήγω 2 Macc 7:30VL.*

καταλεαίνω   fut -λεανῶ (LXX+) *grind down* Da 7:23L.*

καταλέγω   **2.** *reckon, allege* Dt 19:16.*‡

κατάλειψις, -εως, ἡ   (Pla+ *legacy, inheritance*) *heritage, posterity* (no //) Gen 45:7.*

καταλέω   aor κατήλεσα (spur VL -λασα) (Hom+) *grind, crush* Ex 32:20; Dt 9:21; Da 2:34L.*

καταλήγω   (Aeschyl, Aristot+) *stop, cease* 2 Macc 7:30; 9:5; 3 Macc 6:32.*

κατάλημμα, -ατος, τό   (Galen+) *comprehension* (DiogL) Judg 5:13BVL.*

κατάλημψις, -εως, ἡ   (LSJ: -ληψις; Hippocr, Thu, Aristot+) *act of seizing or capturing* Dt 20:19.*

καταλιθοβολέω   (LXX+) *throw stones at, stone* Ex 17:4; Num 14:10.*

κατάλιθος, -ον   (LXX) *set w. stones* Ex 28:17 = 36:17.*

καταλιμπάνω   (alt pres of BDAG: καταλείπω) *lay aside* Gen 39:16; *abandon, forsake* 2 Km 5:21; 3 Km 18:18.*

καταλλαγή   **1.b.** *reconciliation* (of God, to people) 2 Macc 5:20. **2.** *payment, compensation;* Is 9:4 mistrans of מגלל *rolled,* unexpl.*‡

καταλλάσσω 2. *change, exchange.* Jer 31:39R *f.l.* for Gött Ατατ ἠλάλαξε (cj; = MT).‡

καταλογίζομαι (X+) *count, reckon;* (pass) *be reckoned, be considered* Wsd 5:5; Is 14:10; Da 5:17L.*

καταλοχία, -ας, ἡ (h.l.) *registration, enrollment* 2 Ch 31:18 (but *f.l.*; cf. ἐγκαταλοχίζω).*

καταλοχισμός, -οῦ, ὁ (6x, ins, pap+) *register,* (of descent or possession) *enrollment* 1 Ch 4:33; 1 Esdr 5:39.

κατάλυμα 2. *shelter* (for troops; ins), *tent* 2 Km 7:6; 1 Ch 17:5; Jer 40:12; *covert, shelter* (of lion, no //) 32:38.‡

καταλύτης, -ου, ὁ (Polyb+) *lodger, guest* Wsd 5:14.*

καταλύω Jer 45:22R see καταδύ(ν)ω.‡

καταμείγνυμι (Aristoph, X [Anab 7.2.3]+) *combine, mingle* Ex 28:14.*

καταμερίζω (X+) *apportion, allot* Lev 25:46; Num 34:29; Dt 19:3; Josh 13:14; PsSol 17:28; (pass) *be allotted* Num 32:18; 3 Macc 6:31.*

καταμερισμός, -οῦ, ὁ (h.l.) *apportionment* Josh 13:14.*

καταμεστόω (Pherecr 145.48) *fill up* (pf pass ptc) *utterly filled up* 3 Macc 5:46.*

καταμετρέω (7x, Hdt+) *measure out, apportion* Num 34:7ff; Ezk 45:1; (pass) Am 7:17; Ezk 48:14.

καταμηνιαῖος, -ον (dub, h.l.) *monthly;* (subst) *menstrual period* Esth 4:17w VL.*

καταμήνιος, -ον (Hippocr, Aristot+) *monthly;* (neut subst) *menstrual period* Esth 4:17w.*

καταμηνύω (Aeschyl, Hdt+) *inform about, make known* 4 Macc 4:4.*

καταμιμνήσκομαι (h.l.) *remind* 4 Macc 13:12.*

καταμωκάομαι (LXX+) *mock* (τινός) 2 Ch 30:10; Sir 13:7; Jer 45:19.*

καταναγκάζω (Eur+) *coerce, enforce* 1 Macc 2:15.*

καταναλίσκω fut καταναλώσω Dt 7:22; aor κατανάλωσα 1 Ch 21:26; Jer 3:24; pass καταναλώθην Is 59:14. 2. *spend, lavish* EpJer 9.‡

κατανέμω (Hdt+) *allot, divide,* (pass) *graze over, overrun* Ps 79:14.*

κατανένυγμαι pf pass of κατανύσσομαι.

κατανίκημα, -ατος τό (not in HR or LSJ) *victory prize?* Is 63:3VL.*

κατανίσταμαι (Polyb) *rise up (against)* Num 16:3.*

κατανόησις, -εως, ἡ (Pla+) *observation, careful watching* Sir 41:23.*

κατανοίγνυμι aor pass impv κατανοίγητε (Philostrat) *be opened* Ps 4:5VL.*

κατάντημα, -ατος, τό (LXX+) *end, goal* Ps 18:7.*

καταντλέω (Aristoph, Pla+) *pour over, bathe;* (pass, fig) *be flooded or submerged* (by τινί) 4 Macc 7:2.*

κατανύσσομαι pf pass κατανένυγμαι, ptc κατανενυγμένος Ps 29:13 mistrans of דמה *be silent* as if דמם *wail, lament;* cf. Ps 4:5.‡

κατανύω (Hdt, Soph+) *accomplish, complete* (a journey) 2 Macc 9:4.*

κατανωτίζομαι (ins, pap+) *turn one's back; refuse, disdain* Jdth 5:4.*

κατάξας fut of κατάγνυμι.

καταξηραίνω (Pla+) *dry out* (τι) Josh 2:10; Jdth 5:13; Hos 13:15.*

κατάξηρος, -ον (Hippocr, Aristot+) *dried out, withered* Num 11:6.*

κατάξιος, -α, -ον (Soph+) *suitable, appropriate* Esth 8:12r.*‡

καταξιόω 2. *bid, urge* 2 Macc 13:12.‡

καταξύω (Hippocr, Theophr+) *make smooth, plane;* (pass) *be planed smooth* EpJer 7.*

καταπαίζω dep fut καταπαίξεται (Aristoph+) *mock, insult* (τινός) 4 Km 2:23; Jer 2:16; (κατά τινος) 9:4.*

καταπαλαίω (Eur, Pla+) *gain the fall* (in wrestling), *overthrow* (fig) 4 Macc 3:18.*‡

καταπανουργεύομαι (h.l.) *scheme or devise wickedly* Ps 82:4.*

καταπάσσω aor mid κατεπάσομαι (Hippocr, Aristot+) *strew, sprinkle* (act or mid) Esth 4:1; 2 Macc 10:25; 14:15; Job 2:12; Mi 1:10; Jer 6:26.*

καταπάτημα, -ατος, τό (9x, LXX) *trampled-down substance or place* Mi 7:10;

Is 5:5 = Odes 10:5; Da 8:13L. La 2:8R see καταπόντισμα.

καταπάτησις, -εως, ἡ (LXX) *trampling down* 4 Km 13:7; PsSol 2:19.*

κατάπαυμα, -ατος, τό (Hom *Il* 17.38) *respite, repose* Sir 36:12.*

κατάπαυσις Judg 20:43A may arise fr textual confusion and mistrans of מנוחה *without respite* (Soggin, OTL ad loc).‡

καταπαύω **2.b.β.** *provide rest* (for τινί, no //) 2 Ch 15:15.‡

καταπείθω (LXX+) *persuade;* pf pass (cf. BDAG: πείθω) *trust* Ezk 16:15vL. 2 Km 17:16vL makes no sense; error for καταπίπτω?

καταπειράζω (Lysias, Polyb+) *make an attempt* (against τι) 2 Macc 13:18.*

καταπελματόομαι (h.l.) *be worn through in the sole* Josh 9:5.*

καταπέλτης, -ου, ὁ (Aristot, ins+) *catapult;* > *instrument of torture* (DiodS 20.71.2) 4 Macc 8:13; 9:26; 11:9, 26; 18:20.*

καταπενθέω (AnthPal) *wail, lament* Ex 33:4.*

καταπέτομαι aor κατεπετάσθην (Hdt+) *fly down* Pr 27:8.*

καταπήγνυμι aor κατέπηξα (Hom+) *plant, affix, situate* 1 Km 31:10; Hos 5:2; 9:8.*

καταπηδάω (X+) *spring off, dismount* Gen 24:64; 1 Km 25:23.*

κατάπικρος, -ον (LXX+) *bitter, harsh* 2 Km 17:8.*

καταπλάσσω (Hdt+) *plaster over* Job 37:11; (mid) *apply as a plaster* Is 38:21.*

καταπληγμός, -οῦ, ὁ (h.l.) *consternation, astonishment* Sir 21:4.*

κατάπληξις, -εως, ἡ (Hippocr, Thu+) *dread, consternation* 2 Esdr 3:3.*‡

κατάπλους, -ουν (Thu, Polyb+) *sailing down;* (subst) *voyage down* 3 Macc 4:10.*

καταπολεμέω (Thu+) *subdue in war* Josh 10:25.*

κατάπολις, gen **-ιδος** or **-εως** (h.l.; not in HR or LSJ); adj by analogy to ἀπόπολις *banished;* [trag] *in the (each and every) city* 3 Macc 3:16.*

καταπονέω aor pass κατεπονήθην (Heraclitus, Aristot, Polyb, pap+) *torment, wear down, oppress;* (pass) *be worn out or tormented* 3 Macc 2:13; La 3:49G; (ptc) *tormented, worn out, oppressed* 2 Macc 8:2G; 3 Macc 2:2.*‡

κατάπονος, -ον (Theophr+) *wearing, oppressive* 3 Macc 4:14.*

καταπόντισμα, -ατος, τό (not in HR; LSJSup) *what is drowned or destroyed; destruction* La 2:8G (Origen; MT בלע *swallow up, destroy*).

καταποντισμός, -οῦ, ὁ (Isocr+) *drowning;* Ps 51:6 mistrans of בלע *confusion* as if fr בלע *swallow up.*

καταπορεύομαι (Polyb, ins) *go back, return* 2 Macc 11:30; 3 Macc 4:11.*

καταπραΰνω aor κατεπράϋνα (Pla+) *placate, allay, appease* 2 Macc 13:26; Ps 82:2; 88:10; Pr 15:18.*

καταπρίω (Hdt+) *saw up* Sus 59G.*

καταπροδίδωμι (Hdt, Aristoph+) *betray, abandon to the enemy* 4 Macc 2:10.*

καταπρονομεύω (LXX) *carry off* Num 21:1; *plunder, despoil* Judg 2:14B.*

καταπτήσσω fut -πτήξω pf κατέπτηκα (Hom+) *cower, fear* (τι), *be in terror* Josh 2:24; Pr 28:14; 29:9; 30:30; Sir 32:18.*

κατάπτωμα, -ατος, τό (LXX+) *collapsed place, gap* (in fence) Ps 143:14.*

κατάπτωσις, -εως, ἡ (Hippocr+) *fall, collapse* 3 Macc 2:14.*

καταράκτης see καταρρ-.

κατάρασις, -εως, ἡ (LXX) *cursing* Num 23:11; Judg 5:23A; Jer 30:7. Hos 7:6cj mistrans of MT בארבם (?; Wolff Hermeneia ad loc cj בער בם *burn within them*) as if בארדם *in their cursing.**

καταράσσω see καταρράσσω.

κατάρατος, -ον (Eur, Demosth, ins+) *accursed* 2 Macc 12:35; 4 Macc 4:5.*

καταργυρόω (Hdt+) *cover or plate w. silver* Ex 27:17.*

καταρ(ρ)άκτης, -ου, ὁ (11x, adj Soph+: *swooping down*) **1.** *sluice,* in sky (e.g., for rain) Gen 7:11; 4 Km 7:2; Ps 41:8; Mal 3:10. **2.** *portcullis* Jer 20:2f; 36:26. **3.** *sea-bird* (cormorant?) Lev 11:17 = Dt 14:17. (In Lat as loanword w. all these meanings.)

καταρ(ρ)άσσω aor κατέρραξα fut pass καταρ(ρ)αχθήσεται pf pass ptc κατερραγμένος (8x, Hdt+) *hurl down* Sir 46:6; Ps 73:6; (pass) *be overthrown* Ps 36:24. Hos 7:6 cj κατάρασις, q.v.

καταρρεμβεύω (so Gött, LSJ; Ra -ρομβ-; h.l.) *cause to wander* Num 32:13.*

καταρρέω pf κατερρύηκα **2.** *fall down, drop off* (of leaves: X, Theophr) Jer 8:13.‡

καταρρήγνυμι 2 pf ptc (pass sense) κατερρήγως or -ρρώγως (Hdt, Soph+) *break down* Pr 27:9; pf ptc *torn or broken down* Josh 9:4.*

καταρρίπτω (Aeschyl+) *hurl down* La 2:1; (pass ptc) Wsd 17:17.*

κατάρρυτος, -ον (Hdt, Eur+) *watered; flowing* (αἵματι) 2 Macc 12:16.*

κατάρχω (11x, Hom, Hdt+) **1.** (act) *govern, rule* (τινός) Num 16:13; 3 Km 10:22a; Joel 2:17; (ἐν αυτοις) 2 Esdr 19:28. **2.** (mid) *begin, initiate* (prayer or song) 2 Macc 1:23; 12:37; *take the offensive, attack* 4:40; 3 Km 9:19(VL).

κατασήθω aor κατέσησα (Hippocr+) *sift* (through a sieve) Bel 14.*

κατασιγάω (Pla [PHAEDO 107a]+) *keep silent*; (pass) *be silenced* Ezk 27:32VL.*

κατασιωπάω (X+) *reduce to silence* Num 13:30; 2 Esdr 18:11; Job 37:20; 39:17.*

κατασκεδάννυμι aor κατεσκέδασεν (Aristoph+) *sprinkle* Ex 24:8.*

κατασκέπτομαι aor κατεσκέψαντο (25; Polyb+) *reconnoiter, investigate* Num 10:33; 13:2ff; Josh 7:2; Eccl 1:13.

κατασκεύασμα, -ατος, τό (Demosth+) *furnishings* Jdth 15:11R (q.l.; Gött σκεύασμα); *work of craft or art* Sir 32:6.*

κατασκευή, -ῆς, ἡ (Thu+) *outfitting, equipping* Ex 35:24; 2 Ch 26:15; 2 Macc 4:20; *construction* Num 8:4; 1 Ch 29:19; (aesthetic) *arrangement, artistry* 2 Macc 15:39; (sg or pl) *furnishings, fittings* Ex 27:19; 3 Macc 5:45.*

κατασκηνόω **1.a.** (trans, no//; =BDAG 1) *cause to dwell, settle* Num 14:30; Ps 7:6; Jer 7:12. **b.** (also trans, no//) *inhabit* Pr 2:21; 8:12; Mi 7:14.‡

κατάσκιος, -ον (Hes, Hdt+) **1.** *shaded* (= BDAG) Hab 3:3; Zech 1:8. **2.** *overshadowing, shade-giving* (Aeschyl+) Jer 2:20; Ezk 20:28.*‡

κατασμικρύνω (DemetrPhaler) *diminish, reduce,* (pass) *be made or become small* 2 Km 7:19.*

κατασπαταλάω (LXX+) *live self-indulgently* Pr 29:21; Am 6:4.*

κατασπάω (24x, Hdt+) **1.** *pull or tear down* 2 Km 11:25; Tob 13:14S; Pr 15:25; PsSol 2:19; Mi 1:6; La 3:11G; Bel 28Θ; (fig) *demoralize* 2 Ch 32:18. **2.** *breach, violate* 2 Ch 24:7.

κατασπείρω (fig) *scatter as if sowing* 3 Macc 5:26; (but to ill or no effect) Job 18:15.‡

κατασπεύδω (20x, Aeschin+) **1.** *hasten, urge on* (τινά) Ex 5:10; 2 Ch 26:20; Esth 5:5; 1 Macc 13:21; (pass ptc) *urged on* Sir 28:11a. **2.** *disturb, agitate* (no //) Da 4:19. **3.** (intr) *hasten* (no //) Ex 9:19; Dt 33:2; 1 Ch 21:30; 1 Macc 6:57; (ptc) *hastening on* Sir 28:11b.

κατασπουδάζομαι (Hdt+: *be in earnest*) *be frightened* (no //; cf. σπουδάζω) Job 23:15a.*

καταστασιάζω (X+) *stand in opposition, revolt* Ex 38:22.*

κατάστασις, -εως, ἡ (Aeschyl, Hdt+) *confrontation, (legal) pleading* (Aristot, pap+) Wsd 12:12.*‡

κατάστεμα = BDAG: κατάστημα‡

καταστενάζω (LXX+) *mourn, groan* Ex 2:23; 3 Macc 6:34; Jer 22:23; La 1:11; Ezk 9:4; 21:11.*

καταστέφω pf pass ptc κατεστεμμένος (Hippocr, Eur+) *wreathe or crown* 3 Macc 7:16.*‡

καταστηρίζω (Hippocr, Aristot+) *establish, prop in place*; (pass) *be firmly established* Job 20:7.*

καταστραγγίζω (h.l.) *squeeze out* Lev 5:9.*

καταστρατοπεδεύω (X+) *go into (military) camp* Josh 4:19; Jdth 3:10; 7:18; 2 Macc 4:22.*

καταστρέφω **4.** *turn over, yield* (one's life) 2 Macc 9:28.

καταστρώννυμι or **-ννύω** **2.b.** *spread out, spread before* (τινί) Jdth 12:1R (Gött pass; -στρωθῆναι).‡

κατασύρω fut -συρῶ (Da 11:26L rd -συρεῖ) aor κατέσυρα (Hdt+) *overwhelm, lay waste, ravage* Jer 29:10; Da 11:10L, 26L.*‡

κατασφαλίζομαι (LXX+) *make secure* 2 Macc 1:19; (pass) *be secured* 3 Macc 4:9.*

κατασχίζω (Aristoph+) *cut up, tear up* 1 Macc 1:56; Is 63:12G.*

κατατάσσω (Lysias, X+) *order, appoint* Job 7:12; 15:23; 35:10; Jer 19:8G; Ezk 44:14.*

κατατᾰχέω (not in HR; pap, Polyb+) *accelerate, push along* 1 Ch 21:6VL.*

κατατᾰχύνω (dub; not in HR or LSJ) *accelerate, push along* 1 Ch 21:6VL.*

κατατείνω fut κατατενῶ (Hom, Hdt+) *stretch taut* 1 Esdr 8:68VL; > *rack, torture* Lev 25:43ff; 4 Macc 9:13; 11:18.*

κατατέμνω (Hdt+) *gash, mutilate* Lev 21:5; 3 Km 18:28; Hos 7:14; Is 15:2.*

κατατέρπομαι (h.l.) *rejoice, celebrate* Zeph 3:14.*

κατατήκω (Hom+: *dissolve, melt*) *wear away* (Lucian) Mi 4:13.*

κατατίθημι 3. *set aside, act apart from* (τι) Esth 3:13d.*‡

κατατίλλω (Hippocr+) *pull to pieces* 1 Esdr 8:68.*

κατατιτρώσκω (X, Polyb+) *wound severely* (X *Anab* 4.1.10) 4 Macc 6:6.*

κατατολμάω (Polyb+) *recklessly presume* 2 Macc 3:24; 5:15.*

κατατρίβω aor pass κατετρίβη (Pla+) *wear out* (trans) Da 7:25L; (pass intr) Dt 8:4; 29:4; Pr 5:11; *be consumed in* (τι) Sir 26:24VL.*‡

κατατρυφάω (LXX, Lucian) *delight in, rejoice in* Ps 36:4, 11.*

κατατρώγω (CratinusCom, Aristoph+) *eat up, devour* Pr 24:22e.*

κατατυγχάνω (Demosth, Aristot+) *reach one's goal, be successful* Job 3:22.*

καταφαίνω (Hdt+) *appear, seem* Gen 48:17.*

καταφερής, -ες (Hdt+) *going down;* (subst) *sloping (ground)* Josh 7:5.*

καταφέρω 1.b. (pass) *be brought down* Is 28:2; *fall, descend* 2 Km 14:14; Ezk 47:2.‡

καταφθάνω (LXX+) *overtake, come up on* (τινά) Judg 20:42A.*

καταφθονέω (dub; not in LSJ) *be utterly resentful* Bel 12ΘVL.*

καταφλέγω aor κατέφλεξα (8x, Hom+) *burn up, consume* 2 Macc 12:6; (fig) 4 Macc 3:11; Ps 104:32; Wsd 16:18.*

καταφλογίζω (h.l.) *burn fiercely, be all-consuming* Ps 17:9.*

κατάφοβος, -ον (Polyb+) *greatly afraid, terrified* Pr 29:16.*

καταφορά, -ᾶς, ἡ (Hippocr, Theophr, ins+) *downward motion, sinking, descending* PsSol 16:1.*

καταφράσσω (LXX+) (pass) *be fortified, be covered* 1 Macc 6:38.*

καταφρόνησις, -εως, ἡ (Thu+) *contempt, humiliation* 2 Macc 3:18.*

καταφρονητέον (Philostrat+) *one must despise* Sir 22:23G.*

καταφυγή, -ῆς, ἡ (22x, Hdt+) *refuge, place of safety* Ex 17:15; Dt 19:3; 2 Km 22:3 = Ps 17:3; 2 Macc 10:28; Ps 9:10; PsSol 5:2; 15:1; Is 25:12; Da 11:39Θ.

καταφύτευσις, -εως, ἡ (h.l.) *planting* Jer 38:22.*

καταφυτεύω (25x, Strabo+) *transplant, plant* (intr) Jer 1:10; Sir 49:7; (obj field) Pr 31:16; (obj vine, vineyards) Dt 6:11; Ps 79:10; Am 9:14; Is 65:21; (obj trees) Lev 19:23; (obj people [fig]) Ex 15:17; 2 Km 7:10; 2 Macc 1:29; Ps 43:3; Am 9:15; Jer 38:28.

καταχαλάω (h.l.) *let down, lower* Josh 2:15.*

καταχαλκόω (Hdt, DiodS+) *cover or plate w. copper;* pf pass ptc κατακεχαλκωμένος *copper-plated* 2 Ch 4:9.*

καταχέω Job 41:15 mistrans of יָצַק *cast, smelt* (pass) as if *pour out* (act).‡

κατάχρεος, -ον (Polyb+) *indebted to, involved in* Wsd 1:4.*

καταχρίω (Aristot, ins) *coat, smear* Ex 2:3; Wsd 13:14.*

καταχρυσόω (17x, Hdt+) *gild, cover w. gold* Ex 25:11ff; 2 Ch 3:4ff.

κατάχυσις, -εως, ἡ (Hippocr+) *effusion, pouring;* Job 36:16 mistrans of מוּצָק² *distress, narrowness* as if מוּצָק¹ *casting, smelting* (cf. επιχυσις).*

καταχώννυμι (Hdt+) *bury, overwhelm* Zech 9:15.*

καταχωρίζω (X: *arrange*; pap, ins+) *record* 1 Ch 27:24; Esth 2:23; 3 Macc 2:29.*

καταψευσμός, -οῦ, ὁ (h.l.) *calumny, false accusation* Sir 26:5.*

καταψύχω (Aeschyl+) *cool off, rest* (no //) Gen 18:4.*‡

κατεγχειρέω (Philod+) *take in hand, undertake*, > *propose, plot;* (pass ptc subst) *proposed or plotted matter or act* 3 Macc 1:21.*

κατεδέθη aor pass of BDAG: καταδέω.

κατειλέω pf pass ptc κατειλημένος (not in HR; cf. συνειλέω; Hdt, X, Joseph+) *confine, crowd, coop up* 2 Macc 15:19cj (some Lat mss CONCLUSI).

κατεῖπα or -πον (Hdt, Eur+) *speak against, denounce* Num 14:37.*

κατελεέω (Pla+) *treat w. kindness or mercy* (Polyb 2.6.2) 4 Macc 8:10.*

κατεμβλέπω (LXX+) *look in the face* Ex 3:6.*

κατεναντίον = BDAG: κατέναντι.

κατεντευκτής, -οῦ, ὁ (h.l.) *accuser* Job 7:20.*

κατενύχθησεν aor pass of κατανύσσομαι.

κατεπείγω (Hom+) *press hard* (as a creditor) Ex 22:24.*

κατεπικύπτω (h.l.) *stoop over, lean upon* Esth 5:1d.*

κατεπλάγην aor pass of BDAG: καταπλήσσω Josh 5:1; ptc 3 Macc 1:9.

κατεραυνάω (LSJ: -ρευν-, h.l.) *thoroughly search or expose* Jer 30:4vl.*

κατεργάζομαι 2.b. *make, cause to be* (w. adj of qual) PsSol 17:37.‡

κατεργασία, -ας, ἡ (Hippocr, Aristot+) *working out, production, realization* 1 Ch 28:19.*

κάτεργον, -ου, τό (Theophr, pap: *wage, cost of labor*) *resource or equipment* (for tabernacle service, no //) Ex 30:16; 35:21.*

κατεσκάφην aor pass of BDAG: κατασκάπτω Pr 11:11; Joel 1:17; Jer 2:15; fut pass κατασκαφήσομαι Am 3:14; pf pass ptc κατεσκαμμένος 9:11.

κατέστακα or καθέστακα = καθέστηκα pf of καθίστημι Jer 1:10.

κατευθικτέω (h.l.) *hit precisely or accurately* 2 Macc 14:43.*

κατευθύνω 2. (intr, no //) *go straight forward* 1 Km 6:12; Ps 58:5; (fig) *proceed without deviation* Ezk 18:25; *succeed in* (+inf) Judg 12:6; *flourish* Ps 100:7; Sir 29:18. 2 Km 19:18 mistrans of חלצ (hiph? qal?) *wade through* as if *succeed* (cf. Aram; McCarter AB).‡

κατευφημέω (ins+) *praise, applaud* 3 Macc 7:13.*

κατεύχομαι (Aeschyl, Hdt+) 1. *pray fervently* 2 Macc 15:12. 2. *pray against, imprecate, call down curses* 4 Macc 12:19.*

κατέχω 1.b.β. (obj materials) *hold together, cover over* 4 Km 12:13.‡

κατηγόρημα, -ατος, τό (Pla+) *accusation* 2 Macc 4:47vl.*

κατήλεσα aor of καταλέω.

κατηράθην aor pass of BDAG: καταράομαι.

κατηφής, -ές (Hom, Eur+) *obscure, dim* Wsd 17:4.*‡

κατισχύω 3. (trans) a. *strengthen* (τι) 4 Km 22:5; Ezk 30:24 (τινά) Da 10:18L; *cause to prevail* (τινά) Ex 18:23; Dt 1:38; Judg 7:8B; 9:24A; 1 Esdr 7:15; Ezk 3:8. b. *conquer, overpower* 2 Ch 8:3; Is 42:25; Da 11:5L.‡

κατοδυνάω pf pass ptc κατωδυνωμένος or (Ezk 9:4G) κατοδ- (LXX) *make miserable, afflict* Ex 1:14; (pass) *suffer, be afflicted* Tob 8:20S; Ezk 9:4.*

κατοικεσία, -ας, ἡ (LXX+) *dwelling, act or place of inhabiting* Ps 106:36; La 1:7G.*

κατοίκησις 2. *household*, (coll) *residents* (no //) 2 Km 9:12.‡

κατοικία 2. *community of residents, settlement* Jer 3:6; Ezk 48:15.‡

κατοικοδομέω (X+) pf pass ptc κατῳκοδομημένος (subst) *place for building houses* Gen 36:43.*

κάτοικος, -ου, ὁ (Aristot+) *inhabitant* Gen 50:11; Josh 8:20; 1 Macc 1:38; Pr 31:23.*

κατοικτίζω (Aeschyl, Hdt+) *arouse or cause pity* (Soph OEDCOL 1282) 4 Macc 13:27vl.*

κατοινόομαι (not in HR; Pla LEG) only pf pass ptc κατοινωμένος *wine-drenched*, (subst) *drunken person* Hab 2:5.*

κατοίομαι   (Philo) *be insolent;* (pres ptc subst) *insolent person* Hab 2:5vL.*

κατόπισθεν   (25x, Hom+) **1.** *after, behind* (prep w. gen) Gen 37:17; Ruth 2:2; 1 Macc 10:79; Pr 24:27; Zech 6:6; *in place of, after* Da 8:8L. **2.** *next to* Judg 18:12A; 2 Esdr 14:7.

κατοπίσω   (h.l.) *behind* (prep w. gen) Judg 18:22A.*

κατοπτεύω   (Soph, Polyb+) *observe closely* Esth 8:12d.*

κάτοπτρον, -ου, τό   (Aeschyl+) *mirror* Ex 38:26.*

κατόρθωσις, -εως, ἡ   (Hippocr+) *setting straight, setting upright* 2 Ch 3:17; Jdth 11:7; Ps 96:2.*

κατορύσσω   aor pass κατωρύγη vL -ύχθη (10; Hdt+) *bury in the earth* Gen 48:7; Josh 24:32f; Tob 14:6BA, Am 9:2; Jer 13:7.

κατορχέομαι   (Hdt+) *dance in triumphant mockery,* > (Strabo 17.1.17) *dance w. contemptuous or disreputable abandon* Zech 12:10.*

κατοχεύω   (LXX+) *cross-breed* Lev 19:19.*

κατόχιμος, -η, -ον   (pap+) *held (long-term), possessed* Lev 25:46.*

κάτοχος, -ον   (Aeschyl+) *holding fast* Jon 2:7.*

κατώδυνος, -ον   (LXX) *anguished, afflicted* Judg 18:25A; 1 Km 1:10; 22:2; 30:6; 4 Km 4:27.*

κάτωθεν   (8x, Aeschyl+) *from below, underneath* Ex 26:24; Dt 33:13; Is 14:9.

κατῴκισται   pf pass of κατοικίζω Ps 92:1.

κατώτατος   superl of κάτω; *lowest* La 3:55. (subst) *lowest place* Ps 62:10; Odes 12:13; (adv) κατωτάτω (Hdt) Tob 4:19S, impr prep w. gen (cf. seq) *far below* Tob 13:2S.‡

κατώτερον   (neut of κατώτερος; as prep w. gen) *below, to the south of* Gen 35:8.

καυλός, -οῦ, ὁ   (Hom+) *stem (of menorah)* Ex 25:31; 38:13; Num 8:4.*

καυστικός, -ή, -όν   (Aristot+) *burning, capable of burning* 4 Macc 6:27; (comp) 10:14.*

καυτήριον, -ου, τό   (DiodS+) *branding iron* 4 Macc 15:22.*

καυχάομαι   **3.** *talk loudly, shout* Da 5:6L.‡

καύχησις, -εως, ἡ   (10x, Epicurus, Philod, NT+) *boasting* Sir 31:10. 1 Ch 29:13; Pr 16:31; Ezk 16:12, 17, 39; 23:26, 42; 24:25 mistrans of תפארה *decoration, splendor* as if *arrogance, boasting.* Jer 12:13 mistrans of תבואה *produce, harvest* as if תפארת *boasting?*‡

καφουρη   translit of כפורי *bowls* (cf. κεφφουρη/ε) 2 Esdr 8:27.*

καψάκης, -ου, ὁ   (vL καμψ-; ins, pap) *flask* 3 Km 17:12ff; 19:6; Jdth 10:5.*

κέγχρος, -ου, ὁ   (Hes, Hdt+) *millet* Ezk 4:9.*

κέδρινος, -η, -ον   (27x, Hom+) *of cedar* Lev 14:4ff; 2 Km 5:11 = 1 Ch 14:1; 1 Esdr 4:48; SSol 8:9

κεινηθήσεται   itac misspelling of fut pass of κενάω (dub, = κενόω, not in HR or LSJ) Ps 103:5vL.*

κεῖνος   = BDAG: ἐκεῖνος Wsd 12:10vL.*

κειρία   **2.** *bedding,* (pl) *bedclothes* Pr 7:16.*‡

κείρω   fut κερῶ pf pass ptc κεκαρμένος **2.** *cut close,* > *mow, harvest* (hay or grass, no //; κείρω w. respect to agricultural land means *ravage, plunder*) Pr 27:25 (renders נראה *appear, come to be visible,* unexpl).‡

κεκαρμένος   pf pass ptc of κείρω.

κεκατηραμένος   pf pass ptc of καταράομαι, w. false redupl of prefix as well as root (cf. BDAG) Sir 3:16.

κεκλεμμένος   pf pass ptc of κλέπτω.

κεκλιμένος   pf pass ptc of κλίνω.

κεκραμένος   alt pf pass ptc of BDAG: κεράννυμι.

κεκριμένος   pf pass ptc of BDAG: κρίνω.

κενεών, -ῶνος, ὁ   (Hom, X+) **1.** *hollow, soft space between ribs and hip, flank* 4 Macc 6:8. **2.** *hollow* (in land); > *empty space* (in crowd, no //) 2 Macc 14:44.*

κενιει   itac misspelling of καινίζω (3rd sg fut καινιεῖ, q.l. w. Gött) Sir 38:28vL.*

κενολογέω   (Aristoph+) *speak foolishly* Is 8:19.*

κενός   διὰ κενῆς (= BDAG 3εἰς κενόν) *to no purpose, uselessly* 1 Macc 6:12; Ps 24:3; Pr 23:29; Sir 23:11.‡

κενοτάφιον, -ου, τό   (X+) *tomb, cenotaph;* 1 Km 19:13, 16 renders תרפים *household god*—was translator thinking of (rationalizing?) a human-shaped coffin, e.g., from Egypt?*

κεντέω (Hom, Hdt+) *stab, goad* Job 6:4.*

κεπφόομαι aor pass ptc κεπφωθείς (Cicero [I BCE]; fr κέπφος, a type of *seabird*, > [fig, Aristoph] *birdbrain*) *be a birdbrain* Pr 7:22.*

κεράμεος, -α, -ον or **κεραμεοῦς, -ᾶ, -οῦν** (not in HR; Pla, Theophr+) *of clay or earth* Da 2:41 VL.*

κέρας **1.b.** *horn used as musical instrument* (X ANAB 2.2.4) 1 Ch 25:5. **2.b.** (military) *end or wing of an army* 1 Macc 9:1.‡

κερασθείς aor pass ptc of BDAG: κεράννυμι Bel 11G.

κέρασμα, -ατος, τό (Zeno+) *mixture, mixed or poured drink* Ps 74:9; Is 65:11; Jer 31:12G (Ra κερατα but MT נבל *jar*; better κεραμιον [Gött VL, cj], which also accords better w. συγκόπτω).*

κεράστης, -ου, ὁ (Soph+ as adj *horned*) *horned serpent* (= Heb) Pr 23:32.*

κερατίζω (12x, LXX+) *gore* (w. horns), *butt* Ex 21:28ff; Dt 33:17; (fig) 3 Km 22:11 = 2Ch 18:10; Ps 43:6; Jer 27:11; *charge, attack* Da 8:4.

κεράτινος, -η, -ον (23x, X+) *made of horn* Ps 97:6; (fem subst) *horn, trumpet* (= Heb שופר, no //) Judg 3:27; 2 Km 15:10; 2 Ch 15:14; 2 Esdr 14:12.

κερατιστής, -ές (LXX) *given to goring or butting* Ex 21:29, 36.*

κεραυνός, -οῦ, ὁ (Hom, Hdt+) *thunderbolt* 2 Macc 10:30; Job 38:35; Wsd 19:13.*

κεραυνόω (Hdt+) *thunder, hurl a thunderbolt* Is 30:30.*

κέρκος, -ου, ὁ (Aristoph+) *tail* Ex 4:4; Judg 15:4; Pr 26:17.*

κέρκωψ, -ωπος, ὁ (Hdt+) *person w. tail, monkey-like person*, > *scoundrel, trickster* Pr 26:22.*

κεφάλαιον **2.b.** *principal amount* Lev 5:24; Num 5:7. **c.** *sum total, total amount* Num 4:2; 31:26.‡

κεφαλή **2.c.** *capital* (of column or pillar) 3 Km 7:16; 2 Ch 3:15. **d.** *column* (of soldiers), *advance guard* Job 1:17. κατὰ κεφαλήν Num 1:2, 18; 3:27; 1 Ch 23:3, 24 (לגלגלתם) *individually, person by person, by headcount.* Sir 25:15 mistrans of ראש² *poison, venom* as if ראש¹ *head*.‡

κεφαλίς **2.** *extremity, capital* Ex 26:24; Num 3:36.‡

κεφφουρε, κεφφουρη translit of כפורי *bowls* 1 Ch 28:17; 2 Esdr 1:10 (cf. καφουρη).*

κεχρημένος see χράομαι.

κέχυται pf pass of χέω.

κέχωσται pf pass of χόω.

κηδεία, -ας, ἡ (Eur, ApollonRhod, ins+) *care for the dead*, (specif) *funeral* 2 Macc 4:49; 5:10.*

κηδεμονία, -ας, ἡ (Pla, ins+) *care, oversight, service* 4 Macc 4:4, 20.*

κηδεμών, -όνος, ὁ (Hom+) *one who cares; guardian, protector* 2 Macc 4:2.*

κηλιδόω (Eur, Aristot+) *stain, defile* Jer 2:22; Da 11:33L.*

κηλίς, -ῖδος, ἡ (Aeschyl+) *blemish, stain* 2 Macc 6:25; Wsd 13:14.*

κημός, -οῦ, ὁ (Aeschyl, X+) *muzzle* Ps 31:9; Ezk 19:4, 9.*

κηρίον Ezk 20:6, 15 renders צבי *ornament, glory*, unexpl.‡

κηρογονία, -ας, ἡ (h.l.) *shaping of wax, forming of honeycombs* 4 Macc 14:19.*

κηρός, -οῦ, ὁ (7x, Hom+) *wax* Jdth 16:15; Ps 21:15; Mi 1:4; Is 64:1.

κίβδηλος, -ον (Hdt+) *adulterated* Lev 19:19; Dt 22:11; (fig) *fraudulent, crude* Wsd 2:16; (subst) *false god* 15:9.*

κίδαρις, -εως, ἡ (14x, Ctesius+) *Persian-style headdress, turban* Ex 28:4ff; Lev 8:13; 1 Esdr 3:6; Sir 45:12; Zech 3:5; Ezk 21:31.

κίνημα, -ατος, τό (Aristot+) *commotion, disturbance* 1 Macc 13:44, > (bodily) *sensation* 4 Macc 1:35.*

κινητικός, -ή, -όν (Hippocr, Pla, X+) *mobile*; (comp) *more mobile* Wsd 7:24.*

κινύρα, -ας, ἡ (22x, LXX, Joseph) *lyre* (Heb כנור) 1 Km 10:5; 2 Ch 5:12; 1 Macc 3:45; Sir 39:15.*

κιρνάω (Hom+) *mix* Ps 101:10.*

κισσός, -οῦ, ὁ (Soph+) *ivy* 2 Macc 6:7.*

κισσόφυλλον, -ου, τό (LXX+) *ivy leaf* 3 Macc 2:29.*

κιχράω fut κίχρῶ = BDAG: κίχρημι.

κίων, κίονος, ὁ (Hom+) *pillar* (of building) Judg 16:25Bff. 3 Km 15:15 mistrans of קדש

sacred gift as if קדש *tower, pillar* (opp error in Ezk 27:6).*

κλαίω   3 Km 18:45 mistrans of וירכב *and he mounted* as if ויבך *and he wept.*‡

κλαυθμών, -ῶνος, ὁ   (LXX) *place for crying.* 2 Km 5:23f; Ps 83:7 mistrans of בכא *N LOC* as if fr בכה *weep.**

κλαυσθήσονται   fut pass of κλαίω.

κλείς   3. *lock* Bel 11G. 4. *collarbone* (Hom+) Job 31:22 (Heb שכם *shoulder*).‡

κλ(ε)ιτύς, -ύος, ἡ   ([c. accent Ra; c. LSJ, cf. BDAG: κλείω] Hom+) *rear, inner or closed-off portion* Ps 127:3 [Gött vl fem def art; rd ταῖς κλ(ε)ιτέσι].*

κλέπτω   2. *come covertly, act deceitfully* Sus 12G.‡

κλεψιμαῖος, -α, -ον   (LXX+) *stolen*, (subst) *stolen object* Tob 2:13.*

κληδονίζομαι   (LXX+) *be a seeker of omens* Dt 18:10; 4 Km 21:6 = 2 Ch 33:6.*

κληδονισμός, -οῦ, ὁ   (LXX) *conjurer, omen interpreter* Is 2:6.*

κληδών, -όνος, ἡ   (Hom+) *omen* Dt 18:14.*

κληματίς, -ίδος, ἡ   (Thu+) *small branch* Dt 32:32 = Odes 2:32; Is 18:5; (coll sg) *brushwood* Da 3:46.*

κληροδοσία, -ας, ἡ   (DiodS) *hereditary (right of) possession* 1 Macc 10:89; Ps 77:55; Eccl 7:11; Da 11:21L, 34L.*

κληροδοτέω   (LXX+) *give as an inheritance* 2 Esdr 9:12; Sir 17:11; *distribute* (w. cogn acc) Ps 77:55.*

κληρονομέω   3. *dispossess, disinherit* (s.t. of ירש, no //) Dt 12:2; Zech 9:4; Is 17:14.‡

κληρονόμος   3. *dispossessor* (no //; cf. κληρονομέω) Jer 8:10.‡

κληρουχία, -ας, ἡ   (Isocr, ins, pap) *allotment of land* (esp to foreigner or settler) 2 Esdr 21:20vl.*

κληρόω   Is 17:11 mistrans of נחלה *disease* as if נחלה *inheritance* (see also πατήρ).‡

κληρωτί   (LXX) *by lot* Josh 21:4ff.*

κλητέον   (Pla+) *it must be called or named* (Pla Rep 470d) EpJer 39, 44, 63.*

κλητός   2. (fem subst) *summoned assembly* (no //; renders מקרא) fem by attraction to ἑορτή Lev 23:2 or ἡμέρα Ex 12:16; Num 28:25.‡

κλίμα   2. *direction* (e.g., North, East). Judg 20:2A mistrans of פנות *towers*, (fig) *leaders* as if fr פנה *turn in a specific direction* (κατὰ πρόσωπον in B txt as if related to פנים *face*).‡

κλιμακτήρ, -ῆρος, ὁ   (Eur, ins+) *rung* (of ladder), > *step* Ezk 40:22ff; 43:17.*

κλίνω   pf pass ptc κεκλιμένος 3. (trans) *turn, incline* Ps 20:12.‡

κλίτος, -ους, τό   (47x, Lysias) *slope, cliff* (cf. κλειτύς) 2 Km 16:13vl; *side* (no //) Ex 25:12ff; 3 Km 7:39; 2 Ch 29:4; Ps 90:7; Ezk 46:21ff.

κλοιός, -οῦ, ὁ   (22x, Eur+) *collar* (of gold, as ornament, Eur Cycl 184) Gen 41:42; 1 Ch 18:7; Pr 1:9; for animals Judg 8:26A; (of iron) Dt 28:48; (wood, X HG 2.4.41) Jer 34:2; 35:10, 12; (or either) 35:13; (for prisoners) 3 Km 12:4ff; (slaves [fig]) Sir 6:24, 29. Hab 2:6 mistrans of עליו *upon him* as if עלו *his yoke*. Da 8:25Θ mistrans of על *upon, against* as if על *yoke*.*

κλοποφορέω   (h.l.) *rob, steal from* Gen 31:26.*

κλώθω   in our lit, alw pf pass ptc κεκλωσμένος (32; Hdt+ [Hom in compounds]) *spin;* (pf pass ptc) *spun* Ex 25:4; 26:1ff; Lev 14:4ff; Sir 45:10.‡

κλών, κλωνός, ὁ   (Soph+) *twig, slip* Job 40:22; Wsd 4:5. Job 18:13 mistrans of (עורו) בדי *pieces* (of his skin) as if בד *shoot*.

κλῶσμα, -ατος, τό   (ins+) *thread* Num 15:38; Judg 16:9A; Sir 6:30.*

κλωστός, -ή, -όν   (AeneasTact+) *spun* Lev 14:6.*

κνήμη, -ης, ἡ   (Hom+) *leg, shin* Dt 28:35; Judg 15:8B; Ps 146:10; SSol 5:15; Is 47:2; Da 2:33Θ.*

κνημίς, -ῖδος, ἡ   (Hom+) *greave, shin guard* 1 Km 17:6.*

κνήφη, -ης, ἡ   (h.l.) *itch, infection* Dt 28:27.*

κνίδη, -ης, ἡ   (Hippocr, Aristot+) *nettle* Job 31:40.*

κνίζω   (Pind, Hdt+) *scratch, nick* Am 7:14.*

κνώδαλον, -ου, τό   (Hom+) *wild animal, brute* Wsd 11:15; 16:1; 17:9.*

κοθωνός, -οῦ, ὁ (not in LSJ) translit/loanword fr כתנת *tunic* (cf. *VL* χιτῶν) 2 Esdr 2:69.*

κοιλάς, -άδος, ἡ (48x, Polyb+) **1.** *hollow, indentation* Lev 14:37. **2.** *valley* Gen 14:8; Josh 17:16; 1 Ch 11:15; Ps 59:8; SSol 2:1; Hos 1:5; Jer 21:13.

κοίλασμα, -ατος, τό (LXX+) *hollow, pit, indentation* Is 8:14.*

κοιλία SSol 5:14 mistrans of מעים (*exterior*) *stomach, lower torso* as if (*interior*) *stomach, body cavity* (so 5:4); 7:3 mistrans of בטן (*exterior*) *belly* as if (*interior*) *belly, womb.*‡

κοῖλος, -η, -ον (Hom+) *hollow* Ex 27:8; *depressed* Lev 13:32, 34; (fem subst) *hold* (of ship) Jon 1:5; (neut pl) *boots, shoes* (cf. Aelian *NAT AN* 6:32) Josh 9:5.*

κοιλοσταθμέω (LXX) *provide with vaulted ceiling* 3 Km 6:9, 15.*

κοιλόσταθμος, -ον (pap, ins) *with vaulted (or embossed) ceiling* Hg 1:4.*

κοιλότης, -ητος η (Aristot+) *hollow, valley* Wsd 17:18.*

κοίλωμα, -ατος, τό (Aristot+) **1.** *niche, hollow, cavity* 2 Macc 1:19; Ezk 43:14; *indentation, fluting* 3 Km 7:3. **2.** *basin, valley* Gen 23:2; SSol 2:17; 8:14.*

κοιμάω 1.b. *lie down* 2 Km 13:31; (euphem) *have sex* (Hom, Hdt+) Lev 15:18; 2 Km 11:4; EpJer 43. **3.** (fig, pass) *be laid aside for the night* (no //) Ex 23:18; Lev 19:13; Josh 6:11.‡

κοιμίζω (14x, Soph+) *cause to lie down* Gen 24:11; *lay, place* (τι) 2 Km 8:2; 2 Ch 16:14; (τινά) 3 Km 3:20; *lay down* 17:19; *cause to sleep* Judg 16:19; Job 24:7; (fig) *put to death* PsSol 2:31; Na 3:18

κοινολογέομαι (Hdt+) *deliberate together* 1 Macc 14:9; *negotiate* 15:28.*

κοινολογία, -ας, ἡ (Hippocr, Polyb+) *discussion, deliberation* 2 Macc 14:22.*

κοινός 1.a.β. *public, of or related to the state* 2 Macc 15:6.‡

κοινωνέω 4. *communicate w.* (τινί) 3 Macc 4:11; *have dealings w.* (Pla, Aristoph), *join oneself* (πρός τινα *to someone*) 2 Ch 20:35.‡

κοινῶς 2. *together* Tob 2:2S; 5:13BA, 9:6.‡

κοιτάζω (9x, Pind+) *lie down* (mid) Lev 15:20; Ps 103:22; Zech 2:14; Da 4:15Θ; *bed down* (act caus, subj shepherds) SSol 1:7; Jer 40:12.

κοιτασία, -ας, ἡ (h.l.) *sexual contact or activity* Lev 20:15.*

κοίτη 3. *lair, nest* (Eur+) PsSol 17:16; Is 11:8.‡

κολάπτω pf pass ptc κεκολαμμένος (Hippocr, Aristot+) *carve, chisel, engrave* Ex 32:16; 3 Km 7:46, 49; 3 Macc 2:27; Sir 45:11.*

κολαστήριον, -ου, τό (LXX+) *instrument of punishment or torture* 4 Macc 10:4VL.*

κολεός, -οῦ, ὁ (Hom+: κουλεόν, κολεόν) *scabbard* 2 Km 20:8; 1 Ch 21:27; Jer 29:6; Ezk 21:8ff.*

κόλλα, -ης, ἡ (Hdt+) *glue* Is 44:13.*

κόλλησις, -εως, ἡ (Hdt+: *joining by solder or glue*) *steadfast union or friendship* Sir 25:12(VL).*

κολλύρα, -ας, ἡ (Aristoph+) *loaf of bread* 2 Km 13:6VL.*

κολλυρίζω (LXX) *bake* 2 Km 13:6, 8.*

κολλύριον, -ου, τό (LXX) *loaf of bread* (dim of κολλύρα or κολλυρίς) 3 Km 12:24h, i, l, 14:3(VL).*‡

κολλυρίς, -ίδος, ἡ (LXX) *loaf of bread* 2 Km 6:19; 13:6, 8, 10.*

κολοβόκερκος, -ον (h.l.) *w. docked tail* Lev 22:23.*

κολοβόριν, gen **-ινος** (h.l.) *w. nose mutilated or cut off* Lev 21:18.*

κολοκύνθη, -ης, ἡ (Aristot+; VVLL -τη or -θα, =) *gourd plant* Jon 4:6ff.*

κόλπος 3.b. *hollow* (of bottom of chariot) 3 Km 22:35. Hos 8:1 mistrans of חֵךְ *palate, mouth* as if חֵיק *lap, bosom.*‡

κόλπωμα, -ατος, τό (LXX+) *depression, recess* (no //) Ezk 43:13.*

κομιδῇ (Aristoph, Pla+) *completely, altogether* 4 Macc 3:1.*

κόμμα, -ατος, τό (Aristoph+) *coinage* 1 Macc 15:6.*

κόνδυ, -υος, τό (9x, Menand+) *cup* Gen 44:2ff; Is 51:17, 22.*

κονδυλίζω (Hyperid) *beat* (with fists), *oppress, maltreat* Am 2:7; Mal 3:5.*

κονδυλισμός, -οῦ, ὁ   (LXX+) *beating, cruel act* Zeph 2:8.*

κονία, -ας, ἡ   (Hom+) *lime, plaster, whitewash* Dt 27:2, 4; Job 28:4; 38:38; Am 2:1; Is 27:9.*

κονίαμα, -ατος, τό   (Hippocr, Demosth+) *plaster, whitewash* Da 5:1L, 5.*

κόνις, -εως, ἡ   (Hom, Aeschyl+) *dust* 3 Macc 1:18; 4:6.*

κοντός, -οῦ, ὁ   (Hom, Hdt+) *pole, shaft* 1 Km 17:7; *pike* Ezk 39:9.*

κόνυζα, -ης, ἡ   (HecataeusMil, Aristot+) *fleabane* (genus INULA) Is 55:13.*

κοπάζω   2. (trans) *cause to abate or grow calm* (no //) Sir 39:28; 43:23.‡

κοπανίζω   pf pass ptc κεκοπανισμένος (LXX+) *grind* Da 7:7L; (ptc) *ground, milled* (of flour) 3 Km 2:46e; 5:2.*

κοπήσομαι   fut pass of BDAG: κόπτω; *be mourned* Jer 16:4.

κοπόω   (LXX+) *exhaust, weary* 1 Macc 12:44R; (RECTE) Eccl 10:15; (pass ptc) *wearied* Jdth 13:1.*

κόπτω   1.b. *cut down, kill* Judg 1:4B; 20:43A. κόπτω συνθήκην *make a covenant* (Heb) 4 Km 17:15VL.‡

κόπωσις, -εως, ἡ   (h.l.) *weariness, (state or act of) making weary* Eccl 12:12.*

κορέω   fut κορησουσι(ν) by-form of BDAG: κορέννυμι (Hdt+) (intr) *be satisfied* Dt 31:20.*‡

κόριον, -ου, τό   (pap+) *coriander* Ex 16:14, 31; Num 11:7.*

κόρος², -ου, ὁ   (Hom+) *satiety, abundance* Esth 8:12c.*‡

κορύνη, -ης, ἡ   (Hom, Hdt+) *club, mace.* 2 Km 21:16 renders חדשה *new,* unexpl.

κόρυς, -υθος, ἡ   (Hom+) *helmet* Wsd 5:18.*

κορυφή, -ῆς, ἡ   (52x, Hom+) **1.** *head* Gen 49:26; Ps 7:17; Pr 1:9; Ezk 8:3; Da 4:9L. **2.** *top* Ex 17:9; Josh 15:8f; Jdth 4:5; Hos 4:13; Ezk 6:13; *tip* (of fingers) 4 Macc 10:7.

κορώνη, -ης, ἡ   (Hom+) type of *crow, raven* Jer 3:2; EpJer 53.*

κόσκινον, -ου, τό   (Semonides of Amorgos) *sieve* Sir 27:4.*

κόσμιος   2.b. (neut subst) *ornament;* (fig) *adornment, (rhetorical) flourish* Eccl 12:9.*‡

κοσμοπληθής, -ές   (h.l.) *filling the world* 4 Macc 15:31.*

κοσμοποιΐα, -ας, ἡ   (Aristot+) *making of the world, creation* (Strabo 15.1.59) 4 Macc 14:7.*

κοσμοφορέω   (h.l. not in LSJ) *carry (all the species of) the world* 4 Macc 15:31.*

κόσυμβος, -ου, ὁ   (LXX) *fringe, tassel* Ex 28:39; Is 3:18.*

κοσυμβωτός, -ή, -όν   (h.l.) *fringed, tasseled* Ex 28:4.*

κοτύλη, -ης, ἡ   (8x, Hom, Hdt+) *cup, liquid measure* (ca. 0.2*l*) Lev 14:10ff; Ezk 45:14.*

κουρά, -ᾶς, ἡ   (Aeschyl, Hdt+) *cropping, what is cut off* Josh 5:12VL; (specif) *shearing* (of sheep) Dt 18:4; Job 31:20. 2 Esdr 13:15 see κώδιον.

κουρεύς, -έως, ὁ   (Pla+) *barber* Judg 16:19A; Ezk 5:1.*

κουφίζω   Job 21:30 perh s.t. of חשׂך nif'al *be spared* (based on 2 Esdr 9:13).‡

κοῦφος, -η, -ον   (19x, Hom+) **1.** *light, nimble, swift* 2 Km 1:23; 1 Ch 12:9; Sir 11:26; Is 18:2; La 4:19; (adv) Is 5:26; (comp) Jer 4:13. **2.** *inconsequential* 1 Km 18:23; *insubstantial* Wsd 5:11; κ. καρδία *deficient in intellect and character* Sir 19:4.

κόχλαξ, -ακος, ὁ   (Thu+: καχληξ) *pebble* 1 Km 14:14; (coll) *gravel*; > (metonymy) *dry riverbed, gulley* 1 Macc 10:73.*

κραδαίνω   (Hom+) *agitate, cause to quiver or tremble* 3 Macc 2:21; *brandish* 2 Macc 11:8.*

κραιπαλάω   pf ptc κεκραιπαληκώς (Aristoph+) *become drunk* Ps 77:65; Is 24:20; 29:9.*

κρᾶμα, -ατος, τό   (Strabo+) *mixture,* (specif) *mixed wine* SSol 7:3.*

κραταιότης, -ητος, ἡ   (h.l.) *power, strength* Ps 45:4.*

κραταιόω   2. (act trans) *overpower* (τινά) 2 Km 11:25²; (intr) *be(come) strong* 2 Ch 23:1; *prevail* (ὑπέρ τινα) 2 Km 13:14; 3 Km 21:23ff.‡

κραταίωμα, -ατος, τό   (LXX) *strength* Ps 24:14; 27:8; 30:4; 42:2.*

κραταιῶς (adv of κραταιός) *strongly, forcefully* Judg 8:1A; Pr 22:3; *violently, by force* 1 Km 2:16.*

κραταίωσις, -εως, ἡ (LXX) *strength* Jdth 7:22; Ps 59:9; 67:36.*

κρατέω 3c. *prevail, prove superior* 1 Ch 19:2. Job 26:9 mistrans of אחז¹ *cover* as if אחז² *grasp*. Da 5:12Θ s.t. of אחידה *riddle*, fr אחד *grasp, seize* (Heb אחז).‡

κρατήρ, -ῆρος, ὁ (Hom+) **1.** *bowl* (for mixing or drinking) Ex 24:6; Pr 9:2f; (fig) SSol 7:3. **2.** *hollow, blossom* (of flower) Ex 25:31, 34.*

κράτησις, -εως, ἡ (pap+) *right of possession, dominion* Wsd 6:3.*

κρατύνω (Hom+) *strengthen, confirm* Wsd 14:16.*

κραυάζω (spur; not in LSJ) error for κραυγάζω Tob 2:13vLBA.*

κρεάγρα, -ας ἡ (9x, Aristoph+) *meat hook or fork* Ex 27:3; 1 Km 2:13; 1 Ch 28:17; Jer 52:18.

κρεανομέω (Isaeus+) *divide meat, butcher* Lev 8:20.*

κρεμαστός, -ή, -όν (Soph+) *hung, suspended* 3 Km 7:6; Judg 6:2B (neut subst) *elevated niche or ridge* (? no //).

κρεμνάω var of BDAG: κρεμάννυμι/κρεμάζω Job 26:7vL.

κρημνίζω (LXX+) *hurl headlong* 2 Macc 6:10.*

κρήνη, -ης, ἡ (Hom, Hdt+) *well, cistern* 2 Km 2:13; 4:12; 3 Km 3:1; 22:38; 4 Km 20:20; Sir 48:17.*

κρηπίς, -ίδος, ἡ (Hdt+) *bottom, bank* (of river) Josh 3:15; 4:18; 1 Ch 12:16; 1 Macc 9:43; *base* (of altar) 2 Macc 10:26; Joel 2:17.*

κρίκος, -ου, ὁ (13x, Hom, Hdt+) *curtain ring or eyelet* Ex 26:6ff; Job 38:6; Is 58:5.‡

κρίμα **7.** (no //; s.t. of משפט *judgment, decree, custom*) *policy, custom* Lev 18:4; 4 Km 11:14; 2 Esdr 11:7; Ps 88:31; Sir 17:12; Jer 12:1; etc; *pattern, design* 2 Ch 4:7.‡

κρίνον **2.** *cup* (blossom-shaped, for lamps of menorah) Ex 25:31; Num 8:4.‡

κριός **2.** *battering ram* (Polyb 1.48.9) 2 Macc 12:15; PsSol 2:1.‡

κρίσις **4.** *pattern, custom* (no //, s.t. of משפט *judgment, decree, custom, pattern*) 1 Ch 6:17.‡

κριτήριον Judg 5:10B mistrans of מדין *N LOC* as if fr דין *judge*.‡

κρόκη, -ης, ἡ (Hes, Hdt+) *woof* (of fabric) Lev 13:48ff.*

κρόκινος, -η, -ον (Theophr+) *made of saffron* Pr 7:17vL.*

κροκόδειλος, -ου, ὁ (Hdt+) *lizard* Lev 11:29.*

κρόκος, ου, ὁ (Hom+) *saffron* Pr 7:17; SSol 4:14.*

κρόμμυον, -ου, τό (Hom, Hdt+) *onion* Num 11:5.*

κροσσοί, -ῶν οἱ (LXX+) *lappets* (small interlocking or overlapping plates) Ex 28:22, 29a; 36:22.*

κροσσωτός, -όν (Lycophron+) *fringed, tasseled*; (neut subst) *braid, brocade work* Ex 28:14; Ps 44:14.*

κρόταφος, -ου, ὁ (Hom+) *side of forehead, temple* Judg 4:21Bf; 5:26B; Ps 131:4; PsSol 4:16.*

κροτέω (11x, Hom+) *clap* (hands), *applaud* 4 Km 11:12; Ps 46:1; Job 27:23; (in derision) Na 3:19; La 2:15; Ezk 6:11.

κρουνηδόν (LXX+) *gushing or streaming like a spring* 2 Macc 14:45.*

κρύβδην (Hom, Pind+) *secretly* 2 Km 12:12vL.*

κρυβῆ (LXX+) = BDAG: κρυφῇ 1 Km 19:2; 2 Km 12:12; 3 Macc 4:12.*

κρύπτω Pr 2:1; 7:1; 10:14 mistrans of צפן *store up* as if *hide*. But Pr 17:9 renders כסה *cover up, conceal*, > *forgive* (sin or wrong; cf. Ps 31:1 ἐπικαλύπτω).‡

κρυσταλλοειδής, -ές (Epicurus+) *like ice* Wsd 19:21.*

κρύφιος voc κρύφιε **2.** *concealed, latent;* "whoever you may be" (for פלני אלמוני *a certain man*) Ruth 4:1. Ps 9:1; 45:1 renders עלמות unexpl mus t.t. as if fr עלם¹ *be hidden*.‡

κρύφος, -ου, ὁ (Pind: *cloud*) *cave, secret place* (no //) 1 Macc 1:53; 2:31ff.

κτάομαι Ezk 8:3 mistrans of קנאה *jealousy* as if fr קנה *acquire*.‡

κτείνω (Hom, Hdt+) *put to death, kill* 3 Macc 1:2; Pr 24:11; 25:5.*

κτηνοτρόφος, -ον (DiodS, pap) *cattle keeping* Gen 46:32, 34; Num 32:4; (subst) Gen 4:20.*

κτηνώδης, -ες (Aesop, Philo) *like an animal, beastly* Ps 72:22.*

κτῆσις, -εως, ἡ (40x, Soph+) *acquisition, property, possession* Gen 23:4; Judg 6:5B; 4Rg 3:17; Ps 103:24; Pr 1:13; Sir 36:24; Jer 39:7.

κτίζω 2. (human subj) *build, work* Hg 2:9.‡

κτύπος, -ου, ὁ (Hom+) *crash, boom* Wsd 17:17.*

κύαθος, -ου, ὁ (Anacr, Aristoph+) *ladle* Ex 25:29; 38:12; Num 4:7; Jer 52:19.*

κύαμος, -ου, ὁ (Hom+) *bean* 2 Km 17:28; Ezk 4:9.*

κυβερνάω (Hom+) *pilot, steer* Wsd 10:4; (fig) *lead, govern* Pr 12:5; Wsd 14:6; Sus 5.*‡

κύβος, -ου, ὁ (Hdt+) *cake, block* Esth 1:6; Job 38:38.*

κυδοιμός, οῦ, ὁ (Hom+) *uproar, din* (of battle); > *turmoil* (of storm, no //) Job 38:25.*

κῦδος, -εος, τό (Hom+) *glory, fame* Is 14:25.*

κύησις, -εως, ἡ (Pla+) *conception* Ruth 4:13.*

κύθρα cf. χύτρα.‡

κυθρόπους, -οδος (vl χυτρ-, = ; Hes+) *cauldron or pot stand* Lev 11:35.*

κύκλος, -ου, ὁ (Hom+; BDAG: dat as adv) *circle, circular course* Eccl 1:6; Wsd 7:19.*

κυκλόω 3. (caus) *take around, lead around* Ex 13:18.*‡

κύκλωμα, -ατος, τό (Eur+) *anything round: wheel, coil* Ps 139:10; Job 37:12; *round outer edge* 2 Ch 4:2; *rim* (of a square obj, no //) Ezk 43:17; *circumference* (of a city, no //) 48:35.*

κύκλωσις, -εως, ἡ (X+) *surrounding movement, way around* Sir 43:12.*

κύκνειος, -ον (Soph+) *of a swan* 4 Macc 15:21.*

κύκνος, -ου, ὁ (Hom+) *swan* Lev 11:18; Dt 14:16.*

κυλικεῖον, -ου, τό (Aristoph+) *sideboard, cup stand* 1 Macc 15:32.*

κυλίκινος, -ον (dub, not in LSJ) *cup-shaped* Esth 1:7 vl.*

κυλίκιον, -ου, τό (Lysias, Theophr+) *small cup* Esth 1:7.*

κυλίω 1.b. (trans) *roll, tumble* (obj person [no //], from window) 4 Km 9:33.‡

κυμαίνω (Hom+) *surge up* (in waves), *be in tumult* (act & mid) Wsd 5:10; Is 5:30; 17:12; Jer 6:23; (trans) *stir into tumult* 26:7.*‡

κυμάτιον, -ου, τό (ins+) *fluted or grooved molding* Ex 25:11ff.*

κυμβαλίζω (Menand+) *play cymbals* 2 Esdr 22:27.*

κυνηγέω (Aristot+) *hunt* Gen 25:27.*‡

κυνήγιον, -ου, τό (Polyb, DiodS+) *prey* Sir 13:19.*‡

κυνηγός, -οῦ, ὁ (Aeschyl+) *hunter* Gen 10:9; 1 Ch 1:10.*

κυνικός, -ή, -όν (X? Menand+) *dog-like, currish.* 1 Km 25:3 mistrans of כלבי N GENT *Calebite* as if כלב *dog.*

κυνόμυια, -ας, ἡ (9x, Hom+) *fly,* (coll) *flies* Ex 8:17ff; Ps 77:45; 104:31.*

κυοφορία, -ας, ἡ (LXX+) *pregnancy* 4 Macc 15:6; 16:7.*

κυπαρίσσινος, -ον (Hom+) *of cypress wood* 2 Esdr 18:15; Ezk 27:24.*

κυπάρισσος, -ου, ἡ (12x, Hom, Hdt+) *cypress tree* 4 Km 19:23; Job 40:17; Is 37:24; Ezk 27:5; *wood* Ezk 31:3; SSol 1:17; *tree or wood* Is 60:13.

κυπρίζω (LXX) *bloom* SSol 2:13, 15.*

κυπρισμός, οῦ, ὁ (Eustath) *bloom or flower* (of henna? of cypress?) SSol 7:13.*

κύπρος, ου, ἡ (Theophr, Joseph+) *Cypriote myrrh* (Theophr)? *henna* (Sem כֹּפֶר)? *cypress* (so app Joseph BJ 4.469; c. LSJ)? SSol 1:14; 4:13.*

κυρειος itac error for (I) κύριος (adj) Da 4:22ΘVL, 6:27ΘVL.

κυριεία, -ας, ἡ (VVLL κυρία, κυρεία, = ; 8; Aristot+) *power, lordship, mastery, dominion* 1 Macc 8:24R (Gött κυρία); Is 40:10; Da 11:3f.

κυριεύω 3. *seize, overpower* Da 6:25Θ.‡

κύριος κύριος Ezk 2:4vvLL, 14:6R; 26:21R etc renders אדני יהוה *Lord Yahweh* (vl oft αδωναι κυρ.) VEL SIM.‡

κυρτός, -ή, -όν (Hom+) *hunched, hunchbacked* Lev 21:20; 3 Km 21:11.*

κύτος *hollow* (= BDAG), > *body, trunk* (of person), *trunk* (of tree, no //) Da 4:11.‡

κύφω (h.l. = κύπτω) *hang one's head; look down* Job 22:29.*

κυψέλη, -ης, ἡ (Hdt+) *bin, chest* Hg 2:16.*

κώδιον, -ου, τό (Aristoph+) *fleece, sheepskin* Jdth 12:15. 2 Esdr 13:15 κωδιων τη κουρα *fleeces for the shearing* mistrans of לגן השלח *the canal for the garden,* arising fr confusion of גן *garden* and גז *fleece, shearing.*

κώδων, -ωνος, ὁ (Aeschyl+) *bell* Ex 28:33f; 36:33f; 2 Ch 4:13; Sir 45:9.*

κώθων, -ωνος, ὁ (ArchilochusLyr, Aristoph+) *drinking party* (as religious banquet or festival) Esth 8:17; 3 Macc 6:31.*

κωθωνίζω (Aristot+) (pass) *get drunk, drink recklessly* 1 Esdr 4:63; Esth 3:15.*

κωκυτός, -οῦ, ὁ (Hom, Aeschyl+) *shriek, wailing* 3 Macc 6:32.*

κωλέα, -ας, ἡ (Aristoph+ [contr κωλή]) *thigh, leg* 1 Km 9:24.*

κώλυμα, -ατος, τό (Hippocr, Eur+) *hindrance* Job 13:27.*

κωλυτικός, -ή, -όν (X+) *hindering, preventing, impeding* (of τινός) 4 Macc 1:3, 30; 2:6.*

κωμάρχης, -ου, ὁ (X+) *village chief or leader* Esth 2:3.*

κωνώπιον, -ου, τό (LXX+ [Lat since Varo, Horace, Propertius, all I BCE]) *mosquito curtain* Jdth 10:21; 13:9, 15; 16:19.*

κώπη, -ης, ἡ (Hom+) *handle,* > *oar* (Hdt 8.11.1) Ezk 27:6.*

κωπηλάτης, -ου, ὁ (Clearchus+) *rower* (Polyb 34.3.8) Ezk 27:8ff.*

κωφεύω (11x, LXX+) *remain silent* Judg 16:2; 2 Km 13:20; Job 6:24.

Λ

λαβή, -ῆς, ἡ (Alcaeus+) *handle, grip* Judg 3:22.*

λαβίς, -ίδος, ἡ (Hippocr+) *forceps, pair of tongs, clamp* Ex 38:17; Num 4:9; 2 Ch 4:21; Is 6:6.*

λάβρος, -ον (Hom, Hdt+) *stormy, turbulent, furious* Pr 28:3; Job 38:25, 34; (superl) 4 Macc 16:3.*

λάγανον, -ου, τό (8x, LXX+) *flat baked cake* (e.g., tortilla) Ex 29:2; Lev 8:26; 2 Km 6:19; 1 Ch 23:29.

λαγών, -όνος, ἡ (Hippocr, Eur+) *flank* Sir 47:19.*

λάθη aor subj of λανθάνω.

λαθραῖος, -ον (Aeschyl+) *clandestine, secret* Wsd 1:11 (λάθριος vL, =); (adv) 1 Km 24:5; 2 Macc 1:19.*

λάθριος, -ον (Soph+) *secret* Pr 21:14.*

λαιμαργία, -ας, ἡ (Pla+) *gluttony* 4 Macc 1:27.*

λακάνη = λεκάνη

λάλημα, -ατος, τό (Soph+: *talk, prattle*) *byword, example* (no //) 3 Km 9:7; Tob 3:4S; Ezk 23:10; 36:3.*

λαλητός, -ή, -όν (EtymMag: *discussed, talked about*) *able to speak* (no //) Job 38:14.*

λαμβάνω λαμ- ψυχήν (נשא נפש, no //) *desire, apply oneself, aim one's whole effort* Ps 23:4; Hos 4:8. Hab 1:3 *take up,* > *begin* (παραβολήν, cf. ἀναλαμβάνω; no //, s.t. of נשא [abs] *make a beginning,* but cf. BDAG: 1. *take up, find opportunity*).‡

λαμπάδιον, -ου, τό (Pla+) *small torch or lamp* Ex 38:16; 3 Km 7:35; Zech 4:2f.*

λαμπήνη, -ης, ἡ (Soph+) *covered chariot* Judg 5:10A; 1 Km 26:5, 7; Is 66:20.*

λαμπηνικός, -ή, -όν (h.l.) *like a λαμπήνη* Num 7:3.*

λαμπρός 5. (of persons) *illustrious, celebrated;* (subst) *admired person* Sir 31:23.‡

λαμπτήρ, -ῆρος, ὁ (Hom, Eur, X+) *lantern, lamp* Pr 16:28; 20:9a; 21:4; 24:20.*

λάμψις, -εως, ἡ (LXX+) *brightness, shining* (fig) Bar 4:2.*

λανθάνω fut λήσομαι 2 aor ἔλαθον pf λέληθα **2.** *be left over* (no //) 2 Km 17:22;

perh s.t. [based on Is 40:26?] of עדר³ *be missing, be lacking*.‡

λάξ (Hom, Aeschyl+) *w. one's foot* 4 Macc 6:8.*

λαξευτήριον, -ου, τό (h.l.) *chisel, stone-cutting tool* Ps 73:6.*

λαξεύω (11x, LXX) *hew (stone)* Ex 34:1; Jdth 1:2; Is 9:9. Pf pass ptc Λελαξευμένον N LOC (פסגה) Num 23:14R; Dt 3:27; should be so read Num 21:20; 23:14 Gött. Cf. Λαξεύτης Dt 4:49.

λαογραφία, -ας, ἡ (LXX, ins, pap) *enrollment, census (for taxes)* 3 Macc 2:28.*

λαπιστής, -οῦ, ὁ (h.l.) *swaggerer* Sir 20:7.*

λάπτω aor ἔλαψα (Hom+) *lap, lick up* Judg 7:5ff.*

λάρος, -ου, ὁ (Hom+) *seagull* Lev 11:16 = Dt 14:15.*

λατομητός, -ή, -όν (Strabo) *hewn* 4 Km 12:13; 22:6.*

λατρευτός, -ή, -όν (13x, LXX+) *hired, servile* Ex 12:16; Lev 23:7; Num 29:12.

λάτρις, -ιος, ἡ (Theognis, Soph+) *servant, slave* Job 2:9d.*

λαφυρεύω (h.l.) *plunder, loot* Jdth 15:11R.*

λαφυρέω (Aq) *plunder, loot* Jdth 15:11G.*

λάφυρον, -ου, τό (Aeschyl+) (in LXX only pl) *spoil, plunder* 1 Ch 26:27; Jdth 15:7; 2 Macc 8:30.*

λαχανεία, -ας, ἡ (pap+) *growing of vegetables or herbs* Dt 11:10.*

λέαινα, -ης, ἡ (Hdt+) *lioness* Job 4:10; Da 7:4.*

λεαίνω fut λεανῶ aor ἐλέανα (Hom+) *grind small, crush* 2 Km 22:43 = Ps17:43; Job 14:19.*

λέβης, -ητος, ὁ (33x, Hom+) *kettle, basin* Ex 16:3; 1 Km 2:14; 1 Esdr 1:13; Ps 59:10; Sir 13:2; Am 4:2; Jer 1:13.

λεηλατέω (Hdt+) *plunder* 2 Macc 2:21.*

λειοπετρία so Gött; cf. λεωπετρία.

λειτούργημα, -ατος τό (LXX+) *performance (of public ritual or service)* Num 4:32; 7:9.*

λειτουργήσιμος, -ον (h.l.) *used in (religious) service* 1 Ch 28:13.*

λείχω fut λείξω aor ἔλειξα (Hdt+) *lick* 3 Km 20:19; Ps 71:9; Mi 7:17; Is 49:23.*‡

λεκάνη, -ης, ἡ (Aristoph+) *bowl, dish* Judg 5:25(A: λακ-, =); 6:38.*

λέληθα pf of BDAG; λανθάνω; adv of pf pass ptc λεληθότως (Ps-Pla [AXIOCH]+) *secretly* 2 Macc 6:11; 8:1.*

λελογχώς pf ptc of BDAG: λαγχάνω.

λέξις, -εως, ἡ (8x, Pla+) *verbal communication; saying* Sir prol 20; *speech* Job 36:2; *language* Esth 1:22; *text* 2 Macc 2:31; *style or manner (of speaking)* Sir 23:12.

λεοντηδόν (h.l.) *like a lion, in lion-like fashion* 2 Macc 11:11.*

λεοντινον (dub; not in LSJ) *like a lion* 2 Macc 11:11vl.*

λεπίζω (Theophr+) *peel off, strip* Gen 30:37f; Tob 3:17BA, 11:12BA; (fig) *steal* 1 Macc 1:22.*

λέπισμα, -ατος, τό (LXX+) *strip, peeled area* Gen 30:37.*

λέπρα, -ας, ἡ (39x, Hdt+) *skin disease, leprosy (not the modern disease by that name)* Lev 13:2ff; 4 Km 5:11; 2 Ch 26:20ff.‡

λεπρόομαι (pap) *become leprous* 4 Km 5:1, 27; 15:5.*

λεπτός 1.b. *fine, powdery* Ex 30:36; *fine, small* 2 Ch 34:7. συνθετον λεπτον *finely ground and mixed* Ex 30:7; (neut pl subst) *fine particles, dust* Da 2:35L.‡

λεπτύνω aor ἐλέπτυνα (18x; Hippocr+) 1. *make thin* Ps 28:6. 2. *grind down* (no //) 2 Km 22:43(= Ps17:43); Mi 4:13; Is 41:15; *grind or crush into dust* (no //) 4 Km 23:6; 2 Ch 23:17; Da 2:34Θ; 6:25Θ.

λέπυρον, -ου, τό (Batr+: *rind, husk*) *slice (of fruit,* no //) SSol 4:3 = 6:6.*

λέσχη, -ης, ἡ (Hom, Hdt+) *scandal, gossip* Pr 23:29.*

λευκαίνω 2. *become white* (act intr) Lev 13:19; (pass) Ps 50:9.‡

λευκα(ν)θίζω (Hdt+) *become white* Lev 13:38f. SSol 8:5 mistrans of מן־המדבר *from the wilderness*, prob as if hoph ptc of ברר *be pure*.*

λεύκη, -ης, ἡ (Theophr+) *white poplar* Hos 4:13; Is 41:19.*

λευκότης, -ητος, ἡ (Hippocr, Pla) *whiteness* Sir 43:18.*

λεύκωμα, -ατος, τό (6x, Lysias, Aristot+) *white spot or scale* Tob 2:10; 3:17.

λεχώ, -οῦς, ἡ (*VVLL* λεχως, λοχω, -ως, = ; Aeschyl, Eur, ins+) *woman in childbirth* (or immediately after) EpJer 27.*

λεωπετρία, -ας, ἡ (DiodS 3.16.2) *smooth or level stone* Ezk 24:7fR; 26:4R; 14R (Gött λειοπετρία).*

λήγω aor ἔληξα (Hom, Hdt+) *leave off, cease* (from τινός) 2 Macc 9:7, 11, 18; 15:24; 3 Macc 3:16; 6:16.*

λῆμμα **2.** *obligation, burden* (no //, s.t. fr e.g., מַשָּׂא *burden*; λαμβάνω oft renders נשא *take up, carry*) Job 31:23, > *prophetic pronouncement* (no //) 4 Km 9:25; Na 1:1; Hg 2:14; Jer 23:33; La 2:14.‡

ληνός **2.** *tub, trough* Gen 30:38.‡

λήσομαι dep fut of BDAG: λανθάνω.

ληστεύω (Thu+) *rob, plunder* 1 Esdr 4:23.*

ληστήριον, -ου, τό (X, ins, pap+) *band of plunderers* 2 Ch 22:1; 36:5b.*

λιβανόομαι pf pass ptc λιβανωμένος (HerodianGramm) *mix w. incense* 3 Macc 5:45.*

λιγύριον, -ου, τό (Joseph) *jacinth* Ex 28:19 = 36:19; Ezk 28:13.*

λιθοβόλον, -ου, τό (Polyb, DiodS [masc]; Joseph) *stone thrower, catapult* 1 Macc 6:51.*

λίθυς Jer 18:3 mistrans of אָבְנַיִם (dual) *potter's wheel* as if אֲבָנִים *stones*.‡

λιθουργέω (LXX+) *cut or carve stone* Ex 35:33.*

λιθουργικός, -ή, -όν (Lysias, ins) *of a stone mason* Ex 28:11; (pl subst) *masonry* 31:5.*

λιθουργός, -οῦ, ὁ (Aristoph, Thu+) *stone mason* Sir 45:11.*

λιθώδης, -ες (Hdt+) *stony, rocky*; (subst) *rocky ground* Sir 32:20.*

λικμάω fut λικμήσω or Att λικμιῶ (19; Hom+) **1.** *thresh, winnow* Ruth 3:2; Am 9:9. **2.** *scatter* (like chaff) 3 Km 14:15; Job 27:21; Ezk 26:4; Da 2:44Θ, (mid) Wsd 11:18.‡

λικμήτωρ, -ορος, ὁ (*h.l.*) *winnower* (fig) Pr 20:26.*

λικμός, -οῦ, ὁ (LXX+) *winnowing basket* Am 9:9.*

λίκνον, -ου, τό (not in HR; Soph+) *winnowing basket* Am 9:9VL.*

λιμαγχονέω (Hippocr+) *weaken through hunger* Dt 8:3.*

λιμοκτονέω (Hippocr, Pla+) *deprive of food, starve* Pr 10:3.*

λιμώσσω fut λιμώξω (Strabo+) *be famished* Ps 58:7, 15.*

λιπαίνω aor pass (in mid sense) ἐλιπάνθην *anoint oneself* 2 Esdr 19:25. Hab 1:16 mistrans of בְּהֵמָה שָׁמֵן *in them (becomes) fat* as if בָּהֶם הַשְׁמִין *in them he makes fat*.‡

λιπαρός, -ά, -όν (Hom+) *oily or fat*, (of land) *fertile* 2 Esdr 19:35; (of bread) *oiled or* (fig) *rich* Is 30:23; (sg neut subst) *fatness, riches, resources* (no //) Judg 3:29B (BHS note at 3:29 is incorrect; refers only to A).‡

λίπασμα, -ατος, τό (Hippocr+) *fat*; (pl) *fat foods* 1 Esdr 9:51 = 2 Esdr 18:10.*

λιποθυμέω (Hippocr, Plu+) *faint, lose consciousness* 4 Macc 6:26.*

λίσσομαι (Hom, Hdt+) *pray* Job 17:2.*

λιτανεία, -ας, ἡ (LXX+) *petition, entreaty* 2 Macc 3:20; 10:16; 3 Macc 2:21; 5:9.*

λιτός, -ή, -όν (Hippocr, ins+) *simple, frugal* (Polyb 6.48.7) Judg 11:3A.*

λιχήν, -ῆνος, ὁ (Aeschyl+) *canker, sore* Lev 21:20; 22:22.*

λιχνεία, -ας, ἡ (X, Pla+) *gluttony* 3 Macc 6:36.*

λίψ **2.** *south(west) wind* (Hdt+) Ps 77:26.‡

λοβός, -οῦ, ὁ (21x, Hom+) *lobe* (of liver) Ex 29:13, 22; Lev 3:4; (of ear) Ex 29:20; Lev 8:23; Am 3:12.*

λογεῖον, -ου, τό (19x, ins+) *breast pouch* (for oracular stones, no //) Ex 28:15ffR; Lev 8:8R (Gött λόγιον in both books); Sir 45:10 (better: λόγιον; based on Ex passages).*

λογισμός **1.b.** *reckoning, accounting* (Lysias, Demosth) 2 Macc 6:23; Jer 18:11.‡

λογιστής, -οῦ, ὁ (Aristoph, Pla+: *calculator, administrator*) *engineer* (no //) 2 Ch 26:15.*

λόγος **2.a.β.** λόγον ἔχειν *take account of*, > *be anxious about* (Hdt 1.62.2), *consider worthy of notice* Jer 49:16.‡

λοιμεύομαι (h.l.) *be diseased* (fig) Pr 19:19; but mistrans of נצל hiph *extricate, rescue* as if fr ליץ *mock, ridicule* (λοιμός renders לץ *mocker* Pr 19:25).

λοιμότης, -ητος, ἡ (h.l.) *plague;* (fig) *pestilent conduct* Esth 8:12g.*

λουτήρ, -ῆρος, ὁ (14x, CallixenusHist, ins+) *washbasin* Ex 30:18; Lev 8:11; 2 Km 8:8; 2 Ch 4:3ff.

λοφιά, -ᾶς, ἡ (Hom, Hdt+: *mane*) *ridge, crest* Josh 15:2, 5; 18:19.*

λοχάω (Hom+) *lie in wait, ambush* Wsd 14:24.*

λοχεύω (Eur+) *bear young;* (mid) *give birth* Gen 33:13; Ps 77:71.*

λυθρώδης, -ες (LXX+) *blood-defiled* Wsd 11:6.*

λυμαίνομαι (LXX alw deponent) fut λυμανεῖται, -νοῦνται; aor ἐλυμηνάμην.

λυμεών, -ῶνος, ὁ (Soph+) *corrupter* (γυναικῶν Eur *Hipp* 1068) 4 Macc 18:8.*

λύσις 2. *interpretation, explanation* Eccl 8:1; Wsd 8:8; Da 12:8L.*‡

λυσιτέλεια, -ας, ἡ (Polyb+) *gain, advantage* 2 Macc 2:27.*

λυσιτελής, -ές (X+) *useful, advantageous* Sir 28:21.*

λυτρών, -ῶνος, ὁ (AnecdGr) *latrine* 4 Km 10:27.*

λύτρωσις Judg 1:15 mistrans of (Upper and Lower) גלת *Gullah* or *Gulloth* N LOC (cf. BHS ad loc) as if fr גאל *redeem*.‡

λυτρωτός, -ή, -όν (LXX) *subject to redemption* Lev 25:31f.*

λύω 2.c. *solve, resolve* (riddle or puzzle, Pla) *explain, set forth* 1 Esdr 9:46.‡

λῶμα, -ατος, τό (LXX) *hem, border* Ex 28:33f; 36:32ff.*

λωποδυτέω (Aristoph+) *plunder* 1 Esdr 4:24.*

M

μά exclamatory particle (in oaths, Hom+) *in accordance with* (τι) 4 Macc 10:15.*

μαγειρεῖον, -ου, τό (Aristot+) *oven, hearth* Ezk 46:23, 24R.*

μαγειρεύω (Theophr+) *butcher* (fig) La 2:21.*

μαγείρισσα, -ας, ἡ (h.l.) *cook* 1 Km 8:13.*

μάγειρος, -ου, ὁ (Hdt+) *cook, butcher* 1 Km 9:23f; Ezk 46:24G. La 2:20 mistrans of טפחים (h.l.) *healthy children* (?) as if טבחים *cooks.**

μαγικός, -ή, -όν (LXX+) *magical* Wsd 17:7.*

μαγίς, -ίδος, ἡ (Hippocr, Soph+) *loaf* Judg 7:13.*

μαδαρόω (h.l.) *pull out hair* 2 Esdr 23:25.*

μαδάω (Hippocr, Aristoph+) *become bald* Lev 13:40f; *be rubbed bare* (no //) Ezk 29:18.*

μαδεββαν (not in HR) 2 Km 12:31 mistranslit of מלבן (Qere; MT מלכן) *brick mold* as if N LOC.*

μαδων translit of מדון (Qere) *contention* 2 Km 21:20.*

μαελεθ translit of מחלת (unexpl mus t.t.) Ps 52:1; 87:1.*

μάζα, -ας, ἡ (Hes, Hdt+) *cake, lump* Bel 27.*

μαζουρωθ translit of מזרות *constellations* 4 Km 23:5; Job 38:32.*

μαθήσομαι fut of BDAG: μανθάνω, Dt 5:1; Is 29:24.

μαῖα, -ας, ἡ (9x, Hom+: *nurse,* etc) *midwife* Gen 35:17; 38:28; Ex 1:15ff.*‡

μαιμάσσω (LXX+) *be eager, greatly desire* Job 38:8; Jer 4:19.*

μαιόομαι fut pass μαιωθήσομαι (Callim+) *attend a birth, deliver* Ex 1:16; (pass) *be brought to birth* Job 26:5.*

μακαριότης, -ητος, ἡ (Aristot+) *happiness* 4 Macc 4:12.*

μακαριστός, -ή, -όν (Hdt, Aristoph+) *to be considered happy, enviable* 2 Macc 7:24; Pr 14:21; 16:20; 29:18.*

μακροβίωσις, -εως, ἡ (h.l.) *long life* Bar 3:14.*

μακροημέρευσις, -εως, ἡ (LSJSup: ins [IV CE]) *long life* Sir 1:12, 20; 30:22.*

μακροημερεύω (7x, not in LSJ) *live long, prolong one's days* Dt 5:33; 6:2; Judg 2:7; Sir 3:6.

μακροήμερος, -ον (LXX+) *long-lived* Dt 4:40.*

μακροθυμέω **1.b.** (trans, no //) *bear patiently* Bar 4:25.‡

μακρότερον (comp neut acc sg of BDAG: μακρός, as adv) *far away, (too) far* (X ANAB 3.4.16) Dt 12:21.*

μακρότης, -ητος, ἡ (9x, LXX+) *length* (of days, of life) Dt 30:20; 4 Macc 18:19; Ps 20:5; La 5:20; Da 7:12Θ; εἰς μ. ἡμερῶν *forever* Ps 22:6. Eccl 8:12 mistrans of מַאֲרִיךְ *lengthen* as if מֵאֹרֶךְ *from length*.

μακροτονέω (PhiloMech) *extend, prolong, take (too much) time* 2 Macc 8:26.*

μακροχρονίζω (LXX, pap [VI CE]) *extend one's time, last a long time* Dt 17:20R; 32:27.*

μάκρυμμα, -ατος, τό (LXX) *something (to be) put at a distance; abomination* 2 Esdr 9:1, 11.*

μακρύνω aor pass ἐμακρύνθησαν pf ptc μεμακρυγκώς pass μεμακρυμμένος (25x, 13x in Pss; LXX+) **1.** *move far away* (intr) Judg 18:22; 1 Macc 8:23; Ps 54:8; Eccl 7:24; (trans) *move away, remove* Ps 39:12; PsSol 12:4; Is 6:12; Jer 34:10; *put far away* Ps 128:3; (pass) *be far removed* Ps 118:150; Is 49:19. **2.** *take a long time, delay* (+inf) Jdth 2:13; *hold back* (+obj) Ps 21:20; (pass, mid sense) *hold (oneself) back, refrain* Eccl 3:5; *prolong, extend through time* (pass intr) Ps 119:5; (act trans) Eccl 8:13.

μάλα (Hom+) **1.** *indeed, surely, certainly* 2 Km 14:5; 3 Km 1:43; 4 Km 4:14; Tob 7:10S; 4 Macc 13:13; Da 10:21L. **2.** *well, much* Tob 10:6S; 2 Macc 12:18; εὖ μάλα *very well, very much* 2 Macc 8:30; 10:18, 32.*‡

μάλαγμα, -ατος, τό (Pla+) *medicinal plaster, emollient* Wsd 16:12; Is 1:6; Ezk 30:21.*

μαλακοψυχέω (h.l.) *be weak-willed or cowardly* 4 Macc 6:17.*

μαλακύνω (Hippocr, X+) *soften, weaken* Job 23:16.*

μαν see μαναα, BDAG: μάννα.

μαναα (19x; VVLL μαννα, μααvα, μανααν etc, =) translit of מנחה *gift* 4 Km 8:8f; 2 Esdr 23:5; Jer 17:26; Bar 1:10G (RECTE; Ra μάννα) Ezk 46:5ff; Da 2:46Θ.

μάνδρα **2.** *den, lair* (of wild beasts, no //) Ps 9:30; 103:22; SSol 4:8; Am 3:4; Jer 4:7; *den, hiding place* (for people, no //) Judg 6:2A; 1 Km 13:6.‡

μανδραγόρας, -ου, ὁ (X+) *mandrake* Gen 30:14ff; SSol 7:14.*

μανδύας, -ου, ὁ (Aeschyl+) *cloak* Judg 3:16; 1 Km 17:38f; 2 Km 20:8; 10:4 = Ch 19:4.*

μανη translit of מנה *mina* (unit of wt for precious metals) Da 5(preface)L, 25, 26Θ.*

μανιάκης, -ου, ὁ (Polyb+) *necklace* 1 Esdr 3:6; Da 5:7, 16, 29.*

μανιώδης, -ες (Thu+) *crazy, mad* (Eur BACCH 299) 3 Macc 5:45.*

μαντεία, -ας, ἡ (14x, Hdt+) *oracle* (in our lit, alw pagan or false) Num 23:23; 4 Km 17:17; Sir 34:5; Mi 3:6; Is 16:6.

μαντεῖον, -ου, τό (Hom+: *oracle*) *method or means of divination* Ezk 21:27; *oracle* Pr 16:10; *price of divination* (no //) Num 22:7.*

μαραίνω **2.** (act trans) *wither, blight* Job 15:30; *consume, destroy* Wsd 19:21.‡

μαρμάρινος, -η, -ον (Theocr, ins+) *of marble* (DiodS 17.45.3) SSol 5:15.*

μάρμαρος, -ου, ὁ (Hom+: *stone*) *marble* (Theophr+). EpJer 71 mistrans of שש³ *linen* as if שש² *alabaster*.*‡

μαρσίππιον, -ου, τό (Hippocr+) *small sack, purse* Pr 1:14; Sir 18:33; Is 46:6.*

μάρσιππος, -ου, ὁ (19x, X+) *sack, bag* Gen 42:27ff; 43:12ff; 44:1ff; Dt 25:13; Mi 6:11.⁴

μαρτύριον **1.c.** (no //) *physical proof or sign*; (pl) *insignia* 2 Ch 23:11. Pr 29:24 mistrans of עַד *continuing future, forever* as if עֵד *witness*.‡

μασενα translit of משנה *second* ([newer] section of Jerusalem) 4 Km 22:14; = μασανα 2 Ch 34:22.*

μασμαρωθ prob corresp to מחתות *buckets* or מזרקות *basins*; mistranslit? txt? Jer 52:19.*

μασομελ (not in HR) translit of משמאל *from the left* (i.e., *North*) Josh 19:27B (A: ἀπὸ ἀριστερῶν).

μαστιτής, -οῦ, ὁ (h.l.) *wielder of a whip* 4 Macc 9:11VL.*

μαστός Jer 18:14 mistrans of שדי *field* as if fr שד *breast*.‡

ματαιόφρων, -ονος, ὁ   (LXX+) *foolish-minded person* 3 Macc 6:11.*

μαχητής, -οῦ, ὁ   (24x, Hom+, rare in prose) *warrior* Judg 3:29A; 2 Km 15:18; 1 Ch 28:1; Ob 9; Jer 28:30.

μάχιμος, -ον   (Hdt+) *ready to fight, quarrelsome* Pr 21:19; (subst) *soldier, warrior* Josh 5:6; 6:3ff. 4 Km 19:25 mistrans of נצה² *devastated, ruined* as if נצה¹ *quarreling.**

μαχιρ   (HR μαχειρ; MT מכלת [= מאכל *food*?] Origen μαχαλ) translit of מחיר *compensation, equivalent value* 3 Km 5:25.*

μαχμα   (not in HR) mistranslit of מכבר *blanket* 4 Km 8:15.*

μαωζιν   translit of מעזים *fortresses* Da 11:38Θ.*

μαων, μουων   translit of מעון *dwelling* 1 Km 2:32VL (Origen).*

μεγαλαυχία, -ας, ἡ   (Pla+) *boasting* 4 Macc 2:15.*

μεγαλόδοξος, -ον   (Pind, ins+) *great in glory* 3 Macc 6:18; (adv, *h.l.*) 6:39.*

μεγαλοημέρευσις, -εως, ἡ   (*h.l.*) *long life* Sir 30:22VL.*

μεγαλοκράτωρ, -ορος, ὁ   (*h.l.*) *great ruler* 4 Macc 6:2.*

μεγαλομερής, -ές   (Pla, Polyb+) *glorious, magnificent* 3 Macc 5:8; (adv) -μερῶς (ins, Polyb+) *magnificently, lavishly* 2 Macc 4:22, 49G; 3 Macc 6:33.*

μεγαλοποιέω   (Stob) *do great things* Sir 50:22VL.*

μεγαλοπρεπῶς   (Hdt+, X *Anab* 1.4.17) *in exalted fashion, magnificently* 2 Macc 4:49R; 4 Macc 5:24.*

μεγαλοπτέρυγος, -ον   (LXX) *great-winged* Ezk 17:3, 7.*

μεγαλόσαρκος, ον   (*h.l.*) *large of flesh* (Heb *large-phallused, lustful*) Ezk 16:26.*

μεγαλοσθενής, -ές   (Pind+) *very strong* 3 Macc 5:13.*

μεγαλοφρονέω   (X+) *be magnanimous, be courageous* 4 Macc 6:24.*

μεγαλόφρων, -ονος   (Protagorus [V BCE], X+) *magnanimous, high-minded* 4 Macc 6:5; 9:21; *arrogant* (no //, but adv Pla, X) Pr 21:4.*

μεγαλόφωνος, -ον   (not in HR; Hippocr, Aristot+) *loud-voiced, bawling* Sir 26:27(VL).*

μεγαλόψυχος, -ον   (Isocr, Aristot+) *magnanimous* 4 Macc 15:10; (adv) *magnanimously* 3 Macc 6:41.*

μεγάλωμα, -ατος, τό   (*h.l.*) *might, greatness* Jer 31:17.*

μεγαλώνυμος, -ον   (Soph+) *having a great name* (Aristoph *Thesm* 315) Jer 39:19.*

μεγαλωστί   (Hom+) *far and wide* 1 Esdr 5:62.*

μεθαρμόζω   (Aeschyl+) *transpose, correct*; (pass) Wsd 19:18.*

μεθαχαβιν   translit of מתחבאים *keeping themselves hidden* 1 Ch 21:20.*

μεθίστημι   **1.c.** (act, 1 aor) *stand aside, stop, make way* (no //) 3 Km 18:29.*‡

μέθοδος, -ου, ὁ   (Pla+) *stratagem, scheme* Esth 8:12n; 2 Macc 13:18.*

μεθύσκω   aor ἐμέθυσα fut pass μεθυσθήσομαι pf pass ptc μεμεθυσμένος **2.** (trans) *cause to drink freely* Sir 1:16; Jer 38:25; La 3:15; *drench* Ps 64:10; Sir 39:22; (intr) *be filled* Ps 22:5; (pass) 35:9; Hos 14:8. Is 7:20 mistrans of שכיר *hired* as if fr שכר *be drunk.*‡

μεθύω   (only pres and impf; other forms fr μεθύσκω) **2.** *be drenched* (Hom+) Is 58:11.‡

μεθωεσιμ   translit of מתיחשים (hit ptc of יחש *register*) *those who maintain genealogical registers* 2 Esdr 2:62.*

μεῖγμα   = BDAG: μίγμα Sir 38:7.

μείγνυμι   aor εἴμειξα (impr in our edd ἔμιξα pass ἐμίχθην) 2 aor pass ἐμίγην pf pass ptc μεμειγμένος (in our edd -μιγ-, cf. W) *mix, mingle* Gen 30:40; Ex 30:35; Ps 105:35; Pr 14:16. 4 Km 18:23 = Is 36:8 mistrans of I ערב *wager* as if II ערב *mingle.* Cf. also μίσγω.*‡

μειδιάω   (Hom+) *smile* Sir 21:20.*‡

μειερος   (spur; not in HR, LSJ, or Gött app) itac error for μίαρος (Gött μίερος, =) 2 Macc 9:13VL.*

μειράκιον, -ου, τό   (Hippocr, Aristoph, Pla+) *young boy, youth* 2 Macc 7:25; 4 Macc 8:14; 11:24; 14:4.*

μειρακίσκος, -ου, ὁ (Pla+) *boy, lad, youth* 4 Macc 8:1; 11:13.*

μεῖραξ, -ακος, ὁ (Aristoph: ἡ *girl*) *young boy* (LXX+) 4 Macc 14:6, 8.*

μεισουβρις, -εως, ἡ (spur; not in HR or LSJ) *meaning?* 3 Macc 6:9VL.*

μέλαθρον, -ου, τό (Hom+) *beam, timber* 3 Km 6:5; 7:9.*

μελαθρόω (h.l.) *frame w. timbers or beams* 3 Km 7:42.*

μελάνθιον, -ου, τό (Hippocr+) *black cumin* Is 28:25, 27.*

μελανία, -ας, ἡ (X+) *blackness, dark cloud;* (fig) *grief, mourning* (no //, but cf. Rv 6:12) Sir 19:26.*

μελανόομαι pf μεμελάνομαι (LXX, Aëtius) *become black or dark* SSol 1:6; EpJer 21.*

μέλεος, -α, -ον (Hom, Hdt+) *miserable* 4 Macc 16:6.*

μελετάω **2.b.** *declaim, practice orations* Is 38:14 (s.t. of הגה *mumble, twitter* as if *meditate*).‡

μελέτη **2.** *lecture, declamation* Job 37:2. **3.** *practice, usage, pursuit* La 3:62.*‡

μελετητικός, -η, -ον (h.l.) *declaiming, practicing, exercising* Ezk 7:16VL, but mistrans of הגאיות *the valleys* as if fr הגה *speak, consider, read in an undertone* (cf. μελετάω).

μελίζω (7x, Pherecyd, LXX+) *dismember, divide up, cut in pieces* Lev 1:6; Judg 19:29; Mi 3:3.

μελισσών, -ῶνος, ὁ (LXX+) *apiary* 1 Km 14:25f.*

μελον (not in HR) translit of מלון *campground, (temporary) shelter* 4 Km 19:23.*

μέλος **3.** *line of music* Sir 32:6; *song, strain* 3 Macc 5:25 6:32. Ezk 2:10 mistrans of הגה *groan* as if rel to mus t.t. הגיון.‡

μελύνω (spur; not in LSJ) *scribal error for* μεγαλύνω Sir 50:18VL.*

μελχομ translit of מלכם *their king* as if N PERS Am 1:15VL (Aq, Sym); but 3 Km 11:5VL—VVLL μελχο(λ)—translit of מלכם N DEI.*

μελω translit of מלוא *terrace* 3 Km 9:15(VL) 24(VL).

μελῳδέω (Aristoph, Pla+) *chant, sing* 4 Macc 18:15.*

μελῳδία, -ας, ἡ (Eur, Pla+) *melody, song* 4 Macc 15:21.*

μελῳδός, -ή, -όν (Eur, Pla+) *melodious, musical* 4 Macc 10:21.*

μεμήνασιν 3rd pl act pf (pres meaning) of BDAG: μαίνομαι; *be (have gone) insane* Wsd 14:28.*

μεμωκημένος pf pass ptc of μωκάομαι.

μέντοιγε (X+) *nevertheless* Ps 38:7.*

μεριδάρχης, -οῦ, ὁ (pap, Joseph) *district governor* 1 Macc 10:65.*

μεριδαρχία, -ας, ἡ (LXX+) *appointed office* 1 Esdr 1:5, 12; 5:4; 8:28.*

μερίς **3.** *party, faction* Wsd 1:16.‡

μερισμός **1.c.** *allotment; allotted group* (of people, no //) 2 Esdr 6:18.‡

μεριτεύομαι (h.l.) *divide or apportion* Job 40:30.*

μέρος **1.b.γ.** *district, area* Ex 16:35; Judg 18:2A. **1.c.** κατὰ μέρος *part by part,* > *systematically* Pr 29:11. 2 Esdr 4:20 mistrans of Aram הלך *tax* as if חלק *portion, share.*‡

μεσαῖος, -α, -ον (not in HR; AntiphanesCom) *in the middle* (mistrans of בנים *champion? infantryman?* as if fr בין *between*) 1 Km 17:23(VL).*

μέσακλον, -ου, τό (h.l.) *beam of a loom* (? so Heb; cf. ἀντίον) 1 Km 17:7.*

μεσηβρινός, -ή, -όν (Aeschyl+) *midday, noontime* 1 Esdr 9:41; Ps 90:6; Job 5:14; Is 16:3.*

μεσῆλιξ, gen **-ικος** (not in HR; Pollux+) *middle-aged* 1 Km 17:23VL.*

μεσθααλ mistranslit of מלתחה *wardrobe, storeroom* (doublet for οἴκου) 4 Km 10:22.*

μεσόγειος, -ον (Hdt -γαιος, Thu, Pla -γεως +) *inland* (SCIL ὁδός VEL SIM) 2 Macc 8:35.*

μεσοπορέω wrongly -πωρέω (Menand, Theophr+) *be halfway through* Sir 31:21VL.*

μεσοπόρφυρος, -ον (LXX+) *interwoven or decorated with purple* Is 3:21, 24.*

μέσος for ἀνὰ μέσον see ἀνά. EpJer 54 appar mistrans, unexpl.‡

μεσότης, -ητος, ἡ (Pla+) *center, median* Wsd 7:18.*

μεσσαβ translit of מצב *outpost* (cf. ὑπόστασις) 1 Km 14:1, 6.*

μεσσαε (HR: Aq) translit of מסה, > (adv) *alternately* (*h.l.*) 4 Km 11:6VL.*

μεταβάλλω 2. (act) *change* (trans or intr) Ex 7:17; Josh 7:8; Esth 5:1; Job 10:8; Hab 1:11; *exchange, depart from* 3 Macc 1:3; (intr) *come (in payment or exchange)* Is 60:5.‡

μεταβηχας (N LOC in HR) translit of מטבחת *from Tibchath* (N LOC) 1 Ch 18:8.*

μεταβολή, -ῆς, ἡ (8x, Hdt+) 1. *reversal, change* Esth 4:17y; 3 Macc 5:40; Wsd 7:18; Is 30:32. 2. *exchange* (in commerce) Is 47:15.

μεταβολία, -ας, ἡ (*h.l.*) *commercial exchange* Sir 37:11.*

μεταβόλος, -ον (ins, pap) *changeable*; (subst) *peddler, huckster* Is 23:2, 3.*

μεταγενής, -ές (Menand+) *born after*; (comp) μεταγενέστερος *later, subsequent* (to τινός) 1 Esdr 8:1.*

μεταγίνομαι (ins) *come or happen later* 2 Macc 2:1f (*f.l.* for BDAG: μετάγω [pass] *be removed to another place*, Goldstein AB).*

μετάγω 2.b. *"transfer" to another language, translate* (no //) Sir prol 22.‡

μεταδιαιτάω (Lucian) *change one's manner of life* 4 Macc 8:8.*

μεταδιώκω (Hdt+) *pursue, study* 2 Macc 2:31.*

μεταίρω (Eur, ins+) *remove* 4 Km 16:17; 25:11; Ps 79:9; Pr 22:28.*‡

μεταίτιος, -ον (not in HR; Hdt+) *accessory to, sharing responsibility for* (τινός) Esth 8:12e.*

μετακίνησις, -εως, ἡ (Hippocr, Aristot+) 1. *change, alteration* Zech 13:1VL. 2. *removal, displacement* 2 Esdr 9:11.*

μετακιρνάομαι (*h.l.*) *change its nature* Wsd 16:21.*

μετακομίζω (not in HR; Pla+) *convey, bring back* Jdth 11:14.*

μετακρίνομαι (dub, not in LSJ) *bring justice* (?) Wsd 16:21VL.*

μεταλαμβάνω 2.b. *receive as news, > realize, understand* 2 Macc 4:21; 3 Macc 3:1.‡

μεταλλάσσω pf μετήλλαχα (11x, Hdt+) 1. *exchange; quit* or *leave* (life), *die* 1 Esdr 1:29; Esth 2:7; 2 Macc 4:7, 37. 2. *change, alter, transform* (τι into τι) 2 Macc 6:31.‡

μεταλλεύω (Pla+) 1. *mine* Dt 8:9. 2. *change, transform,"undermine"* (?) (appar = μεταλλάσσω, no //) Wsd 4:12; (pass) 16:25.*

μέταλλον, -ου, τό (Hdt+) *mine* 1 Macc 8:3.*

μεταμέλει (act only impers; pass = BDAG: μεταμέλομαι) impf pass μετεμελόμην aor pass μετεμελήθην (not μεταμελέω, c. HR) fut pass μεταμεληθήσομαι (14x; Aeschyl, Hdt, Polyb+) 1. (act) *be a cause of regret or repentance* (to τινί; Pla APOL 38e) Ex 13:17. 2. (pass) *regret, repent* 1 Km 15:35; 1 Macc 11:10; Ps 105:45; Pr 5:11; Wsd 19:2 Zech 11:5; Ezk 14:22; Sir 32:19 rd μεταμέλου (c. Ra, Gött; no μεταμελέω exists [c. LSJ], cf. μέλω).‡

μεταμέλεια, -ας, ἡ (Democr, Thu+) *regret, repentance* PsSol 9:7; Hos 11:8.*

μετάμελος, -ου, ὁ (Thu+) *change of heart, regret, repentance* 4 Km 3:27; 3 Macc 2:24; Pr 11:3.*

μεταναστεύω (Strabo) *flee, depart* Ps 10:1; 61:7; (trans) *remove, cause to flee* 51:7.*

μετανάστης, -ου, ὁ (Hom, Hdt+) *migrant, refugee, fugitive* Jer 30:21VL.*

μετανίστημι (Soph, Thu+) *migrate from, leave behind* 2 Km 15:20; (abs) *migrate, wander* Ps 108:10.*

μεταπαιδεύω (LXX+) *teach differently*; (pass) *learn to be different* 4 Macc 2:7.*

μεταπείθω (Aristoph, X+) *persuade to change* 4 Macc 11:25.*

μεταπίπτω (Heraclitus, Hdt+) *fall out differently; change* 3 Macc 3:8; *change for the worse, spread* (of disease) Lev 13:5ff.*

μετασκευάζω (Aristoph, X+) *refashion, transform* Am 5:8.*

μεταστρέφω 2. (pass) *be turned over to* (τινί), *pass to* (no //, s.t. of הפך niph *be changed, > pass to*) La 5:2.‡

μεταστροφή, -ῆς, ἡ (Pla REP 525c, 532b) *turning, redirection* 3 Km 12:15 = 2 Ch 10:15*

μεταφέρω (Soph, X+) *transfer, convey* 1 Ch 13:3; 1 Esdr 4:48.*

μετάφρασις, -εως, ἡ (Plu) *paraphrase* 2 Macc 2:31.*

μετάφρενον, -ου, τό (Hom+) *back* (usu pl, even for one pers) Dt 32:11; Is 51:23; in

Ps 67:14; 90:4 Heb is *wings* (as in Ps 54:7), unexpl.*

μεταχέω (Diosc, Joseph *AJ* 9.48+: *pour fr one vessel to another*) *irrigate, water* (no //) 4 Macc 1:29.*

μετέρχομαι (Hom, Hdt+) **1.** (intr) *come among* 1 Km 5:8f. **2.** (trans) *seek, pursue* (cf. our *"come after"*) 1 Macc 15:4; 4 Macc 10:21; 18:22; Wsd 14:30.*

μετεωρίζω (10x, Aristoph+) (mid trans) *raise up, lift high* (obj διανοίαν *be haughty*) 2 Macc 5:17; (mid/pass) *be raised up* (in pride) Ps 130:1; (in exultation) Mi 4:1; *soar up, fly* Ezk 10:16; Ob 4.‡

μετεωρισμός, -οῦ, ὁ (7x, Aristot+) **1.** *lifting up* (of mind or eyes, in pride) 2 Macc 5:21; Sir 23:4. **2.** *wave, swell* (of sea) Ps 41:8; Jon 2:4.

μετέωρος, -ον (16x, Hdt+) **1.** *high, upper* Is 17:6; Ezk 3:15; (subst) *eminence, high place* Sir 22:18; Jer 38:35. **2.** *exalted, uplifted* Judg 1:15; Jer 39:17; (subst) *arrogant (person)* 2 Km 22:28; Is 2:12. Job 28:18 mistrans of ראמות *coral* (?) as if fr רום *be high.*

μετήλλαχα see μεταλλάσσω.

μετοικέω (Aeschyl+) *settle in a different place* 2 Km 15:19.*

μετοικία, -ας, ἡ (Aeschyl, Thu+) *deportation* 3 Km 8:47; 1 Ch 5:41; Jer 9:10; 20:4.*

μετουσία, -ας, ἡ (Aristoph, X+) *participation, enjoyment* 4 Macc 2:1.*

μέτρησις, -εως, ἡ (Hdt+) *measurement* 3 Km 7:24.*

μετριάζω (Soph, Thu+) *be moderate;* (of persons, Theophr) *be "so-so," be unwell* 2 Esdr 12:2.*

μετριότης, -ητος, ἡ (not in HR; Hippocr, Thu+) *moderation* Wsd 12:22cj (for μυριο-).*

μέτρον Zech 5:6ff mistrans of איפה; prob here *basket* rather than *measure.*‡

μεχωνωθ (20x) translit of מכנ(ו)ות *supports, (wheeled) stands* 3 Km 7:27ff; 2 Ch 4:14.

μή τι Gen 18:30, 32 modal expression *"(let it) not (be) anything," don't hold it against me* (no //).

μηδαμόθεν (X+) *from nowhere* Wsd 17:9.*

μηθέτερος, -α, -ον (Thu, Pla+) *neither* (of two) Pr 24:21.*

μῆκος **1.b.** (of time) Pr 3:2.‡

μηκύνω **2.** *delay* Ezk 12:25, 28.‡

μῆλον, -ου, τό (Hom+) **1.** *apple, fruit* Gen 30:14; Pr 25:11; SSol 2:3, 5; 7:9; *apple tree* (no //) SSol 8:5; Joel 1:12. **2.** *cheek* (pap, ins+) SSol 4:3; 6:7.*

μηνιαῖος, -α, -ον (10x, Hippocr+) *of one month, a month old* Lev 27:6; Num 3:15ff; 8:16; 26:62.*

μηνίαμα, -ατος, τό (h.l. = μήνιμα) *cause of anger or guilt* Sir 40:4.*

μήνιμα, -ατος, τό (Hom+) *cause of anger or guilt* Dt 14:21VL, Sir 40:4VL.*

μῆνις, gen **μηνίσεως, ἡ** (Hom, Hdt+) *rage, implacable anger* Gen 49:7; Num 35:21; Sir 27:30; 28:5; PsSol 2:23 (only instance of this gen; class μήνιος or μήνιδος).*‡

μηνίσκος, -ου, ὁ (Aristoph+) *crescent (ornament)* Judg 8:21, 26B; Is 3:18.*

μηρίον, -ου, τό (Hom+) *thigh bone* Lev 3:4ff; 4:9; 7:4; Job 15:27.*

μηρός 4 Km 16:14 mistrans of יד (fig) *side or base* as if (lit) *thigh.*‡

μηρυκάομαι (= BDAG: μαρυ-; LXX+) *chew cud, ruminate* Lev 11:26.*‡

μηρυκισμός, -οῦ, ὁ (11x, LXX+) *cud* Lev 11:3ff; Dt 14:6ff.*

μηρύομαι (Hom, Hes+) *spin* (into thread) Pr 31:13.*

μητρῷος, -α, -ον (Aeschyl, X+) *of the mother* 4 Macc 13:19.*

μηχανεύομαι (LXX+) *construct* 2 Ch 26:15; (fig) *devise* 3 Macc 6:22.*

μηχανή **2.** (fig) *contrivance, scheme* 3 Macc 4:19.‡

μηχάνημα, -ατος, τό (Hippocr, trag, X+) **1.** *machine* (esp for war or siege) 4 Macc 7:4. **2.** *subtle contrivance* 1 Macc 13:29.*

μιαίνω **3.** *declare defiled* (no //, but cf. BDAG: καθαρίζω 3.) Lev 13:3. PsSol 2:13 rd ἐμιαίνοσαν (J. Trafton, *Syriac Version*, εμιαινον).‡

μιαιόω impf ἐμιαίωσαν f.l. for ἐμιαίνοσαν (for -σαν w. impf see BDF 84); cf. μιαίνω.

μιαιφονία, -ας, ἡ (Demosth, DiodS+) *bloodthirsty murderousness* 4 Macc 9:9; 10:11.*

μιαιφόνος, -ον (Hom, Hdt+) *bloodthirsty, murderous;* (subst) *bloodstained murderer* 2 Macc 4:38; 12:6.*

μίανσις, -εως, ἡ (Porph) *defilement* Lev 13:44.*

μιαροφαγέω (10x; LXX) *eat defiled or defiling food* 4 Macc 5:3ff; 8:1ff.

μιαροφαγία, -ας, ἡ (LXX) *eating of defiled or defiling food* 4 Macc 5:27; 6:19; 7:6; 11:25.*

μιερός, -ά, -όν 2 Macc 4:19G; 5:16G κτλ later form of BDAG: μιαρός.

μικρολόγος, -ον (Pla+) *attentive to trifles,* > *stingy, penurious* Sir 14:3.*

μικρός La 4:18 mistrans of צַעַד *step, footprint* as if צְ(ע)יר *small, young, insignificant.*‡

μικρότης, -ητος, ἡ (Anaxagoras [V BCE], Pla+) *smallness* PsSol 14:7; 3 Km 12:10, 24r renders קֹמֶן *little finger? phallus?* as if fr קטן *be small.**

μικροῦ (adv subst) = BDAG: παρὰ μικρόν *nearly* Gen 26:10.

μικρύνω see σμικρύνω.

μίλτος, -ου, ἡ (Hdt+) *red ochre* (iron oxide) Wsd 13:14; Jer 22:14.*

μισάνθρωπος, -ον (PhrynicusCom [V BCE], Pla+) *hating humanity* 4 Macc 11:4.*

μισάρετος, -ον (Philo) *hating virtue* 4 Macc 11:4.*

μίσγω (Hom, Hdt) pres only (other tenses fr μείγνυμι) *mix* Hos 4:2; Is 1:22.*

μισητός, -ή, -όν (9x, Aeschyl+) *hated, hateful* Gen 34:30; Pr 24:24; Wsd 14:9; Sir 10:7.

μισθωτός Is 28:1, 3 mistrans of שִׁכּוֹר *drunken* as if שָׂכִיר *hired man.*‡

μισοξενία, -ας, ἡ (h.l.) *hatred of strangers* Wsd 19:13.*

μισοπονηρεύω (dub; not in LSJ) *hate to do evil* 2 Macc 4:49VL.*

μισοπονηρέω (Lysias, Polyb+) *hate evil* 2 Macc 4:49; 8:4.*

μισοπονηρία, -ας, ἡ (Hippocr, Aristot+) *hatred of evil* 2 Macc 3:1.*

μισοπόνηρος, -ον (Demosth+) *hating wrong and wrongdoers* Esth 8:12d.*

μίσυβρις, -ιος, ὁ (h.l.) *hater of insolence* 3 Macc 6:9.*

μνημόσυνον 4. *memorandum* Esth 1:1p; Tob 12:12; 1 Macc 8:22; Mal 3:16. 5. *way to (re)call or make evident* (no //; = Heb זֵכֶר) Ex 3:15; Num 5:15. Lev 2:2ff et al render אַזְכָּרָה (unknown) as if fr זכר *remember.*‡

μνήσκομαι shortened form of BDAG: μιμνήσκομαι, = ; 1 Macc 6:12VL.*

μολόχη, -ης, ἡ (Hes+: μαλα- or μολο-) *mallow tree* Job 24:24.*

μόλυβδος, -ου, ὁ (Simonid, Hdt+) *lead;* = BDAG: μόλιβος (already in Hom, and perh poetic). μόλυβος (Ezk 27:12R) and μόλιβδος (Ezk 22:18VL) are alike false conflations of these two forms of this appar loanword (cf. LSJ, Lat PLUMBUM).

μόλυνσις, -εως, ἡ (LXX+) *defilement* Jer 51:4.*

μολύνω 1 Esdr 8:80R; 2 Macc 14:3R μεμολυσμένος (pf pass ptc) is an error; Gött -μολυμμ- (= BDAG), txt and all mss.‡

μόναρχος, -ου, ὁ (Theognis, Hdt+) *sole ruler* 3 Macc 2:2.*

μονή 3. *continuing existence* 1 Macc 7:38.*‡

μονήμερος, -ον (Aelian, ins) *for one day* Wsd 5:14VL.*

μονία, -ας, ἡ (MaximusAstrologus [I BCE]) *solitude* PsSol 4:18VL.*

μόνιμος, -ον (Soph+) *fixed, stable, steady* Gen 49:26; (subst) *permanence, security* Jer 38:17.*

μονιός, -όν (Callim+) *solitary,* > *wild,* (subst) *solitary wild boar* Ps 79:14.*

μονόζωνος, -ον (10x, LXX+) *lightly armed;* (subst) *light-armed troops* 2 Km 22:30; 4 Km 5:2; Job 29:25.

μονοήμερος, -ον (Batr+) *for one day* Wsd 5:14.*

μονόκερως, -ωτος, τό (8x, Archilochus-Lyr, Aristot) *unicorn* Num 23:22; Ps 21:22; Job 39:9; Ps 77:69 mistrans of רָמִים *lofty* as if רְאֵם *wild ox* (consistently rendered *unicorn* in LXX; cf. Vulg (Gallican Psalter), where Jerome varies from *unicorn* to *rhinoceros* to translit of the Greek).

μονομαχέω (Hdt+) *engage in single combat* 1 Km 17:10; Ps 151:1.*

μόνορχις, gen -εως (LXX+) *w. one testicle* Lev 21:20.*

μόνος **3.** κατὰ μόνας *solely, only* (Polyb 4.15.10) Judg 17:3A.‡

μονότροπος, -ον (Eur+) *alone, solitary* Ps 67:7.*

μονοφαγία, -ας, ἡ (h.l.) *eating alone, > gluttony* 4 Macc 1:27.*

μονοφάγος, -ον (Aristoph+) *eating alone, > gluttonous* 4 Macc 2:7.*

μόνωσις, -εως, ἡ (not in HR; Pla+) *solitariness* PsSol 4:18.*

μονώτατος, -η, -ον (superl/elat of BDAG: μόνος) *sole, only* Esth 3:13e; *completely alone* Judg 3:20; 3 Km 19:10.

μόρον, -ου, τό (Aeschyl, Hippocr+) *blackberry* 1 Macc 6:34.*

μόρος, -ου, ὁ (7x, Hom+) *fate, doom, death* 2 Macc 9:28; 3 Macc 3:1.

μορφή **2.** *attractive appearance, winsomeness* Tob 1:13.‡

μοσφαθαιμ (vl -φαιθαμ) translit of משפתים *saddlebags* Judg 5:16A.*

μοσχάριον, -ου, τό (12x, pap+) *calf* Gen 18:7; Ex 24:5; Am 6:4; Is 11:6.

μόσχευμα, -ατος, τό (Theophr+) *shoot, sprig* (removed and transplanted) Wsd 4:3.*

μοτόω (Hippocr) *stanch a wound* Hos 6:1.*

μουσικός, -ή, -όν (17x; Pind, Hdt, ins+) **1.** *musical, pertaining to music;* **2.** (coll pl subst, X+) *music, songs* Gen 31:27; 1 Esdr 4:63; 5:2; 1 Macc 9:41; Sir 22:6; 32:3ff. **3.** *musical instrument* (no //) 1 Esdr 5:59; 1 Macc 9:39; Da 3:5ff.‡

μοχθέω (15x, Hom+) *toil, labor* 1 Esdr 4:22; Eccl 1:3; 2:11ff; Is 62:8; *exhaust, make weary* (no //) La 3:5.

μοχθηρός, -ά, -όν (Aeschyl+) *distressing, wretched* Sir 26:5; 27:15.*

μόχθος **2.** *result or fruit of such labor* (no // but cf. πόνος) Is 61:8; Jer 3:24.‡

μυαλόομαι (h.l.) *be full of marrow* Ps 65:15.*

μυγαλή, -ῆς, ἡ (Hdt+) *field mouse, shrew* Lev 11:30.*

μυθολόγος, -ου, ὁ (Pla, Aristot+) *storyteller, purveyor of legends* Bar 3:23.*

μυῖα, -ας, ἡ (Hom+) *fly* 4 Km 1:2ff; Eccl 10:1; Wsd 16:9; Is 7:18.*

μυκτήρ, -ῆρος, ὁ (10x, Hdt+) *nostril* Num 11:20; 4 Km 19:28; 4 Macc 6:25; Pr 30:33; *nose* (no //) SSol 7:5; Ezk 16:12.

μυκτηρισμός, -οῦ, ὁ (8x, Menand) *scorn, contempt* 2 Esdr 13:36; Ps 34:16; Job 34:7; PsSol 4:7.

μύλη, -ης, ἡ (Hom+) *millstone, > (pl) molars, teeth* Ps 57:7; Pr 30:14; Job 29:17; Joel 1:6.*

μυξωτήρ, -ῆρος, ὁ (Hdt+) *nostril; > small pipe* (no //) Zech 4:12.*

μυρεψικός, -ή, -όν (Polyb+) *aromatic, perfumed* Ex 30:25, 35; SSol 5:13; 8:2.*

μυρεψός, -οῦ, ὁ or ἡ (9x, Critias, Aristot+) *perfumer* Ex 30:25; 1 Km 8:13; 1 Ch 9:30; SSol 3:6; *apothecary, druggist* Sir 38:8.

μυριοπλάσιος, -ον (X+) *ten thousand-fold;* (neut acc as adv) Ps 67:18; (adv, w. comp adj) *ten thousand times* (more than τινός) Sir 23:19.*

μυριότης, -ητος, ἡ (h.l.) *multitude, mass of ten thousand* Wsd 12:22.*

μυρισμός, -οῦ, ὁ (LXX+) *perfume, ointment* (no //) Jdth 16:7.*

μυρμηκιάω (h.l.) *have warts* Lev 22:22.*

μυρμηκολέων, -οντος, ὁ (h.l.) *ant-lion* Job 4:11.*

μύρμηξ, -ηκος, ὁ (Hes+) *ant* Pr 6:6; 30:25.*

μυροβρεχής, -ές (h.l.) *wet w. perfume or unguent* 3 Macc 4:6.*

μυρσίνη, -ης, ἡ (ArchilochusLyr, Hdt+) *myrtle* 2 Esdr 18:15; Is 41:19; 55:13.*

μύσος, -ους, τό (Aeschyl+) *pollution* 2 Macc 6:19, 25.*

μύσταξ, -ακος, ὁ (Hom+: μασ-; StrattisCom [V BCE]+) *mustache* 2 Km 19:25.*

μύστης, -ου, ὁ (Heraclitus, X+) *initiate* Wsd 12:5; (fem) μύστις, -ιδος ἡ (LXX+) 8:4.*

μυστικῶς (Strabo+ [adj since Hdt]) *secretly* 3 Macc 3:10.*

μυχός, -οῦ, ὁ (Hom+) *deep recess, hidden nook* Wsd 17:4, 13.*

μωκάομαι pf pass ptc μεμωκημένος (Epicurus+) *mimic, ridicule;* pass ptc *ridiculous* Jer 28:18.*

μώκημα, -ατος, τό (h.l.) mockery, mimicry Sir 34:18VL.*

μωκός, -οῦ, ὁ (Aristot+) mocker, mimic Sir 33:6.*

μώμημα, -ατος, τό (h.l.) blame, censure Sir 34:18VL.*

μωμητός, -ή, -όν (Aeschyl+) blameworthy, disgraceful (Heb מום disfigurements, blemish, as alw w. this group) Dt 32:5.*

μωρεύω (h.l.) render or show to be foolish Is 44:25.*

N

ναβαλ 2 Km 3:33f translit of נָבָל fool, disdainful person as if N PERS (cf. 1 Km 25:3ff), but MT v 34 נפל one who falls (cf. VL ναφα); 1 Km 10:5VL translit of נֶבֶל harp.*

νάβλα, -ας, ἡ (14x, Strabo, ins, Joseph; Sem loanword [Heb נֶבֶל]) harp, stringed instrument 1 Km 10:5; 1 Ch 13:8; 1 Macc 13:51.

ναζιρ translit of נזיר nazirite Judg 13:5B.*

ναζιραῖος, -ον (LXX, not in LSJ) consecrated by nazirite vows Judg 13:5A, 7A; 16:17A; (subst) 1 Macc 3:49.*

ναθιναῖος, -ου, ὁ (10x; HR N PROP; not in LSJ) loanword/translit (ναθινιν 2:58; ναθινειμ VL; -ιμ 7:7, 24) of נתינים temple servants 2 Esdr 2:43.*

ναίω (Hom+; only poetic) inhabit, dwell (in) Job 22:12.*

νακκαριμ (HR Ακκαρειμ, N LOC) mistranslit of נקדים shepherds Am 1:1 (cf. νωκηδ)

νᾶμα, -ατος, τό (Aeschyl, Pla+) fluid, juice SSol 8:2.*

νάπη, -ης, ἡ (9x, Hdt+) wooded valley, vale, glen Num 21:20; Josh 18:16; Is 40:12.

ναρκάω (Hom+) grow numb, stiffen Gen 32:26, 33; Job 33:19; Da 11:6L.*

νασιβ translit of נצב official, viceroy 3 Km 16:28e (MT 22:48).*

νασιφ translit of נציב military garrison (or error for נצב prefect, viceroy) 3 Km 4:18.*

ναῦλον, -ου, τό (Aristoph+) passage money, fare Jon 1:3.*

ναυτικός, -ή, -όν (Hdt+) seafaring 3 Km 9:27; (subst) sailor Jon 1:5.*

νάφθας, νάφθα, ὁ (Pers loanword; Strabo+) naphtha Da 3:46.*

ναχαλ translit of נחל wadi, stream Jer 38:40.*

νεάζω (Aeschyl+) be young or of youthful spirit 4 Macc 5:31.*

νεανικός, -ή, -όν (Hippocr, Eur, Pla+) youthful, fresh, vigorous 3 Macc 4:8.*

νεᾶνις, -ιδος, ἡ (37x, Hom+) young woman Ex 2:8; Ruth 2:5; 3 Macc 4:6; Ps 67:26; SSol 1:3; Sir 20:4; Da 11:6Θ.‡

νεβελ translit of נֵבֶל jar 1 Km 1:24; 2 Km 16:1; Hos 3:2.*

νεβρός, -οῦ, ὁ or ἡ (Hom, Hdt+) fawn SSol 2:9, 17; 4:5 = 7:4; 8:14.*

νεελασα translit of נעלסה (niph of עלס) be glad Job 39:13.*

νεεσσαραν (doublet w. συνεχόμενος) translit of נעצר detained 1 Km 21:8.*

νεζερ translit of נזר fillet, diadem 4 Km 11:12.*

νεῖκος, -εος, τό (Hom, Hdt+) strife, quarrel, fight Pr 10:12; Hos 10:11. Job 36:7R; Am 1:11R; 8:7R; Jer 3:5R; La 3:18R; 5:20R etc should be read (w. Gött) νῖκος (q.v.). Ezk 3:8f mistrans of מצח forehead, brow as if מצה quarrel, brawl; (cf. Ra VL).‡

νεκριμαῖος, -α, -ον (Aq, ins [II CE]+) dead; (neut subst) carcass, corpse (of person, no //; cf. θνησιμαῖος) 3 Km 13:30VL.*

νέμω fut νεμήσω aor pass ἐνεμήθην 1. (act) shepherd, tend, pasture Gen 36:24; 1 Km 21:8; Hos 4:16; (mid/pass, = BDAG) be pastured, graze, feed (on) Gen 41:18; Ex 34:3; SSol 4:5; Mi 7:14; Jer 27:19. 2. range, wander Gen 41:3; 2 Macc 10:6; Wsd 19:9.‡

νενησμένος pf pass ptc pf BDAG: νήθω Ex 26:31.

νεογνός, -ή, -όν (HomHymns, Hdt+) newly born 3 Macc 1:20; 5:49.*

νεόκτιστος, -ον (Hdt+) newly made Wsd 11:18.*

νέος   1.c. (pl subst) *first fruits* (no //) Num 28:26; Sir 50:8.‡

νεοσσιά   (4 Macc 14:15) = νοσσιά.

νεοσσός   (Att νεοττός) = BDAG: νοσσός (Gött changes Ra's νεοσσος to νοσσος in Lev).‡

νεόω   (Aeschyl+: *renew*; νεάω [Hes, Aristoph+] *plow up*) *plow up* Jer 4:3.*

νεσσα   translit of נֹצָה *falcon* (?) Job 39:13.*

νεῦμα, -ατος, τό   (Aeschyl, Thu+) *gesture; nod* (X ANAB 5.8.20) 2 Macc 8:18; *signal, gesture* (of eyes, no //) Is 3:16.*

νευρά, -ᾶς, ἡ   (Hom+) *cord of sinew; bowstring* Judg 16:7A, 8, 9A; *whip* 2 Macc 7:1.*

νευρέα, -ας, ἡ   (not in LSJ; = νευρά) Judg 16:7B, 9B.*

νευροκοπέω   (pap, Polyb+) *hamstring* Gen 49:6; Dt 21:4, 6; Josh 11:6, 9.*

νεύω   2. *incline to, face, look toward* Pr 4:25.‡

νεφθαι   (HR as N PROP) play on words νάφθα and νεφθαρ (q.v.) to form intermediate "etymological" step 2 Macc 1:36.*

νεφθαρ   (not in HR) translit of נפטר *escape, be released (from duty)*; as (false) etymology for νάφθα *petroleum* (orig Akk; Strabo+) as if connected with purifying the temple 2Macc1:36.*

νεφρός   2. (fig, Heb) *best or richest part* Dt 32:14.‡

νεχωθα   translit of נְכֹתֹה *his treasury* 4 Km 20:13 = Is 39:2.*

νέωμα, -ατος, τό   (h.l.) *fallow* (but plowed) *land* Jer 4:3.*

νεώς, νεώ, ὁ   (7x, Aeschyl, Pla+) alt form of BDAG: ναός *temple, sanctuary proper* 2 Macc 4:14; 6:2; etc.*

νεωστί   (Hdt+) *just recently, lately* Jdth 4:3.*

νεώτατος   superl of νέος.

νεωτερίζω   (Thu, Pla+) *revolutionize* 4 Macc 3:21.*

νηπιοκτόνος, -ον   (h.l.) *of the killing of children* Wsd 11:7.*

νηπιότης   2. *childhood* Ezk 16:22.‡

νῆσος   2. (fig, Heb) *separate group*, (of people) *community* (no //) Gen 10:5.‡

νηστός, -ή, -όν   (h.l.) *spun* Ex 31:4.*

νίκημα, -ατος, τό   (ins, Polyb+) *victory prize* 1 Esdr 3:9VL.*

νικοποιέω   (dub; not in HR or LSJ) = ἐπινικάω 2 Esdr 3:8VL.*

νῖκος   2 Km 2:26; Job 36:7; Am 11:1; Jer 3:5; La 5:20 etc εἰς νῖκος mistrans of לנצח *in perpetuity, forever* as if Aram (sim sounds also factor) *victory* (pace R. A. Kraft, SEPTUAGINTAL LEXICOGRAPHY [SCS 1; Missoula: Scholars, 1975], 153–56] νῖκος still means *victory*). La 3:18G mistrans of נצח *glory, luster* as if Aram *victory*.‡

νίπτω   3. *cause to pour* (no //) Job 20:23 (renders מטר *rain*).‡

νίτρον, -ου, τό   (Sappho, Aristot+; Hdt+: λίτ-) *sodium carbonate, natron* (Heb נֶתֶר) Jer 2:22.*

νιφετός, -οῦ, ὁ   (Hom, Hdt+) *snow* Dt 32:2; Da 3:68.*

νοερός, -ά, -όν   (Heraclitus, Aristot+) *perceptive, reflective* Wsd 7:22, 23.*

νοέω   4.b. (Hom+) *be intent on, intend to* (+inf) 2 Km 20:15.*‡

νοήμων, -ον, gen **-ονος**   (10x, Hom+) *intelligent, reflective, thoughtful* Pr 1:5; 10:5; Sir 19:29; Da 12:10Θ.*

νόησις, -εως, ἡ   (c. HR; DiogApol [V BCE], Pla+) *intelligence, process of thought* Job 33:3.*

νοητῶς   (adj Parmenides, Pla+, adv LXX+) *intelligently, thoughtfully* Pr 23:1.*

νοθεύω   (Zeno) *corrupt a marriage* Wsd 14:24.*

νόθος, -η, -ον   (Hom, Hdt+) 1. *illegitimate in birth* Wsd 4:3. 2. *spurious, meretricious*; (adv) *falsely, basely* 3 Macc 3:17.*‡

νομάς, gen **-άδος, ὁ** or **ἡ**   (Hdt+) 1. *grazing* Job 1:3; 42:12; (of dogs) *for tending flocks* 30:1. > *pastured, fattened* 1 Km 28:24; 3 Km 2:46e = 5:3; 1 Ch 27:29. 2. *wandering, nomadic*; (subst) *nomad* 2 Macc 12:11. 3. (subst) *channel (for irrigation*; ins) Job 20:17.*

νομή   3. *usage*; ἐν χειρῶν νομαῖς *in action, in combat* (ins) 2 Macc 5:14; more commonly ἐν χ. νόμῳ (fr νόμος but =, Hdt+); ἐν χ. νόμοις (= , no //) VL.‡

νόμιμος   Ezk 16:27 mistrans of חק *portion* as if *pattern, decree*.‡

νομιστέον (Pla, Menand+) *it is to be reckoned or accounted* EpJer 39, 44, 56, 63.*

νομοθέσμως (h.l.) *according to Torah* Pr 31:28.*

νόμος 1. (pl) *customs, usual practices* (X Anab 1.2.15) 3 Macc 5:36.‡

νομός, -οῦ, ὁ (Hdt+) 1. *pasture, field* 3 Macc 4:3. 2. *district, province, nome* 1 Macc 10:30, 38; 11:34, 57; Is 19:2.*

νομοφαγία, -ας, ἡ (spur; not in LSJ) *grazing, eating like an animal* or *licit eating, eating what is customary* 4 Macc 1:27vl.*

νομοφύλαξ, -ακος, ὁ or **ἡ** (Pla+) *guardian of custom or law* 4 Macc 15:32.*

νοσερός, -ά, -όν (Hippocr, Eur+) *diseased* Jer 14:15; 16:4.*

νοσσεύω (Hdt+) 1. *nest* Jer 31:28; Da 4:12L, 21G, (of porcupines) Is 34:15. 2. *build a nest* Ezk 31:6; (fig) *construct* Sir 1:15.*

νοσσιά 1.b. (fig) *dwelling* Num 24:21; Sir 36:27; *lair* (of lion) Na 2:13. c. *cell, compartment* Gen 6:14. Pr 16:16 mistrans of קנה *acquire* as if קֵן *nest*, might be read as *dwelling, chamber brood* or 2. *group of offspring* (cf. Lk 13:34).‡

νοσσοποιέω (LXX+) *make a den or lair* Is 13:22; (mid) *nest on* 4 Macc 14:16vl.*

νόφος, -ου, ὁ (dub; not in HR or LSJ) *cloud* (? cf. BDAG: νέφος) 3 Km 8:53a vl.*

νυκτερινός, -ή, -όν (6x, Aristot+) *at night, nocturnal* Ps 90:5; Pr 7:9; Job 4:13.

νυκτερίς, -ίδος, ἡ (Hom+) *bat* Lev 11:19 = Dt 14:18; Is 2:20; EpJer 21.*

νυκτικόραξ, -ακος, ὁ (Aristot+) *horned owl* Lev 11:17 = Dt 14:17; 1 Km 26:20; Ps 101:7*

νύκτωρ (Hes, Soph+) *by night, at night* 2 Macc 12:6; 13:15; 3 Macc 1:2; Sir 38:27.*

νυμφαγωγός, -όν (Eur+) *leading the bride*, (subst) *trusted friend* (no //, palace honorific?) Gen 21:22, 32; 26:26; *best man* Judg 14:20A.*

νύμφευσις, -εως, ἡ (h.l.) *wedding* SSol 3:11.*

νύσταγμα, -ατος, τό (h.l.) *short sleep, nap* Job 33:15.*

νυσταγμός, -οῦ, ὁ (Hippocr+) *drowsiness, dozing* Ps 131:4; Sir 31:2; Jer 23:31; Da 4:33bL.*

νωθροκάρδιος, -ον (h.l.) *sluggish of mind, stupid, lazy* Pr 12:8.*

νωθρότης, -ητος, ἡ (Hippocr, Aristot+) *sluggishness of movement* 3 Macc 4:5.*

νωκηδ translit of נֹקֵד *shepherd, sheep breeder* (cf. νακκαριμ) 4 Km 3:4.*

νῶτος (cf. BDAG) Ex 37:12, 13 transl Heb כתף *shoulder*, here meaning *side* of the gateway; τὸ κατὰ νώτου ... ἐπὶ τοῦ νώτου τοῦ δευτέρου, *on the one side ... on the other side*. Cf. 3 Km 6:8 ὠμίαν. Is 17:12 may render (so BHS) כביר *powerful*, unexpl. 3 Km 7:19; Job 15:26 mistrans of גב *hub, boss* as if *back*.‡

νωτοφόρος, -ον (X, pap+) *carrying on the back*; (subst) *porter* 2 Ch 2:17; 34:13.*

Ξ

ξανθίζω (Aristoph+) *become yellow* Lev 13:30ff.*

ξανθός, -ή, -όν (Hom+) *yellow* Lev 13:36.*

ξένιος, -α, -ον (8x, Hom+) *pertaining to hospitality*; (sg subst) *hospitality* 2 Macc 6:2; (pl) *gifts of hospitality and friendship* 2 Esdr 1:6; 1 Macc 10:36; Sir 20:29, > *tribute* 2 Km 8:2; Hos 10:6.

ξενισμός, -οῦ, ὁ (Pla, ins+) *entertainment of a stranger, hospitality* Pr 15:17.*‡

ξενιτεία, -ας, ἡ (LXX+) *life in a foreign country* Wsd 18:3.*

ξενολογέω (Isocr, Polyb, ins) *recruit mercenaries* 1 Macc 4:35; 11:38; 15:3.*

ξενοτροφέω (Thu [7.48.5]+) *hire or maintain mercenary troops* 2 Macc 10:14.*

ξεστός, -ή, -όν (Hom+) *hewn, dressed* (of stone, or objects made of stone or wood) 1 Ch 22:2cj, 1 Esdr 6:8cj, 24cj, 1 Macc 13:27; Sir 22:17vl (q.l.); Am 5:11G.*

ξέω (Hom+) *scrape* Job 7:5vl.*

ξηρασία, -ας, ἡ (Hippocr, AntiphoOr, Aristot+) *dryness, desiccation* Judg 6:37ff; 2 Esdr 19:11; Na 1:10; Ezk 17:10; 40:43.*

ξιφηφόρος, -ον (Aeschyl, Eur+) *bearing or wielding a sword* 4 Macc 16:20.*

ξυλάριον, -ου, τό (vl -ληρ- dub; not in LSJ. lxx+) *stick of wood* 3 Km 17:12.*

ξυλοκόπος, -ον (X+) *cutting wood;* (subst) *woodcutter* Dt 29:10; Josh 9:21ff.*

ξυλοπελέκητος (not in HR or LSJ) *f.l.* for ξυλα πελεκητα (so rd w. ms B, mt) 3 Km 10:11vl.*

ξυλοφορία, -ας, ἡ (Lysias) *assessment or provision of wood* (no //) 2 Esdr 20:35.*

ξυλοφόρος, -ον (Epicurus+) *wood-carrying;* (subst) *one who provides wood* (no //) 2 Esdr 23:31.*

ξυλόω pf pass ptc ἐξυλωμένος (Theophr+) *panel, cover w. wood* 2 Ch 3:5; pass ptc *paneled* (ins) Jer 22:14; Ezk 41:16.*

ξύρησις, -εως, ἡ (lxx+) *shaving* (of one's head, in mourning) Is 22:12.*

ξυρόν, -οῦ, τό (7x, Hom+) *razor* Num 6:5; Judg 16:17A; Ps 51:4; Is 7:20; (scribe's) *knife* (no //) Jer 43:23.

ξυστός, -ή, -όν (Hom+) *shaved, planed; dressed* (of stone, no //; better ξεστ-) 1 Ch 22:2; 1 Esdr 6:8, 24; Sir 22:17; Am 5:11R.*

ξύω (Hom+) *scrape away* Job 2:8; 7:5.*

Ο

ὀβολός, -οῦ, ὁ (7x, Aristoph+) *small weight or coin* (orig *nail*) Ex 30:13; 1 Km 2:36; Pr 17:6; Ezk 45:12.

ὀγδοηκοστός, -ή, -όν (Hippocr, Thu+) *eightieth* 2 Macc 1:9.*

ὄγδοος Ps 6:1; 11:1 renders השמינית unexpl mus t.t. (*octave?*).‡

ὁδοιπόρος, -ου, ὁ (Aeschyl+) *traveler* Gen 37:25; Judg 19:17; 2 Km 12:4; Pr 6:11; Sir 26:12; 42:3.*

ὀδυνηρός, -ά, -όν (Mimnermus, Pind, Eur+) *painful, woeful* 3 Km 2:8, 35m, Jer 14:17; 37:17; La 5:17.*

οἰακίζω (Hdt+) *manage, govern* Job 37:10.*

οἴαξ, -ακος, ὁ (Hom, Aeschyl, Pla+) *rudder, tiller* (fig) 4 Macc 7:3.*

οἰκεῖος **2.** *suitable, proper,* (Stoic t.t.) *conformable to Nature* 2 Macc 15:12.‡

οἰκειότης, -ητος, ἡ (Hdt+) *kinship, intimacy* Lev 20:19.*

οἰκειόω (Hdt+: *befriend, reconcile*) *adapt, make suitable* (Polyb+); pf pass ptc *appropriate, suitable* 4 Macc 5:26.*

οἰκέσιος, -ου, ὁ (dub; not in LSJ) *resident?* 4 Km 19:25vl.*

οἰκετικός, -ή, -όν (Pla+) *suited or related to slaves* 3 Macc 2:28.*

οἰκέτις, -ιδος, ἡ (Hippocr, Soph+) *female slave* Ex 21:7; Lev 19:20; Pr 30:23.*

οἰκέω impf ᾤκουν (vl οἴκουν, =) aor ᾤκησα.‡

οἰκητός, -ή, -όν (Soph+) **1.** *inhabited* 2 Macc 9:17; 3 Macc 4:3. **2.** *habitable* Lev 25:29.*

οἰκία **3.b.** κατ᾽ οἰκίαν *at home;* > *proper, usual, assigned* (no //) 2 Macc 13:15.‡

οἰκίδιον, -ου, τό (Aristoph+) *small house, outbuilding* Tob 2:4S; 2 Macc 8:33.*

οἰκίζω (Hdt+) *settle, cause to live* Job 22:8; (pass) *be made habitable* (no //) Sir 10:3; 38:32.*

οἰκίον, -ου, τό (Hom, Hdt+) *house* 2 Macc 8:33vl.*

οἰκογενής, -ή (11x, Pla+) *born in the household* 1 Esdr 3:1; (subst) *member of household, slave* Gen 14:14; Eccl 2:7; Jer 2:14.

οἰκοδομή Ezk 16:61 mistrans of לבנות as *daughters* as if fr בנה *build* (16:31R note [surely correct, though ignored in Gött] οἰκοδομέω and θυγατράσιν is doublet, arising fr opp error).‡

οἰκόπεδον, -ου, τό (Thu+) *building site* Ps 101:7; 108:10; *building* Sir 49:13.*

οἶκος 3 Km 7:13 s.t. of בית *interior* as if *house*. 4 Km 12:10 see ἀνήρ. 2 Ch 23:1 mistrans of ברית *covenant* as if בית *house*.‡

οἰκτίρημα, -ατος, τό (h.l.) mercy, compassion Jer 38:3.*

οἰκτιρμός 2. lament, plea for pity (no //, but class οἰκτίζομαι can mean either pity or bewail) Da 9:18Θ(1).‡

οἴκτιστος, -ον (Hom+) most lamentable 2 Macc 9:28.*

οἶκτος, -ου, ὁ (Hom, Hdt+) pity Esth 3:13f; cry of lamentation 3 Macc 1:4; 5:49; 6:22; Jer 9:18f.*

οἰκτρός, -ά, -όν (Hom, Hdt+) pitiable, lamentable 4 Macc 15:18; Wsd 18:10; Jer 6:26; (superl) οἰκτρότατος most pitiable 3 Macc 5:24.*

οἴμμοι (18x, Hom+ [ὤ μοι, οἴμοι; cf. W]) alas, woe is me Judg 11:35A; 1 Macc 2:7; Ps 119:5; Job 10:15; Joel 1:15; Jer 4:31.

οἶμος, -ου, ὁ (not in HR; Hom+) road, path Jer 38:21cj (surely correct—Heb מסלה highway; Aq, Sym: τρίβος).

οἰμωγή, -ῆς, ἡ (Hom, Hdt+) lament, outcry 3 Macc 6:32.*

οἰμώζω (Hom, Aristoph+) bewail, lament 4 Macc 12:14.*

οἰνοδόχος, -ον (HeroAlex+) wine-carrying; (subst) wine-bearer (no //) Tob 1:22VL.*

οἰνοποτέω (Callim+) drink wine Pr 31:4.*

οἰνοφλυγέω (Philo [EBR 16; =], Pollux) become drunk Dt 21:20.*

οἰνοχοέω (Hom, X+) pour wine Gen 40:13; Da 5:2L.*

οἰνοχόη, -ης, ἡ (Hes, Thu+: vessel for wine) cupbearer (no //) Eccl 2:8.*

οἰνοχόος, -ου, ὁ (Hom+) wine server, cupbearer Gen 40:20; 3 Km 10:5 = 2 Ch 9:4; 2 Esdr 11:11; Tob 1:22BA, Eccl 2:8.*.

οἰνόω pf pass ptc οἰνωμένος (Hom, Hdt+) intoxicate; (pass) become drunk Ezk 23:42VL.*

οἴομαι impf ᾤμην 2. suppose oneself (in a dream), > seem Gen 40:16; 41:1.‡

οἶσθα 2 sg of οἶδα.

οἰστρηλασία, -ας, ἡ (h.l.) maddening torment 4 Macc 2:4.*

οἶστρος, -ου, ὁ (Hom, Hdt+) gadfly, > sting, (fig) anything maddening or tormenting, frenzied desire 4 Macc 2:3; 3:17.*

οιφι (11x) translit of אפה dry measure (approx 40l) Lev 5:11; Ruth 2:17; Ezk 45:13.

οἴχομαι impf ᾠχόμην (31; Hom+) go, depart Gen 12:4; 1 Esdr 9:54; Tob 2:7; 4 Macc 4:1; Job 14:10; Jer 9:9; (pass) be removed, vanish Hos 10:14; Jer 30:1 (Gött 29:8).

οἰωνίζομαι fut οἰωνιοῦμαι impf οἰωνιζόμην aor οἰωνίσαντο (X+) divine from omens Gen 30:27; 44:5ff; Lev 19:26; 4 Km 17:17; 21:6 = 2 Ch 33:6; (ptc subst) diviner Dt 18:10; take as an omen 3 Km 21:33.*

οἰώνισμα, -ατος, τό (Eur+) omen 1 Km 15:23; Jer 14:14; 34:9.*

οἰωνισμός, -οῦ, ὁ (LXX+) omen Gen 44:5, 15; Num 23:23; Sir 34:5.*

οἰωνόβρωτος, -ον (Strabo+) for eating by birds 2 Macc 9:15; 3 Macc 6:34.*

οἰωνός, -οῦ, ὁ (Hom+) large bird (of prey, of omen), > omen Num 24:1.*

ὀκλάζω pf act ptc ὀκλακώς (Soph+) crouch down, sink down 1 Km 4:19; 3 Km 8:54; (trans) bend 19:18.*

ὀκνηρία, -ας, ἡ (LXX+) delay Eccl 10:18.*

ὀκτακισχίλιοι, -αι, -α (9x, Hdt+) eight thousand Num 2:24; 1 Ch 29:7; 1 Macc 5:20.*

ὀκτακόσιοι, -αι, -α (16x, Hdt+) eight hundred Gen 5:17; 2 Km 23:8; 1 Esdr 5:11.

ὀκτάπηχυς, -υ (ins, Polyb+) eight cubits long 3 Km 7:47.*

ὀκτωκαίδεκα (10x, Hdt+) eighteen Judg 10:18A; 2 Esdr 8:18.

ὀκτωκαιδέκατος, -η, -ον (16x, Hom+) eighteenth 3 Km 15:1; 1 Esdr 1:22; Jer 39:1; Da 3:1.

ὄλβος, -ου, ὁ (Hom, Hdt+) prosperity Sir 30:15.*

ὀλέθρευσις, -εως, ἡ (h.l.) destruction, ruin Josh 17:13VL.*

ὀλεθρία, -ας, ἡ (LXX) destruction, ruin Esth 8:12t; 3 Macc 4:2; 5:5.*

ὀλεθροφόρος, -ον (h.l.) bringing death or ruin 4 Macc 8:19.*

ὀλέκω (Hom+) ruin, kill Job 10:16; 32:18; (pass) be destroyed, die 17:1.*

ὀλιγόβιος, -ον (Aristot+) short-lived Job 11:2; 14:1.*‡

ὀλιγοποιέω (h.l.) diminish, make lesser or fewer Sir 48:2.*
ὀλιγοστός superl of BDAG: ὀλίγος.
ὀλιγότης, -ητος, ἡ (Pla+) smallness, fewness Ps 101:24.*
ὀλιγοψυχία, -ας, ἡ (Hippocr) discouragement, loss of heart Ex 6:9; Ps 54:9; PsSol 16:11.*
ὀλιγόω aor pass ὠλιγώθη (11; LXX) make few 4 Km 4:3; reduce, lessen Hab 3:12; (pass) seem small 2 Esdr 19:32; diminish, pass away Judg 10:16B; Ps 11:2; Pr 10:27; Joel 1:10.
ὀλισθάνω (VL -θαίνω, =) fut ὀλισθήσω aor ὠλίσθησα (8x, Hom+) slip and fall Pr 14:19; PsSol 16:1; Sir 9:9; 14:1; (caus, no //) make to fall Sir 3:24.
ὀλίσθημα, -ατος, τό (9x, Pla+) slip, fall Ps 34:6; Sir 20:18; Jer 23:12; -θρημα Da 11:21Θ.
ὀλίσθησις, -εως, ἡ (not in HR; Hippocr, Pla+) slipping and falling Sir 28:26VL.*
ὁλκεῖον, -ου, τό (ins, Polyb+ [ApollonRhod ὁλκήϊον ship's hull]) basin, large bowl Jdth 15:11.
ὁλκή, -ῆς, ἡ (26x, Aeschyl+) weight ("pull" on the scale) Gen 24:22; 2 Km 21:16; 1 Ch 21:25; Sir 8:2. 2 Macc 12:28G; Sir 29:13 see ἀλκή.
ὄλλυμι aor ὤλεσα 3rd pl opt ὀλέσαισαν (VL -ειαν, =) 2 aor mid ὤλετο pf mid ptc ὀλωλώς 2. (mid) perish, cease to exist Pr 2:22; Job 4:11; Jer 10:20R (Gött omits doublet); 29:10.‡
ὁλοκαρπόω (LXX) (pass) be offered 4 Macc 18:11; Sir 45:14.*
ὁλοκάρπωμα, -ατος, τό (LXX) offering, sacrifice Lev 16:24; Num 15:3R (Gött ὁλοκαύτωμα); Wsd 3:6.*
ὁλοκάρπωσις, -εως, ἡ (10x, LXX) offering, sacrifice Gen 8:20; 22:2ff; Lev 9:3; Is 40:16; 43:23.
ὁλόκαυτος, -ον (Callim+) burned completely Lev 6:16.*
ὁλοκαύτωμα Ezk 40:40 mistrans of עוֹלָה (the one) going up as if עוֹלָה whole burnt offering.‡
ὁλοκαύτωσις, -εως, ἡ (83x, LXX) sacrificing of whole animal by burning Ex 29:25;
1 Km 6:14; 1 Ch 21:23; 1 Macc 4:44; Da 3:38; the sacrifice itself Lev 6:3; Num 15:5; 2 Ch 29:27; 2 Esdr 3:2.
ὀλολυγμός, -οῦ, ὁ (Aeschyl+) loud cry, wailing Zeph 1:10; Is 15:8.*
ὁλοπόρφυρος, -ον (X, Plu) completely purple Num 4:7, 13.*
ὁλόρριζος, -ον (Theophr+) w. the whole root,"root and all" Pr 15:6; Job 4:7; (adv) ὁλορριζεί Esth 3:13f.*
ὁλοσφύρητος, -ον (LXX+) of solid beaten metal Sir 50:9.*
ὁλοσχερής, -ές (Hippocr, Theophr+) entire, complete 3 Macc 5:31; (adv) 1 Esdr 6:27; Ezk 22:30.*
ὀλοφύρομαι (Hom, Hdt+) mourn, lament 3 Macc 4:2; 4 Macc 16:5, 12.*
ὀλύρα, -ας, ἡ (Hdt+) type of wheat Ex 9:32; Ezk 4:9.*
ὀλυρίτης, -ες (h.l.) made of ὀλύρα 3 Km 19:6.*
ὁμαλισμός, -οῦ, ὁ (DionysThrax [II BCE]) leveling PsSol 11:4; Mi 7:17; Bar 5:7.*
ὄμβρημα, -ατος, τό (LXX+) rainwater Ps 77:44.*
ὅμηρος, -ου, ὁ (8x, Hdt+) pledge, surety; (neut pl) party of hostages 1 Macc 8:7; 9:53; Is 18:2; (even if only one pers) 1 Macc 1:10.
ὁμιλέω 2. be intimate (w. τινί) Sus 37G, 54Θ.‡
ὁμίχλη, -ης, ἡ (9x, Hom+) 1. mist, fog Ps 147:5; Wsd 2:4; Joel 2:2. 2. gloom, darkness Am 4:13; Is 29:18.‡
ὄμνυμι, ὀμνύω dep fut ὀμοῦμαι pf ὀμώμοκα Pr 30:9 renders תפש take hold of, make use of, > profane (God's name), pious correction.‡
ὁμοεθνής, -ές (Hdt, Polyb+) of the same people or race; (subst) compatriot, (in our lit alw) fellow Jew 2 Macc 4:2; 5:6; 12:5; 15:30f; 3 Macc 4:12; 7:14.*
ὁμοζηλία, -ας, ἡ (h.l.) shared or common zeal 4 Macc 13:25.*
ὁμοιότροπος, -ον (not in HR; Hippocr, Thu+) of the same kind or manner Sir 26:27(VL).*

ὁμοιόψηφος, -ον (dub; not in LSJ) *voting or deciding similarly* 2 Macc 14:20G.*

ὁμολογία 3. *assent, agreement,* > *promise, contract* Lev 22:18; Jer 51:25 (or: mistrans of נדר *vow* as if נדבה *voluntary gift*; cf. seq). 4. > *voluntary offering* (no //, s.t. of נדבה free inclination, > *voluntary offering*) Dt 12:17; Ezk 46:12.‡

ὁμόλογος, -ον (X+) *agreeing, confessing* Sus 60G; (adv) *in agreement,* > *willingly* Hos 14:5.*

ὁμομήτριος, -ον (Hdt+) *having the same mother* Gen 43:29.*

ὁμοπάτριος, -α, -ον (Hdt+) *having the same father* Lev 18:11.*

ὁμορέω (Hdt+) *be neighbors;* (ptc subst) *neighbor* 1 Ch 12:41; Jer 27:40; Ezk 16:26.*

ὅμορος, -ον (Hdt+) *contiguous, neighboring* (land) Num 35:5; (people) 2 Ch 21:16.*

ὁμόσπονδος, -ον (Hdt+) *sharing a common cup;* (fig) *showing loyalty* 3 Macc 3:7.*

ὁμοῦμαι fut of BDAG: ὀμνύω, pf ὀμώμοκα.

ὁμόψηφος, -ον (Hdt, Lysias+) *voting the same or together* 2 Macc 14:20R.*

ὁμόψυχος, -ον (LXX+) *of the same mind or attitude* 2 Macc 14:20.*

ὀμφακίζω (LXX+) *bear sour grapes* Is 18:5.*

ὀμφαλός, -όν (Hom, Hdt+) *navel* SSol 7:3; Job 40:16; (fig) *center, midpoint* (of world [orig designated round stone at Delphi; Pind, Aeschyl, Strabo 9.3.6+]), renders טבור *navel* Judg 9:37; (N LOC *Tabor*) Ezk 38:12.*

ὄναγρος, -ου, ὁ (Strabo+) *wild donkey* Ps 103:11; Sir 13:19; Da 5:21Θ.*

ὀνείδισμα, -ατος, τό (Hdt+) *obj of blame or insult* Ezk 36:3.*

ὄνειρος, -ου, ὁ (Hom, Hdt+) *dream* 2 Macc 15:11; 4 Macc 6:5; Wsd 18:17, 19.*‡

ὀνήσεται fut of BDAG: ὀνίνημι, Sir 30:2.

ὄνησις, -εως, ἡ (Hom+) *advantage, gain* Zech 8:10.*

ὀνοκένταυρος, -ου, ὁ (LXX+) *mythical creature* (lit "*donkey-centaur*") Is 13:22; 34:11, 14.*

ὀνομασία, -ας, ἡ (Pla+) *act of naming* (no //) Sir 23:9.*

ὀνομαστί (Hdt+) *by name* Esth 2:14VL.*

ὀνομαστός, -ή, -όν (22x, Hom+) *of name, famous* Gen 6:4; 2 Km 7:9; Jdth 11:23; Sir 39:2; Zeph 3:19; Is 56:5; Bar 3:26.‡

ὀνοματογραφία, -ας, ἡ (SextEmp) *list of names* Esth 6:11; 8:48.*

ὀντιν(α)οῦν see ὁστισοῦν.

ὄνυξ, -υχος, ὁ (10x, Hom+) 1. *claw, talon* 4 Macc 9:26; Ezk 17:3, 7; Da 7:19; *nail, fingernail* Da 4:33aL, 33Θ. 2. *hoof* (X+) Lev 11:7 = Dt 14:8. 3. *onyx* (precious stone, LXX+) Job 28:16. 4. *aromatic material* (LXX+) Ex 30:34; Sir 24:15.*

ὀνυχίζω aor mid ὠνυχισάμην (Cratinus-Com+) 1. *pare nails* 2 Km 19:25. 2. *split, divide* (hoof, no //) Lev 11:3ff; Dt 14:6ff.*

ὀνύχιον, -ου, τό (Theophr) *type of onyx* Ex 28:20 = 36:20; Ezk 28:13.*

ὀνυχιστήρ, -ῆρος, ὁ (LXX) *hoof* Lev 11:3ff; Dt 14:6ff.*

ὀξέως (Thu+) adv of ὀξύς *quickly, swiftly* Wsd 3:18; 16:11; Joel 4:4; Is 8:1, 3.*

ὀξυγράφος, -ον (LXX, Philo) *swift-writing* Ps 44:2.*

ὀξύθυμος, -ον (Aeschyl, Aristot+) *quick-tempered, quickly angered* Pr 14:17.*

ὀξύνω (8x, Hdt+) *sharpen* Pr 24:22d; Wsd 5:20; Is 44:12. Zech 2:4 mistrans of החריד *frighten* as if החריד *sharpen* (cf. χείρ).

ὀξύς comp ὀξύτερος. Job 16:10 renders חרפה *disgrace,* as if rel to חד *sharp,* חדודה *sharpened.*‡

ὀξυσθενής, -ές (h.l. not in LSJ) *quick and strong* Job 39:23VL.*

ὀξύτης, -ητος, ἡ (Critias, Pla+) *swiftness* Jer 8:16.*

ὀπηνίκα (Soph+) *since, when* Jdth 11:11; 4 Macc 2:21.*

ὀπήτιον, -ου, τό (LXX+) *small awl* Ex 21:6 // Dt 15:17.*

ὄπισθε = BDAG: -θεν Josh 6:13.‡

ὀπίσθιος, -α, -ον (9x, Hdt+) *to the rear part or back side* Ex 26:27; (usu subst) Ex 26:23; 3 Km 7:13 = 2 Ch 4:4; Jer 13:22; (adv) *backwards* 1 Km 4:18 (cf. ἐμπρόσθιος).

ὀπισθότονος, -ου, ὁ (Hippocr, Pla+) *tetanus* Dt 32:24.*

ὀπισθοφανής, -ες (ins) *facing away, looking backward* (adj and adv) Gen 9:23.*

ὀπίσω 2. *beyond, on the other side of* (no //) Tob 1:2S (cf. Vulg POST). 2 Km 2:23 mistrans of אחרי (subst) *back end, butt* (of spear) as if *behind*.‡

ὁπλιστής, -οῦ, ὁ (VettVal+) *warrior* Num 32:21VL.*

ὁπλίτης, -ου, ὁ (Aeschyl, Hdt+) *footsoldier, warrior* (X ANAB 1.1.2) Num 32:21.*

ὁπλοδοτέω (h.l.) *provide w. weapons, arm* 1 Macc 14:32.*

ὁπλοθήκη, -ης, ἡ (ins, DiodS+) *armory* 2 Ch 32:27.*

ὁπλολογέω (Philo FLACC 92) *disarm* (τινά), *gather weapons from* 2 Macc 8:27, 31.*

ὁπλομάχος, -ον (X, Polyb+) *heavily armed, equipped for war* Is 13:4f.*

ὁπλοποιέω (Strabo) *make into a weapon* Wsd 5:17.*

ὁπλοφόρος, -ον (Eur, X+) *bearing weapons, armed*; (subst) *armed man, warrior* 2 Ch 14:7.*

ὀπτάζομαι (h.l.) *appear, be seen* Num 14:14.*

ὀπτασία 3. *(public) appearance* (opp ἡσυχία *retirement*) Esth 4:17w.‡

ὀπωροφυλάκιον, -ου, τό (LXX) *hut for one who guards a garden or orchard* Ps 78:1; Mi 1:6; 3:12; Is 1:8; 24:20.*

ὅρασις 1 Ch 17:17 mistrans of תור *turning* (txt confused; 2 Km 7:19 νόμος, MT תורה [cf. McCarter AB ad loc]) as if הראה *appearance*. Job 37:18 mistrans of ראי *mirror*, fr ראה see.‡

ὁρατής, -οῦ, ὁ (Plu) *one who sees, observer* Job 34:21; 35:13.*

ὁρατικός, -η, -ον (Aristot+) *able to see* (fig) Pr 22:29.*

ὁρατός 2 Km 23:21 = 1 Ch 11:23 mistrans of מראה *handsome* as if *vision*.‡

ὁράω A.1.e. (pres ptc) *seer* (Heb, no //) 2 Km 24:11; 2 Ch 9:29 etc (cf. βλέπω).‡

ὀργανικός, -ή, -όν (Aristot+) *instrumental, effective* (DiodS 17.43.1) 2 Macc 12:15.*

ὄργανον 1. (specif) *musical instrument* 1 Ch 6:17; Ps 151:2; Am 5:23. 2. *(architectural) work, construction* 3 Macc 13:5.‡

ὀργή Am 4:10 mistrans of אף *nostril* as if *anger*.‡

ὀργιάω (LXX+) *be wanton, rampage* Is 5:29VL.*

ὄρθιος, -α, -ον (Hes, Hdt+) *erect, upright* (= BDAG: ὀρθός) 1 Km 28:14.*

ὀρθόω aor pass ὠρθώθην 1.b. (pass, fig) *be upright* 1 Esdr 1:21. 2. *make straight* PsSol 10:3.‡

ὀρθρεύω (Eur+) *lie awake before dawn*; > *arise early* (no //) Tob 9:6BA.*

ὀρθρίζω 2 Ch 36:15 s.t. of שכם hiph *do repeatedly* as if *arise early*.‡

ὀρθρόω (spur; h.l.) *arise early* Ps 118:148VL.*

ὁρίζω fut ὁριῶ 2.b. (abs) *act as or form the boundary* (of a territory) Josh 15:12; 18:20; 23:4; Ezk 47:20.‡

ὁρισμός, -οῦ, ὁ (Aristot+) *marking out*; 1. *definition*, > *stipulation* (no //) Num 30:3ff; Esth 4:17o; 2 Macc 12:25; Da 6:6ffG, 8ffΘ. 2. (= BDAG) *boundary*, > *orbit, fixed course* (of heavenly bodies, 1Cl 20.3) Sir 33:10G; > *season, fixed time* (no //) Ex 8:8.‡

ὁρκισμός, -οῦ, ὁ (Polyb) *oath* Gen 21:31f; 24:41; Lev 5:1; 1 Macc 6:62; Sir 36:7R.*

ὁρκόω (Thu+) *bind by oath* Gen 24:37VL, 4 Km 11:4VL.

ὁρμή 2. *onrush* Pr 3:25; 21:1; > *crowd* (of people, no //) 3 Macc 1:23.‡

ὅρμημα, -ατος, τό (10x, LXX+) 1. *sudden onrush*; (of troops) 1 Macc 4:8; *torrent* Ps 45:5; *swoop*; (of eagle) Dt 28:49. 2. *impulsive aggression* Ex 32:22; *fury* Hos 5:10.‡

ὁρμίσκος, -ου, ὁ (ins) *small necklace* Gen 38:18, 25; Judg 8:26A; Pr 25:11; SSol 1:10; 7:2.*

ὅρμος, -ου, ὁ (Hom+) *harbor* Gen 49:13; 4 Macc 13:6; Ezk 27:11.*

ὀρνίθιον, -ου, τό (13x, Hdt+; dim of BDAG: ὄρνις) *small bird* Lev 14:4ff.*

ὀρνιθοσκοπέομαι (h.l.) *watch birds for omens* Lev 19:26.*

ὁρόδαμνος, -ου, ὁ see ῥαδάμνος (=).

ὅρος 1.b. *specific (limit of) time* 2 Esdr 12:6.*‡

ὀροφοκοιτέω (h.l.; not in HR or LSJ, but VVLL ὀροφοιτέω *roam the mountains* etc make no sense and are otherwise unattested) *nest in thatch of roof* (c. Ra, w. TOTP, NRSV) 4 Macc 14:15.*

ὄροφος, -ου, ὁ (Hom, Hdt+) *reed for thatching,* > *thatched roof* Wsd 17:2.*

ὀροφόω (ins+) *roof, cover w. a roof* 3 Km 7:44vL.*

ὀρόφωμα, -ατος, τό (CallixenusHist, DiodS) *ceiling, canopy* 2 Ch 3:7; Ezk 41:26.*

ὀρτυγομήτρα, -ας, ἡ (Aristot+) *type of rail that migrates w. quail; perh* (no //) *simply quail* (ὄρτυξ does not occur) Ex 16:13; Num 11:31f; Ps 104:40; Wsd 16:2; 19:12.*

ὄρυξ, -υγος, ὁ (Aristot+) *oryx* Dt 14:5.*

ὀρύσσω **4.** *dig into, gouge* (Aristoph Av 442; of a wrestler) Ps 21:17.‡

ὀρφανεία, -ας, ἡ (Pind [-νία]+, pap) *state of being orphaned,* > *bereavement, loss of children* PsSol 4:10; Is 47:8.*

ὀρχέομαι (Hom, Hdt+) *dance* 2 Km 6:16ff = 1 Ch 15:29; Eccl 3:4; Is 13:21.*‡

ὁσιόω fut pass ὁσιωθήσονται (Eur+) *sanctify;* (pass) *be made holy* 2 Km 22:26 = Ps 17:26; Wsd 6:10.*

ὄσπριον, -ου, τό (Hdt+) *pulse, legume;* (pl, as food) *peas, beans* (X Anab 4.4.9) Da 1:12L, 16L.*

ὁστισοῦν, ἡτισοῦν, ὁτιοῦν (Aristoph, Thu+) *any whatsoever* Dt 24:10; 3 Km 10:21vL, 2 Macc 5:10; 14:3; 3 Macc 7:7.*

ὀστρακώδης, -ες (Aristot+) *like a potsherd;* > (of land) *hard, rocky* (rendering N LOC חֶרֶם Judg 1:35B.*

ὀσφραίνομαι aor pass ὠσφράνθη (15; Hdt+) *smell, catch the scent* (τι) Gen 8:21; (τινός) Judg 16:9; Tob 8:3BA, Job 39:25; (ἐν τινί) Am 5:21; (fig) Job 39:25; (abs) Tob 6:17; Ps 113:14; Sir 30:19.

ὀσφρασία, -ας, ἡ (LXX+) *scent* Hos 14:7.*

ὁτιοῦν see ὁστισοῦν.

ὀτρύνω (Hom, Pind, Aeschyl+ [very rare in prose]) *rouse, urge on* 3 Macc 5:46.*

οὐδαμοῦ (Hdt+) *nowhere at all* 3 Km 2:36; Pr 23:5; Job 19:7; 21:9.*

οὐλή, -ῆς, ἡ (Hom+) *scar, mark* Lev 13:2ff; 14:56.*

οὗπερ 2 Macc 4:38 cf. BDAG: οὗ, ὅσπερ.

οὐραγέω (Polyb+) *be the rear guard, bring up the rear* Josh 6:9; (fig) *lag behind* Sir 32:11.*

οὐραγία, -ας, ἡ (Polyb, DiodS) *rear guard* Dt 25:18; Josh 10:19.*

οὐρέω (Hes, Hdt+) *urinate* 1 Km 25:22, 34; 3 Km 12:24m; 20:21; 4 Km 9:8; alw οὐρῶν πρὸς τοίχον *"pissing against a wall,"* i.e., *"male".*

οὔριος, -ου, ὁ (Aeschyl+) *fair wind* (w. ᾠόν); *"wind-egg"* (Aristot), i.e., *sterile and unimpregnated egg, producing no chick* Is 59:5.*

οὖρον, ου, τό (Hdt+) *urine* 4 Km 18:27 = Is 36:12.*

οὗτοι (Hom, Pla+) *indeed not* Num 18:32vL.*

οὐχ οὕτως 4 Km 19:32 mistrans of לכן *therefore* as if לא כן *(it is) not so.*

ουχορεκαινος (or -χερο-; no matter how divided or parsed, not in HR or LSJ) 1 Ch 12:34vvLL mere copyists' cjj.*

ὀφείλω fut ὀφειλήσω (Tob 6:13G; Job 6:20) or ὀφειλέσω (Tob 6:13R).‡

ὀφθαλμοφανής, -ές (Aristot+) *visible;* (adv) Esth 8:13.*

ὀφιόδηκτος, -ον (LXX+) *bitten by a snake* Sir 12:13.*

ὀφιομάχης, -ου, ὁ (LXX, Philo) *one who fights w. snakes* Lev 11:22.*

ὄφλησις, -εως, ἡ (h.l.) *penalty or payment due;* Bar 3:8 prob mistrans of (שאה) מְשֹׁאָה *desolation* as if (נשא) מַשָּׂאָה *secured loan.*

ὀχεία, -ας, ἡ (X+) *impregnation, breeding* Sir 33:6.*

ὀχεῖον, -ου, τό (Aristot+) *breeding stock, stallion* Sir 33:6vL.*

ὀχλαγωγέω (Polyb, Strabo) *draw a crowd, stir up a mob* Am 7:16.*

ὀχλέω **1.b.** (intr) *be on the move, be troublesome* 3 Macc 5:41.*‡

ὀχληρία, -ας, ἡ (dub; h.l.) *troublesomeness* Eccl 7:25vL.*

ὀχυράζω (spur; not in LSJ) *fortify* 1 Macc 6:26vL.*

ὀχυρός, -ά, -όν (64x, Hes+) **1.** *strong* 2 Macc 12:18; 13:19. **2.** *fortified* Ex 1:11; Dt 3:5; Josh 10:20; 1 Macc 1:19; Ps 70:3; Sir 28:14;

Mi 7:12; Is 25:2; Da 11:15; (subst) *stronghold, fortified place* (fem) Is 17:13; (neut) 37:26.‡

ὀχυρόω aor ὠχύρωσεν, pass ὠχυρώθησαν (18; Pla+) *fortify, strengthen* 2 Ch 11:11; 1 Macc 1:62; Jer 28:53; *secure, lock* EpJer 17; (pass) *be strengthened*, (ptc) *fortified, secured* Josh 6:1; (fig) 4 Macc 13:7.

ὀχυρωμάτιον, -ου, τό (h.l.) *small fortification* 1 Macc 16:15.*

ὀχύρωσις, -εως, ἡ (pap, Joseph) *fortifying, (process of) fortification* 1 Macc 10:11; 14:10.*

ὀψίζω (Lysias, X+) *come at night, come late* 1 Km 17:16(VL); Sir 36:27.*

ὄψον, -ου, τό (or ὄψος, -εος; Hom+) *food,* (specif) *fish* (Zen-P) Num 11:22; (pl) *varied dishes* Tob 2:2BA, 7:8BA.*

ὀψοποίημα, -ατος, τό (Geopon) *prepared food;* (pl) *various dishes* Jdth 12:1.*

Π

παγγέωργος, -ου, ὁ (h.l.) *master gardener* (fig) 4 Macc 1:29.*

παγείς aor pass ptc, παγήσομαι fut pass of πήγνυμι.

παγετός, -οῦ, ὁ (Pind+) *frost* Gen 31:40; Sir 3:15; Jer 43:30; Bar 2:25.*

παγκρατής, -ές (Aeschyl+) *all-powerful* 2 Macc 3:22.*

πάγος, -ου, ὁ (Aeschyl+) *frost* Ex 16:14; Job 37:10; Na 3:17; Zech 14:6; Da 3:69.*

παθεινός, -ή, -όν (ins, pap) *suffering* Job 29:25.*

παθοκράτεια, -ας, ἡ (LXX) *control of emotion, self-restraint* 4 Macc 13:5, 16.*

παθοκρατέομαι (h.l.) *be controlled by emotions* 4 Macc 7:20.*

παιάν, -ᾶνος, ὁ (Hom, Aeschyl, Thu+) *paean, song of triumph or war* 2 Macc 15:25.*

παιγνία, -ας, ἡ (Hdt+) *sport, game* Judg 16:27B; Jer 30:10.*

παίγνιον, -ου, τό (Pla+) *plaything* Wsd 15:12; Hab 1:10; *child's game, playful gesture* Wsd 12:26.*

παιδεύω Pr 22:3 mistrans of סתר *hide* as if יסר *teach.*‡

παιδοποιέω (Eur, Pla+) *beget children* 2 Macc 14:25.*

παιδοποιία, -ας, ἡ (Pla+) *begetting of children* 4 Macc 17:6.*

παιδοχαρακτήρ, -ῆρος, ὁ (dub; not in LSJ) *character* (lit *impress, molding*) *of a child* 4 Macc 15:4VL.*

παίω aor ἔπαισα, pf πέπαικα (26; Aeschyl Hdt+) *strike* Ex 12:13; Josh 20:9; Job 16:10; PsSol 8:15; Is 14:6; Jer 5:6; Da 8:7Θ.‡

παλάθη, -ης, ἡ (7x, Hdt+) *cake of dried fruit* 1 Km 25:18; Jdth 10:5; Is 38:21.

παλαιός 1 Km 7:12 mistrans of N LOC יְשָׁנָה (q.l.; MT הַשֵּׁן *the crag,* but cf. 2Ch 13:19) as if fr ישׁן *grow old.*‡

παλαιστή, -ῆς, ἡ or παλαιστής, -οῦ, ὁ (Hippocr, Aristot+) (LXX) *palm's breadth, four inches* Ex 25:25; 3 Km 7:12; 2 Ch 4:5; Ps 38:6; Ezk 40:5, 43; 43:13.*

παλαίστρα, -ας, ἡ (Hdt, Eur, X+) *wrestling school* 2 Macc 4:14.*

παλαίω (Hom+) *wrestle, strive* Gen 32:25f; Esth 1:1e. Judg 20:33A mistrans of מגיח (hiph ptc) *bursting forth,* unexpl.*‡

παλαίωμα, -ατος, τό (LXX) *something gone by or ancient, something worn out;* Job 36:28; 37:18, 21 renders שחק *cloud, dust,* fr שחק *grind down, wear away.*

παλαίωσις, -εως, ἡ (Hippocr, Strabo+) *aging, dilapidation.* Na 2:1 renders בליעל *wickedness* as if prep ב *in* and (unknown) noun.

παλλακή, -ῆς, ἡ (43x, Hdt+) *concubine* Gen 22:24; Judg 8:31; 2 Km 3:7; 1 Esdr 4:29; 2 Macc 4:30; SSol 6:8; Da 5:2Θ.

παλλακίς, -ίδος, ἡ (Hom+) *concubine* Job 19:17.*

πάλλω (Hom+) *sway, shake, brandish;* (pass) *be shaken, fall* (or *hurl oneself*) *headlong* 2 Esdr 9:3, 5.*

παμβασιλεύς, -έως, ὁ (LXX+; fem Eur+) *universal king* Sir 50:15.*

παμβότανον, -ου, τό (h.l.) *whole range of plants* Job 5:25.*‡

παμμ(ε)ιγής, -ές (Aeschyl+; better μιγ-; Gött, W p. 31) *all mixed together* 2 Macc 3:21; 12:13.*

παμμελής, -ές (LXX+) *w. all kinds of melodies* 3 Macc 7:16.*

παμμίαρος, -ον (Aristoph) *completely abominable* (superl h.l.) 4 Macc 10:17.*

παμπληθής, -ές (X, Pla+) *exceedingly numerous* 2 Macc 10:24.*‡

παμποίκιλος, -ον (Hom, Eur, Pla+) *most varied in kind* 4 Macc 15:11.*

παμπόνηρος, -ον (Aristoph, Pla+) *completely bad* 2 Macc 14:27.*

πάμφυλος, -ον (Aristoph, Pla+) *of mixed or all-inclusive nationalities* 2 Macc 8:9; 12:27; 4 Macc 4:11.*

πανάγιος, -ον (LXX) *completely holy* 4 Macc 4:7; 14:7.*‡

πάνδεινος, -ον (Pla+) *completely dreadful* 4 Macc 3:15; 4:7.*

πάνδημος, -ον (Soph+, adv Aeschyl, Hdt+) *of the whole community, general, universal* 2 Macc 3:18; adv πανδημεί *generally, in all-encompassing fashion* Dt 13:17.*

πανεθνεί (Strabo 5.1.3) *as a whole nation* Wsd 19:8.*

πανεπίσκοπος, -ον (LXX+) *all-overseeing, omnipresent* Wsd 7:23.*

πανηγυρίζω (Hdt+) *celebrate a religious festival, observe a holy day* Is 66:10.*

πανηγύριος, -ον (dub; not in LSJ) *assembled? festive?* Na 3:10VL.*

πανηγυρισμός, -οῦ, ὁ (LXX+) *celebration, holiday revel* Wsd 15:12.*

πανθήρ, -ῆρος, ὁ (Hdt+) *panther* Hos 5:14; 13:7.*

πανόδυρτος, -ον (VL -δυρκτ- [dub] = ; AnthPal, ins) *altogether painful or lamentable* 3 Macc 4:2; 6:32.*

πανοικία, -ας, ἡ (dat as adv Hdt+; other cases only LXX) *entire household* Gen 50:8, 22; Ex 1:1; Judg 18:21A; Esth 8:12r; 3 Macc 3:27.*

πανούργευμα, -ατος, τό (LXX) *great deed* Jdth 11:8; Sir 1:6; 42:18.*

πανουργεύομαι (LXX+) *be clever or cunning* 1 Km 23:22.*

πανούργημα, -ατος, τό (Soph+) *clever trick* Sir 1:6VL.*

πανουργία 2. *shrewdness, cleverness* (no //) Pr 1:4; 8:5.‡

πάνσοφος, -ον (trag, Pla+) *utterly wise* 4 Macc 1:12; 2:19; 13:19.*

παντεπίσκοπος, -ον (dub, h.l.) *all-overseeing* Wsd 7:23VL.*

παντεπόπτης, -ες (LXX+) *all-surveying* 2 Macc 9:5.*‡

παντευχία, -ας, ἡ (Pherecr, Eur+) *full armor or equipment* 4 Macc 3:12.*

παντοδαπός, -ή, -όν (Sappho, Aeschyl, Hdt+) *of every kind or type* (also of trees, X ANAB 1.2.22) Job 40:21.*

παντοδύναμος, -ον (LXX) *omnipotent* Wsd 7:23; 11:17; 18:15.*

παντοῖος, -α, -ον (Hom, Hdt+) *numerous, various, manifold* 2 Macc 5:3; 3 Macc 5:22; 7:16; 4 Macc 1:34; Da 2:6L.*

παντοκρατορία, -ας, ἡ (not in HR; h.l.) *omnipotence* Sir 19:20VL.*

παντοτρόφος, -ον (Aeschyl) *nurturing everything* Wsd 16:25.*

παντοφαγία, -ας, ἡ (h.l.) *eating of anything, indiscriminate eating* 4 Macc 1:27.*

πανυπέρτατος, -ον (Hom+) *highest of all, supreme* 3 Macc 1:20.*

πάππος, -ου, ὁ (Hdt+) *grandfather* Sir Prol 7.*

πάπυρος, -ου, ὁ or ἡ (Theophr+) *papyrus* Job 8:11; 40:21; Is 19:6.*

παρά C.1.c.β. *to the point that, w. the result that* (no //) Jer 4:7.‡

παραβάλλω (Hom, Hdt+) 1. *throw, cast* (fodder or grain) Judg 19:21A; Ruth 2:16; (fig, of wisdom) Pr 2:2². 2. *offer, present; turn* (τι to τινί) Pr 2:2¹; 4:20; 5:1, 13; 22:17; (mid) *expose (oneself) to danger, risk* 2 Macc 14:38. 3. *approach, come close to* 1 Macc 3:40VL; 5:5VL.*‡

παραβαπτός, -όν (h.l.) *dyed*; (subst) *dyed object* Ezk 23:15VL.*

παραβασιλεύω (Eunap: *reign simultaneously, be coregent*) *commit treason, subvert the monarchy* 3 Macc 6:24.*

παραβιῶμαι Att fut of BDAG: παραβιάζω Am 6:10.*

παραβιβάζω (LXX, Philo) *set aside,* > *forgive* (sin) 2 Km 12:13; 24:10 (but, > *violate* [laws] Philo *Flacc* 150). Da 11:20Θ renders מעביר *cause to pass by* (s.t.) but txt? (cf. BHS, KB3).

παραβιωτής, -ές (dub; not in LSJ) *using force;* (subst) *forceful or violent person* Am 6:10vL.*

παραβλέπω **2.** *look sideways, glance* Job 20:9; (trans) *glance at* 28:7; *look sideways at* SSol 1:6.‡

παραβολή Ezk 12:22f; 16:44 etc s.t. of משל *proverb, saying* as if *figure, parable*.‡

παραγγέλλω **2.** *summon* (Demosth, pap) 1 Km 10:17.‡

παράγγελμα 1 Km 22:14 mistrans of משמעה *bodyguard* (who are alw within hearing) fr שמע *hear*.

παραγινώσκω (X+) *err in judgment* 3 Macc 1:12vL.*

παράγω aor pass παρήχθην **5.a.** *lead aside,* > *divert, avert* Eccl 11:10. **b.** *induce, mislead;* (pass) *be misled or drawn off* 2 Esdr 9:2.‡

παραγωγή, -ῆς, ἡ (not in HR; Hdt+) *disobedience, perversion* Esth 3:13e vL.*

παράδειγμα, -ατος, τό (Hdt+) *pattern* Ex 25:9; 1 Ch 28:11ff; *example* 3 Macc 2:5; Na 3:6. Jer 8:2; 9:21; 16:4 mistrans of דמן *dung* as if דמי *likeness*.

παραδειγματισμός, -οῦ, ὁ (Polyb+) *exemplary punishment* 3 Macc 4:11; 7:14.*

παραδείκνυμι aor pass ptc παραδειχθείς (X+) *reveal, make manifest* Ex 27:8; Hos 13:4; Ezk 22:2; Bel 8fG.*

παράδεισος **3.** *garden, (enclosed) park* (X *Anab* 1.2.7) Num 24:6; 2 Ch 33:20; Eccl 2:5; Sir 24:30; Joel 2:3; Is 1:30; Sus 7.‡

παραδοξάζω (7x, LXX+) *treat w. distinction* (cf. Heb פלה) 2 Macc 3:30; > *distinguish, mark off* Ex 8:18; 3 Macc 2:9; > *make more extreme* Dt 28:59; Sir 10:13.

παραδρομή, -ῆς, ἡ (Aristot+) *train, group of attendants* 2 Macc 3:28; SSol 7:6.*

παράδωσις, -εως, ἡ (dub; not in LSJ, = BDAG: -δοσις, attracted to spelling of vb?) *handing over* Judg 11:30A.*

παραζεύγνυμι (Eur+) *assign, attach* Jdth 10:17.*

παραζηλόω **2.** *be jealous* Ps 36:1.‡

παραζώνη, -ης, ἡ (h.l.) *belt, girdle* 2 Km 18:11.*

παραζώννυμι (not in HR, Pla+) *wear at the belt* 4 Km 3:21vL.*

παράθεμα, -ατος, τό (LXX) *covering, wrapping* Ex 38:24; 39:9.*

παραθερμαίνω pf pass παρατεθέρμανται (Aristot+) *be warm;* (pass) *be heated* (in anger) Dt 19:6.*

παράθεσις, -εως, ἡ (8x, Hippocr, Polyb+) **1.** *what is set aside;* (sg or pl) *supplies, stores* 2 Ch 11:11; 1 Macc 6:53; Pr 6:8. **2.** *what is set before; dinner* 4 Km 6:23; Pr 15:17.

παραθλίβω (LXX+) *harass, suppress* 4 Km 6:32.*

παραίνεσις, -εως, ἡ (Hdt+) *counsel, encouragement* Wsd 8:9.*

παραινέω impf παρῄνουν (Hdt+) *urge, exhort* 2 Macc 7:25f; 3 Macc 5:17; *recommend, approve* 7:12R.*‡

παραιρέω aor mid παρείλατο (Hdt+) *draw off, remove* Num 11:25.*

παραίτιος, (-α), -ον (Aeschyl, Polyb+) *helping to cause or bring about* (τινός) 2 Macc 11:19.*

παρακαθεύδω (Aelian [*Var Hist* 137]) *sleep beside, guard* Jdth 10:20.*

παρακαθίστημι aor pass ptc παρακατασταθείς *station beside;* (pass ptc) *placed nearby, provided* 2 Macc 12:3.*‡

παρακαλέω 2 Km 24:16; Ps 89:13 mistrans of נחם *repent, change one's mind* as if *be consoled*.‡

παρακαλίζω (dub; not in HR or LSJ) *encourage* Is 13:2vL.*

παρακάλυμμα, -ατος, τό (AntiphanesCom, Plu+) *curtain, screen* Wsd 17:3.

παρακατατίθημι (Hdt, Pla+) *entrust to someone's care or keeping* 2 Macc 3:15; 9:25; Jer 47:7; 48:10.*

παρακλείω (Hdt [6.60]+) *displace, exclude,* > *put out of the way, murder* (Polyb 5.39.3; c. LSJ, Loeb) 2 Macc 4:34.*

παρακλητικός, -ή, -όν (Pla+) *encouraging, heartening* Zech 1:13.*

παρακλήτωρ, -ορος, ὁ (Schol Eur) *comforter, encourager* Job 16:2.*

παρακλίνω (Hom, Hdt+) *turn aside* Sir 47:19vL.*

παρακμάζω (X+) *go past one's prime* Sir 42:9.*

παράκοιτος, -ον (DiodS) *lying beside;* (subst) *sleeping companion, sexual partner* Da 5:2, 3, 23Θ.*

παρακομίζω (6x, Eur+) *convey, deliver* 2 Macc 4:19ff; 9:8ff.*

παρακρούω (Pla+) (mid) *mislead, cheat* Gen 31:7.*

παραλαλέω (Menand+) *insinuate, ridicule* (no //) Ps 43:17.*

παραλαμβάνω 2.c. *take over, take possession of* (territory, e.g., by inheritance) Jer 30:17 (Gött 30:1).‡

παραλία see BDAG: παράλιος‡

παραλλαγή 4 Km 9:20 mistrans of שגעון *madness*, perh as if fr שגה *wander, weave (from side to side)*.*‡

παράλλαξις, -εως, ἡ (Hippocr, Pla+) *change, aberration* Esth 3:13evL; *displacement, cessation* (no //) Da 12:11Θ.*

παραλλάσσω pf pass ptc παρηλλαγμένος 1. *change* Da 6:16Θ; (ptc subst) *change, transformation* 2 Macc 3:16. 2. *pass by, avoid* Pr 4:15. 2 Esdr 1:9 mistrans of מחלף (h.l. unknown) as if fr חלף *change* (vL pf pass ptc of BDAG: παράγω). Esth 3:13e txt?*‡

παραλογισμός, -οῦ, ὁ (Aristot, Polyb+) *deception, trick* Esth 8:12f, n; 2 Macc 1:13; PsSol 4:10, 22.*

παράλυσις, -εως, ἡ (Theophr+) *paralysis;* Ezk 21:15 unexpl.*

παραλύω 2. (no //) *pay* (a penalty) Gen 4:15.‡

παραναγινώσκω (Isocr, Polyb+) *read publicly* 2 Macc 8:23; 3 Macc 1:12.*

παρανακλίνω (h.l.) *lay down alongside* (τινί) Sir 47:19.*

παραναλίσκω aor pass παρανηλώμην (AntiphoOr, DiodS+) *waste;* (pass) *be lost to no purpose* Num 17:27.*

παράνομος 2. *egregious, indecent* (no //, but παρανομία can mean *indecency, behavior unsanctioned by custom*) 3 Macc 5:27.‡

παραξιφίς, -ίδος, ἡ (DiodS, Strabo+) *knife, dagger* (worn beside sword) 2 Km 5:8.*

παράπαν (9x, Hdt+) *completely, absolutely* (alw w. τό) 3 Km 11:10; Zeph 3:6; Ezk 20:9ff.

παραπέμπω (Hom+) 1. *attend to, follow* Esth 3:13d. 2. *dismiss, ignore* 3 Macc 1:26.*‡

παραπέτασμα, -ατος, τό (Hdt+) *curtain, screen* Am 2:8.*

παραπηδάω (X+) *leap forth* 4 Macc 11:1.*

παραπίπτω 2. (trans, w. cogn acc, no //) *commit* (transgression) Ezk 14:13; 15:8.‡

παράπληκτος, -ον (Soph+) *curtain, hanging* Dt 28:34.*

παραπληξία, -ας, ἡ (Hippocr+: *trembling, palsy*) *frenzy, derangement* Dt 28:28.*

παράπλους, -ου, ὁ (Thu, DiodS+) *voyage* (along coast) 3 Macc 4:11.*

παραπομπή, -ῆς, ἡ (Aristot, X+) *escort, procession* 1 Macc 9:37.*

παραπορεύομαι 1.b. *bypass, avoid,* > *disobey* (commandments) 2 Ch 24:20. 3. *pass away* (no //) Zeph 2:2.‡

παραριθμέω (ins, pap, Plu) *count over, check* Tob 9:5S.*

παραρ(ρ)ίπτω or -ριπτέω (Soph+) *throw, toss away* 2 Macc 1:16. 1 Km 2:36 (ספה *associate, connect*), Ps 83:11 (ספף *hit lie at the threshold*) both mistrans as if fr ספה *snatch away*.*

παράρρυμα, -ατος, τό (Soph, X+) *curtain, hanging* Ex 35:11.*

παράσημον, -ου, τό (Aristot+) *emblem, insignium* 3 Macc 2:29.*‡

παρασιωπάω fut παρασιωπήσομαι pass -πηθήσεται (20; Hyperid, Polyb+) 1. *remain silent* Gen 24:21; 1 Km 7:8; Ps 27:1; PsSol 5:2; Hab 1:13. 2. *pass over, leave unmentioned* Ps 108:1. 3. *be silenced* Pr 12:2. Hos 10:11, 13; Am 6:12 mistrans of חרש¹ *plow* as if חרש² *be silent*. 1 Km 23:9 mistrans of חרש² *leave unattended* as if *keep silent*.

παρασκευή 2. *what is prepared, equipment* Ex 39:22G; 2 Macc 15:21.‡

παράστασις, -εως, ἡ (Pla, X+) *exhibition, display* 1 Macc 15:32.*

παραστήκω var of παρίστημι Judg 3:19A.*

παρασυμβάλλω (LXX) *compare,* (pass) *be compared to* Ps 48:13, 21.*

παρασφαλίζομαι (h.l.) *fortify in turn* 2 Esdr 13:8vL.*

παράταξις **1.b.** *battle line* Num 31:5; 2 Ch 20:15; Ezk 17:21. **3.** *row, arrangement* Judg 6:26. Ezk 24:16 mistrans of במגפה *at a blow, by plague, in sudden death* as if fr אגף *troop* (cf. 17:21).‡

παρατάσσω aor παρετάξαντο pf παρατέτακται (80; Hdt+) **1.** (act or mid) *draw up in battle order* Gen 14:8; Josh 24:8; 1 Km 4:2; 2 Esdr 14:2; 2 Macc 1:11; Ps 26:3; Joel 2:5; Zech 10:5; Jer 6:23; (w. cogn acc) 1 Ch 12:39. **2.** *set in order, decree* (no //) Zech 1:6; 8:15.

παρατείνω pres ptc 2 Km 2:29 mistrans of בתרון (h.l.) *ravine? morning?* as if Aram ב(א)תר *after, all the next, succeeding* (ἡμέραν? νύκτα? no //). Ezk 27:13 pres ptc mistrans of N LOC משך *Meshech* as if משך *extend, prolong.*‡

παρατίθημι **1.b.** *provide, furnish* 1 Macc 1:35. **c.** *deposit or set aside for oneself* (no //) 4 Km 5:24.*‡

παρατρέχω (16x, Hom+) **1.** *run with, accompany;* (of attendants to royalty) 1 Km 22:17; 2 Km 15:1; 2 Ch 12:10. **2.** *run by, slip away* 3 Macc 5:15; Wsd 5:9.

παραφορά, -ᾶς, ἡ (Aeschyl+) *derangement, insanity* Eccl 2:12vL, 7:25vL.*

παραφρόνησις, -εως, ἡ (Hippocr+) *derangement, insanity* Zech 12:4.*

παράφρων, -ον (Soph, Pla+) *insane, senseless* Wsd 5:20.*

παραχρῆμα 2 Km 3:12 mistrans of תחתו *in his stead*, Job 40:12 of תחתם *where they stand*, both as if fr הוש (Aram חות) *hurry.*‡

παραχωρέω (Hippocr, Aristoph+) *yield, concede* 2 Macc 2:28; *pay, hand over* (no //) 8:11.*

παρδάλεος, -ον (Diosc) *leopard-like,* > *wild, beastly* 4 Macc 9:28.*

παρείθην 2 aor pass of BDAG: παρίημι.

πάρειμι¹ (εἰμί) **1.b.β.** (impers) *it comes* (+ inf), > "*one can*" 2 Macc 6:9. **3.** *stand by, join* 3 Macc 1:23.‡

πάρειμι² (εἶμι) *pass by, go by;* (ptc subst) *passerby* Pr 9:15; 15:10.*

παρεισπορεύομαι (h.l.) *enter* 2 Macc 8:1.*

παρεκλείπω (AelAristid) *run out, be exhausted* (no //) Jdth 11:12.*

παρεκτείνω (Aristot+) *extend, stretch, reach* (of territory Ezk 47:19; (fig, w. τινί) *measure oneself against* Pr 23:4.*

παρελέγχω (Galen) *rebuke* 2 Macc 4:33vL.*

παρέλκυσις, -εως, ἡ (lexicog) *delay* Job 25:3.*

παρέλκω fut παρελκύσω aor παρείλκυσα (Aristoph+) *keep waiting, put off* Sir 4:1, 3; 29:5, 8.*

παρεμβάλλω fut παρεμβαλῶ aor παρενέβαλον pf παρεμβέβληκα (198; Aristoph+) **1.** (class *interpose* troops in battle, > *arrange* troops, > [Polyb+] *encamp;* LXX almost alw for חנה) *pitch camp, set up (more or less fortified) camp* Gen 32:2; Ex 14:9; Josh 4:3; 1 Km 4:1; 1 Ch 9:27; Ps 33:8; Jer 27:29. **2.** *insert, insinuate, interpose* (oneself, one's own words) Sir 11:8.‡

παρεμβολή **4.** *detachment* (of soldiers), *company* (LXX, EzkTrag) 1 Macc 4:1.‡

παρεμπίπτω (Pla+) *intrude, creep in* Wsd 7:25.*

παρέξ, πάρεξ (18x, Hom+) **1.** prep (w. gen) **a.** *apart from, except for* Ruth 4:4; 3 Km 3:18; Eccl 2:25; Hos 13:4; Is 43:11; **b.** *in addition to, besides* Judg 8:26B; 2 Esdr 1:6. **2.** (conjunctive adv) *rather, only* 1 Km 20:39; Ezk 15:4.

παρεξίστημι pf ptc παρεξεστηκώς (Epicharm+) *be deranged* Hos 9:7.*

παρέξω (dub, h.l.) *at the outside of* (τινός) Lev 8:17vL.*

παρεπιδείκνυμι (LXX+) *point out as well* 2 Macc 15:10.*

πάρεργος, -ον (Eur, Thu, Pla+) *incidental, trifling* 2 Macc 15:19.*

παρεωραμένος pf pass ptc of BDAG: παροράω.

παρηγορέω (Aeschyl, Hdt+) *persuade, exhort* 4 Macc 12:2.*

παρηλλαγμένος pf pass ptc of παραλλάσσω.

παρηνώχλησα   aor of BDAG: παρενοχλέω.

παρθενικός, -ή, -όν   (DiodS) *suited for a maiden* Joel 1:8; *maidenly, virginal* (no //) Esth 2:3.*

παρθένιος, -ον   (Hom+) *virginal* Esth 2:3VL; (neut pl) *signs pertaining to virginity* Dt 22:14ff; Judg 11:37f.*

παρίημι   1 aor παρῆκαν 2 aor subj παρῇς, impv πάρες. **1.b.** *yield to, leave alone, ignore* (τινί) 2 Km 5:23 = 1 Ch 14:14. 1 Km 2:5 mistrans of חדל² *flourish, succeed* as if חדל¹ *give up, leave alone.*‡

πάρινος, -η, -ον   (ins) *of marble* Esth 1:6.*

πάριος, -ον   (LSJ: under πάρος [Hdt+] *gent of Paros*) 1 Ch 29:2 renders אבני שש *alabaster*; perh = πάρινος *marble* (cf. Esth 1:6 שש).

παρίστημι   **1.c.β.** *dispose, prepare* 1 Macc 6:34.‡

πάροδος¹, -ου, ἡ   (Thu, ins+) **1.** *passage, way through* Gen 38:14. **2.** *passing by* Wsd 2:5; 17:9.*‡

πάροδος², -ου, ὁ   (ins; LSJ [not HR] lists as diff fr prec) *passerby* Ezk 16:15, 25; > *traveler, visitor* 2 Km 12:4. 4 Km 25:24 mistrans of עבדי *servants* as if fr עבר *pass through*.*

παροικεσία, -ας, ἡ   (LXX) *sojourning, captivity* Zech 9:12; Ezk 20:38.*

παροικέω   Ezk 21:17 mistrans of מגרי (fr נגר *pour out* or מגר *throw down* as if fr גור *live as a foreigner* (so also MT).‡

παροίκησις, -εως, ἡ   (Thu+) **1.** *neighborhood* Sir 21:28. **2.** *sojourning, living as an alien* (no //, but cf. BDAG: παροικέω) Gen 28:4; 36:7.*

παροικία   Ps 33:5 mistrans of מגורה *horror* (VL θλίψις = MT) as if מגור *place of sojourning*.‡

παροιμιάζω   (Pla+) *speak or recite a proverb* 4 Macc 18:16.*

παροινέω   (Aristoph, X+) *behave drunkenly*, > *act abusively* Is 41:12.*

παροιστράω   (DiodS 34/35.28a) *rage madly* Hos 4:16; Ezk 2:6.*

παρόρασις, -εως, ἡ   (LXX+) *overlooking, neglect, lack of concern* 2 Macc 5:17.*

παροράω   pf pass ptc παρεωραμένος.‡

παρόργισμα, -ατος, τό   (LXX) *provocative or enraging act* 3 Km 16:33; 20:22; 2 Ch 35:19c.*

παρορμάω   (X+) *incite, urge on* 2 Macc 15:17; 4 Macc 12:6.*

παρωθέω   aor ptc παρώσας (Hippocr, Soph+) *displace, reject* 2 Macc 4:11.*

παρωμίς, -ίδος, ἡ   (h.l.) *shoulder strap* Ex 28:14.*

πᾶς, πᾶσα, πᾶν   masc sg acc πᾶν (cf. Aeolic/Doric πάν, Sappho+) Ex 12:44, 1Km 11:8; 1 Ch 27:1; Jer 13:11.‡

πασθήσεται   (dub) fut pass of πασχω? πειθω? Is 4:5VL.*

πάσσαλος, -ου, ὁ   (23x, Hom, Hdt+) *peg, tent peg* Ex 27:19; Judg 4:21; Sir 14:24; Is 33:20.

πάσσω   aor ἔπασον mid ptc πασάμενος pf pass ptc πεπασμένος (Hom+) *sprinkle, scatter* Ex 9:8, 10; 2 Km 16:13; Esth 1:6; 3 Macc 1:18; Ps 147:5; Sir 43:18.*

παστός, -οῦ, ὁ   (ins) *bridal chamber* 1 Macc 1:27; 3 Macc 1:19; 4:6; Ps 18:6; Joel 2:16.*

παστοφόριον, -ου, τό   (13x, pap, ins) *priest's chamber* 1 Ch 9:26; 23:28; 1 Esdr 8:58; 1 Macc 4:38; Is 22:15.

παταχρός, ὁ or -όν, τό   (not in HR or LSJ) translit/loanword (declined, should be accented in our texts) of Aram (orig Pers) פִּתְכְּרָא *statue* (to avoid naming a false god) Is 8:21; 37:38. πάτραρχος (LSJ, h.l.) πάταρχος f.ll.*

πάτημα, -ατος, τό   (LXX+) *what is trampled down* 4 Km 19:26; Ezk 34:19.*

πατήρ   Is 17:11 renders כְּאֵב אָנוּשׁ *incurable anguish* as if כְּאָב אֱנוֹשׁ *like the father of a man*, and supplies κληρόω (q.v.) fr mistrans of נחלה in prec phrase (the note "insert לפניך cf. G" in BHS is nonsense). Judg 6:11, 24 arises fr misreading of אבי העזרי *the Abi-ezrite*; πατρος Αβιεζρι in 6:11A and 8:32A is confl. 2 Ch 2:13 mistrans of אבי part of N PERS as if *my father*.‡

πατητός, -ή, -όν   (LXX+) *trodden upon* Is 63:2.*

πατράδελφος, -ου, ὁ   (Isocr+) *uncle, father's brother* 1 Ch 27:32. Judg 10:1; 2 Km 23:9, 24 mistrans of N PERS.*

πατριά   1 Ch 11:25 mistrans of משמעה *bodyguard* as if משמ *tribe*; cf. ἀκοή, παράγγελμα.‡

πάτριος   see BDAG: πατρίς.

παύλα, -ης, ἡ   (Soph, Thu+) *pause, cessation* 2 Macc 4:6.*

παύσις, -εως, ἡ   (h.l. Hippocr) *cessation, stopping*; Jer 31:2 mistrans of מרדם N LOC as if fr דמם *be still*.

πάχνη, -ης, ἡ   (9x, Hom+) *frost, freezing rain* Ps 77:47; Job 38:24; Wsd 5:14; Da 3:70.

πάχος, -εος, τό   (13x, Hdt+) *thickness* Num 24:8; 3 Km 7:3; Job 15:26; Jer 52:21; (concr) *thick or stout piece* 2 Macc 4:41. Ps 140:7 MT also difficult; did LXX reading begin as translit of פלח *slice*? 3 Km 7:33 = 2 Ch 4:17 mistrans of מעבה *foundry*, 7:43 of עב¹ *canopy, roof* (?), both as if fr עבי *thickness* (7:26!).

παχύνω   3. *make thick or dense*; 2 Km 22:12 mistrans of עָבֵי *clouds* as if עבי *thickness*.‡

παχύς, -εῖα, -ύ   comp παχύτερος (Hom+) *thick* 3 Km 12:10 = 24r = 2 Ch 10:10; (of liquids) Jdth 10:3; 2 Macc 1:20; *fat* Ps 143:14; (subst) *fat animal* Ezk 34:3; > (of land) *rich, fertile* (X) Is 28:1.*

πεδήτης, -ου, ὁ   (Aristoph+) *prisoner in fetters* Wsd 17:2.*

πεδιαν   Hab 3:5VL itac missp of παιδείαν?

πέδιλον, -ου, τό   (Hom, Hdt+) *sandal, shoe* Odes 4:5 = Hab 3:5.*

πεζικός, -ή, -όν   (X+) *on foot* 1 Macc 15:38; 16:5; 3 Macc 1:1.*

πεζομαχία, -ας, ἡ   (Hdt, Thu+) *infantry warfare, fighting on foot* 4 Macc 17:24.*

πεζός   (29x) 2. *traveling on foot* (as opposed to riding) Ex 12:37; Sir 16:10; Bar 5:6; *fighting on foot*, (as opposed to cavalry) *infantry* Judg 20:2; 3 Km 21:10; 1 Esdr 8:51; 1 Macc 6:30.‡

πείθω   2.c. (abs) *be confident* Pr 28:1; pf ptc *trusting, confident* (Hom) Dt 33:12; > *(over)confident, unprepared* (no //) Judg 8:11.‡

πειρατεύω   (Strabo, ins) *attack, raid* Gen 49:19.*

πειρατήριον, -ου, τό   (Eur+) 1. *trial, test* Job 7:1; 10:17. 2. *band of raiders, pirates* Gen 49:19; Ps 17:30; Job 19:12.*

πειρατής, -οῦ, ὁ   (Polyb+) *pirate, raider* Job 16:9; 25:3; Hos 6:9.*

πείρω   pf pass ptc πεπαρμένος (not in HR; Hom+) *pierce* 3 Macc 2:22VL.*

πέλας   (Hom, Hdt+) *nearby*; ο(ἱ) πελας *the neighbor(s)* Pr 27:2.*‡

πελειόομαι, πέλειος   see πελι-.

πελεκάν, -ᾶνος, ὁ   (Aristot+) *pelican* Lev 11:18; Dt 14:18; Ps 101:7.*

πελεκάω   (Hom+) *hew* 3 Km 6:1b.*

πελεκητός, -ή, -όν   (Theophr) *hewn* 3 Km 10:22; to be restored in 10:11f (cf. ms B; MT אלמגים [uncertain meaning], ἀπελ- alw = גזית *rough-hewn*).

πέλεκυς, -εως, ὁ   (Hom+) *double-edged ax, battle ax* 3 Km 6:7; Ps 73:6; Jer 22:7; EpJer 13.*

πελιόομαι   (Ra: πελει-, cf. W, 57. Hippocr, Aristot+) *be bruised*, > *become dark* La 5:10.*

πελιός, -ή, -όν   (Ra: πέλειος, cf. W, 56f. Hippocr, Demosth, Theophr+) *bruised* Pr 23:29. VL πελιδνός (Hippocr, Aristot+) = .*

πέλμα, -ατος, τό   (Hippocr, pap, Polyb+) *sole* (of foot) Esth 4:17d.*

πελταστής, -οῦ ὅ   (Eur, Thu+) *bearing a (small) shield*; (pl) *light-armed troops* 2 Ch 14:7; 17:17.*

πέλτη, -ης, ἡ   (Hdt+) *small (Thracian) shield* (Eur BACCH 783) Ezk 23:24; 27:10; 38:4f; 39:9.*

πέλυξ, -υκος, ὁ   (LXX+) *ax* Jer 23:9; Ezk 9:2.*

πέμμα, -ατος, τό   (Hdt+) *pastry, sweetmeats* Hos 3:1; Ezk 45:24; 46:5ff.*

πενέομαι or πένομαι   aor ἐπενήθην (LXX) *be poor* Ex 30:15; Lev 14:21; 25:25, 35; Dt 24:12; Pr 30:9.*

πενθικός, -ή, -όν   (LXX+ [adv X+]) *for mourning* Ex 33:4; 2 Km 14:2.*‡

πενία, -ας, ἡ   (10x, Hom, Hdt+) *poverty, lack, need* Pr 6:11; 10:4; Job 36:8; PsSol 16:13.

πενταετηρικός, -ή, -όν   (ins, Plu) *quadrennial, every four years* (five inclusive) 2 Macc 4:18.*

πενταετής, -ές   (Hdt+) *of five years, five years old* Lev 27:5f.*

πεντάπηχυς, -υ   (Hdt+) *five cubits (long or) tall* 1 Ch 11:23.*

πενταπλασίως (adj Hdt+) *five times over* Gen 43:34.*

πενταπλοῦς (Hippocr, pap+) *five-fold* 3 Km 6:31.*

πεντεκαίδεκα (8x, Thu+) *fifteen* Ex 27:14; Lev 27:7; Judg 8:10; Hos 3:2.

πεντεκαιεικοσαετής, -ές (7x, LXX+, not in HR) *of twenty-five years, twenty-five years old* Num 4:23ff; 8:24.*

πεντήκοντα Judg 7:11 mistrans of חֲמֻשִׁים *organized into companies (of fifty), ready for war* (cf. Jsh1:14 "εὔζωνοι η") as if *fifty*.‡

πεντηκονταετής, -ές (7x, Pla+) *of fifty years, fifty years old* Num 4:23ff; 8:25.*

πεπαρμένος see πείρω.

πέπειρος, -ον (Theophr+) *ripe* Gen 40:10.*‡

πεπεμμένος see πέσσω.

πεπηγώς see πήγνυμι.

πέπληγα pf of BDAG: πλήσσω, used in pass sense (as in Pla, al) Num 25:14ff; 2 Ch 29:9.

πεπληθυμμένος see πληθύνω.

πεποιθότως (DioChrys) *confidently, trustingly* Zech 14:11.*

πεπραμένος pf pass ptc of BDAG: πιπράσκω.

πεπρησμένος pf pass ptc of BDAG: πίμπρημι Num 5:21.

πέπων, -ονος, ὁ (adj since Homer: *ripe*) *melon* Num 11:5.*

πέρα (Pla, X+) *beyond, further; on the other side* (= BDAG: πέραν) 2 Esdr 6:6; 7:21, 25.*‡

περαίνω fut περανῶ aor mid ἐπερανάμην pass ἐπεράνθην *finish, achieve* 3 Macc 4:11 (VL -ραθ- *ex errore*); Hab 2:5; *accomplish one's purpose* 1 Km 12:21.*

περασμός, -οῦ, ὁ (LXX) *end, limit, conclusion* Eccl 4:8, 16; 12:12.*

περάτης, -ου, ὁ (Philo *MIGR* 20; =) *wanderer, migrant* Gen 14:13.*

περάω (Hom, Hdt+) *traverse, accomplish* Wsd 19:5VL (q.l. cf. AB).*

πέρδιξ, -ικος, ὁ or ἡ (ArchilochusLyr, Aristoph+) *partridge* Sir 11:30; Jer 17:11.*

περιαγκωνίζω (Eustath) *tie the hands behind the back* 4 Macc 6:3.*

περιαντλέω (Diosc+) *pour all over;* (pass) *be inundated or drowned* (fig) 4 Macc 15:32.*

περιάπτω (Pind, X+) *hang around;* (fig) *attach, impute* (qual imputed can be acc, pers dat [Pla *APOL* 35A], or qual dat, pers only implied [Joseph *AJ* 12.260]) 3 Macc 3:7.*‡

περιάργυρος, -ον (7x, Chares [IV BCE]) *silver-plated* EpJer 7ff.*

περιαργυρόω pf pass ptc περιηργυρωμένος (9x, Theopomp, ins+) *plate w. silver* (cf. περιχρυσόω) Ex 27:11; 37:15ff; 38:18ff; Ps 67:14; Is 30:22.*

περιβάλλω **1.b.** (act intr, no //) *reach around* Job 23:9.‡

περιβιόω pf ptc περιβεωκώς (LXX+) *remain alive* 3 Macc 5:18; (caus) *keep alive* (dub, no //) Ex 22:17VL.*

περίβλεπτος, -ον (Eur, X+) *looked at and admired* Pr 31:23.*

περίβλημα, -ατος, τό (Aristot, pap+) *garment, robe* Num 31:20.*

περιβολή, -ῆς, ἡ (Pla+) *robe, cloak* Gen 49:11; 2 Macc 3:26; Sir 11:4; 50:11; Da 7:9L.*

περίβολος, -ου, ὁ (10x, Hdt+) **1.** *enclosing wall* 3 Macc 4:11; Is 54:12; Ezk 40:5. **2.** *enclosure* Da 3:1L, > *(sacred) precinct* 1 Macc 14:48; 2 Macc 1:15; Sir 50:2.

περίγλυφον, -ου, τό (h.l.) *carved figure* 3 Km 6:29VL.*

περιγραφή, -ῆς, ἡ (Aeschyl+) *individual appearance or outward impression* Sir 22:23VL.*

περιδειπνέω (Artem) *supply a funeral meal* 2 Km 3:35.*

περίδειπνον, -ου, τό (Demosth, pap+) *funeral meal* EpJer 32.*

περιδέξιον, -ου, τό (pap) *armlet, bracelet* (for right arm) Ex 35:22; Num 31:50; Is 3:20.*

περιδιπλόω (h.l.) *doubly wrap* (for travel) Jdth 10:5.*

περιδόντα 3 Macc 1:27VL error for either παριδόντα or περιιδόντα (περιοράω).

περιδύω (Hom+) *strip naked* (trans) 4 Macc 6:2.*

περίειμι¹ (εἰμί) pres ptc περιών (Hom, Hdt+) *survive, be alive* Job 27:15; 2 Macc

7:24; 14:10; *be present or extant, remain, exist* Job 27:3; 31:21; 3 Macc 5:18.*

περίειμι² (εἶμι) impf περιήειν (Hdt+) *go around* Wsd 8:18; *excel, have success* Sir 26:21(*VL*).*

περιεκτικός, -ή, -όν (Zeno+) *comprehensive* (superl) *most comprehensive, all-embracing* (Epict 1.9.4) 4 Macc 1:20.*

περιελῶ fut of περιαιρέω.

περιεπλάκην aor pass of περιπλέκω.

περιεργάζομαι (Hdt+) **1.** *take pains about, investigate* Wsd 8:5*VL*. **2.** *meddle* Sir 3:23.*‡

περιεργασία, -ας, ἡ (AelAristid+) = seq Sir 41:24*VL*.*

περιεργία, -ας, ἡ (Pla+) *meddling* Sir 41:24.*

περιέρχομαι 2 Km 14:20 mistrans of סבב piel (*h.l.* in MT) *turn,* > *change (face), cause to look different* as if qal or polel *encircle.*‡

περίζωμα, -ατος τό (10x, Polyb, pap) **1.** *skirt, apron* Gen 3:7; Ruth 3:15. **2.** *girdle, sash* Pr 31:24; Jer 13:1.

περίθεμα, -ατος, τό (LXX, Schol Aristoph) *cover, wrapping* (cf. παράθεμα) Num 17:3f; Judg 8:26B.*

περιίπταμαι (Aristot+; *VL* περιπέτομαι, =) *fly around; hover or flutter around* 4 Macc 14:17.*

περιίστημι 1.c. (pass ptc) *surrounded, hemmed in, hard pressed* 2 Macc 14:9. **d.** *bring around,* > *convert, change* EpJer 36.‡

περικαθαρίζω (LXX) *clean away* Lev 19:23; Is 6:7; *cleanse* Dt 30:6.*

περικάθημαι (8x, Hdt+) *besiege* Judg 9:31B; 4 Km 6:25; 1 Macc 5:3.

περικαθίζω (18x, Hippocr+) *besiege* Dt 20:12; Josh 10:5; 4 Km 6:24; 1 Ch 20:1; 1 Macc 6:19.‡

περικαίω (Hdt+) *scorch;* (fig) *inflame, burn* 4 Macc 16:3.*

περικαλύπτω 2. *embed, set* (no //) Ex 28:20.‡

περικατάλη(μ)πτος, -ον (PhilippedesCom [IV-III BCE]+) *surrounded* (c. LSJ; DiodS 2.50.5) 2 Macc 14:41.*

περικείρω pf pass ptc περικεκαρμένος (Hdt+) *shear around;* (pass ptc) *shorn, shaven* Jer 9:25; 32:23.*

περικλάω (Aristot, Theophr+) *twist off, break off* 4 Macc 7:5; 10:6; Job 30:4; Wsd 4:5.*

περικλύζω (Thu+) *wash all around;* (mid) *bathe oneself* (no //) Jdth 10:3; Tob 6:2BA.*

περικνημίς, -ῖδος, ἡ (DionysHal+) *leggings, trousers* Da 3:21Θ.*

περικομπέω (Joseph) *reverberate, sound all around* Wsd 17:4.*

περικοσμέω (LXX+) *decorate or adorn all around* Ps 143:12.*

περικρατέω (Hippocr+) *hold fast,* > *master, control* (τινός) 4 Macc 1:9; 2:2; 7:17, 22; 14:11.*

περικύκλῳ (24x, LXX+) *all around;* (adv) Ex 28:33; Ezk 36:4; (prep w. gen) Dt 6:14; 4 Km 6:17; 1 Esdr 1:50; Ps 88:8; Is 4:5; Da 9:16.

περιλακίζω (*h.l.*) *tear thoroughly or all around* 4 Macc 10:8.*

περιλαμβάνω (13x, Hdt+) **1.** *encompass, surround* Ps 47:13; Pr 4:8; Is 31:9. **2.** (no //) *embrace* Gen 29:13; 4 Km 4:16; Eccl 3:5; SSol 2:6; Sir 30:20; La 4:5 (RECTE; Gött & Ra -βαλ- but Heb חבק; cf. sim error [-βαλ- and -λαβ-] at Job 22:22); *put one's arms around* Judg 16:29; *fold* (hands) Eccl 4:5.

περίλημμα, -ατος, τό (lexicog) *embrace* Eccl 3:5*VL*.*

περίλη(μ)ψις, -εως, ἡ (Aristot+: *grasping*) *act of embracing* (s.t.; cf. περιλαμβάνω) Eccl 3:5.*

περίλοιπος, -ον (Aristoph+) *remaining, surviving* Am 5:15. Ps 20:13 mistrans of מיתר *bowstring* as if fr יתר *be left over.**

περιλύω (pap, Aq) *loosen, let go slack* 4 Macc 10:7.*

περίμετρον, -ου, τό (Hdt+) *circumference, perimeter* 3 Km 7:3; 3 Macc 4:11; Sir 50:3.*

περινίπτω (Hom+: -νίζω) *bathe;* (mid) *wash oneself* Tob 6:2S.*

περιξύω (LXX+) *scrape away* Wsd 13:11.*

περιοδεύω (pap+) *travel around* 2 Km 24:8; Zech 1:10f; 6:7.*

περίοδος, -ου, ἡ (Hdt+) *journey around* Josh 6:16.*

περιοικοδομέω (Hdt+) *build around, enclose* Jer 52:4; Ezk 26:8; 39:11; (pass) *be enclosed or shut in* Job 19:8.*

περιονυχίζω (h.l.) *pare the nails* Dt 21:12.*

περιοράω (Hdt+) *look around; overlook* 3 Macc 1:27vl.*

περιουσιασμός, -οῦ, ὁ (lxx) *wealth, treasure, abundance* Ps 134:4; Eccl 2:8.*

περιοχή, -ῆς, ἡ (25x, Theophr, Polyb+; BDAG: *passage of Scripture*) **1.** *siege* 4 Km 24:10; Na 3:14; Jer 19:9. **2.** *fortified enclosure* (no //) 1 Km 22:4f; 2 Ch 32:10; Ps 30:22; Jer 28:30. 4 Km 19:24 mistrans of מָצוֹר *Egypt* as if מְצוּרָה*fortified enclosure*; Ezk 12:13; 17:20 mistrans of מְצוֹדָה *net* as if מְצוּרָה *fortified enclosure*. **3.** *sudden reversal, overturning* (= περιπετεία, cf. LSJ); Ob 1 mistrans of צִיר² *messenger* as if צִיר³ *convulsion, upheaval.*‡

περιπαθῶς (lxx+) *in a state of violent emotion* 4 Macc 8:2.*

περίπατος, -ου, ὁ (8x, Aristot+) *passage, walkway* Job 41:24; Ezk 42:4ff; (fig) *orderly progression* 2 Macc 2:30; > *philosophical discourse* Pr 23:31.

περιπεπλεγμένος pf pass ptc of BDAG: περιπλέκτω.

περιπιλέω (h.l.) *completely and thickly cover* 3 Km 6:21vl.*

περιπλήσσω pf pass ptc περιπεπληγμένος (not in HR or LSJ) *strike all around*; (pass ptc) *utterly stricken* 3 Macc 2:22R (Gött περιπλέκτω).*

περιπόλιον, -ου, τό (Thu, ins) *surrounding fortifications* 1 Macc 11:4, 61.*

περιπορεύομαι (Pla+) *go around* Josh 15:3.*

περιπόρφυρος, -ον (CratesCom [IV bce], Polyb+) *edged with purple*, (subst) *purple-trimmed garment* Is 3:21.*

περίπτερος, -ον (CallixenusHist) lit *flying around; encircled by a colonnade* Am 3:15; (pl subst) *sparks* (of fire) SSol 8:6.*

περίπτωμα, -ατος, τό (Pla+) *chance, happenstance* Ruth 2:3; 2 Km 1:6.*

περιρραντίζω (lxx) *sprinkle around*; (pass; act suppl by BDAG: περιρραίνω, cf. Num 19:18, 21) *be sprinkled* Num 19:13, 20.*

περιρρέω (Hom, Hdt+) *flow around, overflow* 4 Macc 9:20.*

περισιαλόω (h.l.) *embroider around* Ex 36:13.*

περισκελής, -ές (lxx) *around the leg*; (sg or pl subst) *leggings or trousers* Ex 28:42; 36:35; Lev 6:3; 16:14; Sir 45:8; Ezk 44:18.*

περισκυθίζω (lxx+) *scalp in Scythian manner* 2 Macc 7:4.*

περισπασμός, -οῦ, ὁ (9x, Polyb+) *distraction* Tob 10:6S; 2 Macc 10:36; Eccl 1:13; 2:23, 26.

περισπόριον, -ου, τό (65x, lxx) *surrounding (tillable) area* Josh 21:2ff; 1 Ch 6:40ff.

περισσεία, -ας, ἡ (12x, ins+) *abundance, surplus*, > *gain, advantage* (no //, but cf. BDAG: περισσός, τὸ περισσόν *advantage* Ro 3:1) Eccl 1:3; 2:11 etc.‡

περισσεύω **1.b.β.ב.** (pejor) *act superior, be overbearing* (no //) Sir 33:30.*‡

περίστασις, -εως, ἡ (Teleclides [V bce], Aristot+) *surrounding, encirclement* Ezk 26:8; > *circumstance, crisis* 2 Macc 4:16.*

περιστέλλω **2.** *lay out and bury* (a corpse); *be buried* (pass) Ezk 29:5.‡

περιστήθιον, -ου, τό (Philo Somn 1.214; Spec 1.94; both of high-priestly garment) *breast band* Ex 28:4.*

περίστησον aor impv of περιίστημι.

περιστολή, -ῆς, ἡ (lxx+) *robe* Ex 33:6; Sir 45:7; (fig) *decorum, restraint, moderation* (Aristeas 284 //καταστολή) PsSol 13:8.*

περιστόμιον, -ου, τό (Polyb+) *collar* (of garment) Ex 28:32; 36:30; Job 30:18; *edge* (of ravine) Ezk 39:11. Job 15:27 mistrans of פִּימָה *fat* as if rel to פֶּה *mouth*.*

περιστρέφω (Hom+) *circle around* Gen 37:7; (mid) *move around,"make the rounds"* (no //) Num 36:7, 9.*

περιστροφή, -ῆς, ἡ (Soph+) *parade, procession* (no //) Sir 50:5.*

περίστυλος, -ον (Hdt+) *surrounded by a colonnade*; (neut subst) *colonnade* (ins, DiodS) 2 Macc 4:46; 3 Macc 5:23; Ezk 40:17f; 42:3, 5.*

περισύρω (Polyb+) *tear away* Gen 30:37; 2 Macc 7:7; 4 Macc 10:7vl.*

περισχίζω (Hdt, Pla+) *divide*, > *part (in two) and surround*; Ezk 47:15; 48:1 mistrans of חֶתְלוֹן (n loc) as if fr חתל *swaddle, enwrap* (only Ezk 16:4).*‡

περισῴζω (X+) *save from death* 1 Km 30:17vL.*

περίτειχος, -ους, τό (LXX) *surrounding or enclosing wall* 4 Km 25:1; Is 26:1.*

περιτήκω pf pass ptc (Ra) περιτετηκμένος or (HR, LSJ)-τηγμένος (Hippocr, Pla+) *melt away (from around)* 4 Macc 9:21vL.*

περιτομή Jer 11:16 mistrans of המולה *uproar, crowd* as if מולה *circumcision*.‡

περιττός   Att for BDAG: περισσός 2 Macc 12:44vLR.*

περιφανής, -ές (Soph, Thu+) *conspicuous* 4 Macc 8:2vL*; adv -φανῶς *conspicuously* 4 Macc 8:2.*

περιφέρεια, -ας, ἡ (Heraclitus, Aristot+) *curvature*; (fig) *perversity* (no //) Eccl 9:3; 10:13.*

περιφερής, -ές (HermippusCom, Pla+) *rounded, curved; all around, enclosing* 2 Macc 13:5; Ezk 41:10.*

περιφέρω **1.c.** *turn around,* > *make dizzy or giddy, confuse* (Joseph *AJ* 17.92) Eccl 7:7.‡

περιφορά, -ᾶς, ἡ (X, Eur, Pla+) *circular motion, movement in circles,* > (fig) *disorientation, confusion* (no //, but cf. παραφορά, περιφέρω) Eccl 2:2, 12; 7:25.*

περιφράσσω pf pass ptc περιπεφραγμένος (Hippocr, Pla+) *fortify or enclose all around* 3 Km 10:22a; 2 Macc 1:34; 12:13; Job 1:10; Sir 28:24; (pass) *be obstructed or sealed off* EpJer 17.*

περίφρων, gen **-ονος** (Hom, Aeschyl+) *haughty,* > (no //) *despising, viewing w. contempt* (τινός) 4 Macc 8:28.*

περιφυτεύω (Hom, Pla) *plant all around* 4 Macc 2:21.*

περιχαλάω (h.l.) *slacken all around, make completely loose or slack* 4 Macc 7:13.*

περιχαλκόω (h.l. but cf. περιχρυσόω, περιαργυρόω) *plate w. copper or bronze* Ex 27:6.*

περιχαρακόω (Aeschin, Polyb+) *surround w. stockade; besiege* Jer 52:4. Pr 4:8 mistrans of סלל¹ *cherish* as if סלל² *heap up, build* (siege mound or road).*

περιχέω aor pass περιεχύθη pf pass περιεκέχυτο (Hom+) *pour out or around* 2 Ch 29:22; (pass) *be poured out profusely* Jdth 13:2; (fig) *close around, envelop* 2 Macc 3:17, 27; Jon 2:6.*

περίχρυσος, -ον (7x, ins) *gilded, gold-plated* EpJer 7, 38; etc.

περιχρυσόω pf pass ptc περικεχρυσωμένος (Agatharchides+) *gild, cover w. gold* 3 Km 10:18; Is 30:22; 40:19 (cf. περιχαλκόω, περιαργυρόω).*

περιψύχω (Hippocr, Aristot+) *chill, be(come) cool;* (fig) *neglect, be aloof from* Sir 30:7.*

περκάζω (Theophr+) *darken, ripen* (of grapes) Sir 51:15; Am 9:13.*

πέσσω fut πέψωσι pass πεφθήσεται aor ἔπεψα pf pass ptc πεπεμμένος (15; Hom+) *cook, bake* Gen 19:3; Is 44:15; (ptc subst) *baker, cook* 1 Km 8:13.

πέταλον, -ου, τό (7x, Hom+ [of metal, ins]) *leaf, thin plate* Ex 28:36; Lev 8:9; 3 Km 6:18(vL), 35.‡

πεταλόω (pap) *plate or leaf* (w. metal) 3 Km 6:22vL.*

πέταμαι   = BDAG: πέτομαι‡

πετάννυμι or πετάομαι   aor pass ἐπετάσθην *spread out,* > (pass) *fly* Dt 4:17; 2 Km 22:11 = Ps 17:11; Ps 54:7; Pr 26:2; Hab 1:8; *flutter* Job 26:11. Ezk 32:10 mistrans of צפף *wield* as if עוף *fly*.*

πέτασος, -ου, ὁ (Theophr+) *broad-brimmed hat* 2 Macc 4:12.*

πετεινός, -ή, -όν (98x, Hom+) *able to fly, winged* Gen 6:20; Ezk 39:4 (neut subst cf. BDAG).‡

πέτευρον, -ου, τό (vL -ταυρ-, = ; Aristoph+) *plank, springboard,* > *trapdoor* (no //) Pr 9:18.*

πέτρινος, -η, -ον (Hdt+) *of stone or rock* Josh 5:2f; 21:40; 24:31.*

πετροβόλος, -ον (X+) *for throwing* Ezk 13:11, 13; (masc subst, Polyb+) *sling, catapult* 1 Km 14:14; Job 41:20; Wsd 5:22.*

πέτρος, -ου, ὁ (Hom+) *stone* 2 Macc 1:16; 4:41.*‡

πεύκη, -ης, ἡ   (Hom+) *pine* (tree or wood) Is 60:13.*

πεύκινος, -η, -ον   (8x, Soph+) *of pine* 3 Km 5:22; 2 Ch 2:7.

πεφθήσομαι   see πέσσω.

πέψις, -εως, ἡ   (Hippocr, Aristot+) *cooking* (cf. πέσσω) Hos 7:4.*

πῆγμα, -ατος, τό   (Aeschyl+) *anything knit together;* (πήγνυμι) *congealing mass* Josh 3:16; *framework* 4 Macc 9:21.*

πήγνυμι   fut πήξω (late pres πήσσω) aor pass ἐπάγην fut παγήσομαι pf pass πέπηγα **1.b.** (pass) *be fixed, be impaled* 2 Esdr 6:11. **3.** (of water) *solidify, freeze* Sir 43:19f; (of other materials) *harden* Job 41:16.‡

πηδαλιουχέω   (Philo+) *pilot, steer* 4 Macc 7:1.*

πηλός   **3.** *mortar* Gen 11:3.‡

πηλουργός, -όν   (LXX+) *working in clay;* (subst) Wsd 15:7.*

πῆξις, -εως, ἡ   (Hippocr, Pla+) *fixity, stiffness* (of elbow; from reclining too long? from relentless eating?) Sir 41:20.*

πήσσω   see πήγνυμι.

πῆχυς   (cf. BDAG) alt gen (sg and pl) πήχεος, πήχεων Ex 30:2; Da 3:1Θ.‡

πιαίνω   fut πιανεῖ pass πιανθήσεται aor impv πιανάτω (8x, Aeschyl+) **1.** *make fat, enrich* Pr 15:30; Sir 26:13; (pass) *become fat, be enriched* Ps 64:13; Is 58:11; Ezk 17:8, > *become wanton, dissipated* Ezk 17:10. **2.** *cherish, honor* Ps 19:4.*

πίθος, -ου, ὁ   (Hom, Hdt+) *large jar or cask* (for wine) Pr 23:27.*

πικρασμός, -οῦ, ὁ   (Philo) *bitterness, embitterment* Esth 4:17o.*

πικρίς, -ίδος, ἡ   (Aristot+) *ox tongue* (plant or herb) Ex 12:8; Num 9:11.*

πικρόω   (AlexAphr) *embitter* Job 27:2VL.*

πίμπρημι   aor (fr related vb πρήθω [HR]) ἔπρησα pf pass ptc πεπρησμένος (Hom, Aeschyl+) **1.** (mid/pass) *be feverish, swell* (w. disease) Num 5:21, 27; (act) *cause to burn or swell* 5:22. **2.** *burn, burn up* (Hom, Soph+) 3 Macc 5:43VL.*‡

πίν(ν)ινος, -ον   (h.l.) *of mother-of-pearl* Esth 1:6.*

πιπι   (not in LSJ) rendering in Gk letters of יהוה *Yahweh*, Origenic mss, e.g., Is 48:14; 59:13; 64:8.

πίπτω   Ezk 23:3 (21VL) mistrans of מעך pu'al *be pressed or squeezed,* unexpl.‡

πιρασμος   itac misspelling of BDAG: πειρ-.

πίσσα, -ης, ἡ   (Hom, Hdt+) *pitch, resin* Sir 13:1; Is 34:9; Da 3:46; Bel 27.*

πιστεύω   Job 39:24 mistrans of אמן *stand still or firm* as if *trust.*‡

πίστις   1 Ch 9:22, 26, 31 mistrans of אמונה *duty* as if *faith, reliability.* SSol 4:8 mistrans of אמנה מראש *from the peak of Amana* (N LOC) as if fr אמן *be faithful.*‡

πιστοποιέω   (LXX) *confirm, make or prove credible or trustworthy* 4 Macc 7:9; 18:17.*

πιστόω   **3.** (act trans) *cause to be faithful or trustworthy* 2 Km 7:25; 1 Ch 17:14; *bind oneself w. oaths* (no // in act) 2 Macc 7:24; 12:25.‡

πίτυρον, -ου, τό   (Hippocr, Theophr+) *husk, bran* (used for magic [Demosth+]) EpJer 42.*

πίτυς, -υος, ἡ   (Hom, Hdt+) *pine tree* Zech 11:2; Ezk 31:8.*

πλαγιάζω   (LXX+) *turn aside, deflect;* (fig, no //, but cf. πλάγιος) *pervert, mislead* Is 29:21; Ezk 14:5.*

πλάγιος, -α, -ον   (21x, Thu+) *sideways; on the side* Sus 18Θ, 26Θ, *in misleading or perverted fashion* (Pind, Polyb+) Lev 26:21ff; (neut pl subst) *sides, flanks* Gen 6:16; Ex 26:13; ἐκ πλαγίων *alongside* Lev 1:11; Ruth 2:14.

πλάνησις, -εως, ἡ   (10x, Thu+) *deception, misleading* Tob 14:6S; PsSol 8:19; Is 19:14; 22:5; Jer 4:11; Ezk 44:13.

πλανῆτις, -ιδος, ἡ   (Lycophron+) *wanderer* Job 2:9d.*

πλάνος, -ου, ὁ   (Soph, Eur+) *going astray; madness, error* Job 19:4; Jer 23:32.*‡

πλάσσω   **3.** *form (as) a mental image, conceive, imagine* 4 Km 19:25.‡

πλάστης, -ου, ὁ   (Pla+) *maker, modeler* 2 Km 22:3VL, Is 64:7VL.*

πλάστιγξ, -ιγγος, ἡ (Soph+) *scale, balance* 2 Macc 9:8; Wsd 11:22.*

πλάτανος, -ου, ἡ (Aristoph+) **1.** *plane tree* Sir 24:14. **2.** *plane-tree wood* Gen 30:37.*

πλάτος **3.** *plane surface, flat portion* Gen 32:26.‡

πλειστάκις (Hippocr, X, Pla+) *very often* Eccl 7:22.*

πλείων see πολύς.‡

πλέκω aor pass ἐπλάκην pf pass ptc πεπλεγμένος (Hom, Hdt+) *twist, plait* Ex 28:14; Is 28:5.*‡

πλεονάκις (10x, Hippocr+) *many times, over and over* Tob 1:6BA, 5:6S; Ps 105:43; Sir 34:12; Is 42:20.

πλεόνασμα, -ατος, τό (pap+) *excess, remainder* Num 31:32.*

πλεονασμός, -οῦ, ὁ (Aristot, pap+) *increase, profit* Lev 25:37; Pr 28:8; Ezk 18:8ff; 22:12.*

πλεοναστός, -ή, -όν (LXX) *numerous* Dt 30:5; 1 Macc 4:35.*

πλεονέκτημα, -ατος, τό (Gorgias of Leontini, X+) *advantage, profit* Is 56:11vL.*

πλεονεξία **2.** *gain, (large) share* Judg 5:19A.‡

πλευρά, -ᾶς, ἡ (28x, Hom+) **1.** *rib* Gen 2:21; Job 40:18; Sir 30:12; (pl) *body* 3 Km 8:19; Pr 22:27. **2.** *side* (of pers) Num 33:55; Is 11:5; (of mountain) 2 Km 13:34; *side chamber* 2 Km 21:14; Ezk 41:5.‡

πλευρόν, -οῦ, τό (19x, Hom+) **1.** *side* (of obj) Ex 27:7; Ps 47:3; (of pers) 4 Macc 6:6; Ezk 4:4; *wall* 3 Km 6:16. **2.** *rib* Da 7:5. Ezk 41:6 mistrans of צלע *side chamber* as if *side, wall*.

πληθύνω pf pass ptc πεπληθυμμένος La 1:1 mistrans of רב(ה) *great, numerous* as if pass of רבה *be(come) numerous.*‡

πληθύς, -ύος, ἡ (Hom, ps-Pla+) *crowd, mass* (of people) 3 Macc 4:17.*

πλημμέλεια **2.** *offering for sin or error* (s.t. of חטאת *sin, offering or penalty for sin*; cf. ἁμαρτία) Lev 5:15; Num 6:12.‡

πλημμελέω pf pass ptc πεπλημμελημένος (34; Pla+) *offend, commit sin* Lev 4:13ff; Josh 7:1; Ps 33:22f; Sir 9:13; Jer 2:3; (pass) *be made to sin, be misled* Is 28:7vL.*

πλημμέλημα, -ατος, τό (Aeschin+) *mistake, transgression* Jer 2:5; *compensation or restitution for transgression* (s.t. of חטאה *sin, offering or penalty for sin*; cf. ἁμαρτία) Num 5:8.*

πλημμελής, -ές (not in HR; Eur, Pla+) *out of place, mistaken* Sir 10:7.*

πλημμέλησις, -εως, ἡ (LXX) *mistake, transgression* Lev 5:19; 2 Esdr 10:19.*

πληρόω **7.** (caus) *make numerous, multiply* (no //) Ps 109:6. **8.** πλ. τὰς χεῖρας (τὴν χ.) *ordination formula for priesthood* (cf. ἐμπίμπλημι) Ex 32:29; Judg 17:5B.‡

πλήρωσις, -εως, ἡ (Hdt+) **1.** *filling, fullness, completion* Dt 33:16; Jdth 8:31; Jer 4:12; Ezk 32:15; (of time) Jer 5:24; Ezk 5:2; Da 10:3Θ. **2.** *setting* (for stone or jewel) Ex 35:27; 1 Ch 29:2.*

πλησιάζω (Soph, X+) *consort w., have sex w.* (τινί) 2 Macc 6:4.*

πλησιέστερον (LXX+; comp adv of BDAG: πλησίον) *nearer, closer* 4 Macc 12:2.*

πλησμονή **2.** *surfeit, excess* Is 1:14; Ezk 16:49.‡

πλήσσω pf πέπληγα (pass sense) 2 Ch 29:9; (ptc) Num 25:14ff; aor pl impv πλήξατε (no // except in compounds) Jer 30:6G (30:23R πλήσατε).‡

πλήσω trans act fut (rare) of πίμπλημι; Ezk 43:26 cf. πληρόω.

πλινθεία, -ας, ἡ (LXX+) *brick-making* Ex 1:14; 5:8ff.*

πλινθεῖον, -ου, τό (Aristoph+) *brickworks* 3 Km 2:46h. 2 Km 12:31 *brickmold;* mistrans, cf. τίθημι, διάγω.*

πλινθεύω (Hdt+) *make bricks* Gen 11:3.*

πλίνθος, -ου, ἡ (11x, Hdt+) *brick* Gen 11:3; Ex 5:16; Jdth 5:11; Mi 7:11; Is 9:9.

πλινθουργία, -ας, ἡ (h.l.) *brick-making* Ex 5:7.*

πλοῖον Is 18:1 mistrans of צְלָצַל *crickets*, unexpl.‡

πλόκιον, -ου, τό (ins, Plu+: *small necklace*) *small braid of hair* (lexicog) SSol 7:6.*

πλωτός, -ή, -όν (Hom, Hdt+) *suitable to sail upon, navigable* (opp πορευτός Polyb 1.42.2) 2 Macc 5:21; *floating* Job 40:31.*

πνευματοφορέομαι (h.l.) *be blown about* Jer 2:24.*

πνεύμων, -ονος, ὁ (Hom, trag: πλεύμων; Aristot+) *lung(s)* 3 Km 22:34 = 2 Ch 18:33.*

πνεύσω, πνεύσομαι fut of BDAG: πνέω.‡

πνιγμός, -οῦ, ὁ (Hippocr, X+) *choking, suffocation* Sir 51:4.*

πόα, -ης, ἡ (Hom+) **1.** *grass, herb* Pr 27:25 (VL ποια, =). **2.** *lye* (no //) Mal 3:2; Jer 2:22.*‡

ποδάγρα, -ας, ἡ (X+) *trap or fetter for the feet* 4 Macc 11:10.*

ποδιστήρ, -ῆρος, ὁ (Aeschyl+) *tripod, stand* (Joseph *AJ* 8.88; =) 2 Ch 4:16.*

ποθεινός, -ή, -όν (Sappho, Eur, Thuc+) *desiring, longing; desirable, desired* Pr 6:8b; (comp) *more ardent, more fervent* 4 Macc 13:26; *more desirable* 15:1.*

ποία see πόα.

ποικίλλω pf pass ptc πεποικιλμένος (Hom+) *embroider* (cloth); (pass ptc) *dressed or adorned in embroidery* Ps 44:10, 14.*

ποίκιλμα, -ατος, τό (Aeschyl+) *embroidered work* Ezk 23:15; 27:16; *variegation, spottedness* (no //) Jer 13:23.*

ποικιλτής, -οῦ, ὁ (7x, Aristot+) *embroiderer* Ex 26:36; 28:6ff; Sir 45:10.

ποικιλτικός, -ή, -όν (LXX+) *embroidered, related to embroidery* Ex 37:21; Job 38:36.*

ποικιλτός, -ή, -όν (Theopomp) *embroidered* Ex 35:35; Judg 5:30B.*

ποικίλως (X+) *in varied fashion* Esth 1:6; 4 Macc 16:3.*

ποιμήν Jer 3:1; 3 mistrans of רֵעַ *companion, lover* as if רֹעֶה *shepherd*.‡

πόκος, -ου, ὁ (9x, Hom+) *wool, fleece* Judg 6:37ff; 4 Km 3:4; Ps 71:6.*

πολεμικός, -όν (18x, Thu+) *for war* Dt 1:41; 1 Km 8:12; 1 Macc 3:3; Zech 9:10; Jer 21:4.

πολέμιος, -ον (39x, Aeschyl, Hdt+) **1.** *hostile, inimical* 1 Ch 18:10; 2 Macc 3:38; *hurtful, dangerous* 15:39; (subst) *enemy* 1 Esdr 4:4; 2 Esdr 8:31; 1 Macc 7:29; 2 Macc 5:6; Wsd 11:3; EpJer 55; (fem) Is 27:4. **2.** *of war, related to war;* (pl subst) *warring activities* Esth 9:16.

πολεμιστής, -οῦ, ὁ (49x, Hom+) *warrior* Num 31:27; Josh 8:1; Jdth 1:16; 1 Macc 13:10; Wsd 18:15; Joel 2:7; Is 3:2; in our lit, most oft in appos, nearly as adj—cf. Josh 17:1; 1 Km 13:15; 1 Ch 28:3; 1 Macc 15:13; Jer 27:30.

πολεμοτροφέω (LXX) *maintain war, keep on fighting* 2 Macc 10:14f; 14:6.*

πολιορκέω pass ptc πολιορκουμένος pf pass πεπολιόρκημαι (26; Hdt+) *besiege* Josh 10:29; 2 Macc 11:6; Is 1:8; (fig) *harass* 1 Esdr 5:69; (pass) *be hard pressed* Job 17:7.

πολιόρκησις, -εως, ἡ (not in HR or LSJ) *state of siege* Sir 50:4.*

πολιός, -ά, -όν (16x, Hom+) *gray, old* Lev 19:32; (fem subst) *old age* Judg 8:32A; 2 Macc 15:13; (pl) *gray hair* Pr 20:29; Hos 7:9 Is 47:2; = *old age* Sir 6:18.

πόλις Ezk 16:7 mistrans of בעדי עדיים w. *the finest ornaments* (but txt? better: בָּעֵדִים *to [the stage of] menstrual periods*) as if בערי ערים *to the city of cities*.‡

πολλαχόθεν (Thu+) *from many aspects* 4 Macc 1:7.*

πολλαχῶς (Isocr+) *in many ways* 3 Macc 1:25; Ezk 16:26.*

πολλοστός, -ή, -όν (Thu, Pla+) *in an extended series,* > *over and over, for a long time* (no //) Pr 5:19; πολ- ἔργοις *having many accomplishments* (no //) 2 Km 23:20.*‡

πολυανδρεῖος, -ον (Ra: -άνδριος [cf. W, p. 51], ins+) *of many men;* **1.** (neut subst) *cemetery* (Strabo 9.4.2, 16; Joseph *BJ* 5.19) 2 Macc 9:4, 14. **2.** *(place for) public assembly* (Plu) 4 Macc 15:20; Ezk 39:11². Ezk 39:11¹ mistrans of גיא *valley* fr confl of גיא and המון *crowd* later in the verse; Jer 2:23; 19:2, 6 mistrans of גיא appar influenced by (earlier!) transl of Ezk (so W, p.179).*

πολύγονος, -ον (Hdt+) *fertile, prolific* 4 Macc 15:5; Wsd 4:3.*

πολύδακρυς, -υ (Hom+) *w. many tears, very tearful* (ins) 3 Macc 5:25.*

πολυέλεος, -ον (10x, LXX) *very merciful* Ex 34:6; 2 Esdr 19:17; 3 Macc 6:9; Ps 85:5; Jon 4:2.

πολυετής, -ές (Eur+) *after many years* Wsd 4:16.*

πολυημερεύω (h.l.) *be long-lived* Dt 11:21.*

πολυήμερος, -ον (Hippocr+) *of many days, long-lived* Dt 22:7; 25:15; 30:18; Da 4:27L.*

πολύθρηνος, -ον (Aeschyl+) *greatly mourning or wailing* 4 Macc 16:10.*

πολυκέφαλος, -ον (Pla+) *many-headed* 4 Macc 7:14.*

πολυμερής, -ές (Aristot+) *of many parts or aspects* Wsd 7:22*

πολυοδία, -ας, ἡ (h.l.) *great or long journey* Is 57:10.*

πολύορκος, -ον (LXX) *frequently swearing, given to oaths* Sir 23:11; (subst) *frequent swearer of oaths* 27:14.*

πολυοχλία, -ας, ἡ (Polyb, ins) *crowd (of people)* Job 31:34; 39:7; Bar 4:34.*

πολύπαις, gen -παιδος (Strabo+) *w. many children* 4 Macc 16:10.*

πολυπειρία, -ας, ἡ (Thu+) *extensive experience* Wsd 8:8; Sir 25:6.*

πολύπειρος, -ον (Parmenides, Aristot+) *very experienced* Sir 21:22; 36:20; (subst) 34:9.*

πολυπλασιάζω (LXX+) *multiply,* (pass) *become numerous* Dt 4:1R (Gött omit); 8:1; 11:8.*

πολυπλάσιος, -α, -ον (AnthPal+) *many times multiplied* 2 Macc 9:16.*‡

πολυπληθέω (LXX) *multiply,* (intr) *become numerous* Ex 5:5; Dt 7:7; (w. ποσιν, dat of ref) *have many (feet)* Lev 11:42.*

πολυπληθύνω (h.l.) *multiply,* (trans) *make numerous* Ex 32:13.*

πολύπλοκος, -ον (Eur+) *complex* 4 Macc 14:13; *ingenious, crafty* Esth 8:12n; 4 Macc 15:24; (subst) *crafty person, schemer* Job 5:13.*

πολυπραγμονέω (Aristoph+) *be curious, inquire* 2 Macc 2:30.*

πολυρήμων, -ον (HR, LSJ: -ρρήμων; LXX+) *wordy, talking (too) much* Job 8:2.*

πολύς **2.b.γ.** (cf. BDAG; comp πλείων) *abundant, very generally present* (no //) EpJer 11.‡

πολυτόκος, -ον (Hippocr, Aristot+) *prolific, giving multiple birth* Ps 143:13.*

πολύφροντις, -ιδος, ἡ (LXX+) *great care or anxiety* Wsd 9:15.*

πολυχρονίζω (LXX+) *prolong through time* Dt 4:26.*

πολυχρόνιος, -ον (Hdt+) *long-enduring, long-lasting* Wsd 2:10; 4:8; EpJer 46; *long-lived* Job 32:9; = *"eternal"* 4 Macc 17:12; γίνομαι πολυχρ- *be (there) a long time* Gen 26:8.*

πολυωρέω (pap, ins) *care for greatly* Dt 30:9; Ps 11:9; 137:3.*

πομπεύω (Hom+) *parade, process* 2 Macc 6:7; Wsd 4:2.*

πονέω **2.** *have pain in* (τι) 3 Km 15:23; La 4:6; (abs) *be wounded* 2 Ch 18:33.‡

πόνος **1.b.** *the result or product of such labor* (Pind, Aeschyl, X) Dt 28:33; Ps 104:44; Job 5:6; Jer 20:5.‡

ποντόβροχος, -ον (h.l.; vvll ποντοβρυχ(ι)ος dub, not in HR or LSJ [cf. LSJ: βρυξ *depth of the sea*]), *sunk or drowned in the sea* 3 Macc 6:4.*

ποντοπορέω (Hom+) *traveling the sea* Pr 30:19.*

πορεία **3.** *gait, style of walking* Is 3:16.‡

πορεῖον, -ου, τό (Pla+) *conveyance, wagon, cart* Gen 45:17; = ποριον Esth 8:14vl.*

πόρευσις, -εως, ἡ (Pla) *journey* Gen 33:14.*

πορευτός, -ή, -όν (Aeschyl+) *passable, safe for travel* Esth 3:13b; *able to be traversed by walking or land vehicles* (opp πλωτός Polyb 1.42.2) 2 Macc 5:21.*

πορία = πορεία Jer 18:15vl.

πορνεῖον, -ου, τό (Aristoph+) *brothel* Ezk 16:25, 31, 39.*

πορνικός, -ή, -όν (AnthPal+) *of or related to prostitution* Pr 7:10; Ezk 16:24.*

πορνοκόπος, -ου, ὁ (Menand) *one who hires or engages a prostitute* Pr 23:21.*

πόρος, -ου, ὁ (Hom+) *means, way* 1 Macc 12:40G; *way, path* (on water or land) 3 Macc 4:18vl.*

πόρπη, -ης, ἡ (Hom+) *brooch, pin* 1 Macc 10:89; 11:58; 14:44.*

πορφυρίς, -ίδος, ἡ (X+) *purple garment* Judg 8:26B.*

πορφυρίων, -ωνος, ὁ (Aristoph+) *purple coot* Lev 11:18; Dt 14:18.*

ποσαπλῶς (adj: Pla+) *how often, how many times* Ps 62:2.*

ποσαχῶς (Aristot+) *in how many ways* Sir 10:31.*

πότερον (12x; acc adv form of BDAG: πότερος [Hom+], used as interrog) *if, whether, perhaps* Job 4:6; 7:1.‡

πότημα, -ατος, τό (Hippocr+) *drink, potion* Jer 28:39.*

ποτιστήριον, -ου, τό (LXX) *watering trough* Gen 24:20; 30:38.*

πούς 4. *footstep, track,* (fig) *sound, pattering* (of rain) 3 Km 18:41; ἐν τοις ποσιν *in (their) footsteps* (Hdt 2.76.1; = Heb) Judg 8:5B; 4 Km 3:9; κατα ποδας *close behind* (Hdt 5.98.4; Heb עָקֵב *heel*) Gen 49:19. **5.** euphem for genitals (Heb, no //) Judg 3:24B.‡

πρᾶγμα 3.b. (pl) *political affairs, public matters* 1 Macc 3:32; ὁ ἐπὶ τῶν πραγ- *public official*; (pl) *administrators, high officials* (Polyb 3.69.4) 3 Macc 13:2. **5.** *actuality* (opp of ἔμφασις *appearance*); ἐν πρ-*"in fact"* 3 Macc 3:8.‡

πραγματεία 3 Km 7:19 renders either חשק *spoke* or חשר *hub* (both *h.l.*), unexpl.‡

πραγματικός, -ή, -όν (pap, Polyb+) *businesslike*; (subst) *agent, official* 1 Esdr 8:22.*

πρᾶξις 5.b. *exaction, collection* (of money) 2 Macc 4:28.‡

πράσινος, -α, -ον (Aristot) *pale green*; π. λιθος *emerald* Gen 2:12.*

πρᾶσις, -εως, ἡ (21x, Hdt+) **1.** *sale, (act of) selling* Lev 25:27; Dt 18:8; 2 Esdr 23:15; 2 Macc 8:34; Sir 27:2; Ezk 27:17; *transaction* Lev 25:50. **2.a.** *market* Gen 42:1; Lev 25:42; 2 Esdr 23:20. **b.** *something for sale* (no //); *property* Lev 25:14, 25; *wares* 2 Esdr 20:32; 23:16. 4 Km 12:6; 8 as if fr מכר *buy,* but prob fr נכר *recognize,* > *acquaintance*; so NJB.

πράσον, -ου, τό (Aristoph+) *leek* Num 11:5.*

πρατός, -ή, -όν (Soph+) *for sale* 2 Macc 11:3.*

πράττω = BDAG: πράσσω

πραΰθυμος, -ον (LXX) *gentle-spirited* Pr 14:30; (subst) 16:19.*

πραΰνω (Hes, Hdt+) *soothe, calm* (τινί, no //) Ps 93:13; (τινά) Pr 18:14.*

πρεπόντως (Aeschyl, Thu, Pla+) *fittingly, properly* (adv of pres ptc of BDAG: πρέπω) 2 Macc 15:12.*

πρεσβεῖον, -ου, τό (Hom, Demosth+: *right of inheritance*) *advanced age* (no //) 3 Macc 6:1; Ps 70:18; *status as elder* (no //) Gen 43:33; Sus 50Θ.

πρέσβυς, -εως, ὁ (16x, Aeschyl+) **1.** *old man* 4 Macc 7:10; Is 13:8. **2.** *ambassador* Num 21:21; 1 Macc 9:70; Ps 67:32; Hos 5:13; Is 21:2; (comp, cf. BDAG) πρεσβύτερος; (superl) πρεσβύτατος (Hom+) *oldest, eldest* 4 Macc 9:11.*‡

πρην (dub, not in LSJ) *f.l.* for πρηνέα (or BDAG: πρίν?) 3 Macc 5:43vL.*

πρηνέα archaic acc of BDAG: πρηνής *prostrate, fallen flat* 3 Macc 5:43.‡

πρήσας aor act ptc of πίμπρημι.

[πρίαμαι] (Hom+) only aor ἐπρίατο, inf πρίασθαι (πριάσασθαι Gen 42:10vL) *buy, purchase* Gen 42:2ff; 43:2, 20; Pr 31:16.*

πρῖνος, -ου, ὁ (Hes, Aristoph+) *oak tree* Sus 58.*

πριστηροειδής, -ές (*h.l.*) *like a saw* (in appearance) Is 41:15.*

πριστοειδής, -ές (dub; not in LSJ) *like something sawn* (?) Is 41:15vL.*

πρίων, -ονος, ὁ (Soph+) *saw* 2 Km 12:31 = 1 Ch 20:3; Am 1:3; Is 10:15; *serrated mountain ridge* Jdth 3:9.*

προαγορεύω (Hdt+) *proclaim publicly* 2 Macc 4:48.*

προάγω 2.a.β. *go forward, proceed* 2 Macc 10:27; 11:10.‡

προαγωνίζομαι (vL -έομαι spur; not in LSJ; Thu, DiodS+) *fight before, be the prior combatant* 4 Macc 17:13.*

προαδικέω (Aristot+) *do wrong previously*; (pass) *be previously wronged* Wsd 18:2.*‡

προαίρεσις, -εως, ἡ (15x, Pla+) **1.** *choice, inclination* Judg 5:2A; Eccl 1:14ff; Jer 8:5. **2.** *policy* 2 Macc 9:27; 11:26.‡

προαλής, -ές (Hom+) *rash, precipitous* Sir 30:8.*

προαναμέλπω (*h.l.*) *first chant or sing* Wsd 18:9.*

προανατάσσω (*h.l.*) *set before oneself, prefer* Ps 136:6.*

προανατέλλω (LXX+) *arise before or previously* Ezk 17:9.*

προαπαγγέλλω (AeneasTact+) *announce or declare previously or beforehand* Ezk 33:9.*

προαποδείκνυμι (Isocr+) *demonstrate or show in advance;* (pass ptc) *previously proven or shown* (to be construed w. "separated from all justice"; not "previously mentioned" [c. NRSV and TOTP], for which no //) 3 Macc 2:25.*

προαποθνήσκω (Hdt, X+) *die previously* 4 Macc 13:18.*

προασπίζω (LXX, Philo [DECAL 114]+) *hold a shield before,* > *defend, protect* 4 Macc 6:21; 9:15; 14:15.*

προάστιον, -ου, τό (Ra:-στειον; Hdt+) *suburb, area outside the wall* Num 35:2, 7.*

προβάλλω 3. *stand in front* (of τινί), *confront, accuse* Pr 22:21.‡

προβασανίζω (Hero, Joseph, Lucian) *torment or torture previously* 4 Macc 8:5; 10:16.*

προβασκάνιον, -ου, τό (LXX, Plu) *amulet or scarecrow* EpJer 69.*

πρόβλημα, -ατος, τό (12x, Soph+: *obstacle, problem*) *riddle* (no //) Judg 14:12ff; *enigma, mystery* (no //) Ps 48:5; 77:2; Hab 2:6; Da 8:23Θ.*

προβλής, gen **-ῆτος** (Hom+) *jutting out* 4 Macc 13:6.*

προβλητός, -ή, -όν (Soph [AJ 830]) *thrown away* Jer 10:9VL.*

προγονικός, -ή, -όν (MetrodorusPhilos+) *ancestral* 2 Macc 8:17; 14:7 (δόξα Polyb 13.6.3).*

προγράφω (Aristoph, Thu+) *write previously* 1 Esdr 6:31G; Da 3:3L; *enroll* 1 Macc 10:36.*‡

προδίδωμι 3. *give up, surrender* (as already lost) 2 Macc 7:37.‡

προδοσία, -ας, ἡ (Hdt+) *abandonment, betrayal* Wsd 17:11, 14.*

προεκφέρω (DemetrPhaler+) *put forth first* Gen 38:28.*

προελέσθαι 2 aor mid inf of προαιρέω.

προενέχω (dub; h.l.) *entangle previously;* (pass) *be previously involved* 2 Macc 5:18VL.*

προεξαποστέλλω (Polyb 3.86.3) *send out first or ahead of time* 2 Macc 12:21.*

προεπιχειρέω (not in HR; Thu+) *be the first to attack* 3 Macc 7:5VL.*

προέσθαι, πρόῃ see προίημι.

προηγέομαι 2. *take the lead* (in battle) 2 Macc 4:40; (in political action) 10:12.*‡

προηγορέω (X [ANAB 5.5.7]+) *be a spokesman or advocate* 2 Macc 4:48.*

προήγορος, -ου, ὁ (LXX+) *spokesman, advocate* 2 Macc 7:2, 4.*

προήκω (Aristoph, Thu+) *go forward;* (ptc) *advancing, advanced* (in age) 4 Macc 5:4.*

προθερίζω (h.l.) *reap first;* pf pass ptc *already harvested* Judg 15:5A.*

προθυμέομαι (11x, Hdt+) *be willing* 1 Macc 1:13; *be eager, zealous* 1 Ch 29:5; 3 Macc 1:8; *do willingly* 1 Ch 29:17.

προθυμέτερος comp of BDAG: πρόθυμος 2 Macc 15:19.‡

πρόθυρον, -ου τό (24x, Hom+) *doorway, porch* Gen 19:6; Judg 19:27; Zech 12:2; Is 66:17. 3 Km 7:36 mistrans of סף¹ *bowl* as if סף² *threshold*.‡

προίημι pres mid προίεμαι subj προῶμαι 2 aor mid inf προϊέσθαι **1.b.** *emit, utter* Pr 17:27. 2. *dismiss, let go, permit* (to leave) Ex 3:19; Pr 5:9; Job 7:19; 27:6. 3. *give* (oneself) *up, devote* (oneself) Pr 30:32.‡

προκαθηγέομαι (Polyb+) *guide, have influence;* (ptc subst) *leader, person of influence* 1 Esdr 6:11.*

προκαθήκω (dub, not in LSJ) = καθήκω 1 Macc 10:39VL.*

προκαθίζω (Hom, Hdt+) *sit in state* 4 Macc 5:1.*

πρόκαιρος, -ον (spur; h.l.) *premature* 4 Macc 15:2VL.*

προκακόω (Schol) *wrong or mistreat previously;* (pass ptc) *previously wronged or mistreated* 4 Macc 17:22.*

προκαταλαμβάνω pf pass προκατείλημπται (36; Thu+) **1.** (mid) *capture first* Judg 1:12; 1 Macc 6:27; (pass) *be captured first; occupy first, take the lead in capturing* 2 Km 12:28 (fig) *be preoccupied with* Ps 76:5; *occupy in advance* Judg 3:28; Jdth 2:10. **2.** (mid) *capture, occupy* (prefix without force, no //) Judg 9:50A; 2 Km 8:4 = 1 Ch 18:4; 2 Ch 13:19; Jdth 7:7; 1 Macc 5:8,

36; 2 Macc 10:36. **3.** (act) *surprise, overtake* (fig) 3 Macc 2:20; Ps 78:8.

προκατασκευάζω (X+) *prepare in advance* Sir prol 35.*

προκατασκιρρόομαι (*h.l.*; vvLL -σκειρ-, -σκηρ- itac) *harden ahead of time*; (pf pass ptc) *hardened long since* 3 Macc 4:1.*

προκαταχωρίζω (pap+) *set aside previously* 3 Macc 2:29vL.*

πρόκλησις, -εως, ἡ (Hdt+) *challenge, wager, titillation* 2 Macc 4:14vL.*

προκουρία, -ας, ἡ (not in LSJ or HR; *h.l.*) *breast shearing? first shearing?* Tob 1:6vL.*

πρόκρημνος, -ον (*h.l.*) *jutting out* 4 Macc 7:5.*

πρόλημψις, -εως, ἡ (not in HR; Epicurus, Polyb+) *preconception, prior principle* Sir 10:21vL.*

προλήνιον, -ου, τό (*h.l.*) *trough or vat fronting a wine press* Is 5:2.*

πρόλοβος, -ου, ὁ (Aristot+) *crop* (of bird) Lev 1:16.*

πρόλογος, -ου, ὁ (Aristoph, Aristot+) *prologue, preface* Sir prol tit vL.*

προμαχέω (X+) *fight in front* Wsd 18:21.*

προμαχῶν, -ῶνις, ὁ (Hdt+) *outer fortification, breastwork* Tob 13:17; Jer 5:10; 40:4; Ezk 4:2.*

προμηνύω (Soph+) *indicate previously* Wsd 18:19.*

προνομεύω (43x, Polyb+) *plunder, capture* Num 24:17; Josh 8:2; 1 Esdr 4:5; Jdth 1:14; 1 Macc 6:3; Sir 48:15; Is 8:3.

προνομή, -ῆς, ἡ (44x, X+) **1.** *forage* Is 6:13 (mistrans of בער[1] *burn* as if בער[2] *graze*). **2.** *plunder, booty* Num 31:11; Josh 7:21; 4 Km 21:14; 1 Macc 7:47; Is 42:22; Da 11:24; *(act of) plundering* 1 Esdr 8:74; Da 11:33L. **3.** (of people) *captivity, slavery* (no //) Jdth 9:4; Pr 12:24; Is 10:2; *forced labor* (no //; cf. φόρος) 3 Km 9:15(vL) = 10:22a.

προνουμηνία, -ας, ἡ (*h.l.*) *eve of the new moon* Jdth 8:6.*

προοδηγός, -οῦ, ὁ (*h.l.*) *foremost guide* 2 Macc 12:36.*

προοίμιον, ου, τό (Aeschyl+) *preface, prelude* Job 27:1; 29:1. 25:2 mistrans of הַמְשֵׁל

(משׁל[2] hiph) *to rule* as if מָשָׁל *proverb, saying* w. ה interrog.*

πρόπαππος, -ου, ὁ (Lysias, Pla+) *great-grandfather* Ex 10:6.*

προπέτεια, -ας, ἡ (Isocr+) *rashness* 2 Km 6:7vL.*

προπίπτω pf ptc προπεπτωκώς (Hom+) *fall forward* Jdth 13:2; *fall prostrate, bow down* Ps 21:30; 71:9; *die* 2 Macc 12:39ff; 15:28.*

προπομπή, -ῆς, ἡ (X+) *escort* 1 Esdr 8:51.*

προπορεύομαι 2. *come forward, advance* (Polyb) Pr 24:34.‡

προπράσσω aor pass ptc προπραχθέντα pf pass ptc προπεπραγμένα (Aristot+) *do ahead of time*; (ptc subst) *things done previously* 1 Esdr 1:31; 3 Macc 6:27.*

προπτύω (*h.l.*) *spit out* 2 Macc 6:20.*

πρόπτωσις, -εως, ἡ (LXX+) *falling forward* (προπίπτω), *prostration* 2 Macc 3:21; 13:12.*

προπύλαιος, -α, -ον, τό (Hdt+) *before the gate*; (neut pl subst) *gateway* Zeph 1:9vL.*

πρόπυλον, -ου, τό (Hdt+) *gateway, entrance* (sg or pl) Am 9:1; Zeph 1:9.*

πρός 2.a. (w. inf) *about to* Ex 1:16; Tob 14:3BA. **2.b.** *plus, in addition to* (τινί, forming large numbers) 2 Macc 11:11 etc; (abs, as adv; Hom, Hdt+) *besides, moreover* SSol 1:16; Sir 29:25. **3.g.** *onto, upon* Judg 6:20.‡

προσαγγέλλω (Pla, pap+) *announce, report* Jdth 10:18; 2 Macc 3:6; 9:24; 10:21; 13:21; 3 Macc 5:10.*

προσανάβασις, -εως, ἡ (Aeschyl+) *ascent, approach* Josh 15:3.*

προσαναλέγω (*h.l.*) *recount in addition* 2 Macc 8:19.*

προσαναπαύω (Polyb+) *cause to rest*; (mid) *find rest upon or beside* (τινί) Wsd 8:16.*

προσανατρέπω (*h.l.*) *further overturn or undo* Sir 13:23.*

προσαναφέρω fut προσανοίσω aor pass inf προσανενεχθῆναι (Polyb, pap, EpArist) *report* Jdth 11:18; Tob 12:15BA; *refer (for approval)* 2 Macc 11:36.*

προσανοικοδομέω (*h.l.*) *build firmly in place*; (pass, fig) *be firmly established* (as protection or bulwark) Sir 3:14.*

προσαξιόω (Polyb, pap) *ask as well or in addition* 3 Macc 7:10.*

προσαπειλέω (dub; only as vl) *further threaten*; (pass) *be threatened more* Sir 13:3vl.*‡

προσαπέρχομαι (spur; not in LSJ) error for προσαγγέλλω (π for γγ) 2 Macc 9:24vl.*

προσαποθνῄσκω (lxx+) *die in addition* Ex 21:29.*

προσαπόλλυμι (Hdt, Eur+) *put to death* 2 Macc 13:4.*

προσαποστέλλω (Thu, ins) *send along* 2 Macc 11:14.*

προσαπωθέω (h.l.) (pass) *be further rejected* Sir 13:21.*

προσαρτίως (h.l.) *recently* 3 Macc 1:19.*

προσασπίζω (spur; not in LSJ) *protect* 4 Macc 14:15vl.*

προσβαίνω (Hom, Hdt+) *ascend, approach* 1 Esdr 4:53; 8:1; Jdth 4:7; 7:10.*‡

προσβάλλω (9x, Hom+) *strike* Da 7:20Θ, *attack* (τινί) 2 Macc 10:17; *hurl* (τι) Jer 26:4vl.

πρόσβασις, -εως, ἡ (Hdt+) *approach* (esp ascending) Josh 15:7; Jdth 4:7; 3 Macc 1:26; (fig) *occasion, opportunity* 2 Macc 4:13.*

προσβλητός, -ή, -όν (lxx+) *overlaid* Jer 10:9.*

προσβολή, -ῆς, ἡ (Aeschyl, Hdt+) *assault, attack* 2 Macc 5:3; 15:19.*

προσγελάω (Hdt+) *smile* (at τινί) 1 Esdr 4:31; Sir 13:6, 11.*

προσγεννάω (spur; not in LSJ) *produce*; (pf pass ptc subst) *offspring* Lev 20:2vl.*

προσγίνομαι (Hdt+) *come to be present, attach oneself* Lev 18:26; 20:2; Num 15:14.*

προσγράφω (X+) *specify in writing*; (pl pass ptc) *written specifications* 1 Esdr 6:32R.*

προσδεηθῆς aor pass subj of BDAG: προσδέομαι *need (further)* Sir 18:32G.

προσδέχομαι 3. *undertake, attempt* (Hippocr) Da 7:25L. Lev 26:43 mistrans of רצה² *make good, compensate for* as if רצה¹ *enjoy*.‡

προσδέω aor προσέδησα pass subj προσδεθῆς (Hdt+) *bind, attach* 4 Macc 9:26; Sir 18:32R.*‡

προσδίδωμι (Soph+) *give in addition* Gen 29:33; Tob 2:12; Ezk 16:33f.*‡

προσεγγίζω 2. (trans) *bring near, carry in* (Lucian) 3 Km 5:1(vl).‡

προσεδρεία, -ας, ἡ (Eur, Thu+) *close attention, assiduous concern* 3 Macc 4:15.*

πρόσειμι¹ (εἰμί) (Hdt+) *be connected w., belong to* Sir 13:24vl.*‡

πρόσειμι² (εἶμι) (Hom, Hdt+) *approach* 4 Macc 6:14; 14:16, 19.*‡

προσεῖδον see προσοράω

προσεῖπον (Hom+) 2 aor of BDAG: προσαγορεύω or προσφωνέω [q.v.]) *speak* Judg 17:2B, *address* (τινί) Pr 7:13; of BDAG: προσλέγω *answer, reply* 2 Macc 7:8*

προσεκκαίω aor προσεξέκαυσα (lxx+) *ignite further* Num 21:30.*

προσεμβριμάομαι (h.l.) *continue to be indignant* Sir 13:3.*

προσεμπίμπρημι (lxx+) *burn through* Ex 22:5.*

προσενέχω (h.l.) *hold fast*; (pass) *be held* (by τινί), *be in the grip (of), be involved (in)* 2 Macc 5:18.*

προσεξηγέομαι (h.l.; vl προσηγ- dub, not in LSJ) *narrate or relate in addition* 2 Macc 15:11.*

προσεπιαπατάω (spur; not in LSJ) *further deceive* Job 36:16vl.*

προσεπικατατείνω (h.l. [vl προσκατ- Hippocr, =) *tighten still more* 4 Macc 9:19.*

προσεπιτιμάω (Polyb+) *further criticize or censure* Sir 13:22.*

προσεπιχειρέω (dub; not in HR or LSJ) *lay hands on, assault, injure* 3 Macc 7:5vl.*

προσερυθριάω (not in LSJ) *redden* (in anger) *against* Tob 2:14S.*

προσέτι (Hdt+) *moreover* 2 Macc 12:14; 4 Macc 14:1; Job 36:16; *how much more* 2 Km 16:11.*

προσέχω aor subj προσχῇς (Ra), προσσχῇς (Gött) Num 16:15; (pres ptc subst) *fastening* (no //, but cf. ἐξέχω) 3 Km 7:17. Ptc adv προσεχόντως (Hippocr, Menand+) *in alert or attentive fashion* Pr 31:25.‡

προσηκόντως (Thu+) *suitably, properly* 4 Macc 6:33.*

προσηλόω (Pla, Demosth, ins+) *rivet, nail, fasten* 3 Macc 4:9.*‡

προσηλυτεύω (h.l.) *live among* (as an alien or convert) Ezk 14:7.*

προσήλυτος, -ου, ὁ (84x, LXX+) **2.** *immigrant, resident alien, stranger* Ex 12:48; Dt 1:16; 1 Ch 22:2; Ps 93:6; Sir 10:22G (q.l. = Heb); Zech 7:10; Jer 7:6. (The boundary between 1. *proselyte* and 2. *alien* is hard to define in a postexilic context—e.g., Tob 1:8S; cf. the added ambiguity of προσκειμαι.)‡

προσημαίνω aor pass ptc προσημανθείς pf pass ptc προσεσημαμμένος (Hdt, Eur+) *declare, announce;* (pass ptc) *announced, declared* 3 Macc 5:13; *aforesaid, previously mentioned* 5:47; 2 Macc 4:23.*

προσημειόομαι (Eustath) *indicate ahead of time* 4 Macc 15:19.*

προσηνής, -ές (Anacr, Hdt+) *soothing* Pr 25:25.*

πρόσθεμα, -ατος τό (Hippocr, pap+) *something added, increase* Lev 19:25; Ezk 41:7.*

πρόσθεσις, -εως, ἡ (Hippocr, Thu+) *addition, application;* Ezk 47:13 mistrans of N GENT יוסף *Joseph* as if ptc of יסף *add.*‡

προσθλίβω (LXX+) *press up against* Num 22:25.*

προσκαθήκω (h.l.; not in HR or LSJ) *be appropriate or suitable* 1 Macc 10:39G.*

προσκαθίστημι (DiodS, pap+) *arrange for or supply in addition* Judg 14:11A.*

προσκαίω aor pass subj προσκαυθῶ (Aristoph, Aristot+) *burn on;* (pass) *become (too) hot, be burned on* Ezk 24:11.*

προσκαταλαμβάνω (Hippocr) *fasten down, secure* Jdth 2:10vL.*

προσκαταλείπω (Thu+) *leave behind, have left over* Ex 36:7.*

πρόσκαυμα, -ατος τό (LXX) *burned-on residue* (mistrans of פארור *heat* as if פרור *pot*) Joel 2:6; Na 2:11.*

πρόσκειμαι **2.** *lie near, be adjacent* (to τινί; Thu, Polyb) Num 21:15.‡

προσκεφάλαιον, -ου, τό (Hippocr, Cratius-Com, Aristot+) *pillow* 1 Esdr 3:8. Ezk 13:18, 20 mistrans of כסת *(magical) band,* unexpl.*‡

προσκήνιον, -ου, τό (ins, Polyb+ [Lat PROSC(A)ENIUM *stage* since Plautus, ca. 200 BCE]) *outer or public area* (*porch* of a building; lit *in front of the screen*) Jdth 10:22.*

πρόσκλησις, -εως, ἡ (Aristoph, Pla+) *summons* 2 Macc 4:14.*‡

προσκολλάω **2.** (hostile) *stick closely to, pursue closely* Judg 20:45A. **3.** (act trans) *cause to stick, attach* Ezk 29:4.‡

προσκρούω (Pla+) *knock or strike against* Job 40:23; Sir 13:2; *collide,* > *stumble,* (fig) *falter* 2 Macc 13:19.*‡

προσκύνησις, -εως, ἡ (Pla+) *act of worship, obeisance* 3 Macc 3:7; Sir 50:21.*

προσκύπτω (Aristoph, Pla+) *stoop to* (τινί), *bend down toward* 2 Macc 7:27.*

προσκυρέω (Aeschyl+) *adjoin, belong to* 1 Macc 10:39.*

προσλογίζομαι (Hdt+) *reckon, calculate* Lev 27:18; Sir 7:16; (pass) *be reckoned* Josh 13:3; Ps 87:5; Bar 3:11.*

προσμαρτυρέω (Isocr, pap+) *testify (to), confirm* (τινί, Polyb 3.89.4) 3 Macc 5:19.*

προσμείγνυμι (Hdt, Soph+) *approach, come to close quarters* (X ANAB 4.2.16) 2 Macc 15:20; Pr 14:13.*

προσμειδιάω (Plu+) *smile at* (τινί) 4 Macc 8:4.*

προσμένω **3.** *await, wait for* (τινά) Tob 2:2S; 3 Macc 7:17.‡

προσμηνύω (dub; SextEmp w. προμ- as VL) *indicate in addition* Wsd 18:19VL.*

προσνέμω (Soph, Pla+) *attribute, assign* 4 Macc 6:33.*

προσνοέω impf προσενόουν (8x, X+) *notice, observe* (τινί) Judg 3:26; Da 7:8Θ; (τι, τινά) Num 23:9; Tob 11:6; Job 20:9; Is 63:5.

πρόσοδος, -ου, ὁ (7x; Pind, Hdt+) **1.** *(right of) approach, access* 2 Macc 14:3. **2.** *revenue, resources* 2 Macc 3:3; 3 Macc 3:16; Pr 28:16.

προσοδύρομαι (h.l.) *lament in addition* Wsd 19:3.*

προσόζω   aor προσώζεσα (Aristoph+) *smell, stink* Ps 37:6.

προσοίγω   aor προσέωξα (LSJ: προσοίγνυμι, but cf. BDF 101 ἀνοίγω; *h.l.*) *shut* (door) Gen 19:6.*

προσοικέω   (Thu, X+) *live or dwell nearby* Ezk 47:22vl.*

προσονομάζω   (Hdt+) *name, call by name* 2 Macc 6:2.*‡

προσοράω   aor προσεῖδον (Hdt+) *look at* Job 6:15; Wsd 17:10.*

προσοχή, -ῆς, ἡ   (Chrysipp+) *attention, care* Wsd 6:18; 12:10; Sir prol 16; 11:18.*

προσοχθίζω   2 Km 1:21 mistrans of געל niph *be defiled* as if qal *be offended*.‡

προσόχθισμα, -ατος, τό   (10x, LXX) *offensive thing, provocation, cause or object of anger* Dt 7:26; 3 Km 11:33; 3 Macc 2:18; Odes 12:10; Sir 27:13.

προσοχυρόω   (LXX) *further fortify* 1 Macc 13:48, 52.*

προσπαίζω   (X, Pla+) **1.** *celebrate, play* Job 21:11. **2.** *mock, make fun of* (τινί) Sir 8:4.*

προσπαρακαλέω   (Thu+) *exhort also or as well* (Polyb 3.64.11) 2 Macc 12:31.*

προσπάσσω   (LXX+) *sprinkle on* Tob 11:11BA.*

προσπίπτω   **2.b.** *fall into, engage in* Pr 25:8. **3.** *arrive (as news)* 2 Macc 5:11; 3 Macc 4:1; ὁ τὰ προσπίπτοντα *reporter, recorder* 1 Esdr 2:13.‡

προσποιέω   **3.** (act) *add on, produce further* Sir 31:30.‡

προσπορεύομαι   2 Esdr 20:29 renders הַנִּבְדָּל *(he who) separates himself*, > *goes over* (from one party to another; cf. 1 Ch 12:9 χωρίζομαι).‡

προσπροάγω   (dub, not in LSJ) *accomplish* (?) 1 Esdr 1:31vl.*

προσπυρόω   (*h.l.*) *further inflame*, (fig) *further incite* 2 Macc 14:11.*

προσραίνω   fut -ρανῶ aor προσέρρανα (Aristoph+) *sprinkle around or on* Lev 4:6; 8:30.*

προσσιελίζω   (*h.l.*) *spit on* Lev 15:8.*

προσταγή, -ῆς, ἡ   (LXX+) *command, directive* Da 3:95L.*

προσταράσσω   (*h.l.*) *trouble further* Sir 4:3.*

προστάς, -άδις, ἡ   (Callixinus [III bce], ins, pap) *porch, vestibule* Judg 3:22.*

προστατέω   (Aeschyl+) *rule, be in charge of* (τινός) 1 Macc 14:47; Sir 45:24.*

προστάττω   pf ptc προστεταχώς Att for BDAG: προστάσσω, 3 Macc 5:37.‡

προστίθημι   **3.** *impose* (of obligations; Aeschyl, Hdt+) 1 Esdr 7:6. 1 Km 26:10; 27:1; Am 3:15 mistrans of ספה niph *be swept away, vanish* as if יסף *do again* (Is 30:1 mt ספה, emend to יסף).‡

προσυμνέω   (Schol) *affirm or celebrate in singing* 2 Macc 15:9vl.*

προσυμπλέκω   (dub, *h.l.*) = συμπροσπλ-, Da 11:10Θvl.*

προσυπομιμνήσκω   (sic, cf. LSJ; Polyb+) *remind also or in addition* 2 Macc 15:9.*

προσυστέλλω   (*h.l.*) *reduce earlier*; (pass ptc) *formerly reduced or abased* 3 Macc 2:29.*

προσυψόω   (Joseph) *raise higher* 1 Macc 12:36.*

προσφαίνω   (not in HR; Aristides [II ce]) *appear w.* (τινί) 2 Macc 3:26R (Gött προφ-).*

προσφέρω   **1.c.** *bring to bear, employ, use*; (mid) *use, consume* (food) Pr 6:8b.‡

προσφύω   (Hom+) *grow later or in addition* Da 7:20L.*

πρόσχεσις, -εως, ἡ   (spur; *h.l.*) *pretext?* (gloss); f.l. for ὑπόσχεσις, 4 Macc 15:2vl.*

προσχέω   fut προσχεεῖς aor προσέχεεν (23; Aristot+) *pour, pour out* Ex 24:6; Dt 12:27; 4 Km 16:13; 2 Ch 29:22; Ezk 43:18.

προσχράομαι   (Pla, Aristot, pap) *put to use* (τινί) Esth 8:12r.*

πρόσχωμα, -ατος, τό   (Aeschyl+: *alluvial deposit*) *earthen siege work, rampart* (alw obj of εκχέω, s.t. of שפך *heap up* as if *pour out*; no //, but προσχώννυμι/-χόω can mean *heap up earth*) 2 Km 20:15; 4 Km 19:32; Da 11:15Θ.*

προσχωρέω   (Hdt+) *go over to, side with, desert to* (τινί) 1 Ch 12:20f; (πρός τινα) 1 Macc 10:26; Jer 21:9.*

προσωθέω   (Hippocr? Polyb? vl for προωθέω) *push forward* 2 Macc 13:6.*

προσωπεῖον, -ου, τό   (VL προσώτιον spur, not in LSJ; VL [itac missp, not in LSJ] -πιον, = ; Theophr+) *mask* 4 Macc 15:15.*

πρόσωπον   **1.b.** (fig) *intention, purpose* (Heb, no //) 2 Ch 32:2. **3.** *front (of pot)* Jer 1:13; *surface, exterior* (no //) Job 41:4. ἀπὸ προσώπου *regarding, because of* (Heb, no //) Jer 51:3. Eccl 10:10 mistrans of פנים *edges* (of cutting tool) as if *face*; cf. ταράσσω.‡

προτείχισμα, -ατος, τό   (9x, Thu+) *outer wall* 2 Km 20:15; 2 Ch 32:5; SSol 2:14; Ezk 40:5. Ezk 42:20; 48:15 mistrans of חל *commons, non-sacral space* as if ח(י)ל *outer wall.*

προτέρημα, -ατος, τό   (Polyb+) *superiority, success* (in war) Judg 4:9.*

πρότερος   **1.a.β.** *before, in front of* (spatial) Ex 33:19; *first, ahead of* (spatial) Num 10:33; Josh 3:14. **3.** *first in time, at the start* (Lat PRIUS) 1 Macc 8:24, 27.‡

προτίθημι   **1.b.** *place in front of* (as an obstacle) Lev 19:14G. **3.b.** *aim for, put first* Ps 53:5; 85:14.‡

προτιμάω   (Heraclitus, Aeschyl, X+) *give foremost honor to* (τι), *prefer* 2 Macc 15:2; 4 Macc 1:15.*

προτομή, -ῆς, ἡ   (AntiphoOr, ins, DiodS+) *image of face or head, figurehead* 3 Km 10:19; *(decapitated) head* 2 Macc 15:35.*

προϋποδείκνυμι   (not in HR; Philo [HER 50]) *explain previously* 3 Macc 2:25VL.*

προϋποτάσσω   pf pass ptc προϋποτεταγμένος (h.l.) *place (previously) under charge or command* 3 Macc 1:2.*

προϋφίστημι   (LXX+) *be present previously* Wsd 19:7.*

προφαίνω   (Hom, Hdt+) *reveal;* (mid/pass) *appear, be revealed* 2 Macc 3:26G; (Ra προσφαίνω) 4 Macc 4:10.*

προφανῶς   (Polyb+ [adj Bacchylides+]) *in conspicuous fashion* Sir 51:13.*

προφασίζομαι   (Thu+) *allege a pretext, make excuses* 4 Km 5:7; Pr 22:13; (w. cogn acc, Pla REP 474e) Ps 140:4.*

προφασιστικός, -ή, -όν   (Philo PROB 19) *specious, (self-)accusing* Dt 22:14, 17.*

προφέρω   **2.** (act) *put forward,* > *propose, suggest* 3 Macc 7:4; (mid) *put (oneself) forward,* > *plead, insist* 3 Macc 1:12; 5:39.‡

προφθάνω   **3.** *outrun, anticipate, come upon* Ps 17:6; Job 30:27; (fig) *take advantage of* (τινά) Sir 19:27; *approach, come near* 4 Km 19:32; Ps 94:2; 118:147; (trans, no //) *extend in front* Ps 67:32.‡

προφυλακή, -ῆς, ἡ   (12x, X+) **1.** *advance guard, sentry party* Num 32:17; 2 Esdr 14:17; Na 2:6; Ezk 26:8; > *vigil, watch* Ex 12:42. **2.** *(act of) guarding, serving as sentries* 2 Esdr 14:16.

προφύλαξ, -ακις, ὁ   (Thu, X) *sentinel, advance guard* 2 Esdr 14:3; 17:3; 1 Macc 12:27.*

προχαλάω   προκεχάλεσται (Aretaeus+) *relax previously;* (pass) *be loosed, be hanging out* (subj γλῶσσα) *already* 4 Macc 10:19.*

πρόχειρος, -ον   (Aeschyl, Pla+) *ready at hand* Pr 11:3.*

προχώρημα, -ατος, τό   (h.l.) *what is passed or voided; excrement* Ezk 32:6.*

προῶμαι   pres mid subj of προίημι.

προωρώμην   cf. BDAG: προοράω.

πρύτανις, -εως, ὁ   (Stesichorus, Aeschyl+) *master, lord* Wsd 13:2.*

πρώην   (Hom, Hdt+) *in the recent past, yesterday* Josh 8:5.*

πρώϊμος   (better: πρόϊμος; cf. BDAG, BDF 35.1) Job 18:13VL.*‡

πρωρεύς, -έως, ὁ   (W: πρῳ-; X+) *forward or bow officer* Jon 1:6; Ezk 27:29.*

πρωταγωνιστής, -οῦ, ὁ   (Aristot+) *leader, one who fights in front* 1 Macc 9:11; 2 Macc 15:30.*

πρώταρχος, -ον   (Aeschyl AG 1192 *primal) primary, chief* (no //) 2 Macc 10:11.*

πρωτοβαθρέω   (h.l.) *seat in the first place* Esth 3:1.*

πρωτοβολέω   (Hippiatr, Plu+) *sprout, produce* (no //, but -βόλος, -ον *budding, fresh*) Ezk 47:12.*

πρωτογένημα, -ατος, τό   (16x, LXX) *first-fruits* Ex 23:16; 4 Km 4:42; Tob 1:6S; Sir 45:20; Ezk 44:30.

πρωτογενής, -ές   (Pla+) *firstborn* Ex 13:2; Pr 31:2.*

πρωτόγονος, -ον (Hom+) *firstborn;* (subst) Sir 36:11; Mi 7:1.*

πρωτοκλήσιον, -ου, τό (h.l.) *first public proclamation* 2 Macc 4:21G.*

πρωτοκλίσιον, -ου, τό (not in LSJ) *first royal banquet* (w. new king) 2 Macc 4:21R.*

πρωτοκουρά, -ᾶς, ἡ (h.l.) *first fleece* Tob 1:6S.*

πρωτοκουρία, -ας, ἡ (h.l.) *first shearing* Tob 1:6BA.*

πρωτολογία, -ας, ἡ (Demades [IV BCE]+) *right of speaking first* (as prosecutor) Pr 18:17.*

πρωτόπλαστος, -ον (LXX, Philo) *first-formed* Wsd 7:1; 10:1.*

πρωτοτοκεῖον, -ου, τό (c. BDAG: -τόκια; cf. W) Dt 21:17G; q.l. also Gen 25:31ff; 27:36; 1 Ch 5:1; and NT Hb 12:16 (so pap46).*

πρωτοτοκεύω (h.l.) *treat as firstborn* Dt 21:16.*

πρωτοτοκέω (LXX) *bear one's firstborn* 1 Km 6:7, 10; Jer 4:31.*

πταῖσμα, -ατος, τό (Hdt+) *failure, fault, difficulty* 1 Km 6:4.*

πταρμός, -οῦ, ὁ (Hippocr, Thu, Aristoph+) *sneeze, sneezing* Job 41:10.*

πτέρνα **2.** (horse's) *hoof* (= עָקֵב) Gen 49:17; Judg 5:22. **3.** *footprint, track* (no //) SSol 1:8.‡

πτερνίζω fut πτερνιεῖ, pf ἐπτέρνικα (LXX, Philo; fr עקב [Mal 3:8f עבק; metathesis? txt?]) *kick, trip up* Jer 9:3 (Philo LEG 2.99), > *defraud, deceive* (Philo LEG 3.190) Gen 27:36; Hos 12:4.*

πτερνισμός, -οῦ, ὁ (LXX) *deception, treachery* 4 Km 10:19; Ps 40:10.*

πτέρνον, -ου, τό (not in LSJ) *heel* (= BDAG: πτέρνα) Sir 26:18G.*

πτερόν, -οῦ, τό (Hom, Hdt+) *feather* Lev 1:16; *wing* Da 7:4ff.*

πτερύγιον **2.** *flap, edge* (of robe) Num 15:38; Ruth 3:9. **3.** *fin* (of fish) Lev 11:9; Dt 14:9.‡

πτέρυξ **2.** *end, farthest edge* (Heb, no //) Job 37:3; Is 11:12; Ezk 7:2 (LSJSup).‡

πτερύσσομαι (DiphilusCom) *flutter, flap* (wings) Ezk 1:23; 3:13.*

πτήσσω aor ἔπτηξα (Hom+) *cower in fear* Dt 1:29; 4 Km 19:26; 1 Macc 12:28; 4 Macc 16:20; (trans, of τι) 3 Macc 6:13.*

πτίλος, -η, -ον (LXX+) *inflamed, infected* (of eyelid) Lev 21:20.*

πτοέω Jer 28:56 mistrans of חתת *break, shatter* as if *terrify*.‡

πτοή, -ῆς, ἡ (Nicander, Plu+) *fear, terror* 1 Macc 3:25; 3 Macc 6:17.*

πτύελος, -ου, ὁ (Hippocr: -αλος; Aristot+) *saliva, spittle* Job 7:19; 30:10.*

πτύξις, -εως, ἡ (LXX+) *fold, corrugation* Job 41:5.*

πτυχή, -ῆς, ἡ (Hom: πτύξ; Pind, Aeschyl+) *plate, fold; leaf* (of folding door) 3 Km 6:34.*

πτῶμα **2.** *fall,* > *disaster, misfortune* Job 33:17; PsSol 3:10; Is 8:14.‡

πύγαργος, -ου, ὁ (vl πυδ- spur, not in LSJ; Hdt+) *white-rumped antelope* Dt 14:5.*

πυθμήν, -ένος, ὁ (Hom+) **1.** *stem, stalk* Gen 40:10ff; 41:5, 22. **2.** *bottom* Pr 14:12; 16:25.*

πυκάζω pf pass ptc πεπυκασμένος (Hom+) **1.** *cover over* 3 Macc 4:5; *overshadow, protect* Hos 14:9. **2.** *deck w. branches or garlands* Ps 117:27; (of branches themselves) *be thick, flourish* (no //) Job 15:32.*

πυκνός, -ή, -όν (Hom, Hdt+) **1.** (= BDAG) *frequent, often-repeated;* (comp) *more frequent, more numerous* 4 Macc 12:12; (superl πυκνότατος) *rapidly succeeding, continuous* 3 Macc 1:28. **2.** *close-fitted, closely joined* 3 Macc 4:10; *dense* Ezk 31:3vL.*‡

πυκνότης, -ητος, ἡ (not in HR; Aristoph+) *density, frequency* 3 Macc 1:28vL.*

πυλωρός, -οῦ, ὁ (29x, Aeschyl+) *gatekeeper, porter* 1 Ch 9:17; 15:18ff; 2 Esdr 2:42; 17:1; Job 38:17.

πυξίον, -ου, τό (Aristoph+) *tablet, slab* (in class. alw of wood) Ex 24:12; SSol 5:14; Hab 2:2; Is 30:8.*

πύξος, -ου, ἡ (Aristot+) *boxwood tree* Is 41:19.*

πῦρ 1 Km 2:28 mistrans of אִשֶּׁה *offering* as if אֵשׁ *fire*.*‡

πυραμίς, -ίδος, ἡ (Hdt+) *pyramid* 1 Macc 13:28.*

πυργόβαρις, -εως, ἡ (LXX) *citadel, fortress* Ps 121:7; PsSol 8:19.*

πυρεῖον, -ου, τό (21x; HomHymns, Soph+: *fire-stick*) *censer* (no //) Ex 27:3; Num 16:6ff; 4 Km 25:15; 2 Ch 4:11; Sir 50:9.

πυρίκαυστος, -ον (Hom+) *burned in fire* Is 1:7; 9:5; 64:11.*

πυρίπνους, -ουν (Lycophron+) *fire-breathing* 3 Macc 6:34VL (q.l.; πυρόπνους dub, not in LSJ. Cf. W, 124–125).*

πυριφλεγής, -ές (Hippocr, Plu+) *flaming w. fire* 3 Macc 3:29; Wsd 18:3.*

πυροβόλον, -ου, τό (LXX, Plu) *fire-throwing catapult* 1 Macc 6:51.*

πυρογενής, -ές (Ausonius [IV CE]) *born from fire* Wsd 17:5VL.*

πυρόπνους cf. πυρίπνους.

πυρός, -οῦ, ὁ (36x, Hom+) *wheat* Gen 30:14; Ruth 2:23; Ps 80:17; Sir 39:26; Joel 1:11; Ezk 4:9.‡

πυροφόρος, -ου, ὁ (Philo, ins) *wheat bearer* (Jerome [cf. W, 124–125] FRUMENTARIUS *forager*, LSJ only of land; Heb שָׂרִיד *survivor*) Ob 18R.*

πυρόω 3. (obj stones) *ignite*, i.e., *strike* (flint) *to produce fire* (no //) 2 Macc 10:3.‡

πύρπνοος, -ον (Aeschyl+) *fire-breathing* Wsd 11:18.*

πυρπολέω (Hom, Hdt+) *attack or destroy w. fire* 4 Macc 7:4.*

πυρράκης, -ου, ὁ (pap) *red or ruddy person* Gen 25:25; 1 Km 16:12; 17:42.*

πυρρίζω (LXX) *become inflamed* Lev 13:19ff; 14:37.*

πυρρόομαι (Aristot; HR only οἱ τρεῖς) *become red* La 4:7.*

πυρρός 4 Km 5:17 doublet of אֲדָמָה *earth* as if also אֲדָמָה *red-brown*.‡

πυρσεύω (Eur, X+) *kindle, ignite* Pr 16:28; Job 20:10.*

πυρσός, -οῦ, ὁ (not in HR; Hom, Hdt+) *signal fire* Judg 20:38A, 40A.*

πυρφόρος, -ον (Pind+) *fire-carrying*; (subst) 1. *fire bearer, torch carrier* (cf. W, 124–125) Ob 18G . 2. *flaming weapon* Job 41:21 (Heb קִידוֹן *short sword*).*

πυρώδης, -ες (Aristoph+) *fiery* Sir 43:4.*

πύρωσις 3. *fever, inflammation* Am 4:9.‡

πυρωτής, -οῦ, ὁ (Aq, Sym) *smith* 2 Esdr 13:8VL.*

πώγων, -ωνος, ὁ (19x, Hdt+) *beard* Lev 13:29f; 1 Km 21:14; 1 Esdr 8:68; Ps 132:2; Is 7:20.

πῶλος Pr 5:19 mistrans of (h.l.) יַעֲלָה (*female*) *ibex* as if *filly*.‡

Ρ

ῥαβδίζω 2. *thresh, beat* (grain; cf. Theophr, of fruit trees) Judg 6:11; Ruth 2:17.*‡

ῥάβδος 2. *shoot* (of a tree) Is 11:1.‡

ῥαγάς, -άδος, ἡ (EphorusCumaeus) *fissure, crevice* Is 7:19.*

ῥάγμα, -ατος, τό (not in LSJ) Doric for ῥῆγμα [q.v.]) Am 6:11.*

ῥαγῶσιν alt fut of ῥήγνυμι.

ῥάδαμνος, -ου ὁ (Theophr+: ὀρόδαμνος) *branch, bough* Job 8:16; 14:7; 15:32; 40:22.*

ῥᾴδιος, -α, -ον (Hom+; adv in BDAG) *easy, painless, light* 2 Macc 2:26; 4:17.*

ραθμ translit of רֹתֶם *broom shrub* 3 Km 19:4.*

ῥαθυμία, -ας, ἡ (Eur, Thu+) *amusement, light-heartedness* 3 Macc 4:8.*

ῥαίνω fut ῥανῶ aor ἔρρανα (13; Hom+) *sprinkle* Ex 29:21; Lev 4:17; Num 19:4; Is 45:8; Ezk 36:25.‡

ῥακώδης, -ες (LXX+) *ragged*; (pl subst, no //) *rags* Pr 23:21.*

ῥάμμα, -ατος, τό (Pind, Diod+) *thread* Judg 16:12A.*

ῥάμνος, -ου, ἡ (EupolisCom, Theophr, Polyb+) *thorn bush* (prob *boxthorn* [= Heb, Diosc, Paus]) Judg 9:14f; Ps 57:10; EpJer 70.*

ῥανίζω (cf. BDAG: ῥαίνω) fut ῥανιῶ (Pollux) *sprinkle* Lev 14:16VL.*

ῥανίς, -ίδος, ἡ (Eur+) *drop* Wsd 11:22.*

ῥαντός, -ή, -όν (Hippocr+) *speckled, spotted* Gen 30:32ff; 31:10ff.*

ῥάξω fut of BDAG: ῥάσσω Is 9:10.

ῥαπτός, -ή, -όν (Hom, X, Strabo+) *stitched together* Ezk 16:16.*

ῥάπτω aor ἔρραψαν (Hom+) *sew together* Gen 3:7; *sew* Eccl 3:7; Job 16:15.*

ῥάσσω fut ῥάξω aor impv ῥάξον aor pass ἐρράχθην.‡

ῥαφιδευτής, -οῦ, ὁ (h.l.) *embroiderer* Ex 27:16.*

ῥαφιδευτός, -ή, -όν (h.l.) *embroidered* Ex 37:21.*

ῥάχις, -εως, ἡ (Hom+) *spine* Job 40:18; *torso* (no //) 1 Km 5:4.*

ῥέγχω (Aeschyl+) *snore* Jon 1:5f.*

ῥεμβασμός, -οῦ, ὁ (h.l.) *wandering, vacillation* Wsd 4:12.*

ῥεμβεύω (h.l.) *roam (through)* Is 23:16.*

ῥέμβομαι (Menand+) *wander about* Pr 7:12.*

ῥεριμμένος alt pf pass ptc of BDAG: ῥίπτω Jer 43:30VL.

ῥεῦμα, -ατος, τό (Aeschyl, Hdt+) *stream* Sir 39:13.*

ῥέω fut ῥεύσω or (Att dep) ῥυήσομαι (Att) aor ἐρρύην.‡

ῥῆγμα 2. *piece, section, fragment* 4 Km 2:12.‡

ῥήγνυμι alt fut ῥαγῶσιν 2 aor pass ἐρράγην 2 pf (pass sense) ἔρρωγα Josh 9:13; ptc ἐρρηγώς Job 32:19. 3. *break through, breach* 2 Esdr 19:11; (pass) *be breached* (of defenses) 4 Km 25:4 // Jer 46:2.‡

ῥηθησομένος fut pass ptc of εἶπον; (subst) *thing that will be said* 1 Macc 14:44.*

ῥητίνη, -ης, ἡ (Hippocr+) *resin* Gen 37:25; 43:11; Jer 8:22; 26:11; 28:8; Ezk 27:17.*

ῥητός, -ή, -όν (Hom+) *specified, particular* Ex 22:8; (subst) *single thing* 9:4.*

ῥῖγος, -εος, τό (Hom, Hdt+) 1. *cold, frost* Da 3:67L. 2. *ague* (Hippocr, Pla) Dt 28:22.*

ῥίζωμα, -ατος, τό (Aeschyl, Theophr+) *root-mass* Ps 51:7; (fig, of the sea) Job 36:30.*

ῥιπιστός, -ή, -όν (h.l.) *ventilated, breezy* Jer 22:14.*

ῥίπτω fut pass ῥιφήσομαι Wsd 5:22; Is 14:19; aor pass ἐρρίφην or ἐρρίφθην, ptc ῥιφής Wsd 11:14; (poetic) pf pass ptc ῥεριμμένος, plpf pass ἔρριπτο 3. *put out* (of harm's way, no //) Judg 9:17A.‡

ῥόα, -ας, ἡ (24x, Hom+) *pomegranate* (tree) Dt 8:8; 1 Km 14:2; SSol 4:13; Hg 2:19; Ezk 19:10; (fruit) Ex 28:33; 3 Km 7:18; Tob 1:7S; SSol 4:3.

ῥόαξ, -ακος, ὁ (not in LSJ) unknown, perh = ῥύαξ (Thu, Pla+) *effusion, runoff;* corresp to מתוך *from within* (cf. ὁλοκαύτωμα) Ezk 40:40.*

ῥοδοφόρος, -ον (LXX+; VL -νος spur) *rose-bearing* 3 Macc 7:17.*

ῥοιζέω (Hom+) *rush* (mid) SSol 4:15; (act caus, no //) *shoot* (an arrow) 4 Km 13:17VL.*

ῥοΐσκος, -ου, ὁ (Joseph AJ 3.160; =) *pomegranate-shaped knob or tassel* Ex 28:33f; 36:32ff; 2 Ch 3:16; 4:13; Sir 45:9.*

ῥόπαλον, -ου, τό (Hom, Hdt+) *mace* Pr 25:18.*

ῥοπή, -ῆς, ἡ (7x, Alcaeus, Aeschyl+) *small weight* (that balances or tips the scale) Wsd 11:22; Is 40:15; > *decisive moment* 3 Macc 5:49; Wsd 18:12. Josh 13:22 *f.l.* for ῥομφαία; cf. Heb.‡

ροποπώλης see ῥωπο-.

ῥοῦς, ῥοῦ, ὁ (Hom+) *current, flow* Sir 4:26.*

ῥοών, -ῶνος, ὁ (h.l.) *pomegranate orchard* Zech 12:11.*

ῥύδην (CratinusCom+) *flowingly,* > *abundantly; furiously* (no //) 2 Macc 3:25.*

ῥυήσομαι Att fut of ῥέω Ps 147:7.

ῥυθμίζω aor ἐρρύθμισα (Eur, X+) *compose, give shape or form* Is 44:13.*

ῥυθμός, -οῦ, ὁ (ArchilochusLyr, Aeschyl, X+) *pattern* Ex 28:15; 4 Km 16:10; *shape* SSol 7:2; *(musical) rhythm* Wsd 17:17; 19:18.*

ῥῦσις, -εως, ἡ (ins) *deliverance* Sir 51:9.*

ῥύστης, -ου, ὁ (LXX+) *rescuer, deliverer* 3 Macc 7:23; Ps 17:3, 49; 69:6; 143:2.*

ῥωμαλέος, -ον (Hdt+) *strong* 2 Macc 12:27.*

ῥώμη, -ης, ἡ (Xenophanes, Hdt+) *strength* 2 Macc 3:26; 3 Macc 2:4; Pr 6:8c.*

ῥώξ, ῥωγός, ὁ (ArchilochusLyr+) 1. *grape* Lev 19:10; Is 65:8. 2. *berry, fruit* Is 17:6.*

ῥωποπώλης, -ου, ὁ (VVLL ῥοπο-, ῥοβο-, =; for spelling see LSJ, W p. 76. LXX+) *dealer in trinkets* 2 Esdr 13:31f.*

Σ

σαβαχα   translit of שבכה *lattice, screening* 4 Km 25:17.*

σαββατίζω   fut -τιῶ **2.** *have rest, lie idle, enjoy sabbatical year* Lev 26:34f; 2 Ch 36:21; 1 Esdr 1:55.‡

σαβεκ   (not in LSJ) translit of סְבַךְ *thicket* Gen 22:13.*

σαβι   translit of צבי *glory, ornament* Da 11:16Θ, 41Θ, 45Θ.*

σαγή, -ῆς, ἡ   (Aeschyl+) *equipment,* (specif) *harness* (of horse) 2 Macc 3:25.*

σάγμα, -ατος, τό   (Eur+) *pack-saddle* Gen 31:34.*

σαδημωθ   translit of שדמות *terraces,* > *flatlands, plains* 4 Km 23:4.*

σαδηρωθ   translit of שדרת archit t.t. unexpl 4 Km 11:8, 15.*

σαθρός, -ά, -όν   (Hdt+) *unsound, weak* Job 41:19; (comp) Wsd 14:1.*

σαθρόω   (LXX+) *make unsound, weaken* Judg 10:8A.*

σαλαμιν   translit of שְׁלָמִים (c. MT) *peace offerings* Josh 22:29.*

σαλεύω   4 Km 17:20 mistrans of ענה piel *humiliate, mortify* as if נוע *shake, tremble.*‡

σάλος   **2.** *stumbling, unsteadiness* (no //) Ps 54:23; 120:3; La 1:8.‡

σαλπιῶ   Att fut of BDAG σαλπίζω Num 10:5.‡

σαμβύκη, -ης, ἡ   (Aristot, Polyb, Strabo+) *stringed musical instrument* (Aram loanword, סבכא or שבכה) Da 3:5ff.*

σανίδωμα, -ατος, τό   (Theophr+) *planking, deck* 3 Macc 4:10.*

σανιδωτός, -ή, -όν   (h.l.) *of boards or planks* Ex 27:8.*

σαπήσομαι   fut pass of BDAG: σήπω.

σαπρία, -ας, ἡ   (10x, LXX+) *decay, rottenness* 2 Macc 9:9; Job 2:9c; 7:5; PsSol 14:7; 16:14; Joel 2:20.

σαπρίζω   Att fut σαπριῶ (Hippocr) *putrefy, rot* Eccl 10:1.*

σάπφειρος   Is 54:11R; Ezk 9:2R = BDAG (so also Gött, W): -φιρος.‡

σαπῶσιν   fr ἐσάπην, aor pass of BDAG: σήπω.

σαράβαρα, -ων τά   (AntiphanesCom; Aram סרבלין, fr Pers) *trousers* (or mantle worn w. trousers) Da 3:21Θ; 3:94.*

σαρκοφαγέω   (Aristot, DiodS+) *eat meat* 4 Macc 5:26.*

σαρκοφαγία, -ας, ἡ   (Aristot, Philo+) *eating of meat* 4 Macc 5:8, 14.*

σατραπ(ε)ία, -ας, ἡ   (Hdt+) *province* (Pers loanword) Josh 13:3; Judg 3:3; 16:18A; 1 Esdr 3:2; Esth 8:9, 12b; 2 Macc 9:25.*

σατράπης, -ου, ὁ   (47x, X+) *governor* (Pers loanword), *prince* Judg 5:3; 1 Km 5:8; 2 Ch 9:14; 1 Esdr 3:2; Da 6:2ff.

σαύρα, -ας, ἡ   (Hdt, Theophr+) *lizard, salamander* Lev 11:30.*

σαυτοῦ   = BDAG: σεαυτοῦ Dt 21:11; 3 Km 20:7.‡

σαφής, -ές   (Hom [adv], Aeschyl+) *clear, evident* 2 Macc 12:40; Wsd 7:22; Sus 48; (comp as adv) 4 Macc 3:6.*

σαφφωθ   translit of שפות (h.l.) *curds* 2 Km 17:29; translit of סף *cup, bowl* (MT ספים, but gender varies; ספות possible) Jer 52:19.*

σαχωλ   (VVLL -ων, -ωχ, =) translit of שֵׂכֶל *insight, comprehension* 2 Esdr 8:18.*

σβεστικός, -ή, -όν   (Aristot+) *able to quench* Wsd 19:20.*

σεθιειμ   (mis)translit of שפים (N PERS? txt?) 1 Ch 26:16VL.*

σειρά, -ᾶς, ἡ   (Hom+: *cord,* = BDAG) **2.** *strand, lock* (of hair) Judg 16:13, 14B, 19B; Pr 5:22.*‡

σειρήν, -ῆνος, ἡ   (Hom+) *siren* Mi 1:8; Is 13:21; *wasp* (? Aristot), *bird* (?), *jackal* (?) Job 30:29; Is 34:13; 43:20; Jer 27:39 (MT *owl* in prophets, *jackal* in Job).*

σειρήνιος, -ον   (Heliod) *siren-like* 4 Macc 15:21.*

σ(ε)ιρομάστης, -ου, ὁ   (better σιρ-; so Num 25:7G, BDAG [cf. σ(ε)ιρος], LSJ, W. Philo Mech, Joseph+) *lance* Num 25:7; Judg 5:8A; 3 Km 18:28; 4 Km 11:10; Joel 4:10.*

σεῖσμα, -ατος, τό   (pap) *shaking* Sir 27:4.*

σελίς, -ίδος, ἡ   (ins, pap+) *column* (of text; Polyb 5.33.3 τρισιν η τετταρσιν ... σελισιν) Jer 43:23.*

σεμνολογέω   (Demosth+) *commend by solemn or exalted speech* 4 Macc 7:9.*

σεμνοτάτος   superl of BDAG: σεμνός.

σεραφιν   (LXX) translit of שׂרפים, *mythological winged and flaming serpents* Is 6:2, 6.*

σερσερωθ   translit of שׁרשׁרות *chains* (rendered χαλαστά in vs 5; end of 16) 2 Ch 3:16.*

σευτλίον, -ου, τό   (Aristoph+: τευτ-) *beet* Is 51:20.*

σημαία, -ας, ἡ   see σημέα.

σημαίνω   aor ἐσήμηνα or -ανα 4. *give a signal* (Aeschyl+) Josh 6:8; 2 Esdr 18:15; Jer 4:5; *command, direct* 1 Esdr 2:2. Judg 7:21; 2 Esdr 3:11 s.t. of רוע hiph *cry out* as if *give a signal*.‡

σημασία, -ας, ἡ   (25x, Aristot+) *sign, indication, signal* Lev 13:2ff; Num 10:5ff; 2 Ch 13:12; 1 Macc 4:40; PsSol 11:1. Num 29:1; 1 Ch 15:28; 2 Esdr 3:12 s.t. of תרועה *(shout of) celebration* as if *signal*.

σημέα, σημαία or σημεία, -ας, ἡ   (cf. LSJ and Polyb [Loeb] for spelling; Polyb+) 1. *military standard* (Polyb 2.32.6) Is 30:17. 2. *body of troops* under one standard (Polyb 1.33.9; 18.32.11), *division or company* Num 2:2.*

σημεῖον   1.a. *marker, signal* (heard or seen) Is 18:3; specif *military standard*, or *pole* (for mounting same) Nu 21:8.‡

σήπη, -ης, ἡ   (Aq) *decay* Sir 19:3.*

σής, σητός, ὁ   (pl σῆτες; Pind, Aristoph+) *moth* Pr 25:20; Job 4:19; 27:18; Sir 42:13; Mi 7:4; Is 33:1; 50:9; 51:8. Pr 14:30; Job 32:22 perh *larva, worm* (no //; not in Philo, c. BDAG), but mistrans of עשׂה *maker* as if עשׁ *moth*.

σήψ, σηπός, ἡ   (Hippocr+) *putrefying sore* Sir 19:3VL.*

σῆψις, -εως, ἡ   (Empedocles, Aristot+) *decay, putrefaction* Is 14:11.*

σθένος, -εος, τό   (Hom, Hdt+) *strength, force* 3 Macc 2:2; Job 4:10; 16:15; 26:14; PsSol 17:14.*

σθένω   (Aeschyl+) *be strong or capable* 3 Macc 3:8.*

σιαγόνιον, -ου, τό   (Hippocr+) *part around the jaw* Dt 18:3.*

σιαγών   Judg 15:19 mistrans of לחי *N LOC* (*Jawbone*) as if simple noun; cf. 15:9A Λεχι (translit of *N LOC*) and 15:19B².‡

σιβύνη   cf. ζιβ-

σιγηρός, -ά, -όν   (Hippocr, Menand) *silent, quiet* Sir 26:14.*

σιδήρε(ι)ος, -η, -ον   (Hom, Hdt+; later -ριος [ins] or contracted to σιδηροῦς [= BDAG]) *made of iron* Job 40:18VL.*

σιδήριον, -ου, τό   (Hdt, ins, pap+) *iron tool* Eccl 10:10; (specif) *ax head* Dt 19:5; 4 Km 6:5f.*

σιδηρόδεσμος, -ον   (h.l.) *binding w. iron* 3 Macc 4:9.*

σίελον or -αλον, -ου, τό   (Hippocr+) *spittle, saliva* 1 Km 21:14; Is 40:15VL (txt: σίελος, =).*

σίκλος, -ου, ὁ   (54x, X+: σίγλος) 1. *shekel* (unit of weight, = ca. 12g) Ex 30:23; Judg 8:26A; 1 Ch 21:25; Is 7:23. 2. *shekel (coin, monetary unit)* 1 Macc 10:40; prob also so read e.g., Num 3:47ff; Ezk 45:12.

σικυήρατον, -ου, τό   (pap) *cucumber bed* Is 1:8; EpJer 69.*

σίκυος, -ου, ὁ   (Aristoph+) *cucumber* Num 11:5G.*

σίκυς, -υος, ὁ   (not in LSJ; fem: Alcaeus+) *cucumber* Num 11:5R.*

σιρομάστης   cf. σειρ-.

σιρῶνος, -ου, ὁ   (not in LSJ or HR; h.l.) translit (but declined, hence true loanword) of שׂהרן *crescent-shaped ornament* (= μηνίσκος Is 3:18) Judg 8:26A (VL σιωνων spur; not in LSJ).*

σισόη, -ης, ἡ   (h.l.) *roll or knot* (?) Lev 19:27.*

σιτέομαι   (Hom, Hdt+) *eat, feed on* 2 Macc 5:27; Pr 4:17.*

σιτίον, ου, τό   (Hdt, Aristoph+) *grain, food* Pr 30:22.*‡

σιτοβολών, -ῶνος, ὁ   (ins+) *granary* Gen 41:56.*

σιτοδεία, -ας, ἡ   (Hdt+) *want of food, famine* Lev 26:26; 2 Esdr 19:15.*

σιτοδοσία, -ας, ἡ   (LXX+) *distribution or allowance of grain* Gen 42:19, 33.*

σιτομετρέω   (Polyb+) *measure out grain* Gen 47:12, 14.*

σῖτον see BDAG: σῖτος

σιτοποιός, -οῦ, ὁ or ἡ (Hdt+) *miller, baker* Gen 40:17.*

σιώπησις, -εως, ἡ (Schol Ptolem) *silence, taciturnity*; SSol 4:1, 3; 6:7 εκτος της σιωπησεως σου mistrans of מבעד לצמתך *from behind your veil* as if *at a distance from your silence*, perh as if צמה *veil* were related to דמה *be silent*.

σκάλλω aor ἔσκαλον (Hdt+) *hoe, dig up*; (fig) *turn over, work through* Ps 76:7.*

σκαμβός, -ή, -όν (LXX+) *bent, bowed, twisted* Ps 100:4.*

σκάφη **1.b.** *trough, bowl* Bel 33.*‡

σκάφος, -εος, τό (Aeschyl, Hdt+) *hull, ship* 2 Macc 12:3, 6.*

σκελίζω (LXX+) *trip, cause to fall* Jer 10:18.*

σκέλος **1.b.** (specif) *lower leg* (below the knee, no //) Da 2:33L.‡

σκεπάζω 1 Km 23:26 mistrans of חפז niph *hurry* as if fr חפה *cover*.‡

σκέπαρνον or -ος, -ου, τό or ὁ (Hom+) *adze* 1 Ch 20:3; Is 44:12.*‡

σκέπασις, -εως, ἡ (h.l.) *shelter, protection* Dt 33:27.*

σκεπαστής, -οῦ, ὁ (LXX) *protector, defender* Ex 15:2; Dt 32:38; Jdth 9:11; 3 Macc 6:9; Ps 70:6; Sir 51:2.*

σκεπεινός, -ή, -όν (LXX+) *sheltered or sheltering*; (subst) *sheltered places, places for concealment* 2 Esdr 14:7.*

σκέπτομαι (Hom+) **1.** *observe* Zech 11:3. **2.** *look for, search out* Gen 41:33; Ex 18:21. **3.** *watch out, take care* Bel 15G–17G.*‡

σκευάζω (Hdt+) *prepare, contrive* 3 Macc 5:31; (pass ptc) Sir 49:1.*

σκευασία, -ας, ἡ (Ps-Pla, Menand, DiodS [5.74.6]+; VL σκεύασις, -εως ἡ dub, h.l. =) *preparation* Eccl 10:1.*

σκεύασμα, -ατος, τό (Schol Soph, Schol Aristoph) *implement, item of furniture* (no //; rd, w. Ra, κατασκεύασμα) Jdth 15:11G.*

σκευαστός, -ή, -όν (Pla+) *made by craft or art* Is 54:17VL.*

σκευοφύλαξ, -ακος, ὁ (not in HR; pap+) *guard of supplies or stores* 1 Km 17:22VL.*

σκήνωμα *dwelling* (=BDAG) Judg 19:9; Ps 25:8; πολεις σκηνωματων *store-cities* 3 Km 9:19; (specif) *tent, hut* Dt 33:18; Ps 105:25; SSol 1:8; pl *(feast of) Booths, Tabernacles* (no //) 2 Macc 10:6.‡

σκήνωσις, -εως, ἡ (DiodS, pap) *dwelling* 2 Macc 14:35.*

σκῆπτρον **3.** *staff* 1 Km 14:27. 1 Km 2:28; 3 Km 8:16 etc mistrans of שבט *tribe* as if *rod, scepter*; becomes calque in NT and other Jewish or Christian lit (Joseph, Test12Patr, I Cl). Cf. φυλή.‡

σκιαγράφος, -ου, ὁ (LXX+) *scene painter, producer of illusion* Wsd 15:4.*

σκιάδιον, -ου, τό (LSJ: -δειον; Aristoph+) *umbrella*, > *fabric roof or sunshade* (on a vehicle) Is 66:20.*

σκιάζω (16x, Hom+) *overshadow, provide shade or shelter* Ex 38:8; 2 Km 20:6; 1 Ch 28:18; Job 36:28; Wsd 19:7; PsSol 11:5; Jon 4:6; Da 4:12L.

σκληρία, -ας, ἡ (not in HR; Philod+) *hardness, hardening*. Eccl 7:25 renders (sim sound) סכלות *foolishness*.

σκληροκάρδιος, -ον (LXX) *stubborn, hard-hearted* Pr 17:20; Sir 16:9VL, Ezk 3:7.*

σκληροπρόσωπος, -ον (fr Aq, Theod) *hard-faced, stubborn* Ezk 2:4VL.*

σκληρός Eccl 7:17 renders (sim sound) סכל *foolish*.‡

σκληρυσμός, -οῦ, ὁ (not in HR; Hippocr+) *hardening*, > *willfulness, stubbornness* Sir 10:21VL.*

σκνίψ, σκνιπός, ὁ nom pl σκνῖφες, σκνῖπες (Aristot+) *small fly or gnat* Ex 8:12ff; Ps 104:31; Wsd 19:10.*

σκολαβρίζω (spur; not in LSJ) prob dittograph fr κολαβρίζω (-ιας [σ]κολ-) Job 5:4VL.*

σκολιάζω (LXX) *be crooked or perverted, proceed in crooked fashion* Pr 10:8; 14:2; 17:16a.*

σκόπελον, -ου, τό (h.l.) *heap, mound* 4 Km 23:17.*

σκοπεύω (X+) *keep watch, watch closely* Ex 33:8; 1 Km 4:13; Pr 5:21; 15:3; SSol 7:5; Job 39:29; Na 2:2.*

σκοπή, ῆς, ἡ (Aeschyl+) *lookout, watch* Sir 37:14.*

σκοπιά, -ᾶς, ἡ (11x, Hom+) *height, hilltop, lookout* Num 23:14; Judg 10:17B; 3 Km 15:22; 2 Ch 20:24; Is 21:8; *"high place,"* site of pagan rites Num 33:52; Hos 5:1 (N LOC in Heb). Is 41:9 mistrans of מקצות *from the ends* as if מצפות *watchtowers*; Sir 40:6R *watch, guard duty*; better κοπιάω (so Gött).

σκοπός **2.** *watchman, sentry* 1 Km 14:16; Sir 37:14; Hos 9:8; Ezk 3:17. Na 3:12 perh mistrans of בכור *firstfruits* as if fr ברי *bodyguard* (cf. 2Kings 11:4, 19).‡

σκορακισμός, -οῦ, ὁ (Plu) *contemptuous behavior* Sir 41:21.

σκόρδον, -ου, τό (Hdt+: σκοροδον; ins+) *garlic* Num 11:5.*

σκορπίδιον, -ου, τό (Polyb) *dart- or arrow-casting catapult* 1 Macc 6:51.*

σκοτάζω (LXX+) **1.** *become dark* Ps 104:28; Mi 6:14; La 4:8; Ezk 31:15. **2.** *be blinded, have sight dimmed* Eccl 12:3; La 5:17.*

σκοτεινός 4 Km 5:24 mistrans of עפל *citadel* as if אפל *dark(ness)*.‡

σκοτομήνη, -ης, ἡ (LXX+) *dark night* Ps 10:2.*

σκυβαλίζω (LXX+) *discard, treat as dung or rubbish*; (pass, fig) Sir 26:28.*

σκυθρωπάζω (Aristoph, X+) *be sad or sullen* Ps 34:14; 37:7; 41:10; 42:2; Pr 15:13; Jer 19:8; 27:13.*

σκυλεία, -ας, ἡ (h.l.) *act of plundering, taking spoil* 1 Macc 4:23.*

σκυλεύω (30x, Hes+) *strip, plunder* Ex 3:22; 1 Ch 10:8; Jdth 2:27; 1 Macc 3:20; Wsd 10:20; Hab 2:8; Is 8:3.

σκυλμός, -οῦ, ὁ (pap [II BCE]+) *violence, abuse* (oft pl) 3 Macc 3:25; 4:6; 7:5.*

σκύμνος, -ου, ὁ (28x, Hom+) *cub* (esp of lion) Gen 49:9; Judg 14:5; 1 Macc 3:4; Ps 16:12; Job 4:11; Hos 13:8; Is 5:29; *young* (of serpent) La 4:3.

σκυτάλη, -ης, ἡ (Thu+) *pole* Ex 30:4f; *spindle* (no //) 2 Km 3:29. 3 Km 12:24b unexpl.*

σκῶλον, -ου, τό (LXX [σκῶλος, ὁ Hom+]) *sharpened stake* (driven into ground); (fig) *hindrance, obstacle* Ex 10:7; Dt 7:16; Judg 8:27B; 11:35A; 2 Ch 28:23; Is 57:14.*

σκώπτω (Hdt+) *mock* Sir 10:10.*

σμαραγδίτης (PhoenixCol) *of emerald, emerald-like* Esth 1:6.*

σμικρύνω (10x, LXX+) *make small, treat as insignificant* (no //) 1 Ch 16:19; Ps 88:46; Hos 4:3; Da 3:37; *reduce, lessen* Sir 17:25; μικ- Sir 35:7VL, = ; (pass) *become small or lesser* Jer 36:6; Bar 2:34.

σμῖλαξ, -ακις, ἡ (Eur+) *bindweed* (reading סבך [VEL SIM] in both texts, c. MT) Na 1:10; Jer 26:14.*

σμιρίτης, -ες (VL. σμιριτος, = ; h.l. fr σμιρις/σμυρις [DioscEpig] *emery*) *of emery* Job 41:7.*

σμύρνινος, -η, -ον (pap) *made or mixed w. myrrh* Esth 2:12.*

σοομ translit of שהם *precious stone* (onyx? lapis lazuli?) 1 Ch 29:2; perh misread as N PERS (cf. MT 24:27).

σοφιστής, -οῦ, ὁ (9x, Hdt+) *wise man, diviner* Ex 7:11 Da 1:20L; 2:14ffL.

σοφόω (h.l.) *make wise* Ps 145:8.*

σπάδων, -οντις, ὁ (Polyb+) *eunuch* Gen 37:36; Is 39:7.*

σπαίρω (Aristot, Polyb[15.33.5]+) *pant, spasm, flop* (like dying fish) 4 Macc 15:15.*

σπάλαξ, -ακος, ἡ (Aristot+, = ἀσπάλαξ) *mole* Lev 11:30VL.*

σπανίζω pf pass ptc ἐσπανισμένος (Aeschyl, Hdt+) *be(come) scarce, be wanting* (act or pass) Jdth 11:12; Job 14:11; *be in want* 4 Km 14:26; (act trans) *exhaust, make scarce* Da 9:24L.*

σπάνιος, -α, -ον (Hdt+) *rare, scarce*; (acc as adv) *seldom* Pr 25:17.*

σπάνις, -εως, ἡ (Hdt+) *scarcity* Jdth 8:9.*

σπάργανον, -ου, τό (Pind, Aeschyl+) *swaddling-band* Wsd 7:4; Ezk 16:4.*

σπαρτίον, -ου, τό (10x, Aristoph+) **1.** *string, cord* Gen 14:23; Josh 2:18; Eccl 4:12. **2.** *measuring cord* Job 38:5; Is 34:11.

σπασμός, -οῦ, ὁ (Hdt+: *spasm, convulsion*) *brandishing, waving* (of drawn sword; no //, but cf. BDAG: σπάω) 2 Macc 5:2.*

σπατάλη, -ης, ἡ (AnthPal, ins) *luxury, self-indulgence* Sir 27:13.*

σπειρηδόν (Polyb [5.4.9], Strabo) *by (military) companies* 2 Macc 5:2; 12:20.*

σπένδω fut σπείσω aor ἔσπεισα (20; Hom+) *pour out (as an offering)* Gen 35:14; Ex 25:29; 2 Km 23:16 = 1 Ch 11:18; 4 Macc 3:16; Sir 50:15; Hos 9:4; Jer 7:18; Ezk 20:28.‡

σπέρμα 3. *time of sowing* (Hes) Gen 8:22.‡

σπερματίζω (LXX+) *produce seed* (no //) Ex 9:31; (pass) *become pregnant* (no //) Lev 12:2.*

σπερματισμός, -οῦ, ὁ (Theophr) *sexual intercourse* (no //) Lev 18:23.*

σπερῶ fut of BDAG: σπείρω.

σπεύδω pf ἔσπευκα Ex 15:15; Judg 20:41; 1 Km 28:21 s.t. of בהל *be terrified* as if *be in haste* (as in Esth 2:9; Pr 28:22; Eccl 5:1 etc; cf. W, p. 144).‡

σπήλαιον Hab 2:15 mistrans of מעור *sexual organ* as if מערה *cave*.‡

σπιλωθέν aor pass ptc of BDAG: σπιλόω Wsd 15:4.*

σπινθήρ, -ῆρος, ὁ (8x, Hom+) *spark* Wsd 2:2; Sir 11:32; Is 1:31.

σπινόω f.l. (not in LSJ) for σπιλόω (Λ misread as N) Wsd 15:4vl.*

σπλαγχνίζω (act) *eat from sacrificial victims* 2 Macc 6:8; (mid, = BDAG) *show compassion* Pr 17:5vl.*‡

σπλαγχνισμός, -οῦ, ὁ (LXX) *eating of (pagan) sacrifices* (esp choice meats—heart, kidneys, etc) 2 Macc 6:7, 21; 7:42.*

σπλαγχνοφάγος, -ον (LXX+) *eating internal organs* Wsd 12:5.*

σποδιά, -ᾶς, ἡ (Hom+) *heap of ashes* Lev 4:12; Num 19:10, 17.*

σποδοειδής, -ες (Hippocr, Aristot+) *ashen, ash-colored* Gen 30:39; 31:10ff.*

σποδόομαι (Hippocr+) *cover w. ashes* (no //) Jdth 4:11.*

σπονδεῖον, -ου, τό (7x, pap) *cup, bowl* (for offerings) Ex 25:29; 1 Ch 28:17; 1 Esdr 2:9; Sir 50:15.

σπονδή, -ῆς, ἡ (64x, Hes+) *offering* (poured out or drunk) Gen 35:14; 4 Km 16:13; Esth 4:17x, 1 Macc 1:45; Is 57:6; Da 9:27.

σπόνδυλος see σφόν-.

σπόριμος, -ον (c. BDAG, subst *fields for sowing*—opp to pasture or desert—not *standing grain*) *for sowing* Gen 1:29; Lev 11:37; Sir 40:22vl.*‡

σπουδάζω Is 21:3; Job 21:6 s.t. of בהל *be terrified* as if *be in haste*; 22:10; 23:16 (trans) *frighten* as if *hasten* (cf. W, p. 144).‡

σπουδαῖος Ezk 41:25 renders עב *canopy* (?), unexpl.*‡

σπουδαιότης, -ητος, ἡ (Ps-Pla, DiodS 1.93.2) *earnestness* 3 Macc 1:9.*

σπουδή 3. (pl) *rivalries, disputes* (Hdt, Aristoph) Da 11:44Θ. Jer 8:15; 15:8 s.t. of בהלה *terror* fr בהל *hurry, be terrified*.‡

στάθμιον, -ου, τό (16x, pap, ins) *weight, small stone* (for balance scale) Lev 19:35; 4 Km 21:13; Pr 11:1; Am 8:5; Ezk 5:1.

σταθμός, -οῦ, ὁ (52x, Hom+) 1. *weight* Gen 43:21; Lev 26:26; Judg 8:26; 3 Km 7:32f; 1 Ch 22:3; 2 Esdr 8:30ff; Job 28:25; Sir 6:15; Ezk 4:10; perh *plummet* Is 28:17; *(standard) measure* Sir 16:25. 2. (X Anab 1.2.5) *stage* (of journey) Num 33:1; *rest station* Jer 9:1. 3. *post, doorpost* Ex 12:7ff; Judg 16:3; 4 Km 12:10; Pr 8:34; Is 57:8.‡

σταθμόω (Hdt+) *measure* 3 Km 6:23.*

σταῖς, σταιτός, τό (Hdt+) *dough* Ex 12:34, 39; 2 Km 13:8; Jer 7:18.*

στακτή, -ῆς, ἡ (10x, AntiphanesCom) *oil of myrrh* Gen 37:25; 3 Km 10:25; Ps 44:9; SSol 1:13; Is 39:2.

σταλαγμός, -οῦ, ὁ (Aeschyl+) *dripping* 4 Macc 9:20.*

σταλάσσω (Sappho, Eur+) *drip* Mi 2:11.*

στάξω fut of BDAG: στάζω.

στάσιμος, -η, -ον (Hippocr, X+) *steady* Sir 26:17.*

στάσις 1.b. *(existing) condition* or *(political) situation* 2 Esdr 19:6; Da 6:8Θ; status ante quo 1 Macc 7:18. 1.c. *place* 1 Ch 28:2; *position, station* 2 Ch 30:16; 2 Esdr 19:3; Is 22:19; Da 8:17; *base, foundation* (no //) 2 Ch 24:13. 1.d. *posture* 3 Macc 1:23. Judg 9:6 mistrans of מֻצָּב *pillar* (?) as if מֻצָּב *station, office*.‡

σταφίς, -ίδος, τό (pap, ins) *raisin* Num 6:3; 1 Km 25:18; 1 Ch 12:41; Hos 3:1; *raisin cluster or bunch* 2 Km 16:1.*

στεας Jer 7:18vL confusion of σταῖς and στέαρ (cf. both in LSJ).*

στεατόομαι (Hippiatr) *be fattened* (no //) Ezk 39:18.*

στεγάζω (Soph, X+) *cover*; (specif) *roof* (a building, Zen-P) 2 Ch 34:11; 2 Esdr 12:8; 13:3, 6; Ps 103:3.*

στεγνός, -ή, όν (Hdt, Eur, X+) *watertight* Pr 31:27.*

στειρόω (Philod, Philo) *make barren*; (pass) *prove barren, be childless* Sir 42:10.*

στέλεχος, -εος, τό (11x, Hdt+) *stem, trunk* Gen 49:21; Job 14:8; Jer 17:8; *column* (of smoke) SSol 3:6.

στέλλω 3. (mid) *make ready; prepare* (*for oneself*) 2 Macc 5:1; Wsd 14:1, > *acquire* 7:14; Pr 31:25. 4. *set out* (on journey, Hdt+) 3 Macc 4:11.‡

στέμφυλον, -ου, τό (Aristoph+) *pressed grapes* (sg or pl) Num 6:4.*

στενακτός, -ή, -όν (Soph+) *mournful, grieving* Ezk 5:15.*

στενός 2. *close; confining* 4 Km 6:1; *constricting* Is 8:22; *severe* 2 Km 24:14 = 1 Ch 21:13; Job 18:11. (adv) *presenting a threat, offering a difficulty* 1 Km 13:6. 23:14, 19; 24:1, 23 mistrans of מצד/מצודה *stronghold* as if fr צרר *be narrow or confining.* Zech 10:11 mistrans of צרה *distress* as if *narrowness.* Is 30:20 לחץ *affliction* as if (vb) *press, crowd.*‡

στενότης, -ητος, ἡ (Hdt+) *narrowness* 2 Macc 12:21.*

στένω (Hom+) *moan, lament* Gen 4:12, 14; Job 10:1; 30:28; Pr 28:28; 29:2.*

στερεοκάρδιος, -ον (fr Theod) *hard-hearted, willful* Ezk 2:4vL.*

στερεός Is 17:5 renders רפאים *giants* (part of N LOC), as if rel to רפה *heal.*‡

στερεόω Is 51:6 mistrans of מלח (h.l. niph) *be dispersed,* unexpl.‡

στερέω (19x, Hom+) *deprive* τινά *of* τινός Gen 48:11 (= BDAG); *cause* τι *to be lacking from* τινός Job 22:7.‡

στερέωμα 3. *foundation, firm place* (fig) 1 Esdr 8:78. Esth 9:29 mistrans of לקים *to establish,* unexpl. Ezk 13:5 corresp to פרץ *breach,* unexpl.‡

στερέωσις, -εως, ἡ (LXX+) *strengthening, making firm* Job 37:18; Sir 28:10.*

στερίσκω (alt pres of BDAG: στερέω; Hdt, Eur+) *deprive* Eccl 4:8.*

στέρνον, -ου, τό (Hom+) *chest, breast* Sir 26:18R.*

στεφάνη, -ης, ἡ (9x, Hom, Hdt+) *rim* Ex 25:25ff; Dt 22:8. Jer 52:8 mistrans of סירות *pots* as if *crowns, garlands.*

στεφανηφορέω (Eur+, ins) *wear a wreathe* Wsd 4:2.*

στέφανος 3.b. *"gift to the crown"* (pap), *royal tax* 1 Macc 10:29.‡

στέφος, -εος, τό (Empedocles, Aeschyl+ [poetic and late prose], = στέφανος) *crown, garland* 3 Macc 4:8.*

στέφω (Hom+) *put around*; (mid) *crown oneself* Wsd 2:8.*

στηθοδεσμίς, -ίδος, ἡ (pap+) *breast band, girdle* Jer 2:32.*

στηθύνιον, -ου, τό (12x, EubulCom, ins+) *breast* Ex 29:26; Lev 7:30ff; Num 6:20.

στηλογραφία, -ας, ἡ (LXX) *inscription* (in Ps titles) Ps 15:1; 55:1; 59:1.*

στηλόω (9x, ins, pap) *erect, set up* (trans) 2 Km 18:17; 4 Km 17:10; (τινά) La 3:12; (abs) *erect a monument* 2 Km 1:19; (mid/pass) *take one's place, stand* Judg 18:16fA, 2 Km 18:30; (pass) *be established or appointed* 3 Km 22:48(vL).

στήλωμα, -ατος, τό (Aq, Theod) *trunk* (of tree) Is 6:13vL.

στήλωσις, -εως, ἡ (ins) *inscription on a tablet* 2 Km 18:18vL.*

στήμων, -ονος, ὁ (Hes, Aristoph+) *warp* (of fabric) Lev 13:48ff.*

στήρ contraction of BDAG: στέαρ Bel 27Θ.*

στήριγμα, -ατος, τό (16x, Eur+) *support* 2 Km 20:19; Tob 8:6; 1 Macc 6:18; 10:23; Sir 3:31; > *prop* 2 Esdr 9:8; Ps 104:16; Ezk 4:16 of bread stacked on a *stick* or *rack.* 4 Km 25:11 mistrans of אמון *craftsman* as if fr לאמן *be* firm, support. For Ps 71:16; 1 Macc 2:43; cf. Introduction.

στηρίζω   4 Km 18:16 mistrans of אמנה *door-post* (h.l.) as if qal pass ptc of לאמן *be firm, support*.‡

στιβαρός   **2.** *bulky, thick* Ezk 3:6. Hab 2:6 (adv) mistrans of עבטים *pledge (for debt)* as if fr עבה *be thick*.‡

στίβι, -ιος, τό   dat (Gött) στίβει (VL στιμμη or στιμμι, = [cf. Lat STIBIUM, STIBI, or STIMMI]; fr Copt STĒM, pap+) *antimony* Jer 4:30.*

στιβίζομαι   (στιμ[μ]-, = ; Strabo [16.4.17]+) *paint* (one's eyes) w. antimony 4 Km 9:30; Ezk 23:40.*

στίγμα, -ατος, τό   (Hdt+) *(tattoo) mark, inlay* SSol 1:11.*‡

στικτός, -ή, -όν   (Soph+) *spotted,* > *tattooed* Lev 19:28.*

στιλβόω   (LXX+) *cause to flash or shine* Ps 7:12.*

στίλβω   aor ἔστιλψα.‡

στίλβωσις, -εως, ἡ   (LXX) *gleam, shining* Ezk 21:15, 20.*

στιμ-   see στιβ-.

στιππύϊνος, -η, -ον   (LXX) *made of flax or linen* Lev 13:47, 59.*

στιππύον, -ου, τό   (ins, pap [Hdt+ στυππεῖον]) *flax, tow* Judg 15:14; 16:9B; Sir 21:9; Is 1:31; Da 3:46.*

στιχίζω   (h.l.) *arrange in rows* Ezk 42:3.*

στίχος, -ου, ὁ   (23x, Aristot+) *row, course* Ex 28:17ff; 36:17ff; 3 Km 6:36; 7:6ff.*

στοιβάζω   plpf pass ptc ἐστοιβασμένος Josh 2:6 (LXX; = BDAG: στιβ-) *heap up, pile up* Lev 6:5; 3 Km 18:33. SSol 2:5 mistrans of רפד *refresh, sustain* as if *spread in a heap*.*

στοιβή, -ῆς, ἡ   (Aristoph+) **1.** *broom bush* Is 55:13. **2.** *heap* (no //) Judg 15:5A; Ruth 3:7.*

στοιχείωσις, -εως, ἡ   (Epicurus+: *elementary exposition, presentation of elements*) *composition of elements* (no //) 2 Macc 7:22.*

στοιχέω   **2.** *come out as expected, be satisfactory or acceptable* (ins) Eccl 11:6.*‡

στολίζω   fut στολιῶ (12; Eur+) *clothe* (τινά) Esth 4:4; Da 5:7L; (mid/pass) *be clothed, clothe oneself* Jdth 10:3; (mid/pass ptc) *wearing, clothed* 1 Esdr 1:2; Esth 8:15; 2 Macc 3:33.

στολισμός, -οῦ, ὁ   (LXX+) *clothing, outfit* 2 Ch 9:4; Sir 19:30; Ezk 42:14.*

στολιστής, -οῦ, ὁ   (LXX+) *person in charge of vestments* 4 Km 10:22.*

στόλος, -ου, ὁ   (Hdt+) **1.** *equipment,* esp *gear for war* 1 Macc 1:17. **2.** *naval fleet* 2 Macc 12:9; 14:1; 3 Macc 7:17.*

στόμα   **1.d.** also *opening* (of e.g., cave) Josh 10:18; (sack) Gen 42:27; of building—στομα εις στ. 4 Km 10:21; 21:16—or even a region—απο στοματος επι στομα 2 Esdr 9:11—*"door to door," (from) one end to the other*.‡

στομίς, -ίδος, ἡ   (LXX+) *mouth cavity* (no //, but renders מתלעות *jawbone*) Pr 30:14VL (q.l.).*

στόμωμα, -ατος, τό   (Aeschyl, Aristot+) *steel* Sir 31:26.*

στόνος, -ου, ὁ   (not in HR; Hom+) *groaning* Job 4:10VL.*

στοργή, -ῆς, ἡ   (Empedocles+) *love (for family and friends), warm affection* 3Macc 5:32; 4 Macc 14:13ff.*

στοχάζομαι   (Pla+) *reckon, calculate* (distance) Dt 19:3; *ascertain, make out* Wsd 13:9; *take into account* Sir 9:14; *have regard for* (τινός) 2 Macc 14:8.*

στοχαστής, -οῦ, ὁ   (LXX, Philo, Joseph) *conjuror, diviner* Is 3:2.*

στραγγαλάω   (Menand) *strangle* Tob 2:3S.*

στραγγαλιά   Ps 124:5 renders עקלקל *twisting (paths),* unexpl.‡

στραγγαλίς, -ίδος, ἡ   (StrattisCom [II BCE]+) *knot,* > *knotted cord* Judg 8:26B.*

στραγγαλιώδης, -ες   (Com) = seq Pr 8:8VL.*

στραγγαλώδης, -ες   (not in LSJ) *knotted, twisted, tortuous* Pr 8:8.*

στραγ(γ)εύομαι   (not in HR; Aristoph, Pla+) *loiter, delay* (oft confused in mss, ins w. στρατεύομαι [ΣΤΡΑΓ-, ΣΤΡΑΤ-]), q.l. at Judg 19:8; 2 Km 15:28 (rendering מהה *delay*).

στραγγίζω   (LXX+) *squeeze out* Lev 1:15.*

στρατεύω   Judg 19:8; 2 Km 15:28 txt error for στραγγεύομαι, q.v.‡

στρατηγέω (Hdt, Aristoph+) *be in command* 2 Macc 10:32; (fig) *(out)strategize* (τινά), > (pass) *be outmaneuvered* 14:31.*

στρατήγημα, -ατος, τό (X, Polyb+) *stratagem,* > *trick, ruse* (Cicero, Plu+) 2 Macc 14:29.*

στρατηγία, -ας, ἡ (Hdt+) *military command* 2 Km 2:35.*

στρατηγός 3. *commander, general* 1 Macc 8:10.‡

στρατιῶτις, -ιδος, ἡ (Aeschyl+: *soldier's wife,* etc) *woman soldier* (no //) 4 Macc 16:14.*

στρατοκῆρυξ, -υκος, ὁ (ins+) *army herald* 3 Km 22:36.*

στρατοπεδεία, -ας, ἡ (X, Polyb+) *camp* (military) Josh 4:3; 2 Macc 13:14.*

στρατοπεδεύω (11x, Hdt+) 1. *encamp* Gen 12:9; Ex 13:20; 2 Macc 9:23; Pr 4:15. 2. *march out to camp* (no //) Dt 1:40.

στρατός, -οῦ, ὁ (Hom, Hdt+) *army* 2 Macc 8:35; 4 Macc 3:8; 4:5, 11.*

στρέβλη, -ης, ἡ (9x, Aeschyl+: *winch*) *rack, instrument of torture* (Polyb+), > *torture, punishment* (pap, DiodS) 4 Macc 7:4; 8:11; Sir 33:27.*

στρεβλωτήριον, -ου, τό (h.l.) *rack* 4 Macc 8:13.*

στρέμμα, -ατος, τό (Hippocr, Demosth+) *twist, strand* Judg 16:9B.*

στρεπτός, -ή, -όν (10x, Hom, Hdt+) *plaited, twisted* Ex 25:11ff; Esth 4:17k; (subst) *braid* Dt 22:12; *molding, wreathe* 3 Km 7:27f.*

στρῆνος, -εος, τό (Lycophron+) *wild cry.* 4 Km 19:28 mistrans of שׁאן *ease, freedom from trouble or concern* as if שׁאן *uproar.**‡

στρίφνος, -ου, ὁ (h.l.) *hard or tough meat* Job 20:18.*

στροβέω (Aeschyl+) *whirl about,* > *distract, distress* Job 9:34; 13:11; 15:23; 33:7.*

στρογγυλόω (Plu+) *be(come) or appear round* 3 Km 7:17vL.*

στρογγύλωσις, -εως, ἡ (Hippocr) *circle, boundary* (of camp, no //) 1 Km 17:20(vL).*

στρουθίζω (Aristoph+) *chirp like a sparrow* Is 10:14vL.*

στρουθός, -ου, ὁ (8x, Hom, Hdt+) *sparrow* Lev 11:16 = Dt 14:15; Job 30:29; Jer 10:22.‡

στροφεύς, -έως, ὁ (Aristoph+) *socket or pivot of door* 3 Km 6:34; 1 Ch 22:3.*

στροφή, -ῆς, ἡ (Aeschyl+) *turning, twisting;* (fig) *intricacy, literary craft* Pr 1:3; Wsd 8:8; Sir 39:2; PsSol 12:2.*

στρόφιγξ, -ιγγος, ὁ (Eur, Pla+) *pin or pivot* (in socket, at top & bottom of door; Theophr, pap) Pr 26:14.*

στρόφος, -ου, ὁ (Hom, Hdt+) *twisted cord;* > *intestinal spasm* Sir 31:20.*

στροφωτός, -ή, -όν (h.l.) *made to hinge on pivots* Ezk 41:24.*

στρυ(ν)φαλίς, -ίδος, ἡ (h.l.) 1 Km 17:18 vvLL for τρυφ-, q.v.*

στρύχνον, -ου, τό (Theophr+) *nightshade* Job 20:18vL.*

στρῶμα, -ατος, τό (Theognis, Aristoph, X+) *bed, bedding* Pr 22:27.*

στρωμνή, -ῆς, ἡ (11x, Aeschyl+) *bed, bedding* Gen 49:4; Jdth 9:3; Ps 6:7; Job 17:13; Am 6:4; Ezk 27:7.

στρωννύω or στρώννυμι fut στρώσω pf ἔστρωκα pass ἔστρωμαι Ezk 28:7R (Gött τιτρώσκω).‡

στυγέω (Hom, Hdt+) *hate, find abhorrent* 2 Macc 5:8; 3 Macc 2:31.*

στῦλος 2 Ch 34:31 mistrans of עֹמֶד *platform, podium* as if עַמּוּד *pillar.*‡

στυράκινος, -η, -ον (Strabo) *of storax wood* Gen 30:37.

συγγελάω (Eur+) *laugh w.* (τινί) Sir 30:10.*

συγγενής 2 Km 3:39 mistrans of רד *helpless* (NRSV) or *gentle* (AB) as if דד *relative;* see also καθίστημι.‡

συγγηρά(σκ)ω (not in HR; Hdt+) *grow old together* Sir 11:16(vL).*

συγγίνομαι (Hdt+) *associate w., have sex w.* Gen 19:5; 39:10; Jdth 12:16; Sus 11Θ, 39Θ.*

συγγινώσκω 2. *be(come) conscious, recognize, conclude* 2 Macc 14:31.*‡

συγγνωστός, -όν (Soph+) *pardonable* Wsd 6:6; 13:8.*

συγγραφεύς, -έως, ὁ (Aristoph+) *author, writer* 2 Macc 2:28.*

συγγραφή 2. *(bill of) indictment, legal complaint* (no //) Job 31:35.‡

συγγυμνασία, -ας, ἡ   (Zeno the Stoic) *shared training* Wsd 8:18.*

συγκαθίζω   Gen 15:11 mistrans of שוב hiph *drive off* (Vulg ABIGO) as if ישב *sit down*.‡

συγκαθυφαίνω   pf pass ptc συγκαθυφασμένος (h.l.) *interwoven* Is 3:23.*

συγκαίω   pf pass συγκέκαυται (8x, Pla+) *burn (up)* Ps 120:6; Pr 24:22e; Jon 4:8; Is 5:11; (mid/pass) *burn, be consumed* Gen 31:40; Job 16:16; Is 5:24.

συγκάλυμμα, -ατος, τό   (LXX) *something (to be) covered* Dt 23:1; 27:20.*

συγκάμπτω   **1.b.** (intr) *bend down* Judg 5:27A; 4 Km 4:35.‡

συγκαταγηράσκω   (Hdt+) *grow old together w.* Tob 8:7.*

συγκατακληρονομέω   (h.l.) *receive* (pass *be given*) *common inheritance* Num 32:30.*

συγκαταμείγνυμι   aor pass subj -μιγῆτε (Eur, X+) *mingle or blend w.* Josh 23:12.*

συγκαταφέρω   (Aristot+) *carry down together*; (pass) *be borne down together* Is 30:30.*

συγκατεσθίω   (LXX+) *consume, devour together* Is 9:17.*

σύγκειμαι   **2.** *be composed, be constituted* Sir 43:26. **3.** *contrive, conspire* (act, no //) 1 Km 22:8.*‡

συγκεκυφώς   pf ptc of BDAG: συγκύπτω Sir 12:11; 19:26.*

συγκεντέω   (Hdt, Polyb+) *stab all together or at once* 2 Macc 12:23; 13:15R (RECTE).

συγκερατίζω   (h.l.) *"lock horns," do battle* (with, μετά or dat) Da 11:40.*

συγκεραυνόω   (ArchilochusLyr, Eur [BACCH 1103]+) *strike (as) w. lightning* 2 Macc 1:16.*

συγκλασμός, -οῦ, ὁ   (h.l.) *breakage* Joel 1:7.*

σύγκλεισμα, -ατος, τό   (LXX) *encircling rim or border* 3 Km 7:16, 21, 22; 4 Km 16:17.*‡

συγκλεισμός   2 Km 5:24 rd συσσεισμός (cf. 1 Ch 14:15) for מצעדה *breeze* (MT צעדה *marching*). Job 28:15 mistrans of סגור *fine (beaten or hammered)* as if fr סגר *enclose*.

συγκλειστός, -ή, -όν   (Aristot+) *closed, closing*; 3 Km 7:15, 36 mistrans of מסגרת (v. 15) *rim and* סגור (v. 36) *hammered thin, finely worked* (cf. συγκλείω) as if fr סגר *enclose, shut in*.

συγκλείω   **3.** *close up* (from within), *secure*; (pass ptc) *made secure, unassailable* 2 Macc 12:7. 3 Km 6:20; 7:35 etc mistrans of סגור *hammered thin, finely worked*, 4 Km 24:14, 16 mistrans of מסגר *metalworker*, as if fr סגר *enclose, shut in*.‡

συγκληρονομέω   (pap [IV CE, cf. LSJSup]) *be joint heir w.* Sir 22:23.*

σύγκλητος, -ον   (Soph+) *summoned, called together*; (pl subst) *representatives, council* Num 16:2.*

συγκλύζω   (VL συγκλύω spur, not in LSJ; LXX+) *wash over, overwhelm* SSol 8:7; Wsd 5:22; Is 43:2.*

σύγκοιτος, -ον   (Pind+) *sharing a bed*; (fem subst) *sexual partner* Mi 7:5.*

συγκολλάω   (Aristoph+) *glue together* Sir 22:9.*

συγκραθῆναι   aor pass inf of BDAG: συγκεράννυμι.

σύγκριμα, -ατος, τό   (19x, Polyb+, no //) **1.** *decree* Judg 18:9A; 1 Macc 1:57; Da 2:25Θ; 4:17Θ, 24Θ. **2.** *composition, concert* Sir 32:5. **3.** *interpretation* Da 4:18Θ; 5:7L; 5:26Θ. **4.** *excuse, rationalization* Sir 32:17.

συγκρίνω   **4.** (mid reflex) *put one another to the test, contend with* (DiodS) 1 Macc 10:71.‡

σύγκρισις, -εως, ἡ   (42x, Pla+) **1.** *comparison* Wsd 7:8. **2.** *interpretation* Gen 40:12, 18; Judg 7:15; Da 2:4ff. **3.** *decision, ruling* Num 9:3; Judg 18:7A (*usual*) *pattern* Num 29:6ff.

συγκροτέω   (Aristoph, X+) *strike together*; *clap* (hands) Num 24:10; (mid, of knees) *knock* Da 5:6Θ.*

συγκρουσμός, -οῦ, ὁ   (LXX+) *collision, clashing together* 1 Macc 6:41.*

συγκρύπτω   (Hippocr, Eur+) *conceal completely*; (mid) *conceal oneself* (from τινά) 2 Macc 14:30; συγκρύφω (not in LSJ) new pres formed fr pf of -κρύπτω; cf. συγκύφω) Sir 19:27R.*

συγκτίζω   aor pass συνεκτίσθην (Hdt+) *co-originate*; (pass) *be created with* Sir 1:14.*

συγκυρέω   (Hom+) *come together*; only ptc/subst συγκυρῶν *contiguous area* Num 21:25; 35:4; Dt 2:37; 1 Macc 11:34.*

συγκύφω (not in LSJ; new pres formed fr pf of BDAG: συγκύπτω [q.v.]; cf. συγκρύπτω, BDAG: στήκω) Sir 19:27G.*

συγχρονίζω (LXX+; vl συγχρονέω, =) spend time (no //) Sir prol 28.*

συγχωρητέον (Soph, Pla+) it must be permitted or granted 2 Macc 2:31.*

συζυγής, -ές (Ra: συνζ-; LXX+) joined, paired, (specif) married; (subst) husband, partner 3 Macc 4:8.*

συζώννυμι (Aristoph) bind on Lev 8:7; 1 Macc 3:3.*

συκάμινον, -ου, τό (Aristot+) mulberry (fruit of BDAG: συκάμινος) Am 7:14.*

συκοφάντης, -ου, ὁ (Aristoph+) denouncer, (false) accuser Ps 71:4; Pr 28:16.*

συκοφαντία, -ας, ἡ (Lysias+) blackmail, extortion Ps 118:134; Eccl 4:1; 5:7; 7:7; Am 2:8.*

συκών, -ῶνος, ὁ (LXX+) fig orchard Am 4:9; Jer 5:17.*

συλλαμβάνω 1.a.β. capture (a place [immovable], no //) 4 Km 14:7; Jer 31:41; Da 11:15Θ; (pass) be captured 4 Km 18:10. 1 Macc 5:27 cf. συνειλέω (Goldstein AB 2 Maccabees, p 500 [on 2 Macc 15:19]).‡

σύλλημψις, -εως, ἡ (Thu+) 1. conception, pregnancy Hos 9:11; Jer 20:17. 2. capture Job 18:10; Jer 18:22; 41:3.*‡

συλλογή, -ῆς, ἡ (Hdt+) gathering, collecting 1 Km 17:40.*

συλλογίζομαι 2. (pass) be reckoned or counted Num 23:9.‡

συλλογισμός, -οῦ, ὁ (Hippocr, Pla+) reckoning Wsd 4:20; (specif) census (no //) Ex 30:12.*

συλλοιδορέω (Julian) join in abusing or reviling (τινά) Jer 36:27R.*

συλλοχάω (h.l.) recruit (soldiers) 1 Macc 4:28.*

συλλοχισμός, -οῦ, ὁ (AsclepiodTact) census list (no //) 1 Ch 9:1.*

συλλύω aor pass συνελύθη (Aeschyl+) reconcile; (pass) be reconciled, settle (w.) 1 Macc 13:47; 2 Macc 11:14; 13:23.*

συμβάλλω 5.c. (caus, hostile) incite, pit (τινά against someone else) Jer 50:3.‡

συμβαστάζω (Appian) carry together; (pass) be comparable (no //; to τινί) Job 28:16, 19.*

συμβιβῶ Att fut of συμβιβάζω Ps 31:8.‡

συμβιόω, fut- βιώσομαι (Pla+) live w. (τινί) Sir 13:5.*

συμβίωσις, -εως, ἡ (Polyb+) shared life Wsd 8:3, 9, 16.*

συμβιωτής, -οῦ, ὁ (EupolisCom, Polyb+) companion, confidante Bel 2; 30G.*

σύμβλημα, -ατος, τό (LXX+) juncture, seam Is 41:7.*

σύμβλησις, -εως, ἡ (LXX) juncture, seam Ex 26:24.*

συμβοηθός, -όν (h.l.) joining to help 3 Km 21:16.*

συμβολή, -ῆς, ἡ (10x, Hdt+) 1. juncture, connection Ex 26:4ff. 2. subscription, contribution (to festival or shared meal) Pr 23:20; Sir 18:32; Is 23:18.

συμβολοκοπέω (LXX) share in festal meals or parties Dt 21:20; Sir 9:9; 18:33.*

σύμβολον, -ου, τό (Hdt+) token, sign, seal Wsd 2:9; 16:6; Hos 4:12.*

συμβόσκομαι (h.l.) graze together Is 11:6.*

συμβουλευτής, -οῦ, ὁ (Pla+) counselor, advisor 1 Esdr 8:11.*

συμβραβεύω (h.l.) become fellow arbitrators 1 Esdr 9:14.*

συμμαίνομαι (not in HR; Menand+) join in madness Pr 20:1vl.*

συμμαχία, -ας, ἡ (16x, Hdt+) 1. alliance 1 Macc 8:17ff; 2 Macc 4:11; Is 16:4. 2. body of allied or expeditionary troops Jdth 3:6; 1 Macc 11:60.

σύμμαχος, -ον (13x, Sappho, Aeschyl, Hdt+) allied, supportive; (subst) ally 1 Macc 8:20; 9:60; (of God, no //) 2 Macc 8:24; 10:16.

συμμ(ε)ιγής, -ές (better -μιγ-; so LSJ, W; Soph, Pla+) commingled, mixed together Da 2:43.*

συμμείγνυμι fut συμμιγήσομαι aor συνέμειξα (for spelling cf. W) 2. mingle or converse w. (τινί) 2 Macc 3:7; Pr 11:15; join forces 2 Macc 13:3; form an alliance Da 11:6Θ. 3. (hostile, X Anab 2.1.2.) engage (the enemy in battle), close with, attack 2 Macc 15:26.‡

σύμμεικτος, -ον   (HR, Ra συμμικ-; cf. W; 16; Hes, Hdt+) *mixed, consolidated* PsSol 17:15; (subst) **a.** *market* (of mixed goods) Ezk 27:16ff. **b.** *army* (of several nationalities) Jdth 1:16; Na 3:17; Jer 27:37; (pl) *soldiers of several nationalities* Jer 32:20; Ezk 27:27.

συμμετέχω   (Eur, X+) *take part in, share in* (τινός; Eur BACCH 63) 2 Macc 5:20.*

συμμετρία, -ας, ἡ   (Democr, Pla+) *due proportion, moderation* PsSol 5:16.*

σύμμετρος, -ον   (Aeschyl+) *suitable, symmetrical* Jer 22:14.*

συμμιαίνω   (Joseph BJ 4.382) *defile or corrupt also or along w.;* (pass) *be corrupted together w.* (τινί) Bar 3:10.*

συμμιγ-, see συμμειγ-.
συμμικτ-, see σύμμεικτ-.

σύμμιξις, -εως, ἡ   (better: -μειξ-; Anaxagoras, Pla+) *mingling.* 4 Km 14:14 = 2 Ch 25:24 mistrans of תערובות *pledges* (w. ברית = *hostages*) as if fr ערב *mingle.**

συμμίσγω   (Hom+, pres only) *meet, join w.* (τινί) 1 Macc 11:22; (hostile) *encounter in battle* 2 Macc 14:14, 16.*

συμμισοπονηρέω   (h.l.) *share hatred of evil* 2 Macc 4:36.*

συμμολύνω   (Philod+) *defile together;* (pass) *be defiled* Da 1:8L.*

συμπάθεια, -ας, ἡ   (Aristot, Polyb+) *affinity, affection, pity* 4 Macc 6:13; 14:13ff; 15:7ff.*

συμπαίζω   (Anacr, Hdt+) *play w.* (τινί) Sir 30:9.*

συμπαραλαμβάνω   **2.** (pass) *be also overtaken* (no //) Gen 19:17 (but pap961 reads συμπεριλαμβάνω [q.v.] RECTE?).‡

συμπαραμένω   **2.** *endure as long as* (τινί) Ps 71:5.‡

συμπαρίστημι   (Soph+) *stand by to help* Ps 93:16.*

συμπατέω   (11x, CratinusCom+) *trample underfoot* 4 Km 7:17, 20; Na 3:14; Da 7:7Θ, 19Θ.

συμπείθω   (X, Pla+) *convince, persuade* 2 Macc 13:26; 3 Macc 7:3.*

συμπεραίνω   (Eur+: *accomplish, conclude*) *cut off, bring to an end* (no //; Heb קצה, cf. Vulg CONCIDISTI) Hab 2:10.*

συμπεριλαμβάνω   **2.** *gather together* Ezk 5:3.*‡

συμπεριφέρω   (Pla, Polyb+) *carry around w.;* (mid) *go around w., live w.* Pr 5:19 Sir 25:1; *accommodate or adapt oneself* 3 Macc 3:20; > *treat w. understanding* (no //) 2 Macc 9:27; Pr 11:29.*

συμπίπτω   2 Km 5:18, 22 = 1 Ch 14:9, 13 mistrans of נטש niph *spread out* as if *be cast aside.*‡

συμπλεκτός, -όν   (LXX+) *plaited, woven together* Ex 36:30.*

συμπλέκω   aor pass συνεπλάκη pf pass ptc συμπεπλεγμένος (13; Thu+) *plait, weave together* Ex 36:12; Ps 57:3; Job 40:17; Ezk 24:17; *join, link* Ex 28:22; Hos 4:14; La 1:14; (pass) *become entangled* Pr 20:3; Na 2:5.

συμπλήρωσις, -εως, ἡ   (Polyb+) *fulfillment, completion* 2 Ch 36:21; 1 Esdr 1:55; Da 9:2Θ.*

συμπλοκή   3 Km 16:28d renders קדש *cult prostitute,* = ἐδιηλλαγμένος (q.v.) 22:47(VL).‡

συμποδίζω   fut συμποδιοῦσιν aor pass συνεποδίσθησαν (12; Aristoph+) *bind one's feet, bind hand and foot* Gen 22:9; Tob 8:3S; Ps 17:40; Zech 13:3; Da 3:20L; (fig) *entangle, ensnare* Pr 20:11. Hos 11:3 mistrans of רגל (tiphel [=hiph]) *teach to walk* as if *trip up.*

συμποιέω   (Aristoph+) *cooperate, assist* 1 Esdr 6:27.*

συμπολεμέω   (Andoc, Thu+) *fight* (w., on behalf of τινί) Josh 10:14, 42.*

συμπονέω   (Aeschyl+) *labor or struggle together* Sir 37:5.*

συμπορπάω   (LXX+) *fasten or pin* (πορπή) *together* Ex 36:13.*

συμπότης, -ου, ὁ   (Hdt+) *drinking companion* 3 Macc 2:25.*

συμπραγματεύομαι   (ins, pap+) *do business together* 3 Macc 3:10.*

συμπροπέμπω   (Hdt+) *accompany* (at the beginning of a journey) Gen 12:20; 18:16.*

συμπροπορεύομαι   (dub; not in LSJ) *go ahead accompanying* Dt 31:8VL.*

συμπρόσειμι (-εἶναι)   (pap+) *coexist, be present together* Ps 93:20; Eccl 8:15.*

συμπροσπλέκω fut pass συμπροσπλακήσομαι (h.l.) *attach (by weaving), join together*; (pass) *become entangled* (cf. συμπλέκω) Da 11:10Θ.*

σύμπτωμα, -ατος, τό (Thu, Pla+) **1.** *chance event, mishap* Ps 90:6; Pr 27:9. **2.** *sign, indication, symptom* 1 Km 6:9; 20:26.*

συμφερόντως (AntiphoSoph, Pla+; adv of pres ptc of BDAG: συμφέρω) *to one's advantage or benefit* 4 Macc 1:17.*

συμφεύγω (Hdt+) *flee (together), take refuge* 1 Macc 10:84; 2 Macc 10:18, 32; 12:6.*

συμφλέγω (Eur+) *burn to ashes, consume with fire* Is 42:25.*

συμφλογίζω (LXX, Is 42:25 Theod) *burn completely*; (pass) *be burned up* 2 Macc 6:11.*

συμφοράζω (Orph, Philod+) *wail* Is 13:8.*

συμφράσσω (Hdt+) *fence in, hem in* (Heb חבט *beat out, thresh*) Is 27:12.*

συμφρονέω (Polyb+) *conspire* 3 Macc 3:2.*

συμφρύγω (Theophr) *thoroughly parch or dry* 4 Macc 3:11; Ps 101:4.*

συμφύρομαι (Eur+) *mix together* Sir 12:14; Hos 4:14; *have sex* PsSol 8:9.*

συμψάω aor pass συνεψή(σ)θην (Hdt+) *sweep away, obliterate*; (pass) *be swept up or away* Jer 22:19; 30:14; 31:33.*

σύν **4.** (+acc) Aquilan rendering of Heb את (sign of dir obj, as if prep *with*) 3 Km 14:8(vL); Eccl 1:14; 2:17; 3:11; 4:1; etc; 9:15 (w. μιμνήσκω, τινός).‡

συναγελάζομαι (Democr, Aristot+) *flock or herd together*; (fig, of people [Polyb 6.5.7] 4 Macc 18:27.*

σύναγμα, -ατος, τό (Hippocr) *collection, collocation* Eccl 12:11.*

συνάγω Judg 7:22A mistrans of N LOC צרד(ת)ה (txt?) as if fr צרר *hem in?* 3 Km 7:10 mistrans of קוה(ה) *measuring line* as if fr קוה *collect*.‡

συναγωγή **1.b.** *collection, pile* (of stones) Job 8:17. **6.b.** (of all Israel) *assembly, host* Ex 17:1. Da 8:25L mistrans of אפס *end, only, without* as if fr אסף *gather*.‡

συνᾴδω (Aristoph+) *sing together* Hos 7:2.*

συναινέω (Hdt+) *approve* 3 Macc 6:41; 7:12G; *consent* 5:21.*‡

συναλγέω (Aeschyl+) *share in suffering* Sir 37:12.*

συναλοάω (Hippocr, Theocr+) *trample to pieces, crush* Da 2:45L.*

συναναμείγνυμι (Hippocr, Theophr+) or **συναναμίσγω** (LXX+) *mix together*; (pass) *be mixed up or associated* Hos 7:8; Ezk 20:18.*

συνανάμ(ε)ιξις, -εως, ἡ (h.l.) *act of mingling*, > *entering into alliance or partnership* Da 11:23Θ.*

συναναστροφή, -ῆς, ἡ (Epicurus, DiodS+) **1.** *cohabitation, companionship* Wsd 8:16; *association, fellowship* 3 Macc 2:31, 33. **2.** *shared conduct of life* (no //) 3 Macc 3:5.*

συναναφέρω fut συνανοίσετε (Aristot+) *carry up w.* Gen 50:25 = Ex 13:19; *offer up together* (no //, but cf. ἀναφέρω 2.) 2 Km 6:18.*

συναναφύρω (LXX+) *mix together* Ezk 22:6.*‡

συναντάω **1.b.** *stand face to face*, > *confront* Judg 8:21B. Judg 15:12B s.t. of פגע *attack, fall upon, meet*.‡

συναντή, -ῆς, ἡ (LXX) *meeting* (= BDAG: συνάντησις) 3 Km 18:16; 4 Km 2:15; 5:26.*

συνάντημα, -ατος, τό (9x, pap+) *event, occurrence* Ex 9:14; 3 Km 8:37; Eccl 2:14f; 3:19.

συναποκλείω (LXX, dub) *close off* 1 Km 1:5vL, 6vL.*

συναποκρύπτω (LXX+) *hide away together*; (pass) *be hidden away* (μετά τινος) EpJer 48.*

συνάπτω aor συνῆψα pf pass ptc συνημμένος (48; Hdt+) **1.** *join, connect* (objects) Ex 26:6ff; Is 5:8; *adjoin* (territories) Josh 17:10; *reach, extend to* Sir 35:16; Is 15:8; (ptc) *reaching to, touching* 2 Esdr 13:19. **2.** *join (in battle), attack* Dt 2:5ff; Judg 20:20B; 2 Km 1:6; 1 Macc 4:14; Da 11:25Θ; (subj πόλεμος, no //) *be joined* 1 Macc (pass) 9:13; (act) 9:47. **3.** (w. cogn acc) *form an alliance* 3 Km 16:20; 4 Km 10:34.

συναρπάζω **1.b.** *grasp, seize, pick up* 2 Macc 4:41.‡

συναρχία, -ας, ἡ (Aristot+) *common government, shared realm* Esth 3:13d.*

συνασπίζω (Eur+) *share a shield*; (fig) *protect, support* 3 Macc 3:10.*

συναύξω (var form of BDAG: συναυξάνω, = ; Hdt+) *grow simultaneously* 2 Macc 4:4; *grow in mutual dependence* 4 Macc 13:27.*

συναφίστημι (Hdt+) *rebel with, prove unfaithful with* Tob 1:5BA.*

σύναψις, -εως, ἡ (Pla+) *union, juncture;* (as cogn acc) *alliance* (no //) 3 Km 16:20; 4 Km 10:34.*

συνδάκνω aor pass συνεδήχθην (X+) *bite hard;* (pass) *smart, sting* (no //) Tob 11:12BA.

συνδειπνέω (X+) *eat together* Gen 43:32; Pr 23:6.*

σύνδειπνος, -ου, ὁ (X+) *table companion* Sir 9:16.*

συνδέομαι (Pla+) *join in prayer* Zeph 2:1vL.*

σύνδεσμος **4.b.** *conspiracy* (no //) 4 Km 11:14; Jer 11:9. 3 Km 14:24 mistrans of קדש *cult prostitute* as if קשר *conspiracy*. Da 5:12Θ mistrans of קטר *ligature*, > *(magic) knot* as if *ligament, sinew* (5:6Θ).‡

συνδήσω fut of BDAG: συνδέω.

συνδιώκω (Thu+) *join in pursuing* 2 Macc 8:25.*

συνδυάζω (X+) *be combined, be in collusion* Ps 140:4.*

συνεγγίζω (Polyb+) *approach, come near* 2 Macc 10:25, 27; 11:5; Sir 35:17.*

σύνεγγυς (Hippocr, Thu+) **1.** (adv) *nearby* Sir 26:12. **2.** (prep w. gen) *near, next to* Dt 3:29; Tob 11:15S; PsSol 16:2; Sir 14:24; 51:6.*

συνεδρεύω (Demosth, Aristot+) *deliberate, sit in council* Sir 11:9; 23:14; 42:12; Sus 28G.*

συνεδρία, -ας, ἡ (Aeschyl+; W argues for συνεδρεία, ins and pap) *meeting, session* Jdth 6:1, 17; 11:9.*

συνεδριάζω (h.l.) *meet in council* Pr 3:32.*

συνεθίζω (Thu+) *accustom* (w. dbl acc) Sir 23:13; (pass) *become accustomed to* (τινί) 23:9, 15.*

συνείκω (Polyb+) *give way, yield* 4 Macc 8:6.*

συνειλέω pf pass ptc συνειλημένος (not in HR; Hdt, X, Joseph+) *crowd together* 1 Macc 5:27cj.*

συνεῖπον (Lysias, X+) *talk together, agree* Sus 38G; Da 2:9L.*

συνεκκεντέω (h.l.) *stab all together* 2 Macc 5:26.*

συνεκλάσθην aor pass of BDAG: συγκλάω.

συνεκπολεμέω (DiodS) *fight with* (w. dat of advantage *on behalf of*) Dt 1:30; 20:4; Wsd 5:20.*

συνεκτρέφω 2 aor pass ptc συνεκτραφείς (Pla+) *raise together;* (pass) *grow up w., be raised w.* 2 Ch 10:8.*

συνεκτρίβω (h.l.) *destroy altogether* Wsd 11:19.*

συνέκτροφος, -ον (h.l.) *reared w.* 1 Macc 1:6.*

συνελαύνω aor συήλασα pass συνηλάσθην plpf pass συνηλάσμην (Hom+) *drive together,* > *drive, compel* 2 Macc 4:42; (pass) *be driven or compelled* 4:26; 5:5.*‡

συνέλευσις (pap, Plu+) *meeting place.* Judg 9:46Bff mistrans of צריח *cellar, vault, cave.*‡

συνέλκω aor συνέλκυσα (Aristoph, Pla+) *pull along,* > *draw together, associate* Ps 27:3.*

συνεξορμάω (Isocr, X+) *set out together* (pap) 1 Esdr 8:11.*

συνεπακολουθέω (Pla+) *follow along, accompany* Num 32:11f.*

συνεπισκέπτομαι 2 aor pass συνεπεσκέπην *survey at the same time, enumerate along w. others in the census* (no //) Num 1:47G, 49; 2:33; 26:62.*

συνεπίσταμαι (Gorgias of Leontini, X+) *know perfectly well* Job 9:35; 19:27.*

συνεπισχύω (X, Polyb+) *join in helping* (τινί) 2 Ch 32:3; Esth 8:12s.*

συνεπιτίθημι (Thu+) **1.** *add or put on more* Num 12:11. **2.** *join together to attack* (= BDAG) Dt 32:27; Ps 3:7; Ob 13; Zech 1:15.*‡

συνερίζω (pap) *contend w.* (τινί), *fight w.* 2 Macc 8:30.*

συνεσπάσθην see συσπάω.

συνεστραμμένος pf pass ptc of συστρέφω 1 Macc 12:50.

συνέταιρος, -ου, ὁ (11x, Sappho, Hdt+) *companion, friend* Judg 15:2A; 1 Esdr 6:3; Da 2:7L; (fem) -ρίς, -ίδος ἡ Judg 11:37f.

συνετμήθην aor pass of BDAG: συντέμνω.

συνέχω aor subj συσχῶ pass inf συσχεθῆναι **1.b.** συνέχων *sustaining, including,* (chiefly) *attendant* 2 Macc 10:10. **2.b.** *hold back, hoard* (grain, no //) Pr 11:26; (pass) *be stopped or shut* PsSol 17:19. 3 Km 20:21 συνεχόμενον καὶ ἐγκαταλελειμμένον s.t. of עצור ועזוב prob *bound or free* as if *sustained or abandoned*.‡

συνζ- see **συζ-**.

συνήγμαι 3rd sg συνῆκται, pf pass of συνάγω.

συνήθης, -ες (Soph, Thu+) *habitual, usual* (= BDAG); (subst, c. HR) *acquaintance, habitual companion* 2 Macc 3:31.*‡

συνηλασ- see **συνελαύνω**.

συνηλικία, -ας, ἡ (ins [IV CE]) *group of contemporaries or comrades* Da 1:10VL.*

συνῆλιξ, gen **-ικος** (c. HR; Aeschyl+) *contemporary, comrade* Da 1:10Θ.*

συνημμένος see **συνάπτω**.

συνηχέω (Aristot+) *resound together* (παρακειμ. τοπους συνηχ- Polyb 2.29.6) 3 Macc 6:17.*

συνθέλω (Aristot+) *consent, agree* Dt 13:9.*

σύνθεμα, -ατος, τό (late form of σύνθημα, q.v.; Hdt, Pla+) *anything agreed upon,* > *agreement* (cf. X ANAB 4.6.20) Eccl 12:11VL.*

σύνθεσις **2.** (pl) *ingredients* (for a compound, no //) Ex 35:28. Ex 31:11; Lev 4:7; 2 Ch 13:11 etc θυμιαμα συνθεσεως, Ex 38:25; Sir 49:1 etc σύνθεσις θυμιάματος all mistrans of קטרת סמים *fragrant or spicy smoke, smoke of incense,* relating סמים *fragrance, incense* (appears only in this phrase) to שים *put, place* (cf. confusion of ס/ש in related vb סמם in MT at 2Kg 9:30; Job 13:27).‡

σύνθετος, -ον (X, Pla+) *mixed, compounded* Ex 30:7.*

συνθήκη, -ης, ἡ (15x, Aeschyl+) *agreement, pact, covenant* 1 Macc 10:26; Wsd 1:16; PsSol 8:10; Is 28:15; Da 11:6.

σύνθημα, -ατος, τό (Hdt, Soph+) *prearranged signal, password* (X ANAB 1.8.16 Ζευς σωτηρ και νικη) 2 Macc 8:23; 13:15. Judg 12:6A corresp to N LOC *Shibboleth,* in context used as password.*

συνίημι **2.** (Hom, Hdt+) *be aware of, pay attention to* Job 31:1; *perceive, take notice of* (τινός) Ps 5:2; > *survey, review* (no //, ἐν τινί) 2 Esdr 8:15. 4 Km 18:7 mistrans of שכל (hiph) *act w. devotion, flourish, have success* as if *understand, perceive*.‡

συνίστημι **A.1.** *array oneself for battle, sustain* (a siege) 1 Esdr 2:17. **B.1.** (aor act intr) *unite, take a stand* (ἐπί *against*) Num 16:3.‡

συνίστωρ, -ορος, ὁ or **ἡ** (Soph+) *confidante* Job 16:19.*

συννεφέω (LSJ: -νέφω, Aristoph+) *gather clouds* Gen 9:14.*

συννεφής, -ές (Eur+) *clouded over* Dt 33:28.*

συννοέω (Soph+) *comprehend, understand* 2 Macc 5:6; 11:13; 14:3.*

σύννους, -ουν (Hippocr, Aristot+) *deep in thought, gloomy* 1 Esdr 8:68.*

σύννυμφος, -ου, ἡ (LXX+) *fellow daughter-in-law, sister-in-law* Ruth 1:15.*

συνοδία, -ας, ἡ (Strabo, ins+) *group of fellow travelers, caravan;* 2 Esdr 17:5, 65 renders יחש (vb or noun) *register by family or genealogy,* appar mistrans (c. BDAG, LSJ), understood as clan groups who were *travelers together out of exile*.‡

σύνοδος¹, -ου, ὁ (Manetho+) *fellow traveler;* Dt 33:14 mistrans of גֶּרֶשׁ *product* as if fr גרש *drive out* (Sam גרוש *those expelled*).*‡

σύνοδος², -ου, ἡ (Hdt+) **1.** *(cultic) assembly or guild* 3 Km 15:13. **2.** *conspiracy* Jer 9:1.*‡

συνοδυνάομαι (h.l.) *suffer together* Sir 30:10.*

συνοίκησις, -εως, ἡ (Hdt+) *cohabitation* (in marriage) Tob 7:14S.*

συνοικίζω (7x, Hdt+) **1.** *allow or cause to live with, give in marriage* (ξυν-) 1 Esdr 8:81; *take in marriage* 89; (pass) *be bound in marriage* Dt 21:13. **2.** (pass) *be united in a city or community* Sir 16:4; Is 62:4VL.

συνολκή, -ῆς, ἡ (LXX+) *gasping, sucking in* Wsd 15:15.*

σύνολος, -ον (8x, Pla+) *in common, general;* τὸ σύνολον (neut acc as adv) *without exception, in any or every case* Esth 8:12; 3 Macc 3:29ff; Sir 9:9.

συνομολογέω (Hdt+) *agree;* (impers pass) *one must agree or concede* 4 Macc 13:1.*‡

συνοράω **3.** *look on together* 2 Macc 7:4.‡

συνούλωσις, -εως, ἡ   (LXX+) *closing and scarring over of a wound* (οὐλή) Jer 40:6.*

συνουσιασμός, -οῦ, ὁ   (LXX+) *sexual intercourse* 4 Macc 2:3; Sir 23:6.*

συνταγή, -ῆς, ἡ   (ins+) *thing prescribed or directed,* > *signal* Judg 20:38A; PsSol 4:5; (of times) *as directed* 2 Esdr 10:14.*

σύνταγμα, -ατος, τό   (Isocr, X+) **1.** *book, treatise* (DiodS 1.3) 2 Macc 2:23. **2.** *body of doctrine* (Plu) Job 15.8.*

συντάσσω   **2.** (mid) *organize themselves, agree together* 1 Esdr 2:12, 19.‡

συντέλεια   **2.** *consummation, fulfillment* (of prophecy) 1 Esdr 2:1. **3.** *destruction, annihilation* (no //, cf. BDAG: συντελέω *bring to an end, destroy* 1 Esdr 1:53; Pr 1:19; Is 1:28 [also no // outside LXX and Test12Patr]) Judg 20:40; 4 Km 13:17; 2 Esdr 9:14; 1 Macc 3:42; Ps 58:13f; Sir 21:9; Am 1:14; Ezk 13:13. 1 Km 8:3 mistrans of בֶּצַע *profit* as if fr בצע piel *bring to an end*; Am 8:8; 9:5 mistrans of כֻּלָּהּ *all of it* (so also Hab 1:9, 15 כֻּלֹּה) as if כָּלָה *annihilation*; Job 30:2 mistrans of כלח *vigor, maturity* as if כלה *annihilation*.‡

συντελέω   **1.b.** (cf. **3.**) *bring to an end,* > *kill* (no //) Tob 8:19S. 1 Km 20:34 mistrans of כלם hiph *disgrace, abuse* as if כלה hiph *bring to an end, destroy*.‡

συντήκω   pf συντέτηκα (not in HR; AntiphoSoph, Eur+) *melt, liquefy,* > (fig) *waste away, pine* 2 Km 13:4vL.*

συντίθημι   **2.b.** (abs) *come to terms, make a covenant* (Pind, Hdt, X+) 3 Km 16:28c.‡

συντίμησις, -εως, ἡ   (pap) *valuation, assessment, worth* Lev 27:4, 18; Num 18:16; 4 Km 12:5; 23:35.*

συντρέφω   (X+) *feed together;* (mid/pass) *be fed together* Da 1:10L, *be brought up together* 4 Macc 13:21, 24.*

συντρίβω   2 Esdr 12:13, 15 mistrans of שׁבר *inspect, examine* as if שׁבר *break*.‡

συντριμμός, -οῦ, ὁ   (LXX) *shattering, destruction* 2 Km 22:5; Am 5:9; Mi 2:8; Zeph 1:10; Jer 4:20.*

σύντριψις, -εως, ἡ   (LXX+) *destruction, crushing defeat* Josh 10:10.*

συντροφία, -ας, ἡ   (Polyb+) *common upbringing* 3 Macc 5:32; 4 Macc 13:22.*

συντροχάζω   (LXX+) *run together;* Eccl 12:6 mistrans of נרץ (רצץ niph) *be cracked or broken* as if fr רוץ *run*.*

συνυφαίνω   (Hom, Hdt+) *weave together* Ex 28:32; 36:10, 17.*

συνυφή, -ῆς, ἡ   (Pla+) *web* Ex 36:27.*

συνῳκηκυῖα   fem pf ptc of BDAG: συνοικέω; *having become married* Sir 42:9.

συνωμότης, -ου, ὁ   (Hdt+) *ally, confederate* Gen 14:13.*

συνωρίς, -ίδος, ἡ   (Aeschyl+) *pair, team* (of horses) Is 21:9.*

σύριγμα, -ατος, τό   (Soph+) *piping, whistling or hissing sound* Jer 18:16.*

συριγμός   = συρισ-, q.l.

σύριγξ, -ιγγος, ἡ   (Hom+) *shepherd's flute or pipe* Da 3:5ff.*

συρίζω   fut συριεῖ aor ἐσύρισαν (13; Aeschyl+) *whistle or hiss* (in dismay or derision) 3 Km 9:8; Job 27:23; Zeph 2:15; Jer 19:8; (in summons) Is 5:26; 7:18; (of wind) Wsd 17:17; (of snake) Jer 26:22.

συρισμός, -οῦ, ὁ   (7x, X, Aristot+) **1.** *piping* Judg 5:16. **2.** *whistle, hissing* (derision or dismay) 2 Ch 29:8; Mi 6:16; Jer 19:8 (συριγ-); (of snake) Wsd 17:9 (συριγ-).

Συριστί   (HRSupp as N PROP; X, pap+) in *Syrian* or *Aram* (cf. BDAG: Ἑβραϊστι, etc) 4 Km 18:26 = Is 36:11; 2 Esdr 4:7; Da 2:4.*

συρράπτω   (Hes, Hdt+) *stitch together* Ezk 13:18; (pass, fig) *hold together* Job 14:12.*

συρράσσω   (Thu+) *dash together, throw down together* Jdth 9:8vL.*

συρρέμβομαι   (DiogL+) *roam together* Pr 13:20vL.*

σύρρηγμα, -ατος, τό   (Plu?) *collision* Jer 18:16vL.*

σύρω   **2.** (intr act) *crawl along* Dt 32:24; Mi 7:17; (pres ptc) *trailing along* Is 28:2.‡

σῦς, συός, ὁ or ἡ   (Hom+, = BDAG: ὗς) *pig* Ps 79:14.*

συσκευάζω   (Thu+) *take control of* Ex 3:22vL.*

συσκήνιος, -ου, ὁ   (h.l.) *tent mate, fellow sojourner* Ex 16:16.*

σύσκηνος, -ου, ὁ   (Thu+: *fellow soldier*) *tent mate, fellow sojourner* Ex 3:22; 16:16VL.*

συσκιάζω   (Hes+) *overshadow, cast shade* Ex 25:20; Num 4:5; Hos 4:13.*

σύσκιος, -ον   (X, Pla+) *thickly shaded* 3 Km 14:23; SSol 1:16; Ezk 6:13.*

συσκοτάζω   (10x, Thu+; class alw impers: *it gets dark*) *become dark or overcast* 3 Km 18:45; Am 8:9; Jer 4:28; Ezk 30:18; (trans, no //) *darken* Am 5:8; Ezk 32:7.

συσπάω   aor pass συνεσπάσθην (X ANAB 1.5.10; Pla+) *pull or draw together;* (pass) *be drawn together, be shriveled* La 5:10.*‡

συσσεισμός, -οῦ, ὁ   (LXX+) *upheaval,* > *earthquake* 3 Km 19:11f; Sir 22:16; *whirlwind* 4 Km 2:1, 11; 1 Ch 14:15; Na 1:3; Jer 23:19.*

συσσείω   aor συνέσεισας (Aristot+) *shake thoroughly* Ps 28:8; 59:4; Job 4:14; Sir 16:19; Hg 2:7.*

συσσύρω   (LXX+) *sweep along* (w. oneself), > *carry off* 2 Macc 5:16.*

συστέλλω   aor pass συνεστάλην 6. *cast down, abase, reduce* 1 Macc 5:3; (pass) 3:6; Judg 8:28B; 3 Macc 5:33; (fig) *be depressed or intimidated* 2 Macc 6:12.‡

σύστημα or -τεμα, -ατος, τό   (8x, Pla+) 1. *army* 1 Ch 11:16; 2 Macc 8:5; *community* (of people) 3 Macc 3:9. 2. *collection, body* (of water, no //) Gen 1:10; Ezk 31:4. Jer 28:32 mistrans of אגם *bulwark* as if אגם *pool.*

συστράτευμα, -ατος, τό   (dub; not in LSJ) *band of soldiers* 4 Km 14:19VL.*

σύστρεμμα, -ατος, τό   (Aristot+) *band* (of soldiers), *troop* (Polyb+) Num 32:14; 2 Km 4:2; 15:12; 2 Esdr 8:3; (of conspirators, no // but cf. συστρέφω) 4 Km 14:19; 15:30.*.

συστρέφω   2.b. *(be) gather(ed) together,* > (Thu+) *conspire* (mid/pass) 2 Km 15:31; 4 Km 9:14; (act, no //) 3 Km 16:9. 3. *turn around, cause to go in a tight circle* Sir 38:29; (pass) *twist up, become knotted* Gen 43:30.‡

συστροφή, -ῆς, ἡ   (Hdt, Pla+) 1. *disorderly mass* Judg 14:8A; *crowd, mob* 1 Macc 14:44; Ps 63:3; Hos 13:12. 2. *conspiracy* 4 Km 15:15; Am 7:10 (no //, but cf. συστρέφω). 3. συστ. πνεύματος *whirlwind* (Theophr+) Sir 43:17;

Hos 4:19. Jer 4:16 mistrans of צור *besiege* as if *collect.* Ezk 13:21 mistrans of מצודה *captured game* as if fr צור *collect.*‡

συστροφία, -ας, ἡ   (Polyb?) *versatility? f.l.* for συντροφία, 3 Macc 5:32VL.*

συσφίγγω   (LXX+) *bind together, bind tightly* Ex 36:28; Lev 8:7; 3 Km 18:46; *shut or clench tightly* Dt 15:7.*

συσχῶ   aor of συνέχω.

συχνός, -ή, -όν   (Hdt, Aristoph+) *great, extensive;* (pl) *many* 2 Macc 5:9.*

σφαγιάζω   (Hdt, Aristoph+) *slaughter* (obj sacrificial offering) 4 Macc 16:20; (pass) 13:12 (both fig, of Abraham and Isaac).*

σφάγιον   2. *victim to be slaughtered* (but specif not as sacrifice) Lev 22:23.‡

σφάζω   aor pass ἐσφάγην (inf Is 14:21; fut pass Num 11:22).‡

σφαιρωτήρ, -ῆρος, ὁ   (8x, pap) 1. *thong* Gen 14:23 (W: better σφυρ-, cf. LSJSup σφαιρ-). 2. *ornamental ball* Ex 25:31ff.*

σφακελίζω   (Hdt+) *be gangrenous, be infected* Lev 26:16; *be convulsed* Dt 28:32.*

σφαλερός, -ά, -όν   (Aeschyl, Hdt+) *causing to trip or fall, perilous* Pr 5:6.*

σφάλμα, -ατος, τό   (Hdt, Eur+) *slip, fall;* (fig) *failure* Pr 29:25.*

σφενδονάω   (Thu+) *sling, throw* 1 Km 17:49; (fig) 25:29.*

σφενδόνη, -ης, ἡ   (Hom+) 1. *sling* 1 Km 17:40; 25:29; 2 Ch 26:14; Jdth 9:7; Pr 26:8; Sir 47:4; Zech 9:15. 2. *bullet, stone* (thrown by a sling, X+) 1 Macc 6:51.*

σφενδονήτης, -ου, ὁ   (Hdt+) *slinger* Judg 20:16; 4 Km 3:25; 1 Ch 12:2; Jdth 6:12; 1 Macc 9:11.*

σφηκία, -ας, ἡ   (so Ra, Gött in Pentateuch; not in LSJ) or σφηκιά, -ᾶς, ἡ (LSJ: Soph+, Ra at Josh 24:12) *nest or swarm of wasps* Ex 23:28; Dt 7:20; Josh 24:12.*

σφήν, σφηνός, ὁ   (Aeschyl, Aristoph+) *wedge* (as instrument of torture) 4 Macc 8:13; 11:10.*

σφηνόω   (Aristot+) *fix w. a wedge* Judg 3:23, 24B; 2 Esdr 17:3.*

σφήξ, -ηκός, ὁ   (Hom+) *wasp* Wsd 12:8.*

σφιγγία, -ας, ἡ   (h.l.) *restraint, constriction, miserliness* Sir 11:18.*

σφίγγω (Hippocr, Aeschyl+) *bind tight, tie up* 4 Km 12:11; (pass) Pr 5:22.*

σφοδρός, -ά, -όν (Hippocr, Thu, Pla+; adv since Hom) *violent* (of wind or the sea) Ex 10:19; 15:10; 2 Esdr 19:11; Wsd 18:5; comp neut as adv σφοδρότερον (fig) *more vehemently* 4 Macc 5:32; 13:22.*‡

σφόνδυλος, -ου, ὁ (Hippocr, Aristoph+; σπόνδ- Strabo+) *vertebra* 4 Macc 10:8; (specif) *cervical vertebra* Lev 5:8.*

σφῦρα, -ης, ἡ (7x, Hom, Hdt+) *hammer* Judg 4:21; Sir 38:28; Is 41:7.

σφυροκόπος, -ον (LXX+) *hammer-wielding* Gen 4:22.*

σχάζω (Hippocr, Pind+) *let fall*; (pass) *fall* Am 3:5.*

σχεδία, -ας, ἡ (Hom+) *raft* 3 Km 5:23 = 2 Ch 2:15; 1 Esdr 5:53; Wsd 14:5f.*

σχεδιάζω (Pla+) *act carelessly* Bar 1:19.*

σχετλιάζω (Aristoph, Theophr+) *complain bitterly, protest angrily* 4 Macc 3:12; 4:7.*

σχέτλιος, -α, -ον (Hom, Hdt+) *headstrong, unflinching* (e.g., from cruelty), > *cruel, evil* (Aeschyl, Hdt+) 2 Macc 15:5.*

σχίδαξ, -ακος, ὁ (DiodS+) *piece of (split) wood* 3 Km 18:33ff.*

σχίζα, -ης, ἡ (11x, Hom+) *lath, shaft,* > *missile, arrow* 1 Km 20:20ff; 1 Macc 10:80.*

σχῖνος, -ου, ὁ (Hdt+) *mastich tree* (a type of sumac) Sus 54.*

σχιστός, -ή, -όν (Soph+) *split (lengthwise)* Is 19:9.*

σχοίη 2 aor opt (as if -μι vb; cf. Smyth, GREEK GRAMMAR 683, 687) of ἔχω; *may he hold (to)* Job 17:9.

σχοινίον 2. *measuring line* Ps 15:6.‡

σχοινισμός, -οῦ, ὁ (pap+) *measurement, allotment* (of land) Josh 17:5.*

σχοῖνος, -ου, ὁ (Hom, Hdt+) 1. *reed, rush* Mi 6:5; Joel 4:18; *pen, stylus* (for writing) Jer 8:8. 2. *measure* (of length) 2 Macc 11:5; Jer 18:15. 3. *bed* (of rushes, Hom+) Ps 138:3.*

σχολάζω 3. (abs) *cease acting, linger* Ps 45:11.‡

σχολαστής, -οῦ, ὁ (LXX+) *person of leisure, idler* Ex 5:17.*

σώζω 1.b.β. (pass) *escape, get away safely* 4 Km 19:37; 2 Ch 20:24.‡

σωματοποιέω (Polyb, DiodS+) *refresh, revive* (Polyb 3.90.4) Ezk 34:4.*

σωματοφύλαξ, -ακος, ὁ (Polyb+) *bodyguard* 1 Esdr 3:4; Jdth 12:7; 3 Macc 2:23.*

σῶος or σῶος, -α, -ον (Hom, Hdt+ [σῶς], X+) *sound; unharmed, safe* 2 Macc 12:24; 3 Macc 2:7; *undamaged, intact* 2 Macc 3:15, 22; Bel 17Θ.*

σωρηδόν (Polyb+) *in heaps* Wsd 18:23.*

σωρηχ translit of שׂרֵק *choice grapes* Is 5:2 (Odes 10:2 σωρηκ).*

σωρός, -οῦ, ὁ (9x, Hes, Hdt+) *heap, pile* Josh 7:26; 2 Ch 31:6ff.

σωτηρία 3. *security, safety* Gen 26:31.‡

σωφερ translit of שׁוֹפָר *ram's horn, trumpet* 1 Ch 15:28.*

Τ

ταινία, -ας, ἡ (Empedocles, X+) *band, strip* (of wood, ins) Ezk 27:5.*

τακείς aor pass ptc of BDAG: τήκω Ps 57:9.

τακτικός, -ή, -όν (X+: *tactical*) (subst) *administrator, overseer* (no //) Da 6:2ff Θ.*

τάλας, -αινα, -αν (Hom+) *wretched, suffering* 4 Macc 8:17; 12:4; Wsd 15:14; Is 6:5.*

ταμίας, -ου, ὁ (Hom, Hdt+) *steward, treasurer* Is 22:15.*

ταμιεύω (Aristoph, Pla+) *dispense*; (mid) *regulate, control* Pr 29:11; *store up* 4 Macc 12:12.*

τἀνδρός 2 Macc 14:28 (crasis) = τοῦ ἀνδρός.

τανύω (Hom+) *stretch out* Job 9:8; *string* (a bow) Sir 43:12.*

τάξις 5. *company of troops, battalion* 2 Macc 8:22.*‡

ταπεινότης, -ητος, ἡ (Hdt+) *humility, abasement* Sir 13:20.*

ταράσσω Eccl 10:10 mistrans of קלל pilpel *whet, sharpen* as if *shake*; cf. πρόσωπον.‡

ταραχώδης, -ες (Hdt+) *terrifying, dreadful* Ps 90:3; Wsd 17:9.*

ταριχεύω (Aeschyl, Hdt+) *preserve* (meat, w. salt; X Anab 5.4.28) EpJer 27.*

ταρσός, -οῦ, ὁ (Hom+) *flat expanse* (of wing) Wsd 5:11; *palm* (of hand) Da 10:10Θvl.*

τάρταρος, -ου, ὁ (Hom, Aeschyl+) *Tartarus* (n loc), *nether world* Pr 30:16; Job 40:20; 41:24.*

τάσσω Att τάττω (2Macc 10:28) **1.** Ezk 11:7G (q.l.; mt שׂים). **3.** *draw up in battle order* (= παρατάσσω, common in class, but act intr abs no //) Judg 20:30ffA; pass ptc *(forces) in battle array* SSol 6:4.‡

ταυρηδόν (Aristoph+) *like a bull, in bull-like fashion,* > *w. open eyes, boldly* (Pla Phaedo 117b) 4 Macc 15:19.*

τάφρος, -ου, ἡ (Hom, Hdt+) *ditch, trench* Mi 5:5.*

ταχύς 2 Esdr 7:6 mistrans of מהיר *diligent, skilled* as if fr מהר *be quick*. Na 1:14 mistrans of קלל *be worthless* as if *be swift.*‡

ταώς, ταῶνος, ὁ (AntiphanesCom, Aristoph+) *peacock* 3 Km 10:22vl.*

τεθέληκα (late) pf of θέλω (earlier ἠθέληκα, fr ἐθέλω) Ps 40:12.

τεθλασμένος pf pass ptc of BDAG: θλάω.

τεθνεώς pf ptc of BDAG: θνήσκω.

τεθωρακισμένος see θωρακίζω.

τείνω pf τέτακα pass ptc τεταμένος (9x, Hom+) *stretch out, spread* Esth 1:6; Pr 7:16; *reach out* 3 Macc 5:25; Ezk 30:22; *draw* (a bow) 1 Ch 5:18; Jer 27:14.

τείσω see τίνω.

τειχήρης, -ες (11x, Hdt+) *walled, fortified* Num 13:19; Josh 19:35; 2 Ch 11:5ff; Jer 4:5.

τειχίζω pf pass ptc τετειχισμένος (11; Hom+) *wall in, fortify* Jdth 4:5; 5:1; (pass ptc) *fortified, walled* Lev 25:29; 1 Km 27:8; Hos 8:14; Ezk 17:4.

τειχιστής, -οῦ, ὁ (lxx+) *builder, mason* 4 Km 12:13; 22:6.*

τεκνοποιέω (7x, X+) *produce a child* Gen 11:30; 16:2; 30:3; Is 65:23; (trans, no //) Jer 36:6; 38:8. Jer 12:2 mistrans of הלך *go on* as if ילד *bear children*.

τεκνοφόνος, -ον (h.l.) *child-murdering* Wsd 14:23.*

τεκταίνω 2 aor mid ἐτεκτηνόμην (13; Hom+) **1.** *work, contrive* (metal) Bar 3:18. **2.** (fig) *devise, plan, scheme* (act or mid) Ps 128:3; Pr 3:29; Ezk 21:36.

τεκτονικός, -ή, -όν (X+) *of carpentry* Ex 31:5.*

τέκτων **2.** (fig) *worker, contriver* (cf. τεκταίνω) Pr 14:22.‡

τελαμών, -ῶνος, ὁ (Hom, Hdt+) *bandage* 3 Km 21:38, 41.*

τέλειος **1.α.γ.** (pl fem subst; agrees w. preceding ὁλοκαυτώσεις?) *perfect or appropriate sacrifices* (no //; renders שְׁלָמִים *peace offerings, communion sacrifices*) Judg 20:26B; 21:4B. 2 Esdr 2:63 mistrans of תֻּמִּים *oracular instrument* as if תם *(be) perfect.*‡

τελειόω **2.b.β.** (act) *fill* (the hands) Lev 8:33; Num 3:3 (cf. Sir 45:15); (pass) *be filled* (w. respect to one's hands), > *consecrate/be consecrated to the priesthood* (Heb, no //) Lev 4:5; 21:10.‡

τελείωσις **3.** *filling in full measure* (no //; t.t. for act of consecration, "filling" the hand of the priest) Ex 29:22, 26; (cf. 29:9, 29 etc); Lev 7:37.‡

τελεσιουργέω (Aristot, Polyb+) *accomplish perfectly* Pr 19:7.*

τελεσφόρος, -ον (Hom+) *bringing fulfillment;* (subst) title of pagan god and priest (trag, ins), > *pagan priestess* (Heb קדשה *cult prostitute*) Dt 23:18.*

τελετή, -ῆς, ἡ (Hdt+) *rite, ritual* (pagan; cf. τελέω 4.) 3 Km 15:12; 3 Macc 2:30; Wsd 12:4; 14:15, 23; Am 7:9.*

τελέω **4.** (pass) *be consecrated to* (τινί), *be initiated* (into a mystery cult, Hdt 4.79) Num 25:3; Ps 105:28; Hos 4:14 (ptc) renders קָדֵשׁ *cult prostitute* as *initiate*.*‡

τελίσκομαι (ins+) *be initiated or dedicated* (in pagan cult; Heb קדש *cult prostitute*) Dt 23:18.*

τελωνέω (pap, Strabo+) *collect taxes;* (pass) *be assessed and/or paid* 1 Macc 13:39.*

τέμενος, -εος or **-ους, τό** (11x, Hom+) *shrine, sacred precinct* 1 Macc 1:47; 2 Macc 1:15; Hos 8:14; Ezk 6:4.

τέμνω fut τεμῶ aor pass ἐτμήθη (10; Hom+) *cut, cleave* Ex 36:10; 4 Km 6:4; Wsd 5:12; *prune, trim* Lev 25:3; Is 5:6; *cut off* 4 Macc 9:17; *hew* (stone) Da 2:34ΘR (Gött ἀποσχίζω, RECTE).

τένων, -οντος, ὁ (Hom, Hippocr, Eur+) *tendon, ligament* 4 Macc 9:28.*

τερατεύομαι (Aristoph+) *talk marvels,* > *talk strangely,* hence *ignorantly or deceivingly* 3 Macc 1:14.*

τερατοποιός, -όν (Proclus) *wonder-working* 2 Macc 15:21; 3 Macc 6:32.*

τερατοσκόπος, -ου, ὁ (Pla, Aristot+) *diviner, interpreter of omens* Dt 18:11; Zech 3:8.*

τερατώδης, -ες (Aristoph+) *portentous, monstrous* Wsd 17:9VL.*

τερέμινθος, -ου, ἡ (9x, = τέρμ- Aristot+, τερέβ- Sir Gött, Is) **1.** *terebinth tree* Gen 14:6; Josh 24:26; Sir 24:16; Is 1:30. **2.** *fruit* (of same), *pistachio nut* Gen 43:11; Is 6:13. Josh 17:9 unexpl.

τέρετρον, -ου, τό (Hom+) *gimlet, awl* Is 44:12.*

τερπνότης, -ητις, ἡ (LXX+) *delight, pleasure* Ps 15:11; 26:4.*

τέρπω aor pass ἐτέρφθην (12; Hom+) *delight, cheer* 2 Macc 15:39; Ps 64:9; Sir 1:12; (pass) *be (made) happy* Ps 34:9; Job 39:13; Wsd 1:13; Zech 2:14.

τέρψις, -εως, ἡ (Hes+) *delight, enjoyment* 3 Km 8:28 (Heb רִנָּה *cry of joy,* LO mss δέησις); 1 Macc 3:45; 3 Macc 4:6; Wsd 8:18; Zeph 3:17.*

τεσσαρακοστός, -ή, -όν (15x, Aristoph, Thu+) *fortieth* Num 33:38; 3 Km 6:1; 1 Macc 1:20.

τεταγμένως adv (X [OEC 8.3] fr pf pass ptc of τάσσω) *in orderly fashion* 1 Macc 6:40.*

τέτακα pf τεταμένος pf pass ptc of τείνω.

τέταχα pf of BDAG: τάσσω.

τετευχ-, τετυχ- see BDAG τυγχάνω.

τετιλμένος pf pass ptc of BDAG: τίλλω Is 18:7.

τέτοκα pf of BDAG: τίκτω, 1 Km 4:20; Job 38:28.

τετράδραχμον, -ου, τό (Ps-Pla, ins) *silver (four-drachma) coin* Job 42:11.*

τετραίνω fut τρήσω aor ἔτρησα pf pass ptc τετρημένος (Hom, Hdt+) *drill, bore* 4 Km 12:10; Pr 23:27; Is 44:12; *pierce* 4 Km 18:21; Job 40:24.*

τετρακισμύριοι, -αι, -α (X+) *forty thousand* Josh 4:13.*

τετρακοσιοστός, -ή, -όν (Dinarchus, pap) *four hundredth* 3 Km 6:1.*

τετραμερής, -ές (Aristot+) *arrayed in four divisions or battalions* 2 Macc 8:21.*

τετράπεδος, -ον (Polyb+) *four-sided or four-faced* (DiodS of stones) 2 Ch 34:11; Jer 52:4R.*

τετραπλάσιος, -α, -ον (Pla+) *four-fold;* adv τετραπλασίονα (h.l.) 2 Km 12:6VL.

τετραπλῶς (adv of BDAG: -πλοῦς) *fourfold, four-sided* 3 Km 6:33.*

τετράποδος, -ον (VL, Polyb+) *of four feet* (in length); *four feet long* 1 Macc 10:11; Jer 52:4G.*‡

τετράστιχος, -ον (LXX) *arranged in four rows* Ex 28:17 = 36:17; Wsd 18:24.*

τετρημένος see τετραίνω.

τετριμμένος see τρίβω.

τετρωμένος see τιτρώσκω.

τεύξομαι fut of τυγχάνω (BDAG).

τέφρα, -ας, ἡ (Hom+) *ashes* Tob 6:16; 8:2; Wsd 2:3; Bel 14Θ.*

τεχνάζω (Hdt+) *contrive* (act or mid) Is 46:5.*

τεχνάομαι (Hom+) *craft, shape craftily* Wsd 13:11.*

τεχνῖτις, -ιδος, ἡ (ins+) *craftswoman* (alw of σοφία) Wsd 7:22; 8:6; 14:2.*

τήγανον, -ου, τό (13x, EupolisCom, Aristoph+) *skillet, pan* Lev 2:5; 2 Km 6:19; 1 Ch 9:31; 2 Macc 7:3; Ezk 4:3.*

τηκτός, -ή, -όν (Hippocr, Eur+) *able to be melted* Wsd 19:21.*

τήκω fut τήξει aor ἔτηξα aor pass ἐτάκην pf ptc τετηκώς **2.** *pine for, waste away for* Wsd 1:16.‡

τηλαύγημα, -ατος, τό (h.l.) *whitened place, whiteness* Lev 13:23.*

τηλαύγησις, -εως, ἡ (h.l.) *brightness, splendor* Ps 17:13.*

τηρέω 4. *watch for, seek opportunity* 2 Macc 14:29; *watch guardedly, watch for opportunity* *to strike* (no //; Heb שׁוף *attack*, rare—ἐκτρίβω Job 9:17; cf. Sa, reversing "head" and "heel" to make sense—i.e., *protect head, heel*) Gen 3:15.‡

τήρησις 3.b. *safekeeping, preservation* 2 Macc 3:40.‡

τιάρα, -ας, ἡ (Hdt+) *tiara, Persian headdress* (X *Anab* 2.5.23) Ezk 23:15; Da 3:21.*

τίθημι 2 aor mid pl impv θέσθε, inf θέσθαι (2 Km 7:23; not in HR, renders שׂים *put, place*). **1.b.ε.ב.** *regard, consider* 2 Macc 7:12. τιθ- (or διατιθ-) in Is 57:8*vl* renders כרת *come to an agreement, make a covenant*; cf. Hdt+ τιθ-: *make a deposit,* > *mortgage.* 2 Km 12:31 renders MT וישׂם *and he put,* but emend (w. 1 Ch 20:3; cf. LXX L mss καὶ διέπρισεν) to וישׂר *and he ripped (it—the city).*‡

τιθηνέω (Theognis+) *nurse, bring up* Sir 30:9; La 4:5; (fig) *foster, cherish* 3 Macc 3:15.*

τιθηνία, -ας, ἡ (h.l.) *act or period of nursing* 4 Macc 16:7.*

τιθηνός, -όν (7x, Eur+) *nursing, fostering;* (subst) *nurse, guardian* Num 11:12; Ruth 4:16; 3 Macc 1:20; Is 49:23.

τίλλω aor pass ἐτίλην pf pass ptc τετιλμένος.‡

τίμημα, -ατος, τό (Aeschyl+) *valuation, price* Lev 27:27.*

τιμογραφέω (h.l.) *assess for taxation* 4 Km 23:35.*

τιμωρία 2. *relief, rescue* (IIdt+) Da 2:18L.‡

τίναγμα, -ατος, τό (AnthPal) *earthquake, storm* (no //, but OL *tempestas storm*) Job 28:26.*

τινάσσω (Hom+) *shake, thresh* Is 28:27*vl.**

τίνω fut τείσω (c. HR which has τίω; Hom, Hdt+) *pay* (the price), *suffer* (penalty), *undergo* (= BDAG) Pr 27:12; (mid) *avenge oneself on, punish* 20:9c; 24:22, 29.*‡

τιτάν, -ᾶνος, ὁ (HR: *n prop*; Hom+) *titan, giant* Jdth 16:6. 2 Km 5:18, 22 mistrans of רפאים *n loc* as if *giants*.*

τιτρώσκω fut τρώσω (Ezk 28:7G; Ra στρώννυμι) aor ἔτρωσα pass ἐτρώθην pf τέτρωκα pass τέτρωμαι.‡

τμηθ- see τέμνω.

τμητός, -ή, -όν (Soph+) *cut, dressed* (of stone) Ex 20:25.*

τοῖος, -α, -ον (Hom, Aeschyl+, rare in prose) *such as;* (neut pl subst) *such things as these* 2 Esdr 5:3.*

τοκάς, -άδος, ἡ (Hom+) *breeding stock* 3 Km 2:46i.*

τοκετός 2. *being born* (no //) Sir 23:14.*‡

τόκος mistrans/(translit) of תוך *oppression, extortion* Ps 54:12; 71:14; cf. Jer 9:5. 4 Km 4:7 mistrans of נשׁיך *your creditors* (fr נשׁא *make loans at interest,* ptc *creditor*) as if נשׁך *interest.* 2. *childbirth* (Hom+; orig meaning, fr τίκτω) Hos 9:11.‡

τολύπη, -ης, ἡ (Soph, Aristoph+) *ball,* > *gourd* (no //) 4 Km 4:39.*

τομή, -ῆς, ἡ (Hom+) *cutting; stump* Job 15:32; *pruning* SSol 2:12.*

τομίς, -ίδος, ἡ (h.l. f.l.—cf. στομίς) *cutter, knife* Pr 30:14.*

τόμος, -ου, ὁ (Aristoph+) *slice, piece,* > (papyrus) *scroll, sheet* 1 Esdr 6:22; Is 8:1.*

τόξευμα, -ατος, τό (13x, Hdt+) *arrow* Gen 49:23; 4 Km 9:16; 2 Macc 10:30; Pr 7:23; Is 7:24.

τοξεύω (8x, Hom+) *shoot* (bow and arrow) 2 Km 11:20; 2 Ch 35:23; Jer 27:14; (ptc subst) *archer* 2 Km 11:24.

τοξικός, -ή, -όν (Aeschyl+) *for or concerning archery;* (neut subst) *arrow slit, gap in wall* (for archers, no //) Judg 5:28B.*

τοξότης, -ου, ὁ (10x, Hom+) *archer* Gen 21:20; 1 Km 31:3; 1 Ch 10:3; Am 2:15.‡

τοπάδιον (not in LSJ) = τοπάζιον Ps 118:127*vl.**

τοπάρχης, -ου, ὁ (13x, DiodS 6.1.10; pap, ins) *regional commander, governor* Gen 41:34; 4 Km 18:24 = Is 36:9; 1 Esdr 3:2; Esth 3:13a; Da 3:2.

τοπαρχία, -ας, ἡ (ins, pap, Joseph *AJ* 13.125; //) *district* 1 Macc 11:28.*

τόπος Jer 30:2 (Gött 29:9) corrup of το πρόσωπον αυτων (Gött cj, q.l.), > το προς αυτων, > ο τοπος αυτων, mistrans of הפנו (hiph of פנה *turn away*) as if פנה *face.*‡

τορευτός, -ή, -όν (Menand, ins) *carved, worked in relief* Ex 25:18ff; 3 Km 10:22; SSol 5:14; 7:3; Jer 10:9.*

τόσος, -η, -ον (Hom+) *so great, so much* (demonstr pron) Sir 11:11; 13:9.*

τραγέλαφος, -ου, ὁ (Aristoph, Pla, Aristot, DiodS 2:51) *goat-deer* (fantastic creature) Dt 14:5; Job 39:1.*

τρανέομαι (h.l. not in HR or LSJ; but Philo OPIF 127 could be same word; later τρανόω) *become clear or articulate* Is 35:6VL.*

τρανός, -ή, -όν (Soph+) *clear, distinct, articulate* Wsd 7:22; 10:21; Is 35:6.*

τραπήσομαι fut pass of τρέπω Sir 39:27.

τραυματίας, -ου, ὁ (85x, Hdt+) **1.** *wounded man* 2 Macc 4:42; 8:24; 11:12. **2.** (s.t. of חלל *pierced [wounded or dead]*) *casualty* (of war, wounded or dead) Judg 9:40; 1 Km 31:1; 1 Macc 1:18; Ezk 30:11; (fig) Ps 68:27; *killed, corpse* (no //) Gen 34:27; Dt 21:1; 2 Km 1:25; 3 Km 11:15; Jdth 2:8; 1 Macc 9:40; Ps 87:6; Ezk 6:7; 32:20ff.

τραυματίζω pf pass ptc Ezk 28:23; 30:4 etc cf. τραυματίας 2.‡

τραχηλιάω (LXX+) *stiffen or arch one's neck,* (fig) *be haughty* Job 15:25.*

τραχύς **2.** (of animals) *harsh, ferocious* 2 Km 17:8; (fig, of παιδεία) Sir 6:20.‡

τραχύτης, -ητος, ἡ (Democr, X+) *ruggedness;* > *formidable disturbance* 3 Macc 1:23.*

τρέπω 2 aor pass ἐτράπην **3.** (mid) *put to flight, rout* Ex 17:13; Num 14:45; (pass) *turn, be routed* Jdth 15:3; 2 Macc 9:2.‡

τρέφω **3.** *let grow* (hair; Eur BACCH 494) Num 6:5.‡

τρέχω fut δραμοῦμαι 4 Km 11:13 mistrans of רצין *guards, courtiers* (Aram pl; read as N PERS 11:4, 19) as if ptc of רוץ *run* in construction w. העם *the people* (emend MT to *and the people*).‡

τρῆσις, -εως, ἡ (not in HR; Hippocr, Pla+) *perforation, orifice* (Heb מקש *snare, trap*) Job 40:24.*

τρήσω, ἔτρησα see τετραίνω.

τριακάς, -άδος, ἡ (Hes, Hdt+) *thirtieth* (day of the month, ZenP) 2 Macc 11:30.*

τριακονταετής, -ές (Hdt+) *of thirty years; thirty years of age* (of person, Pla REP 539a) 1 Ch 23:3.*

τριακοστός, -ή, -όν (16x; Pind, Hdt+) *thirtieth* 3 Km 16:23; 2 Ch 15:19; 1 Macc 1:10; Sir Prol 27; Jer 52:13.

τρίβολος **2.** (pl) *threshing machine* (Philo-Mech+) 2 Km 12:31.*‡

τρίβος, ὁ or ἡ 1 Ch 26:18; Is 3:12R; 30:11; etc (fem in Is 59:8).‡

τρίβω aor ἔτριψα pf pass ptc τετριμμένος (Hom, Hdt+) **1.** *crush or grind* Num 11:8; Is 38:21; *knead* Jer 7:18. **2.** *wear down;* (pass) *be worn smooth* Pr 15:19.*

τριετής, -ές (Hom, Hdt+) *of three years* 2 Macc 4:23; 14:1; *three years old* 2 Ch 31:16; Is 15:5.*‡

τριετίζω (LXX) *live three years,* (ptc) *three-year-old* Gen 15:9; 1 Km 1:24.*

τριημερία, -ας, ἡ (h.l.) *three-day period or interval* Am 4:4.*

τριηραρχία, -ας, ἡ (X+) *command or outfitting of a trireme* 1 Macc 11:28VL.*

τριήρης, -ρεος, ἡ, gen pl -ρέων or -ῶν (Hipponax, Hdt+) *trireme* 2 Macc 4:20.*

τρικυμία, -ας, ἡ (Eur, Pla+) *set of three waves* (κῦμα) or *thrice-great wave* (fig) 4 Macc 7:2.*

τριμερίζω (h.l.) *apportion in thirds, divide into three parts* Dt 19:3.*

τριόδους, -οντος, ὁ (Pind+) *three-pronged fork, trident* 1 Km 2:13.*

τριπλάσιος, -α, -ον (Aristoph+) *three times over* Sir 43:4VL; (adv) Sir 43:4.*

τριπλοῦς, -ῆ, -οῦν (Aeschyl+) *triple, made up of three* Ezk 42:6.*

τρισάθλιος, -α, -ον (Soph [OEDCOL 372], Menand+) *thrice miserable* 4 Macc 16:6.*

τρισαλιτήριος, -ον (LXX) *thrice-guilty, thoroughly evil* Esth 8:12p; 2 Macc 8:34; 15:3.*

τρισκαίδεκα (Hom+) *thirteen* Num 29:14; 3 Km 7:38; 1 Ch 6:45, 47; 26:11.*

τρισκαιδέκατος, -ον (13x, Hom+) *thirteenth* Gen 14:4; Esth 8:12, 12s; 1 Macc 7:43; Jer 1:2.

τρισμύριοι, -αι, -α (Hdt+) *thirty thousand* Esth 1:7.*

τρισσεύω (LXX) *do something for a third time* 3 Km 18:34; *divide into three groups* 2 Km 18:2VL. 1 Km 20:19f mistrans of שלש piel *do on the third day* as if *do for the third time.*

τρισσός, -ή, -όν (Hes, Pla+) *three-fold* Ezk 42:3 (i.e., *three-storied*). 3 Km 9:22; Ezk 23:23 mistrans of שליש(י) *third man* (in chariot crew) as if שלש *three* (23:15 ὄψις τρίσση renders מראה שלשים *likeness of third men in chariots*). 4 Km 11:10 mistrans of שלט *small shield* as if שלש *three*.

τρισσόω (h.l.) *do for a third time* 3 Km 18:34.*

τρισσῶς (adv of τρισσός, Theophr+) *three times over* 1 Km 20:12; Pr 22:20; Ezk 16:30; 41:16; *in three rows* (no //) 3 Km 7:41f.*

τριστάτης, -ου, ὁ (LXX) *third person*; (in a chariot) *warrior* Ex 14:7; 4 Km 9:25; (in the kingdom, after king and queen) *prime minister* 4 Km 7:2ff; 15:25.*

τριταῖος, -α, -ον (Hdt+) *of three days* (agrees w. subj of relevant verb) 1 Km 9:20; 30:13.*

τρίτος 4. γλῶσσα τρίτη *slanderer's tongue* (AB: same expression found in Rabbinic lit) Sir 28:14f.‡

τρίχαπτος, -ου, ὁ (Pherecr, ins+) *fabric of fine hair* (Heb *silk*?) Ezk 16:10, 13.*

τρίχωμα, -ατος, τό (Hdt+) *hair, head of hair* 1 Esdr 8:68; SSol 4:1; 6:5; Ezk 24:17; Da 7:9L.*

τριώροφος, -ον (Hdt+) *of three stories,* (neut pl subst) *third-story rooms* Gen 6:16; 3 Km 6:8; Ezk 41:7*.

τρομέω (VL τρομάζω, misspelling or spur; Hom+) *tremble* (w. anger) 1 Macc 2:24; (w. fear) Esth 5:9VL.*

τρόπαιον, -ου, τό (Aeschyl, Thu+) *trophy, monument* 2 Macc 5:6; 15:6.*

τροπή 2. *rout, (military) reversal* 1 Macc 5:61. 3 Km 22:35 renders מכה *wound,* unexpl (txt? some cogn of τιτρώσκω?).‡

τρόπις, -ιος, ἡ (Hom+) *ship's keel* Wsd 5:10.*

τροπόω fut mid τροπώσομαι aor mid ἐτροπώσατο aor pass ἐτροπώθην pf pass τετρόπωται (29; pap+) *cause to turn away, put to flight* (act or mid) Judg 4:23B; 2 Km 8:1; 1 Ch 19:16; 1 Macc 4:20; Ps 88:24; Da 7:21L; (pass) *be put to flight* Josh 11:6; 3 Km 22:35 = 2 Ch 18:34; 1 Macc 5:44.

τροφεία, -ας, ἡ (ins: *service as wet nurse*) *act of nourishing or rearing* (no //; better

τροφεῖα [τά; so HR] *milk* [of mother]?) 4 Macc 15:13.*

τροφεύω (LXX+) *nurse, suckle* Ex 2:7; (fig, of God), Bar 4:8.*

τροχαντήρ, -ῆρος, ὁ (Galen+) *instrument of torture* (no //; VL -τήριον only here) 4 Macc 8:13.*

τροχηλάτης, -ου, ὁ (not in HR; Soph Oed Tyr 806; Eur Phoen 39) *charioteer* Sir 20:32G.*

τροχιά 2. *rim* (of wheel) Ezk 27:19.‡

τροχιαῖος, -α, -ον (h.l.) *worked by a wheel* 4 Macc 11:10.*

τροχίζω (AntiphoOr, Aristot+) *break on the wheel, torture* 4 Macc 5:3.*

τροχίσκος, -ου, ὁ (Aristot+) *small wheel or disk; earring* (no //) Ezk 16:12.*

τροχός Ps 82:14; Is 17:13 mistrans of גלגל *tumbleweed* as if גלגל *wheel.*‡

τρυγητής, -οῦ, ὁ (pap) *gatherer of grapes* Sir 33:16; Ob 5; Jer 30:3; 31:32.*

τρύγητος, -ου or -ός, -οῦ (14x, Thu+; for accent cf. W) *grape harvest* Lev 26:5; Judg 8:2; Sir 24:27; Am 4:7; Mi 7:1; Is 24:13.

τρυγίας, -ου, ὁ (LXX+) *lees, dregs* Ps 74:9.*

τρυμαλιά 2. *cave, hole* (in cliff or rocks) Judg 6:2B; 15:8B, 11B; Jer 13:4; 16:16; 30:10.*‡

τρυφαλίς, -ίδος, ἡ (not in HR; Aristoph+: τροφ-) *cheese* 1 Km 17:18.*

τρυφερεύομαι (h.l.) *be delicate or dainty* Esth 5:1a.*

τρυφερός 2. *joyous, delightful* (of Sabbath) Is 58:13 (no //, but cf. BDAG: τρυφή).‡

τρυφερότης, -ητος, τό (Aristot+) *delicacy, daintiness* Dt 28:56.*

τρύφημα, -ατος, τό (Eur+) *object of delight*; (pl) *luxuries* Sir 31:3.*

τρύχω (Hom+) *wear out, consume* Wsd 11:11; 14:15.*

τρώγλη, -ης, ἡ (7x, Aristot+) *hole* 4 Km 12:10; Is 2:19; *cave* 1 Km 14:11; Job 30:6; Is 2:21.

τρωθήσομαι, τρῶσαι, τρώσω see τιτρώσκω.

τύκος or τύχος, -ου, ὁ (not in HR; Eur, ins+) *pole-ax* (Heb מטיל *rod* [? h.l.]) Job 40:18VL.*

τυλόω (Hdt+) *make callous;* (pass) *become calloused* Dt 8:4.*

τυμπανίζω 2. *pound as if on a drum* 1 Km 21:14.*‡

τυμπανίστρια, -ας, ἡ (Demosth+) *drum player* Ps 67:26.*

τύμπανον, -ου, τό (21x, Hdt+) **1.** *drum* Gen 31:27; Judg 11:34; 1 Esdr 5:2; Ps 80:3; Is 5:12. **2.** *instrument of torture* 2 Macc 6:19, 28.

τυπόω (Gorgias of Leontini, Pla+) *form, model* Wsd 13:13; Sir 38:30.*

τυραννέω (Soph+) *rule as a tyrant, tyrannize* 4 Macc 5:28; Pr 28:15; Wsd 10:14; 16:4.*

τυραννία, -ας, ἡ (Xenophanes, pap) *tyranny, despotic conduct* 1 Macc 1:4vL.*

τυραννικός, -ή, -όν (Aeschyl+) *despotic, tyrannical* 3 Macc 3:8; 4 Macc 5:27.*

τυραννίς 2. *princess* (fem of τύραννος, no //, but = class ἡ τυραννός *princess*) Esth 1:18.*‡

τύραννος 2. (pl) *nobles, royal household* Da 4:36Θ.‡

τυρός, -οῦ, ὁ (Hom+) *cheese* Job 10:10.*

τυρόω pf pass ptc τετυρωμένος (Sopater-Com [IV BCE]+) *curdle, make into cheese* Job 10:10; (pass intr) *be curdled* Ps 67:16f; 118:70.*

Υ

ὕβρις Job 37:4 s.t. of גאון *loftiness, majesty* as if *arrogance;* could be rendered as **3.** *damage* (caused by natural elements).‡

ὑβρίστια, -ας, ἡ (not in LSJ) *licentiousness, insolence* Jer 27:31vL.*

ὑβριστικός, -ή, -όν (X, Pla+) *wanton, licentious; conducive to wantonness* (no //) Pr 20:1.*

ὑβρίστρια, -ας, ἡ (h.l.) *dissolute or insolent woman* Jer 27:31.*

ὑγιάζω (10x, Hippocr, Aristot+) *heal, restore to health* Hos 6:2; *make fresh* (of water, i.e., not salt or brackish) Ezk 47:8; (intr) *recover* 4 Km 20:7; (of water) *be fresh* Ezk 47:11; (pass) *recover, be made well* Lev 13:18; Josh 5:8; Job 24:23.

ὑγραίνω (Hippocr, X+) *moisten, make wet;* (pass) *be wetted or soaked* Job 24:8.*

ὑγρασία, -ας, ἡ (Aristot+) *moisture;* (specif) *urine* or *excrement* (no //) Ezk 7:17; 21:12. Jer 31:18 corresp to צמא *dryness*(!), but perh rd (ה)אצ *dung,* for which ὑγρασία may itself be evidence—ὑγραίνω (Hippocr) can refer to loosening of bowels.

ὑδραγωγός, -όν (pap+) *conducting water,* ; (subst) *aqueduct* 4 Km 18:17(= Is 36:2) 20:20; Sir 24:30; Is 41:18.*

ὑδρεύω (12x, Hom+) mid *draw or carry water* Gen 24:11; Ruth 2:9; Jdth 7:13.

ὑδρίσκη, -ης, ἡ (ins+) *small jar* 4 Km 2:20.*

ὑδροφόρος, -ον (Hdt+) *carrying water;* (subst) *water carrier* Dt 29:10; Josh 9:21ff.*

ὕδωρ **1.b.** *liquid* (Aristot) 2 Macc 1:20.‡

ὕειος, -α, -ον (9x, Aristoph+) *of pigs* 2 Macc 6:18; Is 65:4; (neut pl, subst) *pigs* 1 Macc 1:47.

ὑετίζω (LXX+) *cause rain* Job 38:26; Jer 14:22.*

υἱός **2.c.β.** υ. τοῦ θανάτου *destined to death* 1 Km 20:31; 2 Km 12:5; υἱοὶ τῆς ἀποικίας *the exiles* 2 Esdr 4:1; υ. . . ἐτῶν *of (such and such) an age* 4 Km 8:17 etc; *offspring* (fig; arrows in a quiver [= Heb]) La 3:13G.‡

ὑλακτέω (Hom+) *bark, howl* (as a dog) Is 56:10.*

ὕλις, -εως, ἡ (ins, pap) *mud* (cf. ἰλύς) Ps 39:3vL; 68:3vL.*

ὑλοτόμος, -ον (Hom+) *cutting wood* Wsd 13:11.*

ὑλώδης, -ες (Thu+) *wooded.* Job 29:5 renders עמדי *with me,* unexpl.*

ὑμέναιος, -ου, ὁ (Hom, Aeschyl+; rare in prose) *wedding song* 3 Macc 4:6.*

ὕμνησις, -εως, ἡ (DiodS 4.7.4) *singing of praise, (act of) praising* Ps 70:6; 117:14.*

ὑμνητός, -ή, -όν (Pind) *sung about, praised in song* Da 3:54L, 56.*

ὑμνογράφος, -ου, ὁ (Philo+) *composer of hymns or psalms* 4 Macc 18:15.*

ὑμνῳδέω (Aeschyl, Pla+) *sing a song* 1 Ch 25:6.*

ὑπαγορεύω   (X+) *define, designate* 1 Esdr 6:29.*

ὑπάγω   **4.** (trans) *take away, draw off* Ex 14:21.‡

ὕπαιθρος, -ον   (Hippocr, AntiphoOr, X+) *in the open air; in public space* Pr 21:9; *in the field or open country* 2 Macc 15:19.*

ὕπαρ, τό   (indecl; Hom, Aeschyl, Pla+) *waking vision, vision of reality* 2 Macc 15:11.*

ὕπαρξις   Jer 9:9 mistrans of מקנה *cattle* as if *property.*‡

ὕπαρχος, -ου, ὁ   (Hdt, Soph+) *district or provincial governor* 1 Esdr 6:26VL.*

ὑπασπιστής, -οῦ, ὁ   (Hdt, Eur+) *shield bearer, guard* 4 Macc 3:12; 9:11.*

ὕπατος, -ου, ὁ   (7x, Hom+) *highest official* 1 Esdr 3:14; Da 3:2; (specif) *consul* (of Rome, Polyb+) 1 Macc 15:16.

ὑπεκρέω   (Pla, Aristot+) *slip out, slip away* 3 Macc 5:34.*

ὑπεξαιρέω   (Hdt+) *remove;* (mid) *reserve to oneself, put aside, exclude* Gen 39:9.*

ὑπεράγαν   (Eur [written as two words], Strabo+) *beyond measure* 2 Macc 10:34; 13:25G.*‡

ὑπεραγόντως   (ins) *preeminently, surpassingly* 2 Macc 7:20.*

ὑπεράγω   (Polyb+) *be preeminent* 1 Macc 6:43; Sir 33:23; 36:22.*

ὑπεραινετός, -όν   (LXX) *highly praised* Da 3:52; Odes 8:54.*

ὑπεραίρω   (Aeschyl, X+) **1.** *exalt, make great;* (mid) *act arrogantly, give oneself airs* 2 Macc 5:23; (pass) *be exalted* 2 Ch 32:23. **2.** *surpass, go beyond* Pr 31:29; (pass) Ps 71:16. **3.** *go above, overwhelm* Ps 37:5; *be beyond, be too much for* Sir 48:13.*‡

ὑπεράλλομαι   (Hom+) *jump over;* (fig) *leap into prominence* Sir 38:33.*

ὑπεράνω   **2.** (adv, of time) *beyond, from now on* Hg 2:15.‡

ὑπεράνωθεν   (LXX) **1.** (adv) *from up above* Ps 77:23. **2.** (prep w. gen) *from above* Ezk 1:25.*

ὑπέραρσις, -εως, ἡ   (h.l.) *lifting up, exaltation;* Ezk 47:11 mistrans of גבא *pool* as if fr גבה *be high.**

ὑπερασπισμός   La 3:65 mistrans of מגנה *insolence* (or fr מֵגֵן *gift, return*?) as if fr מָגֵן *shield.*‡

ὑπερασπιστεία, -ας, ἡ   (dub) *protection* 4 Macc 15:29VL.*

ὑπερασπίστρια, -ας, ἡ   (h.l.) *protectress* 4 Macc 15:29.*

ὑπερασπιῶ   fut of BDAG: ὑπερασπίζω.

ὑπερβαίνω   **1.b.** *surpass, pass by* 2 Km 18:23. **3.** *step over* 1 Km 5:5; 2 Km 22:30 = Ps 17:30; *pass over,* > (fig) *forgive* (sin) Mi 7:18.‡

ὑπερβάλλω   **2.** *postpone, wait out* Sir 5:7.‡

ὑπερδυναμόω   (h.l.) *overpower* Ps 64:3.*

ὑπερείδω   aor ὑπήρεισα (Pind, Aristot+) *prop up* Job 8:15; *place under* (as support) Pr 9:1.*

ὑπερεκχέω   (DiodS [11.89.4]+) mid/pass *overflow* Pr 5:16; Joel 2:24; 4:13.*

ὑπερένδοξος, -ον   (pap [V CE]) *highly glorified* Da 3:53; Odes 8:56.*

ὑπερέχω   **1.b.** (intr abs) *extend too far* (no //) 3 Km 8:8 = 2 Ch 5:9.‡

ὑπερησπικώς   pf ptc of BDAG: ὑπερασπίζω.

ὑπερηφανεύω   (7x, LXX+) *behave arrogantly* 2 Esdr 19:16; Ps 9:23; Job 22:29; Sir 10:9; PsSol 2:1; Da 5:20Θ.

ὑπερηφανία   **2.** *splendor, magnificence* (no // but cf. seq) Esth 4:17w.‡

ὑπερήφανος   **2.** *sumptuous, splendid* (Pla+) Esth 4:17k.‡

ὑπέρθυρον, -ου, τό   (Hom+) *lintel* (of door or gate) Is 6:4.*

ὑπερισχύω   (16x, Theophr, pap) **1.** *be strong, be overpowering, prevail* Gen 49:26; 2 Km 24:4; 1 Esdr 3:5; Da 3:22Θ; (w. gen) *be stronger than* Josh 17:18; 1 Esdr 4:3; *overpower* Da 11:23Θ. **2.** (trans) *rule, overpower* 1 Esdr 4:2.

ὑπέρκειμαι   (Hippocr, Isocr, Aristot, Polyb+) *be superior to* (τινά), *surpass* Pr 31:29; Ezk 16:47.*

ὑπερκεράω   (Polyb+) *outflank, attack the wings* (lit *horns*) Jdth 15:5; 1 Macc 7:46.*

ὑπερκρατέω   (Joseph) *overpower* 3 Km 16:22.*

ὑπερκύκλῳ   (dub, not in LSJ) *all around* Ezk 32:23VL.*

ὑπερμαχέω   (Soph+) *defend, fight on behalf of* 1 Macc 16:3.*

ὑπέρμαχος 2. (as [fem] adj, no //) *defending* Wsd 10:20.‡

ὑπερμεγέθης, -ες (Hdt, X+) *exceedingly great or difficult* 1 Ch 20:6; Da 4:37aL.*

ὑπερμήκης, -ες (Hdt+) *very tall* Num 13:32.*

ὑπέρογκος 2 Km 13:2 s.t. of פלא niph *be (too) difficult* as if *be extraordinary or excessive*; sim Da 5:12L.‡

ὑπεροῖδα (dub; not in LSJ) *ignore?* (only vvll for ὑπεροράω) Esth 4:17g vl, 4 Macc 9:6vl.*

ὕπερον, -ου, τό (Hes, Hdt+) *pestle* Pr 23:31.*

ὑπερόρασις, -εως, ἡ (MAnt 8.26) *disdain* Num 22:30.*

ὑπεροράω pf pass ptc ὑπερεωρομένος *disdained, despised* Na 3:11.‡

ὑπεροχή 3. *preeminent instance or example* (no //) 2 Macc 13:6.‡

ὑπέροψις, -εως, ἡ (h.l.) *oversight, (act of) overlooking* Lev 20:4.*

ὑπερτήκω (Strabo 3.2.8.) *melt excessively, vaporize*; (pass) *be vaporized or destroyed* 4 Macc 7:12.*

ὑπερτιμάω (Soph+) *greatly admire* 4 Macc 8:5.*

ὑπερυμνητός, -όν (LXX) *highly praised in song* Da 3:53; 3:54Θ; Odes 8:53, 55, 56.*

ὑπερφερής, -ές (h.l.) *surpassing, overbearing* Da 2:31.*

ὑπερφέρω (Hdt+) *be surpassing or excessive* (intr) 1 Esdr 8:72; Da 7:7L; *surpass* (trans) Da 7:20L, 24Θ.*

ὑπέρφοβος, -ον (X, Menand) *very terrible* Da 7:19L.*

ὑπερφωνέω (LXX+) *sing loudly, outdo one another in singing* Jdth 15:14.*

ὑπερχαρής, -ές (Polyb+) *overjoyed* Esth 5:9; 3 Macc 7:20.*

ὑπερχέω aor pass ὑπερεχύθην (Hippocr, Aristot+) *overflow, pour over* La 3:54.*

ὑπέρχομαι (Hom, Hdt+) *go under or into* 3 Macc 4:6.*

ὑπεύθυνος, -ον (Hdt+) *answerable, accountable* Pr 1:23.*

ὑπευθύνω (not in LSJ) *render an account, be answerable* Pr 1:23vl.*

ὑπευλαβέομαι (h.l.) *be wary of or hesitant to* (+ inf) 2 Macc 14:18.*

ὑπήρεισα see ὑπερείδω.

ὑπνόω (26x, Hdt+) 1. *sleep, fall asleep* 1 Km 26:12; Ps 3:6; Sir 46:20; Joel 1:13; Jer 14:9; (trans) *put to sleep* Gen 2:21. 2. *die* (no //); w. cogn acc Ps 75:6; Jer 28:39; (abs) PsSol 16:1; cf. Ps 12:4.‡

ὑπνώδης, -ες (Eur, Pla+) *drowsy, sleepy*; (subst) *sleeper* Pr 23:21.*

ὑπό B.1.b.β. *at the base of, close to* Ex 19:17; Dt 4:11, 49; 3 Km 19:13. B.1.b.γ. *through, across* (no //) Ex 3:1 (cf. BDAG, Ezk 13:18G vl).‡

ὑποβάλλω 2. *lay a foundation for* (τι) 1 Esdr 2:14.‡

ὑποβλέπω (Hippocr, Aristot+) *look askance at, eye angrily* 1 Km 18:9; Sir 37:10.*

ὑπόγειος, -ον (Hdt+; vvll -γαιον, γεων, =) *subterranean* Jer 45:11.*

ὑπογράφω (Thu+) *indicate, suggest* 1 Macc 8:25, 27; *write below* or *dictate* (letter, decree) 3 Macc 2:30; (pf pass ptc) *thing dictated* Esth 8:13; *thing copied below* 1 Esdr 2:12, 19; 2 Macc 9:18; 11:17; 3 Macc 6:41; *thing (here) indicated* 2 Macc 9:25.*

ὑπόγυος, -ον (Hippocr, X+) *imminent, about to happen* 2 Macc 12:31.*

ὑποδεικνύς, -ῦσα, -ύν pres ptc of BDAG: ὑποδείκνυμι.‡

ὑποδύτης, -ου, ὁ (ins, pap, DiodS+) *undergarment* Ex 28:31ff; 36:30ff; Lev 8:7.*

ὑποδύω (Hom, Hdt+; BDAG: ὑποδύομαι) *slip in under* Jdth 6:13; Ezk 16:10vl.*‡

ὑπόθεμα, -ατος, τό (PhiloMech+) *base* Ex 25:38.*

ὑπόθεσις, -εως, ἡ (X, Pla+) *starting point, premise* 4 Macc 1:12.*

ὑποθραύομαι (h.l. dub) *break down* 2 Macc 9:11vl.*

ὑποκαίω (Hdt+) *set fire underneath, heat from below* 4 Macc 11:18; Am 4:2; Jer 1:13; Ezk 24:5; Da 3:25L, 46L.*

ὑποκαλύπτω (not in LSJ, but cf. LSJ: ὑποκάλυμμα) *fold or drape over* (as a cover) Ex 26:12.*

ὑποκάτω 2. *at the base of, close to* (cf. ὑπό, no //) 1 Km 7:11.‡

ὑποκάτωθεν 1.b. *down below* Judg 7:8A.‡

ὑποκρίνομαι 2. (trans) *deceive* PsSol 4:22.‡

ὑπολαμβάνω 4.b. *ponder, think about* (τι, no //) Ps 47:10. 5. *seize, rush upon* (Hdt) Ps 16:12. Job 2:4; 4:1; 6:1 & oft, Da 3:9L; 3:95L s.t. of ענה *answer*, > *testify*; see Ra note at Da 3:9Θ.‡

ὑπόλημψις, -εως, ἡ (Pla+) *prejudice, assumption* (Vulg SUSPICIO) Sir 3:24.*

ὑπόλοιπος, -ον (Hdt+) *remaining, surviving* (subst) Is 11:11.*

ὑπολυπέομαι (h.l.) *be grieved* 2 Macc 4:37VL.*

ὑπόλυσις, -εως, ἡ (LXX+) *dissolution, collapse* Na 2:11.*

ὑπομαστίδιον, ου, τό (h.l. not in HR or LSJ) *nursing child* 3 Macc 3:27; (VVLL -τιος, -θιος *nursing* Conon, Joseph, ins; ὑπομάζιος [=] DiodS 34.2.11).*

ὑπομιμνήσκω 3 Km 4:3 pres ptc s.t. of מזכיר *recorder, chronicler* fr זכר hiph *remind*.‡

ὑπόμνημα, -ατος, τό (Thu+) *memorandum, record* 2 Km 8:16; 1 Esdr 2:19G (= 2:17R); 2 Esdr 6:2.*

ὑπομνηματίζομαι (Polyb+) *record in annals*; (pass) *be recorded* 1 Esdr 6:22.*

ὑπομνηματισμός, -οῦ, ὁ (Polyb, pap, ins+) *record, memorandum* 1 Esdr 2:17R; 2 Esdr 4:15; 2 Macc 4:23; *memoir* 2 Macc 2:13.*

ὑπομνηματογράφος, -ου, ὁ (ins, pap, Strabo+) *court recorder or annalist* 1 Ch 18:15; 2 Ch 34:8; Is 36:3, 22.*

ὑπονόημα, -ατος, τό (Hippocr) *supposition, consideration* Sir 25:7.*

ὑπονοθεύω (CatCodAstr) *obtain* (a position) *by corrupt means*; (pass) *be displaced by corrupt means* 2 Macc 4:7, 26.

ὑπόνοια 2. *hidden meaning* (X, Pla+) Da 4:19L (but 4:33bG *suspicion, anxiety* [= BDAG]).‡

ὑπονομεύω (Dinarchus+) *be undermined by intrigue* 2 Macc 4:26VL.*

ὑπονύσσω (Theocr+) *prod, goad* Is 58:3.*

ὑποπίπτω (Thu, Pla+) 1. *fall before* (τινί), *submit to* Jdth 16:6; ἀπόκρισις ὑποπίπτουσα *submissive answer* (no //) Pr 15:1. 2. *befall, happen*; 1 Esdr 8:17 *occur, enter one's mind, come to one's attention*; κατὰ τὰ ὑποπίπτοντά μοι *"as I see fit, in my own way"* Sus 52G.*‡

ὑποπτεύω 2. *view with apprehension or anxiety* Ps 118:39; Sir 9:13.*‡

ὕποπτος, -ον (Aeschyl, Thu+) *suspecting, suspicious* 2 Macc 3:32; 12:4.*

ὑποπυρρίζω (Diosc+) *become red* Lev 13:24.*

ὑπορράπτω aor ὑπέρραψεν (Eur+) *mend* Sir 50:1.*

ὑπορρίπτω (LSJ: cj Polyb 29.8.3; Plu+) *throw down* 4 Macc 6:25.*

ὑποσημαίνω (Thu+) *give a signal*, > *indicate* 1 Esdr 6:6R.*

ὑποσκελίζω (7x, Pla+) *trip up* Ps 16:13; Pr 10:8; Jer 23:12.

ὑποσκέλισμα, -ατος, τό (h.l.) *fall* (from tripping) Pr 24:17.*

ὑποσκελισμός, -οῦ, ὁ (h.l. dub) *act of falling* (from tripping) Pr 11:3VL.*

ὑπόστασις, -εως ἡ (Hippocr+) 1. *firm stratum, place to stand* Ps 68:3; *foundation* Na 2:8. 2. *substance* Wsd 16:21; *(actual) existence* Dt 11:6; Judg 6:4; Ps 38:6, 8; 88:48; Job 22:20; Jer 10:17; Ezk 26:11. 3. *origin, coming into existence* Ps 138:15. 4. *promise, expectation* Ruth 1:12; Ezk 19:5. 5. *plan, outline* Jer 23:22; Ezk 43:11; *plan, project* PsSol 15:5. Dt 1:12 mistrans of מַשָּׂא *burden* as if מַשֵּׂאָה *lifting up*. 1 Km 13:21 mistrans of לְהַצִּיב (fr נצב, *set in place*) *to set or mount* (an ox goad, which is simply rendered *likewise*; cf. Lucianic VL); 13:23; 14:4 mistrans of מצב *outpost* (also fr נצב *set in place*), cf. 14:1; μεσσαβ.*‡

ὑποστέλλω Hab 2:4 renders עֻפְּלָה *presumption* (?), perh as 2.b. *shrink back, be fearful*.‡

ὑπόστημα, -ατος, τό (Hippocr, Aristot+: *sediment, support*, etc) *base, camp* (no //) 2 Km 23:14 = 1 Ch 11:16VL; *council, assembly* (no //; cf. σύστημα) Jer 23:18.*

ὑποστήριγμα, -ατος, τό (Joseph AJ 8.176; =) *undergirding support* 3 Km 2:35e; 7:11; 10:12; Jer 5:10. Da 11:7Θ renders מָעוֹן *stronghold, fortress*, unexpl.*

ὑποστηρίζω   (LXX+) *undergird, support* Ps 36:17; 144:14.*

ὑποστρώννυμι   aor ὑπέστρωσαν (Hom+) *spread beneath* 4 Macc 9:19; Is 58:5; Ezk 27:30; (fig, w. σεαυτον) *submit to* (τινί) Sir 4:27.*‡

ὑποσχάζω   (h.l.) *trip up* Sir 12:17.*

ὑπόσχεσις, -εως, ἡ   (Hom+) *promise* 4 Macc 15:2; Wsd 12:21.*

ὑποτάσσω   **1.b.β.** (abs) *yield, submit* 2 Macc 13:23; (pl pres ptc) *subjects, subordinates* (Polyb+) 3 Km 10:15.‡

ὑποτίθημι   **1.c.** (act) *put under* Gen 47:29; Ex 17:12; ὑπ. τὸ ξίφος *fall on one's sword* (no //) 2 Macc 14:41. **3.** *make a venture, hazard* 1 Macc 6:46.‡

ὑποτίτθιος, -ον   (pap, ins+) *under the breast*; (subst) *nursing child* Hos 14:1.*

ὑποτομεύς, -έως ὁ   (h.l.) *cutting instrument* (Heb *ax*) 2 Km 12:31VL.*

ὑπουργός, -όν   (Hippocr, X+) *helpful* subst *assistant* Josh 1:1.*

ὑποφαίνω   (Hom, Pla, pap+) *show itself*, (of day) *begin to dawn* (X ANAB 3.2.1) 2 Macc 10:35; 13:17.*

ὑπόφαυσις, -εως, ἡ   (Hdt+) *narrow opening* Ezk 41:16.*

ὑπόφρικος, -ον   (h.l.) *shuddering* 3 Macc 6:20.*

ὑποφυλλίς, -ίδος, ἡ   (dub, h.l.) = ἐπιφ- Ob 5VL.*

ὑποχείριος, -ον   (16x, Hdt+) *in(to) one's power, under one's authority* Gen 14:20; Josh 6:2; 2 Macc 12:28; Wsd 12:9; (subst) *dependent* Josh 9:25; Wsd 14:15; Is 58:3; Bar 2:4.

ὑποχόνδριον, -ου, τό   (Hippocr, Aristot+) *stomach, area beneath the sternum* (χόνδρος *cartilage*) 1 Km 31:3.*

ὑπόχρεως, -ου, ὁ   (Demosth+) *debtor* 1 Km 22:2; Is 50:1.*

ὑποχυτήρ, -ῆρος, ὁ   (lexicog) *pourer* (for lamp oil) Jer 52:19.*

ὕποψ, -οπος, ὁ   or ὕπωψ, -ωπος (not in LSJ LSJSup; h.l.; both spur) *kind of bird* Dt 14:17VVLL.*

ὑπτιάζω   (Soph+) *turn or extend* (hands) *w. palms upward* Job 11:13.*

ὕπτιος, -α, -ον   (Hom, Hdt+) *smooth, sluggish* Job 14:19.*

ὑπώπιον, -ου, τό   (Hom, Eur+) *blow under the eye, black eye* Pr 20:30.*

ὑσσώπιος, -ον   (dub; not in LSJ) *of hyssop*; (subst) *hyssop branch* Num 19:18VL.*

ὑστεροβουλία, -ας, ἡ   (h.l.) *deliberation after the fact, "second thoughts," regret* Pr 31:3.*

ὕστερος, -α, -ον   (18x, Hom+) *latter, later* (opp πρότερος) 1 Ch 29:29; ἐφ' ὑστέρῳ *later, in the end* Wsd 19:11; cf. EpJer 71; (neut as adv) *later, finally* 2 Macc 6:15; Pr 5:4; Sir 1:23; Jer 27:17; (w. gen, as prep) *after, following* 2 Macc 5:20; Jer 36:2; (superl) ὕστατος, -η, -ον *last, final* 3 Macc 5:49.‡

ὑφαίνω   aor ὕψανε pf pass ptc ὑφασμένος.‡

ὑφαιρέω   2 aor ὑφειλάμην (Hom, Hdt+) *omit* (no //; but *subtract, deduct* and ὑφαίρεμα *omission*) Eccl 2:10; (mid) *make off with* Job 21:18; 27:20; *steal, filch* EpJer 9.*

ὑφάντης, -ου, ὁ   (Pla+) *weaver* Ex 26:1; 28:32; 37:3, 5.*

ὑφάπτω   aor ὑφῆψα (Hdt, Eur+) *ignite or set on fire* (from below) 2 Macc 8:33; 12:9; 14:41.*

ὕφασμα, -ατος, τό   (Hom+) *woven cloth* Job 38:36; *webbing* Ex 28:8, 17; 36:17, 28; Judg 16:14.*

ὑφασμένος   pf pass ptc of BDAG: ὑφαίνω Lev 19:19.

ὑφίστημι   **3.** (act) *place under, set (secretly) in place* Zech 9:8; (intr) *place oneself (under or beneath), settle, submit* Judg 9:15B; *remain, stay* 1 Km 30:10; 2 Km 2:23.‡

ὑφοράω   (Thu+) mid *be suspicious, suspect* (X MEM 2.7.12) 2 Macc 7:24; 3 Macc 3:23.*

ὑψαυχενέω   (LXX+) *carry one's neck high*, > *proceed arrogantly* 2 Macc 15:6; 3 Macc 3:19.*

ὑψηλοκάρδιος, -ον   (Eccl 7:8 Sym) *high-hearted, proud* Pr 16:5.*

ὑψηλός   **4.** (neut subst) *high place, elevated place* (Pla, X+) 3 Km 3:2; 11:5; 2 Ch 11:15; Hab 3:19; Jer 19:5.‡

ὑψόω   **1.b.** *erect, build (up)* 2 Esdr 9:9; *bring up, raise* (children, no //) Is 51:18.

2 Esdr 8:25 s.t. of רום hiph (fig) *offer, present* as if (lit) *lift up.* 2 Esdr 10:1 s.t. of רבה hiph *do copiously or persistently* as if *make great.* Pr 3:35 corresp to MT מְרִים unexpl; perh emend either (w. LXX) to מֵרְמִים (fr רום) *exalting,* > *reveling in* (so McKane OTL ad loc) or to מֹרִים (fr מרה *be bitter*) *obstinate* (so NRSV).‡

ὕψωσις, -εως, ἡ (Strabo+) *lifting high, exaltation* Ps 149:6.*

ὕω (Hom, Hdt+) *rain,* (trans) *cause to fall* Ex 9:18; 16:4.*

Φ

φαζ translit of פז *gold* (or *chrysolite/topaz*) SSol 5:11.*

φαιδρός, -α, -ον (Aeschyl+) *bright, beaming, cheerful* (X ANAB 2.6.11) 4 Macc 13:13.*

φαιός, -ά, -όν (Pla+) *gray* Gen 30:32ff.*

φακός, -οῦ, ὁ (10x, Hdt+) **1.** *lentil* Gen 25:34; 2 Km 17:28; Ezk 4:9. **2.** *gourd-like container* 1 Km 10:1; 4 Km 9:1.

φάλαγξ, -αγγος, ἡ (Hom+) *rank, battle line* 1 Macc 6:35ff; 9:12; 10:82.*

φαλακρός, -ά, -όν (Hdt+) *bald* Lev 13:40; Ezk 29:18; (subst) *bald man* 4 Km 2:23.*

φαλακρόω (Hdt+) *shave bald* Ezk 27:31vL.*

φαλάκρωμα, -ατος, τό (10x, LXX+) *bald head, baldness* Lev 13:42f; Am 8:10; Is 3:24.

φαλτ(ε)ια translit of פלתי (cf. φελεθθι) 1 Ch 18:17.*

φάμενος aor mid ptc of BDAG: φήμι.

φαντάζω (Aeschyl, Hdt+) **1.** (mid/pass, = BDAG) *appear, become visible* Wsd 6:16. **2.** (mid/pass) *present an image to oneself, imagine* Sir 34:5.*‡

φαντασία **2.** *appearance* Hab 2:18 (renders מורה *teaching* [cf. identical phrase in Is 9:14] as if מראה *appearance*), 19 (renders יורה *teach*); 3:10 (appar rendering of ידינו *our hands,* reading ר for ד, otherwise unclear). Zech 10:1 mistrans of חזיז *storm* as if fr חזה *see.*‡

φαντασιοκοπέω (h.l.) *play a role, act in pretense* Sir 4:30.*

φαρασιν translit of פרצים *gaps, breaches* (N LOC) 1 Ch 14:11.*

φαρες translit of Aram פרס (unit of weight) *half shekel* Da 5(preface)L; 5:25Θ, 28Θ.*

φαρέτρα, -ας, ἡ (10x, Hom+) *quiver* for arrows Gen 27:3; Ps 10:2; Job 30:11; Sir 26:12; Is 22:6.

φαρμακεύω (Hippocr, Hdt+) **1.** (act) *administer poison* 2 Macc 10:13. **2.** (mid) *practice magic* 2 Ch 33:6; (ptc subst) *magician, practitioner of spells* Ps 57:6.*‡

φαρουριμ translit of פרורים *courts* 4 Km 23:11.*

φάρυγξ, -υγγος, ὁ or ἡ (9x, Hom+) *throat* 1 Km 17:35; Pr 5:3; SSol 5:16; Jer 2:25.

φασεκ (19x, LXX) *Passover* (translit of Heb פסח) 2 Ch 30:1ff; Jer 38:8; φασεχ 2 Ch 35:1ff.*

φάσμα, -ατος, τό (Hdt+) *apparition, delusion* Job 20:8; Wsd 17:4; Is 28:7; *portent* Num 16:30.*

φατνόω (LXX) *make a coffered ceiling* 3 Km 7:40; pf pass ptc Ezk 41:16.*

φάτνωμα, -ατος, τό (Aeschyl, Polyb+) *coffered ceiling* 2 Macc 1:16; Zeph 2:14; Ezk 41:20; (pl) *mullions of same* (so also Polyb 10.27.10; c. LSJ) SSol 1:17; Am 8:3.*‡

φάτνωσις, -εως, ἡ (Sym) *coffered work* (in a ceiling) 3 Km 6:9vL.*

φαυλίζω (16x, Pla+) *despise, consider worthless* Gen 25:34; 2 Km 12:9; Jdth 1:11; Pr 21:12; Mal 1:6; Is 33:19.

φαύλισμα, -ατος, τό (h.l.) *contemptible act* Zeph 3:11.*

φαυλισμός, -οῦ, ὁ (LXX) *contempt, contemptibility* Hos 7:16; Is 28:11; 51:7.*

φαυλίστριος, -α, -ον (h.l.) *contemptuous* Zeph 2:15.*

φαυλότης, -ητος, ἡ (Pla+) *meanness, worthlessness* Wsd 4:12.*

φαῦσις, -εως ἡ (LXX+) **1.** *light* Ps 73:16. **2.** *illumination* Gen 1:14f; Jdth 13:13.*

φείδομαι peculiar to LXX is use w. preps: ἀπό 1 Km 15:3; ἐπί 2 Km 21:7; Jdth 2:11; Job 6:10;

φειδώ Zech 11:6; Jer 15:5; περί 2 Km 12:6; Sir 16:8; ὑπέρ Jon 4:10. Ezk 24:21 mistrans of מחמל *yearning, desire* fr חמל *feel for*, > *pity, spare*.‡

φειδώ, -οῦς, ἡ (Hom+) *sparing, refraining* Esth 3:13f; Wsd 12:18; PsSol 5:13.*

φειδωλός, -ή, -όν (Hes, Pla+) *sparing, miserly* 4 Macc 2:9.*

φελεθθι (-ττι, -τθι; 7; not in HR) translit of פלתי unexpl (honorific for king's guard? cf. כרתי, χερεθθι) 2 Km 8:18; 3 Km 1:38; 1 Ch 18:17.

φελμουνι translit of פלמני *someone in particular, a certain one* Da 8:13.

φερνή, -ῆς, ἡ (Hdt+) **1.** *dowry* Josh 16:10; 2 Macc 1:14. **2.** *bridal price* (no //) Gen 34:12; Ex 22:15f.*

φερνίζω fut φερνιῶ (pap) *pay the bridal price* (no //), *obtain as a wife* Ex 22:15.*

φέρω fut οἴσω pass ἐνεχθήσομαι aor ἤνεγκα ptc ἐνέγκας inf ἐνεγκεῖν pass ἠνέχθην ptc ἐνεχθείς 2 pf ἐνήνοχα **2.a.** *bring praise or tribute/sacrifice* (cf. ἀναφέρω); w. obj expressed Ps 28:1; 75:12; 95:7; unexpressed PsSol 1:6. **3.e.** (mid/pass) *conduct oneself, bear oneself* Gen 49:3. **9.** βαρέως φέρειν *bear w. difficulty, be displeased* 2 Macc 14:27; δυσφόρως φ. *endure w. difficulty, be distressed or troubled* 14:28. **11.** (of body of water) *bear upon, face* (in a direction) Josh 15:2.‡

φεύγω Job 30:3 mistrans of ערק *gnaw* as if Aram ערק/קרק *flee*.‡

φευκτός, -ή, -όν (Soph+) *avoidable* Wsd 17:9.*

φημί aor mid ptc φάμενος.‡

φθάνω 2.b. *attain*, > *manage to* (+ inf) 3 Km 12:18. 2 Km 20:13 mistrans of יגה hoph (h.l.) *be carried off* as if fr נגע *reach, (to) arrive*.‡

φθάρμα, -ατος, τό (Joseph BJ 5:443 [coll pl] *trash, scum*) *corrupted thing or act* Lev 22:25.*

φθέγμα, -ατος, τό (Aeschyl+) *sound* (of speech) Job 6:26; Wsd 1:11.*

φθειρίζω fut φθειριῶ (Aristot+: [mid] *delouse oneself*) *delouse*; (fig) *depopulate* Jer 50:12.*

φθίνω (Hom+; vL φθινύθω, =) *decay* (of moon); *wane* Job 31:26.*

φθονερός, -ά, -όν (Theognis, Hdt+) *envious* Sir 14:10.*

φιάλη SSol 5:13; 6:2 mistrans of ערוגה *bed* (of plants or herbs) as if *bowl*, unexpl.‡

φιλαμαρτήμων, -ον (h.l.) *loving sin* Pr 17:19.*

φιλανθρωπέω (Polyb, ins+) *treat favorably, act kindly to* (τι) 2 Macc 13:23.*

φιλαρχία, -ας, ἡ (Theophr, Polyb+) *love of or lust for power* 4 Macc 2:15.*

φιλελεήμων, -ον (ins) *loving mercy* Tob 14:9BA.*

φιλεχθρέω (Proclus) *be fond of or inclined to hostility* Pr 3:30.*

φιληκοΐα, -ας, ἡ (Isocr+) *delight in listening* 4 Macc 15:21.*

φιλιάζω (LXX+) *befriend, act as a friend* Judg (τινός) 14:20B; (τινί) 5:30A; 2 Ch 19:2; 20:37; 1 Esdr 3:22; (abs) Sir 37:1.*

φιλογέωργος, -ον (X, Aristot+) *loving to farm* 2 Ch 26:10.*

φιλογύναιος, -ον (Theopomp, Aristot+) *loving women* 3 Km 11:1 (vL -γυνης, -ες [AntiphanesCom, Polyb+], =).*

φιλοδοξία, -ας, ἡ (ins, Polyb+) *love of honor or fame* Esth 4:17d; 4 Macc 1:26.*

φιλόκοσμος, -ον (LXX+) *fond of decoration or make-up* EpJer 8.*

φιλομαθέω (Pla+) *love learning* Sir prol 5, 34.*

φιλομαθής, -ές (Pla+) *in love w. learning, eager for knowledge* Sir prol 13.*

φιλομήτωρ, gen **-ορος** (Philo, Plu+) *loving one's mother* 4 Macc 15:10.*

φιλονεικέω (Thu+) *be contentious, love argument or strife* Pr 10:12.*

φιλοπολίτης, -ες (Plu+) *loving one's compatriots* 2 Macc 14:37.*

φιλοπονέω pf pass ptc πεφιλοπονημένος (X+) *love to labor or strive, be industrious*; (pf pass ptc) *lovingly worked through* Sir prol 20.*‡

φιλοπονία, -ας, ἡ (Pla+) *devoted labor or industry* Sir prol 30.*

φιλοσοφέω (Hdt, Pla+) *love knowledge or wisdom, be a philosopher* 4 Macc 5:7, 11; 7:21; 8:1.*

φιλοτεκνία, -ας, ἡ (Plu+) *love of one's children* 4 Macc 14:13ff.*

φιλοτιμία 2. *love of honor, ambition* Wsd 14:18*‡

φιλότιμος, -ον (Aeschyl+: *loving honor, seeking admiration*) 1. *honorable, worthy of emulation* Wsd 18:3; (adv) 2 Macc 2:21. 2. *great, intense* (no //) 3 Macc 4:15; (adv) Sus 12Θ.*

φιλοφρονέω (Hdt+) *incline toward;* (mid/pass) *be pleased,* > *indulge oneself* 2 Macc 2:25.*

φιλόψυχος, -ον (Eur+: *loving one's own life*) *loving the (human) soul* (no //) Wsd 11:26.*

φίλτρον, -ου, τό (Aeschyl+) *love charm or potion, spell* (fig) 4 Macc 13:19, 27; 15:13.*

φιμός, -οῦ, ὁ (Aeschyl+) *muzzle* Job 30:28; Sir 20:29; *bridle* Is 37:29.*

φλεγμαίνω aor ἐφλέγμανεν (Aristoph+) *swell, inflame* Is 1:6; Na 3:19.*

φλεγμονή, -ῆς, ἡ (Hippocr+) *inflammation* (fig) 4 Macc 3:17.*

φλέξ, φλέγος, ἡ (dub; not in LSJ) *flame* (cf. φλόξ) Judg 3:22VL.*

φλιά, -ᾶς, ἡ (12x, Hom+) *doorpost* Ex 12:7; Dt 6:9; 1 Km 1:9; Ezk 43:8.

φλόγινος, -η, -ον (DiodS+) *burning, flaming* Gen 3:24.*

φλοιός, -οῦ, ὁ (Hom, Hdt+) *bark* Wsd 13:11.*

φλόξ Judg 3:22 mistrans of להב *blade* (?) as if *flame.*‡

φλυκτίς, -ίδος, ἡ (Hippocr+) *blister, pustule* Ex 9:9f.*

φοβερίζω (CatCodAstr) *frighten, terrify* 2 Esdr 10:3; 16:9ff; Da 4:5Θ.*

φοβερισμός, -οῦ, ὁ (h.l.) *terror, terrifying deed* Ps 87:17.*

φοβεροειδής, -ές (h.l.) *terrifying in aspect or appearance* 3 Macc 6:18.*

φοιβάω (Eur, Callim+) *play the prophet, seek oracular ecstasy* (cf. Longinus [III CE 8.4 φοιβάζω, rel to **Phoebus** Apollo) Dt 14:1; as transl of גדד hiph *gash oneself* (cf. 3 Km 18:28).

φοῖνιξ 3. *date* (fruit itself; Epicharm+) 2 Km 16:1f; 2 Ch 3:5.‡

φονευτής, -οῦ, ὁ (17x, LXX+ [CF. BDAG]) *murderer, killer* Num 35:11ff; Josh 20:3; Pr 22:13; Is 1:21; υἱὸς φονευτοῦ 4 Km 6:32 *murderer,* cf. υἱός.‡

φονεύω 3 Km 21:40 mistrans of חרץ *determine* as if הרג *kill* or (prob) רצח *murder.*‡

φονή, -ῆς, ἡ (Hom+; alw pl) *carnage, bloodshed, murder* Wsd 12:5.*

φονοκτονέω (LXX) *defile w. murder* Num 35:33; (pass) *be defiled w. murder* Ps 105:38.

φονοκτονία, -ας, ἡ (h.l.) *defiling murder* 1 Macc 1:24.*

φονώδης, -ες (Hippocr, Theophr+) *bloodthirsty, deadly* 4 Macc 10:17.*

φοράζω (dub, not in LSJ but cf. συμφοράζω) *carry along* 1 Ch 22:4VL.*

φορβεά, -ῆς, ἡ (X, pap+) *halter* Job 40:25.*

φορεῖον, -ου, τό (Dinarchus, Polyb+) *litter, palanquin* 2 Macc 3:27; 9:8; SSol 3:9.*

φορεύς, -έως, ὁ (Hom+: *carrier* [animal or person]) *carrying pole* (no //) Ex 27:6f.*

φορθομμιν translit of פרתמים *nobles* Da 1:3Θ.*

φορολογέω (Polyb, ins+) *levy tribute* 1 Esdr 2:22; (pass) *be subject to or pay tribute* 2 Ch 36:4a.*

φορολόγητος, -ον, ὁ (h.l.) *tributary, one who pays tribute* Dt 20:11.*

φορολογία, -ας, ἡ (pap, ins) *tribute* 1 Esdr 2:15; 6:28; 8:22; 1 Macc 1:29.*

φορολόγος, -ου, ὁ (pap+) *tribute or tax collector;* Job 3:18; 39:7 s.t. of נגש *taskmaster, overseer* as if *tax collector.* 2 Esdr 4:7, 18, 23; 5:5 mistrans of נשתון (*official*) *letter,* unexpl.*

φόρος 2. *forced levy* (Plu) Judg 1:28ff; 3 Km 4:6; 2 Ch 8:8; 2 Esdr 7:24; La 1:1.‡

φορτίζω (Hes+, NT) *load, burden;* Ezk 16:33 mistrans of שכר *bribe, persuade w. gifts* as if *load down.**‡

φουρ translit of פור *lot* Esth 9:24VL.*

φραζων translit of פרזון *rural people, rustics, peasants* (as if N PERS?) Judg 5:7A.*

φρέαρ 3. *pool, (tar)pit* Gen 14:10.‡

φρενόω (Aeschyl+) *instruct;* (pass, LXX+) *be elated or excited* (by τινί) 2 Macc 11:4.*

φρικασμός, -οῦ, ὁ (h.l.) *trembling* (in fear) 2 Macc 3:17.*

φρικτός, -ή, -όν (Callim+) *frightful, horrible* Wsd 8:15; (subst) *horrible things* Jer 5:30; 18:13; 23:14; (adv) *horribly* Wsd 6:5.*

φρικώδης, -ες (Hippocr, Aristoph+) *causing shuddering horror;* (subst) *horrible thing* Hos 6:10.*

φρίττω Att for BDAG: φρίσσω Odes 12:4.‡

φρονέω w. μέγα *think lofty thoughts, think presumptuously;* (comp) *think more arrogantly* Esth 8:12c.‡

φροντιστέον (Eur+) *it must be thought out or considered* 2 Macc 2:29.*

φρουρά 3. *garrison, (frontier) post* 2 Macc 12:18.‡

φρούριον, -ου, τό (Aeschyl, Thu+) *garrison, fort* (X Anab 1.4.15) 2 Macc 10:32f; 13:19.*

φρουρόω (dub; not in LSJ. Gött -ρέω) *guard, garrison* Jdth 3:6R.*

φρύαγμα, -ατος, τό (6x, Aeschyl+) *snorting* (of a horse), > *pride, insolence* 3 Macc 6:16; Hos 4:18; Ezk 7:24. Jer 12:5 mistrans of גאון *height,* > *wild place* as if *arrogance.*

φρυάττω Att for BDAG: φρυάσσω.‡

φρύγιον, -ου, τό (EtymMag) *hearth, drying rack* Ps 101:4.*

φρύγω (Hdt+) *parch, roast;* (only pf pass ptc) *parched, roasted* Lev 2:14; 23:14.*

φυγαδεία, -ας, ἡ (Polyb 6.14.3; VettVal) *banishment, flight into exile* Ezk 17:21; *refuge* (no //; renders Aram אשתדור *sedition*) 2 Esdr 4:15VL, 19VL (q.l.; cf. W, p.43).*

φυγαδεῖον, -ου, τό (h.l.) *place of refuge* Num 35:15G (RECTE; cf. W, p.43).*

φυγαδευτήριον, -ου, τό (LXX) 1. *(city of) refuge* Num 35:6ff; Josh 20:2; 1 Ch 6:42ff. 2. *place of refuge* Josh 20:3; 1 Macc 1:53; 10:14.*

φυγάδιον, -ου, τό (dub, cf. W p.43; LXX) *place of refuge* Num 35:15R; 2 Esdr 4:15, 19.*

φυγάς, -άδος, ὁ (9x, Hdt+) *fugitive;* (of an outcast or runaway) 2 Macc 4:26; Pr 28:17; Wsd 10:10; Is 16:4; (of a routed enemy) Ex 23:27.

φυή, -ῆς, ἡ (Hom+) *growth, form, stature* Da 4:15Θ, 23Θ, 26Θ; ἀνέβη φυή τοῖς τείχεσιν "the walls were rebuilt to their original dimensions" 2 Esdr 14:1.*

φῦκος, -εος, τό (Hom+: *seaweed*) *orchil, rouge* (from seaweed; Aristoph+) Wsd 13:14.*

φύλαγμα, -ατος, τό (8x, LXX+) *observance, obligation* Lev 8:35; 1 Macc 8:26; Mal 3:14. Zeph 1:12 mistrans of שֶׁמֶר *dregs* as if fr שָׁמַר *guard, keep.*

φυλακή 2.b. *watch* as group or division of personnel Num 8:26²; 2 Ch 35:2; (also prob Ac 12:10), *corps of guards, garrison* Ezk 23:24. 3.b. *captivity* Da 4:17aL, 25L; ἐν φυλ- *under guard* 1 Macc 13:12. 5. *responsibility, task* (no //; s.t. of משמרת *obligation* fr שמר *guard, keep*) Num 1:53; 3:7ff; 3 Km 2:3; 1 Ch 9:19; Ezk 40:45.‡

φυλάκισσα, -ης, ἡ (h.l. [class φυλακίς]) *guard, watcher* SSol 1:6.*

φυλάρχης, -ου, ὁ (ins, Philo) *head of a tribe* (= BDAG: φύλαρχος) 2 Macc 8:32.*

φυλάττω Att for BDAG: φυλάσσω.‡

φυλή Ezk 19:11, 14 mistrans of שבט *scepter* as if *tribe* (cf. σκῆπτρον).‡

φῦλον, -ου, τό (Hom, Hdt+) *race, nation* 3 Macc 4:14; 5:5.*

φύρασις, -εως, ἡ (LXX+) *mixing, kneading* Hos 7:4.*

φυράω pf pass ptc πεφυραμένος (13; Hdt+) *mix, knead* Gen 18:6; 1 Km 28:24; 1 Ch 23:29.

φύρδην adv (Aeschyl, X+) *in confusion or turmoil* 2 Macc 4:41.*

φυρμός, -οῦ, ὁ (DiodS+) *disorder, confusion* Ezk 7:23; *mixture* PsSol 2:13.*

φύρω pf pass πέφυρμαι (8x, Hom+) *saturate, steep;* (only pass) *be saturated or soaked* 2 Km 20:12; 3 Macc 4:6; Job 7:5; Is 14:19.

φυσάω (Hom+) *blow out, blow (on)* Wsd 11:18; Sir 28:12; 43:4; Is 54:16.*

φυσητήρ, -ῆρος, ὁ (Hdt+) *bellows* Job 32:19; Jer 6:29.*

φύτευμα, -ατος, τό (Pind, Soph+) *something planted, planting* Is 17:10; 60:21; 61:3.*

φυτεύω 2. *fix, embed* (no //); pass ptc *fixed, embedded, secured* Eccl 12:11.‡

φωράω (Soph, X+) *search for a thief;* (pass) *be detected or caught as a criminal* 3 Macc 3:29; Pr 26:19.*

φῶς Ezk 41:11; (c. MT), 42:7, 10, 12 mistrans of גדר(ת) *stone wall,* unexpl.‡

φωταγωγέω (Iambl: *draw down light from above*) *illuminate the way* (for τινά), *guide by light* (no //) 4 Macc 17:5.*

φωτίζω 2 Esdr 2:63; 17:65 mistrans of אורים *oracular instruments* as if fr אור *be light*.‡

X

χαβραθα translit of כִּבְרַת *some distance* as if N LOC Gen 35:16; 48:7 (cf. δεβραθα).*

χαιρετίζω (LXX+) *offer greeting* Tob 5:9S; 7:1.*

χαιροκαίνως (dub; not in HR or LSJ) *recently* (?) 1 Ch 12:34VL.*

χαίρω Pr 6:16 mistrans of שׁשׁ *six* as if שׂושׂ *rejoice*.‡

χαλαστόν, -οῦ, τό (pap [V CE]) *ornamental chain* (cf. σερσερωθ) 2 Ch 3:5, 16.*

χαλάω 2. (γλῶσσαν) *stick out* (no //) Is 57:4.‡

χαλβάνη, -ης, ἡ (Theophr+) *galbanum* Ex 30:34; (= Heb חלבנה), Sir 24:15.*

Χαλδαϊστί (HR as N PROP; Philo LEGAT 1.4.: *Aramaic, the language of Judaism*) *Babylonian* (cf. Συριστί, etc) Da 2:26L.*

χαλεπαίνω (Hom, Hdt+) *become harsh or severe,* > *become angry* (X ANAB 1.4.12) 4 Macc 9:10; 16:22.*

χάλιξ, -ικος, ὁ or ἡ (Aristoph, Thu+) *pebble, stone* Job 8:17; 21:33; Sir 22:18G.*‡

χαλκεῖος, -η, -ον (8x, Hom+) *made of copper or bronze* Judg 16:21B; 1 Esdr 1:38; Job 6:12; Sir 28:20. 2 Ch 35:13; 1 Esdr 1:13; Job 41:23 read χαλκίον (W p. 48; p. 285, n. 30).

χάλκεος = BDAG: χαλκοῦς.

χαλκοπλάστης, -ου, ὁ (h.l.) *copper-shaper* Wsd 15:9.*

χαλκός 2.b. *kettle* 1 Km 2:14VL, Is 36:16VL. La 3:7 s.t. of נחשת *fetter* as if *bronze*.*‡

χαμαιλέων, -οντος, ὁ (Aristot+) *chameleon* Lev 11:30; Zeph 2:14.*

χαμαιπετής, -ές (Aeschyl+) *fallen to the ground, lying prostrate* 1 Esdr 8:88.*

χαμανιμ 2 Esdr 8:27 mistranslit; εις την οδον χαμανιμ corresp to לְדַרְכְּמֹנִים *in drachmae or darics* (MT לאדרכנים) which was read as כמנים, fr דרך כמנים *road*.

χάος, -ους, τό (Hes+) *abyss* Mi 1:6; Zech 14:4.*

χαρα (Gött καρρα *wagons, carts*) 1 Esdr 5:53 renders שמן *oil,* unexpl.*

χαραδριός, -οῦ, ὁ (Aristoph+) *plover* Lev 11:19; Dt 14:18.*

χαρακοβολία, -ας, ἡ (h.l.) *setting up of a palisade* Ezk 17:17.*

χαρακτήρ 3.b. more generally, *sum of such traits, character* in our sense 4 Macc 15:4.‡

χαράσσω aor ἐχάραξα (Hes, Hdt+) *sharpen, whet,* > *provoke, anger* 4 Km 17:11; *engrave,* > *write* Sir 50:27; *stamp,* > *brand* 3 Macc 2:29.*

χαρίεις, -εσσα, -εν (Hom, Pla+) *gracious, elegant, accomplished* 4 Macc 8:3.*

χαριστήριον, -ου, τό (X, Polyb, ins+: *thank offering*) *generous gift or reward* (no //) 2 Macc 12:45.*

χαρμονή, -ῆς, ἡ (Soph+) *joy, delight* 3 Macc 6:31; Job 3:7; 20:5; 40:20; Jer 38:13.*

χαρμοσύνη, -ης, ἡ (LXX+) *celebration, occasion for joy* Lev 22:29; 1 Km 18:6; Jdth 8:6; Jer 31:33; 40:11; Bar 2:23; 4:23.*

χαροποιός, -όν (LXX+) *making glad* Gen 49:12G.*

χαροπός, -όν (Hom+) *bright, flashing* Gen 49:12R.*

χαροῦμαι (late) fut of BDAG: χαίρω Zech 4:10.

χαρσιθ translit of חַרְסִית (Qere; Kethib חרסות) *potsherd* or *clay pit* Jer 19:2.*

χαρτηρία, -ας, ἡ (h.l.) *supply of,* or *place to store, papyrus rolls* 3 Macc 4:20.*

χαρτίον, -ου, τό (13x, dim of BDAG: χάρτης; ins, pap+) *small papyrus roll* Jer 43:2ff.*

χάσκω aor ἔχανε (Hom+) *gape open* Gen 4:11; (trans) *open wide* 1 Esdr 4:19, 31; Ezk 2:8.*

χαῦνος, -ον (Pind, Pla+) *porous, empty* Wsd 2:3.*

χαυών acc pl -ῶνας (LXX; loanword fr Heb כון) *cake* Jer 7:18; 51:19.*

χεῖλος 3. *language* (Heb, no //) Gen 11:1.‡

χειμέριος, -ον (Hom, Hdt+) *wintry* Wsd 16:29.*

χείρ Heb idioms (all no //): *portion, allotment* 2 Km 19:44; so also Jer 6:3 (emend to τὴν χεῖρα w. ms S); על־יד, > ἀνὰ χεῖρα *at the hand of,* > *alongside* 2 Km 15:2 etc; ἐπὶ χεῖρας *alongside* 1 Ch 6:16; *as assistant* 2 Esdr 23:13; *as instituted by* 2 Esdr 3:10. 3 Km 7:18ff s.t. of יד *axle,* 10:19 *armrest,* SSol 5:5 *handle,* as if *hand.* 1 Km 15:12; 2 Km 8:3; 18:18; 1 Ch 18:3; Ezk 21:24 mistrans of יד (fig) *phallus* (cf. Ugar), > *(stone) pillar* as if *hand.* Zech 2:4 mistrans of לידות (fr ידה *throw*) as if fr יד *hand.*‡

χειρίζω (Hippocr, pap, Polyb+) *handle, administer* Esth 8:12e.*

χείριστος, -η, -ον irreg superl of κακός (comp BDAG: χείρων).‡

χειρονομία, -ας, ἡ (h.l.; appar = Hdt+: ἐν χειρῶν νόμῳ) *military engagement, "fair fight"* 3 Macc 1:5.*

χειροπέδη, -ης, ἡ (8x, ins, pap+) *fetter, handcuff* Ps 149:8; Job 36:8; Na 3:10; Is 45:14; Da 4:17aL.

χειρόω (Aeschyl, Hdt+) mid *destroy, kill* 2 Macc 4:34, 42; 3 Macc 7:15; Job 3:8; 13:15; 30:24.*

χελεθθι see χερ-.

χελιδών, -όνος, ἡ (Hom, Hdt+) *swallow* Odes 11:14 = Is 38:14; Jer 8:7; EpJer 21.*

χελύνιον, -ου, τό (Hippocr+) *jaw.* Dt 34:7R (q.l.) mistrans of לח *vigor* as if לחי *jaw* (cf. Vulg DENTES).*

χελώνη, -ης, ἡ (Hdt+: *tortoise*) *mound, heap* (no //; *tomb*?) Hos 12:12.*

χελωνίς, -έως, ἡ (Posidon+: *tortoise-shaped object*) *footstool* Jdth 14:15.*

χερεθ Jer 37:16 corresp to חניות (Kethib), perh חנות (h.l.) *cellar*?, unexpl.

χερεθθι (-λεθθι; 7; not in HR) translit of כרתי unexpl (honorific for king's guard? cf. פלתי, φελεθθι) 2 Km 8:18; 3 Km 1:38; 1 Ch 18:17.

χεροκένως (h.l.) *in empty-handed fashion* 1 Ch 12:34VL.*

χερσαῖος, -α, -ον (Aeschyl, Hdt+) *suited or accustomed to dry land* Lev 11:29; (subst) *land animal* Wsd 19:19.*

χέρσος, -ον (7x, Hom+) *dry, barren;* (fem subst) *barren land* Wsd 10:7; Hos 10:4; Is 5:6.

χεττι (not in HR) mistranslit of כרתי *king's guard* 2 Km 15:18 (cf. χερεθθι).

χεττιιν 4 Km 23:7 renders בתים perh *garments* (so L mss), unexpl.

χέω impf ἐχέομαι aor pass ἐχύθην pf mid/pass κέχυμαι 2. (act) *pour, cast* (metal) Mal 3:3; 3 Km 7:24VL.‡

χηλή, -ῆς, ἡ (Hes+) *cloven hoof* Lev 11:3 = Dt 14:6.*

χηρεία, -ας, ἡ (Thu+) *widowhood* Mi 1:16; Is 47:9; 54:4.*‡

χήρευσις, -εως, ἡ (6x, LXX) *widowhood* Gen 38:14; Jdth 8:5.

χηρεύω (Hom+) *be deprived or bereft* 2 Km 13:20; Jer 28:5; *be a widow* Jdth 8:4.*‡

χθιζός, -ή, -όν (Hom, Hdt+) *of yesterday* Job 8:9.*

χθών, χθονός, ἡ (Hom+) *earth, soil* 3 Km 14:15.*

χίδρον, -ου, τό (Aristoph+) *groat, hulled kernel* Lev 2:14, 16; 23:14.*

χιλιαρχία, -ας, ἡ (X+) *unit of 1,000 soldiers* (= Roman cohort, actually about 600) Num 31:48; 1 Macc 5:13.*

χιλιοπλασίως (h.l.) *a thousand times over* Dt 1:11.*

χίμαιρα, -ας, ἡ (Hom+) *young goat* Lev 4:28f; 5:6.*

χίμαρος, -ου, ὁ (56x, Aristoph+) *young goat* Lev 4:23; Num 7:16; 2 Ch 29:21; Ps 49:9.‡

χιονόομαι (VL in DiogL) *be turned snow white* (?) Ps 67:15.*

χίρ itac misspelling of χείρ 1 Ch 17:23VL.*

χλαῖνα, -ης, ἡ (Hom, Hdt+) *cloak* Pr 31:22.*

χλεύασμα, -ατος, τό (LXX) *object of mockery* Job 12:4.*

χλευασμός, -οῦ, ὁ (Demosth, Polyb+) *object of mockery* Ps 78:4; Jer 20:8.*

χλιδών, -ῶνος, ὁ (Aristoph+) *bracelet, anklet* Num 31:50; 2 Km 1:10; 8:7; Jdth 10:4; Sir 21:21; Is 3:20.*

χλόη, -ης ἡ (12x, Hdt+) *young green growth* (of plants) 2 Km 23:4; Ps 22:2; Job 38:27; Da 4:15Θ, 32L.

χλοηφόρος, -ον   (Eur+) *green-growing* Wsd 19:7.*

χλωρίζω   (LXX+) *become green* Lev 13:49; 14:37.*

χλωροβοτάνη, -ης, ἡ   (dub; *h.l.*) *green plant* 4 Km 19:26VL.*

χλωρότης, -ητος, ἡ   (Plu) *pale (green-)yellow* Ps 67:14.*

χοεύς acc pl χοεῖς   see χοῦς¹.

χοθωνωθ   translit of כתנות *chiton, inner garment* 2 Esdr 17:70, 72.*

χοιρογρύλλιος, -ου, ὁ   (LXX) *coney* Lev 11:6; Dt 14:7; Ps 103:18; Pr 30:26.*

χοιρόγρυλλος, -ου, ὁ   (pap) *coney* Lev 11:6VL.*

χολέρα, -ας, ἡ   (Hippocr+) *nausea, dysentery* Num 11:20; Sir 31:20; 37:30.*

χολή   **1.b.** *poison, venom* (of a snake) Job 20:14. **3.** *gall bladder* Tob 6:5.‡

χόλος, -ου, ὁ   (Hom+) *bile,* > *bitter anger* 3 Macc 5:1, 30; Eccl 5:16; Wsd 18:22.*

χονδρίτης, -ου, ὁ   (LXX+) *cake of coarse grain* Gen 40:16.*

χορεία, -ας, ἡ   (Eur+) *choral dance* Jdth 15:13.*

χορηγία, -ας, ἡ   (Thu+) **1.** *expense of public services* 1 Esdr 4:54f; *public festival* 2 Macc 4:14. **2.** *abundance, extravagance* 3 Macc 5:2, 10. 2 Esdr 5:3; 9 mistrans of אשרן *structure* (?), unexpl.*

χορηγός, -οῦ, ὁ   (Alcman, Hdt+) *leader* (of procession), > *patron* 2 Macc 1:25.*

χορίδιον, -ου, τό   (dub, not in LSJ) *little chorus* (of spectators?) 4 Macc 15:20VL.*

χόριον, -ου, τό   (Hippocr, Aristot+) *placenta* Dt 28:57.*

χορτασία, -ας, ἡ   (LXX+) *act of feeding or being fed* Pr 24:15.*

χορτομανέω   (*h.l.*) *go to seed, grow rank* Pr 24:31.*

χορτώδης, -ες   (LXX+) *grasslike* 2 Macc 5:27.*

χοῦς¹, χοός, ὁ   acc pl χοεῖς (Hippocr, Aristoph+) *measure* (= ca. 1.2*l*) Lev 19:36; 3 Km 7:24.*

χοῦς²   (= BDAG) 2 Esdr 14:4 s.t. of עפר *rubble* as if *dust*.‡

χόω   aor inf χῶσαι pf κέχωσται (Hdt+) *fill with earth* Tob 8:18 (no //; class χοῦν τάφον means *heap up burial mound*; cf. 3 Km 20:15VL [pf pass] *he has been buried*).*

χράομαι   **1.c.** (mid/pass of BDAG: κίχρημι *lend*) *have use of,* > *make use of* (a woman), *consort* or *have sex w.* (τινί) Pr 5:5; (fig) 10:26; > *borrow*; pf pass ptc *borrowed* 4 Km 6:5.‡

χρεία   **4.b.** οἱ πρὸς ταῖς χρ-, οἱ ἐπὶ τῶν χρ- *functionaries, officials* Jdth 12:10; 1 Macc 12:45.‡

χρεμετίζω   (Hom+) *neigh, whinny* (of horses) Sir 33:6; (fig) Jer 5:8; 38:7.*

χρεμετισμός, -οῦ, ὁ   (Aristoph+) *neighing, whinnying* Am 6:7; Jer 8:6, 16; (fig) 13:27.*‡

χρεοκοπέω   (DiodS, Strabo+) *cut down or minimize a debt*; (mid) *deprive oneself of or remit a debt obligation* 4 Macc 2:8.*

χρέος, -ους, τό   (Hom+) *obligation, debt* Dt 15:2f; 1 Km 2:20; Wsd 15:8.*

χρηματισμός   **2.** *document* (DiodS 14.13.8) 2 Macc 11:17.‡

χρηματιστήριον, -ου, τό   (DiodS [1.1.3]+) *treasury* 1 Esdr 3:15.*

χρησιμεύω   (Theophr+) *be useful* Wsd 4:3; Sir 13:4.*

χρησιμολογέω   (Philod?) *speak upliftingly or for edification* Jer 45:4VL.*

χρήσιμος   Zech 6:10, 14 mistrans of טוֹבִיָּה (N PERS) as if טוֹבִיָּה *her goods*.‡

χρῆσις   **4.** *loan* (Aristot, Polyb) 1 Km 1:28.*‡

χρησμολογέω   (Aristoph+) *speak oracles, prophesy* (DiodS 16.26.6) Jer 45:4.*

χρηστοήθεια, -ας, ἡ   (DemetrPhaler) *being good-hearted, generosity of spirit* Sir 37:11.*

χρία   Job 9:33VL = BDAG: χρεία; cf. 13:20VL.*‡

χρῖσις, -εως, ἡ   (14x, Aristot, pap+) *anointing* Ex 29:21; Lev 7:35; Num 4:16; Ps 151:4.‡

χρῖσμα   **2.** *coating,* (of plaster for a wall, DiodS) *glazing* Sir 38:30.‡

χριστός, -ή, -όν   (50x, Aeschyl+) **1.** *for anointing* (ἔλαιον) Lev 21:10, 12. **2.** *anointed* (no //) Lev 4:5; 2 Macc 1:10 (both of priests); (subst) *anointed one; king, messiah* 1 Km 2:10;

χρίω   ψαλτῳδέω   183

Ps 2:2; Sir 46:19; Am 4:13; Da 9:25Θ, 26L; (pl) prophets 1 Ch 16:22 = Ps 104:15.‡

χρίω pf pass ptc κεχρισμένος **2.** *coat, paint* Jer 22:14.‡

χρονίσκος, -ου, ὁ (h.l.) *brief time* 2 Macc 11:1.*

χρυσαυγέω (h.l.) *gleam like gold* Job 37:22.*

χρυσοειδής, -ές (X+) *appearing to be gold, like gold* 1 Esdr 8:57.*

χρυσοτόρευτος, -ον (h.l.) *embossed in gold* Ex 25:18vL.*

χρυσουργός, -οῦ, ὁ (LXX+) *goldsmith* Wsd 15:9.*

χρυσοφορέω (Hdt, Aristot+) *wear gold* (ornaments or cloth) 1 Macc 14:43.*

χρυσοχάλινος, -ον (Hdt+) *w. gold-studded bridle* 2 Esdr 3:6; 2 Macc 10:29.*

χρυσοχόος, -ου, ὁ (Hom+) *smelter of gold, goldsmith* Is 40:19; 46:6; Jer 10:9, 14; 28:17; EpJer 45.*‡

χρύσωμα, -ατος, τό (7x, Eur+) *gold cup (or dish)* 1 Esdr 3:6; 1 Macc 11:58.

χυδαῖος, -α, -ον (Polyb+) *common, > numerous, abundant* Ex 1:7.*

χυλός, -οῦ, ὁ (Hippocr, Pla+) *juice, fluid* 4 Macc 6:25.*

χύμα, -ατος, τό (Aristot+) *what is poured, >* (fig) *flood, torrent* 2 Macc 2:24. 3 Km 5:9 mistrans of רהב *breadth* as if fr רבב *be abundant.**

χύσις, -εως, ἡ (Hom+) **1.** *heap* 1 Km 5:6vL. **2.** *pouring* (Strabo: *casting*) 3 Km 7:11vL.*

χυτός, -ή, -όν (Hom, Hdt+) *poured, cast* (of metal) 2 Ch 4:2; Job 40:18.*

χύτρα, -ας, ἡ (7x, Aristoph+) *earthen pot* Num 11:8; Sir 13:2; Mi 3:3; κύθρα 1 Km 2:14.

χυτρόκαυλος, -ου, ὁ (4x, ins+: -γαυλος) *bucket, basin* 3 Km 7:24ff.*

χυτρόπους see κυθρο-.

χωθαρ translit of כתרת *capital (of column)* 4 Km 25:17; χωθαρεθ = , 2 Ch 4:12f.*

χωλαίνω fut χωλανεῖτε aor ἐχώλανα aor pass -λάνθη (Pla+) *limp, be(come) lame* 3 Km 18:21; Ps 17:46; (pass) *be lamed* 2 Km 4:4.*

χῶμα, -ατος, τό (13x, Hdt+) *mound, heap* Ex 8:12f; Josh 8:28; Job 14:19; Hab 1:10; Is 25:2.

χωμαριμ translit of כמרים *(pagan) priests* 4 Km 23:5.*

χωματίζω (pap) *embank or fortify w. earthen mounds or dikes* Josh 11:13.*

χωνεία, -ας, ἡ (not in HR; Polyb+) *smelting, casting* Job 38:38vL.*

χώνευσις, -εως, ἡ (pap) *smelting, casting* Ex 39:4; 2 Ch 4:3.*

χωνευτήριον, -ου, τό (LXX) *smelting furnace* 3 Km 8:51; Wsd 3:6; Zech 11:13; Mal 3:2.*

χωνευτής, -οῦ, ὁ (LXX+) *smelter, caster of metal* Judg 17:4A.*

χωνεύω (21x, pap, ins) *smelt, cast* Ex 26:37; 3 Km 7:3; 2 Ch 4:3; Mal 3:3; Is 40:19.

χώρα 6. *spot, location* (on a human body, Hom+) Lev 13:23ff. 3 Km 7:16ff mistrans of ליות *garlands,* unexpl.‡

χωρέω 1.c. (of a story or event) *come out, reach a conclusion* 2 Macc 3:40; 13:26.‡

χώρημα, -ατος, τό (Galen+) *receptacle* Ezk 32:6vL.*

χωρισμός 2. *separation* Lev 12:2; 18:19.‡

χωροβατέω (pap+) *pace off, survey* Josh 18:8f.*

χῶσαι see χόω.

Ψ

ψαλίς, -ίδος, ἡ (Aristoph+) *band, ring* Ex 27:10f; 30:4; 37:6.*

ψάλλω fut ψαλῶ aor impv ψάλατε.‡

ψαλμός 3. *mocking or taunting song* (no //) La 3:14.‡

ψαλμῳδός, -οῦ, ὁ (LXX) *psalm singer* 1 Macc 11:70vL, Sir 47:9vL, 50:18vL.*

ψαλτήριον, -ου, τό (26x, Aristot+) *lyre, harp* Gen 4:21; 2 Esdr 22:27; Ps 32:2; Job 21:12; Wsd 19:18; Is 5:12; Da 3:5.

ψάλτης, -ου, ὁ (Menand+) *harpist* 1 Esdr 5:41.*

ψαλτός, -ή, -όν (h.l.) *sung as psalms, sung to the harp* Ps 118:54.*

ψαλτῳδέω (h.l.) *sing psalms* 2 Ch 5:13.*

ψαλτῳδός, -οῦ, ὁ   (13x, LXX) *psalm singer* 1 Ch 6:18; 1 Esdr 5:41; Sir 47:9; 50:18.

ψάμμος, -ου, ἡ   (Hom+) *sand* Odes 12:9; Wsd 7:9.*

ψαμμωτός, -ή, -όν   (h.l.) *of stucco or plaster* Sir 22:17.*

ψαρός, -ά, -όν   (Aristoph+) *dappled, spotted* Zech 1:8; 6:3, 7.*

ψαύω   (Hom, Hdt+) *touch, lay hands on* (τινός) 4 Macc 17:1.*

ψέγω   aor ἔψεξα (Aeschyl+) *censure, criticize* 1 Macc 11:5vL, 11vL.*

ψεκάς, -άδος, ἡ   (Aeschyl, Hdt+) *droplet*; (pl) *drizzle, rain* SSol 5:2; Job 24:8.*

ψέλιον, -ου, τό   (9x, Hdt+) **1.** *armband, bracelet* Gen 24:22ff; Jdth 10:4; Is 3:20. **2.** *iron implement* (pap) Job 40:26.

ψελλίζω   (Pla+) *stammer, speak inarticulately* Is 29:24; 32:4.*

ψευδής   **1.c.** *fallacious, unreal*; (pl subst) *false ones* (i.e., *idols*) 2 Ch 30:14.‡

ψευδοθύριον, -ου, τό   (h.l.) *false or secret door* Bel 21G.*

ψευδοθυρίς, -ίδος, ἡ   (h.l.) *false or secret door* Bel 15G.*

ψευδολογέω   (Isocr+) *speak falsely, lie* Da 11:27L.*

ψηλαφάω   Zech 3:9 mistrans of מוש‎² *remove* as if מוש‎¹ *handle, touch*.‡

ψηλάφησις, -εως, ἡ   (Hippocr, Epicurus+) *touching, feeling* Wsd 15:15.*

ψηλαφητός, -ή, -όν   (h.l.) *requiring groping, profound* (darkness) Ex 10:21.*

ψήφισμα, -ατος, τό   (Aeschyl, Thu+) *decree* 2 Macc 6:8; 10:8; 12:4; 15:36; *proposal, resolve* Esth 3:7; 9:24.*

ψηφολογέω   (h.l.) *pave in mosaic* Tob 13:17.*

ψῆφος   **3.** (fig) *reckoning, counting up, calculation* Eccl 7:25 (renders חשבן‎ *account, result*; 7:27 λογισμός). **4.** *sharp stone* (used as a knife, no //) Ex 4:25.‡

ψιθυρίζω   (Aristoph, Pla+) *whisper* 2 Km 12:19; > *gossip or slander* Ps 40:8; Sir 21:28.*

ψίθυρος, -ον   (Pind, Soph+) *slandering* PsSol 12:3; (subst) *slanderer, gossip* Sir 5:14; 28:13; PsSol 12:1, 4.*

ψιλή, -ῆς, ἡ   (ins [III BCE], CallixenusHist) *carpet* Josh 7:21.*

ψιλόω   (Hes, Hdt+) *pull out, strip away* Ezk 44:20.*

ψόα or ψύα, -ας, ἡ   (also ψοία 2 Km 2:23vL) (Hippocr, Clearch+) *pelvic muscles* Lev 3:9; 2 Km 2:23; 3:27; 20:10; Ps 37:8.*

ψογίζω   aor ἐψόγισα (LXX+) *censure, criticize* 1 Macc 11:5, 11.*

ψόγος, -ου, ὁ   (Aeschyl+) *fault, censure* Gen 37:2; 3 Macc 2:27; 3:7; Ps 30:14; Jer 20:10.*

ψοφέω   (Soph, Eur, X+) *make a noise; stamp* (w. feet, no //) Ezk 6:11.*

ψύα   see ψόα.

ψυγμός, -οῦ, ὁ   (pap, ins+) *drying, place for drying* Num 11:32; Ezk 26:5, 14; 47:10.*

ψυκτήρ, -ῆρος, ὁ   (Eur, Pla+) *wine cooler* (large vessel for immersing jars in ice or cold water) 2 Esdr 1:9.*

ψύλλος, -ου, ὁ or -η, -ης, ἡ)   (Epicharmus, Aristoph+) *flea* 1 Km 24:15.*

ψυχαγωγία, -ας, ἡ   (Pla+) *entertainment, amusement* (of poetry: complement of διδασκαλία, Strabo, 1.1.10) 2 Macc 2:25.*

ψυχή   **1.d.** (s.t.) *soul as power or desire for dominion* Ps 26:12; *as power of thought or intention* 1 Ch 17:2 (cf. *spirit, zeal* [Pind, Hdt+] 2 Macc 7:12); ἐπὶ ψυχῇ *on one's mind* 22:7. Num 5:2; Hg 2:13; Ezk 44:25 mistrans of נפש‎ *dead body* as if *soul*; cf. εἰς ψυχήν *so as to die* Gen 37:21; τίθημι τὴν ψ. ἐν χειρί μου *take my life in my hands* Judg 12:3; ἐν ψυχῇ *risking life/death* 2 Km 23:17 = 1 Ch 11:19; La 5:9; κατὰ τὴν ψυχήν *for the purpose of (saving) life* 3 Km 19:3; περὶ ψυχῆς *a matter of life or death* 1 Macc 12:51; ψυχῇ *for the sake of life itself* Dt 16:8; ἀπὸ ψυχῆς *at the expense of one's life or vitality* Sir 14:4; ζητεῖν τὴν ψυχήν *seek to kill* Jer 25:17; ψυχας κατεσθιων *devouring lives* Ezk 22:25. Ps 68:2; Pr 25:25; Hab 2:5 mistrans of נפש‎ *throat, neck* as if *soul*. Job 24:7 emend to BDAG: ψῦχος *cold* (so Gött app, ad loc) = MT קרה‎ *cold*, cf. 37:9.‡

ψυχικός, -ή, -όν   (Diocles, Aristot+) *mental, spiritual* 4 Macc 1:32; adv -κῶς (LXX+) *in heartfelt manner* (no //) 2 Macc 4:37; 14:24.*‡

ψυχουλκέομαι   (h.l.) *have life or vitality drain off* 3 Macc 5:25.*

ψύχω   **1.b.** (act intr) *cool off, refresh oneself* Jer 6:7. **2.** *let dry* Jer 8:2; ψύχω ψυγμούς *spread out to dry* renders שטח *spread out* Num 11:32; > *spread, strew* (s.t. of שטח, no //) 2 Km 17:19. 4 Km 19:24 mistrans of קרתי (קור) *dig for water* as if fr קרר *keep cool* (cf. Jer 6:7).*‡

ψωμός, -οῦ ὁ   (12x, Hom+) *bit, piece* (in our lit, alw of bread) Judg 19:5B; Ps 147:6; Pr 9:13.

ψώρα, -ης, ἡ   (Hdt+) *itch, mange, scab* Lev 21:20; 26:16; Dt 28:27.*

ψωραγριάω   (h.l.) *suffer from itch or mange* Lev 22:22.*

Ω

ᾤα, -ας, ἡ   (LXX+) *border, collar* Ex 28:32; 36:30; Ps 132:2.*

ὠδίνησεν   aor act of BDAG: ὠδίνω.

ᾠδός, -οῦ, ὁ   (Eur+) *singer* 3 Km 10:12 = 2 Ch 9:11; 4 Km 11:14 = 2 Ch 23:13.*

ὠθέω   fut ὤσω aor ἔωσα pass ptc ὠσθείς pf pass ptc ὠσμένος **1.b.** *force, compel* (no //) Jer 41:11. **2.** *expel, push away* Is 30:22.‡

ᾤκησα, ᾤκουν   see οἰκέω.

ὤλετο   see ὄλλυμι; vL ὤχετο (spur, Λ, > X) Jer 10:20.

ὡμαλισμένος   pf pass ptc of BDAG: ὁμαλίζω Sir 21:10.

ᾤμην   1st sg impf of οἴομαι, *I seemed* Gen 40:16; 2 sg ᾤου *you supposed* Is 57:8; ᾤετο *he seemed* Gen 41:1; aor subj ᾠήθη *he supposed* Esth 8:12o.

ὠμία, -ας, ἡ   (LXX+) *shoulder* 1 Km 9:2; (fig) *support, joist* (?), *angle, corner* (of building or machine) 3 Km 6:8; 7:17ff; 4 Km 11:11 = 2 Ch 23:10.*

ὠμίον, -ου, τό   (ins) *small shoulder* Job 18:13vL.*

ὠμόλινον, -ου, τό   (Aeschyl+) *flax, raw rough cloth* Sir 40:4.*‡

ὠμός   Jer 38:21 f.l. for οἶμος (q.v.), Heb מסלה *road*. Dt 33:12 mistrans of כתף *mountain slope* as if *shoulder*. Mal 2:3 mistrans of זרע *seed* as if זרוע *arm*.‡

ὠμός, -ή, -όν   (Hom+) **1.** *raw* Ex 12:9. **2.** *harsh, savage, cruel* 2 Macc 4:25; 7:27; 4 Macc 9:30; 18:20.*

ὠμότης, -ητος, ἡ   (Soph+) *savagery, cruelty* 2 Macc 12:5; 3 Macc 5:20; 6:24; 7:5.*

ὠμοτοκέω   (LXX+) *miscarry* Job 21:10.*

ὠμόφρων, -ον   (Aeschyl+) *cruel or harsh in mind* 4 Macc 9:15.*

ὠνάσθης   2 aor pass (= mid; *enjoy* τινός, not *be enjoyed*) of BDAG: ὀνίημι Tob 3:8BA.

ὥρα   **4.** *the proper time*, > *something beautiful, beauty* (Menand+), *springtime* Is 52:7.‡

ὡράθην   late (DiodS 20.6.1. ἐωράθη) aor pass of BDAG: ὁράω.

ὡραΐζω   (CratinusCom+) pass *enjoy beauty, take delight* Sir 25:1.*

ὡραιόομαι   (LXX) *be beautiful* 2 Km 1:16; SSol 1:10; 7:2, 7.*

ὡραιότης, -ητις, ἡ   (7x, X+) **1.** *beauty* Ps 44:4; Is 44:13. **2.** *ripeness, bounty* Ps 49:11.

ὡραϊσμός, -οῦ, ὁ   (LXX+) *elegance, adornment* Jer 4:30.*

ὤρυμα, -ατος, τό   (h.l.) *roaring* Ezk 19:7.*

ὡσανεί   (Aristot, Polyb+) *as it were* Esth 1:1i.*

ὤσω   fut, ὠσθείς aor pass ptc, ὠσμένος pf pass ptc of ὠθέω.

ὠτότμητος, -ον   (LXX) *w. ears cropped or cut off* Lev 21:18; 22:23.*

ὠφέλεια   **2.** *gain,* > *profit, plunder* (Polyb 2.3.8) 2 Macc 8:20.‡

ὠφέλημα, -ατος, τό   (Aeschyl+) *benefit, use* Jer 16:19.*

ᾤχετο, ᾠχόμην   see οἴχομαι.

ὤχρα, -ας, ἡ   (Aristot+: *yellow ochre*) *mildew* (no //) Dt 28:22.

Appendix I: Word Lists

I. Precise Parallels: This list contains words from extrabiblical texts that are closely comparable to the LXX usages cited. Words in bold indicate instances where the LXX may help us more precisely interpret the secular text cited.

ἀβλαβής
ἀναδέω
ἀναδίδωμι
ἀνακρούω
ἀνατέλλω
ἀπάντημα
ἀποσπάω
αὐγή
αὐτομολέω
ἄφθορος
βαρυθυμέω
βολή
γαλέαγρα
γένεσις
γυναικῶν
δάκτυλος
δάνος
δαπάνημα
δέρρις
δημαγωγία
δήμιος
διακόπτω
διαρρήγνυμι
διατίθημι
διεγείρω
δρεπανηφόρος
ἔγγραπτος
εἰκότως
ἐκβάλλω
ἐκβιάζω
ἔκλειψις
ἐκπίπτω
ἔκταξις
ἔνεδρος

ἐνέχω
ἔνθεν
ἔξαιμος
ἐξοπλησία
ἐξυμνέω
ἐπεγγελάω
ἐπιβάλλω
ἐπιεικέως
ἐπίθεσις
ἐπικίνδυνος
ἐπιρρίπτω
ἐπιρρώνυμι
ἐπισκευάζω
ἐπιστρατεία
ἐρυμνός
εὐανδρία
εὔκαιρος
εὐκοπία
εὐνομία
εὕρεμα (2)
ἕως
ζευγίζω
ζεύγνυμι
ζυμίτης
θανατόω
θερμασία
θύρσος
ἴλη
ἱππικός
ἰσχύς
κακίζω
κατακύπτω
καταπέλτης
κατατιτρώσκω

κατελεέω
κατοινόομαι
καταρχέομαι
κέρας
κλητέον
κλοιός
κοσμοποιΐα
κριός
κώπη
κωπηλάτης
λιτός
λόγος
λυμεών
μακρότερον
μανιώδης
μαρμάρινος
μεγαλοπρεπῶς
μεγαλώνυμος
μεταμέλει
μεταστροφή
μόνος
νεῦμα
νόμος
ξενοτροφέω
ὀμφαλός
ὁπλίτης
ὀργανικός
ὀρύσσω
ὄσπριον
παντοδαπός
παράδεισος
παρακλείω
πέλτη
περικατάλημπτος

περιστολή
περιφέρω
πολυανδρεῖος
πορευτός
ποῦς
πρᾶγμα
προγονικός
προηγορέω
προσμαρτυρέω
προσμείγνυμι
προσπαρακαλέω
προφασίζομαι
πτερνίζω
σελίς
σημαία
σταθμός
συγκεραυνόω
συμμείγνυμι
συμμετέχω
συναγελάζομαι
συνηχέω
σύνθεμα
σύνθημα
σύνταγμα
σωματοποιέω
ταριχεύω
ταυρηδόν
τελέω
τιάρα
τοπάρχης
τρέφω
τρισάθλιος
τροχηλάτης
ὑποφαίνω

ὑφοράομαι
φαιδρός
φάτνωμα

φρούριον
φυγαδεία
χαλεπαίνω

χρηματισμός
χρησμολογέω
ψυχαγωγία

ὠφέλεια

II. Transliterations: This list contains non-Greek words that have been transliterated from their Hebrew or Aramaic source text. Words in bold are mistransliterations of the words in or inferred from the MT, suggesting copyists' errors in the transmission of the LXX.

αβακ
αβαρκηνιν
αββους
αβεδηριν
αβιρα
αγαθ
αγανωθ
αγουρ
αδων, αδωναι
αδωρηεμ
αθουκιιν
αιδαδ
αιλ, κτλ
αιν
αλαιμωθ
αλωθ
αμμαδαρωθ
αμασενιθ
αματταρι
αμαφεθ
αμμαζειβη
αρ
αρααβ
αραβωθ
αραφωθ
αριηλ
αριωθ
ασαραμελ
ασαρημωθ
ασεδεκ
ασελισι
ασηρωθ
ασιδα
ασιρ
αφεσιμ (see ἄφεσις)
αφφουσωθ
αφφω
αχουχ
βααλταμ
βαδδιν
βακελλεθ
βαμα
βαρακηνιμ
βαρουχ
βαρχαβωθ

βεδεκ
βεζεκ
βεθ
βερ(σ)εχθαν
βιζα
βιρα
γαβης
γαβιν
γαβις
γαι
γαρεμ
γεδδουρ
γεδωρ
γομορ
γωλαθ
γωληλα
δαβιρ
δεβραθα
ελλουλιμ
ελμωνι
ελωαι
ενφωθ
εργαβ
ερσουβα
εσεφιν
εφαδανω
εφουδ, -ωδ,-ωθ
εφραθ
ζακχω
ζεμα
ηδω
θααλα
θαιηλαθα
θαλπιωθ
θαννουριμ
θαρσις
θεε, θειμ
θεεβουλαθω
θεκελ
θεννουριμ
θεραφιν
θραελ
θωδαθα
ιααρ
ιαμιβιν

ιαμιν
ιγλααμ
ἵλεως
ιν
ιρ
ισανα
καδημιμ
καδησιμ
καρασιμ
καφουρη, κεφφ-
μαδεββαν
μαδων
μαελεθ
μαζουρωθ
μαναα
μανη
μασενα
μασμαρωθ
μασομελ
μαχιρ
μαχμα
μαωζιν
μαων
μεθαχαβιν
μεθωεσιμ
μελον
μελχομ
μελω
μεσθααλ
μεσσαβ
μεσσαε
μεταβηχας
μεχωνωθ
μοσφαθαιμ
ναβαλ
ναζιρ
ναθινιμ κτλ
νακκαριμ
νασιβ
νασιφ
ναχαλ
νεβελ
νεελασα
νεεσαραν
νεζερ

νεσσα
νεφθαρ
νεχωθα
νωκηδ
οιφι
πιπι
ραθμ
σαβαχα
σαβεκ
σαβι
σαδημωθ
σαδηρωθ
σαλαμιν
σαφφωθ
σαχωλ
σεραφιν
σερσερωθ
σοομ
σωρηχ
σωφερ
φαζ
φαλτεια
φαρασιν
φαρες
φαρουριμ
φασεκ
φελεθθι
φελμουνι
φορθομμιν
φουρ
φραζων
χαβραθα
χαμανιμ
χαρσιθ
χερεθ
χερεθθι
χεττι
χεττιιν
χοθωνωθ
χωθαρ
χωμαριμ

III. Words Not Known To Occur Outside the LXX Itself

A. *Hapax legomena* (*h.l.*): This list contains words whose sole known occurrence in Greek literature is in the LXX. Words in bold are not included in LSJ.

ἀβατόω
ἀβοηθησία
ἀβουλεύτως
ἁγιαστία
ἀγριομυρίκη
ἀγχιστευτής
ἀδελφοπρεπῶς
ἀδιεξέταστος
Ἀζωτιστί
αἰνιγματιστής
αἱρετίς
ἀκαταπάτητος
ἀκατάποτος
ἀκουσιάζομαι
ἀλλοφυλέω
ἀλλόφωνος
ἀμείδητος
ἀμνησικακία
ἀμορίτης
ἀμφιβολεύς
ἀναβαθμίς
ἀναγνεία
ἀνάμειξις
ἄναξις
ἀναπτέρωσις
ἀνατιναγμός
ἀνδρογύναιος
ἀνείκαστος
ἀντάμειψις
ἀπατητής
ἀπενεόομαι
ἀπευθανατίζω
ἁπλοσύνη
ἀποδεκατίζω
ἀποκακέω
ἀποκάλυμμα
ἀποκέντησις
ἀπόκλεισμα
ἀπόκλειστος
ἀπόλλω
ἀποπαρθενόω
ἀποπρατίζομαι
ἀποστρεβλόω
ἀπωσμός
ἀργυροκοπέω
ἀργυρολόγητος
ἀργυροχόος
ἀρθρέμβολος
ἀροτρόπους
ἀρρενωδῶς

ἀρχιδεσμώτης
ἀρχιοινοχοΐα
ἀσθενόψυχος
ἀσιτί
ἀσφαλτόπισσα,
  -αλτόω
ἀττάκης
αὐγέω
αὐλαῖος
αὐλάρχης, -χία
ἀφεύκτως
βαθύγλωσσος
βαθύφωνος
βαθύχειλος
βακχύριον
βαρύγλωσσος
βαρυκάρδιος
βαρυωπέω
βόμβησις
βοοζύγιον
βούκεντρον
βραχυτελής
βυθοτρεφής
γασβαρηνός
γαυριόομαι
γελοιασμός
γλωσσότμητος
γλωσσοχαριτέω
γνόφερος
γνοφόω
γόγγυσις
γομφιασμός
γοννορυέω
δειλιαίνω
δευτερολογέω
διάγγελμα
διαιτέω
διακάμπτω
διακριβάζομαι
διακρίβεια
διαλοιδόρησις
διαμαχίζομαι
διαπαρατηρέομαι
διαραντός
διάσταλσις
διαστράπτω
διασυρίζω
διασφραγίζομαι
διαφόρημα
διγομία

διεμπίμπλημι
διεξίπταμαι
δίθυμος
διορθρίζω
δοξικός
δοξολογέω
δυνάστευμα
δυσαίακτος
δυσδιήγητος
δυσπέτημα
δωροδεκτής
δωρολήμπτης
ἐγκαίνισις, -νωσις
ἐγκαταλοχίζω
ἐγκλοιόομαι
ἐγκότημα
ἐθνηδόν
ἐθνοπάτωρ
ἐθνόπληθος
εἰδέχθεια
εἰσσπάομαι
ἑκατοστεύω
ἐκβεβηλόω
ἐκβρασμός
ἐκζητητής
ἐκθλιβή
ἐκκήρυκτος
ἐκκόλαμμα
ἐκλιμία
ἐκλογιστία
ἐκλοχίζω
ἐκλύτρωσις
ἐκμυελίζω
ἐκουσιασμός
ἐκπολιτεύω
ἔκπρακτος
ἐκριζωτής
ἐκσαρκίζω
ἐκσιφωνίζω
ἐκσπερματίζω
ἐκσπονδυλίζω
ἐκτριβή
ἐκφυγή
ἐκφύρω
ἐκχολάω
ἐλεημοποιός
ἐλευστέον
ἐμβρίμημα
ἐμμολύνομαι
ἐμπαραγίνομαι

ἐμπληθύνω
ἔμπνευσις
ἐμποδοστατέω,
  -στάτης
ἐμπορπόω
ἔμπτυσμα
ἔννευμα
ἐννοσσοποιέομαι
ἐνσιτέομαι
ἐνσκολιεύομαι
ἐντιναγμός
ἐντότερος
ἔντριτος
ἐνυποτάσσω
ἐξατιμόομαι
ἐξέλευσις
ἐξερεύνησις
ἔξοικος
ἐξολέθρευμα
ἐξουδένωμα
ἔξωσμα
ἑόρτασμα
ἐπακρόασις
ἐπανδρόω
ἐπαξονέω
ἐπαρυστήρ
ἐπευθυμέω
ἐπευλαβέομαι
ἐπιγεμίζω
ἐπιγνωμοσύνη
ἐπίγνωστος
ἐπιεικεύομαι
ἐπικαινίζω
ἐπικαρπολογέομαι
ἐπικραταιόω
ἐπίκυφος
ἐπιρρωγολογέομαι
ἐπισπλαγχνίζομαι
ἐπιστήριγμα
ἐπισυνέχω
ἑπταμήτωρ
ἑπταπλοῦς
ἐργοδιωκτέω
ἐρημίτης
εὐδράνεια
εὐκοσμέω
εὐπόρφυρος
εὐσυναλλάκτως
ἐχθρία
ζῶσις

ἡδυσμός
ἡπατοσκοπέομαι
θραυσμός
θωρακισμός
ἱεροστάτης
ἱεροσύλημα
ἱερόψυχος
ἱματιοφύλαξ
ἰσάστερος
ἰσηγορεύομαι
καθήλωμα
κάθιδρος
καθίπταμαι
κακόμοχθος
καρπόβρωτος
καρτεροψυχία
καταβάσιος
καταγογγύζω
κατάκλιτος
κατακροτέω
καταμερισμός
καταμιμνήσκομαι
καταπανουργέομαι
καταπελματόομαι
καταπληγμός
κατάπολις
καταρρεμβεύω
καταστραγγίζω
κατατέρπομαι
καταφλογίζω
καταφύτευσις
καταχαλάω
καταψευσμός
κατεντευκτής
κατεπικύπτω
κατευθικτέω
κατοπίσω
κηρογονία
κλοποφορέω
κνήφη
κοιτασία
κολοβόριν
κολοβόκερκος
κόπωσις
κοσμοπληθής
κοσμοφορέω
κοσυμβωτός
κοθωνός
κραταιότης
κύφω
λαμπηνικός
λαξευτήριον
λαπιστής
λαφυρεύω, -ρέω
λειτουργήσιμος

λεοντηδόν
λικμήτωρ
λοιμεύομαι
λοιμότης
μαγείρισσα
μαδαρόω
μακροβίωσις
μαλακοψυχέω
μαστιτής
μεγαλοημέρευσις
μεγαλοκράτωρ
μεγαλόσαρκος
μεγάλωμα
μελαθρόω
μελετήτικος
μεριτεύομαι
μέσακλον
μεταβολία
μετακιρνάομαι
μηνίαμα
μισοξενία
μίσυβρις
μονοφαγία
μυαλόομαι
μυριότης
μυρμηκιάω
μυρμηκολέων
μυροβρεχής
μωρεύω
νέωμα
νηπιοκτόνος
νηστός
νομοθέσμως
νύμφευσις
νύσταγμα
νωθροκάρδιος
οἰκτίρημα
οἰστρηλασία
ὀλέθρευσις
ὀλεθροφόρος
ὀλιγοποιέω
ὀλυρίτης
ὁμοζηλία
ὀξυσθενής
ὁπλοδοτέω
ὀπτάζομαι
ὀρνιθοσκοπέομαι
ὀροφοκοιτέω
ὄφλησις
ὀχυρωμάτιον
παγγέωργος
παθοκρατέομαι
παμβότανον
παντοφαγία
παραζώνη

παρανακλίνω
παρασφαλίζομαι
παρεισπορεύομαι
πάριος
παρωμίς
περίγλυφον
περιδιπλόω
περιλακίζω
περιονυχίζω
περισιαλόω
περιχαλάω
περιχαλκόω
πίννιμος
πλινθουργία
πνευματοφορεύομαι
πολιόρκησις
πολυημερεύω
πολυοδία
πολυπληθύνω
ποντόβροχος
πριστειροειδής
προαναμέλπω
προανατάσσω
προθερίζω
προκατασκιρρόομαι
πρόκρημνος
προλήνιον
προνουμηνία
προοδηγός
προπτύω
προσαναλέγω
προσανατρέπω
προσανοικοδομέω
προσαπωθέω
προσαρτίως
προσεμβριμάομαι
προσενέχω
προσεξηγέομαι
προσεπικατατείνω
προσερυθριάω
προσηλυτεύω
προσκαθήκω
προσοδύρομαι
προσοίγω
προσπυρόω
προσσιελίζω
προσταράσσω
προσυστέλλω
προϋποτάσσω
προχώρημα
πρωτοβαθρέω
πρωτοκλήσιον
πρωτοκλίσιον
πρωτοκουρά, -ρία
πρωτοτοκεύω

πτέρνον
ῥαφιδευτής, -τός
ῥεμβασμός
ῥεμβέω
ῥιπιστός
ῥόαξ
ῥοών
σανιδωτός
σιδηρόδεσμος
σιρῶνος
σισόη
σκέπασις
σκόπελον
σκυλεία
σμιρίτης
σοφόω
στιχίζω
στραγγαλώδης
στρεβλωτήριον
στρίφνος
στροφωτός
συγκαθυφαίνω
συγκατακληρονομέω
συγκερατίζω
συγκλασμός
συγκύφω
συλλοχάω
συμβοηθός
συμβόσκομαι
συμβραβεύω
συμμισοπονηρέω
συμπροσπλέκω
συνανάμειξις
συνεδριάζω
συνεκκεντέω
συνεκτρίβω
συνέκτροφος
συνοδυνάομαι
συσκήνιος
σφιγγία
τεκνοφόνος
τηλαύγημα, -γησις
τιθηνία
τιμογραφέω
τριμερία
τριμερίζω
τρισσόω
τροχιαῖος
τρυφερεύομαι
ὑβρίστια
ὑπέραρσις
ὑπερασπίστρια
ὑπερδυναμόω
ὑπέροψις
ὑπερφερής

Appendix I: Word Lists

ὑπευλαβέομαι
ὑποκαλύπτω
ὑπομαστίδιον
ὑποσκέλισμα
ὑποσχάζω
ὑπόφρικος
ὑστεροβουλία
φαντασιακοπέω
φαύλισμα
φαυλίστριος

φιλαμαρτήμων
φοβερισμός
φοβεροειδής
φονοκτονία
φορολόγητος
φρικασμός
φυγαδεῖον
φυγάδιον
φυλάκισσα
χαλκοπλάστης

χαρακοβολία
χαρτηρία
χειρονομία
χιλιοπλασίως
χορτομανέω
χρονίσκος
χρυσαυγέω
χρυσοτόρευτος
ψαλτός
ψαλτωδέω

ψαμμωτός
ψευδοθύριον, -θυρίς
ψηλαφητός
ψηφολογέω
ψυχουλκέομαι
ψωραγριάω
ὤρυμα

B. LXX Words: This list contains words that occur multiple times, but never (with the exceptions stated in the Introduction) outside the LXX. Words in bold are not included in LSJ.

ἀγαλλίαμα
ἀγαυρίαμα, -ριάομαι
ἁγιαστήριον
ἀδελφιδός
ἄκαν
ἀκριβασμός
ἀληρός
ἀλισγέω
ἀλλοφυλισμός
ἀμνάς
ἀμφίασις
ἀναφαλάντωμα
ἀναφορεύς
ἀνεκλιπής
ἀπαντή
ἀπάνωθεν
ἀπόδομα
ἀποικεσία
ἀποκαθαρίζω
ἀποκιδαρόω
ἀποκρυφή
ἀποπεμπτόω
ἀποσκοπεύω
ἀποσυνάγω
ἀρτός
ἀρχιπατριώτης
ἀρχίφυλος
ἀσυνθεσία, -θετέω
ἀτεκνόω
αὔγασμα
ἀφόρισμα
ἀχρειότης
βάδος
βδελυγμός
βηρύλλιον
βουνίζω
γαζαρηνός
γαμβρεύω
γλύκασμα
γομφιάζω
γραμματοεισαγωγεύς

γρηγόρησις
δειλανδρέω
δειλόψυχος
δεινάζω
δεκαπλασιάζω
δευτερόω
διαρτίζω
διασάφησις
διάψαλμα
διδυμεύω
δίμετρον
δωροκοπέω
ἐγκάθετος
ἐγκαινισμός
ἐγκαταπαίζω
ἐγκισσάω
ἐκδικάω
ἐκκαθαρίζω
ἐκλικμάω
ἐκμελίζω
ἔκνηψις
ἐκουσιάζομαι
ἐλαττονόω
ἔμπαιγμα
ἐμφραγμός
ἐντιμόομαι
ἐξακονάω
ἑξακοσιοστός
ἐξηγορία
ἐξηλιάζω
ἐξίλασμα
ἐξιχνιασμός
ἐξολέθρευσις
ἐξομβρέω
ἐξουδένωσις
ἐπανατρυγάω
ἐπαρυστρίς
ἐπευκτός
ἐπικαταράομαι
ἐπιλημπτεύομαι
ἐπιμύλιον

ἐπισκεπάζω
ἐπιστοιβάζω
ἐπιφαυλίζω
ἐπιφυλλίζω
ἐπορχίζομαι
ἐρημικός
ἐρυθροδανόω
ἐσχατίζω
ἔτασις, -σμός
εὐιλατεύω
ἔφισος
ζυμωτός
ζωοποίησις
ἥγησις
ἠρεμάζω
θελητής, -τός
θλιμμός
θνησιμαῖος
θρύλημα
θυσίασμα
Ἰουδαϊστί
ἰταμία
καλλιόομαι
καμιναία
κάρπωμα (?)
καρπωτός
καρυΐσκος
κατάβρωμα, -βρωσις
καταδυναστεία
καταθλάω
κατακάλυμμα
κατακάρπωσις
καταλιθοβολέω
κατάλιθος
καταπάτημα, -τησις
καταπρονομεύω
κατάρασις
κατοδυνάω
κατώδυνος
κερατιστής
κλαυθμών

κληδονόμος
κληρωτί
κοιλοσταθμέω
κολλυρίζω, -ριον, -ρίς
κοσύμβος
κραταίωμα, -ωσις
κυπρίζω
κωφεύω
λαξεύω
λυτρωτός
λῶμα
μακροημερεύω
μάκρυμμα
μεγαλοπτέρυγος
μιαροφαγέω, -ία
ναζιραῖος
ναθιναῖος
ὀλεθρία
ὀλιγόω
ὀλοκαρπόω, -πωμα, -πωσις
ὀλοκαύτωσις
ὀνυχιστήρ
ὀπωροφυλάκιον
παθοκράτεια
παλαιστή
παλαίωμα
πανάγιος
πανοικία
πανούργευμα
παντοδύναμος
παράθεμα
παρασυμβάλλω
παροικεσία
παρόργισμα
παταχρός
πενέομαι
περασμός
περικαθαρίζω
περιουσιασμός
περιρραντίζω

περισκελής	προσοχυρόω	σύγκλεισμα	φαυλισμός
περισπόριον	πρωτογένημα	σύμβλησις	φονοκτονέω
περίτειχος	πρωτοτοκέω	συμβολοκοπέω	φυγαδευτήριον
πιστοποιέω	πτερνισμός	συναντή	φυγάδιον
πλεοναστός	πυργόβαρις	συντριμμός	χαυῶν
πλημμέλησις	πυρρίζω	τετράστιχος	χήρευσις
πολεμοτροφέω	σκεπαστής	τριετίζω	χλεύασμα
πολυέλεος	σκληροκάρδιος	τρισαλιτήριος	χοιρογρύλλιος
πολύορκος	σκολιάζω	τρισσεύω	χωνευτήριον
πολυπληθέω	σπλαγχνισμός	τριστάτης	ψαλμῳδός
ποτιστήριον	στηλογραφία	ὑπεραίνετος	ψαλτῳδός
πραΰθυμος	στίλβωσις	ὑπεράνωθεν	ὡραιόομαι
πρόσκαυμα	στιππύινος	ὑπερυμνητός	ὠτότμητος
προσόχθισμα	συγκάλυμμα	φατνόω	

IV. LXX+: This list contains words whose first known use is in the LXX, although they are also found in later secular Greek texts outside the LXX.

A. Words with multiple non-LXX instances

ἀγαθόω	ἀνταπόκρισις	ἀρχιδεσμοφύλαξ	διαπληκτίζομαι
ἀγαθύνω	ἀντικρίνομαι	ἀρχιευνοῦχος	διάπτωσις
ἀγκωνίσκος	ἀντίπτωμα	ἀρχιμάγειρος	διασκιρτάω
ἀγύναιος	ἀντίψυχος	ἀρχιοινοχόος	διαφλέγω
ἀδιάτρεπτος	ἀνυψόω	ἀρχισιτοποιός	διαφρύγω
ἀδρανής	ἄπαρσις	ἀρχιστράτηγος	διαφωτίζω
ἀδρειόω	ἀπάτησις	ἀσταθής	διεκκύπτω
ἀδυναμέω	ἀπέκτασις	ἄστεγος	διεμβάλλω
ἀθεία	ἀπελέκητος	ἀτράπελος	διηχέω
ἀθλοθετέω	ἀπληστεύομαι	αὐθεντία	διορθωτής
ἀθῳόω	ἀπόβλημα	αὐθωρί	διπλοΐς
ἀκάθεκτος	ἀπογαλακτίζω	αὐτοδέσποτος	διυφαίνω
ἀκαταμάχητος	ἀποκρυβή	ἀφαίρεμα	διχοτόμημα
ἀκηδιάω	ἀποκωφόομαι	ἀφόδευμα	διώροφος
ἀκηλίδωτος	ἀποξαίνω	ἀφόμοιος	διωστήρ
ἀκιδωτός	ἀποπιάζω	βεβήλωσις	δορατοφόρος
ἀκριβάζω	ἀποποιέω	βιβλιοφυλάκιον	δόρκων
ἄλιμος	ἀποπομπαῖος	βοτρύδιον	δοτός
ἀμάσητος	ἀποσάσσω	γαλακτοτροφία	δυσνοέω
ἀμνησία	ἀποσκηνόω	γαυρίαμα	δυσσέβημα
ἀμόλυντος	ἀποσκορακίζω,	γελοιάζω, -αστής	ἐγκηδεύω
ἀμφοτεροδέξιος	-κισμός	γενεσιάρχης	ἔγκοπος
ἀναβίωσις	ἀποσταλάζω	γενεσιουργός	ἐγκρατέω
ἀνάνευσις	ἀποτροπιάζομαι	γενέτις	ἔγκτητος
ἀναποδισμός	ἀποτρυγάω	γλυκάζω, -ασμός	ἐγρήγορος
ἀνατροφή	ἀποτύφλωσις	γλωσσοτομέω	ἐδικητής
ἀνατυπόω	ἀπτόητος	δᾳδουχία	εἰσκύπτω
ἀναφράσσω	ἀπώρυξ	δαψιλέομαι	εἰσοδιάζω
ἀνεμόφθορος	ἀρεταλογία	δεκαμηνιαῖος	ἐκδεκτέον
ἀνεξικακία	ἀρκεύθινος	δευτέριος	ἔκλαμπρος
ἀνεπιστρέπτως	ἁρμόνιος	δευτερονόμιον	ἐκπαίζω
ἀνέφικτος	ἀροτρίασις	διακαθιζάνω	ἐκπεριπορεύομαι
ἀντανακλάω	ἀρτοκοπικός	διανθίζω	ἐκπικραίνω

ἐκτιναγμός
ἔκτριψις
ἐκτύπωσις
ἐκφαυλίζω
ἐμβίωσις
ἐμμελέτημα
ἐναγκάλισμα
ἐναλλαγή
ἐνάρμοστος
ἐνενηκοταετής
ἐνεξουσιάζω
ἐνεχύρασμα
ἔνθεσμος
ἐντίναγμα, -νάσσω
ἐντομίς
ἐνυπνιαστής
ἐξάδελφος
ἔξαρθρος
ἐξεικονίζω
ἐξευμενίζω
ἐξίλασις, -ασμός
ἐξιχνιάζω
ἐξυπνόω
ἐπαίτησις
ἐπάρδω
ἐπιβρέχω
ἐπιγλύφω
ἐπιδιπλόω
ἐπιλυπέω
ἐπιπροστίθημι
ἐπισπουδάζω
ἐπισυστρέφω
ἐπόζω
ἐπωρεύω
ἐργατεία
ἔσθησις
ἐσώτατος
ἑτεροκλινῶς
εὐεκτέω
εὐθίκτως
εὐκληματέω
εὐπάρευφος
εὐπειθέω
ἐφύβριστος
ἐχθρεύω
ἡμισεύω
θηριάλωτος
θυΐσκη
ἰδιόγραφος
ἱλαρόω, -ρύνω
ἱμάντωσις
ἴνδαλμα
ἰσοδύναμος
ἰσοπολίτις
καθαγιάζω

κάθισις
καθοδηγέω
καθυφαίνω
κακοποίησις
κάλλυνθρον
καρδιόω
κάρρον
καταβλέπω
καταβόησις
καταδεσμεύω
κατακενόω
καταλεαίνω
καταμωκάομαι
κατάντημα
καταπείθω
κατάπικρος
κατάπτωμα
κατασπαταλάω
καταστενάζω
κατασφαλίζομαι
καταφθάνω
καταφράσσω
κατεμβλέπω
κατοικεσία
κατοχεύω
κερατίζω
κινύρα
κισσόφυλον
κλεψιμαῖος
κληδονίζομαι
κληροδοτέω
κοίλασμα
κόλπωμα
κονδυλισμός
κοπανίζω
κοπόω
κρημνίζω
κροσσοί
κρουνηδόν
κρυβῆ
κυοφορία
κωνώπιον
λάγανον
λάμψις
λαογραφία
λατρευτός
λειτύργημα
λέπισμα
λιθουργέω
λικμός
λιτανεία
λυθρώδης
μαγικός
μαιμάσσω
μακροημέρευσις

μακροήμερος
μακρότης
μακροχρονίζω
μακρύνω
ματαιόφρων
μεῖραξ
μελανόομαι
μελισσῶν
μεριδαρχία
μεσοπόρφυρος
μεταπαιδεύω
μηρυκάομαι
μηρυκισμός
μηχανεύομαι
μόλυνσις
μονόζωνος
μόνορχις
μυρισμός
νοσσοποιέω
ξενιτεία
ξυλάριον
ξύρησις
οἰωνισμός
ὀκνηρία
ὁλοσφύρητος
ὄμβρημα
ὁμόψυχος
ὀμφακίζω
ὀνοκένταυρος
ὀξυγράφος
ὀπήτιον
ὁρατής
ὀργιάω
ὅρμημα
ὀσφρασία
ὀφιόδηκτος
ὀφιομάχης
παμβασιλεύς
παμμελής
πανεπίσκοπος
πανηγουρισμός
πανουργεύομαι
παντεπόπτης
παραβιβάζω
παραδοξάζω
παραθλίβω
παρακλήτωρ
παρέκλυσις
παρεπιδείκνυμι
παρόρασις
πάτημα, -ητός
πέλυξ
πεντεκαιεικοσαετής
περιβιόω
περίθεμα

περικομπέω
περικοσμέω
περικύκλῳ
περιξύω
περιπαθῶς
περισκυθίζω
περιστήθιον
περιστολή
πηλουργός
πλαγιάζω
πλινθεία
ποικιλτικός
πολυπλασιάζω
πολυρήμων
πολύφροντις
πολυχρονίζω
προανατέλλω
προασπίζω
προβασκάνιον
προήγορος
προκακόω
πρόπτωσις
προσαποθνήσκω
προσβλητός
προσεκκαίω
προσεμπίμπρημι
προσήλυτος
προσημειόομαι
προσθλίβω
προσπάσσω
προσταγή
προσυψόω
προϋφίστημι
πρωτόπλαστος
πτερνίζω
πτίλος
πτύξις
πυροβόλον
ῥακώδης
ῥοδοφόρος
ῥύστης
ῥωποπώλης
σαθρόω
σαπρία
σιτοδοσία
σκαμβός
σκελίζω
σκεπεινός
σκιαγράφος
σκορακισμός
σκοτάζω
σκοτομήνη
σκυβαλίζω
σμικρύνω
σπερματίζω

σπλαγχνοφάγος
στερέωσις
στιλβόω
στολισμός, -ιστής
στομίς
στοχαστής
στραγγίζω
συγκατεσθίω
συγκλύζω
συγκρουσμός
συγχρονίζω
συζυγής
συκῶν
σύμβλημα
συμπλεκτός
συμπορπάω

συναναφύρω
συναποκρύπτω
σύννυμφος
συνολκή
συνούλωσις
συνουσιασμός
σύντριψις
συντροχάζω
συσσεισμός
συσσύρω
συσφίγγω
σφυροκόπος
σχολαστής
τειχιστής
τερπνοτής
τραχηλιάω

τροφεύω
τρυγίας
ὑετίζω
ὑπερηφανεύω
ὑπερφωνέω
ὑπόλυσις
ὑποστηρίζω
ὑποχυτήρ
ὑψαυχενέω
φαλάκρωμα
φαῦσις
φιλεχθρέω
φιλιάζω
φιλόκοσμος
φονευτής
φύλαγμα

φύρασις
χαιρετίζω
χαρμοσύνη
χαροποιός
χλωρίζω
χλωρότης
χονδρίτης
χορτασία
χορτώδης
χρυσουργός
χωνευτής
ψογίζω
ᾠά
ὠμία
ὠμοτοκέω
ὡραϊσμός

B. Words with a single non-LXX instance

ἀγαθόω
ἀναλημπτήρ
ἀνεργεία
ἄνισχυς
ἀπάντημα
ἀπειράγαθος
ἀπερικάθαρτος
ἀπολεπίζω
ἀποστάτις
γονορρυής
γυναικῶν
δεκαπλασιάζω, -σίων
δεκάχορδος
δευτέρωσις
διαπειράζω
διατίλλω

δυσάθλιος
ἑβδομηκοστός
ἐμπλατύνω
ἐνδελεχέω
ἐνθρονίζω
ἐντρύφημα
ἐξιππάζομαι
ἐπιφυτεύω
ἐπιχαρής
ἐρεθιστής
ἐφαμαρτάνω
ἠθολογέω
θηριόβρωτος
θλαδίας
ἰσονομέω
κακοφροσύνη

κατάπαυμα
κατατρυφάω
κεπφόομαι
λεωπετρία
μακροημέρευσις
ὀνοματογραφία
ὁπλολογέω
πανεθνεί
παραβασιλεύω
παρακαθεύδω
παροιστράω
παῦσις
περάτης
προεξαποστέλλω
προφασιστικός
πρώταρχος

ῥοισκός
συμμιαίνω
συμφλογίζω
τερατοποιός
ὕμνησις
ὑπερόρασις
ὑπερτήκω
ὑποστήριγμα
ὑψηλοκάρδιος
φθάρμα
φωταγωγέω
Χαλδαϊστί
χιονόομαι
χρηστοήθεια

V. No //: This list contains words with LXX meaning which have no parallel in secular Greek texts.

ἄβατος
ἄβυσσος
ἀγαθώς
ἀγκύλη
ἀγκών
ἀγνοέω
ἀγρός
ἀδρύνομαι
ἀδυνατέω
αἱμοβόρος
αἰσχύνη
ἀκατέργαστος
ἄκαυστος
ἀκόλαστος
ἀκολουθία

ἀκοντιστής
ἀκοπιαστῶς
ἀκροφύλαξ
ἄλλαγμα
ἀλλάσσω
ἀλογέω
ἁμαρτάνω
ἀμβλύνω
ἀμερής
ἀνά
ἀναβιβάζω
ἀναγνώστης
ἀναλαμβάνω
ἀναλημπτέον
ἀναμιμνήσκω

ἀναφορά
ἀνθομολόγησις
ἀνθράκινος
ἀνομέω
ἀντανίστημι
ἀνταπόκρισις
ἀντιβάλλω
ἀντικαθίζω
ἀντιστηρίζω
ἄντρον
ἄξων
ἀπαγγέλλω
ἀπαίρω
ἁπαλότης
ἀπαντάω

ἀπάντημα
ἅπαξ
ἀπεκδίδωμι
ἀπερείδω
ἀπηλιώτης
ἁπλόω
ἀποβάπτω
ἀποικία
ἀποικισμός
ἀποκάθημαι
ἀποκαθίστημι
ἀποκαλύπτω
ἀποκοσμέω
ἀπομερίζω
ἀπονοέομαι

ἀποξενόω
ἀποπλάνησις
ἀποπομπή (?)
ἀποσκληρύνω
ἀποστατέω
ἀποστολή
ἀποτρίβω
ἀποφέρω
ἀποφθέγγομαι
ἀπώλεια
ἀριστερός
ἀρχή
ἄρχων
ἀσθενέω
ἀτέλεστος
ἀτίμητος
αὐγάζω
αὐθεντία
αὖλαξ
αὐλίζω
αὔρα
αὐταρκέω
ἀφαίρεσις
ἁφή
ἀφήγημα
ἀφορισμός
βάλλω
βάμμα
βαρύνω
βασιλεύω
βδελύσσομαι
βεβαίωσις
βία
βίβλος
βλέπω
βομβέω
βόσκημα
βότρυς
γένημα
γεωμετρικός
γλῶσσα
γραμματεία -τικός
γύμνωσις
γυρόω
δακτυλήθρα
δαψιλέομαι
δεκάς
δεσμός
δῆλος
δημηγορέω
δῆμος
διάζομαι
διακαθίζω
διακλάω
διανόησις

διαπειράζω
διαρκέω
διασκεδάζω
διασκευή
διαστέλλω
διατάσσω
διατείνω
δίδυμος
διέξοδος
διηγέομαι, -γημα,
 -γησις
δίφραξ
διφρεύω
δόξασμα, -αστός
δορυφορία
δροσίζω
δυναστεία
ἐγγαστρίμυθος
ἐγχειρίδιος
ἕδρα
εἰρηνικός
ἐκδίδωμι
ἐκζέω
ἔκθεσις
ἔκθυμος
ἐκκενόω
ἐκκλησιαστής
ἐκκλίνω
ἐκλύω
ἑκούσιος
ἐκπεράω
ἐκπετάννυμι
ἐκπολεμέω
ἐκπορνεύω
ἐκρέω
ἐκτήκω
ἐκτινάσσω
ἔκτριψις
ἐκχέω
ἐλέγχω
ἕλκω
ἐμπλόκιον
ἐμφέρω
ἐνδέω
ἔνθεμα
ἐνθυμέομαι
ἐνοικειόω
ἐνσείω
ἐντήκω
ἐντομίς
ἐντρύφημα
ἐνώπιος
ἐνώτιον
ἐξάλειψις
ἐξαλλάσσω

ἐξάρχω
ἐξελίσσω
ἐξέρπω
ἐξιλάσκομαι
ἕξις
ἐξοδεύω, -όδιος, -οδος
ἐξουσιάζω
ἐπαγωγή
ἐπανορθόω, -θωσις
ἐπάνω
ἐπάνωθεν
ἐπαρκέω
ἐπεισφέρω
ἐπέκεινα
ἐπεξέρχομαι
ἐπιβάθρα
ἐπιβιβάζω
ἐπιδέω
ἐπίθεμα
ἐπίθεσις
ἐπικοινωνέω
ἐπικοσμέω
ἐπικρατέω, -τησις
ἐπικρούω
ἐπίλημπτος
ἐπιμαίνω
ἐπίμεικτος
ἐπιπορεύομαι
ἐπίσκεψις
ἐπισπουδαστής
ἐπιστρέφω
ἐπιτάφιος
ἐπιφέρω
ἐπιχαρής
ἐπίχειρον
ἐπιψάλλω
ἐπιψοφέω
ἐπονείδιστος
ἐποπτικός
ἐπωμίς
ἐρεύγομαι
ἐσχάρα
ἑτεροκλινῶς
ἔτι
εὖγε
εὐκοσμία
εὐπορέω
ἐφαμαρτάνω
ἐφοδεύω
ζάω
ζήλωσις
ἥγημα
ἡμίθνητος
ἠχέω
θέμα

θήρευμα
θλάω
θῦμα
ἰδιόγραφος
ἱερεία
ἱκανόω
ἰσονομέω
ἱστίον
ἰσχύς
ἴχνος
καθιζάνω
καθίστημι
καινουργός
κάλυμμα
κατάδεσμος
καταδιώκω
κατάλειψις
κατάλυμα
καταπαύω
κατασκηνόω
κατασπεύδω
κατασπουδάζομαι
καταψύχω
κάτεργον
κατευθύνω
κατοίκησις
κείρω
κενεών
κεράτινος
κλητός
κλίτος
κοιμάω
κόλπωμα
κοπάζω
κρεμαστός
κρύφος
κυδοιμός
κύκλωμα
κυλίω
κύτος
λάλημα
λαμβάνω
λανθάνω
λεπτύνω
λέπυρον
λῆμμα
λιπαρός
λογεῖον
λογιστής
μαδάω
μακροθυμέω
μάνδρα
μαντεῖον
μαρτύριον
μεγαλόφρων

μεθίστημι
μερισμός
μετάγω
μεταλλεύω
μεταχέω
μὴ τι
μῆλον
μιαίνω
μνημόσυνον
μουσικός
μοχθέω, -θος
μυκτήρ
μυξωτήρ
μυρισμός
νεός
νεῦμα
νῆσος
νίπτω
νυμφάγωγος
ξυλοφορία, -φορος
ξυρόν
οἰκία
οἰκίζω
οἰκτριμός
οἰνοδόχος
οἰνοχόη
ὀλισθάνω
ὀνομασία
ὀνυχίζω
ὀπίσω
ὁράω
ὀρθρεύω
ὁρισμός
ὁρμή
ὀρτογαμήτρα
πανουργία
πιαρά
παραβασιλεύω
παραλαλέω
παράλλαξις
παραλύω
παράνομος
παραπίπτω
παραπληξία
παραπορεύομαι
παρατάσσω
παρατείνω
παρατίθημι
παραχωρέω
παρεκλείπω
παρθενικός
παροίκησις
πείθω
περιβάλλω
περικαλύπτω

περικλύζω
περιλαμβάνω
περίλημψις
περιοχή
περισσεία
περισσεύω
περιστρέφω
περιστροφή
περιφέρεια
περιφορά
περίφρων
πέτευρον
πλαγιάζω
πλείων, πολύς
πληρόω
πόα
ποίκιλμα
πολλοστός
ποῦς
πρᾶσις
πραΰνω
πρεσβεῖον
πρόβλημα
προκαταλαμβάνω
προνομή
προσέχω
πρόσχωμα
πρόσωπον
προφθάνω
πρώταρχος
πρωτοβολέω
πτέρνα
πτέρυξ
πυκάζω
πυρεῖον
πυρόω
ῥακώδης
ῥάχις
ῥίπτω
ῥύδην
σάλος
σής
σκέλος
σκεύασμα
σκήνωμα
σκυτάλη
σμικρύνω
σπασμός
σπερματίζω, -τισμός
σποδόομαι
στάσις
στεατόομαι
στοιβή
στοιχείωσις
στομίς

στρατιῶτις
στρατοπεδεύω
στρογγύλωσις
συγγραφή
σύγκειμαι
σύγκριμα
συγχρονίζω
συλλαμβάνω
συλλογισμός
συλλοχισμός
συμβαστάζω
συμπαραλαμβάνω
συμπεραίνω
συμπεριφέρω
σύν
συναναστροφή
συναναφέρω
συνάπτω
σύναψις
συνδάκνω
σύνδεσμος
συνεπισκέπτομαι
συνέχω
σύνθεσις
συνίημι
συντέλεια
συντελέω
συσκοτάζω
σύστημα
σύστρεμμα
συστρέφω
συστροφή
τακτικός
τάσσω
τεκνοποιέω
τέλειος, -ειόω, -είωσις
τηρέω
τίναγμα
τοκετός
τολύπη
τοξικός
τραυματίας
τρισσῶς
τροχαντήρ
τροχίσκος
τρυφερός
τυρρανίς
ὑβριστικός
ὑγρασία
ὑπερέχω
ὑπερηφανία
ὑπεροχή
ὑπνόω
ὑπό
ὑποκάτω

ὑπολαμβάνω
ὑποπίπτω
ὑπόστημα
ὑποτίθημι
ὑφαιρέω
ὑψόω
φείδομαι
φερνή, -νίζω
φιλότιμος
φιλόψυχος
φορεύς
φυτεύω
φωταγωγέω
χαλάω
χαριστήριον
χεῖλος
χείρ
χελώνη
χόω
χριστός
ψαλμός
ψῆφος
ψοφέω
ψυχή
ψυχικός
ὠθέω
ὦχρα

VI. Words with stereotypical translations (s.t.):
This list contains words consistently used by LXX translators to render a single Hebrew root, regardless of the semantic range of the Hebrew or Greek terms.

ἄβυσσος
ἀδικία
ἀδολεσχέω, -σχία
ἀλήθεια
ἁμάρτημα, -τία
ἀναμιμνήσκω
ἀνήρ
ἄνθρωπος
ἀπαντάω
ἀποτίνω
ἄρσις
γίνομαι
δεξιός
δήλωσις
δικαίωμα
δουλεία
ἐγκάθημαι
ἐγκαταλείπω

ἐκλείχω
ἔλεος
ἐν
ἐπινικάω
ἐπισκέπτομαι
ἐπίσκεψις
ἐπισκοπή
εὐώνυμος
θάλασσα
θυγάτηρ
ἱκανός
κακόω
κληρονομέω
κληρονόμος
κουφίζω
κρατέω
κρίμα
κρίσις

λαμβάνω
λῆμμα
μελετάω
μεταστρέφω
οἶκος
ὁμολογία
ὁράω
ὀρθρίζω
παραβολή
περίλημψις
πλημμέλεια, -λημα
πρόσχωμα
σημαίνω
σημασία
σπεύδω
σπουδάζω
σπουδή
στερεός

συναντάω
συνέχω
τραυματίας
ὕβρις
ὑπέρογκος
ὑπολαμβάνω
ὑπομιμνήσκω
ὑψόω
φορολόγος
φυλακή
χαλκός
χείρ
χοῦς²
ψυχή
ψύχω

VII. Mistranslations:
This list of words represents cases in which the LXX translators misconstrued the meaning of their sources' words, through a confusion of roots or a misunderstanding of meaning of the source. (For words in bold, the mistranslation is unexplained—that is, no suggestion can be offered as to the intention or understanding of the translator with respect to the presumed Hebrew text.)

ἀγάπησις
ἀγχιστεία, -στεύω
ἀδικέω, -κος
αἴρω
αἰσθητικός
αἰσχύνω
αἰχμάλωτος
ἀκοή
ἀκρίς
ἀλλοιόω
ἀλλοίωσις
ἄλσος
ἀλώπηξ
ἀμφιέννυμι
ἀναβάλλω
ἀνάβασις
ἀναπτύσσω
ἀνατολή
ἀναφαίνω
ἄνεσις
ἀνήρ
ἀνθέμιον
ἀντάλλαγμα

ἀντίλημψις
ἀπαλότης
ἀπατάω
ἀπειλή
ἀποβλέπω
ἀποδίδωμι
ἀποκαλύπτω
ἀποκεντέω
ἀπόκλειστος
ἀποκλείω
ἀποκρίνω
ἀπόσπασμα, -σπάω
ἀποτάσσω
ἀποτομή
ἀποτρίβω
ἀργύριον
ἀρήν
ἀροτριάω
ἄρουρα
ἀρχή
ἄρχω
ἀσθενέω
ἀστραπή

αὐλή
αὔριον
αὐχμώδης
βόθρος
βρῶμα
γίγας
γνώριμος, -ιστής
γνωστής
γράφω
δείδω
δειλία
δεσμεύω
δεσμώτης
δευτερόω
δέω
δῆγμα
διάβασις
διάγγελμα
διαγράφω
δίαιτα
διαρρήγνυμι
διασκορπισμός
διαστέλλω

διασώζω
διαφθείρω
διαχέω
διαχωρίζω
διδάσκω
διψάω
δουλεία
δύναμις
δυσμή
ἐγκαθίζω
ἐγκαινίζω
ἐγρήγορος
ἐγχειρίζω
εἶπον
εἰρήνη
ἐκκενόω
ἐκνεύω
ἐκνήφω
ἐκρίπτω
ἐκτινάσσω
ἐλεέω
ἕλκω
ἐλπίζω

ἐλπίς	ἴσος	μάχιμος	περιστόμιον
ἐμπήγνυμι	ἰσότης	μεθύσκω	περισχίζω
ἐμπιμπλάω	ἰσχύς	μείγνυμι	περιτομή
ἐν	κάθαρσις	μελετήτικος	περιχαρακόω
ἐνδιαβάλλω	καθέδρα	μέλος	πετάννυμι
ἔνεδρον	καθηλόω	μέρος	**πίπτω**
ἐντέλλω	καθίζω	μεσαῖος	πιστεύω
ἐξανάστασις	**καθίστημι**	**μέσος**	πίστις
ἐξεγείρω	κάλαμος	μετέωρος	πλευρόν
ἕξις	καλέω	μέτρον	πληθύνω
ἐξίστημι	κάλλος	μηρός	**πλοῖον**
ἐξουδένωμα	**κάμινος**	μικρός, -ότης	ποιμήν
ἔξωθεν	καταβαίνω, -βασις	μισθωτός	πόλις
ἐξωθέω	**κατάγω**	μονόκερως	πολυανδρεῖος
ἐπαινέω	**κατάδυσις**	νεῖκος	πραγματεία
ἐπαίρω	κατακυλίω	νῖκος	πρᾶσις
ἐπακούω	καταλαμβάνω	νόμιμος	πρόθυρον
ἔπαρσις	**καταλλαγή**	νοσσία	πρόνομη
ἐπήκοος	κατανύσσομαι	νῶτος	προοίμιον
ἐπιγινώσκω	κατάπαυσις	οἰκοδομή	προσδέχομαι
ἐπιδέξιος	καταποντισμός	οἶκος	πρόσθεσις
ἐπιδίδωμι	κατάρασις	ὁλοκαύτωμα	πρόσκαυμα
ἐπιθύμημα	καταχέω	ὀξύνω	**προσκεφάλαιον**
ἐπικαλέω	κατάχυσις	ὀξύς	προσοχθίζω
ἐπικρούω	κατευθύνω	ὀπίσω	προστίθημι
ἐπιλέγω	καύχησις	ὅρασις	πρόσωπον
ἐπιξενόομαι	**κείρω**	ὁρατός	προτείχισμα
ἐπισκέπτομαι	κεφαλή	ὀργή	πτοέω
ἐπιστρέφω	**κηρίον**	οὐχ οὕτως	πῦρ
ἐπιφανής	κίων	ὄφλησις	**πυροφόρος**
ἐπιφυλλίζω, -λλίς	κλαίω	παιδεύω	πύρφορος
ἐπίχυσις	κλαυθμών	παλαιός, -αιόω	πῶλος
ἐπωμίς	κληρόω	**παλαίω**	σαλεύω
ἐρημόω	κλίμα	παλαίωσις	σής
ἐσώτατος	κλοιός	παράγγελμα	σιαγών
ἑτοιμάζω, -μασία	κλών	παράδειγμα	σιώπησις
ἕτοιμος	κοιλία	παρακαλέω	σκεπάζω
εὐδοκέω	κόλπος	παραλλαγή, -λλάσσω	σκῆπτρον
εὔηχος	**κορύνη**	παραρίπτω	σκοπία, -πός
εὐλογέω	κρατέω	παρασιωπάω	σκοτεινός
εὐφραίνω	κριτήριον	παράταξις	σπήλαιον
ἐχθρός	κρύπτω	παρατείνω	**σπουδαῖος**
ἡγέομαι	κτάομαι	παραχρῆμα	στάσις
ἧλος	κυνικός	παρίημι	στενός
ἧπαρ	κώδιον	πάροδος	**στερεόω**
ἠχέω	λευκανθίζω	παροικέω, -κία	**στερέωμα**
θάρσος	λίθος	πατήρ	στεφάνη
θελητής	λιπαίνω	πατραδελφός	στήριγμα, -ρίζω
θεμελιόω	λοιμεύομαι	πατρία	στιβαρός
θερισμός	λύτρωσις	παῦσις	στοιβάζω
θέσις	μάγειρος	πάχος, -χύνω	**στραγγαλία**
θήρα	μακρότης	πεντήκοντα	στρῆνος
θυσία	μάρμαρος	περιέρχομαι	στύλος
ἰατρεύω, -τρός	μαρτύριον	περίλοιπος	συγγενής
ἱκανός	μαστός	περιοχή	συγκαθίζω

συγκλεισμός, -στός
συγκλείω
σύμμιξις
συμπίπτω
συμποδίζω
συνάγω, -γωγή
σύνδεσμος
συνέλευσις
σύνθεσις
συνίημι
συνοδία
σύνοδος¹
συντέλεια, -λέω
συντρίβω
συντροχάζω

σύστημα
συστροφή
ταράσσω
ταχύς
τεκνοποιέω
τέλειος
τερέμινθος
τιτάν
τόκος
τόπος
τρέχω
τρισσεύω, -σσός
τροπή
τροχός
ὑλώδης

ὕπαρξις
ὑπέραρσις
ὑπερασπισμός
ὑπόστασις
ὑποστήριγμα
φαντασία
φείδομαι
φεύγω
φθάνω
φιάλη
φλόξ
φονεύω
φορολόγος
φορτίζω
φρύαγμα

φυγαδεῖα
φύλαγμα
φυλή
φῶς
φωτίζω
χαίρω
χείρ
χορηγία
χρησιμός
χύμα
χώρα
ψηλαφάω
ψυχή
ψύχω
ὦμος

VIII. Textual Variants: This list contains verses in the LXX in which the analysis of the indicated word suggests textual emendation for one or both LXX editions. In many cases the suggested emendation follows the indicated word.

Gen 19:17 συμπαραλαμβάνω; 25:31–34; 27:36 πρωτοτοκέω; 49:12 χαροπός, -ποιός
Ex 12:22 θιγγάνω; 28:15ff λογεῖον; 39:22 ἀποσκευή, παρασκευή
Lev 8:8 λογεῖον; 11:19 γλαύξ; 13:22 διάχυσις; 19:14 προτίθημι; 19:19 δίφορος; 25:13, 16 ἔγκτησις, κτῆσις
Nu 1:47 συνεπισκέπτω; 7:88 ἐγκαίνισις, -νωσις; 11:5 σίκυος, σίκυς; 15:3 ὁλοκάρπωμα; 22:24 αὔλαξ; 32:13 καταρρεμβέω; 35:2, 7 προάστιον; 35:15 φυγαδεῖον, -γάδιον
Dt 4:1 πολυπλασιάζω; 15:18 ἐφέτειος, -τιος; 17:18 δίφρος; 17:20 μακροχρονίζω; 18:11 ἐπαείδω; 21:17 πρωτοτοκεῖον; 22:9 δίφορος; 23:22 ἁμαρτία; 24:20 ἐλαιαλογέω; 34:7 χελύνιον
Josh 13:22 ῥοπή
Judg 5:16B ἀγέλη; 5:26A κατακοπή; 11:2 ἑταίρα; 19:8 στραγγεύομαι; 20:48A ἀποκλείω
1 Km 4:21 βαρχαβωθ; 13:20 θέριστρον; 25:35 αἱρετίζω
2 Km 5:24 συγκλεισμός; 12:31 διάγω; 15:28 στραγγεύομαι; 18:14 ἄρχω; 19:19 διάβασις
3 Km 10:11ff πελεκητός
4 Km 5:17 πυρρός
1 Ch 4:21 αββους; 5:1 πρωτοτοκεῖον; 22:2 ξεστός
2 Ch 23:18 εγχειρίζω; 25:16 βουλεύομαι; 31:18 ἐγκαταλοχίζω, καταλοχία
1 Esdr 1:33 ἀποκαθίστημι, ἀφίστημι; 2:17 (19) ὑπόμνημα, ὑπομνηματισμός; 5:53 κάρρον, χαρά; 5:69 ἐπικοιμάομαι; 6:6 ἀποσημαίνω, ὑποσ-; 6:8, 24 ξεστός; 6:32 (31) προγράφω, προσγ-; 8:80 μολύνω
2 Esdr 4:15, 19 φυγαδεῖα; 14:4 ἀχθοφόρος, ἐχθρός
Jdth 3:6 φρουρέω; 10:3 διαξαίνω, διατάσσω; 12:1 καταστρώννυμι; 13:1 ἀποκλείω; 15:11 λαφρεύω, -φρέω, κατασεύασμα, σκεύασμα; 16:17 ἐπανιστάνομαι
Tob 1:22S ἐκλογιστής; 11:8S ἐμπάσσω, ἐμπλάσσω
1 Macc 2:7 εκαθιοαν (sic); 5:27 συλλαμβάνω, συνειλέω; 6:40 ἐκτάσσω; 7:42, 47 ἐκτείνω; 8:24 κυριεία; 10:39 προσκαθήκω; 12:40 πόρος; 12:44 κοπόω; 13:37 βαίνη, βάις; 13:43 ἑλέπολις
2 Macc 2:1 μεταγίνομαι; 3:19 διακύπτω, διεκκύπτω; 3:26 προφαίνω, προσφ-; 4:9 ἐπιχωρέω, ἐφηβία, -βεῖον; 4:13 μολύνω; 4:21 πρωτοκλήσιον, -κλίσιον; 4:29 μεγαλομερής; 4:49

μεγαλομερής, μεγαλοπρεπῶς; 5:25 ἐξοπλησία; 6:4 ἐπιπληρόω; 6:13 ἐπιτίμιον, -τιμος; 8:2 καταπονέω; 8:7 διαχέω, διηχέω; 9:12 ἰσόθεος; 10:30 διακόπτω, διεξίπταμαι; 12:13 γεφυρόω; 12:28 ἀλκή, ὁλκή; 12:43 ἀνδρολογία; 13:15 συγκεντέω; 13:25 ὑπεράγαν; 14:17 βραχέως; 14:20 ὁμοιόψηφος, ὁμόψηφος; 14:38 ἐκτενία; 15:19 καταλαμβάνω, κατειλέω

3 Macc 2:22 περιπλήσσω; 2:31 ἐπιβάθρα, -θρον; 3:1 ἐκχολάω; 3:16 κατάπολις; 4:2 ἄλεκτος, ἄληκτος; 5:2 δράκος, δράξ; 5:20 ἐπιτέλλω; 6:34 πυρίπνους; 6:41 ἐκτενία; 7:12 παραινέω, συναινέω

4 Macc 7:9 ἁγιαστία; 14:15 ὀροφοκοιτέω; 15:13 τροφεία

Ps 54:12 τόκος; 127:3 κλ(ε)ιτύς

Odes 3:3 ἑτοιμάζω

Pr 3:35 ὑψόω; 12:10 βουλεύομαι; 14:33 ἔνεδρος; 28:24 ἀποβιάζομαι; 30:14 στόμις, τόμις

Eccl 2:3 ἕλκος

Job 19:26 ἀνατλέω, ἀνέτλην; 24:7 ψυχή; 24:21 γύναιον, ἀγύναιος; 31:10 ἀλέω; 36:7 (Am 1:11, Jr 3:5, etc.) νεῖκος, νῖκος; 40:2 ἱκανός; 41:23 χάλκειος

Wsd 2:23 ἀϊδιότης, ἰδιότης; 12:22 μετριότης; 19:5 περάω

Sir 3:19 ἐπίδοξος; 3:25 ἀμοιρέω; 9:12; 11:22 εὐοδία; 10:8 ἔκπρακτος; 10:22Gött προσήλυτος; 10:27R δεξαζόμενος; 18:32 προσδεηθής, προσδέω; 19:27 συγκρύπτω, -κύφω; 20:32 τροχηλάτης; 22:17 γλύμμα, ψαμμωτός, ξεστός, ξυστός; 22:18 χάλιξ; 26:5 δέομαι; 26:18 εὔσταθμος, πτέρνον; 26:27 διαιτάω, διαρτάω; 27:22 ἀφίστημι; 29:13 ἀλκή, ὁλκή; 31:2 ἐκνήφω; 32:9 ἐξισάζω; 32:19 μεταμέλει; 36:7 (33:10) ὁρισμός, ὁρκισμός; 37:11 ἐπέτειος, ἐφέτιος; 38:28 κενιει; 40:6 σκοπία; 41:26 κάλυψις; 45:10 λογεῖον; 48:10 καταγράφω; 51:15 ἐξανθέω

PsSol 2:13 μιαίνω; 14:8 ἐπιστατός; 17:6 ἀλάλαγμα

Hos 7:6 κατάρασις, -ράσσω

Am 1:11 (Jb 36:7, etc.) νεῖκος, νῖκος; 5:11 ξέστος

Mi 1:10 καταγέλως; 5:1 ἐμφραγμός

Na 3:7 ἀποπηδάω

Ob 18 πυροφόρος, πύρφ-

Mal 2:3 ἔνυστρον

Is 30:14 ἀποσυρίζω, -σύρω; 40:25 ἰσόω; 55:12 διδάσκω; 63:12 κατασχίζω

Jer 3:5 (Jb 36:7) νεῖκος, νῖκος; 5:31 ἐπικρατέω, -κροτέω; 10:20 ὄλλυμι; 19:8 κατατάσσω; 19:14 διάπτωσις; 23:3 ἐκ-, ἐπιλαμβάνω; 26:28 ἀθωόω; 28:33 αμητος; 29:11 ἐπίχειρον; 30:2 (29:9) τόπος; 30:10 (29:17) ἐγχειρίζω; 30:23 (30:6) πλήσσω, ἔπληξα; 31:12 κέρασμα; 31:39 καταλλάσσω; 33:1 ἀρχή; 36:27 συλλοιδορέω; 38:21 οἶμος, ὦμος; 39:33 ἐκ-, ἐπιλαμβάνω; 45:22 καταδύνω; 52:4 τετράποδος

Bar 1:10 μαναα

La 1:6 ἐξαίρω; 1:7 κατοικεσία; 2:6 διαπετάννυμι, διασπάω; 2:8 καταπόντισμα, καταπάτημα; 2:13 ἰσόω; 3:13 υἱός; 3:11 κατασπάω; 3:49 καταπονέω; 4:5 περιλαμβάνω

Ezk 5:16 ἔκλειψις, ἐξάλειψις; 11:7 τάσσω; 14:6, etc. Κύριος Κύριος; 16:31 οἰκοδομή; 17:6 ἀπορρώξ; 24:3 ἐγχέω; 24:7, etc. λεωπετρία; 27:12 μόλυβδος; 28:7 στρώννυμι, τιτρώσκω; 44:18 βία, βιζα; 45:14 γομορ; 46:23f μαγειρεῖον, μάγειρος; 47:3 ἄφεσις

Sus 50L Ra ἀποκρίνω

Da 2:34Θ ἀποσχίζω, τέμνω; 11:26 κατασύρω

IX. Textual conjectures for the Masoretic Text: This list contains all words the analysis of which suggests an emendation of MT for the underlying Hebrew.

ἀνατρέπω	ἄφεσις	ἐχθές	σαλαμιν
ἀποτάσσω	ἀφορίζω	θαιηλαθα	σμῖλαξ
ἄξων	βεζεκ	θεμελιόω	συγκλεισμός
ἀποστροφή	γομορ	θραελ	τίθημι
αρααβ	διάβασις	καδημιμ	τρέχω
ἀρήν	διάγω	κατάρασις	ὑγρασία
αριηλ	ἐκνεύω	παλαιός	ὑψόω
ασαρημωθ	ἕλκω	πόλις	φῶς
ασεδεκ	ἐμπίμπλημι	προστίθημι	χαμανιμ
αφεσιμ	ἐπαίρω	πτερνίζω	

Appendix II: Comparative Index of Words in This Lexicon and BDAG

In the following list, words in plain type receive adequate coverage in BDAG and thus are not included in this lexicon. Words in bold type are in this lexicon but are not included in BDAG. Italicized words are treated in BDAG, with this lexicon providing additional information pertaining to the LXX. Words in this latter category are also marked with the double dagger symbol (‡) in the applicable lexical entries. Words marked with the dagger symbol (†) occur in the LXX only as variant readings and are not in the text of either edition. Many of these variants are not found either in BDAG or other LXX lexica. Square brackets indicate that BDAG uses a different form of the word from what appears in this lexicon.

A
ἀ
αβακ
αβαρκηνιν
ἀβασίλευτος
ἄβατος
ἀβατόω
αββους
αβεδηριν
αβιρα
ἀβλαβής
ἀβοηθησία
ἀβοήθητος
ἀβουλεύτως
ἀβουλία
ἄβρα
ἀβροχία
ἄβρωτος
ἄβυσσος
αγαθ
ἀγαθοποιέω
ἀγαθοποιός
ἀγαθός
ἀγαθότης
ἀγαθόω
ἀγαθύνω
ἀγαθῶς
ἀγαθωσύνη

ἀγαλλίαμα
ἀγαλλίασις
ἀγαλλιάω
ἄγαλμα
ἄγαμος
ἄγαν
ἀγανακτέω
αγανωθ†
ἀγαπάω
ἀγάπη
ἀγάπησις
ἀγαπητός
ἀγαυρίαμα
ἀγαυριάομαι
ἀγγεῖον
ἀγγελία
ἀγγέλλω
ἄγγελος
ἄγγος
ἄγε
ἀγείοχα (see ἄγω)
ἀγελαῖος
ἀγέλη
ἀγεληδόν
ἀγερωχία
ἀγέρωχος
ἀγήοχα (see ἄγω)
ἁγιάζω
ἁγίασμα

ἁγιασμός
ἁγιαστήριον
ἁγιαστία
ἅγιος
ἁγιότης
ἁγιωσύνη
ἀγκάλη
ἀγκαλίς
ἄγκιστρον
ἀγκύλη
ἀγκών
ἀγκωνίσκος
ἁγνεία
ἁγνισμός
ἁγνίζω
ἅγνισμα
ἁγνισμός
ἀγνοέω
ἀγνόημα
ἄγνοια
ἀγνός
ἄγνος
ἀγνωσία
ἄγνωστος
ἄγονος
ἀγορά
ἀγοράζω
ἀγορανομία
ἀγορασμός

ἀγοραστής
αγουρ
ἀγρεύω
ἀγριαίνω
ἀγριομυρίκη
ἄγριος
ἀγριότης
ἀγριόω
ἄγροικος
ἀγρός
ἀγρυπνέω
ἀγρυπνία
ἄγρωστις
ἀγυιά
ἀγύναιος
ἀγχιστεία
ἀγχιστεύς
ἀγχιστευτής
ἀγχιστεύω
ἄγχω
ἄγω
ἀγωγή
ἀγωγός†
ἀγών
ἀγωνία
ἀγωνιάω
ἀγωνίζομαι
ἀγωνιστής
ἀδαμάντινος

ἀδάμας	ἄζυμος	αἱμωδιάω	ἀκάρδιος
ἀδάμαστος	Ἀζωτιστί	αιν	ἀκαριαῖος
ἄδεια	ἀηδία	αἴνεσις	ἀκαρπία
ἄδειπνος	ἀήρ	αἰνετός	ἄκαρπος
ἀδελφή	ἀθανασία	αἰνέω	ἀκατάγνωστος
ἀδελφιδός	ἀθάνατος	αἴνιγμα	ἀκατακάλυπτος
ἀδελφιδοῦς†	ἀθέμιτος	αἰνιγματιστής	ἀκατάλυτος
ἀδελφικῶς	ἀθεῖα†	αἶνος	ἀκαταμάχητος
ἀδελφοκτόνος	ἀθεσία	αἴξ	ἀκαταπάτητος
ἀδελφοπρεπῶς	ἄθεσμος	αἰπόλιον	ἀκατάποτος
ἀδελφός	ἀθέσμως	αἰπόλος	ἀκατασκεύαστος
ἀδελφότης	ἀθετέω	αἵρεσις	ἀκαταστασία
ἀδεῶς	ἀθέτημα	αἱρετίζω	ἀκαταστατέω
ἄδηλος	ἀθέτησις	αἱρετίς	ἀκατάστατος
ᾅδης	ἀθεώρητος	αἱρετός	ἀκατάσχετος
ἀδιάκριτος	ἀθλέω	αἱρέω	ἀκατέργαστος
ἀδιαλείπτως	ἀθλητής	αἴρω	ἄκαυστος
ἀδιάλυτος	ἄθλιος	αἰσθάνομαι	ἀκέραιος
ἀδιάπτωτος	ἀθλοθετέω	αἴσθησις	ἀκηδία
ἀδιάστρεπτος†	ἄθλον	αἰσθητήριον	ἀκηδιάω
ἀδιάστροφος	ἀθλοφόρος	αἰσθητικός	ἀκηλίδωτος
ἀδιάτρεπτος	αθουκιν	αἴσθομαι	ἀκιδωτός
ἀδιάφορος†	ἀθροίζω	αἴσχιστος	ἀκινάκης
ἀδιεξέταστος	ἄθροισμα	αἰσχρός	ἀκίνητος
ἀδικέω	ἀθρόος	αἰσχρῶς	ἀκίς
ἀδίκημα	ἀθυμέω	αἰσχύνη	ἀκλεής
ἀδικία	ἀθυμία	αἰσχυντηρός	ἀκληρέω
ἄδικος	ἄθυτος	αἰσχύνω	ἄκλητος
ἀδίκως	ἀθῷος	αἰτέω	ἀκλινής
ἀδόκητος	ἀθῳόω	αἴτημα	ἀκμάζω
ἀδόκιμος	αἴγειος	αἴτησις	ἀκμαῖος
ἀδολεσχέω	αἰγιαλός	αἰτία	ἀκμή
ἀδολεσχία	αἰγίδιον	αἰτιάομαι	ἄκμων
ἀδόλως	αιδαδ	αἴτιος	ἀκοή
ἀδοξέω	αἰδέομαι	αἰφνίδιος	ἀκοίμητος
ἀδοξία	αἰδήμων	αἰφνιδίως	ἀκοινώνητος
ἄδοξος	ἀΐδιος	αἰχμαλωσία	ἀκολασία
ἀδρανής	ἀϊδιότης	αἰχμάλωσις†	ἀκόλαστος
ἁδρός	αἰδοῖον	αἰχμαλωτεύω	ἀκολουθέω
ἀδρύνομαι	αἰδώς	αἰχμαλωτίζω	ἀκολουθία
ἀδυναμέω	αἰεί	αἰχμαλωτίς	ἀκόλουθος
ἀδυναμία	αἰθάλη	αἰχμάλωτος	ἀκολούθως
ἀδυνατέω	αἰθής	αἰών	ἀκονάω
ἀδύνατος	αἰθρίζω†	αἰώνιος	ἀκοντίζω
ἄδυτος†	αἴθριος, αἴθριον	ἀκαθαρσία	ἀκοντιστής
ᾄδω	αἰκία	ἀκάθαρτος	ἀκοπιά(σ)τως
αδων	αἰκίζομαι	ἀκάθεκτος†	ἄκοσμος
αδωναι, αδωναιε	αἰκισμός	ἄκαιρος	ἀκουσιάζομαι
αδωρημεμ	αιλ, αιλαμ,	ἀκαίρως	ἀκούσιος
ἀεί	αιλαμμω(θ), αιλευ	ἀκακία	ἀκουστής
ἀειγενής†	αἴλουρος	ἄκακος	ἀκουστός
ἀέναος	αἷμα	ἀκάλυπτος	ἀκουτίζω
ἀεργός	αἱμάσσω	ἄκαν	ἀκούω
ἀέρινος†	αἱμοβόρος	ἄκανθα	ἄκρα
ἀετός	αἱμορροέω	ἀκάνθινος	ἀκρασία

ἀκρατής
ἄκρατος
ἀκριβάζω
ἀκριβασμός
ἀκρίβεια
ἀκριβής
ἀκριβόω
ἀκριβῶς
ἀκρίς
ἄκριτος
ἀκρόαμα
ἀκροάομαι
ἀκρόασις
ἀκροατής
ἀκροβυστία
ἀκρογωνιαῖος
ἀκρόδρυα
ἀκρόπολις
ἄκρος [ἄκρον]
ἀκρότομος
ἀκροφύλαξ
ἀκρωτηριάζω
ἀκρωτήριον
ἀκτίς
ἀκύμα(ν)τος
ἄκυρος
ἀκυρόω
ἀκώλυτος
ἄκων
ἀλάβαστρος
ἀλαζονεία
ἀλαζονεύομαι
ἀλαζών
αλαιμωθ
ἀλάλαγμα†
ἀλαλαγμός
ἀλαλάζω
ἄλαλος
ἅλας
ἀλάστωρ
ἀλγέω
ἀλγηδών
ἄλγημα
ἀλγηρός
ἄλγος
ἀλεεύς
ἄλειμμα
ἀλεῖται, ἀλοῦνται [ἅλλομαι]
ἀλείφω
ἀλεκτρυών
ἄλεκτος
ἀλέκτωρ
ἄλευρον
ἀλέω

ἀλήθεια
ἀληθεύω
ἀληθής
ἀληθινός
ἀληθινῶς
ἀλήθω
ἀληθῶς
ἄληκτος
ἀλιαίετος
ἁλιεύς
ἁλιεύω
ἁλίζω
ἄλιμος
ἀλισγέω
ἁλίσκομαι
ἀλιτήριος
ἀλκή
ἀλλά
ἀλλαγή
ἄλλαγμα
ἀλλάσσω
ἀλλαχῇ
ἀλλαχόθεν
αλληλουια
ἀλλογενής
ἀλλόγλωσσος
ἀλλοεθνής
ἄλλοθεν
ἀλλοιόω
ἀλλοίωσις
ἅλλομαι
ἄλλος
ἄλλοτε
ἀλλότριος
ἀλλοτριότης
ἀλλοτριόω
ἀλλοτρίωσις
ἀλλοφυλέω
ἀλλοφυλισμός
ἀλλόφυλος
ἀλλόφωνος
ἄλλως
ἅλμα
ἅλμη
ἁλμυρίς
ἁλμυρός
ἀλοάω
ἀλογέω
ἀλογιστία
ἀλόγιστος
ἄλογος
ἀλόγως
ἀλοητός
ἀλοιφή
ἀλοῦνται (see ἀλεῖται)

ἅλς
ἄλσος
ἀλσώδης
ἀλυκός
ἀλυσιδωτός
ἅλυσις
ἄλφιτον
ἀλφός
ἅλω (see ἁλίσκομαι)
αλωθ
αλωμων†
ἄλων
ἀλώπηξ
ἅλως
ἅλωσις
ἅμα
ἀμαδαρωθ (see ἀμμαδαρωθ)
ἀμαθία
ἅμαξα
ἀμάραντος
ἀμαρία
ἁμαρτάνω
ἁμάρτημα
ἁμαρτία
ἁμαρτωλός
αμασενιθ
ἀμάσητος
αματταρι
ἀμαυρός
ἀμαυρόω
αμαφεθ
ἀμάω
ἀμβλάκημα
ἀμβλακία
ἀμβλύνω
ἀμβλυωπέω
ἀμβρόσιος
ἀμέθυστος
ἀμείδητος
ἀμειξία
ἀμέλγω
ἀμελέω
ἄμελξις
ἀμελῶς
ἄμεμπτος
ἀμέμπτως
ἀμερής
ἀμέριμνος
ἀμεσσαῖος†
ἀμετάθετος
ἀμέτρητος
αμην
ἄμηνις†
ἀμητός (ἄμητος)

ἀμήχανος
ἀμίαντος
ἀμίνον (see ἀμείνον)
ἀμιξία (see ἀμειξία)
ἀμισθί
ἀμ(μ)αδαρωθ
αμμαζειβη, αμμασβη†
ἄμμος
ἀμμώδης
ἀμνάς
ἀμνημονέω
ἀμνησία
ἀμνησικακία
ἀμνήστευτος
ἀμνηστία
ἀμνός
ἀμοιρέω
ἄμοιρος
ἀμόλυντος
ἀμόρα
ἀμορίτης
ἄμορφος
ἄμπελος
ἀμπελουργός
ἀμπελών
ἀμπλάκημα† (see ἀμβλ-)
ἀμύγδαλον
ἀμύθητος
ἄμυνα
ἀμύνομαι
ἀμφιάζω
ἀμφίασις
ἀμφιβάλλω
ἀμφίβληστρον
ἀμφιβολεύς
ἀμφιέννυμι
ἀμφιλαφής
ἀμφίταπος
ἄμφοδον
ἀμφοτεροδέξιος
ἀμφότεροι
ἄμωμος
ἄν
ἀνά
ἀναβαθμίς
ἀναβαθμός
ἀναβαίνω
ἀναβάλλω
ἀνάβασις
ἀναβαστάζω
ἀναβάτης
ἀναβιβάζω
ἀναβίωσις
ἀναβλαστάνω

ἀναβλέπω
ἀνάβλεψις
ἀναβοάω
ἀναβολή
ἀναβράσσω
ἀναγγέλλω
ἀναγινώσκω
ἀναγκάζω
ἀναγκαῖος
ἀνάγκη
ἀνάγλυφος†
ἀναγνεία
ἀναγνωρίζομαι
ἀνάγνωσις
ἀναγνώστης
ἀναγορεύω
ἀναγραφή
ἀναγράφω
ἀνάγω
ἀνάγωγος
ἀναδείκνυμι
ἀνάδειξις
ἀναδενδράς
ἀναδέχομαι
ἀναδέω†
ἀναδίδωμι
ἀνάδυσις
ἀναδύω†
ἀναζεύγνυμι
ἀναζέω
ἀναζητέω
ἀναζυγή
ἀναζώννυμι
ἀναζωπυρέω
ἀναθάλλω
ἀνάθεμα
ἀναθεματίζω
ἀνάθημα
ἀναίδεια
ἀναιδής
ἀναιδῶς
ἀναίρεσις
ἀναιρέω
ἀναίτιος
ἀναιτίως
ἀνακαινίζω
ἀνακαίω
ἀνακαλέω
ἀνακαλύπτω
ἀνακάμπτω
ἀνάκειμαι
ἀνακηρύσσω
ἀνακλάω
ἀνακλίνω
ἀνάκλισις

ἀνάκλιτον
ἀνακοινόω
ἀνακομίζω
ἀνακόπτω
ἀνακράζω
ἀνακρίνω
ἀνάκρισις
ἀνακρούω
ἀνακύπτω
ἀναλαμβάνω
ἀναλάμπω
ἀνάληγητος
ἀναλέγω
ἀνάλημμα
ἀναλημπτέος
ἀναλημπτήρ
ἀνάλημψις
ἀναλίσκω
ἀναλογίζομαι
ἀναλόγως
ἀναλύω
ἀνάλωσις
ἀναμάρτητος
ἀναμ(ε)ίγνυμι
ἀνάμειξις
ἀναμένω
ἀναμιμνῄσκω
ἀνάμνησις
ἀναμοχλεύω
ἀναμφισβητήτως
ἄνανδρος
ἀνανεάζω
ἀνανεόω
ἀνάνευσις
ἀνανεύω
ἀνανέωσις
ἀναντλέω
ἀναξηραίνω
ἀνάξιος
ἄναξις
ἀναξίως
ἀνάπαλιν
ἀνάπαυλα
ἀνάπαυμα
ἀνάπαυσις
ἀναπαύω
ἀναπείθω
ἀνάπειρος
ἀναπείρω
ἀναπετάννυμι
ἀναπηδάω
ἀναπηδύω
ἀναπίπτω
ἀναπλάσσω
ἀναπληρόω

ἀναπλήρωσις
ἀναπνέω
ἀναπνοή
ἀναποδίζω
ἀναποδισμός
ἀναποιέω
ἀναπτερόω
ἀναπτέρωσις
ἀναπτύσσω
ἀνάπτω
ἀναρίθμητος
ἀναρπάζω
ἀναρρήγνυμι
ἀνασεσωμένοι†
ἀνασκάπτω
ἀνασπάω
ἀνάστασις
ἀναστατόω
ἀναστέλλω
ἀναστενάζω
ἀνάστημα
ἀναστρατοπεδεύω
ἀναστρέφω
ἀναστροφή
ἀνασύρω
ἀνασχίζω
ἀνασῴζω
ἀνατείνω
ἀνατέλλω
ἀνατέμνω
ἀνατίθημι
ἀνατίκτω
ἀνατιναγμός
ἀνατλάω
ἀνατλῶν (see
    ἀνέτλην)
ἀνατολή
ἀνατρέπω
ἀνατρέφω
ἀνατρέχω
ἀνατροπή
ἀνατροφή
ἀνατυπόω
ἀναφαίνω
ἀναφαιρέω
ἀναφάλαντος
ἀναφαλάντωμα
ἀναφέρω
ἀναφθη [ἀνάπτω]
ἀναφορά
ἀναφορεύς
ἀναφράσσω
ἀναφυράω†
ἀναφύω
ἀναφωνέω

ἀναχαίνω
ἀναχέω
ἀναχωρέω
ἀνάψυξις
ἀναψυχή
ἀναψύχω
ἀνδραγαθέω
ἀνδραγάθησις†
ἀνδραγαθία
ἀνδράποδον
ἀνδρεία
ἀνδρεῖος
ἀνδρειόω
ἀνδριοῦμαι
    [ἀνδρίζομαι]
ἀνδρίζομαι
ἀνδρογύναιος
ἀνδρόγυνος
ἀνδρολογία
ἀνδροφονέω
ἀνδροφόνος
ἀνδρόω
ἀνδρωδῶς
ἀνεγείρω
ἀνέγκλητος
ἀνείκαστος
ἀνειλέω
ἀνειμένος (see ἀνίημι)
ἄνειμι
ἀνεκλιπής
ἀνελεημόνως
ἀνελεήμων
ἀνέλπιστος
ἄνεμος
ἀνεμοφθορία
ἀνεμόφθορος
ἀνεμπόδιστος
ἀνενήνοχα (see
    ἀναφέρω)
ἀνεξέλεγκτος
ἀνεξικακία
ἀνεξιχνίαστος
ἀνεπίγραφος†
ἀνεπιεικής
ἀνεπιστρέπτως
ἀνεργεία†
ἀνερευνάω
ἀνέρχομαι
ἄνεσις
ἀνέστραπται (see
    ἀνεστράφη)
ἀνετάζω
ἀνέτλην
ἀνετράπην (see
    ἀνατρέπω)

Appendix II: Comparative Index of Words in This Lexicon and BDAG

ἄνευ	ἄνομος	ἀντίον	ἄοκνος
ἀνευρίσκω	ἀνόμως	ἀντίπαλος	ἀορασία
ἀνέφικτος	ἀνόνητος	**ἀντιπαραβάλλω**	ἀόρατος
ἀνέχυσε	ἀνορθόω	**ἀντιπαράγω**	**ἀπαγγελία**
ἀνέχω	**ἀνορύσσω**	**ἀντιπαραγωγή**	ἀπαγγέλλω
ἀνεψιός	ἀνόσιος	**ἀντιπαρατάσσω**	**ἀπαγορεύω**
ἄνηβος	ἀνοσίως	ἀντιπαρέρχομαι	ἀπάγχω
ἀνήκεστος	**ἄνους**	**ἀντιπεριβάλλω**†	ἀπάγω
ἀνήκοος	ἀνοχή	ἀντιπίπτω	**ἀπαγωγή**
ἀνήκω	ἀνταγωνίζομαι	**ἀντιποιέω**	**ἀπαδικέω**
ἀνήλατος	**ἀνταγωνιστής**	**ἀντιπολεμέω**	**ἀπαιδευσία**
ἀνηλεής	**ἀνταίρω**	**ἀντιπολιτεύομαι**	ἀπαίδευτος
ἀνήνυτος	ἀντακούω	**ἀντιπράττω**	ἀπαίρω
ἀνήρ	ἀντάλλαγμα	**ἀντιπρόσωπος**	ἀπαιτέω
ἀνῃρημένος (see	**ἀνταλλάσσω**	**ἀντίπτωμα**	**ἀπαίτησις**
ἀναιρέω)	**ἀντάμειψις**	**ἀντίρρησις**	**ἀπαλείφω**
ἀνθαιρέομαι	ἀντανειρέω	**ἀντιρρητορεύω**	**ἀπαλλάσσω**
ἀνθέμιον	**ἀντανακλάω**	**ἀντιστήριγμα**	**ἀπαλλοτριόω**
ἀνθέω	**ἀντανίστημι**	**ἀντιστηρίζω**	**ἀπαλλοτρίωσις**
ἄνθημα	ἀνταποδίδωμι	**ἀντισχύω**†	**ἁπαλός**
ἄνθινος	ἀνταπόδομα	ἀντιτάσσω	**ἁπαλότης**
ἀνθίστημι	ἀνταπόδοσις	ἀντιτίθημι	**ἁπαλύνω**
ἀνθομολογέομαι	**ἀνταποθνῄσκω**	**ἀντιφιλοσοφέω**	**ἀπαμαυρόω**
ἀνθομολόγησις	ἀνταποκρίνομαι	**ἀντιφωνέω**	**ἀπαμύνω**
ἄνθος	**ἀνταπόκρισις**	ἀντίψυχος [ἀντίψυχον]	ἀπαναίνομαι
ἀνθρακιά	**ἀνταποστέλλω**	ἀντλέω	**ἀπαναισχυντέω**
ἀνθράκινος	**ἀνταποτίνω**	ἀντοφθαλμέω	**ἀπανίστημι**
ἀνθράκιον	ἀντεῖπον	**ἄντρον**	ἀπαντάω
ἄνθραξ	**ἀντερείδω**	**ἀντρώδης**	**ἀπαντή**
ἀνθρωπάρεσκος	ἀντέχω	ἄνυδρος	**ἀπάντημα**
ἀνθρώπινος	**ἀντηχέω**	ἀνυπέρβλητος	ἀπάντησις
ἄνθρωπος	ἀντί	**ἀνυπερθέτως**	**ἀπάνωθεν**
ἀνθρωπότης	ἀντιβάλλω	**ἀνυπόδετος**	ἅπαξ
ἀνθυφαιρέω	ἀντίγραφον	ἀνυπόκριτος	**ἀπαραίτητος**
ἀνίατος	ἀντιγράφω	ἀνυπομόνητος	**ἀπαραλλάκτως**
ἀνιερόω	**ἀντιδίδωμι**	ἀνυπόνητος	**ἀπαραπόδιστος**
ἀνίημι	**ἀντιδικέω**	ἀνυπόστατος	**ἀπαρασήμαντος**
ἀνίκητος	ἀντίδικος	ἀνυψόω	**ἀπαρέσκω**
ἀνίπταμαι	**ἀντιδοκέω**†	ἀνύω	ἀπαρνέομαι
ἀνίστημι	**ἀντιδοξέω**	ἄνω	**ἄπαρσις**
ἀνίσχυς	ἀντίζηλος	ἄνωθεν	**ἀπαρτία**
ἄνοδος†	**ἀντίθετος**	ἀνώνυμος	**ἀπαρχή**
ἀνοέω†	**ἀντικαθίζω**	ἀνώτατος	**ἀπάρχομαι**
ἀνόητος	ἀντικαθίστημι	ἀνώτερος	ἅπας
ἄνοια	**ἀντικαταλλάσσομαι**	ἀνωφελής	**ἀπασπάζομαι**
ἄνοιγμα†	ἀντίκειμαι	**ἀξία**	ἀπατάω
ἀνοίγω	**ἀντικρίνομαι**	ἀξίνη	ἀπάτη
ἀνοικοδομέω	ἄντικρυς	ἀξιόπιστος	**ἀπατηλός**†
ἀνοίκητος†	ἀντιλαμβάνω	ἄξιος	**ἀπάτησις**
ἄνοικτος	**ἀντιλάμπω**	ἀξιόω	**ἀπατητής**†
ἀνομβρέω	ἀντιλέγω	**ἀξίωμα**	**ἀπαύγασμα**
ἀνομέω	ἀντιλή(μ)πτωρ	ἀξίως	**ἀπαυτομολέω**
ἀνόμημα	ἀντίλημψις	**ἄξων**	ἀπεῖδον
ἀνομία	ἀντιλογία	**ἀοίδιμος**	ἀπείθεια
ἀνόμοιος	**ἀντιμαρτυρέω**	ἀοίκητος	ἀπειθέω

ἀπειθής
ἀπεικάζω
ἀπείκασμα
ἀπειλέω
ἀπειλή
ἄπειμι¹ (εἶναι)
ἄπειμι² (ἰέναι)
ἀπεῖπον
ἀπειράγαθος
ἀπείργω
ἄπειρος
ἀπεκδίδωμι
ἀπέκτασις
ἀπεκχέω†
ἀπελαύνω
ἀπελέγχω
ἀπελέκητος
ἀπελευθερόω
ἀπελπίζω
ἀπέναντι
ἀπεναντίον
ἀπενεόομαι
ἀπένθητος
ἀπέραντος
ἀπερείδω
ἀπερικάθαρτος
ἀπερίσπαστος
ἀπερίτμητος
ἀπέρχομαι
ἀπευθανατίζω
ἀπεχθάνομαι
ἀπέχθεια
ἀπεχθής
ἀπέχω
ἀπεω (see ἀπωθέω)
ἀπηλιώτης
ἀπήμαντος
ἀπηνής
ἄπιος
ἀπιστέω
ἀπιστία
ἄπιστος
ἄπλαστος
ἄπλατος, ἄπλετος
ἀπληστεύομαι
ἀπληστία
ἄπληστος
ἀπλοσύνη
ἁπλότης
ἁπλοῦς
ἁπλόω
ἁπλῶς
ἄπνους
ἀπό
ἀποβαίνω

ἀποβάλλω
ἀποβάπτω
ἀποβιάζομαι
ἀποβλέπω
ἀπόβλημα
ἀπογαλακτίζω
ἀπογεύομαι
ἀπογινώσκω
ἀπόγονος
ἀπογραφή
ἀπογράφω
ἀποδείκνυμι
ἀπόδειξις
ἀποδειροτομέω
ἀποδεκατίζω
ἀποδεκατόω
ἀποδεσμεύω
ἀπόδεσμος
ἀποδέχομαι
ἀποδέω
ἀποδιαστέλλω
ἀποδιδράσκω
ἀποδίδωμι
ἀποδιώκω
ἀποδοκιμάζω
ἀπόδομα
ἀπόδοσις
ἀποδοχεῖον
ἀποδύρομαι
ἀποθαυμάζω
ἀποθερίζω
ἀποθήκη
ἀποθησαυρίζω
ἀποθλίβω
ἀποθνήσκω
ἀποικεσία
ἀποικία
ἀποικίζω
ἀποικισμός
ἀποίχομαι
ἀποκαθαίρω
ἀποκαθαρίζω
ἀποκάθημαι
ἀποκαθίστημι
ἀποκαίω
ἀποκακέω
ἀποκάλυμα
ἀποκαλύπτω
ἀποκάλυψις
ἀπόκειμαι
ἀποκενόω
ἀποκεντέω
ἀποκέντησις
ἀποκεφαλίζω
ἀποκιδαρόω

ἀποκλαίω
ἀπόκλεισμα
ἀπόκλειστος†
ἀποκλείω
ἀποκλίνω
ἀποκλύζω
ἀποκνίζω
ἀποκομίζω
ἀποκόπτω
ἀποκοσμέω
ἀπόκρημνος
ἀποκρίνω [-ομαι]
ἀπόκρισις
ἀποκρυβή
ἀποκρύπτω
ἀποκρυφή
ἀπόκρυφος
ἀποκτείνω
ἀποκυέω
ἀποκυλίω
ἀποκωλύω
ἀποκωφόομαι
ἀπολακτίζω
ἀπολαμβάνω
ἀπόλαυσις
ἀπολαύω
ἀπολέγω
ἀπολείπω
ἀπολεπίζω
ἀπολήγω
ἀπολιθόω
ἀπόλλυμι
ἀπόλλω
ἀπολογέομαι
ἀπολόγημα
ἀπολογία
ἀπόλοιπος
ἀπολούω
ἀπόλυσις
ἀπολυτρόω
ἀπολύτρωσις
ἀπολύω
ἀπομαίνομαι
ἀπομαρτυρέω
ἀπομάσσω
ἀπομάχομαι
ἀπομέμφομαι
ἀπομερίζω
ἀπόμοιρα
ἀπονέμω
ἀπονίπτω
ἀπονοέομαι
ἀπόνοια
ἄπονος
ἀποξαίνω

ἀποξενόω
ἀποξέω†
ἀποξηραίνω
ἀποξύω
ἀποπαρθενόω
ἀποπειράομαι
ἀποπεμπτόω
ἀποπηδάω
ἀποπιάζω
ἀποπίπτω
ἀποπλανάω
ἀποπλάνησις
ἀποπλύνω
ἀποπνέω
ἀποπνίγω
ἀποποιέω
ἀποπομπαῖος
ἀποπομπή
ἀποπρατίζομαι
ἀποπτύω
ἀπόπτωμα
ἀπορνίζομαι
ἀπορέω
ἀπορία
ἀπορρέω
ἀπορρήγνυμι
ἀπόρρητος
ἀπορρίπτω
ἀπόρροια
ἀπορρώξ
ἀποσάσσω
ἀποσβέννυμι
ἀποσείω
ἀποσημαίνω†
ἀποσιωπάω
ἀποσκαρίζω
ἀποσκεδάννυμι
ἀποσκευάζω
ἀποσκευή
ἀποσκηνόω
ἀποσκληρύνω
ἀποσκοπεύω
ἀποσκοπέω
ἀποσκορακίζω
ἀποσκορακισμός
ἀποσκυθίζω
ἀποσοβέω
ἀπόσπασμα
ἀποσπάω
ἀποστάζω
ἀποσταλάζω
ἀποστασία
ἀποστάσιον
ἀπόστασις
ἀποστατέω

ἀποστάτης	ἀποψύχω	αριηλ	ἀρχηγός
ἀποστάτις	ἄπρακτος	ἀριθμέω	ἀρχῆθεν
ἀποστέλλω	ἀπρεπής	ἀριθμητός	ἀρχιδεσμοφύλαξ
ἀποστενόω	ἀπρονοήτως	ἀριθμός	ἀρχιδεσμώτης
ἀποστέργω	ἀπρόπτωτος	ἀριστάω	ἀρχιεράομαι
ἀποστερέω	ἀπροσδεής	ἀριστεία	ἀρχιερατεύω
ἀποστολή	ἀπροσδόκητος	ἀριστερός	ἀρχιερεύς
ἀποστρεβλόω	ἀπροσδοκήτως	ἀριστεύω	ἀρχιερωσύνη
ἀποστρέφω	ἀπρόσκοπος	ἄριστος [ἀγαθός]	ἀρχιευνοῦχος
ἀποστροφή	ἄπταιστος	ἄριστον	ἀρχιμάγειρος
ἀποστύφω	ἀπτόητος	αριωθ	ἀρχιοινοχοΐα
ἀποσυμμείγνυμι†	ἅπτομαι	ἀρκεύθινος	ἀρχιοινοχόος
ἀποσυνάγω	ἅπτω	ἄρκευθος	ἀρχιπατριώτης
ἀποσυρίζω	ἄπυρος	ἀρκέω	ἀρχισιτοποιός
ἀποσύρω	ἀπωθέω	ἄρκος	ἀρχιστράτηγος
ἀποσφάζω	ἀπώλεια	ἅρμα	ἀρχισωματοφύλαξ
ἀποσφενδονάω	ἀπῶρυξ	ἁρματηλάτης	ἀρχιτεκτονέω
ἀποσφράγισμα	ἀπωσμός	ἁρμόζω	ἀρχιτεκτονία
ἀποσχίζω	ἀπωτέρω	ἁρμονία	ἀρχιτέκτων
ἀποτάσσω	αρ†	ἁρμόνιος	ἀρχίφυλος
ἀποτείνω	ἆρα	ἁρμός	ἄρχω
ἀποτελέω	ἄρα	ἀρνέομαι	ἄρχων
ἀποτέμνω	ἀρά	ἀρνίον	ἀρωδιός†
ἀποτηγανίζω	αρααβ	ἀροτήρ	ἄρωμα
ἀποτίθημι	αραβωθ	ἀροτρίασις	ἀσάλευτος
ἀποτίκτω	ἀράομαι	ἀροτριάω	ασαραμελ, σαραμελ
ἀποτίναγμα	ἀραρότως	ἄροτρον	ασαρημωθ
ἀποτινάσσω	αραφωθ	ἀροτρόπους	ἀσβόλη
ἀποτιννύω	ἀράχνη	ἄρουρα	ἀσέβεια
ἀποτίνω	ἀργέω	ἁρπαγή	ἀσεβέω
ἀποτομή	ἀργία	ἅρπαγμα	ἀσέβημα
ἀπότομος	ἀργός	ἁρπάζω	ἀσεβής
ἀποτόμως	ἀργυρικός	ἅρπαξ	ασεδεκ
ἀποτρέμω†	ἀργύριον	ἀρραβών	ἀσέλγεια
ἀποτρέπω	ἀργυροκοπέω	ἀρρενωδῶς	ασελισι
ἀποτρέχω	ἀργυροκόπος	ἄρρηκτος	ἄσημος
ἀποτρίβω	ἀργυρολόγητος	ἄρριζος	ἄσηπτος
ἀποτροπιάζομαι	ἄργυρος	ἀρρωστέω	ασηρωθ
ἀποτρυγάω	ἀργυροῦς	ἀρρώστημα	ἀσθένεια
ἀποτυγχάνω	ἀργυροχόος	ἀρρωστία	ἀσθενέω
ἀποτυμπανίζω	ἀργύρωμα	ἄρρωστος	ἀσθενής
ἀποτυφλόω	ἀργυρώνητος	ἀρσενικός	ἀσθενόψυχος
ἀποτύφλωσις	ἀρδαλόω	ἄρσην	ἄσθμα
ἀποφαίνω [-ομαι]	ἄρδην	ἄρσις	ἀσθμαίνω
ἀποφέρω	ἀρεσκεία	ἀρτάβη	ασιδα
ἀποφεύγω	ἀρέσκω	ἀρτήρ	ἀσίδηρος
ἀποφθέγγομαι	ἀρεστός	ἄρτι	ἀσινής
ἀπόφθεγμα	ἀρεταλογία	ἀρτίως	ασιρ
ἀποφορίζω†	ἀρεταλόγιον†	ἀρτοκοπικός	ἀσιτέω
ἀποφράσσω	ἀρετή	ἀρτός	ἀσιτί
ἀποφυσάω	ἀρήγω	ἄρτος	ἀσκέω
ἀποχέω, ἀποχύννω	ἀρήν	ἀρχαῖος	ἄσκησις
ἀποχωρέω	ἀρθρέμβολον	ἀρχή	ἀσκητής
ἀποχώρησις	ἀρθρέμβολος	ἀρχηγενέτης†	ἀσκοπυτίνη
ἀποχωρίζω	ἄρθρον	ἀρχηγέτης	ἀσκός

ᾆσμα
ἀσμενίζω
ἄσμενος
ἀσμένως
ἀσπάζομαι
ἀσπάλαθος
ἀσπάλαξ
ἀσπιδίσκη
ἀσπίς2
ἀσταθής
ἄστεγος
ἀστεῖος
ἀστείως
ἄστεκτος
ἀστήρ
ἀστοχέω
ἀστραγάλος
ἀστραπή
ἀστράπτω
ἀστρολόγος
ἄστρον
ἀστυγείτων
ἀστυγής†
ἀσυλία
ἄσυλος
ἀσύμφορος
ἀσύμφωνος
ἀσυνετέω†
ἀσύνετος
ἀσυνθεσία
ἀσυνθετέω
ἀσύνθετος
ἀσυρής
ἀσφάλεια
ἀσφαλής
ἀσφαλίζω
ἀσφαλτόπισσα
ἄσφαλτος
ἀσφαλτόω
ἀσφαλῶς
ἀσχημονέω
ἀσχημοσύνη
ἀσχήμων
ἀσχολέω
ἀσχολία
ἀσωτία
ἄσωτος
ἄτακτος
ἀταξία
ἀτάρ
ἀταραξία
ἀτάραχος
ἄταφος
ἄτε
ἀτείχιστος

ἀτεκνία
ἄτεκνος
ἀτεκνόω
ἀτέλεια
ἀτέλεστος
ἀτελής
ἀτενίζω
ἄτερ
ἀτιμάζω
ἀτιμασμός†
ἀτίμητος
ἀτιμία
ἄτιμος
ἀτιμόω
ἀτιμώρητος
ἀτμίς
ἀτμός†
ἀτονέω†
ἀτοπία
ἄτοπος
ἄτρακτος
ἀτράπελος†
ἀτραπός
ἀτρύγητος†
ἄτρυγος
ἄτρωτος
ἀττάκης
ἀττέλεβος
ἀτυχέω
ἀτυχία
αὐγάζω
αὔγασμα
αὐγέω
αὐγή
αὐθάδεια
αὐθάδης
αὐθαιρέτως
αὐθέντης
αὐθεντία
αὐθημερινός
αὐθημερόν
αὐθωρί
αὐλαία
αὐλαῖος
αὖλαξ
αὐλάρχης
αὐλαρχία
αὐλή
αὐλίζω [αὐλίζομαι]
αὐλός
αὐλών
αυναvειν
αὐξάνω
αὔξησις
αὔξω

αὔρα
αὔριον
αὐστηρία
αὐστηρός
αὐστότηρον
αὐτάρκεια
αὐταρκέω
αὐτάρκης
αὐτίκα
αὐτοδέσποτος
αὐτόθεν
αὐτόθι
αὐτοκράτωρ
αὐτόματος
αὐτομολέω
αὐτός
αὐτοσχεδίως
αὐτοῦ
αὐτόχθων
αὐχήν
αὐχμός
αὐχμώδης
ἀφαγνίζω
ἀφαίρεμα
ἀφαίρεσις
ἀφαιρέω
ἀφάλλομαι
ἀφανής
ἀφανίζω
ἀφανισμός
ἀφάπτω
ἀφασία
ἀφεγγής
ἄφεδρος
ἀφειδῶς
ἀφελπίζω
ἄφεμα
ἄφεσις
ἀφέστιος†
ἀφεύκτως
ἀφή
ἀφηγέομαι
ἀφήγημα
ἀφθαρσία
ἄφθαρτος
ἄφθονος
ἄφθορος
ἀφιερόω
ἀφίημι
ἀφικνέομαι
ἄφιξις
ἀφίστημι
ἄφνω
ἀφοβία
ἄφοβος

ἀφόβως
ἀφόδευμα
ἀφοδεύω
ἄφοδος
ἀφόμοιος
ἀφομοιόω
ἀφοράω
ἀφόρητος
ἀφορία
ἀφορίζω
ἀφόρισμα
ἀφορισμός
ἀφορμή
ἀφορολόγητος
ἀφρονεύομαι
ἀφρόνως
ἀφροσύνη
ἄφρων
ἀφυλάκτως
ἀφυστερέω
αφφουσωθ
αφφω
ἄφωνος
ἀχανής
ἄχαρις
ἀχάριστος
ἀχαρίστως
ἀχάτης
ἀχθοφόρος
ἄχι
αχουχ
ἀχρεῖος
ἀχρειότης
ἀχρειόω
ἄχρηστος
ἄχρις/ἄχρι
ἄχυρον
ἀψευδής
ἄψυχος
ἀωρία
ἄωρος

B

βααλταμ
βαδδιν
βαδίζω
βάδος
βαθέως
βαθμός
βάθος
βαθύγλωσσος†
βαθύνω
βαθύς
βαθύφωνος

βαθύχειλος
βαΐνη
βαίνω
βάϊς
βακελ(λ)εθ†
βακτηρία
βακχούριον
βάλανος
βαλλάντιον
βάλλω
βαμα
βάμμα
βαπτίζω
βαπτός
βάπτω
βαρ
βάραθρον
βαρακηνιμ
βαρβαρόομαι
βάρβαρος
βαρβάρως
βαρέω
βαρέως
βάρις
βαρκοννιμ
βάρος
βαρουχ†
βαρύγλωσσος
βαρυηχής
βαρυθυμέω
βαρύθυμος
βαρυκάρδιος
βαρύνω
βαρύς
βαρυωπέω
βαρχαβωθ
βασανίζω
βασανισμός
βασανιστήριον
βάσανος
βασιλεία
βασίλειος
βασιλεύς
βασιλεύω
βασιλικός
*βασιλίσκος*2
βασίλισσα
βάσις
βασκαίνω
βασκανία
βάσκανος
βάσταγμα
βαστάζω
βάτος
βάτραχος

βαφή
βδέλλα
βδέλυγμα
βδελυγμός
βδελυκτός
βδελυρός
βδελύσσομαι
βέβαιος
βεβαιόω
βεβαίως
βεβαίωσις
βέβηλος
βεβηλόω
βεβήλωσις
βεδεκ
βεζεκ†
βεθ
βέλος
βελοστασία†
βελόστασις
βέλτιστος
βελτίων
βερ(σ)εχθαν
βῆμα
βηρύλλιον
βήρυλλος
βία
βιάζω
βίαιος
βιαίως
βιβάζω
βιβλιαφόρος
βιβλιοθήκη
βιβλίον
βιβλιοφυλάκιον
βίβλος
βιβρώσκω
βιζα†
βίκος
βίος
βιοτεύω
βιότης
βιόω
βιρα
βίωσις
βλαβερός
βλάβη
βλάπτω
βλαστάνω
βλάστημα
βλαστός
βλασφημέω
βλασφημία
βλάσφημος
βλέπω

βλέφαρον
βοάω
βοή
βοήθεια
βοηθέω
βοήθημα
βοηθός
βόθρος
βόθυνος
βοΐδιον
βόλβιτον
βολή
βολίς
βομβέω
βόμβησις
βοοζύγιον
βορά
βόρβορος
βορέας
βορρᾶς
βόσκημα
βόσκω
βόστρυχος
βοτάνη
βοτρύδιον
βότρυς
βούβαλος
βούκεντρον
βουκόλιον
βουλευτήριον
βουλευτής
βουλευτικός
βουλεύω
βουλή
βούλημα
βούλομαι
βουνίζω
βουνός
βοῦς
βούτομον
βούτυρον
βραβεύω
βραγχιάω
βραγχνιάω†
βραδέως
βραδύγλωσσος
βραδύνω
βραχέως
βραχίων
βραχύς
βραχυτελής
βρέφος
βρέχω
βρίθω
βρόμος

βροντάω
βροντή
βροτός
βροῦχος
βροχή
βρόχος
βρυγμός
βρύχω
βρῶμα
βρώσιμος
βρῶσις
βρωτός
βύβλινος
βύβλος [βίβλος]
βυθίζω
βυθός
βυθοτρεφής
βύρσα
βύσσινος
βύσσος
βύω
βῶλαξ
βῶλος
βωμός

Γ

γαβης
γαβιν
γαβις
γάζα
γαζαρηνός
γαζοφυλάκιον
γαζοφύλαξ
γαι
γαῖα
γαῖσος
γάλα
γαλαθηνός
γαλακτοποτέω
γαλακτοτροφία
γαλεάγρα
γαλή
γαληνός
γαμβρεύω
γαμβρός
γαμετή
γαμέω
γαμικός
γάμος
γάρ
γαρεμ
γασβαρηνός
γαστήρ
γαστριμαργία

γαστρίμαργος
γαυρίαμα
γαυριάω
γαυριόομαι
γαυρόω
γε
γεδδουρ
γεδωρ
γεῖσος, γεῖσον
γειτνιάω
γείτων
γειώρας
γελάω
γελοιάζω
γελοιασμός
γελοιαστής
γελοῖος
γέλως
γεμίζω
γέμω
γενεά
γενεαλογέω
γενέθλιος
γένειον
γενεσιάρχης
γενεσιουργός
γένεσις
γενέτις
γενετή
γενέτις
γένημα
γενικός
γενναῖος
γενναιότης
γενναίως
γεννάω
γέννημα
γέννησις
γεννητός
γεννήτωρ†
γένος
γεραιός
γεραίρω
γέρας
γερουσία
γέρων
γεῦμα
γεύω [-ομαι]
γεῦσις
γέφυρα
γεφυρόω†
γεώδης
γεωμετρία
γεωμετρικός
γεωργέω

γεωργία
γεώργιον
γεωργός
γῆ
γηγενής
γῆρας
γηράσκω
γηροβοσκέω
γίγαρτον
γίγας
γίνομαι
γινώσκω
γιώρας
γλαύξ
γλεῦκος
γλυκάζω
γλυκαίνω
γλύκασμα
γλυκασμός
γλύκειος†
γλυκερός
γλυκύς
γλυκύτης
γλύμμα
γλυπτός
γλυφή
γλύφω
γλῶσσα
γλωσσόκομον
γλωσσότμητος
γλωσσοτομέω
γλωσσοχαριτέω
γλωσσώδης
γνάθος
γναφεύς
γνήσιος
γνησίως
γνοφερός
γνόφος
γνοφόω
γνοφώδης
γνώμη
γνωρίζω
γνώριμος
γνωριστής
γνῶσις
γνωστέον
γνώστης
γνωστός
γνωστῶς
γογγύζω
γόγγυσις
γογγυσμός
γοερός
γοητεία

γομορ
γόμος
γομφιάζω
γομφιασμός
γονεῖς
γονορρυέω†
γονορρυής
γόνος
γόνυ
γόος
γοῦν
γράμμα
γραμματεία
γραμματεύς
γραμματεύω
γραμματικός
γραμματοεισαγωγεύς
γραπτός
γραφεῖον
γραφή
γραφικός
γραφίς
γράφω
γρηγορέω
γρηγόρησις
γρύζω
γρύψ
γυμνάζω
γυμνασία
γυμνάσιον
γυμνός
γυμνότης
γυμνόω
γύμνωσις
γυναικίος [γυναικεῖος]
γυναικῶν
γύναιον
γυνή
γυναικός
γῦρος
γυρόω
γύψ
γωλαθ
γωληλα
γωνία
γωνιαῖος

Δ

δαβιρ
δαδουχία
δαιμόνιον
δαίμων
δάκνω
δάκρυον

δακρύω
δακτυλήθρα
δακτύλιος
δάκτυλος
δαλός
δαμάζω
δάμαλις
δαν(ε)ίζω
δάνειον
δανεισμός
δανειστής
δάνος
δαπανάω
δαπάνη
δαπάνημα
δάσος
δασύπους
δασύς
δαψιλεύομαι
δαψιλής
δέ
-δε†
δεβραθα
δέησις
δεῖ
δειγματίζω
δείδω
δείκνυμι
δειλαίνω
δείλαιος
δειλανδρέω
δείλη
δειλία
δ(ε)ιλιάζω†
δειλιαίνω
δειλιάω
δειλινός
δειλόομαι
δειλός
δειλόψυχος
δεῖμα
δεινάζω
δεινός
δεινῶς
δειπνέω
δεῖπνον
δέκα
δεκάδαρχος
δεκαέξ
δεκαμηνιαῖος
δεκάμηνος
δεκάπηχυς
δεκαπλασιάζω
δεκαπλασίων
δεκαπλασίως

δεκάς†
δέκατος
δεκατόω
δεκάχορδος
δεκτέον†
δεκτός
δέλτος
δένδρον
δένδρος
δενδροτομέω
δεξαμενή
δεξιάζω
δεξιός
δέομαι
δέος
δέρμα
δερμάτινος
δέρρις
δέρω
δέσις
δεσμεύω
δέσμη
δέσμιος
δεσμός
δεσμοφύλαξ
δεσμωτήριον
δεσμώτης
δεσπόζω
δεσποτεία
δεσποτεύω
δεσπότης
δεῦρο
δεῦτε
δευτερεύω
δευτέριος
δευτερολογέω
δευτερονόμιον
δεύτερος
δευτερόω
δευτέρωσις
δέχομαι
δέω
δή
δῆγμα
δήλαιος, cf. δείλαιος
δῆλος
δηλόω
δήλωσις
δημαγωγέω†
δημαγωγία
δημεύω
δημηγορέω
δήμιος
δημιουργέω
δημιουργός

δῆμος
δημόσιος
δημοτελής
δημότης
διά
διαβάθρα
διαβαίνω
διαβάλλω
διάβασις
διάβημα
διαβιάζομαι
διαβιβάζω
διαβιόω
διαβοάω
διαβολή
διάβολος
διαβουλεύομαι
διαβουλή†
διαβούλιον
διαγγέλλω
διάγγελμα
διαγίνομαι
διαγινώσκω
διαγλύφω
διάγνωσις
διαγογγύζω
διαγορεύω
διαγραφή
διαγράφω
διάγω
διαγωγή
διαδέχομαι
διαδέω
διάδηλος
διάδημα
διαδιδράσκω
διαδίδωμι
διάδοχος
διαδύνω
διαζάω
διάζομαι
διαθερμαίνω
διάθεσις
διαθήκη
διαθρύπτω
διαίρεσις
διαιρέω
δίαιτα
διαιτάω
διαιτέω
διακαθιζάνω
διακαθίζω
διακαίω
διακάμπτω
διακαρτερέω

διακατέχω
διάκειμαι
διάκενος
διακινδυνεύω
διακινέω
διακλάω
διακλείω†
διακλέπτω
διακολυμβάω
διακομίζω
διακονία
διάκονος
διακοπή
διακόπτω
διακόσιοι
διακοσμέω
διακόσμησις
διακούω
διακρατέω
διακριβάζομαι
διακρίβεια†
διακριβόω
διακρίνω
διάκρισις
διακρύπτω†
διακυβερνάω
διακύπτω
διακωλύω
διαλαμβάνω
διαλανθάνω
διαλέγομαι
διαλείπω
διάλεκτος
διάλευκος
διάλημψις
διαλιμπάνω
διαλλαγή
διαλλάσσω [-ομαι]
διάλλομαι
διαλογή
διαλογίζομαι
διαλογισμός
διάλογος†
διαλοιδόρησις
διάλυσις
διαλυτός†
διαλύω
διαμαρτάνω
διαμαρτυρέω
διαμαρτυρία
διαμαρτύρομαι
διαμασάομαι
διαμαχίζομαι
διαμάχομαι
διαμελίζω

διαμένω
διαμερίζω
διαμερισμός
διαμετρέω
διαμέτρησις
διαναπαύω
διαναφέρω†
διανέμω
διανεύω
διανήθω
διανθίζω
διανίστημι
διανοέομαι
διανόημα
διανόησις
διάνοια
διανοίγω
διανυκτερεύω
διανύω
διαξαίνω
διαπαρατηρέομαι
διαπαρθενεύω
διαπαύω
διαπειλέω
διαπειράζω
διαπείρω
διαπέμπω
διαπεράω
διαπετάννυμι
διαπέτομαι, διίπταμαι
διάπηγον†
διαπίπτω
διαπλατύνω
διαπληκτίζομαι
διαπνέω
διαπονέω
[διαπονέομαι]
διαπορεύομαι
διάπρασις
διαπράσσω
διαπρεπής
διαπρέπω†
διαπρίω
διάπτωσις
διάπυρος
διαπυρόω
διαραντός†
διαριθμέω
διαρκέω
διαρπαγή
διαρπάζω
διαρραίνω
διαρρέω
διαρρήγνυμι
διαρρίπτω

διαρρυθμίζω	διατρίβω	**διεξίπταμαι**†	**διοράω**
διαρτάω	**διατροπόω**†	**διεξοδεύω**	**διοργίζομαι**
διαρτίζω	διατροφή	*διέξοδος*	διορθόω
διασαλεύω	**διατυπόω**	διέπω	**διορθρίζω**
διασαφέω	*διαφαίνω*	**διερεθίζω**	**διορθωτής**
διασαφηνίζω†	διαφανής	**διερευνάω**	*διορίζω*
διασάφησις	**διαφαύσκω**	διερμηνεύω	**διόρυγμα**
διασαφίζω†	**διαφείδομαι**†	*διέρχομαι*	διορύσσω
διασείω	*διαφέρω*	**δίεσις**	διότι
διασκάπτω	διαφεύγω	**διετηρίς**	**δίπηχυς**
διασκεδάζω, -άννυμι	*διαφθείρω*	διετής	**διπλασιάζω**
διασκευάζω	διαφθορά	**διευλαβέομαι**	**διπλασιασμός**
διασκευή	**διαφλέγω**	*διηγέομαι*	**διπλάσιος**
διασκιρτάω	**διαφοβέω**†	*διήγημα*	**διπλοίς**
διασκορπίζω	**διαφόβημα**	*διήγησις*	διπλοῦς
διασκορπισμός	διαφορά	**διηθέω**	διπλόω
δίασμα	διαφορέω	**διήκω**	δίς
διασπασμός	διαφόρημα	**διηλόω**	**δίσκος**
διασπάω	*διάφορος*	διηνεκῶς	**δισμύριοι**
διασπείρω	**διαφρύγω**†	**διηχέω**	δισσός
διασπορά	*διαφυλάσσω*	**δίθυμος**	δισσῶς
διάσταλσις	**διαφωνέω**	**δίημι**	δίστομος
διάστασις	**διαφώσκω**	διικνέομαι	**δισχιλιάς**†
διαστέλλω	**διαφωτίζω**	**διίπταμαι, -ομαι** (see διαπέτομαι)	δισχίλιοι
διάστημα	διαχέω		**διτάλαντος**
διαστηρίζω†	διαχρίω	*διίστημι*	διυλίζω
διαστολή	**διάχρυσος**	δικάζω	**διυφαίνω**
διαστράπτω	**διάχυσις**	**δικαιοκρίτης**	**διφθέρα**
διαστρέφω	*διαχωρίζω*	**δικαιολογία**	**δίφορος**†
διαστροφή	**διάψαλμα**	*δίκαιος*	**δίφραξ**
διαστρώννυμι	διαψεύδω	δικαιοσύνη	**διφρεύω**
διασυρίζω	**διαψιθυρίζω**	δικαιόω	**δίφρος**
διασφαγή	*δίγλωσσος*	δικαίωμα	*δίχα*
διασφάλλω	**διγομία**	δικαίως	**διχηλεύω**†
διασφραγίζομαι†	διδακτός	δικαίωσις	διχηλέω
διασχίζω	διδασκαλία	**δικαστήριον**	**διχομηνία**
διασῴζω	διδάσκαλος	δικαστής	διχοστασία
διαταγή	*διδάσκω*	*δίκη*	διχοτομέω
διάταγμα	διδαχή	*δίκτυον*	**διχοτόμημα**
διάταξις	δίδραχμον	**δικτυόω**	**δίψα**
διατάσσω	**διδυμεύω**	**δικτυωτός**	*διψάω*
διατείνω	*δίδυμος* [Δίδυμος]	**διμαφουν**†	δίψος
διατελέω	*δίδωμι*	**διμερής**	**διψώδης**
διατήκω	**διεγγυάω**	**δίμετρον**	*διωγμός*
διατηρέω	*διεγείρω*	**δίνη**	**διωθέω**
διατήρησις	**διεκβάλλω**	διό	διώκω
διατίθημι	**διεκβολή**	διοδεύω	**διώροφος**
διατίλλω	**διεκκύπτω**	**δίοδος**	**διῶρυξ**
διατόνιον	*διελαύνω*	**διοικέω**	**διωστήρ**
διατόρευμα†	*διελέγχω*	διοίκησις	δόγμα
διατρεπής†	**διεμβάλλω**	**διοικητής**	δογματίζω
διατρέπω	**διεμπίμπλημι**	**διοικοδομέω**	δοκέω
διατρέφω	**διεξάγω**	**διόλλυμι**	δοκιμάζω
διατρέχω	δίεξειμι (διεξιέναι)	**διόλου**	δοκιμασία
διατριβή	*διεξέρχομαι*	διόπερ	**δοκιμαστής**

δοκίμιον	δυναμόω	δῶρον	ἐγκεντρίζω
δόκιμος	**δυναστεία**		ἐγκεντρισμός†
δοκός	**δυνάστευμα**	**E**	ἐγκηδεύω
δόκωσις	δυναστεύω		ἐγκισσάω
δόλιος	δυνάστης	ἔα	*ἐγκλείω*
δολιότης	ἐάν	**ἔγκληρος**	
δολιόω	δυνατός	ἐάνπερ	**ἐγκλοιόομαι**
δόλος	δυνατῶς	**ἔαρ**	**ἐγκοίλιος**
δολόω	*δύνω*	ἑαυτοῦ	**ἔγκοιλος**
δόμα	δύο	*ἐάω*	**ἐγκολαπτός**
δόμος	**δυσάθλιος**	ἑβδομάς	**ἐγκολάπτω**
δόξα	**δυσαίακτος**	ἑβδομήκοντα	**ἐγκολλάω**
δοξάζω	**δυσάλυκτος**	ἑβδομηκοντάκις	**ἔγκοπος**
δόξασμα	δυσβάστακτος	**ἑβδομηκοστός**	**ἐγκοσμέω**
δοξαστός	**δυσγένεια**†	ἕβδομος	**ἐγκοτέω**
δοξικός	**δυσδιήγητος**	**ἐγγαστρίμυθος**	**ἐγκότημα**
δοξολογέω	**δυσημερία**	**ἐγγελάω**†	ἐγκράτεια
δορά	δύσις	*ἐγγεννάω* (see ἐνγ-)	ἐγκρατεύομαι
δορατοφόρος	**δυσκατάπαυστος**	*ἐγγίζω*	**ἐγκρατέω**
δοριάλωτος	**δυσκλεής**	**ἐγγίνομαι**†	ἐγκρατής
δορκάδιον	**δυσκολία**	**ἐγγίων**	ἐγκρίς
δορκάς	δύσκολος	**ἐγγλύφω**	**ἐγκρούω**
δόρκων	**δύσκωφος**	**ἔγγονος**†	ἐγκρύπτω
δόρυ	**δυσμένεια**	**ἔγγραπτος**	**ἐγκρυφίας**
δορυφορία	δυσμενής	**ἐγγραφή**	**ἐγκτάομαι**
δορυφόρος	*δυσμή*	ἐγγράφω	**ἔγκτημα**†
δόσις	**δυσνοέω**	**ἐγγυάω**	**ἔγκτησις**
δότης	**δυσπέτημα**	**ἐγγύη**	**ἔγκτητος**
δοτός	**δυσπολιόρκητος**	**ἐγγύθεν**	**ἐγκύκλιος**
δουλεία	**δυσπρόσιτος**	ἔγγυος	**ἐγκυλίω**
δουλεύω	**δυσσέβεια**	ἐγγύς	**ἔγκυος**
δούλη	**δυσσεβέω**	ἐγείρω	**ἐγκύπτω**
δοῦλος	**δυσσέβημα**	*ἔγερσις*	**ἐγκωμιάζω**
δοῦλος	**δυσσεβής**	ἐγκάθετος	**ἐγκώμιον**
δουλόω	**δυστοκέω**	ἐγκάθημαι	**ἐγρήγορος**
δοχή	δυσφημέω	**ἐγκαθίζω**	**ἐγχάσκω**
δράγμα	δυσφημία	*ἐγκαίνια*	ἐγχειρέω
δράκος	**δύσφημος**	*ἐγκαινίζω*	**ἐγχείρημα**
δράκων	**δυσφορέω**	**ἐγκαίνισις**†	**ἐγχειρίδιος**
δρᾶμα	**δύσφορος**	**ἐγκαινισμός**	**ἐγχειρίζω**†
δράξ	**δυσχέρεια**	**ἐγκαίνωσις**	**ἐγχειρόω**†
δραπέτης	δυσχερής	**ἐγκαίω**	**ἐγχέω**
δράσσομαι	δύσχρηστος	ἐγκαλέω	ἐγχρίω
δραχμή	**δυσώδης**	**ἐγκαλύπτω**†	**ἐγχρονίζω**
δράω	δύω	ἔγκαρπος	**ἐγχρυσόω**†
δρεπανηφόρος	δώδεκα	**ἐγκαρτερέω**	ἐγχώριος
δρέπανον	**δωδεκαετής**	**ἐγκατακρύπτω**	ἐγώ
δρομεύς	**δωδεκάμηνος**	ἐγκατάλειμμα	**ἔγωγε**
δρόμος	δωδέκατος	ἐγκαταλείπω	ἐδαφίζω
δροσίζω	δῶμα	ἐγκαταλιμπάνω	ἔδαφος
δρόσος	δωρεά	**ἐγκαταλοχίζω**†	**ἔδεσμα**
δρυμός	δωρέομαι	**ἐγκαταπαίζω**	**ἕδρα**
δρῦς	δώρημα	**ἔγκατον**	**ἑδράζω**
δύναμαι	**δωροδεκτής**	ἐγκαυχάομαι	**ἔδρασμα**†
δύναμις	δωροκοπέω	ἔγκειμαι	**ἐθελοκωφέω**
	δωρολήμπτης		

ἐθίζω	εἰσκύπτω	ἐκδιδάσκω	ἐκκοσμέω†
ἐθισμός	**εἰσοδιάζω**	**ἐκδιδύσκω**	*ἐκκρεμάννυμι*
ἐθνάρχης	**εἰσόδιον**	*ἐκδίδωμι*	**ἐκκρούω**
ἐθνηδόν	εἴσοδος	ἐκδιηγέομαι	**ἐκκύπτω**
ἐθνοπάτωρ	**εἰσοράω**	**ἐκδικάζω**	ἐκλαλέω
ἐθνόπληθης	**εἰσπέμπω**	**ἐκδικάω**	ἐκλαμβάνω
ἔθνος	εἰσπηδάω	*ἐκδικέω*	**ἔκλαμπρος**
ἔθος	**εἰσπλέω**	ἐκδίκησις	ἐκλάμπω
εἰ	εἰσπορεύομαι	**ἐκδικητής**	**ἔκλαμψις**
εἰδέχθεια	**εἰσσπάομαι**	ἔκδικος	ἐκλατομέω
εἴδησις	εἰστρέχω	ἐκδιώκω	ἐκλέγω
εἶδον	εἰσφέρω	ἔκδοτος	*ἐκλείπω*
εἶδος	**εἰσφορά**	*ἐκδύνω* [ἐκδύω]	**ἐκλείχω**
εἰδώλιον	εἶτα	ἐκεῖ	**ἔκλειψις**
εἰδωλόθυτος	εἴτε	ἐκεῖθεν	**ἐκλεκτέον**†
εἴδωλον	*εἴτοι* [εἰ τοί]	ἐκεῖνος	ἐκλεκτός
εἴθε	εἴωθα	ἐκεῖσε	**ἐκλευκαίνω**
εἰκάζω	ἐκ	**ἐκζέω**	**ἔκλευκος**
εἰκάς	ἕκαστος	ἐκζητέω	**ἐκλικμάω**
εἰκῇ	ἑκάτερος	**ἐκζητητής**	**ἐκλιμία**
εἰκοσαετής	**ἑκατέρωθεν**	ἐκθαμβέω	**ἐκλιμπάνω**
εἴκοσι	ἑκατόν	ἔκθαμβος	ἐκλογή
εἰκοστός	ἑκατονταετής	ἐκθαυμάζω	**ἐκλογίζομαι**
εἰκότως	ἑκατονταπλασίων	**ἔκθεμα**	**ἐκλογιότης**†
εἴκω	ἑκατοντάρχης	**ἐκθερίζω**	**ἐκλογιστής**
εἰκών	ἑκατόνταρχος	**ἔκθεσις**	**ἐκλογιστία**
εἰλέω	**ἐκατοντάς**	**ἔκθεσμος**	**ἐκλοχίζω**
εἰλικρινής	**ἑκατοστεύω**	**ἐκθηλάζω**	**ἔκλυσις**
εἰμι (εἶναι)	**ἑκατοστός**	**ἐκθλιβή**	**ἐκλύτρωσις**
εἰμι (ἰέναι)	*ἐκβαίνω*	**ἐκθλίβω**	*ἐκλύω*
εἵνεκεν	ἐκβάλλω	**ἔκθλιψις**†	**ἐκμαρτυρέω**
εἴπερ	ἔκβασις	**ἔκθυμος**	ἐκμάσσω
εἶπον	**ἐκβασσεύω**†	ἐκκαθαίρω	**ἐκμελετάω**
εἴργω	**ἐκβεβηλόω**†	**ἐκκαθαρίζω**	**ἐκμελίζω**
εἰρηνεύω	**ἐκβιάζω**	**ἐκκαίδεκα**	**ἐκμελῶς**†
εἰρήνη	*ἐκβλαστάνω*	**ἐκκαιδέκατος**	**ἐκμετρέω**
εἰρηνικός	**ἐκβλύζω**	*ἐκκαίω*	**ἐκμιαίνω**
εἰρηνοποιέω	**ἐκβοάω**	**ἐκκαλέω**	**ἐκμυελίζω**
εἱρκτή	ἐκβολή	**ἐκκαλύπτω**	ἐκμυκτηρίζω
εἰρωνεία	ἔκβολος	**ἐκκενόω**	*ἐκνεύω*
εἷς μία ἕν	**ἐκβράζω**	*ἐκκεντέω*	*ἐκνήφω*
εἰς	**ἐκβρασμός**	**ἐκκήρυκτος**	**ἔκνηψις**
εἰσάγω	**ἐκγελάω**	**ἐκκινέω**	**ἐκουσιάζομαι**
εἰσαγωγή†	**ἐκγεννάω**	ἐκκλάω	**ἐκουσιασμός**
εἰσακούω	ἔκγονος	ἐκκλησία	*ἐκούσιος*
εἰσβάλλω	ἐκγράφω	*ἐκκλησιάζω*	ἐκουσίως
εἰσβλέπω	ἐκδανείζω	ἐκκλησιαστής	**ἐκπαιδεύω**
εἰσδέχομαι	ἐκδειματόω	**ἔκκλητος**	**ἐκπαίζω**
εἰσδύνω	**ἐκδεκτέον**	*ἐκκλίνω*	ἐκπειράζω
εἴσειμι	ἐκδέρω	**ἐκκλύζω**	ἐκπέμπω
εἰσέρχομαι	*ἐκδέχομαι*	**ἐκκόλαμμα**	ἐκπεράω
εἰσηγέομαι†	**ἐκδέω**	**ἐκκολαπτός**†	**ἐκπεριπορεύομαι**
εἰσηγορεύομαι†	ἔκδηλος	ἐκκολάπτω	*ἐκπετάννυμι*
εἰσκολάπτω†	**ἐκδημία**	**ἐκκομιδή**	ἐκπέτομαι
εἰσκυκλέω	ἐκδιαιτάω	ἐκκόπτω	ἐκπηδάω

ἐκπιάζω, ἐκπιέζω	ἐκτίνω	ἐλαττόω	ἐμμένω
ἐκπικραίνω	ἐκτοκίζω	ἐλάττωμα	ἐμμέσῳ
ἐκπίνω	ἐκτομίας	ἐλάττωσις	ἐμμολύνομαι
ἐκπίπτω	ἐκτομίς†	ἐλαύνω	ἔμμονος
ἐκπληρόω	ἐκτοπίζω	ἔλαφος	ἐμός
ἐκπλήρωσις	ἐκτός	ἐλαφρός	ἔμπαιγμα
ἐκπλήσσω	ἕκτος	ἐλάχιστος	ἐμπαιγμός
ἐκπλύνω	ἐκτρεπής†	ἐλεάω	ἐμπαίζω
ἐκποιέω	ἐκτρέπω	ἐλεγμός	ἐμπαίκτης
ἐκπολεμέω	ἐκτρέφω	ἔλεγξις	ἐμπαραγίνομαι
ἐκπολιορκέω	ἐκτρέχω	ἔλεγχος	ἐμπαρρησιάζω†
ἐκπολιτεύω	ἐκτριβή	ἐλέγχω	ἐμπάσσω†
ἐκπορεύομαι	ἐκτρίβω	ἐλεεινός	ἐμπειρέω
ἐκπορθέω	ἔκτριψις	ἐλεέω	ἐμπειρία
ἐκπορνεύω	ἐκτρυγάω	ἐλεημοποιός	ἔμπειρος
ἔκπρακτος†	ἐκτρώγω	ἐλεημοσύνη	ἐμπεριπατέω
ἐκπρεπής	ἔκτρωμα	ἐλεήμων	ἐμπήγνυμι
ἐκπρίαμαι	ἐκτυπόω	ἔλεος	ἐμπηδάω
ἐκπρίω	ἐκτύπωμα	ἐλεόπολις (see	ἐμπι(μ)πλάω
ἐκπυρόω	ἐκτύπωσις	ἐλέπολις)	[ἐμπί(μ)πλημι]
ἐκρέω	ἐκτυφλόω	ἐλέπολις	ἐμπίμπρημι
ἔκρηγμα	ἐκφαίνω	ἐλευθερία	ἐμπίπτω
ἐκρήγνυμι	ἐκφαυλίζω	ἐλεύθερος	ἐμπιστεύω
ἐκριζόω	ἐκφέρω	ἐλευθερόω	ἐμπλάσσω
ἐκριζωτής	ἐκφεύγω	ἐλευστέον	ἐμπλατύνω
ἐκρίπτω	ἐκφλέγω	ἐλεφαντάρχης	ἐμπλέκω
ἔκρυσις	ἐκφοβέω	ἐλεφάντινος	ἐμπληθύνω
ἐκσαρκίζω	ἔκφοβος	ἐλέφας	ἐμπλόκιον
ἐκσιφωνίζω	ἐκφορά	ἑλικτός	ἔμπνευσις
ἐκσοβέω	ἐκφόριον	ἕλιξ	ἐμπνέω
ἐκσπάω	ἐκφυγή	ἑλίσσω	ἔμπνους
ἐκσπερματίζω	ἐκφύρω	ἕλκος	ἐμποδίζω
ἐκσπονδυλίζω	ἐκφυσάω	ἕλκω	ἐμποδιστικός
ἔκστασις	ἔκφυσημα†	ἐλλείπω	ἐμποδοστατέω
ἐκστραγγίζω†	ἐκφωνέω	ἐλλιπής	ἐμποδοστάτης
ἐκστρατεύω	ἐκχέω	ελλουλιμ	ἐμποιέω
ἐκστρέφω	ἐκχολάω	ελμωνι	ἐμπολάω
ἐκσυρίζω	ἔκχυσις	ἕλος	ἐμπολιορκέω†
ἐκσύρω	ἐκχωρέω	ἐλπίζω	ἔμπονος
ἐκταράσσω	ἐκχωρίζω	ἐλπίς	ἐμπορεύομαι
ἔκταξις†	ἐκψύχω	ελωαι	ἐμπορία
ἔκτασις	ἑκών	ἐμαυτοῦ	ἐμπόριον
ἐκτάσσω	ἐλαία	ἐμβαίνω	ἔμπορος
ἐκτείνω	ἐλαιαλογέω	ἐμβάλλω	ἐμπορπάω
ἐκτελέω	ἐλάϊνος	ἐμβατεύω	ἔμπροσθεν
ἐκτέμνω	ἔλαιον	ἐμβιβάζω	ἐμπρόσθιος
ἐκτένεια	ἐλαιών	ἐμβίωσις	ἔμπτυσμα
ἐκτενής	ἔλασμα	ἐμβλέπω	ἐμπτύω
ἐκτενία	ελασσ- (see ελαττ-)	ἐμβολή	ἐμπυρίζω
ἐκτενῶς	ἐλάσσων	ἐμβριμάομαι	ἐμπυρισμός
ἐκτήκω	ἐλάτη	ἐμβρίμημα	ἐμπυριστής
ἐκτίθημι	ἐλάτινος	ἔμετος	ἔμπυρος
ἐκτίκτω	ἐλατός	ἐμέω	ἐμφαίνω
ἐκτιναγμός	ἐλαττονέω	ἐμμανής	ἐμφανής
ἐκτινάσσω	ἐλαττονόω	ἐμμελέτημα	ἐμφανίζω

ἐμφανισμός
ἐμφανῶς
ἔμφασις
ἐμφέρω
ἔμφοβος
ἐμφραγμός
ἐμφράσσω
ἐμφυράω†
ἐμφυσάω
ἐμφυσιόω
ἔμφυτος
ἐν
ἕν
ἐναγκαλίζομαι
ἐναγκάλισμα
ἐναγωνίζομαι
ἐναθλέω
ἐνακούω
ἐναλλαγή
ἐναλλάξ
ἐνάλλομαι
ἔναντι
ἐναντίον
ἐναντιόομαι
ἐναντίος
ἐναπερείδομαι
ἐναποθνῄσκω
ἐναποσφραγίζω
ἔναρα†
ἐνάρετος
ἐναρίθμιος
ἐναρμόζω
ἐνάρμοστος†
ἐνάρχομαι
ἐνατενίζω
ἔνατος
ἐναφίημι
ἐνγεννάω† [ἐγγεννάω]
ἐνδεής
ἔνδεια
ἐνδείκνυμι
ἐνδείκτης
ἔνδεκα
ἐνδέκατος
ἐνδελεχέω
ἐνδελεχής,
  ἐνδελεχιστός†
ἐνδελεχίζω
ἐνδελεχισμός
ἔνδεσμος
ἐνδέχομαι
ἐνδέω¹
ἐνδέω²
ἐνδιαβάλλω
ἐνδιαλλάσσω†

ἐνδιατρίβω
ἐνδιδύσκω
ἐνδίδωμι
ἐνδογενής
ἔνδοθεν
ἔνδον
ἐνδοξάζομαι
ἔνδοξος
ἐνδόξως
ἐνδόσθια
ἐνδυάζω†
ἔνδυμα
ἔνδυσις
ἐνδύω
ἐνέδρα
ἐνεδρεύω
ἔνεδρον
ἔνεδρος†
ἐνεῖδον
ἐνειλέω
ἔνειμι (ἐνεῖναι)
ἐνείρω
ἕνεκα
ἐνεμπίμπλημι†
ἐνεμπορεύομαι†
ἐνενήκοντα
ἐνενηκονταετής
ἐνεξουσιάζω
ἐνεός
ἐνεργάζομαι
ἐνέργεια
ἐνεργέω
ἐνεργός
ἐνευλογέω
ἐνευφραίνομαι
ἐνεχυράζω
ἐνεχύρασμα
ἐνεχυρασμός
ἐνέχυρον
ἐνέχω
ἐνῆλιξ
ἐνῆχος†
ἔνθα
ἐνθάδε
ἔνθεμα
ἐνθέμιον
ἔνθεν
ἔνθεσμος
ἐνθουσιάζω
ἐνθρονίζω
ἐνθρύπτω
ἐνθυμέομαι
ἐνθύμημα
ἐνθύμιος
ἐνιαύσιος

ἐνιαυτός
ἐνίημι
ἐνικός†
ἔνιοι
ἐνίοτε
ἐνίστημι
ἐνισχύω
ενκτησις (see εγκ-)
ἐννακισχίλιοι
ἐννακόσιοι
ἐννέα
ἐννεακαίδεκα
ἐννεακαιδέκατος
ἐννέμω
ἔννευμα
ἐννεύω
ἐννοέω
ἐννόημα
ἔννοια
ἔννομος
ἐννόμως
ἐννοσσεύω
ἐννοσσοποιέομαι
ἔννυχος
ἐνοικειόω
ἐνοικέω
ἐνοικίζω
ἔνοικος
ἐνοπλίζω
ἔνοπλος
ἐνοράω
ἐνόρκιος
ἔνορκος
ἐνοχλέω
ἔνοχος
ἐνπροσθέσ(ε)ιος†
ἐνσείω
ἐνσιτέομαι
ἐνσκολιεύομαι
ἔνταλμα
ἐντάσσω
ἐνταῦθα
ἐνταφιάζω
ἐνταφιαστής
ἐντείνω
ἐντέλλω
ἔντερον
ἐντεῦθεν
ἔντευξις
ἐντήκω
ἐντίθημι
ἐντιμόομαι
ἔντιμος
ἐντίμως
ἐντίναγμα†

ἐντιναγμός
ἐντινάσσω
ἐντολή
ἐντομίς
ἐντός
ἐντότερος†
ἐντρέπω
ἐντρεχής
ἔντριτος
ἔντρομος
ἐντροπή
ἐντρυφάω
ἐντρύφημα
ἐντυγχάνω
ἐντυχία
ἔνυδρος
ἐνυπνιάζω
ἐνυπνιαστής
ἐνύπνιον
ἐνυποκρίνομαι†
ἐνυποτάσσω
ἔνυστρον
ἐνυψόω†
ενφωθ
ἐνώπιος [ἐνώπιον]
ἐνωτίζομαι
ἐνώτιον
ἐξ
ἕξ
ἐξαγγέλλω
ἐξαγοράζω
ἐξαγορεύω
ἐξαγορία
ἐξαγριαίνω
ἐξάγω
ἐξάδελφος
ἔξαιμος
ἐξαίρετος
ἐξαιρέω
ἐξαίρω
ἐξαίσιος
ἐξαίφνης
ἑξάκις
ἑξακισχίλιοι
ἐξακολουθέω
ἐξακονάω
ἑξακόσιοι
ἑξακοσιοστός
ἐξακριβάζομαι
ἐξάλειπτρον
ἐξαλείφω
ἐξάλειψις
ἐξαλλάσσω
ἐξαλλοιόω
ἐξάλλομαι

Appendix II: Comparative Index of Words in This Lexicon and BDAG

ἔξαλλος	ἔξεστιν	ἐξορίζω†	ἐπάν
ἐξαλλοτριόω	ἐξετάζω	ἐξορκίζω	ἐπανάγω
ἐξαμαρτάνω	**ἐξέτασις**	**ἐξορμάω**	**ἐπαναγωγή**†
ἐξάμηνος	ἐξετασμός	ἐξορύσσω	**ἐπαναιρέω**
ἐξαναλίσκω	**ἐξετάστεον**	ἐξουδενέω	**ἐπανακαινίζω**
ἐξανάστασις	**ἐξευμενίζω**	**ἐξουδένημα**	**ἐπανακαλέω**†
ἐξανατέλλω	**ἐξεύρεσις**	ἐξουδενόω	*ἐπαναπαύω* [-ομαι]
ἐξανθέω	**ἐξευρίσκω**	**ἐξουδένωμα**	**ἐπανάστασις**
ἐξανίστημι	**ἐξευφραίνομαι**†	**ἐξουδένωσις**	**ἐπαναστρέφω**
ἐξαντλέω	*ἐξέχω*	ἐξουθενέω	**ἐπανατρυγάω**
ἐξαπατάω	ἐξηγέομαι	ἐξουθενόω	**ἐπανδρόω**
ἐξάπινα	ἐξήγησις	ἐξουσία	ἐπανέρχομαι
ἐξαπίνης	**ἐξηγητής**	ἐξουσιάζω	ἐπανήκω
ἐξαπόλλυμι	**ἐξηγορία**	**ἐξουσιαστής**†	**ἐπανθέω**
ἐξαπορέω	ἐξήκοντα	ἐξοχή	ἐπανιστάνομαι
ἐξαποστέλλω	**ἐξηκονταετής**	**ἐξυβρίζω**	[ἐπανίστημι]
ἐξαποστολή	**ἐξηκοστός**	**ἐξυμνέω**	**ἐπάνοδος**
ἐξάπτω	**ἐξηλιάζω**	ἐξυπνίζω	**ἐπανορθόω**
ἔξαρθρος	**ἐξημερόω**	ἔξυπνος	*ἐπανόρθωσις*
ἐξαρθρόω	ἑξῆς	**ἐξυπνόω**	*ἐπάνω*
ἐξαριθμέω	ἐξηχέω	**ἐξυψόω**	*ἐπάνωθεν*
ἐξαρκέω	**ἐξικνέομαι**	ἔξω	**ἐπαξονέω**
ἐξαρνέομαι	**ἐξίλασις**	ἔξωθεν	**ἐπαοιδή**
ἐξαρπάζω	*ἐξιλάσκομαι*	ἔξωθέω	**ἐπαοιδός**
ἔξαρσις	**ἐξίλασμα**	**ἔξωσμα**	**ἐπαποστέλλω**
ἐξαρτάω	ἐξιλασμός	**ἐξώτατος**	**ἐπάρδω**
ἐξάρχω	**ἐξιππάζομαι**	ἐξώτερος	**ἐπαρήγω**
ἐξασθενέω	**ἐξίπταμαι**	**ἐξωτέρω**	*ἐπαρκέω*
ἐξασκέω	*ἕξις*	ἔοικα	**ἐπαρκῶς**†
ἐξαστράπτω	**ἐξισάζω**	ἑορτάζω	**ἔπαρμα**
ἐξατιμόομαι	**ἐξισόω**	**ἑόρτασμα**	**ἔπαρξις**†
ἐξαφίημι	*ἐξίστημι*	ἑορτή	**ἔπαρσις**
ἐξαφίστημι†	**ἐξιχνεύω**	ἐπαγγελία	**ἐπαρυστήρ**
ἐξεγείρω	**ἐξιχνιάζω**	ἐπαγγέλλω	**ἐπαρυστρίς**
ἐξέγερσις	**ἐξιχνιασμός**	*ἐπάγω*	**ἔπαρχος**
ἐξέδρα	**ἐξοδεύω**	**ἐπαγωγή**	**ἐπάρχω**
ἐξεικονίζω	**ἐξοδία**	**ἐπαγωγός**	**ἐπασθμαίνω**
ἔξειμι (ἐξιέναι)	**ἐξοδιάζω**	**ἐπαείδω**	**ἔπαυλις**
ἐξεκκλησιάζω	**ἐξόδιος**	**ἐπαινεστός**	**ἐπαύξω**
ἐξελαύνω	*ἔξοδος*	**ἐπαινετός**	**ἐπαύριον**
ἐξελέγχω	**ἐξοικοδομέω**†	[Ἐπαινετός]	ἐπαφίημι
ἐξέλευσις	**ἔξοικος**	ἐπαινέω	**ἐπεγγελάω**
ἐξελίσσω	**ἐξοκέλλω**	ἔπαινος	ἐπεγείρω
ἐξέλκω	**ἐξολέθρευμα**	ἐπαίρω	ἐπεί
ἐξεμέω	**ἐξολέθρευσις**	ἐπαισχύνομαι	*ἐπείγω*
ἐξεραυνάω	ἐξολεθρεύω	ἐπαιτέω	ἐπειδή
ἐξεργάζομαι	**ἐξολλύω (-όλλυμι)**	**ἐπαίτησις**	*ἐπεῖδον*
ἐξεργαστικός	**ἐξομβρέω**	**ἐπαίτιος**†	**ἔπειμι** (inf. ἐπεῖναι)
ἐξερεύγομαι	**ἐξόμνυμι**	ἐπακολουθέω	*ἔπειμι* (ἐπιέναι)
ἐξερευνάω	ἐξομοιόω	**ἐπακουστός**	ἐπεισέρχομαι
[ἐξεραυνάω]	ἐξομολογέω	ἐπακούω	**ἐπεισφέρω**
ἐξερεύνησις	*ἐξομολόγησις*	**ἐπακρόασις**	ἔπειτα
ἐξερημόω	**ἐξόπισθεν**	**ἐπαλγέστερος**	*ἐπέκεινα*
ἐξέρπω	**ἐξοπλησία**	ἔπαλξις	**ἐπέκτασις**†
ἐξέρχομαι	ἐξοπλίζω	ἐπαμύνω	**ἐπεκχέω**

ἐπελπίζω	-εδέησα)	ἐπικουφίζω	ἐπιορκέω
ἐπενδύτης	ἐπιδέχομαι	ἐπίκουφος†	ἐπιορκία
ἐπεξέρχομαι	ἐπιδέω (aor -έδησα)	ἐπικραταιόω	ἐπίορκος
ἐπερείδω	ἐπίδηλος	ἐπικράτεια	ἐπιπαραγίνομαι
ἐπέρχομαι	ἐπιδιαιρέω	ἐπικρατέω	ἐπιπαρέρχομαι†
ἐπερωτάω	ἐπιδίδωμι	ἐπικράτησις	ἐπιπείθω†
ἐπερώτημα	ἐπιδιηγέομαι†	ἐπικρεμάννυμι	ἐπίπεμπτος
ἐπερώτησις	ἐπιδιπλόω	ἐπικρίνω	ἐπιπέμπω
ἐπέτειος†	ἐπιδιώκω	ἐπικροτέω	ἐπιπίπτω
ἐπευθυμέω	ἐπίδοξος	ἐπικρούω	ἐπίπληξις
ἐπευκτός	ἐπιδύνω [ἐπιδύω]	ἐπικρύπτω†	ἐπιπληρόω
ἐπευλαβέομαι†	ἐπιείκεια	ἐπίκτητος	ἐπιποθέω
ἐπεύχομαι	ἐπιεικεύομαι	ἐπικυλίω	ἐπίποκος†
ἐπέχω	ἐπιεικής	ἐπικύπτω†	ἐπιπολάζω
ἐπήκοος	ἐπιεικέως	ἐπίκυφος	ἐπιπολαῖος
ἐπήλυτος	ἐπιζάω	ἐπιλαμβάνομαι	ἐπίπονος
ἐπί	ἐπιζεύγνυμι	ἐπιλάμπω	ἐπιπορεύομαι
ἐπιβάθρα	ἐπιζήμιον	ἐπιλανθάνω	ἐπιπροστίθημι
ἐπίβαθρον	ἐπιζητέω	ἐπιλέγω	ἐπιρραίνω
ἐπιβαίνω	ἐπιθανάτιος	ἐπίλεκτος	ἐπιρραντίζω
ἐπιβάλλω	ἐπιθαυμάζω†	ἐπιλημπτεύομαι	ἐπιρρέω
ἐπίβασις	ἐπίθεμα	ἐπίλημπτος	ἐπιρ(ρ)ίπτω
ἐπιβάτης	ἐπίθεσις	ἐπιλησμονή	ἐπιρρωγολογέομαι
ἐπιβιβάζω	ἐπιθεωρέω	ἐπιλογίζομαι	ἐπιρρώννυμι
ἐπιβιόω	ἐπιθυμέω	ἐπίλοιπος	ἐπίσαγμα
ἐπιβλέπω	ἐπιθύμημα	ἐπιλυπέω	ἐπισάσσω
ἐπίβλημα	ἐπιθυμητής	ἐπιμαίνω	ἐπισείω
ἐπιβοάω	ἐπιθυμητός	ἐπιμαρτύρομαι	ἐπισημαίνω
ἐπιβοηθέω	ἐπιθυμία	ἐπιμ(ε)ίγνυμι	ἐπίσημον
ἐπιβόλαιον	ἐπιθύω	ἐπίμ(ε)ικτος	ἐπίσημος
ἐπιβολή	ἐπικάθημαι	ἐπιμ(ε)ιξία†	ἐπισιτίζομαι
ἐπιβουλεύω	ἐπικαθίζω	ἐπίμ(ε)ιξις†	ἐπισιτισμός
ἐπιβουλή	ἐπικαινίζω	ἐπιμέλεια	ἐπισκάζω
ἐπίβουλος	ἐπίκαιρος	ἐπιμελέστερον	ἐπισκεπάζω
ἐπιβρέχω	ἐπικαλέω	[ἐπιμελῶς]	ἐπισκέπτομαι
ἐπιβρίθω	ἐπικάλυμμα	ἐπιμέλομαι	ἐπισκευάζω [-ομαι]
ἐπιγαμβρεύω	ἐπικαλύπτω	[ἐπιμελέυμαι]	ἐπίσκεψις
ἐπιγαμία	ἐπικαρπολογέομαι	ἐπιμελῶς	ἐπισκιάζω
ἐπιγελάω	ἐπικαταλαμβάνω	ἐπιμένω	ἐπισκοπέω
ἐπιγεμίζω	ἐπικαταράομαι	ἐπιμερίζω†	ἐπισκοπή
ἐπιγίνομαι	ἐπικατάρατος	ἐπιμήκης	ἐπίσκοπος
ἐπιγινώσκω	ἐπίκειμαι	ἐπιμιμνήσκομαι	ἐπισκορακίζω†
ἐπιγλύφω†	ἐπικερδής	ἐπιμίξ	ἔπισος†
ἐπιγνωμοσύνη	ἐπικίνδυνος	ἐπιμονή	ἐπίσπαστρον
ἐπιγνώμων	ἐπικινέω	ἐπίμοχθος	ἐπισπάω
ἐπίγνωσις	ἐπικληρόω†	ἐπιμύλιον	ἐπισπεύδω
ἐπίγνωστος	ἐπίκλησις	ἐπινεύω	ἐπισπλαγχνίζομαι
ἐπιγονή	ἐπίκλητος	ἐπινεφής	ἐπισπουδάζω
ἐπιγράφω	ἐπικλίνω	ἐπινικάω†	ἐπισπουδαστής
ἐπιδεής	ἐπικλύζω	ἐπινίκιος	ἐπίσταμαι
ἐπιδείκνυμι	ἐπικοιμάομαι	ἐπινοέω	ἐπιστατέω
ἐπίδειξις	ἐπικοινωνέω	ἐπίνοια	ἐπιστάτης
ἐπιδέκατος	ἐπικοπή	ἐπινύσσω†	ἐπιστατός†
ἐπιδέξιος	ἐπικοσμέω	ἐπινυστάζω	ἐπιστήμη
ἐπιδέομαι (aor	ἐπικουρία	ἐπιξενόομαι	ἐπιστήμων

Appendix II: Comparative Index of Words in This Lexicon and BDAG 221

ἐπιστήριγμα	ἐπιφανής	ἐπωμίς	ἐρυσίβη
ἐπιστηρίζω	**ἐπιφαυλίζω**†	ἐπώνυμος	ἔρχομαι
ἐπιστοιβάζω	ἐπιφαύσκω	ἐπωρύω	ἐρῶ
ἐπιστολή	[ἐπιφώσκω]	**ἐραστής**	ἐρωδιός
ἐπιστρατεία	ἐπιφέρω	ἐράω	ἔρως
ἐπιστρατεύω	**ἐπιφημίζω**	**εργαβ**	ἐρωτάω
ἐπιστράτηγος	**ἐπιφυλλίζω**	ἐργάζομαι	**ἐρώτημα**
ἐπιστρατοπεδεύω	**ἐπιφυλλίς**	**ἐργαλεῖον**	**εσεφιν**
ἐπιστραφής†	**ἐπιφύω**	ἐργασία	ἐσθής
ἐπιστρέφω	**ἐπιφυτεύω**	**ἐργάσιμος**	**ἔσθησις**
ἐπιστροφή	ἐπιφωνέω	**ἐργατεία**	ἐσθίω
ἐπισυνάγω	**ἐπιχαίρω**	ἐργατεύομαι	ἔσοπτρον
ἐπισυναγωγή	**ἐπιχαρής**	ἐργάτης	ἑσπέρα
ἐπισυνέχω	**ἐπίχαρις**†	**ἐργάτις**	ἑσπερινός
ἐπισυνίημι†	**ἐπίχαρμα**	**ἐργοδιωκτέω**	**ἑστία**
ἐπισυνίστημι	**ἐπίχαρτος**	**ἐργοδιώκτης**	**ἑστιατορία**
ἐπισυντελέω†	ἐπιχειρέω	**ἐργολαβία**	**ἐσχάρα**
ἐπισύστασις	**ἐπιχείρημα**	ἔργον	**ἐσχαρίς**†
ἐπισυστρέφω	**ἐπίχειρον**	ἐρεθίζω	**ἐσχαρίτης**
ἐπισφαλής	ἐπιχέω	**ἐρεθισμός**	**ἐσχατίζω**
ἐπισφραγίζω	ἐπιχορηγέω	**ἐρεθιστής**	**ἐσχατογήρως**
ἐπισχύω	**ἐπίχυσις**	ἐρείδω	ἔσχατος
ἐπιταγή	ἐπιχωρέω	**ἔρεισμα**	ἔσω
ἐπίταγμα	**ἐπιχώρησις**	**ἐρεοῦς**	ἔσωθεν
ἐπιταράσσω	**ἐπιψάλλω**	**ἔρετης**†	**ἐσώτατος**
ἐπίτασις	**ἐπιψοφέω**	ἐρεύγομαι	ἐσώτερος
ἐπιτάσσω	**ἔποδος** (see ἐφ-)	**ἔρευνα**	ἐτάζω
ἐπιταφή†	**ἐπόζω**	ἐρευνάω [ἐραυνάω]	**ἑταίρα**
ἐπιτάφιος	**ἐποίκιον**	ἐρημία	**ἑταιρίζω**
ἐπιτείνω	**ἐποικτείρω**†	**ἐρημικός**	**ἑταῖρος**
ἐπιτελέω	**ἕπομαι**	**ἐρημίτης**	**ἔτασις**
ἐπιτέλλω†	**ἐπονείδιστος**	ἔρημος	**ἐτασμός**
ἐπιτέμνω	ἐπονομάζω	ἐρημόω	**ἑτερόζυγος**
ἐπιτερπής	**ἐποξύνω**	ἐρήμωσις	**ἑτεροκλινῶς**
ἐπιτήδειος	**ἐπόπτης**	ἐρίζω	**ἑτεροκωφέω**†
ἐπιτήδευμα	**ἐποπτικός**	ἐριθεύομαι	ἕτερος
ἐπιτηδεύω	**ἐποργίζομαι**	**ἔριθος**	**ἑτέρωθεν**
ἐπιτηρέω	ἔπος	ἐρικτός	ἔτι
ἐπιτίθημι	**ἐποτρύνω**	ἔριον	ἑτοιμάζω
ἐπιτιμάω	ἐπουράνιος	ἔρις	ἑτοιμασία
ἐπιτίμησις	**ἔποψ**	ἐρίφιον	ἕτοιμος
ἐπιτιμία	ἑπτά	ἔριφος	ἑτοίμως
ἐπιτίμιον	**ἑπταετής**	ἑρμηνεία	ἔτος
ἐπίτιμος	**ἑπτακαίδεκα**	ἑρμηνευτής	εὖ
ἐπιτομή	**ἑπτακαιδέκατος**	ἑρμηνεύω	**εὐαγγελία**
ἐπιτρέπω	ἑπτάκι [ἑπτάκις]	ἑρπετόν	εὐαγγέλιον
ἐπιτρέχω	ἑπτακισχίλιοι	**ἕρπω**	εὐαγγελίζω
ἐπιτρίβω†	ἑπτακόσιοι	ερ(σ)ουβα†	**εὐάλωτος**
ἐπίτριψις†	**ἑπτάμηνος**	ἐρυθαίνω	**εὐανδρία**
ἐπιτροπή	**ἑπταμήτωρ**	**ἐρύθημα**	**εὐαπάντητος**
ἐπίτροπος	**ἑπταπλάσιος**	ἐρυθριάω	εὐαρεστέω
ἐπιτυγχάνω	ἑπταπλασίων	**ἐρυθροδανόω**	εὐάρεστος
ἐπιτυχία	ἑπταπλασίως	ἐρυθρός	**εὐάρμοστος**
ἐπιφαίνω	**ἑπταπλοῦς**†	**ἐρυμνός**	εὖγε
ἐπιφάνεια	**ἑπτάπυργος**	**ἐρυμνότης**	**εὐγένεια**

εὐγενής
εὐγενίζω
ευγενναισας†
εὐγενῶς
εὐγνωμοσύνη
εὔγνωστος
εὐδία
εὐδοκέω
εὐδοκία
εὐδοκιμέω
εὐδόκιμος
εὐδοξία†
εὐδράνεια
εὐειδής
εὐεκτέω
εὔελπις
εὐεξία
εὐεπίβατος†
εὐεργεσία
εὐεργετέω
εὐεργέτημα
εὐεργέτης
εὐεργετικός
εὔζωνος
εὐήθης
εὐήκοος
εὐημερέω
εὐημερία
εὔηχος
εὐθαλέω
εὐθαλής
εὐθαρσέως†
εὐθαρσής
εὔθετος
εὐθέως
εὐθηνέω
εὐθηνία
εὐθής
εὐθίκτως
εὔθραυστος
εὔθυμος
εὔθυνα
εὐθύνω
εὐθύς
εὐθύς
εὐθύτης
εὐιλατεύω
εὐίλατος
εὐκαιρία
εὔκαιρος
εὐκατάλλακτος
εὐκαταφρόνητος
εὐκίνητος
εὐκλεής
εὔκλεια
εὐκληματέω

εὔκληρος†
εὔκολος
εὐκοπία
εὔκοπος
εὐκοσμέω
εὐκοσμία
εὔκυκλος
εὐλάβεια
εὐλαβέομαι
εὐλαβῶς [εὐλαβής]
εὔλαλος
εὐλογέω
εὐλογητός
εὐλογία
ευλογιν†
εὐλογιστία
εὐμαθῶς
εὐμεγέθης
εὐμελής
εὐμένεια
εὐμενής
εὐμετάβολος
εὐμήκης
εὐμορφία
εὔμορφος
εὐνοέω
εὔνοια
εὐνομία
εὔνους
εὐνοῦχος
εὐοδία
εὔοδος
εὐοδόω
εὔοπτος
εὐπαθέω
εὐπάρυφος
εὐπείθεια
εὐπειθέω
εὐπορέω
εὐπόρφυρος†
εὐπραξία
εὐπρέπεια
εὐπρεπής
εὐπρεπῶς
εὐπροσήγορος
εὐπρόσωπος
εὕρεμα
εὕρεσις
εὑρετής
εὑρετός
εὑρίσκω
εὖρος
εὔρυθμος
ευρυμνοτης†
εὐρύς
εὐρυχωρία

εὐρύχωρος
εὔρωστος
εὐρωτιάω
εὐσέβεια
εὐσεβέω
εὐσεβής
εὔσημος
εὔσκιος
εὔσπλαγχνος
εὐστάθεια
εὐσταθέω
εὐσταθής
εὔσταθμος†
εὔστοχος
εὐστροφία
εὐσυναλλάκτως
εὐσχημοσύνη
εὐσχήμων
εὐτακτέω
εὐτάκτως
εὐταξία
εὐτεκνία
εὐτελής
εὔτηκτος
εὐτολμία
εὐτονία
εὔτονος
εὐτόνως
εὐτρεπίζω
εὐτρεπῶς
εὐτυχία†
εὐφημέω
εὔφθαρτος
εὐφραίνω
εὐφρονεύομαι†
εὐφροσύνη
εὐψύσυνος
εὐφυής
εὐχαρής†
εὔχαρις
εὐχαριστέω
εὐχαριστία
εὐχάριστος
εὐχαριστήριον†
εὐχερής
εὐχή
εὔχομαι
εὐχρηστία
εὔχρηστος
εὐψυχία
εὔψυχος
εὐώδης
εὐωδία
εὐωδιάζω
εὐώνυμος
εὐωχέω

εὐωχία
εφαδανω
ἐφάλλομαι
ἐφαμαρτάνω
ἐφάπτω
ἐφαρμόζω
ἐφέλκω
ἐφέστιος†
ἐφέτειος†
ἐφέτιος
ἐφηβεῖον
ἐφηβία†
ἔφηβος
ἔφηλος
ἐφημερία
ἐφθός
ἐφικτός
ἔφιππος
ἐφίπταμαι
ἔφισος
ἐφίστημι
ἐφοδεύω
ἐφοδιάζω
ἐφόδιον
ἔφοδος¹†
ἔφοδος²
ἐφοράω
ἐφορμάω†
εφουδ
εφραθ
ἐφύβριστος
ἐχθές
ἔχθιστος
ἔχθρα
ἐχθραίνω
ἐχθρεύω
ἐχθρία†
ἐχθρός
ἐχῖνος
ἔχις
ἔχω
ἔψεμα
ἕψω
ἑωθινός
ἕωλος
ἕως¹
ἕως²
ἑωσφόρος

Z

ζακχω
ζάω
ζέα
ζεμα
ζευγίζω

ζεύγνυμι
ζεῦγος
ζέω
ζῆλος
ζηλοτυπία
ζηλόω
ζήλωσις
ζηλωτής
ζηλωτός
ζημία
ζημιόω
ζητέω
ζητι†
ζιβύνη
ζυγός
ζυγόω
ζῦθος
ζύμη
ζυμίτης
ζυμόω
ζυμωτός
ζωγραφέω
ζωγραφία
ζωγρεία
ζωγρέω
ζωγρίας
ζωή
ζωμός
ζώνη
ζώννυμι
ζωογονέω
ζῷον
ζωοποιέω
ζωοποίησις
ζωόω
ζωπυρέω
ζώπυρον
ζῶσις
ζωτικός

Η

ἤ
ἦ
ἡγεμονία
ἡγεμονικός
ἡγεμών
ἡγέομαι
ἥγημα
ἥγησις
ἡγητέον
ἡγνέσθω†
ἡδέως
ἤδη
ἥδομαι
ἡδονή

ἡδύνω
ἡδυπάθεια
ἡδύς
ἥδυσμα
ἡδυσμός
ἡδύφωνος
ἤδω
ἠθολογέω
ἦθος
ἥκω
ἤλεκτρος
ἡλιάζω
ἡλικία
ἡλικιώτης
ἥλιος
ἧλος
ἡμέρα
ἥμερος
ἡμερόω
ἡμέτερος
ἡμίεφθος
ἡμιθανής
ἡμίθνητος
ἡμίονος
ἡμίσευμα
ἡμισεύω
ἥμισυς
ἡνία
ἡνίκα
ἡνίοχος
ἤνυστρον
ἧπαρ
ἡπατοσκοπέομαι
ἤπερ
ἡπιότης
ἠρεμάζω
ἡσυχάζω
ἡσυχῇ
ἡσυχία
ἡσύχιος
ἥσυχος
ἤτοι
ἡττάω [-ομαι]
ἥττημα
ἥττων
ἠχέω
ἦχος
ἤχος
ἠχώ

Θ

θααλα
θαιηλαθα
θάλαμος
θάλασσα

θαλάσσιος
θαλλός
θάλλω
θαλπιωθ
θάλπω
θαμβέω
θάμβος
θανατηφόρος
θάνατος
θανατόω
θανάτωσις
θαννουριμ
θάπτω
θαραφιν
θαρραλέος
θαρρέω [θαρσέω]
θαρσις
θάρσος
θαρσύνω
θᾶττον
θαῦμα
θαυμάζω
θαυμάσιος
θαυμασμός
θαυμαστός
θαυμαστόω
θαυμαστῶς
θέα
θεάομαι
θεε
θεεβουλαθω
θειμ
θεῖον
θεῖος
θειότης
θεκελ
θέλημα
θέλησις
θελητής
θελητός
θέλω
θέμα
θεμέλιον/θεμέλιος
θεμελιόω
θεμελίωσις
θέμις
θεμιτός
θεννουριμ
θεόκτιστος
θεομαχέω
θεός
θεοσέβεια
θεοσεβής
θεοτόκος
θεράπαινα
θεραπεία

θεραπεύω
θεράπων
θεραφιν
θερίζω
θερινός
θερισμός
θεριστής
θέριστρον
θερμαίνω
θερμασία
θερμαστρίς
θέρμη
θερμός
θερμότης
θέρος
θέσις
θεσμός
θεωρέω
θεωρητός
θεωρία
θεωρός
θήκη
θηλάζω
θηλυκός
θηλυμανής
θῆλυς
θήρ
θήρα
θήρευμα
θηρευτής
θηρεύω
θηριάλωτος
θηριόβρωτος
θηρίον
θηριόω
θηριώδης
θησαυρίζω
θησαύρισμα
θησαυρός
θησαυροφύλαξ
θίασος
θίβις
θιγγάνω
θιμωνία
θίς
θλαδίας
θλάσμα
θλάω
θλίβεσθαι [θλίβω]
θλιμμός
θλῖψις
θνησιμαῖος
θνῄσκω
θνητός
θοβρος†
θοῖνα

θολερός
θορυβέω
θόρυβος
θραελ
θράσος
θρασυκάρδιος
θρασύνω
θρασύς
θραῦμα†
θραῦσις
θραῦσμα
θραυσμός
θραύω
θρεπτός
θρηνέω
θρήνημα
θρῆνος
θρησκεία
θρησκεύω
θρίξ
θροέω
θρονίζω
θρόνος
θροῦς
θρυλέω
θρύλημα
θρύπτω
θυγάτηρ
θύελλα
θυΐα
θυΐσκη
θυλάκιον
θύλακος
θῦμα
θυμήρης
θυμιάζω†
θυμίαμα
θυμιατήριον
θυμιάω
θυμός
θυμόω
θυμώδης
θύρα
θυρεός
θυρεοφόρος
θυρίς
θυρόω
θύρσος
θύρωμα
θυρωρός
θυσία
θυσιάζω
θυσίασμα
θυσιαστήριον
θύω

θωδαθα
θωρακίζω
θωρακισμός
θώραξ

I

ιααρ
ἴαμα
ιαμιβιν
ιαμιν
ἰάομαι
ἴασις
ἴασπις
ἰατής
ἰατρεία
ἰατρεῖον
ἰατρεύω
ἰατρός
ἶβις
ιγλααμ
ἰγνύα
ἰδέ
ἰδέα
ἰδιόγραφος
ἰδιοποιέω
ἴδιος
ἰδιότης
ἰδιώτης
ἰδιωτικός
ἰδού
ἰδρόω
ἰδρύω
ἱδρώς
ἱέραξ
ἱερατεία
ἱεράτευμα
ἱερατεύω
ἱερατικός
ἱερεία
ιερευμα†
ἱερεύς
ἱερόδουλος
ἱερόν
ἱεροπρεπής
ἱερός
ἱεροστάτης
ἱεροσυλέω
ἱεροσύλημα
ἱεροσυλία
ἱερόσυλος
ἱερουργία
ἱεροψάλτης
ἱερόψυχος
ἱέρωμα

ἱερωσύνη
ἴθι
ἱκανός
ἱκανόω
ἱκανῶς
ἱκετεία
ικετετον†
ἱκετεύω
ἱκετηρία
ἱκέτης
ἰκμάς
ἴκτερος
ἴκτηρ†
ἰκτῖνος
ἱλαρός
ἱλαρότης
ἱλαρόω
ἱλαρύνω
ἱλάσκομαι
ἱλασμός
ἱλαστήριον
ἱλατεύω
ἵλεως
ἴλη
ἰλύς
ἱμάντωσις
ἱμάς
ἱμάτιον
ἱματιοφύλαξ
ἱματισμός
ἱμείρομαι (see ὁμείρομαι)
ιν
ἵνα
ἴνδαλμα
ἰξευτής
ἰοβόλος
ἰόομαι
ἰός
ἰουδαΐζω
Ἰουδαϊστί
ἱππάζομαι
ἱππάρχης
ἱππάρχος†
ἱππασία
ἱππεύς
ἱππεύω
ἱππικός
ἱππόδρομος
ἵππος
ιρ
ἶρις
ισανα
ἰσάστερος
ἰσηγορέομαι

ἰσοδυναμέω
ἰσοδύναμος
ἰσόθεος
ἰσόμοιρος
ἰσονομέω
ἰσόπεδος
ἰσοπολίτης
ἰσοπολῖτις
ἴσος
ἰσότης
ἰσόψυχος
ἰσόω
ἰστάνω [ἵστημι]
ἵστημι
ἱστίον
ἱστορέω
ἱστορία
ἱστός
ἰσχίον
ἰσχνόφωνος
ἰσχυρός
ἰσχυρόω
ἰσχυρῶς
ἰσχύς
ἰσχύω
ἴσως
ἰταμία
ἰταμός
ἰτέα
ἰχθυηρός
ἰχθυϊκός†
ἰχθύς
ἰχνευτής
ἰχνεύω
ἴχνος
ἰχώρ

K

κάβος
κἀγώ
καδημιμ
καδησιμ
κάδιον
κάδος
καθά
καθαγιάζω
καθαίρεσις
καθαιρέω
καθαίρω
καθάπερ
καθαρ(ε)ιότης
καθαρίζω
καθαριόω
καθάρισις†

Appendix II: Comparative Index of Words in This Lexicon and BDAG

καθαρισμός
καθαρός
καθαρότης
καθάρσιος
κάθαρσις
καθέδρα
καθέζομαι
καθεῖς
κάθεμα
καθεύδω
καθηγεμών
καθήκω
καθηλόω
καθήλωμα†
κάθημαι
καθημερινός
καθίγω
κάθιδρος
καθιδρύω
καθιζάνω
καθίζω
καθίημι
καθίπταμαι
κάθισις
καθίστημι
καθό
καθοδηγέω
κάθοδος
καθόλου
καθομολογέω
καθοπλίζω
καθοράω
καθόρμιον
καθότι
καθυβρίζω
καθυμνέω
καθύπερθε(ν)
καθυπνόω
καθυστερέω
καθυφαίνω
καθώς
καί
καινίζω
καινός
καινότης
καινουργός
καίπερ
καίριος
καιρός
καίτοι
καίω
κἀκεῖ
κἀκεῖνος
κακηγορέω
κακία

κακίζω
κακοήθεια
κακοήθης
κακολογέω
κακόμοχθος
κακοπάθεια
κακοπαθέω
κακοποιέω
κακοποίησις
κακοποιός
κακοπραγία
κακός
κακοτεχνέω
κακότεχνος
κακότης†
κακουργία
κακοῦργος
κακουχέω
κακοφροσύνη
κακόφρων
κακόω
κακῶς
κάκωσις
καλαβώτης
κάλαθος
καλαμάομαι
καλάμη
καλάμινος
καλαμίσκος
κάλαμος
καλέω
καλλιόομαι
καλλίπαις
καλλίων
καλλονή
κάλλος
κάλλυνθρον
καλλωπίζω
καλοκἀγαθία
καλός
κάλος
κάλπη
κάλυμμα
κάλυξ
καλυπτήρ
καλύπτω
κάλυψις
καλώδιον
καλῶς
κάμαξ
καμάρα
κάματος†
κἀμέ
καμηλοπάρδαλις
κάμηλος

καμιναία
κάμινος
καμμύω
κάμνω
κἀμοί
κἀμοῦ
καμπή
κάμπη
κάμπτω
καμπύλος
κἄν
κάνθαρος
κανθός
κανοῦν
κανών
κάπηλος
καπνίζω
καπνοδόχη†
καπνός
κάππαρις
κάπτω
καρασιμ
καρδία
καρδιόω
καρόω
καρπάσινος
καρπίζω
κάρπιμος
καρπόβρωτος
καρπός¹
καρπός²
καρποφορέω
καρποφόρος
καρπόω
κάρπωμα
κάρπωσις
καρπωτός
κάρρον†
κάρταλλος
καρτερέω
καρτερία
καρτερός
καρτεροψυχία
καρύα
καρύϊνος
καρυΐσκος
κάρυον
καρυωτός
κάρφος
κασία
κασσιτέρινος
κασσίτερος
κατά
καταβαίνω
καταβάλλω

καταβαρύνω
καταβάσιος
κατάβασις
καταβιάζω
καταβιβάζω
καταβιβρώσκω
καταβιόω
καταβλάπτω
καταβλέπω
καταβοάω
καταβόησις
καταβολή
καταβόσκω
κατάβρωμα
κατάβρωσις
κατάγαιος
καταγγέλλω
καταγέλαστος
καταγελάω
κατάγελως
καταγηράσκω
καταγίνομαι
καταγινώσκω
κατάγνυμι
κατάγνωσις
καταγογγύζω
καταγράφω
κατάγω
καταδαμάζω
καταδαπανάω
καταδείκνυμι
καταδέομαι
καταδεσμεύω
κατάδεσμος
καταδέχομαι
καταδέω
καταδιαιρέω
καταδικάζω
καταδίκη
καταδιώκω
καταδολεσχέω
καταδουλόω
καταδρομή
καταδυναστεία
καταδυναστεύω
καταδύ(ν)ω
κατάδυσις
καταθαρσέω
καταθλάω
καταθύμιος
καταιγίς
καταιδέομαι
καταικίζω
καταισχύνω
κατακαίω

κατακάλυμμα
κατακαλύπτω
κατακάμπτω
κατάκαρπος
κατακάρπωσις
κατάκαυμα
κατακαυχάομαι
κατάκειμαι
κατακενόω
κατακεντέω
κατακλάω
κατάκλειστος
κατακλείω
κατακληροδοτέω
κατακληρονομέω
κατακληρόω
κατακλίνω
κατάκλιστρος†
κατάκλιτος
κατακλύζω
κατακλυσμός
κατακολουθέω
κατακονδυλίζω
κατακοντίζω
κατακοπή
κατάκοπος
κατακόπτω
κατακοσμέω
κατακρατέω
κατακρημνίζω
κατακρίνω
κατακροτέω
κατακρούω
κατακρύπτω
κατακτάομαι
κατακτείνω
κατακυλίω
κατακύπτω
κατακυριεύω
καταλαλέω
καταλαλιά
καταλαμβάνω
καταλάμπω
καταλγήγω† (see καταλήγω)
καταλεαίνω
καταλέγω
κατάλειμμα
καταλείπω
κατάλειψις
καταλέω
καταλήγω
κατάλημμα†
κατάλημψις
καταλιθοβολέω

κατάλιθος
καταλιμπάνω
καταλλαγή
καταλλάσσω
καταλογίζομαι
κατάλοιπος
καταλοχία
καταλοχισμός
κατάλυμα
κατάλυσις
καταλύτης
καταλύω
καταμανθάνω
καταμαρτυρέω
καταμείγνυμι
καταμένω
καταμερίζω
καταμερισμός
καταμεστόω
καταμετρέω
καταμηναῖος†
καταμήνιος
καταμηνύω
καταμιμνήσκομαι
καταμωκάομαι
καταναγκάζω
καταναλίσκω
κατανέμω
κατανίκημα†
κατανίσταμαι
κατανοέω
κατανόησις
κατανοίγνυμι†
κατανταω
κατάντημα
καταντλέω
κατάνυξις
κατανύσσομαι
κατανύω
κατανωτίζομαι
καταξαίνω
καταξηραίνω
κατάξηρος
κατάξιος
καταξιόω
καταξύω
καταπαίζω
καταπαλαίω
καταπανουργεύομαι
καταπάσσω
καταπατέω
καταπάτημα
καταπάτησις
καταπαυμα
κατάπαυσις

καταπαύω
καταπείθω†
καταπειράζω
καταπελματόομαι
καταπέλτης
καταπενθέω
καταπέτασμα
καταπέτομαι
καταπήγνυμι
καταπηδάω
κατάπικρος
καταπίνω
καταπίπτω
καταπιστεύω
καταπλάσσω
καταπληγμός
κατάπληξις
καταπλήσσω
κατάπλους
καταπολεμέω
κατάπολις†
καταπονέω
κατάπονος
καταποντίζω
καταπόντισμα†
καταποντισμός
καταπορεύομαι
καταπραΰνω
καταπρίω
καταπροδίδωμι
καταπρονομεύω
καταπτήσσω
κατάπτωμα
κατάπτωσις
κατάρα
καταράομαι
κατάρασις
κατάρατος
καταργέω
καταργυρόω
καταριθμέω
καταρ(ρ)άκτης
καταρ(ρ)άσσω
καταρρεμβεύω
καταρρέω
καταρρήγνυμι
καταρρίπτω
κατάρρυτος
καταρτίζω
κατάρχω
κατασβέννυμι
κατασείω
κατασήθω
κατασιγάω†
κατασιωπάω

κατασκάπτω
κατασκεδάννυμι
κατασκέπτομαι
κατασκευάζω
κατασκεύασμα
κατασκευή
κατασκηνόω
κατασκήνωσις
κατάσκιος
κατασκοπεύω
κατασκοπέω
κατάσκοπος
κατασμικρύνω
κατασοφίζομαι
κατασπαταλάω
κατασπάω
κατασπείρω
κατασπεύδω
κατασπουδάζομαι
καταστασιάζω
κατάστασις
κατατέλλω
κατάστεμα
[*κατάστημα*]
καταστενάζω
καταστέφω
καταστηρίζω
καταστολή
καταστραγγίζω
καταστρατοπεδεύω
καταστρέφω
καταστροφή
καταστρώννυμι
κατασύρω
κατασφάζω
κατασφαλίζομαι
κατασφραγίζω
κατάσχεσις
κατασχίζω
κατατάσσω
καταταχέω†
καταταχύνω†
κατατείνω
κατατέμνω
κατατέρπομαι
κατατήκω
κατατίθημι
κατατίλλω
κατατιτρώσκω
κατατολμάω
κατατοξεύω
κατατρέχω
κατατρίβω
κατατρυφάω
κατατρώγω

κατατυγχάνω
καταυγάζω
καταφαίνω
καταφερής
καταφέρω
καταφεύγω
καταφθάνω
καταφθείρω
καταφθονέω
καταφθορά
καταφιλέω
καταφλέγω
καταφλογίζω
κατάφοβος
καταφορά
καταφράσσω
καταφρονέω
καταφρόνησις
καταφρονήτεον†
καταφρονητής
καταφυγή
καταφύτευσις
καταφυτεύω
καταχαίρω
καταχαλάω
καταχαλκόω
καταχέω
καταχράομαι
κατάχρεος
καταχρίω
καταχρυσόω
κατάχυσις
καταχώννυμι
καταχωρίζω
καταψεύδομαι
καταψευσμός
καταψύχω
κατεγχειρέω
κατειλέω
κατεῖπα or –ον
κατελεέω
κατεμβλέπω
κατέναντι
κατεναντίον
κατεντευκτής
κατενώπιον
κατεπείγω
κατεπίθυμος
κατεπικύπτω
κατεραυνάω†
κατεργάζομαι
κατεργασία
κάτεργον
κατέρχομαι
κατεσθίω

κατευθικτέω
κατευθύνω
κατευλογέω
κατευοδόω
κατευφημέω
κατεύχομαι
κατέχω
κατηγορέω
κατηγόρημα†
κατήγορος
κατηφής
κατιόω
κατισχύω
κατοδυνάω
κατοικεσία
κατοικέω
κατοίκησις
κατοικητήριον
κατοικία
κατοικίζω
κατοικοδομέω
κάτοικος
κατοικτίζω†
κατοικτίρω
κατοινόομαι
κατοίομαι
κατόπισθεν
κατοπίσω
κατοπτεύω
κάτοπτρον
κατορθόω
κατόρθωσις
κατορύσσω
κατορχέομαι
κατοχεύω
κατόχιμος
κάτοχος
κάτω
κατώδυνος
κάτωθεν
κατώτατος
κατώτερον
καυλός
καῦμα
καῦσις
καυστικός
καύσων
καυτήριον
καυχάομαι
καύχημα
καύχησις
καφουρη
καψάκης
κέγχρος
κέδρινος

κέδρος
κεῖμαι
κεινηθήσεται (cf.
 BDAG κενόω
κεῖνος†
κειρία
κείρω
κέλευσμα
κελεύω
κενεών
κενοδοξέω
κενοδοξία
κενολογέω
κενός
κενοτάφιον
κενόω
κεντέω
κέντρον
κεπφόομαι
κεράμεος, κεραμεοῦς†
κεραμεύς
κεραμικός
κεράμιον
κέραμος
κεράννυμι
κέρας
κέρασμα
κεράστης
κερατίζω
κεράτινος
κερατιστής
κεραυνός
κεραυνόω
κέρκος
κέρκωψ
κεφάλαιον
κεφαλαιόω
κεφαλή
κεφαλίς
κεφφουρε, κεφφουρη
κηδεία
κηδεμονία
κηδεμών
κηδεύω
κηλιδόω
κηλίς
κημός
κῆπος
κηρίον
κηρογονία
κηρός
κήρυγμα
κῆρυξ
κηρύσσω
κῆτος

κίβδηλος
κιβωτός
κίδαρις
κιθάρα
κιθαρίζω
κινδυνεύω
κίνδυνος
κινέω
κίνημα
κίνησις
κινητικός
κιννάμωμον
κινύρα
κιρνάω
κισσάω
κισσός
κισσόφυλλον
κιχράω [κίχρημι]
κίων
κλάδος
κλαίω
κλάσμα
κλαυθμός
κλαυθμών
κλάω
κλεῖθρον
κλείς
κλ(ε)ιτύς
κλείω
κλέμμα
κλέος
κλέπτης
κλέπτω
κλεψιμαῖος
κληδονίζομαι
κληδονισμός
κληδών
κλῆμα
κληματίς
κληροδοσία
κληροδοτέω
κληρονομέω
κληρονομία
κληρονόμος
κλῆρος
κληρουχία†
κληρόω
κληρωτί
κλῆσις
κλητέος
κλητός
κλίβανος
κλίμα
κλιμακτήρ
κλῖμαξ

κλίνη	κολλύρα†	κόσμος	κρόμμυον
κλίνω	κολλυρίζω	κοσμοφορέω	κροσσοί
κλισία	κολλύριον	κόσυμβος	κροσσωτός
κλίτος	κολλυρίς	κοσυμβωτός	κρόταφος
κλοιός	κολοβόκερκος	κοτύλη	κροτέω
κλοπή	κολοβόριν	κουρά	κρουνηδόν
κλοποφορέω	κολοβόω	κουρεύς	κρούω
κλύδων	**κολοκύνθη**	κουφίζω	**κρύβδην†**
κλυδωνίζομαι	κόλπος	**κοῦφος**	**κρυβῇ**
κλώθω	**κόλπωμα**	κόφινος	κρυπτός
κλών	κολυμβάω	**κόχλαξ**	κρύπτω
κλῶσμα	κολυμβήθρα	**κραδαίνω**	**κρυσταλλοειδής**
κλωστός	κόμη	κράζω	κρύσταλλος
κνήμη	**κομιδῇ**	**κραιπαλάω**	κρυφαῖος
κνημίς	κομίζω	**κρᾶμα**	κρυφῇ
κνήφη	**κόμμα**	κρανίον	κρύφιος
κνίδη	κόμπος	κράσπεδον	**κρύφος**
κνίζω	**κόνδυ**	κραταιός	κτάομαι
κνώδαλον	**κονδυλίζω**	**κραταιότης**	**κτείνω**
κοθωνός	**κονδυλισμός**	κραταιόω	κτῆμα
κοιλάς	**κονία**	**κραταίωμα**	κτῆνος
κοίλασμα	**κονίαμα**	**κραταιῶς**	**κτηνοτρόφος**
κοιλία	κονιάω	**κραταίωσις**	**κτηνώδης**
κοῖλος	κονιορτός	κρατέω	**κτῆσις**
κοιλοσταθμέω	**κόνις**	**κρατήρ**	κτίζω
κοιλόσταθμος	**κοντός**	**κράτησις**	κτίσις
κοιλότης	**κόνυζα**	κράτιστος	κτίσμα
κοίλωμα	κοπάζω	κράτος	κτίστης
κοιμάω	**κοπανίζω**	**κρατύνω**	**κτύπος**
κοίμησις	κοπετός	**κραυάζω [κραυγάζω]**	**κύαθος**
κοιμίζω	κοπή	κραυγή	**κύαμος**
κοινολογέομαι	κοπιάω	**κρεάγρα**	κυβερνάω
κοινολογία	κόπος	**κρεανομέω**	κυβέρνησις
κοινός	**κοπόω**	κρέας	κυβερνήτης
κοινόω	κοπρία	κρείσσων	**κύβος**
κοινωνέω	κόπριον	**κρεμαστός**	**κυδοιμός**
κοινωνία	κόπρος	κρεμάω [κρεμάννυμι]	**κῦδος**
κοινωνός	κόπτω	**κρημνίζω**	κυέω
κοινῶς	**κόπωσις**	κρημνός	**κύησις**
κοιτάζω	κόραξ	**κρήνη**	κύθρα
κοιτασία	κοράσιον	**κρηπίς**	**κυθρόπους**
κοίτη	κορέω [κορέννυμι]	κριθή	κυκλεύω
κοιτών	κόρη	κρίθινος	κυκλόθεν
κόκκινος	**κόριον**	κρίκος	**κύκλος**
κόκκος	κόρος¹	κρίμα	κυκλόω
κολαβρίζω	**κόρος²**	κρίνον	κύκλῳ
κολάζω	**κορύνη**	κρίνω	**κύκλωμα**
κολακεύω	**κόρυς**	κριός	**κύκλωσις**
κολάπτω	κορυφή	κρίσις	**κύκνειος**
κόλασις	**κορώνη**	κριτήριον	**κύκνος**
κολαστήριον†	**κόσκινον**	κριτής	**κυλικεῖον**
κολεός	κοσμέω	**κρόκη**	**κυλίκινος†**
κόλλα	κόσμιος	**κρόκινος†**	**κυλίκιον**
κολλάω	**κοσμοπληθής**	**κροκόδειλος**	κυλίω
κόλλησις	**κοσμοποιΐα**	**κρόκος**	κῦμα

κυμαίνω
κυμάτιον
κυμβαλίζω
κύμβαλον
κύμινον
κυνηγέω
κυνήγιον
κυνηγός
κυνικός
κυνόμυια
κυοφορέω
κυοφορία
κυπαρίσσινος
κυπάρισσος
κυπρίζω
κυπρισμός
κύπρος
κύπτω
κυρία
κυριεία
κυριεύω
κύριος¹
κύριος²
κυρόω
κυρτός
κύτος
κύφω
κυψέλη
κύω
κύων
κώδιον
κώδων
κώθων
κωθωνίζω
κωκυτός
κωλέα
κῶλον
κώλυμα
κωλυτικός
κωλύω
κωμάρχης
κώμη
κῶμος
κωνώπιον
κώπη
κωπηλάτης
κωφεύω
κωφός
κωφόω

Λ

λαβή
λαβίς
λάβρος

λάγανον
λαγών
λαγχάνω
λάθρα
λαθραῖος
λάθριος
λαῖλαψ
λαιμαργία
λακάνη (see λεκάνη)
λάκκος
λακτίζω
λαλέω
λάλημα
λαλητός
λαλιά
λαμβάνω
λαμπάδιον
λαμπάς
λαμπήνη
λαμπηνικός
λαμπρός
λαμπρότης
λαμπτήρ
λάμπω
λάμψις
λανθάνω
λάξ
λαξευτήριον
λαξευτός
λαξεύω
λαογραφία
λαός
λαπιστής
λάπτω
λάρος
λάρυγξ
λατομέω
λατομητός
λατόμος
λατρεία
λατρευτός
λατρεύω
λάτρις
λαύω
λαφυρεύω
λαφυρέω
λάφυρον
λαχανεία
λάχανον
λέαινα
λεαίνω
λέβης
λέγω
λεηλατέω
λεῖμμα

λειοπετρία (see λεωπετρία)
λεῖος
λειποτακτέω
λείπω
λειτουργέω
λειτούργημα
λειτουργήσιμος
λειτουργία
λειτουργικός
λειτουργός
λείχω
λεκάνη
λεληθότως
λέξις
λεοντηδόν
λεοντινον†
λεπίζω
λεπίς
λέπισμα
λέπρα
λεπράω
λεπρόομαι
λεπρός
λεπτός
λεπτύνω
λέπυρον
λέσχη
λευκαίνω
λευκα(ν)θίζω
λεύκη
λευκός
λευκότης
λεύκωμα
λεχώ
λέων
λεωπετρία
λήγω
λήθη
λῆμμα
λῆμψις
ληνός
λῆρος
ληρώδης
ληστεύω
ληστήριον
ληστής
λίαν
λιβανόομαι
λίβανος
λιβανωτός
λιγύριον
λιθάζω
λίθινος
λιθοβολέω

λιθοβόλον
λίθος
λιθουργέω
λιθουργικός
λιθουργός
λιθώδης
λικμάω
λικμήτωρ
λικμός
λίκνον†
λιμαγχονέω
λιμήν
λίμνη
λιμοκτονέω
λιμός
λιμώσσω
λινοκαλάμη
λίνον
λινοῦς
λιπαίνω
λιπαρός
λίπασμα
λιποθυμέω
λίσσομαι
λιτανεία
λιτανεύω
λιτός
λιχήν
λιχνεία
λίψ
λοβός
λογεῖον
λογίζομαι
λόγιον
λογισμός
λογιστής
λόγος
λόγχη
λοιδορέω
λοιδορία
λοίδορος
λοιμεύομαι
λοιμός
λοιμός
λοιμότης
λοιπός
λουτήρ
λουτρόν
λούω
λοφιά
λοχάω
λοχεύω
λυθρώδης
λύκος
λυμαίνομαι

λυμεών	μακρόθυμος	μάταιος	μέθυσος
λυπέω	μακρός	ματαιότης	*μεθύω*
λύπη	**μακρότερον**	**ματαιόφρων**	**μεθωεσιμ**
λυπηρός	**μακρότης**	ματαιόω	**μεῖγμα**
λύσις	**μακροτονέω**	ματαίως	*μείγνυμι* [μίγνυμι]
λυσιτέλεια	**μακροχρονίζω**	μάτην	*μειδιάω*
λυσιτελέω	μακροχρόνιος	μάχαιρα	**μειερος**†
λυσιτελής	**μάκρυμμα**	μάχη	*μείζων*
λύτρον	**μακρύνω**	**μαχητής**	*μειόω*
λυτρόω	*μάλα*	**μάχιμος**	**μειράκιον**
λυτρών	**μάλαγμα**	μαχιρ	**μειρακίσκος**
λύτρωσις	μαλακία	**μαχμα**	**μεῖραξ**
λυτρωτής	μαλακίζομαι	μάχομαι	**μεισουβρις**†
λυτρωτός	μαλακός	**μαωζιν**	**μέλαθρον**
λυχνία	**μαλακοψυχέω**	**μαων**	**μελαθρόω**
λύχνος	**μαλακύνω**	μεγαλαυχέω	**μελάνθιον**
λύω	*μάλιστα*	**μεγαλαυχία**	**μελανία**
λῶμα	*μᾶλλον*	μεγαλεῖος	**μελανόομαι**
λωποδυτέω	μάμμη	μεγαλεσότης	*μέλας*
	μαν	**μεγαλόδοξος**	*μέλει*
Μ	**μαναα**	**μεγαλοημέρευσις**†	*μέλεος*
	μάνδρα	**μεγαλοκράτωρ**	*μελετάω*
μά	**μανδραγόρας**	**μεγαλομερής**	*μελέτη*
μαγειρεῖον	**μανδύας**	**μεγαλοποιέω**†	**μελετήτικος**†
μαγειρεύω	**μανη**	μεγαλοπρέπεια	μέλι
μαγείρισσα	μανθάνω	μεγαλοπρεπής	**μελίζω**
μάγειρος	μανία	**μεγαλοπρεπῶς**	μέλισσα
μαγικός	**μανιάκης**	**μεγαλοπτέρυγος**	**μελισσών**
μαγίς	**μανιώδης**	μεγαλορρημονέω	*μέλλω*
μάγος	*μαννα*	**μεγαλόσαρκος**	**μελον**
μαδαρόω	**μαντεία**	**μεγαλοσθενής**	*μέλος*
μαδάω	**μαντεῖον**	μεγαλοφρονέω	**μελύνω**†
μαδεββαν	μαντεύομαι	**μεγαλόφρων**	**μελχομ**†
μαδων	*μάντις*	**μεγαλόφωνος**	**μελω**†
μαελεθ	*μαραίνω*	**μεγαλόψυχος**	**μελῳδέω**
μάζα	**μαρμάρινος**	μεγαλύνω	**μελῳδία**
μαζουρωθ	*μάρμαρος*	**μεγάλωμα**	**μελῳδός**
μάθημα	**μαρσίππιον**	**μεγαλώνυμος**	μέμφομαι
μαῖα	**μάρσιππος**	μεγάλως	*μέμψις*
μαιμάσσω	μαρτυρέω	**μεγαλωστί**	*μέν*
μαίνομαι	μαρτυρία	μεγαλωσύνη	*μέντοι*
μαιόομαι	μαρτύριον	*μέγας*	**μέντοιγε**
μακαρίζω	μαρτύρομαι	μέγεθος	*μένω*
μακάριος	μάρτυς	μεγιστάν	**μεριδάρχης**
μακαριότης	μαρυκάομαι, cf.	μέγιστος	**μεριδαρχία**
μακαριστός	μηρυκάομαι	**μεθαρμόζω**	μερίζω
μακράν	μασάομαι	**μεθαχαβιν**	μέριμνα
μακρόβιος	**μασενα**, μασανα	μεθερμηνεύω	μεριμνάω
μακροβίωσις	**μασμαρωθ**	μέθη	*μερίς*
μακροημέρευσις	**μασομελ**	*μεθίστημι*	*μερισμός*
μακροημερεύω	μαστιγόω	μεθοδεύω	**μεριτεύομαι**
μακροήμερος	μαστίζω	**μέθοδος**	*μέρος*
μακρόθεν	μάστιξ	μεθόριον	μεσάζω
μακροθυμέω	**μαστιτής**†	*μεθύσκω*	**μεσαῖος**†
μακροθυμία	*μαστός*	μέθυσμα	**μέσακλον**

μεσῆλιξ†
μεσημβρινός
μεσημβρία
μεσθααλ
μεσίτης
μεσόγειος
μεσονύκτιον
μεσοπορέω†
μεσοπόρφυρος
μέσος
μεσότης
μεσόω
μεσσαβ
μεσσαε†
μεστός
μεστόω
μετά
μεταβαίνω
μεταβάλλω
μεταβηχας
μεταβολή
μεταβολία
μεταβόλος
μεταγενής
μεταγίνομαι
μετάγω
μεταδιαιτάω
μεταδίδωμι
μεταδιώκω
μετάθεσις
μεταίρω
μεταίτιος
μετακαλέω
μετακινέω
μετακίνησις
μετακιρνάομαι
μετακομίζω
μετακρίνομαι†
μεταλαμβάνω
μεταλλάσσω
μεταλλεύω
μέταλλον
μεταμέλει
 [μεταμέλομαι]
μεταμέλεια
μετάμελος
μεταναστεύω
μετανάστης†
μετανίστημι
μετανοέω
μετάνοια
μεταξύ
μεταπαιδεύω
μεταπείθω
μεταπέμπω

μεταπίπτω
μετασκευάζω
μεταστρέφω
μεταστροφή
μετασχηματίζω
μετατίθημι
μετατρέπω
μεταφέρω
μετάφρασις
μετάφρενον
μεταφυτεύω†
μεταχέω
μετέπειτα
μετέρχομαι
μετέχω
μετεωρίζω [-ομαι]
μετεωρισμός
μετέωρος
μετοικεσία
μετοικέω
μετοικία
μετοικίζω
μετουσία
μετοχή
μέτοχος
μετρέω
μέτρησις
μετρητής
μετριάζω
μέτριος
μετριότης†
μετρίως
μέτρον
μέτωπον
μέχρι
μέχρις
μεχωνωθ
μή τι
μηδαμόθεν
μηδαμῶς
μηδέ
μηδείς
μηδέποτε
μηθείς
μηθέτερος
μηκέτι
μῆκος
μηκύνω
μῆλον
μηλωτή
μήν
μήν
μηνιαῖος
μηνίαμα
μήνιμα†

μηνιάω
μῆνις
μηνίσκος
μηνίω
μηνύω
μήποτε
μήπως
μηρίον
μηρός
μηρυκάομαι
 [μαρυκάομαι]
μηρυκισμός
μηρύομαι
μήτε
μήτηρ
μήτι
μήτρα
μητρόπολις
μητρῷος
μηχανάομαι
μηχανεύομαι
μηχανή
μηχάνημα
μιαίνω
μιαιόω†
μιαιφονία
μιαιφόνος
μίανσις
μιαρός (cf. μιερός)
μιαροφαγέω
μιαροφαγία
μίασμα
μιασμός
μιερός [μιαρός]
μ(ε)ίγνυμι
μικρολόγος
μικρός
μικρότης
μικροῦ
μικρύνω (see
 σμικρύνω)
μικρῶς
μίλτος
μιμέομαι
μίμημα
μιμνήσκω
μισάνθρωπος
μισάρετος
μίσγω
μισέω
μισητός
μίσθιος
μισθός
μισθόω
μίσθωμα

μισθωτός
μισοξενία
μισοπονηρεύω†
μισοπονηρέω
μισοπονηρία
μισοπόνηρος
μῖσος
μίσυβρις
μίτρα
μνᾶ
μνεία
μνῆμα
μνημεῖον
μνήμη
μνημονεύω
μνημόσυνον
μνησικακέω
μνησίκακος
μνήσκομαι†
 [μιμνήσκομαι]
μνηστεύω
μογιλάλος
μόγις
μοιχαλίς
μοιχάω
μοιχεία
μοιχεύω
μοιχός
μόλιβδος [μόλιβος]
μόλιβος
μόλις
μολόχη
μόλυβδος [μόλιβος]
μόλυβος [μόλιβος]
μόλυνσις
μολύνω
μολυσμός
μονάζω
μόναρχος
μονή
μονήμερος†
μονία†
μόνιμος
μονιός
μονογενής
μονόζωνος
μονοήμερος
μονόκερως
μονομαχέω
μόνον
μόνορχις
μόνος
μονότροπος
μονοφαγία
μονοφάγος

μόνωσις
μονώτατος [μόνος]
μόρον
μόρος
μορφή
μοσφαθαιμ
μοσχάριον
μόσχευμα
μόσχος
μοτόω
μουσικός
μοχθέω
μοχθηρός
μόχθος
μοχλός
μυαλόομαι
μυγαλή
μυελός
μυέω
μυθολόγος
μῦθος
μυῖα
μυκτήρ
μυκτηρίζω
μυκτηρισμός
μύλη
μύλος
μυλών
μυξωτήρ
μυρεψικός
μυρεψός
μυριάς
μύριοι
μυριοπλάσιος
μυριότης
μυρισμός
μυρμηκιάω
μυρμηκολέων
μύρμηξ
μυροβρεχής
μύρον
μυρσίνη
μῦς
μυσερός
μύσος
μύσταξ
μυστήριον
μύστης
μυστικῶς
μυχός
μωκάομαι
μώκημα†
μωκός
μώλωψ
μωμάομαι

μώμημα†
μωμητός
μῶμος
μωραίνω
μωρεύω
μωρία
μωρός

N

ναβαλ
νάβλα
ναζιρ
ναζιραῖος
ναθιναῖος, ναθινιμ, ναθινιν
ναί
ναίω
νακκαριμ
νᾶμα
ναός
νάπη
νάρδος
ναρκάω
νασιβ
νασιφ
ναῦλον
ναῦς
ναυτικός
νάφθα(ς)
ναχαλ
νεάζω
νεανίας
νεανικός
νεᾶνις
νεανίσκος
νεβελ
νεβρός
νεελασα
νεεσσαραν
νεζερ
νεῖκος
νεκριμαῖος
νεκρός
νέμω
νεογνός
νεόκτιστος
νέος
νεοσσιά
νεοσσός [νοσσός]
νεότης
νεόφυτος
νεόω
νεσσα
νεῦμα

νευρά
νευρέα (see νευρά)
νευροκοπέω
νεῦρον
νεύω
νεφέλη
νεφθαι
νεφθαρ
νέφος
νεφρός
νεχωθα
νέωμα
νεώς
νεωστί
νεωτερίζω
νεωτερικός
νή
νήθω
νηκτός
νηπιοκτόνος
νήπιος
νηπιότης
νῆσος
νηστεία
νηστεύω
νῆστις
νηστός
νήχω
νικάω
νίκη
νίκημα†
νικάω
νικοποιέω†
νῖκος
νίπτω
νίτρον
νιφετός
νοερός
νοέω
νόημα
νοήμων
νόησις
νοητῶς
νοθεύω
νόθος
νομάς
νομή
νομίζω
νομικός
νόμιμος
νομίμως
νόμισμα
νομιστέον
νομοθεσία
νομοθέσμως

νομοθετέω
νομοθέτης
νόμος
νομός
νομοφαγία†
νομοφύλαξ
νοσερός
νοσέω
νόσος
νοσσεύω
νοσσιά
νοσσίον
νοσσοποιέω
νοσφίζω
νότος
νόφος†
νουθεσία
νουθετέω
νουθέτημα
νουθέτησις
νουμηνία
νοῦς
νυκτερινός
νυκτερίς
νυκτικόραξ
νύκτωρ
νυμφαγωγός
νύμφευσις
νύμφη
νυμφίος
νυμφών
νῦν
νυνί
νύξ
νύσσω
νύσταγμα
νυσταγμός
νυστάζω
νωθροκάρδιος
νωθρός
νωθρότης
νωκηδ
νῶτος
νωτοφόρος

Ξ

ξαίνω
ξανθίζω
ξανθός
ξενίζω
ξένιος
ξενισμός
ξενιτεία
ξενολογέω

Appendix II: Comparative Index of Words in This Lexicon and BDAG   233

ξένος	οἰκέσιος†	ὀκνέω	ὁμείρομαι
ξενοτροφέω	οἰκέτης	**ὀκνηρία**	**ὅμηρος**
ξεστός	**οἰκετικός**	ὀκνηρός	*ὁμιλέω*
ξέω†	**οἰκέτις**	**ὀκτακισχίλιοι**	*ὁμιλία*
ξηραίνω	*οἰκέω*	**ὀκτακόσιοι**	*ὁμίχλη*
ξηρασία	οἴκημα	**ὀκτάπηχυς**	ὅμμα
ξηρός	οἴκησις	ὀκτώ	*ὄμνυμι* [ὀμνύω]
ξιφηφόρος	οἰκητήριον	**ὀκτωκαίδεκα**	**ὁμοεθνής**
ξίφος	**οἰκητός**	**ὀκτωκαιδέκατος**	**ὁμοζηλία**
ξυλάριον	οἰκήτωρ	ὄλβος	ὁμοθυμαδόν
ξύλινος	*οἰκία*	**ὀλέθρευσις†**	ὁμοιοπαθής
ξυλοκόπος	**οἰκίδιον**	**ὀλεθρία**	ὅμοιος
ξύλον	**οἰκίζω**	**ὀλέθριος**	ὁμοιότης
ξυλοπελεκητος†	**οἰκίον†**	ὄλεθρος	**ὁμοιότροπος†**
ξυλοφορία	**οἰκογενής**	**ὀλεθροφόρος**	**ὁμοιόψηφος†**
ξυλοφόρος	οἰκοδομέω	**ὀλέκω**	ὁμοιόω
ξυλόω	*οἰκοδομή*	*ὀλιγόβιος*	ὁμοίωμα
ξυράω	οἰκοδόμος	**ὀλιγοποιέω**	ὁμοίως
ξύρησις	οἰκονομέω	*ὀλίγος*	ὁμοίωσις
ξυρόν	οἰκονομία	**ὀλιγοστός**	ὁμολογέω
ξυστός	οἰκονόμος	**ὀλιγότης**	*ὁμολογία*
ξύω	**οἰκόπεδον**	*ὀλιγοχρόνιος*	**ὁμόλογος**
	οἶκος	ὀλιγοψυχέω	ὁμολογουμένως
Ο	οἰκτίρημα	**ὀλιγοψυχία**	ὁμολόγως
	οἰκτιρμός	ὀλιγόψυχος	**ὁμομήτριος**
ὁ, ἡ, τό	οἰκτίρμων	**ὀλιγόω**	ὁμονοέω
ὀβελίσκος	οἰκτίρω	*ὀλιγωρέω*	ὁμόνοια
ὀβολός	**οἴκτιστος**	**ὀλισθάνω**	**ὁμοπάτριος**
ὀγδοήκοντα	**οἶκτος**	**ὀλίσθησις†**	ὁμορέω
ὀγδοηκοστός	**οἰκτρός**	**ὀλίσθ(ρ)ημα**	**ὅμορος**
ὄγδοος	**οἴμμοι**	**ὀλκεῖον**	**ὁμόσπονδος**
ὅδε	**οἶμος†**	**ὀλκή**	ὁμοῦ
ὁδεύω	**οἰμωγή**	*ὄλλυμι*	ὁμόφυλος
ὁδηγέω	**οἰμώζω**	**ὁλοκαρπόω**	**ὁμόψηφος**
ὁδηγός	**οἰνοδόχος†**	**ὁλοκάρπωμα**	**ὁμόψυχος**
ὁδοιπορία	**οἰνοποτέω**	**ὁλοκάρπωσις**	**ὀμφακίζω**
ὁδοιπόρος	οἰνοπότης	ὁλόκαυστος	ὀμφαλός
ὁδοποιέω	*οἶνος*	*ὁλοκαύτωμα*	ὄμφαξ
ὁδός	οἰνοφλυγέω	**ὁλοκαύτωσις**	ὅμως
ὀδούς	**οἰνοχοέω**	ὁλόκληρος	**ὄναγρος**
ὀδυνάω	**οἰνοχόη**	**ὀλολυγμός**	ὀνειδίζω
ὀδύνη	**οἰνοχόος**	**ὀλολύζω**	**ὀνείδισμα**
ὀδυνηρός	**οἰνόω**	**ὁλοπόρφυρος**	ὀνειδισμός
ὀδυρμός	*οἴομαι*	**ὁλόρριζος, ὁλορριζεί**	ὄνειδος
ὀδύρομαι	οἰος	ὅλος	ὄνειρος
ὄζος	**οἰστρηλασία**	**ὁλοσφύρητος**	**ὄνησις**
ὄζω	**οἴστρος**	**ὁλοσχερής**	ὀνίνημι
ὅθεν	οιφι	**ὀλοφύρομαι**	**ὀνοκένταυρος**
ὀθόνιον	**οἴχομαι**	ὄλυνθος	ὄνομα
οἰακίζω	**οἰωνίζομαι**	**ὀλύρα**	ὀνομάζω
οἴαξ	**οἰώνισμα**	**ὀλυρίτης**	**ὀνομασία**
οἶδα (εἰδέναι, εἰδεῖν)	**οἰωνισμός**	ὁμαλίζω	**ὀνομαστί†**
οἰκεῖος	**οἰωνόβρωτος**	**ὁμαλισμός**	*ὀνομαστός*
οἰκειότης	οἰωνός	**ὄμβρημα**	**ὀνοματογραφία**
οἰκειόω	**ὀκλάζω**	ὄμβρος	ὄνος

ὄντως
ὄνυξ
ὀνυχίζω
ὀνύχιον
ὀνυχιστήρ
ὀξέως
ὄξος
ὀξυγράφος
ὀξύθυμος
ὀξύνω
ὀξύς
ὀξυσθενής†
ὀξύτης
ὀπή
ὀπηνίκα
ὀπήτιον
ὄπισθε [ὄπισθεν]
ὀπίσθιος
ὀπισθότονος
ὀπισθοφανής
ὀπίσω
ὁπλή
ὁπλίζω
ὁπλιστής†
ὁπλίτης
ὁπλοδοτέω
ὁπλοθήκη
ὁπλολογέω
ὁπλομάχος
ὅπλον
ὁπλοποιέω
ὁπλοφόρος
ὁποῖος
ὁπόταν
ὁπότε
ὅπου
ὀπτάζομαι
ὀπτάνομαι
ὀπτασία
ὀπτάω
ὀπτός
ὀπώρα
ὀπωροφυλάκιον
ὅπως
ὅραμα
ὅρασις
ὁρατής
ὁρατικός
ὁρατός
ὁράω
ὀργανικός
ὄργανον
ὀργή
ὀργιάω†
ὀργίζω

ὀργίλος
ὀργίλως
ὀρεινός
ὄρεξις
ὄρθιος
ὀρθός
ὀρθοτομέω
ὀρθόω
ὀρθρεύω
ὀρθρίζω
ὀρθρινός
ὄρθριος
ὄρθρος
ὀρθρόω†
ὀρθῶς
ὁρίζω
ὅριον
ὁρισμός
ὁρκίζω
ὁρκισμός
ὅρκος
ὁρκόω†
ὁρκωμοσία
ὁρμάω
ὁρμή
ὅρμημα
ὁρμίσκος
ὅρμος
ὄρνεον
ὀρνίθιον
ὀρνιθοσκοπέομαι
ὄρνις
ὀρόδαμνος (see ῥάδαμνος)
ὅρος
ὄρος
ὀροφο(κο)ιτέω
ὄροφος
ὀροφόω†
ὀρόφωμα
ὀρτυγαμήτρα
ὄρυξ
ὀρύσσω
ὀρφαν(ε)ία
ὀρφανός
ὀρχέομαι
ὅς, ἥ, ὅ
ὅσιος
ὁσιότης
ὁσιόω
ὁσίως
ὀσμή
ὅσος
ὅσπερ
ὄσπριον

ὅστις
ὁστισοῦν
ὀστοῦν
ὀστράκινος
ὄστρακον
ὀστρακώδης
ὀσφραίνομαι
ὀσφρασία
ὀσφύς
ὅταν
ὅτε
ὅτι
ὁτιοῦν (see ὁστισοῦν)
ὀτρύνω
οὐ
οὐ
οὐαί
οὐδαμοῦ
οὐδαμῶς
οὐδέ
οὐδείς
οὐδέποτε
οὐδέπω
οὐδείς
οὐκ
οὐκέτι
οὐλή
οὖν
οὗπερ [ὅσπερ]
οὔπω
οὐρά
οὐραγέω
οὐραγία
οὐράνιος
οὐρανόθεν
οὐρανός
οὐρέω
οὔριος
οὖρον
οὖς
οὐσία
οὔτε
οὔτοι†
οὗτος
οὕτω(ς)
οὐχ
οὐχί
ουχοκεραινος†
ὀφείλημι
ὀφείλω
ὄφελος
ὀφθαλμός
ὀφθαλμοφανής
ὀφιόδηκτος
ὀφιομάχης

ὄφις
ὄφλησις
ὀφρύς
ὀχεία
ὀχεῖον†
ὀχλαγωγέω
ὀχλέω
ὀχληρία†
ὄχλος
ὀχυράζω†
ὀχυρός
ὀχυρόω
ὀχύρωμα
ὀχυρωμάτιον
ὀχύρωσις
ὀψάριον
ὀψέ
ὀψία
ὀψίζω
ὄψιμος
ὄψις
ὄψον, -ος, -εος
ὀψοποίημα
ὀψώνιον

Π

παγγέωργος
παγετός
παγιδεύω
παγίς
παγκρατής
πάγος
παθεινός
παθοκράτεια
παθοκρατέομαι
πάθυς
παιάν
παιγνία
παίγνιον
παιδάριον
παιδεία
παιδευτής
παιδεύω
παιδίον
παιδίσκη
παιδοποιέω
παιδοποιία
παιδοχαρακτήρ†
παίζω
παῖς
παίω
παλάθη
πάλαι
παλαιός

παλαιόω	παντοφαγία	παρακαθίστημι	παραπορεύομαι
παλαιστή(ς)	πάντως	παρακαλέω	παράπτωμα
παλαίστρα	πάνυ	**παρακαλίζω**†	παράπτωσις
παλαίω	**πανυπέρτατος**	**παρακάλυμμα**	**παραριθμέω**
παλαίωμα	**πάππος**	παρακαλύπτω	παραρρέω
παλαίωσις	**πάπυρος**	παρακαταθήκη	**παραρ(ρ)ίπτω**, or -πτέω
πάλιν	*παρά*	**παρακατατίθημι**	
παλλακή	παραβαίνω	παράκειμαι	**παράρρυμα**
παλλακίς	*παραβάλλω*	παρακελεύω	*παράσημον*
πάλλω	**παραβαπτός**†	**παρακλείω**	[παράσημος]
παμβασιλεύς	**παραβασιλεύω**	παράκλησις	**παρασιωπάω**
παμβότανον	παραβασιλεύω ... παράβασις	**παρακλητικός**	παρασκευάζω
παμμ(ε)ιγής	παραβιάζομαι	**παρακλήτωρ**	*παρασκευή*
παμμελής	**παραβιβάζω**	**παρακλίνω**†	**παράστασις**
παμμίαρος	**παραβιωτής**†	**παρακμάζω**	**παραστήκω**
παμπληθής	*παραβλέπω*	**παράκοιτος**	**παρασυμβάλλω**
παμποίκιλος	*παραβολή*	παρακολουθέω	**παρασφαλίζομαι**†
παμπόνηρος	*παραγγέλλω*	**παρακομίζω**	*παράταξις*
πάμφυλος	*παράγγελμα*	παρακούω	**παρατάσσω**
πανάγιος	παραγίνομαι	**παρακρούω**	*παρατείνω*
πάνδεινος	**παραγινώσκω**†	παρακύπτω	παρατηρέω
πάνδημος	*παράγω*	**παραλαλέω**	*παρατίθημι*
πανεθνεί	**παραγωγή**†	παραλαμβάνω	**παρατρέχω**
πανεπίσκοπος	**παράδειγμα**	παραλείπω	παραυτίκα
πανηγυρίζω	παραδειγματίζω	*παραλία* [παράλιος]	παραφέρω
πανήγυρις	**παραδειγματισμός**	παράλιος	**παραφορά**†
πανηγύριος†	**παραδείκνυμι**	*παραλλαγή*	παραφρονέω
πανηγυρισμός	*παράδεισος*	**παράλλαξις**	**παραφρόνησις**
πανθήρ	παραδέχομαι	*παραλλάσσω*	**παράφρων**
πανόδυρτος	παραδίδωμι	παραλογίζομαι	παραφυάς
πανοικία	**παραδοξάζω**	**παραλογισμός**	*παραχρῆμα*
πανοπλία	παράδοξος	**παράλυσις**	**παραχωρέω**
πανούργευμα	παράδοσις	*παραλύω*	**παρδάλεος**
πανουργεύομαι	**παραδρομή**	παραμένω	πάρδαλις
πανούργημα	**παράδωσις**	παραμυθέομαι	παρεδρεύω
πανουργία	**παραζεύγνυμι**	παραμυθία	**πάρεδρος**
πανοῦργος	*παραζηλόω*	παραμύθιον	παρεῖδον
πάνσοφος	**παραζώνη**	**παραναγινώσκω**	*πάρειμι* (παρεῖναι)
πανταχῆ	παραζώνη	**παρανακλίνω**	**πάρειμι** (παριέναι)
πανταχόθεν	**παραζώννυμι**†	**παραναλίσκω**	**παρεισπορεύομαι**
πανταχοῦ	παραθαλάσσιος	παρανομέω	**παρεκλείπω**
παντελής	παραθαρσύνω	παρανομία	**παρεκτείνω**
παντελῶς	**παράθεμα**	*παράνομος*	**παρελέγχω**†
παντεπίσκοπος†	παραθερμαίνω	**παραξιφίς**	**παρέλκυσις**
παντεπόπτης	**παράθεσις**	*παράπαν*	**παρέλκω**
παντευχία	παραθήκη	παραπέμπω	*παρεμβάλλω*
πάντη	**παραθλίβω**	**παραπέτασμα**	*παρεμβολή*
παντοδαπός	**παραίνεσις**	παραπηδάω	**παρεμπίπτω**
παντοδύναμος	*παραινέω*	παραπικραίνω	παρενοχλέω
πάντοθεν	**παραιρέω**	παραπικρασμός	**παρέξ, πάρεξ**
παντοῖος	παραιτέομαι	*παραπίπτω*	**παρεξίστημι**
παντοκρατορία†	*παραίτιος*	**παράπληκτος**	**παρεπιδείκνυμι**
παντοκράτωρ	**παρακαθεύδω**	**παραπληξία**	παρεπίδημος
πάντοτε	παρακάθημαι	**παράπλους**	**πάρεργος**
παντοτρόφος	παρακαθίζω	**παραπομπή**	παρέρχομαι

παρέχω	πατρῷος	πεντάκις	**περιεργασία**†
παρηγορέω	**παύλα**	πεντακισχίλιοι	**περιεργία**
παρηγορία	**παύσις**	πεντακόσιοι	*περιέρχομαι*
παρθενία	παύω	**πεντάπηχυς**	περιέχω
παρθενικός	**πάχνη**	**πενταπλασίως**	**περίζωμα**
παρθένιος	**πάχος**	**πενταπλοῦς**	περιζώννυμι
παρθένος	*παχύνω*	πέντε	**περίθεμα**
παρίημι	**παχύς**	**πεντεκαίδεκα**	**περιΐπταμαι**
πάρινος	πεδάω	πεντεκαιδέκατος	*περιΐστημι*
πάριος	πέδη	**πεντεκαιεικοσαετής**	περικαθαίρω
παρίστημι	**πεδήτης**	πεντήκοντα	**περικαθαρίζω**
παροδεύω	**πέδιλον**	**πεντηκονταετής**	περικάθαρμα
πάροδος[1]	πεδ(ε)ινός	πεντηκόνταρχος	**περικάθημαι**
πάροδος[2]	πεδίον	πεντηκοστός	περικαθίζω
παροικεσία	**πεζικός**	*πέπειρος*	**περικαίω**
παροικέω	**πεζομαχία**	πεποίθησις	*περικαλύπτω*
παροίκησις	*πεζός*	**πεποιθότως**	**περικατάλη(μ)πτος**
παροικία	πειθαρχέω	**πέπων**	περίκειμαι
πάροικος	πείθω	*πέρα* [πέραν]	**περικείρω**
παροιμία	πεινάω	**περαίνω**	περικεφαλαία
παροιμιάζω	πεῖρα	πέρας	**περικλάω**
παροινέω	πειρασμός	**περασμός**	**περικλύζω**
παροιστράω	**πειρατεύω**	περάτης	**περικνημίς**
παροξύνω	**πειρατήριον**	περάω	**περικομπέω**
παροξυσμός	**πειρατής**	**πέρδιξ**	**περικοσμέω**
παρόρασις	πειράω/πειράζω	περί	**περικρατέω**
παροράω	**πείρω**	**περιαγκωνίζω**	περικυκλόω
παροργίζω	πέλαγος	περιάγω	**περικύκλῳ**
παρόργισμα	*πέλας*	περιαιρέω	**περιλακίζω**
παροργισμός	**πελειόομαι** (see πελι-)	**περιαντλέω**	**περιλαμβάνω**
παρορμάω	πέλειος	*περιάπτω*	περιλείπομαι
παρουσία	**πελεκάν**	**περιάργυρος**	**περίλημμα**†
παρρησία	**πελεκάω**	**περιαργυρόω**	**περίλη(μ)ψις**
παρρησιάζομαι	**πελεκητός**	περιαστράπτω	**περίλοιπος**
παρωθέω	**πέλεκυς**	περιβάλλω	περίλυπος
παρωμίς	**πελιόομαι**	**περιβιόω**	**περιλύω**
πᾶς, πᾶσα, πᾶν	πελιός	**περίβλεπτος**	περιμένω
πάσσαλος	πέλμα	περιβλέπω	**περίμετρον**
πάσσω	**πελταστής**	**περίβλημα**	**περινίπτω**
παστός	**πέλτη**	περιβόητος	**περιξύω**
παστοφόριον	**πέλυξ**	περιβόλαιον	**περιοδεύω**
πασχα	**πέμμα**	**περιβολή**	**περίοδος**
πάσχω	πέμπτος	**περίβολος**	**περιοικοδομέω**
πατάσσω	πέμπω	περιγίνομαι	*περίοικος*
παταχρός	**πενέομαι/πένομαι**	**περίγλυφον**†	**περιονυχίζω**
πατέω	πένης	**περιγραφή**†	**περιοράω**†
πάτημα	πενθερά	**περιδειπνέω**	**περιουσιασμός**
πατήρ	πενθερός	**περίδειπνον**	περιούσιος
πατητός	πενθέω	**περιδέξιον**	*περιοχή*
πατράδελφος	*πενθικός*	**περιδιπλόω**	**περιπαθῶς**
πατριά	πένθος	**περιδύω**	περιπατέω
πατριάρχης	**πενία**	**περίειμι**[1] (**περιεῖναι**)	**περίπατος**
πατρικός	πενιχρός	**περίειμι**[2] (**περιιέναι**)	περιπίπτω
πάτριος	**πενταετηρικός**	**περιεκτικός**	**περιπιλέω**†
πατρίς	**πενταετής**	*περιεργάζομαι*	περιπλέκω

Appendix II: Comparative Index of Words in This Lexicon and BDAG

περιπλήσσω	περιχαρής	**πιπι**†	**πλημμέλησις**
περιποιέω	**περιχέω**	πιπράσκω	*πλήμμυρα*
περιποίησις	**περίχρυσος**	*πίπτω*	*πλήν*
περιπόλιον	**περιχρυσόω**	**πίσσα**	*πλήρης*
περιπορεύομαι	περίχωρος	*πιστεύω*	*πληροφορέω*
περιπόρφυρος	περίψημα	*πίστις*	*πληρόω*
περίπτερος	**περιψύχω**	**πιστοποιέω**	*πλήρωμα*
περίπτωμα	**περκάζω**	πιστός	**πλήρωσις**
περιρραίνω	**πέσσω**	πιστόω	**πλησιάζω**
περιρραντίζω	*πέταλον*	πιστῶς	**πλησιέστερον**
περιρρέω	**πεταλόω**†	**πίτυρον**	πλησίον
περιρρήγνυμι	*πέταμαι [πέτομαι]*	**πίτυς**	*πλησμονή*
περισιαλόω	**πετάννυμι**	πίων	*πλήσσω*
περισκελής	**πέτασος**	**πλαγιάζω**	**πλινθεία**
περισκυθίζω	*πετεινός [πετεινόν]*	**πλάγιος**	**πλινθεῖον**
περισπασμός	**πέτευρον**	πλανάω	**πλινθεύω**
περισπάω	πέτομαι	πλάνη	**πλίνθος**
περισπόριον	πέτρα	**πλάνησις**	**πλινθουργία**
περισσεία	**πέτρινος**	πλανήτης	*πλοῖον*
περίσσευμα	**πετροβόλος**	**πλανῆτις**	πλόκαμος
περισσεύω	*πέτρος [Πέτρος]*	πλάνος	πλοκή
περισσός	**πεύκη**	πλάξ	**πλόκιον**
περισσῶς	**πεύκινος**	πλάσμα	πλοῦς
περίστασις	**πέψις**	πλάσσω	πλούσιος
περιστέλλω	πηγή	**πλάστης**†	πλουτέω
περιστερά	**πῆγμα**	**πλάστιγξ**	πλουτίζω
περιστήθιον	*πήγνυμι*	**πλάτανος**	πλοῦτος
περιστολή	**πηδαλιουχέω**	πλάτος	πλύνω
περιστόμιον	πηδάω	πλατύνω	**πλωτός**
περιστρέφω	πηλίκος	πλατύς	πνεῦμα
περιστροφή	πήλινος	πλατυσμός	**πνευματοφορέομαι**
περίστυλος	πηλός	**πλειστάκις**	πνευματοφόρος
περισύρω	πηλουργός	πλεῖστος	**πνεύμων**
περισχίζω	**πῆξις**	πλείων	*πνέω*, fut πνευσω
περισῴζω	**πήσσω** (see πήγνυμι)	πλέκω	**πνιγμός**
περιτειχίζω	πήρα	πλεονάζω	πνίγω
περίτειχος	πηρόω	**πλεονάκις**	πνοή
περιτέμνω	πῆχυς	**πλεόνασμα**	**πόα**
περιτήκω†	πιάζω	πλεονασμός	ποδάγρα
περιτίθημι	**πιαίνω**	**πλεοναστός**	ποδήρης
περιτομή	πιέζω	πλεονεκτέω	**ποδιστήρ**
περιτρέπω	πίθηκος	**πλεονέκτημα**†	**ποθεινός**
περιτρέχω	**πίθος**	πλεονέκτης	πόθεν
περιφανής	πικραίνω	πλεονεξία	πόθεω
περιφέρεια	**πικρασμός**	πλευρά	*πόα [ποία]*
περιφερής	πικρία	**πλευρόν**	ποιέω
περιφέρω	**πικρίς**	πλέω	ποίημα
περιφορά	πικρός	πληγή	ποίησις
περιφράσσω	**πικρόω**†	πλῆθος	ποιητής
περιφρονέω	πικρῶς	πληθύνω	ποικιλία
περίφρων	πίμπλημι	**πληθύς**	**ποικίλλω**
περιφυτεύω	*πίμπρημι*	πληθύνω	**ποίκιλμα**
περιχαλάω	**πίν(ν)ινος**	*πλημμέλεια*	ποικίλος
περιχαλκόω	πίνω	**πλημμελέω**	ποικιλτής
περιχαρακόω	πιότης	**πλημμέλημα**	**ποικιλτικός**
		πλημμελής	

ποικιλτός	*πολύς*	**ποτιστήριον**	**προανατέλλω**
ποικίλως	πολυτελής	ποτόν	**προαπαγγέλλω**
ποιμαίνω	**πολυτόκος**	πότος	**προαποδείκνυμι**
ποιμενικός	πολυτρόπος	που	**προαποθνήσκω**
ποιμήν	**πολύφροντις**	ποῦ	**προασπίζω**
ποίμνη	**πολυχρονίζω**	πούς	**προάστ(ε)ιον**
ποίμνιον	**πολυχρόνιος**	πρᾶγμα	προβαίνω
ποῖος	**πολυωρέω**	πραγματεία	*προβάλλω*
πόκος	πόμα	πραγματεύομαι	**προβασανίζω**
πολεμέω	**πομπεύω**	**πραγματικός**	**προβασκάνιον**
πολεμικός	*πονέω*	πράκτωρ	προβατικός
πολέμιος	πονηρεύομαι	*πρᾶξις*	πρόβατον
πολεμιστής	πονηρία	**πρᾶος**	προβιβάζω
πόλεμος	πονηρός	πρασιά	προβλέπω
πολεμοτροφέω	*πόνος*	**πράσινος**	**πρόβλημα**
πολιά	**ποντόβροχος**	**πρᾶσις**	**προβλής**
πολιορκέω	**ποντοπορέω**	**πράσον**	**προβλητός**†
πολιόρκησις†	πόντος	πράσσω	προγίνομαι
πολιορκία	*πορεία*	**πράττω** [πράσσω]	προγινώσκω
πολιός	**πορεῖον**	**πρατός**	πρόγνωσις
πόλις	**πόρευσις**	**πραΰθυμος**	**προγονικός**
πολιτεία	**πορευτός**	**πραΰνω**	πρόγονος
πολίτευμα	πορεύω	πραΰς	*προγράφω*
πολιτεύομαι	πορθέω	πραΰτης	πρόδηλος
πολίτης	*πορία* (see πορεία)	**πρεπόντως**	προδηλόω
πολλάκις	πορίζω	πρέπω	*προδίδωμι*
πολλαχόθεν	πορισμός	πρεσβεία	**προδοσία**
πολλαχῶς	πορνεία	**πρεσβεῖον**	προδότης
πολλοστός	**πορνεῖον**	πρεσβευτής	πρόδρομος
πολυανδρεῖος	πορνεύω	**πρέσβυς**	προεῖδον
πολύγονος	πόρνη	*πρεσβύτερος* (see	**προεκφέρω**
πολύδακρυς	**πορνικός**	πρέσβυς)	**προενέχω**
πολυέλεος	**πορνοκόπος**	πρεσβύτης	**προεξαποστέλλω**
πολυετής	**πόρος**	πρεσβῦτις	**προεπιχειρέω**†
πολυημερεύω	πόρνος	πρήθω	προέρχομαι
πολυήμερος	**πόρπη**	**πρηνή**†	προετοιμάζω
πολύθρηνος	πόρρω	*πρηνέα* [πρηνής]	*προηγέομαι*
πολυκέφαλος	πόρρωθεν	**πρίαμαι**	**προηγορέω**
πολυμερής	πορφύρα	πρίζω	**προήγορος**
πολυλογία	**πορφυρίς**	πρίν	**προήκω**
πολυμερής	**πορφυρίων**	**πρῖνος**	**προθερίζω**
πολυοδία	πορφυροῦς	**πριστηροειδής**	πρόθεσις
πολύορκος	ποσάκις	**πριστοειδής**†	**προθυμέομαι**
πολυοχλία	**ποσαπλῶς**	πρίω	*προθυμέτερος*
πολύπαις	**ποσαχῶς**	πρίων	[πρόθυμος]
πολυπειρία	*πύσις*	*πρό*	προθυμία
πολύπειρος	πόσος	**προαγορεύω**	πρόθυμος
πολυπλασιάζω	ποταμός	*προάγω*	προθύμως
πολυπλάσιος	ποταπός	**προαγωνίζομαι**	*πρόθυρον*
πολυπλήθεια	ποτέ	*προαδικέω*	*προΐημι*
πολυπληθέω	πότε	*προαίρεσις*	πρόϊμος
πολυπληθύνω	*πότερον*	προαιρέω	προΐστημι
πολύπλοκος	**πότημα**	**προαλής**	**προκαθηγέομαι**
πολυπραγμονέω	ποτήριον	**προαναμέλπω**	**προκαθήκω**†
πολυρήμων	ποτίζω	**προανατάσσω**	προκάθημαι

Appendix II: Comparative Index of Words in This Lexicon and BDAG

προκαθίζω
πρόκαιρος†
προκακόω
προκαλέω
προκαταλαμβάνω
προκατασκευάζω
προκατασκιρρόομαι
προκαταχωρίζω†
πρόκειμαι
πρόκλησις†
προκοπή
προκουρία†
πρόκρημνος
προκρίνω
προλαμβάνω
προλέγω
πρόλημψις†
προλήνιον
πρόλοβος
πρόλογος†
προμαχέω
προμαχών
προμηνύω
προνοέω
πρόνοια
προνομεύω
προνομή
προνουμηνία
προοδηγός
πρόοιδα
προοίμιον
προοράω
πρόπαππος
προπάτωρ
προπέμπω
προπέτεια†
προπετής
προπίπτω
προπομπή
προπορεύομαι
προπράσσω
προπτύω
πρόπτωσις
προπύλαιος†
πρόπυλον
πρός
προσάββατον
προσαγγέλλω
προσαγορεύω
προσάγω
προσαιτέω
προσαναβαίνω
προσανάβασις
προσαναλέγω
προσαναπαύω

προσαναπληρόω
προσανατρέπω
προσαναφέρω
προσανοικοδομέω
προσαξιόω
προσαπειλέω†
προσαπέρχομαι†
προσαποθνήσκω
προσαπόλλυμι
προσαποστέλλω
προσαπωθέω
προσαρτίως
προσασπίζω†
προσβαίνω
προσβάλλω
πρόσβασις
προσβλητός
προσβολή
προσγελάω
προσγεννάω†
προσγίνομαι
προσγράφω
προσδεκτός
προσδέομαι
προσδέχομαι
προσδέω
προσδίδωμι
προσδοκάω
προσδοκία
προσεγγίζω
προσεδρεία
προσεδρεύω
προσεῖδον
πρόσειμι¹ (προσεῖναι)
πρόσειμι² (προσιέναι)
προσεῖπον
προσεκκαίω
προσεμβριμάομαι
προσεμπίμπρημι
προσενέχω
προσεξηγέομαι
προσεπιαπιτάω†
προσεπικατατείνω
προσεπιτιμάω
προσεπιχειρέω†
προσερυθριάω
προσέρχομαι
προσέτι
προσευχή
προσεύχομαι
προσέχω
προσηκόντως
προσήκω
προσηλόω
προσηλυτεύω

προσήλυτος
προσημαίνω
προσημειόομαι
προσηνής
πρόσθεμα
πρόσθεσις
προσθλίβω
προσκαθήκω†
προσκαθίστημι
πρόσκαιρος
προσκαίω
προσκαλέω
προσκαρτερέω
προσκαταλαμβάνω†
προσκαταλείπω
πρόσκαυμα
πρόσκειμαι
προσκεφάλαιον
προσκήνιον
πρόσκλησις
προσκλίνω
προσκολλάω
πρόσκομμα
προσκόπτω
προσκρούω
προσκυνέω
προσκύνησις
προσκύπτω
προσκυρέω
προσλαλέω
προσλαμβάνω
προσλέγω
προσλογίζομαι
προσμαρτυρέω
προσμείγνυμι
προσμειδιάω
προσμένω
προσμηνύω†
προσνέμω
προσνοέω
πρόσοδος
προσοδύρομαι
προσόζω
προσοίγω
προσοικέω†
προσονομάζω
προσοράω
προσοχή
προσοχθίζω
προσόχθισμα
προσοχυρόω
πρόσοψις
προσπαίζω
προσπαρακαλέω
προσπάσσω

προσπίπτω
προσποιέω
προσπορεύομαι
προσπροάγω†
προσπυρόω
προσραίνω
προσσιελίζω
προσταγή
πρόσταγμα
προσταράσσω
προστάς
προστατέω
προστάτης
προστάττω
[προστάσσω]
προστίθημι
πρόστιμον
προστρέχω
προσυμνέω†
προσυμπλέκω†
προσυπομιμνήσκω
προσυστέλλω
προσυψόω
προσφαίνω
πρόσφατος
προσφάτως
προσφέρω
προσφιλής
προσφορά
προσφύω
προσφωνέω
προσχαίρω
πρόσχεσις†
προσχέω
προσχράομαι
πρόσχωμα
προσχωρέω
προσωθέω
προσωπεῖον
πρόσωπον
προτάσσω
προτείνω
προτείχισμα
προτέρημα
πρότερος
προτίθημι
προτιμάω
προτομή
προτρέπω
προτρέχω
προϋπάρχω
προϋποδείκνυμι†
προϋποτάσσω
προϋφίστημι
προφαίνω

προφανῶς	πτερύγιον	πυρρός	ῥητός
προφασίζομαι	πτέρυξ	**πυρσεύω**	**ῥῖγος**
πρόφασις	**πτερύσσομαι**	**πυρσός**	**ῥίζα**
προφασιστικός	πτερωτός	**πυρφόρος**	**ῥιζόω**
προφέρω	**πτήσσω**	**πυρώδης**	**ῥίζωμα**
προφητεία	**πτίλος**	*πύρωσις*	**ῥιπίζω**
προφητεύω	πτοέω	**πυρωτής**	**ῥιπιστός**
προφήτης	**πτοή**	**πώγων**	*ῥίπτω*
προφῆτις	πτόησις	πωλέω	**ῥίς**
προφθάνω	**πτύελος**	*πῶλος*	**ῥόα**
προφυλακή	πτύσσω	πώποτε	**ῥόαξ**
προφύλαξ	**πτύξις**	πωρόω	**ῥόδον**
προφυλάσσω	**πτυχή**	πῶς	**ῥοδοφόρος**
προχαλάω	πτύω	πώς	**ῥοιζέω**
προχειρίζω	*πτῶμα*		ῥοῖζος
πρόχειρος	πτῶσις	**Ρ**	**ῥοῖσκος**
προχώρημα	πτωχεία		ῥομφαία
πρύτανις	πτωχεύω	*ῥαβδίζω*	**ῥόπαλον**
πρώην	πτωχίζω	*ῥάβδος*	*ῥοπή*
πρωΐ	πτωχός	**ῥαγάς**	**ῥοποπώλης** (see
πρωία	**πύγαργος**	**ῥάγμα**	ῥωποπώλης)
πρωΐθεν	πυγμή	**ῥάδαμνος**	**ῥοῦς**
πρώϊμος† [πρόϊμος]	**πυθμήν**	**ῥάδιος**	**ῥοών**
πρωϊνός	**πυκάζω**	ραθμ	**ῥύδην**
πρωρεύς	*πυκνός*	ῥαθυμέω	**ῥυθμίζω**
πρωταγωνιστής	**πυκνότης**†	**ῥαθυμία**	**ῥυθμός**
πρώταρχος	πύλη	*ῥαίνω*	**ῥύμη**
πρωτεύω	πυλών	ῥάκος	**ῥύομαι**
πρωτοβαθρέω	**πυλωρός**	**ῥακώδης**	**ῥυπαρός**
πρωτοβολέω	πυνθάνομαι	**ῥάμμα**	**ῥύπος**
πρωτογένημα	**πυξίον**	**ῥάμνος**	**ῥύσις**
πρωτογενής	**πύξος**	**ῥανίζω**†	**ῥῦσις**
πρωτόγονος	*πῦρ*	**ῥανίς**	**ῥύστης**
πρωτοκλήσιον†	πυρά	ῥαντίζω	**ῥωμαλέος**
πρωτοκλίσιον	**πυραμίς**	ῥαντισμός	**ῥώμη**
πρωτοκουρά	**πυργόβαρις**	**ῥαντός**	**ῥώννυμι**
πρωτοκουρία	πύργος	ῥαπίζω	**ῥώξ**
πρωτολογία	**πυρεῖον**	**ῥάπισμα**	ῥωποπώλης
πρωτόπλαστος	πυρετός	**ῥαπτός**	
πρῶτος	**πυρίκαυστος**	**ῥάπτω**	**Σ**
πρωτοστάτης	πύρινος	*ῥάσσω*	
πρωτοτοκεῖον†	πυρίπνους	**ῥαφιδευτής**	**σαβαχα**
πρωτοτοκεύω	πυριφλεγής	**ῥαφιδευτός**	σαβαωθ
πρωτοτοκέω	**πυροβόλον**	**ῥάχις**	*σαββατίζω*
πρωτοτόκια	**πυρογενής**†	**ῥέγχω**	σάββατον
πρωτότοκος	**πυρόπνους** (see	**ῥεμβασμός**	**σαβεκ**
πταῖσμα	πυρίπνους)	**ῥεμβεύω**	**σαβι**
πταίω, ἐπταιχώς	*πυρός*	**ῥέμβομαι**	**σαγή**
πταρμός	**πυροφόρος**	ῥεῦμα	σαγήνη
πτέρνα	*πυρόω*	*ῥέω*	**σάγμα**
πτερνίζω	**πύρπνοος**	*ῥῆγμα*	**σαθρός**
πτερνισμός	**πυρπολέω**	*ῥήγνυμι*	**σαθρόω**
πτέρνον†	**πυρράκης**	ῥῆμα	σάκκος
πτερόν	**πυρρίζω**	ῥῆσις	**σαλαμιν**
πτεροφυέω	**πυρρόομαι**	**ῥητίνη**	*σαλεύω*

Appendix II: Comparative Index of Words in This Lexicon and BDAG 241

σάλος
σάλπιγξ
σαλπίζω, σαλπιῶ
σαμβύκη
σανδάλιον
σανίδωμα
σανιδωτός
σανίς
σαπρία
σαπρίζω
σάπφειρος [σάπφιρος]
σαράβαρα
σαραμελ (see ασαραμελ)
σάρδιον
σάρκινος
σαρκοφαγέω
σαρκοφαγία
σάρξ
σαταν/σατανᾶς
σάτον
σατραπ(ε)ία
σατράπης
σαύρα
σαυτοῦ
σαφής
σαφφωθ
σαφῶς
σαχωλ
σβέννυμι
σβεστικός
σεαυτοῦ
σέβασμα
σέβω
σεθιειμ†
σειρά
σειρήν
σειρήνιος
σ(ε)ιρομάστης
σεῖσμα
σεισμός
σείω
σελήνη
σελίς
σεμίδαλις
σεμνολογέω
σεμνός
σεμνότης
σεμνῶς
σεραφιν
σερσερωθ
σευτλίον
σηκός
σημαία
σημαίνω

σημασία
σημέα
σημεῖον
σημειόω
σημείωσις
σήμερον
σήπη
σήπω
σής
σητόβρωτος
σήψ†
σήψις
σθένος
σθένω
σιαγόνιον
σιαγών
σιγάω
σιγή
σιγηρός
σιδήρ(ε)ιος†
σιδήριον
σιδηρόδεσμος
σίδηρος
σιδηροῦς
σίελον
σικερα
σίκλος
σικυήρατον
σίκυος
σίκυς
σινδών
σειρομάστης (see σιρομάστης)
σιρῶνος
σισόη
σιτευτός
σιτέομαι
σιτίον
σιτοβολών
σιτοδεία
σιτοδοσία
σιτομετρέω
σῖτον [σῖτος]
σιτοποιός
σιωπάω
σιωπή
σιώπησις
σκάλλω
σκαμβός
σκανδαλίζω
σκάνδαλον
σκάπτω
σκάφη
σκάφος
σκελίζω

σκέλος
σκεπάζω
σκέπαρνον
σκέπασις
σκεπαστής
σκεπεινός
σκέπη
σκέπτομαι
σκευάζω
σκευασία
σκεύασμα†
σκευαστός†
σκεῦος
σκευοφύλαξ†
σκηνή
σκηνοπηγία
σκῆνος
σκηνόω
σκήνωμα
σκήνωσις
σκῆπτρον
σκιά
σκιαγράφος
σκιάδ(ε)ιον
σκιάζω
σκιρτάω
σκληρία
σκληροκαρδία
σκληροκάρδιος
σκληροπρόσωπος†
σκληρός
σκληρότης
σκληροτράχηλος
σκληρύνω
σκληρυσμός†
σκνίψ
σκολαβρίζω†
σκολιάζω
σκολιός
σκολιότης
σκόλοψ
σκόπελον
σκοπεύω
σκοπέω
σκοπή
σκοπιά
σκοπός
σκορακισμός
σκόρδον
σκορπίδιον
σκορπίζω
σκορπίος
σκορπισμός
σκοτάζω
σκοτεινός

σκοτία
σκοτίζω
σκοτομήνη
σκότος
σκοτόω
σκυβαλίζω
σκύβαλον
σκυθρωπάζω
σκυθρωπός
σκυλεία
σκυλεύω
σκυλμός
σκῦλον
σκύμνος
σκυτάλη
σκώληξ
σκῶλον
σκώπτω
σμαραγδίτης
σμάραγδος
σμῆγμα
σμικρύνω
σμῖλαξ
σμιρίτης
σμύρνα
σμύρνινος
σοβέω
σοομ
σορός
σός, σή, σόν
σοφία
σοφίζω
σοφιστής
σοφός
σοφόω
σπάδων
σπαίρω
σπάλαξ†
σπανίζω
σπάνιος
σπάνις
σπαράσσω
σπάργανον
σπαργανόω
σπαρτίον
σπασμός
σπαταλάω
σπατάλη
σπάω
σπεῖρα
σπειρηδόν
σπείρω
σπένδω
σπέρμα
σπερματίζω

σπερματισμός
σπεύδω
σπήλαιον
σπιθαμή
σπιλόω
σπινθήρ
σπινόω†
σπλαγχνίζω [-ομαι]
σπλαγχνισμός
σπλάγχνον
σπλαγχνοφάγος
σποδιά
σποδοειδής
σποδόομαι
σποδός
σπονδεῖον
σπονδή
σπόνδυλος
σπορά
σπόριμος
σπόρος
σπουδάζω
σπουδαῖος
σπουδαιότης
σπουδαίως
σπουδή
σταγών
στάδιον
στάζω
στάθμιον
σταθμός
σταθμάω
σταῖς
στακτή
σταλαγμός
σταλάσσω
στάμνος
στασιάζω
στάσιμος
στάσις
σταυρόω
σταφίς
σταφυλή
στάχυς
στέαρ
στεας†
στεατόομαι
στεγάζω
στέγη
στεγνός
στέγω
στεῖρα
στειρόω
στέλεχος
στέλλω

στέμφυλον
στεναγμός
στενάζω
στενακτός
στενός
στενότης
στενοχωρέω
στενοχωρία
στένω
στέργω
στερεοκάρδιος†
στερεός
στερεόω
στερέω
στερέωμα
στερέωσις
στερίσκω
στέρνον
στεφάνη
στεφανηφορέω
στέφανος
στεφανόω
στέφος
στέφω
στηθοδεσμίς
στῆθος
στηθύνιον
στήκω
στήλη
στηλογραφία
στηλόω
στήλωμα†
στήλωσις†
στήμων
στῆρ
στήριγμα
στηρίζω
στιβαρός
στίβι
στιβίζομαι
στίγμα
στιγμή
στικτός
στιλβόω
στίλβω
στίλβωσις
στιμ(μ)ίζομαι (see στιβίζομαι)
στιππύινος
στιππύον
στιχίζω
στίχος
στοά
στοιβάζω
στοιβή

στοιχεῖον
στοιχείωσις
στοιχέω
στολή
στολίζω
στολισμός
στολιστής
στόλος
στόμα
στομίς†
στόμωμα
στόνος†
στοργή
στοχάζομαι
στοχαστής
στραγγαλάω
στραγγαλιά
στραγγαλίς
στραγγαλιώδης†
στραγγαλώδης
στραγ(γ)εύομαι†
στραγγίζω
στρατεία
στράτευμα
στρατεύω
στρατηγέω
στρατήγημα
στρατηγία
στρατηγός
στρατιά
στρατιώτης
στρατιῶτις
στρατοκήρυξ
στρατοπεδεία
στρατοπεδεύω
στρατόπεδον
στρατός
στρέβλη
στρεβλός
στρεβλόω
στρεβλωτήριον
στρέμμα
στρεπτός
στρέφω
στρῆνος
στρίφνος
στροβέω
στρογγυλόω†
στρογγύλος
στρογγύλωσις†
στρουθίζω†
στρουθίον
στρουθός
στροφεύς
στροφή

στρόφιγξ
στρόφος
στροφωτός
στρυ(ν)φαλίς†
στρύχνον†
στρῶμα
στρωμνή
στρωννύω, στρώννυμι
στυγέω
στυγνάζω
στυγνός
στῦλος
στυράκινος
σύ
συγγελάω
συγγένεια
συγγενής
συγγηρά(σκ)ω†
συγγίνομαι
συγγινώσκω
συγγνώμη
συγγνωμονέω
συγγνωστός
συγγραφεύς
συγγραφή
συγγράφω
συγγυμνασία
συγκάθημαι
συγκαθίζω
συγκαθυφαίνω
συγκαίω
συγκαλέω
συγκάλλυμα
συγκαλύπτω
συγκάμπτω
συγκαταβαίνω
συγκαταγηράσκω
συγκατακληρονομέω
συγκαταμ(ε)ίγνυμι
συγκατατίθημι
συγκαταφέρω
συγκατεσθίω
σύγκειμαι
συγκεντέω
συγκεράννυμι
συγκερατίζω
συγκεραυνόω
συγκλασμός
συγκλάω
σύγκλεισμα
συγκλεισμός
συγκλειστός
συγκλείω
συγκληρονομέω
σύγκλητος

Appendix II: Comparative Index of Words in This Lexicon and BDAG

συγκλύζω
σύγκοιτος
συγκολλάω
συγκομίζω
συγκόπτω
σύγκρασις
σύγκριμα
συγκρίνω
σύγκρισις
συγκροτέω
συγκρουσμός
συγκρύπτω, συγκρύφω
συγκτίζω
συγκύπτω
συγκυρέω
συγκύφω†
συγχαίρω
συγχέω
συγχρονίζω
σύγχυσις
συγχωρέω
συγχωρητέον
συζεύγνυμι
συζυγής
συζώννυμι
συκάμινον
συκάμινος
συκῆ
σῦκον
συκοφαντέω
συκοφάντης
συκοφαντία
συκῶν
συλάω
συλλαλέω
συλλαμβάνω
συλλέγω
σύλλημψις [σύλληψις]
συλλογή
συλλογίζομαι
συλλογισμός
συλλοιδορέω
συλλοχάω
συλλοχισμός
συλλυπέω
συλλύω
συμβαίνω
συμβάλλω
συμβαστάζω
συμβιβάζω
συμβιόω
συμβίωσις
συμβιωτής
σύμβλημα
σύμβλησις

συμβοηθός
συμβολή
συμβολοκοπέω
σύμβολον
συμβόσκομαι
συμβουλευτής
συμβουλεύω
συμβουλία
συμβούλιον
σύμβουλος
συμβραβεύω
συμμαίνομαι†
συμμαχία
σύμμαχος
συμμ(ε)ιγής
συμμείγνυμι
σύμμεικτος
συμμετέχω
συμμετρία
σύμμετρος
συμμιαίνω
σύμμιξις
συμμίσγω
συμμισοπονηρέω
συμμολύνω
συμπάθεια
συμπαθέω
συμπαθής
συμπαίζω
συμπαραγίνομαι
συμπαραλαμβάνω
συμπαραμένω
συμπάρειμι (-εἶναι)
συμπαρίστημι
σύμπας
συμπατέω
συμπείθω
συμπεραίνω
συμπεριλαμβάνω
συμπεριφέρω
συμπίνω
συμπίπτω
συμπλεκτός
συμπλέκω
συμπλήρωσις
συμπλοκή
συμποδίζω
συμποιέω
συμπολεμέω
συμπονέω
συμπορεύομαι
συμπορπάω
συμποσία
συμπόσιον
συμπότης

συμπραγματεύομαι
συμπροπέμπω
συμπροπορεύομαι†
συμπρόσειμι (-εἶναι)
συμπροσπλέκω
σύμπτωμα
συμφερόντως
συμφέρω
συμφεύγω
σύμφημι
συμφλέγω
συμφλογίζω
συμφορά
συμφοράζω
σύμφορος
συμφράσσω
συμφρονέω
συμφρύγω
συμφύρομαι
σύμφυτος
συμφύω
συμφωνέω
συμφωνία
σύμφωνος
συμψάω
σύν
συναγελάζομαι
σύναγμα
συνάγω
συναγωγή
συνάδω
συναθροίζω
συναινέω
συνακολουθέω
συναλγέω
συνάλλαγμα
συναλοάω
συναναβαίνω
συνανάκειμαι
συναναμείγνυμι
συνανάμ(ε)ιξις
συναναμίσγω (see
  συναναμείγνυμι)
συναναπαύομαι
συναναστρέφω
συναναστροφή
συναναφέρω
συναναφύρω
συναντάω
συναντή
συνάντημα
συνάντησις
συναντιλαμβάνομαι
συναπάγω
συναποθνῄσκω

συναποκλείω†
συναποκρύπτω
συναπόλλυμι
συναποστέλλω
συνάπτω
συναριθμέω
συναρπάζω
συναρχία
συνασπίζω
συναυλίζομαι
συναύξω
συναφίστημι
σύναψις
συνδάκνω
συνδειπνέω
σύνδειπνος
συνδέομαι†
σύνδεσμος
συνδέω
συνδιώκω
σύνδουλος
συνδρομή
συνδυάζω
συνεγγίζω
σύνεγγυς
συνεγείρω
συνεδρεύω
συνεδρία
συνεδριάζω
συνέδριον
σύνεδρος
συνεθίζω
συνείδησις
συνεῖδον
συνείκω
συνειλέω†
σύνειμι (-εἶναι)
συνεῖπον
συνεισέρχομαι
συνεκκεντέω
συνεκπολεμέω
συνεκπορεύομαι
συνεκτρέφω
συνεκτρίβω
συνέκτροφος
συνελαύνω
συνέλευσις
συνέλκω
συνεξέρχομαι
συνεξορμάω
συνεπακολουθέω
συνεπισκέπτομαι
συνεπίσταμαι
συνεπισχύω
συνεπιτίθημι

συνέπομαι	σύνταγμα	συστράτευμα†	σῶμα
συνεργέω	σύνταξις	σύστρεμμα	σωματικός
συνεργός	συνταράσσω	συστρέφω	**σωματοποιέω**
συνερίζω	συντάσσω	συστροφή	**σωματοφύλαξ**
συνέρχομαι	συντέλεια	**συστροφία**†	**σῶος**
συνεσθίω	συντελέω	**συσφίγγω**	σωρεύω
σύνεσις	συντέμνω	**συχνός**	**σωρηδόν**
συνέταιρος, συνεταιρίς	**συντήκω**†	σφαγή	**σωρηκ/σωρηχ**
συνετίζω	συντηρέω	**σφαγιάζω**	**σωρός**
συνετός	συντίθημι	σφάγιον	σωτήρ
συνετῶς	**συντίμησις**	σφάζω	σωτηρία
συνευδοκέω	σύντομος	**σφαιρωτήρ**	σωτήριος
συνευφραίνομαι	συντόμως	**σφακελίζω**	**σωφερ**
συνέχω	**συντρέφω**	**σφαλερός**	σωφρόνως
συνζυγής (see συζυγής)	συντρέχω	σφάλλω	σωφροσύνη
	συντριβή	**σφάλμα**	σώφρων
συνήθεια	συντρίβω	**σφενδονάω**	
συνήθης	σύντριμμα	**σφενδόνη**	**T**
συνηλικία†	**συντριμμός**	**σφενδονήτης**	
συνήλιξ	**σύντριψις**	**σφηκία**, σφηκιά	**τάγμα**
συνηχέω	**συντροφία**	σφήν	**ταινία**
συνθέλω	σύντροφος	**σφηνόω**	**τακτικός**
σύνθεμα†	**συντροχάζω**	σφήξ	τακτός
σύνθεσις	συντυγχάνω	**σφιγγία**	ταλαιπωρέω
σύνθετος	**συνυφαίνω**	**σφίγγω**	ταλαιπωρία
συνθήκη	**συνυφή**	σφόδρα	ταλαίπωρος
σύνθημα	**συνωμότης**	σφοδρός	**τάλαντον**
συνθλάω	**συνωρίς**	σφοδρῶς	**τάλας**
συνθλίβω	**σύριγμα**	σφόνδυλος	**ταμίας**
συνίημι	**συριγμός** (see συρισμός)	σφραγίζω	ταμιεῖον
συνίστημι		σφραγίς	**ταμιεύω**
συνίστωρ	**σύριγξ**	σφῦρα	τανύω
συννεφέω	**συρίζω**	σφυροκοπέω	τάξις
συννεφής	**συρισμός**	σφυροκόπος	ταπεινός
συννοέω	Συριστί	**σχάζω**	**ταπεινότης**
σύννους	συρράπτω	**σχεδία**	ταπεινοφρονέω
σύννυμφος	**συρράσσω**†	**σχεδιάζω**	ταπεινόφρων
συνοδεύω	**συρρέμβομαι**†	σχεδόν	ταπεινόω
συνοδία	**σύρρηγμα**†	**σχετλιάζω**	ταπείνωσις
σύνοδος¹	σύρω	**σχέτλιος**	ταράσσω
σύνοδος²	σῦς	σχῆμα	ταραχή
συνοδυνάομαι	**συσκευάζω**†	σχηματίζω	τάραχος
σύνοιδα	**συσκήνιος**	**σχίδαξ**	**ταραχώδης**
συνοικέω	**σύσκηνος**	**σχίζα**	**ταριχεύω**
συνοίκησις	**συσκιάζω**	**σχῖνος**	**ταρσός**
συνοικίζω	**σύσκιος**	σχισμή	**τάρταρος**
συνοικοδομέω	**συσκοτάζω**	**σχιστός**	τάσσω
συνολκή	συσπάω	σχοινίον	**ταυρηδόν**
σύνολος	**συσσεισμός**	σχοίνισμα	ταῦρος
συνομολογέω	**συσσείω**	**σχοινισμός**	ταφή
συνοράω	σύσσημον	**σχοῖνος**	τάφος
συνούλωσις	**συσσωρεύω**	σχολάζω	**τάφρος**
συνουσιασμός	σύστασις	**σχολαστής**	τάχα
συνοχή	συστέλλω	σχολή	ταχέως
συνταγή	**σύστημα**, σύστεμα	σώζω	ταχινός

τάχος
ταχύνω
ταχύς
ταώς†
τε
τέγος
τείνω
τειχήρης
τειχίζω
τειχιστής
τεῖχος
τεκμήριον
τέκνον
τεκνοποιέω
τεκνοφόνος
τεκταίνω
τεκτονικός
τέκτων
τελαμών
τέλειος
τελειότης
τελειόω
τελείως
τελείωσις
τέλεον
τελεσιουργέω
τελεσφορέω
τελεσφόρος
τελετή
τελευταῖος
τελευτάω
τελευτή
τελέω
τελίσκομαι
τέλος
τελωνέω
τέμενος
τέμνω
τένων
τέρας
τερατεύομαι
τερατοποιός
τερατοσκόπος
τερατώδης†
τερέμινθος
τέρετρον
τέρμα
τερπνός
τερπνότης
τέρπω
τέρψις
τεσσαράκοντα
τεσσαρακοστός
τέσσαρες
τεσσαρεσκαιδέκατος

τεταγμένως
τέταρτος
τετράγωνος
τετράδραχμον
τεταίνω
τετρακισμύριοι
τετρακισχίλιοι
τετρακόσιοι
τετρακοσιοστός
τετραμερής
τετράμηνος
τετράπεδος
τετραπλάσιος†
τετραπλῶς
τετράποδος
τετράπους
τετράς
τετράστιχος
τέφρα
τεχνάζω
τεχνάομαι
τέχνη
τεχνίτης
τεχνῖτις
τηγανίζω
τήγανον
τηκτός
τήκω
τηλαύγημα
τηλαυγής
τηλαύγησις
τηλικοῦτος
τηρέω
τήρησις
τιάρα
τίθημι
τιθηνέω
τιθηνία
τιθηνός
τίκτω
τίλλω
τιμάω
τιμή
τίμημα
τίμιος
τιμογραφέω
τιμωρέω
τιμωρητής
τιμωρία
τίναγμα
τινάσσω†
τίνω
τίς
τις
τιτάν

τιτρώσκω
τμητός
τοι
τοιγαροῦν
τοίνυν
τοῖος
τοιόσδε
τοιοῦτος
τοῖχος
τοκάς
τοκετός
τόκος
τόλμα
τολμάω
τολμηρός
τολύπη
τομή
τομίς
τόμος
τόνος
τόξευμα
τοξεύω
τοξικός
τόξον
τοξότης
τοπάδιον† (see τοπάζιον)
τοπάζιον
τοπάρχης
τοπαρχία
τόπος
τορευτός
τόσος
τοσοῦτος
τότε
τραγέλαφος
τράγος
τρανέομαι†
τρανός
τράπεζα
τραῦμα
τραυματίας
τραυματίζω
τραχηλιάω
τράχηλος
τραχύς
τραχύτης
τρεῖς
τρέμω
τρέπω
τρέφω
τρέχω
τρῆσις
τριακάς
τριάκοντα

τριακονταετής
τριακόσιοι
τριακοστός
τρίβολος
τρίβος
τρίβω
τριετής
τριετίζω
τριημερία
τριηραρχία†
τριήρης
τρικυμία
τριμερίζω
τρίμηνος
τριόδους
τριπλάσιος
τριπλοῦς
τρίς
τρισάθλιος
τρισαλιτήριος
τρισκαίδεκα
τρισκαιδέκατος
τρισμύριοι
τρισσεύω
τρισσός
τρισσόω
τρισσῶς
τριστάτης
τρισχίλιοι
τριταῖος
τρίτος
τρίχαπτος
τρίχινος
τρίχωμα
τριώροφος
τρομέω
τρόμος
τρόπαιον
τροπή
τρόπις
τρόπος
τροπόω
τροφεία
τροφεύω
τροφή
τροφός
τροφοφορέω
τροχαντήρ
τροχηλάτης†
τροχιά
τροχιαῖος
τροχίζω
τροχίσκος
τροχός
τρυβλίον

τρυγάω
τρυγητής
τρύγητος/-τός
τρυγίας
τρυγών
τρυμαλιά
τρυπάω
τρυφαλίς
τρυφάω
τρυφερεύομαι
τρυφερός
τρυφερότης
τρυφή
τρύφημα
τρύχω
τρώγλη
τρώγω
τυγχάνω
τύκος†
τυλόω
τυμπανίζω
τυμπανίστρια
τύμπανον
τύπος
τυπόω
τύπτω
τυραννέω
τυραννία†
τυραννικός
τυραννίς
τύραννος
τυρός
τυρόω
τυφλός
τυφλόω
τῦφος
τύχη

Υ

ὕαινα
ὑακίνθινος
ὑάκινθος
ὕαλος
ὑβρίζω
ὕβρις
ὑβριστής
ὑβρίστια†
ὑβριστικός
ὑβρίστρια
ὑγιάζω
ὑγιαίνω
ὑγίεια
ὑγιής
ὑγραίνω

ὑγρασία
ὑγρός
ὑδραγωγός
ὑδρεύω
ὑδρία
ὑδρίσκη
ὑδροποτέω
ὑδροφόρος
ὕδωρ
ὕειος
ὑετίζω
ὑετός
υἱός
ὑλακτέω
ὕλη
ὕλις†
ὑλοτόμος
ὑλώδης
ὑμεῖς
ὑμέναιος
ὑμέτερος
ὑμνέω
ὕμνησις
ὑμνητός
ὑμνογράφος
ὕμνος
ὑμνωδέω
ὑπαγορεύω
ὑπάγω
ὕπαιθρος
ὑπακοή
ὑπακούω
ὕπανδρος
ὑπαντάω
ὑπάντησις
ὕπαρ
ὕπαρος
ὕπαρξις
ὕπαρχος†
ὑπάρχω
ὑπασπιστής
ὕπατος
ὑπείκω
ὑπεκρέω
ὑπεναντίος
ὑπεξαιρέω
ὑπέρ
ὑπεράγαν
ὑπεραγόντως
ὑπεράγω
ὑπεραινετός
ὑπεραίρω
ὑπεράλλομαι
ὑπεράνω
ὑπεράνωθεν

ὑπέραρσις
ὑπερασπίζω
ὑπερασπισμός
ὑπερασπιστεία†
ὑπερασπιστής
ὑπερασπίστρια
ὑπερβαίνω
ὑπερβαλλόντως
ὑπερβάλλω
ὑπερβολή
ὑπερδυναμόω
ὑπερεῖδον
ὑπερείδω
ὑπερεκχέω
ὑπερένδοξος
ὑπερέχω
ὑπερηφανεύω
ὑπερηφανέω
ὑπερηφανία
ὑπερήφανος
ὑπέρθυρον
ὑπερισχύω
ὑπέρκειμαι
ὑπερκεράω
ὑπερκρατέω
ὑπερκύκλω†
ὑπερμαχέω
ὑπέρμαχος
ὑπερμεγέθης
ὑπερμήκης
ὑπέρογκος
ὑπεροῖδα†
ὕπερον
ὑπερόρασις
ὑπεροράω
ὑπεροχή
ὑπέρυψις
ὑπερπλεονάζω
ὑπερτήκω
ὑπερτίθημι
ὑπερτιμάω
ὑπερυμνητός
ὑπερυψόω
ὑπερφερής
ὑπερφέρω
ὑπέρφοβος
ὑπερφρονέω
ὑπερφωνέω
ὑπερχαρής
ὑπερχέω
ὑπέρχομαι
ὑπερῷον
ὑπερῷος
ὑπεύθυνος
ὑπευθύνω†

ὑπευλαβέομαι
ὑπέχω
ὑπήκοος
ὑπηρεσία
ὑπηρετέω
ὑπηρέτης
ὑπισχνέομαι
ὕπνος
ὑπνόω
ὑπνώδης
ὑπό
ὑποβάλλω
ὑποβλέπω
ὑπόγειος
ὑπογραμμός
ὑπογράφω
ὑπόγυος
ὑπόδειγμα
ὑποδείκνυμι/-νύω
ὑποδέχομαι
ὑποδέω
ὑπόδημα
ὑποδύτης
ὑποδύω [-ομαι]
ὑποζύγιον
ὑποζώννυμι
ὑπόθεμα
ὑπόθεσις
ὑποθραύομαι†
ὑποκαίω
ὑποκαλύπτω
ὑποκάτω
ὑποκάτωθεν
ὑπόκειμαι
ὑποκρίνομαι
ὑπόκρισις
ὑποκριτής
ὑπολαμβάνω
ὑπόλειμμα
ὑπολείπω
ὑπόλημψις
ὑπολήνιον
ὑπόλοιπος
ὑπολυπέομαι†
ὑπόλυσις
ὑπολύω
ὑπομαστίδιον
ὑπομένω
ὑπομιμνῄσκω
ὑπόμνημα
ὑπομνηματίζομαι
ὑπομνηματισμός
ὑπομνηματογράφος
ὑπόμνησις
ὑπομονή

ὑπονοέω
ὑπονόημα
ὑπονοθεύω
ὑπόνοια
ὑπονομεύω†
ὑπονύσσω
ὑποπίπτω
ὑποπόδιον
ὑποπτεύω
ὕποπτος
ὑποπυρρίζω
ὑπορράπτω
ὑπορρίπτω
ὑποσημαίνω
ὑποσκελίζω
ὑποσκέλισμα
ὑποσκελισμός†
ὑπόστασις
ὑποστέλλω
ὑπόστημα
ὑποστήριγμα
ὑποστηρίζω
ὑποστρέφω
ὑποστρώννυμι
ὑποσχάζω
ὑπόσχεσις
ὑποτάσσω
ὑποτίθημι
ὑποτίτθιος
ὑποτομεύς†
ὑπουργός
ὑποφαίνω
ὑπόφαυσις
ὑποφέρω
ὑπόφρικος
ὑποφυλλίς†
ὑποχείριος
ὑποχόνδριον
ὑπόχρεως
ὑποχυτήρ
ὑποχωρέω
ὕποψ, -ωψ†
ὑποψία
ὑπτιάζω
ὕπτιος
ὑπώπιον
ὗς, ὑός
ὑσσώπιος†
ὕσσωπος
ὑστερέω
ὑστέρημα
ὑστεροβουλία
ὕστερος
ὑφαίνω
ὑφαιρέω

ὑφάντης
ὑφαντός
ὑφάπτω
ὕφασμα
ὑφίστημι
ὑφοράω
ὑψαυχενέω
ὑψηλοκάρδιος
ὑψηλός
ὕψιστος
ὕψος
ὑψόω
ὕψωμα
ὕψωσις
ὕω

Φ

φαζ
φαιδρός
φαίνω
φαιός
φακός
φάλαγξ
φαλακρός
φαλακρόω†
φαλάκρωμα
φαλτ(ε)ια†
φανερός
φανερόω
φανερῶς
φαντάζω
φαντασία
φαντασιοκοπέω
φάντασμα
φάραγξ
φαρασιν
φαρες
φαρέτρα
φαρμακεία
φαρμακεύω
φάρμακον
φαρμακός
φαρουριμ
φάρυγξ
φασεκ
φασεχ
φάσις
φάσκω
φάσμα
φάτνη
φατνόω
φάτνωμα
φάτνωσις†
φαυλίζω

φαύλισμα
φαυλισμός
φαυλίστριος
φαῦλος
φαυλότης
φαῦσις
φέγγος
φείδομαι
φειδώ
φειδωλός
φελεθθι
φελμουνι
φερνή
φερνίζω
φέρω
φεύγω
φευκτός
φήμη
φημί
φημίζω
φθάνω
φθάρμα
φθαρτός
φθέγγομαι
φθέγμα
φθειρίζω
φθείρω
φθίνω
φθόγγος
φθονερός
φθονέω
φθόνος
φθορά
φθορεύς
φιάλη
φιλάγαθος
φιλαδελφία
φιλάδελφος
φιλαμαρτήμων
φιλανθρωπέω
φιλανθρωπία
φιλάνθρωπος
φιλανθρώπως
φιλαργυρέω
φιλαργυρία
φιλάργυρος
φιλαρχία
φιλελεήμων
φιλεχθρέω
φιλέω
φιληκοΐα
φίλημα
φιλία
φιλιάζω
φιλογέωργος

φιλογύναιος
φιλοδοξία
φιλόκοσμος
φιλομαθέω
φιλομαθής
φιλομήτωρ
φιλονεικέω
φιλονεικία
φιλόνεικος
φιλοπολίτης
φιλοπονέω
φιλοπονία
φίλος
φιλοσοφέω
φιλοσοφία
φιλόσοφος
φιλοστοργία
φιλόστοργος
φιλοστόργως
φιλοτεκνία
φιλότεκνος
φιλοτιμία
φιλότιμος
φιλοφρονέω
φιλοφρόνως
φιλόψυχος
φίλτρον
φιμός
φιμόω
φλεγμαίνω
φλεγμονή
φλέγω
φλέξ†
φλέψ
φλεβός
φλιά
φλογίζω
φλόγινος
φλοιός
φλόξ
φλύαρος
φλυκτίς
φοβερίζω
φοβερισμός
φοβεροειδής
φοβερός
φοβέω
φόβητρον
φόβος
φοιβάω
φοινικοῦς
φοῖνιξ
φονευτής
φονεύω
φονή

φονοκτονέω
φονοκτονία
φόνος
φονώδης
φοράζω
φορβεά
φορεῖον
φορεύς
φορέω
φορθομμιν
φορολογέω
φορολόγητος
φορολογία
φορολόγος
φόρος
φορτίζω
φορτίον
φουρ†
φραγμός
φράζω
φραζων
φράσσω
φρέαρ
φρενόω
φρήν
φρικασμός
φρίκη
φρικτός
φρικώδης
φρίττω [φρίσσω]
φρονέω
φρόνημα
φρόνησις
φρόνιμος
φροντίζω
φροντίς
φροντιστέον
φρουρά
φρουρέω
φρούριον
φρουρόω
φρύαγμα
φρυάττω [φρυάσσω]
φρύγανον
φρύγιον
φρύγω
φυγαδεῖα
φυγαδεῖον
φυγαδευτήριον
φυγαδεύω
φυγάδιον
φυγάς
φυγή
φυή
φῦκος

φύλαγμα
φυλακή
φυλακίζω
φυλάκισσα
φύλαξ
φυλάρχης
φύλαρχος
φυλάττω [φυλάσσω]
φυλή
φύλλον
φῦλον
φύραμα
φύρασις
φυράω
φύρδην
φυρμός
φύρω
φυσάω
φυσητήρ
φυσιόω
φύσις
φυτεία
φύτευμα
φυτεύω
φυτός
φυτόν
φύω
φωνέω
φωνή
φωράω
φῶς
φωστήρ
φωταγωγέω
φωτεινός
φωτίζω
φωτισμός

X

χαβραθα
χαιρετίζω
χαιροκαίνως†
χαίρω
χάλαζα
χαλαστόν
χαλάω
χαλβάνη
Χαλδαϊστί
χαλεπαίνω
χαλεπός
χαλινός
χάλιξ
χαλκεῖος
χαλκεύς
χαλκεύω

χαλκίον
χαλκοπλάστης
χαλκός
χαλκοῦς
χαμαί
χαμαιλέων
χαμαιπετής
χαμανιμ
χάος
χαρά
χαρα
χαραδριός
χαρακοβολία
χαρακόω
χαρακτήρ
χαράκωσις
χάραξ
χαράσσω
χαρίεις
χαρίζομαι
χάρις
χαριστήριον
χαριτόω
χαρμονή
χαρμοσύνη
χαροποιός
χαροπός
χαρσιθ
χαρτηρία
χάρτης
χαρτίον
χάσκω
χάσμα
χαῦνος
χαυών
χεῖλος
χειμάζω
χείμαρρος/ους
χειμερινός
χειμέριος
χειμών
χείρ
χειραγωγέω
χειρίζω
χείριστος [χείρων]
χειρίστως
χειρόγραφον
χειρονομία
χειροπέδη
χειροποίητος
χειροτονία
χειρόω
χείρων
χελεθθι (see χερεθθι)
χελιδών

χελύνιον
χελώνη
χελωνίς
χερεθ
χερεθθι
χεροκένως†
χερουβ
χερσαῖος
χέρσος
χερσόω
χεττι
χεττιιν
χέω
χηλή
χήρα
χηρεία
χήρευσις
χηρεύω
χθιζός
χθών
χίδρον
χιλιαρχία
χιλίαρχος
χιλιάς
χίλιοι
χιλιοπλασίως
χίμαιρα
χίμαρος
χιονόομαι
χίρ† (see χείρ)
χιτών
χιών
χλαῖνα
χλαμύς
χλευάζω
χλεύασμα
χλευασμός
χλιδών
χλόη
χλοηφόρος
χλωρίζω
χλωροβοτάνη†
χλωρός
χλωρότης
χνοῦς
χοθωνωθ
χοῖνιξ
χοιρογρύλλιος
χοιρόγρυλλος†
χολάω
χολέρα
χολή
χόλος
χονδρίτης
χορδή

χορεία	χρυσοειδής	ψαλμωδός†	ψυχρός
χορεύω	χρυσόλιθος	ψαλτήριον	ψύχω
χορηγέω	χρυσός	ψάλτης	ψωμίζω
χορηγία	χρυσουργός	ψαλτός	ψωμός
χορηγός	χρυσοτόρευτος†	ψαλτωδέω	ψώρα
χορίδιον†	χρυσοῦς	ψαλτωδός	ψωραγριάω
χόριον	χρυσοφορέω	ψάμμος	
χορός	χρυσοχάλινος	ψαμμωτός	**Ω**
χορτάζω	χρυσοχόος	ψαρός	
χορτασία	χρυσόω	ψαύω	ὦ
χόρτασμα	**χρύσωμα**	ψέγω†	ᾧα
χορτομανέω	χρῶμα	ψεκάς	ὧδε
χόρτος	χρώς	ψέλιον	ᾠδή
χορτώδης	χυδαῖος	ψελλίζω	ὠδίν
χοῦς, χοός	χυλός	ψευδής	ὠδίνω
χοῦς, χοός	χύμα	ψευδοθύριον	ᾠδός
χόω	χύσις†	ψευδοθυρίς	ὠθέω
χράομαι	χυτός	ψευδολογέω	ὠμία
χρεία	χύτρα	ψεύδομαι	ὤμιον†
χρεμετίζω	χυτρόκαυλος	ψευδομαρτυρέω	ὠμόλινον
χρεμετισμός	χυτρόπους (see κυθρο-)	ψευδομάρτυς	ὦμος
χρεοκοπέω		ψευδοπροφήτης	ὠμός
χρέος	χωθαρ(εθ)	ψεῦδος	ὠμότης
χρεοφειλέτης	χωλαίνω	ψεύστης	ὠμοτοκέω
χρή	χωλός	ψηλαφάω	ὠμόφρων
χρῄζω	χῶμα	ψηλάφησις	ᾠόν
χρῆμα	χωμαριμ	ψηλαφητός	ὥρα
χρηματίζω	χωματίζω	ψήφισμα	ὡραΐζω
χρηματισμός	χωνεία†	ψηφολογέω	ὡραιόομαι
χρηματιστήριον	χώνευμα	ψῆφος	ὡραῖος
χρησιμεύω	χώνευσις	ψιθυρίζω	ὡραιότης
χρησιμολογέω	χωνευτήριον	ψιθυρισμός	ὡραϊσμός
χρήσιμος	χωνευτής	ψίθυρος	ὥριμος
χρῆσις	χωνευτός	ψιλή	ὥρυμα
χρηστεύομαι	**χωνεύω**	ψιλόω	ὠρύομαι
χρηστοήθεια	χώρα	ψόα	ὡς
χρηστός	χωρέω	ψογίζω	ὥς
χρηστότης	**χώρημα†**	ψόγος	ὡσανεί
χρία [χρεία]	χωρίζω	ψοφέω	ὡσαύτως
χρῖσις	χωρίον	ψόφος	ὡσεί
χρῖσμα	χωρίς	ψύα	ὥσπερ
χριστός [Χριστός]	χωρισμός	ψυγμός	ὥστε
χρίω	**χωροβατέω**	ψυκτήρ	ὠτίον
χρόα		ψύλλος	ὠτότμητος
χρονίζω	**Ψ**	ψυχαγωγία	ὠφέλεια
χρονίσκος		ψυχή	ὠφελέω
χρόνος	ψαλίς	ψυχικός	ὠφέλημα
χρυσαυγέω	ψάλλω	ψῦχος	ὤχρα
χρυσίον	ψαλμός	ψυχουλκέομαι	

Appendix III: Septuagint—English Bible Parallels

Table A: Comparison of Septuagint Book Titles with English Bible Titles

Γενεσις	Genesis	Ιωβ	Job
Εξοδος	Exodus	Σοφια Σαλωμωνος	Wisdom of Solomon
Λευιτικον	Leviticus	Σοφια Σιραχ	Sirach (Ecclesiasticus)
Αριθμοι	Numbers	Ψαλμοι Σολομωντος	Psalms of Solomon
Δευτερονομιον	Deuteronomy	Ωσηε	Hosea
Ιησους	Joshua	Αμως	Amos
Κριται	Judges	Μιχαιας	Micah
Ρουθ	Ruth	Ιωηλ	Joel
Βασιλειων Α'-Β'	1–2 Kingdoms (1–2 Samuel)	Αβδιου	Obadiah
		Ιωνας	Johan
Βασιλειων Γ'- Δ'	3–4 Kingdoms (1–2 Kings)	Ναουμ	Nahum
		Αμβακουμ	Habakkuk
Παραλειπομενων Α'- Β'	1–2 Chronicles	Σοφονιας	Zephaniah
Εσδρας Α'	1 Esdras	Αγγαιος	Haggai
Εσδρας Β'	2 Esdras (Ezra & Nehemiah)	Ζαχαριας	Zechariah
		Μαλαχιας	Malachi
Εδθηρ	Esther (with additions)	Ησαιας	Isaiah
Ιουδιθ	Judith	Ιερεμιας	Jeremiah
Τοβιτ	Tobit	Βαρουχ	Baruch
Μακκαβαιων Α'-Δ'	1–4 Maccabees	Θρηνοι	Lamentations
Ψαλμοι	Psalms	Επιστολη Ιερεμιου	Epistle of Jeremiah
Οδαι	Odes	Ιεζεκιηλ	Ezekiel
Παροιμιαι	Proverbs	Σουσαννα	Susanna
Εκκλησιαστης	Ecclesiastes	Δανιηλ	Daniel (with additions)
Ασμα	Song of Solomon	Βηλ και Δρακων	Bel and the Dragon

Table B: Comparison of English Bible References with Septuagint References

Those familiar with the English Bible (EB) who wish to find a parallel verse in the Septuagint must first overcome the difficulty that not only are the names of the books sometimes different, but often the chapters and verses within the books don't match up precisely. Although several English names of the biblical books derive from the Greek titles (e.g., Genesis, Exodus, Deuteronomy, Psalms, and Ecclesiastes), the EB is, by and large, based on the Hebrew Bible (HB), and its books, chapters, and verses parallel the HB more closely than they do the LXX.

The following table provides a complete set of parallel references for the EB and the LXX, wherever these two differ.

When the EB reference matches the corresponding LXX reference, there is no reference on the chart.

In some cases, the LXX has no corresponding verse in the EB or vice versa. This lack of a corresponding verse is indicated by a series of dashes (--------). Sometimes (frequently) the wording in the LXX is not reflected exactly in the wording in the EB since the EB is based on the HB, not on the LXX. The importance of this fact is that one should not expect, even if the verses align, that the translation in an EB is an accurate translation of the LXX for that same verse or verses. These differences are, of course, the major reason for the importance of this book.

Since the books of the Apocrypha are not represented in the HB, and since the chapter and verse numbers of the apocryphal books in the EB match those of the LXX, these books are not represented in the table. The sole exception relates to the Book of Daniel and will be discussed below.

In some cases, portions of verses are either not represented at all in one version or are represented differently in the EB than they are in the LXX. In those cases, the verse in question (whether LXX or EB) is followed with a letter of the alphabet in parentheses that indicates whether the first, second, third, etc., fraction of the verse is represented differently in the other version. Thus Gn 31:44(a) in the LXX, that is, only the first part of the LXX verse, is represented in the entire comparable verse in the EB, whereas the second part of the LXX verse, Gn 31:44(b), is found in the EB in the second part of Gen 31:50, that is, 31:50(b).

Often LXX verses or portions of verses not found in the EB have been numbered in such a way as to supplement the verse numbering of the HB rather than break the flow of its chapter and verse numbers. Thus material represented in the LXX that is not found in the same location in the EB will often be numbered with the same number as the previous matching verse, but with alphabetical characters (not in parentheses) following the number. Thus verses numbered 24a, 24b, 24c, etc., all of which are distinct from EB v. 24, represent material found in the LXX *between* EB verses 24 and 25. So, for example, the table indicates that the LXX version of Ex 28:29a (a distinct unit of text from Ex 28:29) is found in the HB in 28:23–28. Since the LXX includes this material in 29a, vv. 23–28 are missing from the LXX verse numbers, leaving the chapter with the following peculiar succession of verses: 22, 29, 29a, 30, etc.

Rarely, differences in the arrangement of verses between LXX and EB are dealt with in the LXX simply by retaining the numbering scheme of the HB but arranging the verses in the order in which they are found in the LXX text. This occurs, for example, in ΠΑΡΟΙΜΙΑΙ (Proverbs) 24–31, where the material from EB Prov 30:1–14 is inserted between LXX Prov 24:1–22e and 24:23–34, with the HB/EB numbering retained in the LXX despite the break in the numberic succession of verses.

Although the EB most often follows the chapter and verse numbers of the HB, there are several places where the EB numbering has diverged from both the LXX and the HB. When this occurs, the LXX reference is italicized in the table. Thus the material in Ex 7:26–29 (LXX and HB) corresponds with Ex 8:1–4 in the EB.

As noted above, the books of the Aprocrypha are not found in this table except for the Book of Daniel. The sole exception relates to one of the three additions to Daniel, the Prayer of Azaria and the Song of the Three Hebrew Children (LXX Daniel 3:26–90), which is included in the midst of the chapter in a way that diverges from the Heb numbering scheme.

The Psalms present a unique challenge in that for many of them, both in the LXX and HB, the opening notation (or superscription) is numbered as the first verse of the Psalm. Each subsequent verse, then, is numbered one digit higher than the corresponding verse in the EB, where the superscriptions are not numbered. This situation should always be kept in mind when comparing LXX/HB references to the Psalms with EB references. The pattern is so frequent throughout the Psalms that individual instances are not spelled out in this table. To further complicate matters, Pss 10–112 are numbered one digit lower in the LXX than in the HB or EB, owing to the fact that two of the HB Psalms (Pss 9–10) are represented by a single LXX Psalm (Ps 9). There are several other differences in the numbering of the Psalms represented in the table. Should all of the changes in the number of Psalms be desired in full detail, the SBL Handbook of Style (Peabody, Mass.: Hendrickson. 1999), 174–75 may be consulted.

Septuagint (italic = Heb. Bible)	English Bible	Septuagint (italic = Heb. Bible)	English Bible
Γενεσις	Genesis	39:14	39:35
31:44(a)	31:44	39:15	39:38
31:44(b)	31:50(b)	39:16	39:37
31:46(a)	31:46	39:17	39:36
31:46(b)	31:48(a)	39:18	39:41
31:48	31:51, 52(a), 48(b)	39:19	39:40(a)
31:50	31:50(a)	39:20	39:34
31:52	31:52(b)	--------	39:39
32:1	31:55	39:21	39:40(b)
32:2–33	32:2–32	39:22	39:42
35:16(a)	35:21	39:23	39:43
35:16(b)	35:16	40:6b	40:8
		--------	40:7, 8
Εξοδος	Exodus	--------	40:11
7:26–29	8:1–4	--------	40:28
8:1–28	8:5–32		
20:13–15	20:14, 15, 13	Λευιτικον	Leviticus
21:16,17	21:17, 16	*5:20–26*	6:1–7
21:37	22:1	*6:1–23*	6:8–30
22:1–30	22:2–31		
--------	25:6	Αριθμοι	Numbers
28:29a	28:23–28	1:24–35	1:26–37
--------	32:9	1:36–37	1:24–25
--------	35:8	6:23(b)	6:27
35:12a	35:15, 17	10:34–35	10:35–36
--------	35:18	10:36	10:34
--------	36:10–33	*17:1–15*	16:36–50
36:8b–38	39:1–31	*17:16–28*	17:1–13
37:1–2	36:8(b)–9	26:15–23	26:19–27
37:3–6	36:35–38	26:24–27	26:15–18
37:7–21	38:9–23	26:28–31	26:44–47
38:1–17	37:1–24	26:32–47	26:28–43
38:18	36:34	*30:1*	29:40
38:22–24	38:1–7	*30:2–17*	30:1–16
38:25	37:29		
38:26	38:8	Δευτερονομιον	Deuteronomy
38:27	40:30–32	*13:1*	12:32
39:1–7	38:24–29	*13:2–19*	14:1–18
39:8	38:31	*23:1*	22:30
39:9	38:30	*23:2–26*	23:1–25
39:11	39:32	*28:69*	29:1
39:13	39:33	*29:1–28*	29:2–29

Ιησους	Joshua	────────	11:3(b)
────────	8:26	11:5	11:7
9:2a–f	8:30–35	11:6	11:5
19: 47	19:48	11:7	11:8
19:48	19:47	11:8	11:6
24:29	24:31	11:43(b)	12:2
24:30–31	24:29–30	12:24a–f	────────
		12:24g–n	14:1–18
Βασιλειων Α'	1 Samuel	12:24o–z	12:1–24
21:1	20:42(b)	────────	14:19, 20
21:2–16	21:1–15	16:28d–g	22:47–50
24:1	23:29	*18:34(a)*	18:33(b)
24:2–23	24:1–22	*21:20*	20:21
		22:21(b)	22:22(a)
Βασιλειων Β'	2 Samuel	*22:44*	22:43(c)
19:1	18:33	*22:45–54*	22:44–53
19:2–44	19:1–43		
		Βασιλειων Δ'	2 Kings
Βασιλειων Γ'	1 Kings	*12:1*	11:21
2:35c	3:1	*12:2–22*	12:1–21
2:35f–g	9:24–25		
2:35h	9:23	Παραλειπομενων Α'	1 Chronicles
2:46a	4:20	────────	1:11–23
2:46f–g	4:24–25	*5:27–41*	6:1–15
2:46k	4:21	*6:1–66*	6:16–81
4:17, 18, 19	4:18, 19, 17	*12:4*	12:4(a)
5:1	4:27–28	*12:5*	12:4(b)
5:2–3	4:22–23	*12:6–41*	12:5–40
5:9–14a	4:29–34	────────	16:24
5:14b	9:16, 17		
5:15–30	5:1–16	Παραλειπομενων Β'	2 Chronicles
5:32	5:18(b)	*1:18*	2:1
6:1a, b	5:17–18(a)	*2:1–17*	2:2–18
────────	6:11–13	*13:23*	14:1
6:1c–d; 2:35c	6:37–38	*14:1–14*	14:2–15
6:3b	6:14	────────	27:8
7:1–6	7:13–18		
7:7	7:21	Εσδρας Β'	Ezra/Nehemiah
7:8–9	7:19–20	2 Esdras 1–10	Ezra 1–10
────────	7:22	2 Esdras 11–23	Nehemiah 1–13
7:10–11	7:23–24	────────	3:7, 8(a)
7:12	7:26	*13:33–37*	4:1–5(a)
7:13	7:25	*14:1–17*	4:7–23(a)
────────	7:31	*17:69–73*	7:68–72 (Heb)
7:32	7:47	*20:1*	9:38
7:33	7:46	*20:2–40*	10:1–39
7:34–37	7:48–51		11:16, 20–21, 23(b),
7:38	7:1(a)		28–29, 32–35
7:39–49	7:2–12	────────	12:4–7(a)
7:50	7:1(b)	────────	
8:53a	8:12–13		
────────	8:41(b), 42(a)	Εσθηρ	Esther
10:22a	9:15	1:1a–r	?
10:22b, c	9:20–22	1:1s	1:1
11:1	11:3(a)	────────	4:6
		────────	9:5, 30

Appendix III: Septuagint—English Bible Parallels

Ιωβ	Job
--------	23:14
40:25–32	41:1–8
41:1–26	41:9–34

Ψαλμοι	Psalms
9:22–39	10:1–18
chs. 10–112	chs. 11–113
113:1–8	114:1–8
113:9–26	115:1–18
114:1–9	116:1–9
115:1–10	116:10–19
116–145	117–146
146:1–11	147:1–11
147:1–9	147:12–20

Παροιμιαι	Proverbs
--------	4:7
--------	8:33
--------	11:4
--------	15:31
--------	16:1–3
15:27a	16:6
15:28a	16:7
15:29a, b	16:8, 9
16:9	16:4
--------	18:23, 24
--------	19:1, 2
--------	20:14–19
20:9a–c	20:20–22
--------	21:5
--------	22:6
--------	23:23
24:22a–e	--------

For the following sections in Proverbs, the LXX verse numbers match those of the EB but are not always in numeric order. The LXX order is as follows:

24:1–22e
30:1–14
24:23–34
30:15–33
31:1–9
25:1–28
26:1–28
27:1–27
28:1–28
29:1–27
31:10–31

Εκκλησιαστης	Ecclesiastes
4:17	5:1
5:1–19	5:2–20

Ασμα	Song of Songs
6:13	7:1
7:1–13	7:2–14

Ησαιας	Isaiah
--------	2:22
9:1	8:23
9:2–21	9:1–20
--------	40:7
40:7, 8	40:8
--------	56:12
63:19(a)	63:19
63:19(b)	64:1
64:2–11	64:1–12

Ιερεμιας	Jeremiah
--------	2:1, 2(a)
--------	7:1, 2(a)
--------	8:10(b)–12
8:23	9:1
9:1–25	9:2–26
--------	10:6–8
(between 10:4 and 5)	10:9
--------	10:10
--------	11:7
11:8	11:8(a)
--------	11:8(b)
--------	17:1–4
25:14	25:13(c); 49:34(a)
--------	25:14
25:15–19	49:35–39
25:20	49:34(b)
26:1	--------
26:2–25	46:2–25
--------	46:26
26:27–28	46:27–28
27:1–46	50:1–46
28:1–64	51:1–64
29:1–7	47:1–7
30:1–16	49:7–22
30:17–21	49:1–5
30:23–28	49:28–33
30:29–33	49:23–27
31:1–44	48:1–44
--------	48:45–47
32:13b	25:13(b)
32:15–38	25:15–38
33	26
--------	27:1
34:1	--------
34:2–6	27:2–6
--------	27:7
34:8–12	27:8–12
--------	27:13
34:14–16	27:14–16

--------	27:17	32:21b	32:19
34:18–20	27:18–20	--------	33:25(a)–27(a)
--------	27:21	--------	40:30
34:22	27:22(a)	--------	40:38(b)–39(a)
--------	27:22(b)	42:19, 18	42:18, 19
35:1–17	28:1–17		
36:1–13	29:1–13	**Δανιηλ**	**Daniel**
36:14	29:14(a)	3:24–25	--------
--------	29:14(b)	3:26–90 (Prayer of Azaria	--------
36:15	29:15	and Song of the Three	
--------	29:16–20	Children)	
36:21–32	29:21–32	3:91–97	3:24–30
37:1–9	30:1–9	not in Ra	4:1–3
--------	30:10–11	not in Theod	4:37(a–c)
37:12–14	30:12–14	not in Ra	5:14–15
--------	30:15	6:1	5:31
37:16–24	30:16–24	6:2–29	6:1–28
38:1–34	31:1–34	not in Ra	5:18–22
38:35	31:37		
38:36	31:35	**Ωσηε**	**Hosea**
38:37	31:36	2:1–2	1:10–11
38:38–40	31:38–40	2:3–25	2:1–23
ch. 39	ch. 32	12:1	11:12
40:1–13	33:1–13	12:2–15	12:1–14
--------	33:14–26	14:1	13:16
chs. 41–45	chs. 34–38	14:2–10	14:1–9
46:1–3	39:1–3		
--------	39:4–13	**Ιωηλ**	**Joel**
46:14–18	39:14–18	3:1–5	2:28–32
51:1–30	44:1–30	4:1–21	3:1–21
51:31–35	45:1–5		
--------	46:1	**Αμως**	**Amos**
--------	46:26	2:1	1:17
--------	51:44(b)–49(a)	2:2–11	2:1–10
--------	52:2–3		
--------	52:28–30	**Μιχαιας**	**Micah**
		4:14	5:1
Θρηνοι	**Lamentations**	5:1–14	5:2–15
--------	3:22–24		
--------	3:29	**Ναουμ**	**Nahum**
		2:1	1:15
Ιεζεκιηλ	**Ezekiel**	2:2–14	2:1–13
--------	1:14		
--------	1:25(b)–26(a)	**Ζαχαριας**	**Zecharaiah**
--------	7:5(b)	2:1–4	1:18–21
--------	7:6(b)	2:5–17	2:1–13
7:3	7:6(a)		
7:4–6	7:7–9	**Μαλαχιας**	**Malachi**
7:7–9	7:3–5(a)	3:19–21	4:1–3
--------	10:14	3:22–23	4:5–6
21:1–5	20:45–49	3:24	4:4
21:6–37	21:1–32		
--------	27:31–32(b)